I0823880

The Complete Letters of Constance Fenimore Woolson

UNIVERSITY PRESS OF FLORIDA

Florida A&M University, Tallahassee
Florida Atlantic University, Boca Raton
Florida Gulf Coast University, Ft. Myers
Florida International University, Miami
Florida State University, Tallahassee
New College of Florida, Sarasota
University of Central Florida, Orlando
University of Florida, Gainesville
University of North Florida, Jacksonville
University of South Florida, Tampa
University of West Florida, Pensacola

The Complete Letters of *Constance Fenimore Woolson*

EDITED BY

SHARON L. DEAN

University Press of Florida

Gainesville · Tallahassee · Tampa · Boca Raton

Pensacola · Orlando · Miami · Jacksonville · Ft. Myers · Sarasota

Printed in the United States of America. This book is printed on Glatfelter Natures Book, a paper certified under the standards of the Forestry Stewardship Council (FSC). It is a recycled stock that contains 30 percent post-consumer waste and is acid-free.

17 16 15 14 13 12 6 5 4 3 2 1

Library of Congress Cataloging-in-Publication Data

Woolson, Constance Fenimore, 1840–1894.
The complete letters of Constance Fenimore Woolson / Edited by Sharon L. Dean.
p. cm.
Includes bibliographical references and index.
ISBN 978-0-8130-3989-3 (alk. paper)
1. Woolson, Constance Fenimore, 1840–1894—Correspondence. 2. Woolson, Constance Fenimore, 1840–1894—Biography. 3. Authors, American—19th century—Biography. 4. Women and literature—United States—History—19th century. I. Dean, Sharon L., 1943– II. Title.
PS3363.A44 2012
813'.4—dc23
2012009830

University Press of Florida
15 Northwest 15th Street
Gainesville, FL 32611-2079
http://www.upf.com

For

The Constance Fenimore Woolson Society

Contents

Preface

> As I was much separated from my sister, our letters were much . . . We promised each other to be safety valves and also promised each other to destroy letters as soon as answered. Therefore, when she was taken, I was the only person who had no letters. How I missed her clear, strong, interesting letters! . . . And *my* kind of letter amused her; she said I told her things that no one else told her. Oh, that awful silence!
>
> Clara Benedict to Miss May Harris (Benedict/CFW, 387)

Constance Fenimore Woolson's letters, gathered for the first time in *The Complete Letters of Constance Fenimore Woolson,* remove Woolson not only from the "awful silence" that her sister Clara Benedict wrote of in her letter to May Harris, but also from the shadow of Henry James, with whom many scholars have associated her to the exclusion of the array of people, places, and ideas that shaped her large and varied life. Using this edition, scholars can now explore what David Barton and Nigel Hall have called the "social practice" of letter writing. They will be able to explore her relationship to family and friends, to writers and royalty, to artists and musicians, to the rich and the less affluent, to the eccentric and the ordinary. They will be able to read her body of work against her perceptions on politics and popular culture, art and economics, medicine and the environment. And they will hear the candor of a woman who shared her deepest thoughts not only with women friends but also with men to whom she wrote with extraordinary ease.

Material developments in the nineteenth century allowed letter writing like Woolson's to flourish. Stationery became available and affordable, and the easier-to-use steel pen replaced the quill, though in Woolson's case she often had to revert to the quill because of persistent pain in her hand, wrist, and arm. The Postal Act of 1792 created a national postal service in the United States and the Congressional Acts of 1845 and 1851 lowered the cost of stamps. In the first of her surviving letters, written in the late 1840s, the young Connie, who had received no valentines, asks an older friend if she had received any. While this may sound to the modern reader like the sad musings of a lonely girl, it should be, instead, a simple reminder that sending valentines became common only when postal rates declined. The steamship enabled Woolson and many like her to travel abroad, and the postal system enabled them to remain in contact with family and friends and with publishers to whom some sent manuscripts about their travels. As Mary Suzanne Schriber has traced, by the late nineteenth century many public letters from American women living abroad had progressed from using the voice of an amateur instructing readers in manners and civility to the voice of a committed and confident artist. Hotel letterhead began to appear and the fact that Woolson used it only at the end of her life when she was visiting Greece and Cairo reveals her preferred habit of staying not in hotels but in rooms of her own. Over and over again, Woolson wrote from Europe about how much she valued the letters and gifts she received through the mail, and she often complained that larger packages of books cost an exorbitant fee. Her letters reveal, as well, the role of banks in the international postal system. Woolson was in contact with a variety of bankers, who always knew her whereabouts and could forward letters. The return addresses at the head of Woolson's letters document the numerous places to which those letters were sent or forwarded. Some years, such as 1875 and 1881, must have been exhausting for a woman who longed for a permanent home.

As valuable as I hope this edition of letters will be in tracing Woolson's responses to the many places she wandered through, it cannot replicate the experience of reading the letters in their original form. We read differently if we read a magazine like *Appletons' Journal* firsthand or on the *Making of America* website. Woolson's letters make clear how much she worked at revisions between the magazine serialization of her novels and the book form. But not only are the texts different, so, too, the experience of reading any edition of letters is different from reading the original. In print editions, readers miss the feel of the paper, whether expensive or fragile, whether black-bordered mourning paper or a decorative card, and miss the way a writer positions the letter on the page. They also miss the personality of the handwriting and of changes in handwriting, which in Woolson's case is especially interesting because her handwriting changes significantly as her pain increases. Some contemporary editions of letters replicate idiosyncrasies with textual markings now made possible by word processing tools. An attentive reader may be able to surmise that a series of strikethroughs indicate that a writer is struggling to find a way to express him- or herself, as I would speculate about only two of Woolson's letters, one written to Henry James on February 12, 1882, and the other to Samuel Mather written on November 20, 1893. In other cases, Woolson's quill may have slipped because her wrist was sore or because her dog jumped on her writing table. However valuable textual markings are to indicate the quirks of a particular letter-writer, they are never the real thing.

Editorial decisions rightly vary depending on whose letters are being edited for what audience. An editor must ask whether to use what scholars call "plain-text editing" that takes advantage of available technologies to replicate such things as strikethroughs, blanked-out words, multiple underlinings, carets, and ampersands or "clear-text editing" that reproduces a visually clean text but changes, for example, ampersands to *and*, *&c* to *etc.*, and underlining to italics. Should obvious errors be silently corrected? Should punctuation be modernized? Should return addresses and signatures be standardized? Should footnotes be extensive or minimal and where should the footnote number be placed? Woolson's letters present difficulties not only because they are scattered in nearly forty places, but also because many of them survive only in fragments and many of the fragments survive with no original but only as they have been transcribed by her niece Clare Benedict. Someone, almost certainly Benedict, typed these letters.[1] Benedict then published these transcripts and other letters for which no transcripts survive in her three-volume *Five Generations.* To complicate this further, she published only excerpts and excerpts from a single letter may appear in different parts of her three volumes or be repeated within these volumes. Benedict pasted fragments of original letters, sometimes but not always ones she quoted in *Five Generations,* into books related to Woolson, thus obscuring the pasted side of the letter. As much as she thought she was serving her aunt's reputation, Benedict's decisions have made the process of gathering Woolson's letters akin to piecing together a complicated jigsaw puzzle when many of the pieces are missing.

Only a few letters that Benedict used in *Five Generations* have survived in their original form. The letters that she typed before publishing them are almost all to Woolson's niece and Benedict's cousin, Kate Mather. I can only speculate that the originals of these letters survive in unidentified fragments tipped into books or that they disappeared because neither Mather nor Benedict married and there were no direct descendents to preserve them. However, many original letters to Kate's brother, Samuel Mather, do survive, preserved at the Western Reserve Historical Society in Cleveland or by his granddaughter Molly Anderson. Though as complete as an exhaustive search has uncovered, this edition of letters is necessarily fragmented. Using it, readers will not experience Woolson's "clear, strong, interesting" letters the way her sister Clara Benedict did or even the way I did as I read through the originals. But this collection will, at least in part, break her "awful silence."

Notes

1. The handwriting on the edges of the transcripts seems to be Benedict's and most of the cut-up fragments of original letters are tipped into books in the Benedict collection at Western Reserve Historical Society. Although one could argue that this is not sufficient evidence, for the sake of clarity, I am attributing this work to Benedict.

A Note on the Text

Because many of Woolson's letters are fragmented and corrupted, Woolson scholarship will benefit most from an edition of letters that favors most of the apparatus of plain-text editing but that also uses the consistency and standardization of clear-text editing techniques. With this in mind, I have made the following editorial decisions.

- Return addresses: Woolson generally placed these flush right with some variations of line breaks. I have made the position and punctuation of addresses and dates consistent both as a space-saver and as an aid to scholars who until now have not had a way of tracing her whereabouts, but I have preserved her inconsistent habit of abbreviating or spelling out in full. Woolson's habit of leaving out the year when she dated letters has forced me to use internal evidence to present these letters in chronological order. Envelopes have sometimes helped, but few of these survive. I have reproduced the dates Woolson wrote on her letters and put the year in brackets when I am confident of it and in brackets with a question mark when I am not. When a year is evident but a month is not, I have placed the letter as close within the chronology of the year as seems likely. I have also included a section for letters impossible to date and have divided these letters by their early, middle, or late composition.
- Signatures: I have maintained the varied wording and punctuation that Woolson used as a lead-in to her signature, but again as a space-saver have placed her signatures all flush right even though she followed the habit of many of her contemporaries and wrote closing comments in margins or at the head of the letter. I have also consistently placed a period after her signature as was her usual habit even if the overwriting makes this illegible or if the original of the letter does not survive.
- Punctuation with quotations: To minimize distractions for the reader, I have regularized the position of periods and commas to appear inside closing quotation marks. Woolson followed neither British nor American conventions, often even placing the comma underneath the quotation mark.
- Punctuation with abbreviations: To avoid the appearance of editing errors and to make the letters that survive only in typed transcriptions or book

versions consistent with originals, I have adopted Woolson's usual practice for abbreviations. Thus, I have maintained periods with *ms.* or *mss.* (manuscript), *Col.*, *Prof.*, and *Rev*. I have eliminated periods with *Mr, Mrs, Dr, Mt, St* (Street and Saint). Woolson could be so inconsistent that, for example, in a single paragraph she might use or omit the period after *Mr.* even with the same person's name.

- Punctuation with superscripts: Nineteenth-century practice often added an underline and a ditto mark beneath a superscript. I have eliminated these difficult-to-reproduce markings.
- Paragraphs: Like others of her day, Woolson sometimes signaled the end of a paragraph with a dash or by starting a new line flush left. She used numerous dashes, most of which do not indicate paragraph breaks. In a single letter, she might indent some paragraphs, start some flush left whether the preceding paragraph ends flush right or mid-line, or leave a long space before starting a new paragraph on the same line as the old. To avoid ambiguity, I have indented all paragraphs.
- Strikethroughs, overwriting, and carets: Despite increasing pain, Woolson did not often need to strike through a word. When she did, she sometimes used a single and sometimes a double line. If she scribbled through a word, I have indicated this with a double strikethrough so that what is barely legible in the manuscript will be legible to the reader of this edition. I have not indicated words that are so illegible that even the letter recipient would not be able to decipher them. Nor have I used carets because these marks can be distracting and because, if Woolson changed her mind about wording, a struck-through word has been recorded. In some letters, a tiny section of the paper has been excised (perhaps an artifact of the preservation process) and words lost. These excisions, indicated in brackets where they occur, do not appear to have been deliberate on either Woolson's or Clare Benedict's part.

In all other matters I have followed Woolson's text and have used bracketed insertions only when there is danger of misreading. I have reproduced

- erratic use of commas, which sometimes appear with parentheses and dashes, sometimes not;
- variations in spelling, capitalization, and usage: for example, *and/&*; *South/south*; *traveling/travelling*; *to day/to-day/today*; *Menton/Mentone*; *Bellosguardo/Bellos Guardo*; *fete/fête*.

Other decisions:

- The correct spelling of one of Woolson's bankers is *Macquay and Hooker,* though some scholars have misinterpreted Woolson's handwriting to read *Magnay and Hooker.* Throughout, I have used the correct spelling and her numerous references to financial matters will allow someone to trace the state of her finances at the end of her life.
- Throughout, I have, of course, used originals as available. When the only available copy is her niece Clare Benedict's, I have reproduced that from whichever is the fullest version, Benedict's typescript or her books, and I have retained her inconsistent use of ellipses. Although these ellipses are probably Benedict's, I have not made this judgment by putting them between brackets. To be consistent with Woolson's habits, I have changed Benedict's italics to underscoring when Woolson is emphasizing something and to quotation marks when Woolson is using a title. Also to be consistent with Woolson's habits, I have inserted periods with her salutations and signatures and eliminated them with *Mr, Mrs,* and *Dr.* Because brackets or other editorial symbols are intrusive, I have not recorded differences between original letters and Benedict's typed transcripts or book versions. Interested readers can trace a letter's location by using the footnote reference. In the Addendum of Letters, I have included a sample to illustrate the differences between an original and Benedict's versions.
- To reduce the need for repetitive footnotes, an Appendix of Names follows the letters. Readers should consult this for a list of first names that Woolson frequently used.

Acknowledgments

The task of finding and collating letters that Woolson rarely dated by year has been enormous, and I could not have completed it without the help and encouragement of numerous people. Kristin Comment began the project with me and purchased and transcribed many of the early letters. With Kathleen Diffley's prompting, Victoria Brehm and Cheryl Torsney helped me comb through folders of material at Western Reserve Historical Society. Vicky also helped me with proofreading and provided detailed advice on the introduction and design of the book. Kevin O'Donnell secured copies of letters from WRHS; Joan Weimer alerted me to the fact that the now privately owned letters to Samuel Mather are copied on microfilm there; Rochelle Johnson discovered a letter at the eleventh hour; Susan Goodman pointed me to a Howells source at the Houghton Library; and Geraldine Murphy offered assistance checking material in New York City. Anne Boyd Rioux photographed letters at the Library of Congress and gave helpful feedback throughout my process of editing; John Pearson demonstrated his admirable work ethic when he spent a few days at my home transcribing letters; and Alice Hall Petry's edition of Woolson's letters to John Hay saved me hours of tracking down obscure name references. Librarians and archivists throughout the country and in Canada, Rome, and Switzerland were prompt in sending material, showing enthusiasm for the project; Holly Klump of Regina Library, Rivier College, helped me secure an elusive source; Sr. Lucille Thibodeau of Rivier College, Bill Weißker, and Silke Weißker-Vorgias helped with translations. Karen Kilcup and Pierre Walker supported this project during the review process and the staff at the University Press of Florida helped to bring the manuscript into print. Special thanks to Amy Gorelick, Associate Director, University Press of Florida, who advocated for publication; Nicole McGrath, who tirelessly helped pursue permissions; and Nevil Parker, who guided the manuscript through the editorial process. Helena Berg's copyediting was invaluable. Special thanks as well go to Woolson family members: Gary Woolson for providing information on Clare Benedict and on Woolson's brother Charly's suicide; Samuel Mather's granddaughter Molly Anderson and great-granddaughter Connie Anderson, who shared Woolson's letters to him that were preserved by his daughter, Constance Mather Bishop. Connie was especially helpful proofreading these letters and supplying me with family information. Finally, my deepest appreciation and love to my husband, Ron, who never complained when I denied him computer time or a walk in the woods.

Sources

Grateful acknowledgment to all those who provided access to Woolson's letters. Sources are abbreviated as follows.

American Antiquarian: With permission from American Antiquarian Society, James Fenimore Cooper Papers.

Anderson: With permission from Molly Anderson, private collector.

Barnard: With permission from Barnard College Archives, Overbury Collection, File 8.

Basel: With Permission from Cooper Library, Department of English, University of Basel, Switzerland.

Beinecke: Daniel Cady Eaton Collection, Mss. 581, and E. C. Stedman Collection, Yale Collection of American Literature, Beinecke Rare Book and Manuscript Library.

Benedict/Abroad: Benedict, Clare. *Five Generations*. Vol. 3, *The Benedicts Abroad*. London: Ellis, 1929–30, 1932.

Benedict/CFW: Benedict, Clare. *Five Generations*. Vol. 2, *Constance Fenimore Woolson*. London: Ellis, 1929–30, 1932.

Benedict/Voices: Benedict, Clare. *Five Generations*. Vol. 1, *Voices Out of the Past*. London: Ellis, 1929–30, 1932.

Beverly: Beverly Historical Society and Museum, Beverly, Mass.

Brigham Young: With permission from Brigham Young University, Perry Special Collections, Vault MSS2.

Brown: With permission from John Hay Papers, John Hay Library, Brown University. Alice Hall Petry also edited Woolson's letters to John and Clara Hay: "'Always, Your Attached Friend': The Unpublished Letters of Constance Fenimore Woolson to John and Clara Hay." *Books at Brown*, 29–30 (1982–83): 11–107. My transcriptions are from the originals.

Claremont: With permission from Fiske Free Library Historical Collection, Claremont, N.H.

Colby: With permission from Colby College Special Collections, Waterville, Maine.

Columbia: E. C. Stedman Collection, Rare Book and Manuscript Library, Columbia University.

Cornell: Daniel Willard Fiske Papers, #13-1-1165; George Hyde Clarke Collection #77-83853; Courtesy of Division of Rare and Manuscript Collections, Cornell University Libraries.

Duke: With permission from Paul Hamilton Hayne Collection, Rare Book, Manuscript, and Special Collections Library, Duke University.

Emory: Joel Chandler Harris Collection, Manuscript, Archives, and Rare Book Library, Emory University, Atlanta, Ga.

Hayes: With permission from William Dean Howells Collection, Rutherford B. Hayes Presidential Center, Fremont, Ohio.

Houghton: By permission of the Houghton Library, Harvard University: Thomas Bailey Aldrich, MS Am 1429 (4842, 4843); Elinor Howells MS Am 1784.5 (25); William Dean Howells, MS Am 1784 (558); Winifred Howells's autograph album MS Am 1784.7(5); Henry James, MS Am 1429; MS Am 1094 (496, 497, 498, 498a).

Huntington: This item is reproduced by permission of The Huntington Library, San Marino, California.

Johns Hopkins: With permission from Department of Rare Books and Manuscripts, Sheridan Libraries, Johns Hopkins University.

Knox: With permission from Special Collections and Archives, Knox College Library, Galesburg, Ill.

LOC: Library of Congress, Harry Payne Whitney Collection, MSS45468; R. R. Bowker Collection, MSS13433.

Massachusetts: With permission from Grenville H. Norcross Autograph Collection, Massachusetts Historical Society, Boston, Mass.

McGill: With permission from Leon Edel Papers, Rare Books and Special Collections, McGill University Library.

Morgan: William Wilberforce Baldwin Collection, MA 3564, The Morgan Library and Museum, N.Y., N.Y.

NYPL: New York Public Library, Richard Watson Gilder papers and Lee Kohns collections, Manuscripts and Archives Division, Astor, Lenox and Tilden Foundations.

Non-Catholic Cemetery: With the kind permission of The Non-Catholic Cemetery in Rome, Italy, previously called the Protestant Cemetery.

Pennsylvania: With permission from University of Pennsylvania, Elsa Noble Collection, Mss. 155883767, Rare Book and Manuscript Library.

Petry: See Brown.

Phillips Exeter: Edwin Fay Rice Autograph Collection, Class of 1945 Library, Phillips Exeter Academy.

Princeton: With permission from Archives of Charles Scribner's Sons and General Mss [misc], Manuscripts Division, Department of Rare Books and Special Collections, Princeton University Library.

Rollins: With permission from Department of College Archives and Special Collections, Olin Library, Rollins College, Winter Park, Fla.

Schlesinger: With permission from Strickland Autograph Collection, Schlesinger Library, Radcliffe Institute, Harvard University.

Virginia: Special Collections, University of Virginia Library.

Wisconsin: With permission from University of Wisconsin–Madison, Department of Special Collections University of Wisconsin, Madison, Wis.

Woolson: With permission from Gary W. Woolson, private collector.

WRHS/Benedict: With permission from Clare Benedict Collection, Mss. 4830 Western Reserve Historical Society, Cleveland, Ohio.

WRHS/Mather: With permission from Samuel Mather Family Papers, Mss. 3735, Western Reserve Historical Society, Cleveland, Ohio.

WRHS/Wickham: With permission from Gertrude Van Rensselaer Wickham Collection, Mss. 1085, Western Reserve Historical Society, Cleveland, Ohio.

Chronology

Note: Harper's refers to the publishing company Harper & Bros.; *Harper's* refers to *Harper's New Monthly Magazine.*

1840: Woolson born on March 5th in Claremont, N.H., the fifth daughter of Charles and Hannah Cooper Pomeroy Woolson. Between March 21 and Apr. 3, sisters Julia (age 2), Gertrude (age 4), and Ann (age 5) die of scarlet fever. In winter, moves with parents and sisters Georgiana (age 9) and Emma (age 7) to Cleveland, Ohio, stopping first in Cooperstown to visit Cooper relatives.

1840s: Sister Clara born (1843). Sister Alida born (1845; dies 1846). Brother Charles Jarvis Jr. born (1846). Late 1840s attends Miss Hayden's school in Cleveland.

1850s: Attends Cleveland Female Seminary. Sister Georgiana marries Samuel Livingston Mather (1850). Samuel Mather born (1851). Sister Emma marries Rev. Timothy Carter (1851). Carter dies (1851). Emma dies (1852). Katharine Livingston Mather born (1853). Georgiana dies (1853). Begins summer visits to Mackinac Island, Mich. Visits to Wisconsin and to Zoar Community in Ohio likely occur in the 1850s. Graduates Madame Chegaray's School, N.Y. (1858).

1861–66: Works for the Union cause during the Civil War, spending part of her time in New York and part in Cleveland.

1867: Sister Clara marries George Benedict Jr.

1869: Father, Charles Jarvis Woolson Sr. dies, possibly of a heart condition.

1870–71: George Benedict Jr. killed in train crash (1871). Spends time in Cleveland, with relatives in Cooperstown, and in New York City where she stays on 49 West 32nd Street. Publishes sketches "The Happy Valley" (*Harper's,* July 1870); "Fairy Island" (*Putnam's,* July 1870), "The Haunted Lake" (*Harper's,* Dec. 1871). Publishes essays "Spots" (*Lippincott's,* May 1871), "Extremities. The Head and Hands" (*Harper's Bazar,* Oct. 21, 1871) "Extremities. The Feet." (*Harper's Bazar,* Nov. 18, 1871). Publishes poems "Charles Dickens. Christmas, 1870" (*Harper's Bazar,* Dec. 31, 1870). Publishes stories "An October Idyl" (*Harper's,* Nov. 1870), "A Day of Mystery" (*Appletons',* Sept. 9, 1871), "Cicely's Christmas" (*Appletons',* Dec. 30, 1871). Begins publishing "Letters from Gotham" in George Benedict's *Daily Cleveland Herald* (Dec. 24, 1870, Jan. 10, 1871, Jan. 14, 1871, Jan. 21, 1871, Jan. 28, 1871, Feb. 4, 1871).

1872: Spends time in Cleveland at 131 St. Clair St. Publishes travel narratives "In Search of the Picturesque" (*Harper's*, July), "American Cities—Detroit" (*Appletons'*, July 27), "Round by Propeller, (*Harper's*, Sept.). Publishes poems "The Herald's Cry" (*Lippincott's*, Jan.), "Walpurgis Night" (*Old and New*, Jan.), "Love Unexpressed" (*Appletons'*, March 9), "The Heart of June" (*Galaxy*, June), "Longing" (*Appletons'*, June 22), "Off Thunder Bay" (*Harper's*, July), "Corn Fields" (*Harper's*, Aug.), "Floating. Otsego Lake, September, 1872" (*New York Evening Mail*, Sept. 14), "Ideal. (The artist speaks.)" (*Atlantic Monthly*, Oct.), "October's Song" (*Harper's*, Oct.), "Lake Erie in September" (*Appletons'*, Oct. 12), "Christmas in the City" (*Appletons'*, Dec. 28). Publishes stories "A Merry Christmas" (*Harper's*, Jan.), "Margaret Morris" (*Appletons'*, Apr. 13), "Weighed in the Balance" (*Appletons'*, June 1), "One Versus Two" (*Lippincott's*, Aug.), "Lily and Diamond" (*Appletons'*, Nov. 2).

1873: Stays at 131 St. Clair Street in Cleveland and at 61 West 17th Street in New York City. Wins thousand-dollar prize from D. Lothrop & Co. for *The Old Stone House*, a novel for children. Publishes travel narratives "The Wine Islands of Lake Erie" (*Harper's*, June), "Mackinac Island" (*Appletons'*, March 8; Appletons' *Picturesque America*, vol. 1), "The Bones of Our Ancestors" (*Harper's*, Sept.), "Lakeshore Relics" (*Lippincott's*, Nov.), "Lake Superior" (Appletons' *Picturesque America*, vol. 1), "The South Shore of Lake Erie" (Appletons' *Picturesque America*, vol. 1). Publishes poems, "Commonplace" (*Lippincott's*, Feb.), "February" (*Appletons'*, Feb. 8), "The Greatest of All is Charity" (*Harper's Bazar*, Feb. 8), "March" (*Harper's*, March), "Two Ways" (*Ohio Farmer*, Apr. 12, *Atlantic Monthly*, June), "Heliotrope" (*Harper's*, July), "Sail-Rock, Lake Superior" (*Appletons'*, July 12), "Kentucky Belle" (*Appletons'*, Sept. 6), "Hero Worship" (*Harper's*, Oct.), "Cleopatra" (*Appletons'*, Oct. 4), "Memory" (*Appletons'*, Nov. 8), "The Haunting Face" (*Appletons'*, Dec. 6). Publishes stories "King Log" (*Appletons'*, Jan. 18), "On the Iron Mountain," (*Appletons'*, Feb. 15), "Ballast Island" (*Appletons'*, June 28), "Solomon" (*Atlantic Monthly*, Oct.), "St. Clair Flats" (*Appletons'*, Oct. 4).

1874: Travels to St. Augustine by Apr., where she meets E. C. Stedman and begins a correspondence with him. Writes to William Dean Howells about her first submissions to *Atlantic Monthly*. Begins serious study of ferns. Travels, via Charleston, to Asheville, N.C., in June. Briefly leaves her mother for a trip to New York. Remains in Asheville until Oct. then returns via Chattanooga and Atlanta to St. Augustine, stopping along the way at various Civil War battlefields, a habit she continues throughout her time in the South. Publishes travel narratives "A Voyage to the Unknown River" (*Appletons'*, May 16); "The Ancient City I & II" begins serialization in *Harper's* (Dec. 1874–Jan. 1875). Publishes essay "Euterpe in America" (*Lippincott's*, Nov.). Publishes poems "Yellow Jessamine" (*Appletons'*, March 21), "Dolores"

(*Appletons'*, July 11), "At the Smithy" (*Appletons'*, Sept. 5), "The Florida Beach" (*Galaxy*, Oct.), "Indian Summer" (*Appletons'*, Oct. 17), "Pine-Barrens" (*Harper's*, Dec.), "Matanzas River" (*Harper's*, Dec.). Publishes stories "A Flower of the Snow" (*Galaxy*, Jan.), "The Story of Huron Grand Harbor" (*Appletons'*, Apr. 18), "Misery Landing" (*Harper's*, May), "The Waldenburg Road" (*Appletons'*, July 4), "Duets" (*Harper's*, Sept.), "Peter the Parson" (*Scribner's*, Sept.), "The Lady of Little Fishing" (*Massachusetts Plowman*, Sept.; *New England Journal of Agriculture*, Sept.; *Atlantic Monthly*, Sept.), "Jeannette" (*Scribner's*, Dec.), "The Old Agency" (*Galaxy*, Dec.).

1875: Begins correspondence with Paul Hamilton Hayne, whom she never meets in person. Winters in St. Augustine. Stays in Charleston, S.C., in Apr. and May, in Cleveland Springs, Shelby, N.C., in June and July, and in Goshen, Va., in Aug. and Sept. Returns via Charleston to St. Augustine, arriving there in Dec. Visits Greenbriar resort in White Sulphur Springs, W.Va., and Harpers Ferry in late Aug. or early Sept. Osgood publishes first collection of stories *Castle Nowhere: Lake Country Sketches* ("Castle Nowhere," "Peter the Parson," "Jeannette," "The Old Agency," "Misery Landing," "Solomon," "Wilhelmina," "St. Clair Flats," "The Lady of Little Fishing"). Publishes travel narratives "The Ancient City, II" (*Harper's*, Jan.) "The French Broad" (*Harper's*, Apr.), "Up the Ashley and Cooper" (*Harper's*, Dec.). Publishes essay "Southern Men and Women" (*Cleveland Herald*, Rpt. *New York Times* July 31). Publishes poems "The Legend of Maria Sanchez Creek" (*Harper's*, Jan.), "A Fire in the Forest" (*Appletons'*, Dec. 4). Publishes stories "Wilhelmina" (*Atlantic Monthly*, Jan.), "Miss Elisabetha" (*Appletons'*, March 13).

1876: Spends time in St. Augustine in Jan. and Feb. then travels in Apr. via Savannah to Summerville, S.C., and stays into May. Travels north to Cooperstown for first visit in three and a half years. Leaves Cooperstown in Oct. or Nov., stopping in Wilmington, N.C., in Nov. and Dec. Publishes travel narrative "The Oklawaha" (*Harper's*, Jan.). Publishes poems "On a Homely Woman, Dead" (*Appletons'*, Apr. 1), "Tom" (*Appletons'*, May 20), "To George Eliot" (*The New Century for Woman*, May 20), "Only the Brakesman" (*Appletons'*, n.s., July), "Forgotten" (*Harper's*, July), "To Jean Ingelow" (*The New Century for Woman*, July 8), "Four-Leaved Clover" (*Harper's Bazar*, July 8), "On the Border" (*Appletons'*, n.s., Sept.), "Morris Island" (*Appletons'*, n.s., Dec.). Publishes stories "Crowder's Cove" (*Appletons'*, March 18), "Old Gardiston" (*Harper's*, Apr.), "In the Cotton Country" (*Appletons'*, Apr. 29), "Felipa" (*Lippincott's*, June), "Mission Endeavor" (*Harper's*, Nov.), "The Old Five" (*Appletons'*, n.s., Nov.).

1877: In Jan. and Feb., writes from St. Augustine to nephew Sam Mather expressing worry about brother Charly's emotional health; conceals this worry from her mother. Spends much of the year in Yonkers, N.Y., where sister Clara has a house. Enjoys visits in N.Y. from E. C. Stedman and his wife. Writes frequently to noted botanist D. C. Eaton about collecting ferns. Publishes reviews in Contributors' Club section of *Atlantic Monthly*: *Mercy Philbrick's Choice* (May), *That Lass o' Lowrie's* (Sept.), *Samuel Brohl et Cie* (Nov.). Publishes poems "Two Women. 1862" (*Appletons'*, n.s., Jan. & Feb.), "Mizpah. Genesis XXXI. 49" (*Appletons'*, n.s., June), "'I, Too!'" (*Appletons'*, n.s., Sept.). Publishes stories "Rodman the Keeper" (*Atlantic Monthly*, March), "Sister St. Luke" (*Galaxy*, Apr.), "Keller Hill" (*Appletons'*, n.s., May), "Barnaby Pass" (*Harper's*, July), "Raspberry Island. Told to me by Dora" (*Harper's*, Oct.).

1878: Spends Jan. through May in St. Augustine and Hibernia, Fla., then whereabouts unknown, though could be in Yonkers with mother and sister Clara. Begins work on first novel, *Anne*. Publishes essays and reviews for *Atlantic Monthly*'s Contributors' Club: "Comparison of Prose and Poetry" (June), "Farjeon" (July), "South Carolina Gentleman" (Aug.), review of *Esther Pennefather* (Oct.). Publishes poems "To Certain Biographers" (*Appletons'*, n.s., Sept.), "An Intercepted Letter" (*Harper's Bazar*, Sept. 7), "In Remembrance" (*New York Evening Post*, Oct. 18). Publishes stories "Matches Morganatic" (*Harper's*, March), "King David" (*Scribner's*, Apr.), "Up in the Blue Ridge" (*Appletons'*, n.s., Aug.), "Bro" (*Appletons'*, n.s., Nov.).

1879: Leaves Yonkers in Jan. After death of mother on Feb. 13, spends March in Washington, D.C., the summer in Cooperstown, and Oct. in Cleveland. Sails in Nov. on the steamship *Gallia* for Europe via Queenstown, Ireland, and Liverpool. Enjoys museums and cathedrals of London despite the cold weather, then travels to Menton, France, stopping for only a day in Paris. Begins correspondence with John and Clara Hay. Stops publishing poetry and publishes fewer travel narratives, concentrating on short fiction and novels. Publishes reviews in *Atlantic Monthly*'s Contributors' Club (*The Europeans*, Jan. and Feb.), *L'Idée de Jean Têterol* (Feb.), *Far from the Madding Crowd* (Feb.). Publishes biographical essay "Henry Middleton: President of the First Continental Congress" (*Pennsylvania Magazine of History and Biography*). Publishes stories "Miss Vedder" (*Harper's*, March), "Black Point" (*Harper's*, June), "Mrs. Edward Pinckney" (*Christian Union*, Aug. 6).

1880: Spends Jan. to March in Menton, then spends late March to May in Florence, where meets Henry James and explores art treasures with him. Spends part of June in Venice, then travels to Switzerland, staying in Lucerne in July and Aug. and Geneva in the fall. Returns to Florence by Dec. Writes concerns to Sam Mather about brother Charly's desire to invest in California land. Publishes collection *Rodman the Keeper: Southern Sketches* with Appletons' ("Rodman the Keeper," "Sister

St. Luke," "Miss Elisabetha," "Old Gardiston," "The South Devil," "In the Cotton Country," "Felipa," "'Bro,'" "King David," "Up in the Blue Ridge"). Begins serialization of novel *Anne* in *Harper's* (Dec. 1880–May 1882). Publishes travel narrative "Pictures of Travel: The Last Summer of the St. Gotthard" (*Christian Union,* Sept. 1). Publishes stories "The South Devil" (*Atlantic Monthly,* Feb.), "'Miss Grief'" (*Lippincott's,* May), "A Florentine Experiment" (*Atlantic Monthly,* Oct.), "The Old Palace Keeper" (*Christian Union,* Oct. 14).

1881: Leaves Florence for Siena in Jan., then spends the remainder of Jan. through May in Rome. Returns to Switzerland in July and Aug., where drafts "At the Château of Corinne." Spends time in Geneva, Engelberg, and Lucerne. Travels through Turin, Milan, Padua, Venice, Florence, Rome, and Naples, arriving in Sorrento by Dec. Whereabouts unknown for the remainder of the year, but probably in Switzerland and Italy. As working on serialization of *Anne,* publishes only one other piece, the travel narrative "The Roman May, and a Walk" (*Christian Union,* July 27).

1882: Spends Jan. into Apr. in Sorrento, where enjoys a visit from nephew, Sam Mather, and his new wife, Flora Stone Mather; visits Paestum and Salerno with them. Returns to Florence in May and then to Baden-Baden, where writes for an uninterrupted six weeks. Visits Dresden at the end of Aug. and Cologne in Sept. Arrives in London in Sept., where remains for the rest of the year. Publishes book version of *Anne* with Harper's. Begins serialization of novel *For the Major* (*Harper's,* Nov. 1882–Apr. 1883). Publishes stories "In Venice" (*Atlantic Monthly,* Apr.) and "The Street of the Hyacinth" (*Century,* June).

1883: Spends time in Paris in late 1882 or early 1883, where goes to the theater with geologist Clarence King. Arrives in Florence in Jan., where sees William Dean Howells and meets Vernon Lee. In Apr. flees the society of Florence for Venice, where lives in an apartment in the Gritti Palace above John Addington Symonds. Leaves Venice for Engelberg and Baden-Baden in July and Aug. and arrives in London late in the year. Brother Charly commits suicide in Los Angeles on Aug. 20. *For the Major* continues serialization in *Harper's* and book version appears (Harper's). British company Sampson and Low publishes *Anne* and *For the Major.* Works on travel narrative "At Mentone."

1884: Lives in Sloane St., London, where is ill for three months, partially because she is mourning suicide of her brother. In June or July leaves London proper for Hampstead Heath. Spends time in Dover in Sept., in Salisbury in Oct., and in Vienna in Nov. and Dec. Publishes travel narrative "At Mentone" (*Harper's,* Jan. and Feb.) and poem "Mentone" (*Harper's* Jan.).

1885: Few letters survive, but they show her living in Vienna in Apr. and Leamington, Warwickshire, in Sept. where she remains through Dec. Begins serialization of *East Angels* (*Harper's* Jan. 1885–May 1886).

1886: Lives in Portman Square, London, in Feb. and March, then returns to Florence, stopping first in Strasbourg, Lucerne, and Venice in Apr. Spends three months on Lake Leman (Geneva) in Switzerland. Fears the revisions for the book version of *East Angels* has been lost at sea and so spends frantic time rewriting until news arrives that the manuscript is safe. Spends time in Chamonix and Geneva in July and Aug. Begins long residence on Bellosguardo Hill in Florence, in the Villa Castellani in Oct. and Nov. and in the Villa Brichieri in Dec. Begins correspondence with Dr. William Wilberforce Baldwin, often focusing on her health. Letters to nephew Sam Mather begin to show concerns about money. Harper's reissues *Rodman the Keeper*. Harper's and Sampson and Low publish book version of *East Angels*.

1887: Continues to live in Villa Brichieri, where Henry James also rents rooms in Apr. and May. Becomes godmother to child of Frank and Lizzie Boott Duveneck. Publishes story "At the Château of Corinne" (*Harper's*, Oct.).

1888: Continues to live in Villa Brichieri. Spends time in Oct. in Geneva where she regularly has visits from Henry James, who is also in Geneva. Publishes stories "Neptune's Shore" (*Harper's*, Oct.), "A Pink Villa" (*Harper's*, Nov.), "The Front Yard" (*Harper's*, Dec.).

1889: Remains at the Villa Brichieri until July, then travels to Venice, where niece Kate Mather visits. Returns to the Villa Brichieri in Aug. Visits Paris Exhibition sometime during the year. Expresses concern to Sam Mather that she has drawn on her capital. Arrives in Richmond, Eng. by Oct., then returns again to the Villa Brichieri, which she vacates in Dec. *Harper's* serializes *Jupiter Lights* (Jan. to Sept.); Harper's and Samson and Low publish book version.

1890: Travels in Jan. to Corfu and Cairo with sister Clara, then remains alone in Cairo. Travel includes a trip to Jerusalem and other sites in the Holy Land. At the end of Apr., returns, via Wales, to Eng., where remains in Cheltenham until the end of the year. Negotiates with Harper's, which has first bid on all her work, to write a new travel narrative. Poem "In March" appears in *Current Literature* 4:3 (March).

1891: Continues to live in Cheltenham and enjoys visits from her sister Clara and her nieces Clare Benedict and Kate Mather, as well as from Henry James. Moves to Oxford in July. In Nov., attends the fiftieth performance of Henry James's *The American* and comments on the "crowded & brilliant house." Negotiates various financial matters with Sam Mather. Wrestles with severe head pain for several months at the end of the year. Publishes travel narrative "Cairo in 1890" (*Harper's*, Oct. and Nov.).

1892: Despite continued pain and illness, works on novel *Horace Chase*. Publishes travel narrative "Corfu and the Ionian Sea" (*Harper's*, Aug.). Publishes stories "Dorothy" (*Harper's*, March), "In Sloane Street" (*Harper's Bazar*, June 11), "A Christmas Party" (*Harper's*, Dec.).

1893: Asks Sam Mather for advice on how a businessman like Horace Chase would talk. *Harper's* is able to make changes she requests as it serializes the novel (Jan. to Aug.). Leaves England for Venice in June, stopping first in Paris where she visits with Henry James. Lives in Casa Biondetti until finding more suitable rooms in Casa Semitecolo on the Grand Canal. Completes book manuscript of *Horace Chase*. Plans to begin a new novel on Jan. 1st.

1894: Suffering from illness, jumps to her death from the window of Casa Semitecolo on Jan. 24th. Harper's and Osgood, McIlvaine & Co. publish book version of *Horace Chase*. Stories "A Transplanted Boy" (*Harper's*, Feb.) and "A Waitress" (*Harper's*, June) published posthumously.

1895: Harper's publishes posthumous collection *The Front Yard and Other Italian Stories* ("The Front Yard," "Neptune's Shore," "A Pink Villa," "The Street of the Hyacinth," "A Christmas Party," "In Venice").

1896: Harper's publishes posthumous collections *Mentone, Cairo, and Corfu* and *Dorothy and Other Italian Stories* ("Dorothy," "A Transplanted Boy," "A Florentine Experiment," "A Waitress," "At the Château of Corinne").

Posthumous writings collected by Clare Benedict in *Five Generations*, 3 vols. (Ellis, 1929–30, 1932). Works that appear only in the 1932 volume are designated 1932.

Poems: "Alas!" (II, 1932), "Contrast" (II, 1932), "Clara 'Bright Illustrious'" (III), "Detroit River" (II, 1932), "'Gentleman Waife'" (I, II 1932), "Gettysburg. 1876" (III; also published in 1889 in *American War Ballads and Lyrics*, Putnam), "In Memoriam" (II), "Martins On the Telegraph Wire" (II), "Mackinac—Revisited" (I, II, 1932), "Plum's Picture" (III), "St. Augustine Light" (I), "We Shall Meet Them Again" (II, 1932).

Essays and Sketches: "A Brief Sketch of the Life of Charles Jarvis Woolson" (I), "The Piazza of St. John's Gate" (II, 1932), "The Villa Medici" (II, 1932).

Other: Undated poems "The God of February" and "In the December Twilight" archived in "Miss Woolson's Poetry Book" at Western Reserve Historical Society. Also at WRHS, comic poem "Haj You Chorgotten." Story "Hepzibah's Story" edited by Robert Gingras and published in *Resources for American Literary Study* 10 (1980): 33–45.

Introduction: Twenty Years a Wanderer

On July 4, 1893, Constance Woolson wrote from Venice to her niece Kate Mather, "It is a curious fate that has made the most domestic woman in the world,—the one most fond of a home, a fixed home, and all her own things about her,—that has made such a woman a wanderer for nearly twenty years." On this Fourth of July, her last, she had seen American flags flying from the balconies of expatriates, yet had forgotten the date herself until the flags reminded her of home. Home remained good to her, her popularity in the United States guaranteeing her publication in one of the nation's premier outlets, *Harper's New Monthly Magazine,* and earning her a cover photo on *Harper's Bazar*. By 1893, she had been living in Europe for thirteen years and planned eventually to return to America. But, she lamented to Kate: "I am so tired of changing, and sometimes so disheartened at the thought of all the labor that must be gone through before a new place is any where near comfortable,—that it seems as if, after I am settled this time, I shall never have the strength or courage to move again." She had recently left Oxford, England, for Venice and was staying in unsatisfactory rooms at the Casa Biondetti, editing the book version of her last novel, *Horace Chase,* and looking for an apartment where she could have her own things brought from storage in Florence. By mid-October, Woolson found more suitable rooms in the Casa Semitecolo and rediscovered her joy in Venetian life.

Despite frequent complaints about the effort of moving, Woolson was nurtured on movement and travel. In 1839, her parents, Charles Jarvis and Hannah Cooper Pomeroy Woolson, had journeyed as far west as Milwaukee, Wisconsin, stopping in Cooperstown, New York, along the way to visit Hannah's Cooper relatives. When they returned in the late summer, Hannah was pregnant with her sixth daughter, Constance, who was born on March 5, 1840. By April 3rd, three of the little daughters had died of scarlet fever, leaving Constance with two older sisters, Georgiana and Emma. When winter arrived, the family left forever the scene of so much pain to settle in Cleveland, Ohio, where they had friends and opportunity.

As a child, Woolson enjoyed the permanence of a "fixed home" that her letters suggest was idyllic despite the lingering sorrow over so many deaths. More children were born to Jarvis and Hannah—Clara, Alida, who died within a year of her birth, and Charles Jarvis Jr. An array of dogs were also treated as family members. Together, they frequently traveled by wagon, by train, by boat: to Cooperstown, to Mackinac Island, Michigan, to the Ohio religious community at Zoar. Woolson loved the adventure of travel. In her first surviving letter, written while she was still a child in Cleveland's Miss Hayden's School, she quizzes an older girl named Louisa, who was at boarding school in New York: Does Louisa like being away? Does she have a "*fire* in [her] room" or is she "like most boarding-school girls frozen to death?" Does she "sleep in a large room with a great many girls, or in a small one with one girl?" Did she receive any valentines? Was there a show on Washington's Birthday? Did she leave school at Christmas? Even in childhood, Woolson wanted to see, to learn, to go "away from home for a time." And go away she did. She attended Madame Chegaray's School in New York City, years later describing for poet and critic Edmund Clarence Stedman her impressions of the mostly Southern girls who were her classmates.

No letters survive from Woolson's time at school or from the years surrounding the Civil War, which she seems to have spent in Cleveland, but later letters indicate that, her friendship with Southern girls aside, she remained "a red hot abolitionist, Republican and hard-money advocate" (Hayne, Apr. 17, 1876). Throughout her life, she was fascinated with a war whose scenes of battle she never witnessed. The romance and excitement she remembered sometimes caused her to forget the pain and resentment that must have shaped the memories of so many Southerners. One with whom she shared her thoughts of the war was poet Paul Hamilton Hayne, who had fought for the Confederacy. On July 23, 1875, she wrote, "So you were at Sumter.—And I (lately) was on Morris Island! What days they were! After all, we *lived* then. It is in vain for our generation to hope to be any other than 'people who remember.' Sometimes even now, I wake early, and think I hear the distant call of the newsboy far down the street, 'Extra! Extra! All about the last battle!'—And then how we rushed out to get it, how we devoured it, and then hurried down to the 'Soldier's Aid' rooms to do the little that was open to us faraway ones to do,—prepare boxes of supplies for the soldiers." Woolson prepared these supplies for Union soldiers, but at war's end she honored the heroes of the Confederate side and the soldiers from both sides whose unmarked graves she visited when she lived in the South.

Before she moved south where she could visit these graves, Woolson ventured to New York City where she wrote a series of "Letters from Gotham" for the *Daily Cleveland Herald*, the newspaper edited by her sister Clara's husband, George Benedict, and his father. These "Letters" capture images of the city that she later turned into thematic undercurrents of her fiction: the great divide between rich and poor; the marginalization of minorities, in this case New York's Jewish population; the architectural magnificence that destroyed the natural landscape. They portray the city's excess—of clothing, of food, of frenetic activity—but they also celebrate the extraordinary amount of culture available to New Yorkers in libraries, theaters, music halls, and museums. From descriptions of florist shops to iced-in rivers to the 3,500 congregants at the church services of Henry Ward Beecher, the "Letters" are detailed, energetic, and amazed.

Had Woolson remained in New York, she could have become a successful journalist, but her father's death in 1869 was followed in 1871 by George Benedict's death in a train crash. Her sister Emma, Emma's husband, and her sister Georgiana had also died. Although Woolson remained close to Georgiana's widowed husband, Samuel Livingston Mather, he had his own young children to tend. More problematic, Woolson's only brother, Charly, was in constant need of economic support. His emotional state was so precarious that he remained a worry until he committed suicide in 1883.[1] Concerned about Charly, still in mourning for Jarvis Woolson and George Benedict, Woolson, her mother, her widowed sister Clara, and Clara's child Clare lived for a time with relatives in Cooperstown, but Hannah's health and the economic depression of 1873 prompted them to move south.

Woolson's twenty years of wandering began with that move. Her letters offer a window framing the cultures of places where she traveled and lived, from the reconstructing South to a reunified Italy and a colonized Egypt. Beginning with the letters from the South, readers can travel with Woolson through a remarkable number of places that were constructing and reconstructing themselves in the second half of the nineteenth century. Charleston in 1875 was "charming," "the most picturesque city" Woolson visited (Sam Mather, Apr. 25), but just a year later it had become so volatile with the tensions of Reconstruction that she feared to enter it (Eaton, Dec. 10, 1876). Greenbriar in White Sulphur Springs, West Virginia, was insufferably fashionable; isolated areas like Asheville or Shelby, North Carolina, were breathtakingly beautiful. Woolson's response to Asheville illustrates especially well how unspoiled were the more remote destinations. She described the area in many letters, one of the most remarkable to Elizabeth Gwinn Mather, the second wife of Samuel Livingston Mather. The letter narrates a harrowing stage ride during a storm along the French Broad River, which was "rushing and roaring within ten feet of [the stage], and the rocky road just wide enough for [the] wheels" (Dec. 4, 1874). When the storm abated the next day, the "great peaks" of the Smoky Mountains arose "purple and misty," and the river appeared as "the most beautiful small river" Woolson had ever seen.

Because of her growing sense of well-being in the arms of nature and her aversion to a fashionable society that she satirized in her travel writing, by 1875 Woolson seemed ready to embrace an isolated writing life in close contact with nature. In August of that year, she decided to stay, alone, in Goshen, Virginia, in the Appalachian Mountains because she "never was in a better place for writing; mountain air, & absolutely no interruptions" (Hayne, Aug. 26, 1875). Her publications in early

1876 suggest that she had some success, probably with three of her short stories that focus on Civil War themes, "Crowder's Cove," "Old Gardiston," and "In the Cotton Country." She was learning during these years that she would concentrate on fiction, not poetry; that despite writing an award-winning children's book (*The Old Stone House*), she did not like working in this genre; and that she did not like the "mere beauty at the expense of power" she thought too many women writers displayed (Hayne, May 1, 1875). Her isolation in Goshen may have helped her to think through the kind of writer she wished to be, but, even more, it taught her something about the kind of life she wanted to lead. By November, she had begun to feel a "great isolation and loneliness" after being five weeks in a "little cottage-room at some distance from the hotel, entirely alone" during a bout of bad weather (Hayne, All Saint's Day 1875?). As much as she felt overwhelmed by society, she needed human contact as well as privacy to function. Nature and activity within nature were crucial for her, but desolate isolation was debilitating.

After her lonely weeks in Goshen, Woolson returned to St. Augustine and increasingly concentrated on writing short stories and drafting her novel *Anne*. She continued to travel, and her letters reveal visits to Savannah, Georgia; Summerville, South Carolina; Wilmington, North Carolina; and journeys north to Cooperstown, New York. For over six months in 1877 she stayed in a house her sister Clara secured in Yonkers, then she and her mother returned to the warm climate of the South. In December 1879, they again visited Yonkers, and there in brutally cold weather they discussed where in the South they would spend the rest of the winter months. Whatever they decided, their plans were cut short when Hannah died on February 13th. The next letter that survives, dated March 14th from Washington, D. C., shows Woolson gathered with Clara, Clare, and her niece Kate Mather, with no plans for where she would go next. But by November she had booked passage on the Steamship *Gallia* to begin a decade and a half of travel through Europe.

After landing in England in 1880, Woolson continued her habit of grounding herself in the natural environment. She traveled first with Clara and Clare to Menton, France, where she quickly purchased a botany book, having become an avid fern collector when she lived in the South. The three stayed in Menton for only a few months, but long enough for Woolson to gather material for the only long travel narrative that she published in the 1880s, "At Mentone." Once she left Menton, she traveled so widely that her early introduction to Europe must have been exhausting. Her 1880 letters show her in Menton, Florence, Venice, Lucerne, Geneva, and Florence a second time. In 1881, she was in Florence, Siena, Geneva, Engelberg, and Lucerne and in 1882 in Sorrento, Paestum, Salerno, Florence, Baden-Baden, Dresden, Cologne, and London. Despite the months she spent in Switzerland, she used it as the setting for only one of her stories, "At the Château of Corrine," which she drafted in 1881 but did not publish until 1887. Rather, she looked backward in her second novel, *For the Major,* to the mountains she had loved in North Carolina and began to use her favorite Italian cities, especially Florence and Venice, for her short fiction.

When Woolson began her travels in Europe, she accompanied Clara and Clare, but she soon decided to remain alone in the cities she, unlike Clara, loved. She stayed, for example, in Rome through the winter of 1881, though her stubbornness reduced "everybody at home to serious preparations for [her] funeral" (Stedman, Aug. 11, 1881). Increasingly, she created a sense of home by securing rooms for extended periods of time. The longest and happiest was the period from December 1886 to December 1889 in the Villa Brichieri on Bellosguardo Hill in Florence. From here she recalled the swamps and orange groves of Florida in her novel *East Angels* and the coast of Georgia and the banks of Lake Superior in *Jupiter Lights.* Here, as well, she enjoyed the friendship of Henry James, who also rented rooms in the Villa Brichieri in April and May of 1887.

Although some writers today portray Woolson as a woman craving James's attention and haunting his imagination, others see their relationship as based on an equal commitment to their craft. They seem to have corresponded frequently, but only four letters survive because both believed that letters should remain private. James, especially, raised questions about privacy in his story "The Aspern Papers," which skewers a "publishing scoundrel" who wanted to edit the letters of a dead writer. Although James advocated burning personal letters and likely burned many of those written to and by Woolson, he reviewed as many as fifteen collections of letters himself. The scoundrel in him and us compels us to read letters that were meant to remain private. Intersecting the private and the public, letters from the past represent the gossip networks we have multiplied in today's technological world. By today's standards, Woolson gossips lightly: Tolstoy, she has on good authority, neglects his wife and children; Frances Hodgson Burnett, the author of *Little Lord Fauntleroy,* tries to seem younger than she is; British writer Ouida makes a fool out of herself with too many lovers and fails to support her mother; Rudyard Kipling is too young to marry.

Beyond providing gossip about the once-famous, Woolson's letters help us to tease out the ordinary concerns of a far from ordinary woman. They show us someone who eschewed fashion but could be a bit of a fashionista herself when she described fellow writer Elizabeth Stuart Phelps as a dress reformer who wore clothes without beauty, the point being "to look as man-ish as possible" (Stedman, Jan. 20, 1875). But when Woolson succumbed to the pressure to buy herself an expensive dress, she regretted it. Though hers was a gilded age, her pocketbook was not. Her letters provide clues to how women of small means traveling alone were treated, how they judged what places were safe to walk in, how they negotiated rooms of their own separate from expensive public hotels. And they show the private anguish of a woman who knew too well that she lived on the underside of the huge divide between the upper and middle classes of the Gilded Age. When financial worries or exhaustion and illness depressed her, she turned as do so many today to prescription drugs. Although she knew the danger of drug abuse, having seen her brother's emotional problems exacerbated by morphine, she contacted a strange doctor rather than her trusted physician in the final days of her life, begging for morphine to help her through sleepless nights brought on by illness and despair.

Woolson's letters remind us that the nineteenth century, like our own, was fraught not only with social and gender inequity, but also with practices that were destroying the natural landscape. Woolson watched industrialism transform the forested city of her childhood and pollute the rivers so much that Ohio's Cuyahoga caught on fire. She bemoaned the rising tourism that eventually brought "grandees" to St. Augustine, "those old New York City families who come down from the Dutch times & have 'Van' in their names somewhere; people who have been rich for generations and absolutely know nothing of their own country outside of the 'City,' although very familiar of course with Europe!" (Hayne, All Saint's Day, 1875?). She saw railroads come to Florida, and she knew that conspicuous wealth would alter forever the landscape of Asheville, North Carolina, when George Vanderbilt chose it as the setting for Biltmore, his 250-room mansion. As she wrote in her novel *Horace Chase*, the one "solace" of the Civil War "was the check it gave to the advance of those horrible railroads. . . . [W]hen you perceive that your last acre of primitive forest is forever gone, then you will repent. And you will begin to cultivate wildness."

Not only do Woolson's letters uncover a backstory about her world, they also show how the act of letter writing itself helped her to maintain a connection to those she cared about. Her letters take on a different tone depending on the correspondent. Those to Dr. William Wilberforce Baldwin, the favorite physician of American and British expatriates, share her battles with depression as do many of her letters to family. For financial advice, she turned to her nephew Sam Mather, who was making a fortune in iron mining. Her correspondence with him also reminded her of the days when Cleveland was her home and he the boy she saw reflected in photographs of his own children that she frequently asked him to send. Other letters to family or to her girlhood friend Arabella Carter Washburn reminisce about life at home. Those in the 1870s to Paul Hamilton Hayne show her supporting his efforts to write poetry that would appeal to a northern audience even as she is deciding whether to concentrate her own writing on poetry or fiction. Clarence Stedman, who eventually edited a multivolume anthology of American literature that included Woolson's story "The Lady of Little Fishing," became a trusted friend to whom she wrote about her literary taste, and Henry Mills Alden, an editor at Harper's, expressed in his work thoughts on spirituality she shared. Woolson's correspondence with politician and Lincoln biographer John Hay and his wife Clara developed in the 1880s after Sam Mather married Clara Hay's sister, Flora Stone. Her letters to the Hays contain much social gossip, but also reflect a deep interest in Lincoln and his Civil War presidency. Woolson's letters to Henry James show her esteem for a man whose work she found her "true country, [her] real home" (May 7, 1883), and those to and about William Dean Howells, the influential editor of *Atlantic Monthly*, suggest that he was an enigma whose goodwill she needed to cultivate.

When she sailed for Europe, Woolson had published over fifty poems, more than a dozen travel narratives, a collection of nine of her nearly forty short stories, and had drafted her first novel for adults. Her literary reputation was building and as a result she found it even harder to escape society in Europe than she had in the United States. No paparazzi followed her about, but she succumbed to the nineteenth-century equivalent by having photographs taken, a portrait medallion made of her profile, and a bust cast by the sculptor Richard Greenough. As much as this notoriety pained Woolson, it also gave her access to some of the most cultured people of the day. They took her to plays and museums, they loaned her books, they introduced her to Oxford dons and American diplomats. But because she had no fixed cultural circle, she could also declare herself free from the trappings of received opinion. Her letters show how she learned about the pronouncements of art critics like John Ruskin, then made her own decisions about what she liked and did not like—nude statues, for example, displaying a form she did not appreciate because, she quipped, she had no experience with nude bodies. This ability to declare her own taste is even more apparent in her comments on the literature of her day. She read the work of writers we continue to revere: Dickens, George Eliot, Robert and Elizabeth Barrett Browning, Dostoyevsky, Turgenev, Ibsen. On February 12, 1882, she wrote to Henry James an extraordinary analysis of his *Portrait of a Lady*, arguing that he did not allow us to know if Isabel Archer ever loved her husband and that in his future writing he should commit himself to a portrait of a woman who knows how to love. She had opinions on mass-market literature as well, and her letters from both the United States and Europe contain assessments of once-popular writers like Oliver Bell Bunce, Henry Lynden Flash, Katherine Macquoid, and Sarah Piatt.

Woolson's comments on her own writing and her negotiations with publishers reveal how much power they wielded on her professional life: early on Appletons' reneged on promised royalties and Harper's asked her not to write so much about the Civil War lest she offend southern readers; later an unnamed publisher wooed her to contract only with them but she refused because Harper's treated her well; others asked her to write for the lucrative children's market she disparaged. Whether she was writing about a northern school teacher who fails to understand the freed slaves he was trying to teach ("King David"), an androgynous child who raises questions about gender identity ("Felipa"), an impoverished American wife of an Italian peasant ("The Front Yard"), the marginalization of women writers and artists ("'Miss Grief,'" "The Street of the Hyacinth"), or the fruits of imperialism in Egypt ("Cairo in 1890"), Woolson rose to fame without ever selling out to the demands of the marketplace.

Fame and the glamour of Europe were not, however, enough, so Woolson's letters from Europe express an increasing sense of homelessness. To Stedman, she wrote, "I should never be anything but American. [. . .] The Lake-country & Mackinac, the beautiful South, the farming-country of Ohio—these are the scenes that I belong to" (April 30, 1883). To Henry James, she confided, "I suppose there never was a woman so ill-fitted to do without a home as I am. I am constantly trying to make temporary homes out of impossible rooms at hotels & pensions" (Aug. 30, 1882). By 1889, the glow of Florence had faded, and Woolson was becoming tired and depressed. With the financial help of Clara and her nephew Sam, she was able to sail for Corfu and then Egypt, remaining in Cairo until mid-April, 1890. Where Clara cut short her visit because she found Cairo "perfectly detestable, & [had] but one wish: namely—to get away" (Sam Mather, Jan. 31, 1890), Woolson adored the city and all she saw in its vicinity. On January 18th, she wrote to Dr. Baldwin that her "imaginations of Egypt,—vivid and highly colored as they were,—[fell] far below the reality. The picturesqueness of everything, the queerness of everything, the solemnity, the age, the color—all [was] extraordinary." All of Woolson's letters from Cairo voice the same energy and enthusiasm, whether she is describing the Nile, the Holy Land, or the minarets and narrow streets of the old city. Returning from Cairo, she shared with Henry Mills Alden a profound recognition: "Traveling—the actual seeing of far countries and their customs—gives one a much wider vision; it then becomes very difficult to go back to the narrow ideas which one once had, & which one's best friends, perhaps, still retain" (May 11, 1890).

Woolson's trip to Cairo gave her a new burst of energy when she returned to England, first to Cheltenham and then Oxford. From Cairo, she had written to Alden, "I shall do no travel sketches in [the] future. They take an immense amount of time, and, when done, what are they! It is a pity, for if I could put down the joy, the heavenly delight which the strangeness & beauty of the East gave me, it would be a book of heaven!" (Jan. 17, 1890). But her memories of the trip so haunted her that she contracted with Harper's to write travel narratives about Corfu and Cairo.

She also began work on her last novel, *Horace Chase*, in which she would look backward to her memories of Asheville and St. Augustine. She remembered her favorite places in Italy as she set "Dorothy" in Florence and "A Christmas Party" in Venice. Although she had not lived in London since 1884, she published "In Sloane Street," the only story she set in England, in 1892. The story seems inspired partly by her memory of living in Sloane Street in 1884 and partly by an 1890 train accident that her friend Dr. Baldwin saw and that surely reminded her of the death of her brother-in-law George Benedict years earlier.

Woolson's publication schedule in the 1890s reveals a productive period. But it was also physically exhausting and her letters are filled with complaints about her health and her fear that she had to keep writing at an unsustainable pace to make the money she needed. Yet to hear only depression and exhaustion in these letters is to miss the times she enjoyed crew races at Oxford, or rowed herself on the Thames, or rambled through Thomas Gray's country churchyard at Stoke Poges. That the English weather made these days too few prompted her to decide to find rooms once again in Venice, this time for an extended stay. Having made her decision, she wrote in 1893 to an unknown recipient, that she found that she was "still capable of joy."

For seven months in Venice, Woolson did find moments of joy. Her rooms at the Casa Biondetti were unsatisfactory, but by October she found more suitable ones in the Casa Semitecolo. She enjoyed gossiping about the visiting royalty, borrowed books from her friend Daniel Curtis's extensive library, attended the theater, spent evenings floating in a gondola along the lagoons, and bought a dog she named Othello, the Moor of Venice. Although she still found the society of Venice delightful, she turned down a Christmas invitation, preferring to remain alone and reminisce about the Christmases of her youth. She composed one of her last surviving letters to Henry Mills Alden on January 1, 1894, and in it prefigures what was almost certainly her suicide on January 24th.[2] She has, she tells Alden, abandoned her plan to write another novel. She is "finishing up the fringes and edges of [her] literary work," convinced that she "shall do very little more." Some have speculated that she succumbed because she felt betrayed by Henry James, but nothing in her letters confirms this. A year earlier she had expressed confidence in her publishers at Harper's and the fact that they brought out her work posthumously suggests that they did not abandon her. She may have suffered financial losses during the bank failures of 1893–94, but her letters indicate that she felt her own money was safe. More likely, she simply grew too tired to persevere in a world where she could not escape to the peace and security of "a convent" because "there are no worldly convents." Ill and discouraged, she chose death, plunging from her window to the pavement below the Casa Semitecolo. When we read Woolson's private letters and her body of public writing, we can imagine her, ever the wit even in her despair, writing, as she said in her last letter to Alden, her "new effusions on another star, and [sending] them back to [us] by telepathy."

Notes

1. Charles Jarvis Woolson Jr. is listed in a ledger at the Los Angeles County Recorder's Office (Register of Deaths, Sept. 1877 to Jan. 1888, Book I, Health Department) as having committed suicide by poison.

2. Woolson's death was initially reported as a suicide until the family protested. The letter from Marie Holas appended to this edition of letters supports an interpretation of suicide.

Selected Bibliography

For a full bibliography, see the Constance Fenimore Woolson Society's website at http://blogs.bgsu.edu/cfwoolson/.

Barton, David, and Nigel Hall, eds. *Letter Writing as Social Practice.* Philadelphia: John Benjamins, 2000.

Boyd, Anne E. *Writing for Immortality: Women Writers and the Emergence of High Literary Culture in America.* Baltimore: Johns Hopkins University Press, 2004.

Brehm, Victoria, ed. *Constance Fenimore Woolson's Nineteenth Century.* Detroit: Wayne State University Press, 2001.

Brehm, Victoria, and Sharon L. Dean, eds. *Constance Fenimore Woolson: Selected Stories and Travel Narratives.* Knoxville: University of Tennessee Press, 2004.

Dean, Sharon L. *Constance Fenimore Woolson: Homeward Bound.* Knoxville: University of Tennessee Press, 1995.

———. *Constance Fenimore Woolson and Edith Wharton: Perspectives on Landscape and Art.* Knoxville: University of Tennessee Press, 2002.

Diffley, Kathleen, ed. *To Live and Die: Collected Stories of the Civil War.* Durham: Duke University Press, 2004.

Edel, Leon. *The Life of Henry James.* 5 vols. Philadelphia: Lippincott, 1943–80.

Elsden, Annamaria Formichella. *Roman Fever: Domesticity and Nationalism in Nineteenth-Century American Women's Writing.* Columbus: Ohio State University Press, 2004.

Gordon, Lyndall. *A Private Life of Henry James.* New York: Norton, 1998.

Henkins, David M. *The Postal Age: The Emergence of Modern Communications in Nineteenth-Century America.* Chicago: University of Chicago Press, 2006.

Lodge, David. *Author, Author.* New York: Viking, 2004.

Maguire, Elizabeth. *The Open Door.* New York: Other Press, 2008.

Moore, Rayburn S. *Constance F. Woolson.* New Haven, Conn.: Twayne, 1963.

———, ed. *For the Major and Selected Short Stories.* New Haven, Conn.: College and University Press, 1967.

O'Donnell, Kevin, and Helen Hollingsworth. *Seekers of Scenery: Travel Writing from Southern Appalachia, 1840–1900.* Knoxville: University of Tennessee Press, 2004.

Petry, Alice Hall. "'Always, Your Attached Friend': The Unpublished Letters of Constance Fenimore Woolson to John and Clara Hay." *Books at Brown,* 29–30 (1982–83): 11–107. John Hay Papers, John Hay Library, Brown University.

Schriber, Mary Suzanne. *Writing Home: American Women Abroad, 1830–1920.* Charlottesville: University Press of Virginia, 1997.

Tennant, Emma. *Felony.* London: Jonathan Cape, 2002.

Tóibín, Colm. *The Master*. New York: Scribner, 2004.

Torsney, Cheryl B. *Constance Fenimore Woolson: The Grief of Artistry*. Athens: University Press of Georgia, 1989.

Torsney, Cheryl B., ed. *Critical Essays on Constance Fenimore Woolson*. New York: Macmillan, G. K. Hall, 1992.

Weimer, Joan, ed. *Women Artists, Women Exiles: "'Miss Grief'" and Other Stories*. By Constance Fenimore Woolson. New Brunswick, N.J.: Rutgers University Press, 1988.

Letters

To Louisa (Benedict/CFW, 15–16)[1]

My dear Louisa.

Sister Emma told me when she first came home that you wished me to write to you, and although it is a good while since then, yet I thought "better late than never," and have determined to write you a good long letter. How do you like being at boarding school? Sister Emma has been on a journey in the country for her health. She has been quite sick ever since she came from New York. She took a bad cold and has had some trouble with her lungs. We hope the journey has done her some good. Sister Emma is very kind to us children; she gives me music lessons. Clara, Charley and I, still go to Miss Hayden's school; I should like to go to boarding school very much. I always liked the idea of going away from home for a time. I expect to go to Wisconsin next summer on a visit which I think will be delightful.

Has there been any cold weather in New York this winter, and have you had a fire in your room, or like most boarding-school girls frozen to death? Do you sleep in a large room with a great many girls, or in a small one with one girl? Do'nt I puzzle you with such a host of questions? . . . Do all your school go out to walk together. . . . Was there any great show in New York on Washington's Birthday? In the morning I thought there was going to be grand doings, so I took Clara and Charley out with me. We found a good place and pretty soon the soldiers came by. Then we went across the street and waited for them half an hour at least and as they did not come, I went home, for I was half frozen. Did you have any Valentines? I did not have one. Did you go away from school Christmas day, and did you enjoy yourself? . . . I only hope now, my dear Louisa, that you will write to me, if you have any time, even if it should be but a short note.

Yours ever,
Constance Woolson.

Notes

1. Benedict identifies Louisa as a childhood friend of Woolson's. Since both Woolson and her younger siblings are still attending Miss Hayden's School, this is her earliest surviving letter, written in the late 1840s. Throughout this edition, readers should consult the appendix for unannotated names.

To Flora Payne Whitney (Benedict/CFW, 16–17)[1]

[1863/64?]

"Seems to me if I had a friend in exile across the ocean"—In exile! I wish I could be in "exile" too, if I could visit the most beautiful and famous places the world can show! You are the most fortunate young lady I know, and ought to be the happiest. I envy you to that extent that the tenth commandment makes me shudder, for although I am willing to settle down after thirty years are told, I do not care to be forced into quiescence yet awhile. But whether we will or no, we are quiet to the depths of stagnation . . . But as you express a desire to hear the "news," I will scrape up whatever is afloat, although it must sound very flat if read in Florence la Bella or on the beautiful Rhine. And, by the way, for my sake, please note every inch of the enchanted river, for I am Rhine-mad, and shall be waiting with several thousand questions on the subject or ever you take off your bonnet. . . . [2] Shall you bring home any books? If so, do bring some French works. I have forgotten everything I ever knew about the language, but of course you can speak it fluently? Well, Flo, this is a stupid letter, but what can one say of this stupid place to a person visiting the fairest corners of the earth? Of one thing rest assured—that is, that I was truly glad to hear from you, and I shall be still more glad to see you home again . . . Come home prepared to find a string of questions and a heartfelt welcome from

Your friend,
Constance.

Notes

1. Flora was in Europe in 1863 and '64.
2. "Or" may be Benedict's mistake for "if."

To Arabella Carter, later Washburn (Benedict/Voices, 271)[1]

Here I am, perched up on the old red lounge in Gramp's favourite corner room. We came down yesterday by rail, having made a start the day before with the horses and concluded the weather was too uncertain to risk such a long ride. Gramp did not feel at home in the nice buggy and harness; that was easy to see! He missed the antediluvian relic in which he had so long been accustomed to rampage through the country. I made him take the pretty white robe also, which was another grief. So we dined at Richfield and returned home the same day, discovering Gram and Sarah Hayden carousing over oyster soup and evidently discomfited at our arrival. Indeed the domestic horizon looked so threatening that we concluded, if we were going to Zoar at all, we had better start the next morning. So we did and passed over the Pittsburg road and the famous Tuscarawas Branch with the usual enjoyment, especially of the tunnel, where, of course, we stopped and breathed coal smoke for ten minutes. We sent our bags up to the Hotel by the old white horse, and Father and I walked. The afternoon was perfectly delightful, warm, hazy, and the trees were gloriously coloured. The light yellow and orange tints had blown away but the oaks were gorgeous and I think I like them the best. We found the Hotel perfectly quiet and cleaner than I ever saw it. Everything has evidently just been washed and scrubbed. Everybody seems very glad to see us, and this morning the chickens were unexceptionable and the bretzels delicious. The town is just the same. Everything is as usual, even the toothache! If you were only here I could enjoy myself very much, as the weather is warm and the flat in good condition. I would challenge you to a row to the Island this very minute. I presume you would not go, as I fancy we are more particular about our hands than we used to be! If you would not row, you might sit in the stern of my boat—see how good-natured I am.

"Horse at the door." I must go and be murdered! Farewell.[2]

Notes

1. The letter appears to have been written when the Woolsons still visited Zoar, before the death of Woolson's father in 1869.

2. Woolson feared horses.

To Miss Arabella Carter, later Washburn (Benedict/CFW, 17–18)[1]

. . . There is no danger of my thinking of, and liking you less now that you are going to be married. But I have felt such a conviction that you would some day lose your interest in me, and also all outside things, that I thought best to prepare for the worst . . . I don't mean to say that you will even come actually to dislike me, but you will probably take a middle course. You have been the best friend I ever had and have done and said countless kind things for me. I shall never change . . . and if, after all, things should not turn out as I fear, and "Mrs Washburn" continues the same friend that "Belle" has been for so many years, don't you suppose I shall be glad and grateful? Of course I shall. Time will show. . . . You don't know how I rejoice in your happiness, Belle. I am so, so glad for you. A man's true, earnest love is a great gift. If you do not accept it and enjoy it, I shall—shake you! Why can't you fling all your misgivings to the winds and be simply happy? The glory of your life has come to you. Everything else is trivial compared to it. You and he are really alone in the world together. Two souls that love always are. Do give up your past life and duties and BE HAPPY!

Notes

1. Beginning in 1870/71, Benedict refers to Arabella Carter as Mrs. Washburn; therefore, this letter was written prior to those years.

To Arabella Carter Washburn (Benedict/CFW, 18–19)[1]

New York.

. . . After your long silence you could not have chosen a better moment for your letter. It came two minutes after I had said "Good-Bye" to Clara and George and it was so welcome that unconsciously my wrath at your procrastination faded away. There was a little danger of my feeling the void of loneliness after ten days of Clara and constant excitement in the way of music and glittering shows, and your letter dropped down at the very moment it was wanted. I think you have been very bad not to write for so long. You may say, perhaps, that I did not write to you when you were abroad, but that is a very different case, for then you had the constant companionship of your husband, whereas I am a desolate spinster . . . Since you were so———as to marry, I have drawn myself into my shell and although I have, here and everywhere, plenty of nice acquaintances, I have no longer a friend such as you were in those days. I suppose I shall never have such a friend again. For that dash you may substitute "mean," "sensible," "selfish" or "wise," whichever you please. For my part I highly approve of you in the character of Wife and Mother, but for all that I am none the less lonely.

"The October Idyll" was wordy, but I am only feeling my way, now. I shall do better in time, but I never cease to wonder at my success. If you think it is easy to advance, even so short a distance as I have, just try it.

Notes

1. The references to "An October Idyl" (*Harper's New Monthly Magazine,* Nov. 1870) and to Clara and George identify this date as sometime between 1870 and George Benedict's death in 1871. Benedict may have added the extra *l* in "Idyl." Readers should consult the Chronology when titles of Woolson's works are easy to identify by the letter's date.

To Messrs. Roberts Brothers (McGill)

Saturday, Nov. 12th, [1870]
Messrs. Roberts Brothers.
Boston.

I have commenced the translation of one of George Sand's stories entitled "La Mare au Diable."[1]—Will you be so kind as to inform me whether this work of translating the series is open to all competitors, and also if there is danger of my volume being a duplicate.

Of course I am well aware that any translation must stand entirely upon its own merits, but before finishing it, I shall be greatly obliged if you will answer, addressing

Miss Constance F. Woolson

N° 49 West 32d St
New York City

Notes

1. George Sand published *The Devil's Pool* in 1846.

To Mary L. Booth (Princeton)

N° 49 West 32d St
Thursday, Feb. 2d, 1871
Miss Mary L. Booth.

Dear Madame.

Your note enclosing the cheque for fifty dollars reached me this morning and I am much obliged to you.

I would rather not have my name appear with the article, but if it is necessary, please give only "Constance Fenimore," as I have taken that for a nom de plume.[1]

Truly yours
Constance Fenimore Woolson.

Notes

1. Woolson is referring to one of two essays "Extremities. The Head and Hands" or "Extremities. The Feet" published in the Oct. 21 and Nov. 21, 1871 issues of *Harper's Bazar*, the magazine Mary Booth edited.

To Messrs. Roberts Brothers (McGill)

Feb. 25th, 1871
Messrs. Roberts Brothers.

I have completed my translation of "La Mare Au Diable," by George Sand, and am now engaged in copying it.[1] This morning I noticed the enclosed paragraph, among the book notices in the "Cleveland Herald."—Will this make any difference in your acceptance of my translation; provided, of course, that my version pleases you.—

I have taken the greatest pains with it, and cannot but feel almost sure of its merits.

Respectfully &c—
Miss Constance F. Woolson.
N° 131 St Clair St
Cleveland
Ohio

Notes

1. Woolson never published a translation of George Sand's 1846 novel *The Devil's Pool.*

To Unknown Recipient (Hayes)[1]

131 St Clair St
Cleveland. Ohio
Aug. 24th, 1871

Coming back to the intense heat of Cleveland, how often have I sighed for the Island, and envied you both, dear friends, for the fresh air and the blue waters of the beautiful Straits; walking through the noisy streets with the sun glaring up from the pavement, how often have I thought of the path through the cedars on the hill, the blue-green spruces of the British Landing, the swaying harebells on the precipice, the rings of juniper and the many-fingered larches, the last two so inseparably connected with Mackinac in my mind that I am quite willing to believe they grow no where else in all the whole wide world.—I try to solace myself, however, with the delicious fruits with which the market overflows. If it were possible, I should try to send you a store of the best; but by sad experience I have learned the reverse. Ripe fruit will not travel, and Stewards know not honesty. We have kept house in Mackinac, and we know!—An exception, however, may be made in favor of grapes; do you like them? If yes, when they are ripe, may I send you some?—

We had a pleasant sail through Huron, and after spending a day in Detroit, reached home on Monday evening by cars. After all, one of the sweetest pleasures of traveling is the home-coming, don't you think so?—It is so pleasant to be missed! Our darling little Plum stood on the piazza as we drove up to the cottage, the breeze lifting her red-golden curls from her white shoulders; and her blue eyes like stars; as she recognized us, she began to dance up and down, chanting in a little monotone "They're pum home,—they're pum home! I'se so glard."—

Then came a train of friends with "how do you do," and "have you enjoyed yourselves"; next, unpacking, and reading the accumulated letters awaiting us; then a little aimless wandering round as though we were travelers still; and finally a settling down into well worn habits,—a lifting up of the old burdens, (not too heavy,—you know; only ballast to keep us steady)—and home life is started again to go on no one knows how long.

Benedene has the idylic Scene. I gave it to her as soon as I arrived and we read it together. Then she carried it away and I have not seen it since, but I hope she will allow me to take it again, as I want to give it a fair study. Although this one reading was, of course, hasty, still I can say that I like the stray leaf from your summer book very much; it seems to me that you have caught the sunny atmosphere of a

Mackinac summer morning, the bright presence of a group of fresh young minds, and the very spirit of a sparkling original conversation, hovering from topic to topic as such conversations always do,—perhaps their greatest charm. Such is the general impression left upon my mind by the one reading,—but I warn you that when I obtain the Ms. again, ~~an~~ I shall study it critically and go hunting for faults! If I find any, shall I tell you? And I must thank you for so gracefully bringing in my name. I had no suspicion of any such compliment and was surprised and pleased. Some persons do not care for notice, but I like it,—*dearly*.—My poor name! It has never had half a chance for life. Most people think it, and its owner, far too stiff for common use. I presume Benedene has already sent you her own thanks. She looks as lovely as a damask rose this summer.—

I have not begun to work yet but this afternoon will see the old blank book in place, with a roll of lead pencils! Some charming letters (*with* enclosures) were waiting for me when I returned, and I feel inspired to go on.—This I throw in, as part of my high pressure system for you. On the whole, how glad you must be that I do not *live* in Mackinac!

Give my love to the Island. It is a haunted place to me; every path has its spirit, every rock its lingering associations. I was there when I was sixteen and seventeen; twenty and twenty five, and,—but the two last times—perhaps it is as well not to be *too* explicit!

I hope to hear from you, both or one, as you please—If there is anything I can do for you I shall be so much pleased if you will call upon me.

With kindest regards from my Mother, I am your attached friend
Constance Fenimore Woolson.

If you see the Hulberts, please mention our safe arrival, &c. &c.

Notes

1. Because this letter, with no salutation, is filed in the William Dean Howells collection at the Hayes Presidential Library, it may be to him, but the tone seems too familiar for 1871.

To Edward Everett Hale (Pennsylvania)

131 St Clair St
Cleveland. Ohio
Dec. 1st, 1871
Rev. E. E. Hale.

Dear Sir.

I received your letter on my way to church yesterday, and it brightens all the Thanksgiving services. I thank you for it.

As regards the "sharpness," perhaps it was not so much that you were sharp, as that I was soft; even a touch will disturb a jelly, you know.

I knew nothing of the author of the newspaper article I sent you; but I feel very sorry for {him / her} since {he / she} had lived to be called a "stark fool" by Mr Hale himself.—But, if I should write out what I recently heard from an army officer who used to attend your church in Boston, I am sure you could not help being pleased; honest and appreciative praise is always pleasant, no matter how well we deserve it. I am, unfortunately, very shy, and therefore when I go east in the spring to visit the bones of my ancestors at Mt Woolaston, (if there is any such place,), I shall be obliged to content myself with a distant view in the church, to verify the officer's pleasant sayings.[1]

I am glad to know that some of my articles are to appear in the "Old and New." I believe I once asked you to place a Nom de Plume after "Mint, Anise and Cinnamon." If not too late, I retract the request; it shall bear my true signature.

I hope you will accept "Talk." I should so much like to have it appear in the "Old and New."

I send back the "Swallow," in the hope that you may yet give it a resting place. At the time when Mr Bryant's translation appeared, it excited some attention among the Italian scholars here on account of the home versions. One of our editors made up an article on the subject which I send.—it explains itself.[2]

As the article had only a local circulation, I thought it might make no difference with my verses. If, however, the newspapers type has spoiled them for the "Old & New," then, I suppose,—these poor little rhymes must come sadly home again.

You speak of "my friend Mr Alden."—He little suspects what a friend he has out here in the Forest City! His cordial words, kind letters,—and sympathy when my brother was killed at New Hamburg last winter, I can never forget.[3] He may extend the same kindness to all his contributors, but that makes no difference in its value. It was a great deal to me,—it came at the right time,—and he has my gratitude and earnest good wishes.

In return for the brightness you gave to my Thanksgiving, I wish that you may have a very happy Christmas.

Truly yours
Constance Fenimore Woolson.

Notes

1. See Woolson's sketch "The Bones of Our Ancestors," *Harper's New Monthly Magazine*, Sept. 1873.

2. Hale's magazine *Old and New* merged with *Scribner's* in 1875. I have found no record of anything by Woolson titled "Mint, Anise and Cinnamon," "Talk," or "Swallow." Bryant is likely William Cullen Bryant.

3. Woolson is referring to her brother-in-law George Benedict, who was killed in a train accident.

To Jane Averell Carter (Benedict/CFW, 37)[1]

[1871?]

Nothing could have exceeded the kindness of the Mathers. It has actually made me think better of everybody—of the whole world—to find such real and generous goodness a fact. Proved by actions; not by words merely. And it touches me much to think that in helping C. they are all (Clara and the Mathers) helping me as well; wishing to save me from anxiety as much as they can. It is a good world, after all, isn't it?

Notes

1. The letter was likely written after the death of Clara Woolson Benedict's husband in 1871.

To Edward Everett Hale (Pennsylvania)

N° 131 St Clair St
Cleveland. Ohio
May 29th, [1872?]
Rev. E. E. Hale.

Dear Sir.

I am glad to hear that my "Walpurgis Night" is in type; I do not understand exactly what the phrase means, but it looks right, and I have a sanguine temperament.—

Perhaps I ought to apologize for sending so many inquiries after the verses, but it is less than a year since I made my first attempt in writing for the magazines, and I have always supposed that the Mss. of unknown contributors were in imminent peril of wastebasket oblivion and destruction.

I shall be proud to see <u>my</u> verses in "Old and New" and I do not think Editors are so cruel after all;—Although my cousin Miss S. F. Cooper <u>did</u> assure me solemnly last summer that they were from necessity "Iron-hearted despots,"—and advised me never to enter the circle where they reign.

Truly yours
Constance Fenimore Woolson.

To Mary L. Booth (Woolson)

131 St Clair St
Cleveland. Ohio
Jan. 27th, 1973

Dear Miss Booth.

Your note enclosing the cheque came this morning.—Thank you.[1]

I am glad you liked the verses well enough to print them; I did not think you would.—

I see you have been giving a reception to Miss Faithful.[2] How pleasant!—I mean the Reception, not Miss F.—of whose greatness I have but a vague understanding.—Such meetings can only be held in New York.—I shall live there sometime—if I live long enough.

Truly Yours
Constance F. Woolson.

Notes

1. The payment is likely for Woolson's poem "The Greatest of All is Charity," published in *Harper's Bazar*, Feb. 8, 1873, the magazine Mary Booth edited.

2. Britain's Emily Faithfull (1835–95) founded a printing company where only women could publish. The misspelling is Woolson's.

To R. R. Bowker (LOC)

131 St Clair St
Cleveland. Ohio
May 31st, 1873

Dear Sir.

The "Evening Mail" is my only New York daily; I read it regularly and faithfully. Many times, therefore, during the last two years, (which period embraces my whole existence as a writer) when reading your magazine criticisms, I have sighed over the adjectives that fell to my lot.—Now, however, on returning from a journey down the Ohio River, and looking over the "Mails" piled up during my absence, I find in your notices of the "Harper" and "Atlantic" for June, the enclosed lines.

As, with all the sighing, I have never doubted the justice of your censure, so now I do not doubt the praise.—Seriously, Sir, I thank you.

By the way, although it was against myself, I could not help laughing over your paragraph on my poor "Commonplace" in "Lippincott" for last February. It was happy, terse, and to the point, and in spite of myself, I enjoyed it.

It must be charming to be a critic. The criticisms in the "Mail" always seem honest; they are not made to order.

Yours, &c
Constance Fenimore Woolson.

To William Dean Howells (Houghton)

N° 61 West 17th St
New York City
Oct 27th, [1873?]
Mr W. D. Howells.

I send "Wilhelmina" reconstructed, having taken out 1308 words of "sister-in-law"; the Ms. looks longer than the first copy because it is not so closely written.

Will you be so kind as to send me a line here, acknowledging its arrival? I expect to leave next week for Florida, and shall have no settled address for some time.

I have received no cheque for "Solomon." I mention it thinking it may have been lost.

It has given me great pleasure to enter within the "Atlantic" circle. You may be amused to know that my three models, whose styles I study and admire, are

George Eliot
Bret Harte
W. D. Howells

Quite unlike, are they not?

Yours Truly
Constance F. Woolson.

To Edmund Clarence Stedman (Beinecke)

St Augustine. Fla.
April 13th, [1874]

Dear Mr Stedman.

This evening's mail brings me your letter which pleases me so much that I am answering it right away by the light of my one miserable candle so that it may go tomorrow. Yes. "The Florida Beach" came back. I have sent it to the "Galaxy." By the way, since I saw you that seventy-five dollar cheque due me from the "Galaxy" office has arrived safely; I mention it because you offered to stir them up about it.[1]—I should be ever so glad if you can stir up Mr Gilder to publish "Jeannette." Not that it is a good story; but it is weary waiting for a first appearance. They had a story of mine which they don't like, "Peter the Parson"; in my opinion it is the most powerful thing I have ever written.— —Our mutual friend has gone, and Waife has not been seen since he left. The little Argo lies desolate under the dock. However I have sung her praises in a sketch which the ever-cordial and kindly Appleton will publish.—The M. Friend promised to send me your "Lord's Day Gale" which I am most desirous to see.[2] It will probably reach here tomorrow.—Supposing I should take a fancy to tell you what I think of it?— —I have kept track of your homeward journey through the friendly "Arcadian,"—and what a fresh little paper it is!—We ordered it on trial for a few months, but I see I shall have to become a regular subscriber.— — —It is warm here now; my sister has gone and we feel lonely. Nobody walks on the glacis now,—nobody on the sea wall. The Plaega is deserted.[3] The hotels will close this month.—I have not been out on the pine barrens for some time, since the snakes are out, I am told, in battle array. I shall not soon forget your high treason at Ponce de Leon Spring,—the way you looked around, and then calmly said,—"Well,—take it altogether,—on all sides,—it is about the ugliest place I ever saw!"—The joke is that we had all thought so in our hearts all winter, but never dared say so, as it was our only walk.—We shall stay here a month or so longer, I presume.—I shall take great pleasure in reading your article on Tennyson, when, (Alas, when!) I get the magazine. I am curious to see what you will say on some points.—

Excuse the scrawling writing.

Sincerely Your Friend
Constance F. Woolson.

I have so carefully put away your address that I cannot find it, and therefore send this to the care of Mr Gilder.

Notes

1. Woolson is referring to a check for her poem "A Flower of the Snow," published in *The Galaxy* in Jan. 1874; that magazine published a second poem, "The Florida Beach," in Oct. 1874.

2. Woolson is punning on Dickens's novel *Our Mutual Friend* (1864–65). Gentleman Waife is a character in Woolson's travel sketch "A Voyage to the Unknown River" (*Appletons' Journal,* May 1874) and the "little Argo," the name of the boat in that sketch. Stedman's "The Lord's Day Gale" appeared in *Atlantic Monthly,* April 1874.

3. Plaega: playground.

To Edmund Clarence Stedman (Columbia)

Asheville
Buncombe Co. North Carolina
June 12th [1874]

Dear Mr Stedman.

Here we are, up in your "Scribner" mountains, and find them better than the lavender magazine represented. Purple peaks all around, any number of "Gaps" to visit, the wonders of each said to be "more remarkable than anything in Switzerland," &c&c. The element of danger is supplied by rattlesnakes, who,—however, live up on the stone ledges, (like "Elsie Venner," you remember.) and do not come to town "very often"![1]—In St Augustine it was all sailing; here it ~~was~~ is all horseback riding.—I have never lived among real mountains before, and already I feel an affection for Mt Pisgah which I can see from my window. I think, too, that I shall become great friends with the Black Mountain.—For pastime there are two rushing rivers, the lovely French-Broad, and the Swananoa. The mountain springs, too, are bewitching. I cannot pass one without drinking, and go about with a cup slung from my belt. You remember the "Ponce de Leon"? Six months of that charming fountain have given me an abiding thirst.—

In Charleston I purchased the Scribners containing your two articles on Tennyson; also the complete edition of your poems. Our Mutual Friend had previously sent me "The Lord's Day Gale," and the "Scribner" for last November with your article on Mrs Browning. Now then shall I tell you what I think?—I like the "Lord's Day Gale" best.—It seems to me so strong, and yet so simple; like the people it describes.—So briny of the ocean,—so full of sea-storm flavor.—Next to that "Paw in Wall Street."—Then a number,—"Bohemia," "Refuge in Nature," "John Brown," "Surf," "The Protest of Faith," "Horace Greeley," "Spoken at Sea," and "The Undiscovered Country." I must tell you, though, that I have not yet read the two long poems, the "Blameless Prince," and "Alice of Monmouth."—I have, for summer reading, those two, and Geo Eliot's "Legend of Jubal."— — In the "Lord's Day Gale" I was especially impressed by the third verse.—Also the eleventh, twelfth, and thirteenth. In the seventeenth verse that, "a night and day,—a day and night,"—was quite a study for me.—Will you tell me, when you are writing, who "Hypatia" is? I mean the modern one, of course.—[2]

I was charmed with the Tennyson articles, both, and all of both. But do you know I have no recollection of the "Ulysses" you praise so strongly. I must hunt up a copy and read it. How clear sighted your showing up of Rossetti as compared with Tennyson. I, for one, had become confused by the hue and cry after the poets of the Rosetti school, and you define the difference, which I felt, but could not express, even to myself. (But you yourself are in the American hue and cry, after "Joaquin" Miller! I suppose you will say he had the "wilding flavor.")—I was amused at the criticism of a church paper on these two articles. "Mr Stedman," it said, "seems to appreciate Tennyson and praises him highly; the latter, let us assure Mr Stedman, was not necessary. Tennyson holds the King's place &c&c." Now what amused me was this; I know that editor; he is a man of fifty or over, and belongs to the generation that adored Tennyson and saw no flaw. It is only within the last ten years or so, that a younger people have begun to "mistrust the quality of his genius," and "revise the laudatory judgments formerly pronounced" upon him.—That editor is probably entirely ignorant of the new school arising around him. He read poetry when he was young, and now reads none, but holds steadfastly to his youthful decisions and beliefs.—It pleases me that you like "St Agnes" and "In Galahad,"—my favorites.—As outside touches, that was very good about "a group of sturdy refined, comfortable fellows &c&c."—And this, which is so true, only we had never thought of it ourselves: "the great novelists of our day who correspond to the dramatists of a past age"—. By the way, I have never read anything of Landor.—And who pray is "Darley"?[3]—But you will tire of all this.—And so I wo'nt say anything more, not even about the Browning article.—Please remember how far away I am from everything and everybody. These articles of yours have been very charming to me, and I have studied them not a little.

We shall probably remain here all summer. Indeed, my Mother declares that she intends to stay until the railroad is finished. Which will be sometime in the next century. The stage ride to get here is something fearful.

I only like the Arcadian because it has so much literary gossip. A man who lives in the centre of everything do'nt care about that, naturally. I have never lived in that delightful "centre," you know!

I received a very pleasant letter from Mr Gilder, finally accepting a second story.[4] I suspect I am indebted to you for the cordiality of its tone. Thank you.

With regards to Mrs Stedman (and I wish I could have come to her little dinner that night) I am

Sincerely Your Friend,
Constance F. Woolson.

Notes

1. An 1861 novel by Oliver Wendell Holmes.

2. Hypatia of Alexandria (350–70?–415 AD) was one of the first women mathematicians. I have been unable to locate Stedman's "modern" Hypatia in his poem of that title.

3. George Darley (1795–1846), Irish poet, dramatist, and mathematician.

4. Richard Watson Gilder, editor of *Scribner's*, accepted Woolson's stories "Peter the Parson" (Sept. 1874) and "Jeannette" (Dec. 1874).

To Edmund Clarence Stedman (Columbia)

Asheville
Buncombe Co. N.C.
Aug 21st [1874]

My dear Sir.

Thanks for the Tribune notice received last evening. ["L. G. Mc"?] is ever so kind, and altogether I feel comforted.[1] Would you believe it,—the people here have never even seen one of George Eliot's novels,—have never so much as heard the names of Bret Harte or Joaquin Miller,—and speak of Addison as one of the "modern writers!"—One of them, having by chance come across one of my stories, gravely began comparing it to portions of the "Children of the Abbey"![2]—And you must not suppose either that these people are without culture; far from it. Many of them are from old Charleston families, honored Southern names; having become impoverished by the war, they have moved up here to their former summer residences, all they have left of their old estates.—In addition I have been reduced very low by a book which has been presented to me, "The Living Writers of the South." Had you any idea that there were 166 men and 75 women in Dixie at this moment, each and all "eminent in the literature of the 19th century?" The following verse is the first of eight entitled "What She brought Me," by a man named "Flash" of New Orleans ("far beyond any other American poet," my book says)—and several persons have here said they could not read it without tears![3]

"This faded flower that you see
 Was given me a year ago
By one whose dainty little hand
 Is whiter than the snow."

I never before was so far from my base, and really if I do'nt have some literary supplies before long, I shall starve.

What! Write that novel in three months?—No indeed! Nor in six. Nor in four times six perhaps.—But you can do me a great favor if you will. Do you know of any good critic who will look over a Ms. poem, and give me a fair opinion?—Of course I wish to pay for the work and should consider it a regular business transaction.—The truth is I have not the courage to bring out a poem on which no eyes have looked save my own. The thirty or forty now afloat have run the gauntlet, being small and slim; but the grown up fellow now in my hands frightens me.—Would it not be possible for me to get a fair impartial criticism without betraying who I am?—That is what I should prefer. Could you not send me a line of credentials which I could enclose with my Ms. to the critic, and the address merely of my P.O.

Box here?—Probably your influence and name would induce the critic to look over the work, and at the same time, you would not be bothered as you know nothing of the Ms. and only endorse me, personally. I suppose there are men in N.Y. who do such things; but I do'nt know them.—Do'nt send me the name of any high and mighty person; just some good honest steady going critic who is used to criticizing and reviewing.—I am writing in great haste to catch the stage, so can only say that the mountains continue grand and all is well. Am studying ferns.—Have just sent to N.Y. for the magazines; can get nothing here.

With Regard
Yours Truly
Constance F. W.

Notes

1. Woolson is speaking of a review in the New York *Tribune.*
2. A 1796 romance written by Irish novelist Regina Maria Roche.
3. James Wood Davidson's *Living Writers of the South* appeared in 1869. Flash is New Orleans poet Henry Lynden Flash.

To Edmund Clarence Stedman? (Columbia)[1]

[Sept. 6th, 1874]

do not be afraid to make it strong and dramatic." But I am afraid. That is the very point of the difficulty. I shall write it,—and run!—Probably to Australia.—

I have been amusing myself collecting ferns all summer; do you know anything about them? I have a microscope and go climbing around up and down the rocks searching out their plumy green. Mr Pell has been pretending to rusticate at Milford in company with several hundred city people. I hear from the Army people at St Augustine quite frequently. They are alive still.

I have your little photograph stuck up on my wall; but must say it looks like a Brigand with that full beard.—

Very Truly your friend
Constance F. Woolson.
Sept 7th

I wonder if you meant all you said about the stories.—The reason I am so curious is because I have had a contest about them; one person, a literary man too, has given me up as hopelessly lost,—altogether gone astray into the hard realistic tendencies of the day. "Solomon" was bad, it seems. But "Peter" is a great deal "badder." I think of going to live on a desert island. Will you make me a visit once a year?—

Notes

1. Only this fragment, likely to Stedman, survives.

To Edmund Clarence Stedman (Columbia)

Asheville
Sept. 28th [1874]

Dear Mr Stedman.

After three nights without sleep and three days of wearisome traveling including the "last straw" in the shape of a twenty-five mile stageride over the Blue Ridge, I yet read that long letter of yours within ten minutes after my arrival, hat and gloves still on! Does'nt that tell the story?—Now that I am back in this quaint old Eagle Hotel, with a bright fire burning on the little hearth, and the simple-minded Moravian family, who are our hosts, coming and going with their primitive questions and ways, I am half inclined to believe the New York visit a dream.[1] I do'nt know how to express to you my sense of the great kindness I received from Mrs Stedman and yourself during this visit. But you are only carrying out and on the same remarkable kindness you have steadily shown ever since our short acquaintance at St Augustine. Nobody begins to do so much for me as you do. I have been really touched by it, and you seem to me the most generous person in the world, when, with all your crowding duties, plans, cares, and occupations, you still find time to give me so much aid.—I only want to find fault with you in one little thing; you must give up the notion that I have any satire about me, at least in what I say. I have none. When I ask you a question, I ask for information pur et simple.[2] You have a way of looking at me sometimes as though you doubted whether I spoke in good faith.—I should not object to possessing satire if nature had given it; but she has not.—I found that out long ago.—One does not like to be misjudged, you know.—

I think you ought to be a very happy man, for you have such a delightful home. Many times on the long way down here I thought of those rooms and all their comfort and beauty; especially did I dwell on that little book-lined sanctum of yours. I never saw anything in the way of a home that so entirely suited <u>me</u>; there is just room enough for cosy comfort and no room for the terrible household care that wears out a woman's strength and light heartedness.—I am glad that I met Mrs Stoddard and Mrs Dodge; but I could not help thinking that evening how glad <u>you</u> must be in your inmost soul that your wife was not a writer. How much prettier and lovelier a thousand times over was Mrs Stedman in every motion look and tone than the best we other three could do! What <u>is</u> the reason that if we take up a pen we seem to lose so much in other ways?—Mrs Dodge is "fine looking"; but—anyone would know she was literary. Why must it inevitably be so?—But perhaps it is "compensation"; as we gain money, or fame, just so surely must we lose that which in our hearts we prize a great deal more.

Mr Bowker's criticism I suspect you already know. He found what seemed to me almost no fault at all, merely pointing out a few halting places, and little errors of form &c&c, which I should have corrected myself in any case, as the Ms. I sent him was a first copy, scarcely altered from the original writing-out, which itself shows hardly an erasure. I sent it to him to decide the (to me) great question, can I or can I not write verse. If he had been very severe, I think I should have felt better contented, for now I am as much at sea as ever. He said the poem was "worthy of the author of 'Peter the Parson' and 'Little Fishing.'" And then he advised me to lay it aside for a year!—I have followed your advice as to the Osgood letter, in a measure. Almost, but not absolutely.—And I shall really begin this winter on that novel. And, finally, I think you are right, and I will leave off climbing twenty trees at once! At the same time, I owe it to myself to say that all these various styles have been tentative; I really wanted to find out what I could do best.—

In spite of all I said to you, I do <u>not</u> plead guilty to imitating Harte. I only meant that his style had impressed me so deeply that it would be a wonder if something did not show to others how much he was to me. But Charlotte Bronte, George Eliot, and George Sand are equally powerful with me. Also Dickens. Harte coming last was the sensation of the hour; that was all.—

I do'nt know any book I shall purchase with more satisfaction than this forthcoming one of yours; I am tired of carrying around the crumpled magazines containing the Tennyson and Browning (Madame) articles, and yet I wo'nt leave these behind anywhere for I read them over often.—you would be surprised to know how often. I think I have always had a stronger taste of critical writings than for any other kind; ten years ago, for instance, I would read notices in the Atlantic before even [excision] the stories. And "ten years ago" you know, we were supposed to like stories! . . .

Mother has been perfectly well during my absence and as the climate suits her so charmingly we shall probably remain here until the frosts clear out the low countries for us. The trees are turning already and, as a Troy banker with a turn for verse once wrote to Father, "The seasons come and go,—Scarce apprehended; though bright have been its flowers,—Summer is ended!"

I shall write to Cooperstown for that autograph of Uncle Fenimore and send it to your son.—Come to Florida if you possibly can, and bring Madame. I am conceited enough to think we should become real friends, for she has, I know, sincerity. And how rare that is!—If women would ever say what they mean I should like them better. As it is I am afraid of them; afraid of their "ridicule-behind-one's-back," I mean.

My sister has just sent us fifteen new novels! I am going to read only one,—"Alcestis."[3]

Very Sincerely Yours
Constance F. Woolson.

Notes

1. The Moravian sect first developed as a fifteenth-century reform movement within the Catholic church. Under persecution in the eighteenth-century, Moravians emigrated to Germany where they influenced John Wesley and the Methodist movement. Settlements in the United States were concentrated in North Carolina. Moravians emphasize the Bible and personal faith and morality over church doctrine.

2. pur et simple: pure and simple.

3. In *Victorian Poets* (1875), Stedman discussed Robert Browning's translation of Euripides' "Alcestis."

To James R. Osgood (Massachusetts)

Asheville
Buncombe Co. N.C.
Oct. 22nd [1874]
Mr James R. Osgood.

Dear Sir.

I received your very pleasant letter, and shall endeavor to send you the new story in time.[1] You say "by January"; do you mean the first of January, or can I have the month?—They have just sent me from Scribner's, the proof sheets of "Jeannette," one of the three unpublished stories; so I suppose that will be out in time. But as to the other two, I know nothing. If they are not published before, can I wait for the February numbers, which will be out January the fifteenth?—I shall, of course, write to the editors who hold the Mss.—but I should like to know how much time I can give them.—If you prefer it, I can withdraw the stories without waiting for their publication in the magazines, although, of course, I do not wish to do so unless necessary.—If you will be so kind as to send me a line immediately, it will reach me before I leave the mountains; we are going slowly southward, but have not decided where we shall spend the winter.—Possibly, St Augustine. Please look at "Jeannette" when it comes out, and see if you like it well enough to include it in the volume?—I like it; but that is because it is such an accurate picture of Mackinac.

Very Truly Yours,
Constance F. Woolson.

Notes

1. Woolson is negotiating what stories to include in *Castle Nowhere: Lake Country Sketches* (Osgood 1875).

To Daniel C. Eaton (Beinecke)

Asheville
Buncombe Co. North Carolina
Oct. 29th, [1874]
Prof. Daniel C. Eaton.

Dear Sir.

While spending the summer among these mountains with my invalid Mother, I have been amusing myself trying to study ferns; "Gray's New Manual," and "Moore's British Ferns" have been my only teachers.[1] Seeing your name in the former, I take the liberty of writing in order to ask you the name of the enclosed specimen; it is very common about here, a large fern,—but from June 6th until a few days ago when frost came, it has refused to show me a seed, so, of course, I cannot place it.—I have collected on the mountains and along the French Broad river this summer the Polypody; Maidenhair; Bracken; Cheilanthes—; Pellaea;—Asplenium-ebeneum, and felix-femina;—Phegopteris-polypodioides;—Aspidium marginale, and Polystichum-acrostichoides; Cytopteris-bulbifera; and the unknown one enclosed. In a few weeks we shall leave for Florida and as I am desirous to pursue the study there, may I ask you to send me the name of the best fern book for the south; I see the Manual is only for the northern states. I do not wish to purchase Dr Chapman's "Flora," unless there is nothing else.[2] Is there no American book especially on Ferns?—I was obliged to try the Manual containing 700 pages that I cared nothing for, in order to get the 16 pages on Ferns!—Has Chapman's "Flora" much information about ferns,—and plates of them?—If you will be so very kind as to answer immediately, I shall receive the letter here; if that is not possible, please direct to St Augustine, Florida, addressing,

Miss Constance Fenimore Woolson.

Notes

1. Asa Gray first published his *New Manual of Botany* in 1848; Thomas Moore (1821–87) published *British Ferns* in 1855.

2. Woolson did purchase A. W. Chapman's *Flora of the Southern United States*. Her 1872 edition with her marginal notes is archived at Rollins College.

To Elizabeth Gwinn Mather (Rollins)[1]

St Augustine. Fla.
Dec. 4th [1874?]

Dear Libbie.

I have long been wishing to write to you, but what with moving about, hunting for comfortable quarters, and always and ever the same unending pen work which must be done, I find myself behind hand in what I wish to do. As I can do nothing after nightfall, you can understand how short the days seem. We left Asheville one bright morning in a covered wagon, scarlet in hue, called the "Palmetto"; all our trunks, six in number, were strapped in and on it, and the mulatto boy who drove us, rode in a crook-back position all the way. However, he said he did not mind it, and whistled and sang to himself the entire journey. We decided to go westward after all, as the North Carolina railroad connects with nothing, and the metropolis of "Statesville" where we would have been obliged to wait over, was too well remembered from last June. We came south via Chattanooga and Atlanta; a roundabout way reminding me of old Mrs Carter's, "Arabella child, when you go out to the Varian's, please stop in at Dr Terry's and get that medicine." However, it was very pleasant, and we both wished to see Chattanooga. We traveled in our wagon two days down the beautiful French Broad river; the road is the narrowest I ever saw, cut out of the solid rock, with the great cliffs on one side and the foaming rushing water on the other. In some places it is a real cañon, and the little slice of blue sky far above seems very far away. Fortunately we met few persons, and those we did meet, tall mountaineers in their blue jean suits, turned their great clumsy wagons half over, or into the river, to make way for us, a native politeness I appreciated, from the bottom of my heart. I think if you could have seen us the afternoon of the first day, you would have been horrified; about four o'clock rain came down in torrents, and it grew dark rapidly down in our gorge with the great cliffs on each side; we had yet five miles to go, nor were we sure exactly where our stopping place was. Finally it became entirely dark, the rain pouring in torrents meanwhile. Fortunately, it was not cold, and Mother, muffled in waterproofs, was as quiet and placid on her back seat as she was when Kate and I took her around Lake Otsego in a similar storm. Not so my anxious self. On the front seat, by the side of the mulatto boy I took my station, and did'nt I watch the road, the rocks, the horses!—The river was rushing and roaring within ten feet of us, and the rocky road just wide enough for our wheels. I think nothing ever shone out so beautifully as the glow of Mrs McDowill's pitchpine fire through her low windows as we turned the last curve. For lights they brought out flaming brands from the hearth, and rejoiced I was when Mother was established in a rocking chair and all her wet wraps off. Take cold? Not she! Said she never felt better in her life, eat a hearty supper, slept soundly in the odd little bedroom, and was ready to start at seven the next morning. All that day we rode along the river and through the Great Smoky Mountains; it was real Indian summer weather and the great peaks were purple and misty. As to the river, it is the most beautiful small river I have ever seen; I mean small as compared with the Hudson or the Mississippi.[2] In time it must be famous. The only incident was the meeting of the stage going to Asheville, and a few moments after, the finding of the mail bag in the road. We thought that the best thing we could do was to take it on with us, and as the way was smoother, we drove rapidly for about half an hour, when a distant shouting reached our ears. We stopped, and presently a panting man came in sight behind; it was the driver of the stage who had missed his bag about the time we picked it up, and had been running after us all that way! We slept that night at Wolf Creek, a town consisting of one farm house; and then, taking the cars, rolled into Chattanooga on the evening of the second day. We had lovely warm weather while there, and went up to the top of Lookout Mountain, Mother riding comfortably in a carriage up the fine military road, and I walking most of the way looking for ferns. We were very much impressed by the view from Lookout; not that it is more extensive than others we have seen this summer, but on account of the memories of the terrible battlefields in every direction. Up those very heights where we were standing had swarmed the ranks of the blue and the gray, down in that beautiful valley below us they had died, poor fellows, by thousands, on the long blue line of Missionary Ridge opposite were those batteries which had cut to pieces so fearfully our Ohio regiments, and all the way down to Chickamauga, ten miles distant, every step was fought for till the little creek we saw ran red. Was it not at Chickamauga that Howard Burnham was killed? As if to give emphasis to these thoughts, there on a green slope below us gleamed the low headstones of fourteen thousand of our soldiers, gathered from the hill sides around. And now all was calm and peaceful, the river curving around the little town, the blue distant peaks visible in seven different states; the only signs of the past were those graves, and the old earthworks and rifle pits in every direction. The ride to Atlanta along the identical track fought over by Sherman and Johnston, was almost startling from the names called in at the car door; Dalton, Resaca, Ringgold, Allatoona, Kenesaw, &c, all names of the most terrible battles our western troops took part in. How they brought back the war! Those days of excitement, when we watched for the "extra," to see whether we had gained or lost. At Atlanta, Mother and I went out to see the Confederate monument to the Georgia dead.[3] It is a massive structure, but, like the one in Richmond, not to be compared with those we have at the north. There too we found the ranks of low headboards as far as we could see, thousands upon thousands. I cannot describe it, but certainly there is something very impressive in these poor soldiers' graves. So many of them were young, all died painful deaths, and almost all left broken hearts behind them, fathers and mothers who lost their boys, young wives who lost their husbands.—From Atlanta, (which is a bright thriving town) to Macon, and thence to Savannah,—so we went "marching through Georgia."[4] We saw Julia Closson who is looking very well this fall; her youngest child, "Nelly," is a little beauty,—resembling Dr Terry, I think. Then on we came by cars to Jacksonville, and thence by boat to our landing, Tocoi, where an important little locomotive was "tooting" on the dock. Think of it,—a railroad to the "ancient city"![5] It will soon be "ancient" no longer. Indeed, it changes daily, I am sorry to say. But the climate is certainly delicious. To day, for instance, we are sitting with open windows, there is a lovely breeze blowing in from the ocean, and the soft Florida sky is as blue as June in Ohio. We have better rooms than we had last year, Mother possessing a pleasant little piazza commanding a view over the water; this piazza is a great resource to her in the afternoons. In the mornings she walks on the sea wall; then she embroiders, then dinner and a nap, then the piazza, a little reading, then tea, the mail. Bézique and bed. When Clara arrives, Bézique will be varied by cribbage. I only know Bézique, and it took me a long time to learn that! This living south has its disadvantages. . . . But Mother is well here. That is the whole story. Health is everything.[6]

But I have so much to be thankful for in Mother's renewed health, and in the success that has come to me, limited of course, but very great when you think that it lifts all pecuniary cares off my mind. With the money I earn by my pen, Mother and I are entirely comfortable in our quiet way; without it, we should be very much cramped, and every day an anxiety. To be sure, our income is small, but if it is sufficient for our wants, that is all that is necessary. Do you remember Mr Micawber' s sayings; "Suppose a man's income be twenty shillings: he spends twenty shillings and sixpence,—Want! He spends nineteen shillings and sixpence,—Affluence!"—[7]

Ellen Terry [excision]

I think she is really unkind never to write to me. Do you ever hear anything of my old friend Mary Bratenell. Clara writes that Jane Carter has charming rooms in New York, and looks well; yet says she is far from happy, being troubled with business cares! What a commentary on riches! How is Mr Mather's club going on?—And are your Cleveland people going to make Mr Payne president?[8] I suppose "the Payne Boys" and "Leonard" are going on in the same old way. We read every word of the "Cleveland Herald," so we know something of the city affairs, the charming columns about the "Fire Department Investigation," and all the other [excision] you personally, my dear

Notes

1. Portions of this letter also appear in Benedict/Voices, 251–52 and in Benedict/Abroad, 748–49, where the letter is identified, incorrectly, as being addressed to Samuel Livingston Mather.

2. Woolson eventually published a travel sketch on "The French Broad" (*Harper's New Monthly Magazine*, Apr. 1875). This indicates that the correct year for the letter is 1874, not 1875 as listed in Victoria Brehm and Sharon L. Dean, eds. *Constance Fenimore Woolson: Selected Stories and Travel Narratives* (Knoxville: University of Tennessee Press, 2004): 85–87.

3. A Howard Burnham of Longmeadow, Massachusetts, was killed at Chickamauga. Woolson is referring to the Chattanooga National Cemetery and the Oakland Cemetery,

Atlanta. Confederate General Joseph Johnston (1807–91) and Union General William Sherman (1820–91) fought in Georgia. She is also echoing Union Col. Thomas Berry, who said of the Battle of Chickamauga (Sept. 18–20, 1863) that the "creek ran red with blood."

4. This song by Henry Clay Work (1832–84) honors Sherman's Atlanta march.

5. The railroad arrived in St. Augustine in 1876.

6. The main text of the letter stops here. The fragments following are pasted into *Rodman the Keeper* at Rollins College. The handwriting and type of ink indicate that the fragments were cut from this letter.

7. The quotation is from Dickens's *David Copperfield* (1849–50). A portion of this letter follows this paragraph in Benedict/Voices (229) and Benedict/Abroad (739). It reads as follows:

> I have been studying ferns and have become quite an enthusiast. This winter I am going to learn to play chess! Do'nt you see how I am providing for a solitary old age!! . . . Now I am going out to walk on the pine barrens and to see the sunset.

8. Henry Payne was a member of the Ohio Democratic Electoral Commission for the 1876 presidential election.

To Daniel C. Eaton (Beinecke)

St Augustine. Florida
Dec. 12th, [1874]
Prof. Daniel C. Eaton.

Dear Sir.

Your kind note encourages me to send another fern. What is it?—It grows in the swamps near here, and is so large I can only forward a fragment.—Thanks for the check list; but it only convinces me that the "Flora" must be purchased.[1] "Nineteen ferns in Florida,"—and to not be sure about any of them!—I have just ordered the "Flora" and Gray's first "Lessons." It will give me pleasure to forward to you specimens of the sea weeds that are found here; to get them, one is obliged to sail over to the "North Beach," or to the outside of Anastasia Island. I have not yet been over; but we go frequently during the season.—On our way down from North Carolina, I found the pretty little "Asplenium Trichomanes" on the spurs of the Great Smoky range in Tennessee; the "Polypodium Incanum," on the very top of Lookout Mountain; and since I have arrived here I have found both "Woodwardia Virginica," and "Woodwardia Angustifolia," in swampy ground along the pine barrens.—They are so unlike that in spite of the book, I can hardly believe they belong to the same family.—

Truly yours
Constance Fenimore Woolson.

Notes

1. A. W. Chapman's *Flora of the Southern United States* and Asa Gray's *First Lessons in Botany and Vegetable Physiology* (1857).

To Arabella Carter Washburn (Benedict/Voices, 230–31; Benedict/Abroad, 740–41)[1]

. . . The life here is so fresh, so new, so full of a certain wild freedom. I walk miles through the hummocks, where it looks as though no one had ever walked before, gathering wild flowers everywhere, or sitting down under the pine trees to rest in the shade. Yes, shade! For it is so warm that shade is desirable. Then on other days I take a row boat and go prowling down the inlet into all sorts of creeks that go no one knows where; I wind through dense forest where the trees meet overhead, and the long grey moss brushes my solitary boat as I pass. I go far up the Sebastian River as utterly alone as Robinson Crusoe. I meet alligators, porpoises, pelicans, cranes, and even deer, but not a human soul. Then again I often sail out with the numerous gentlemen who have nothing else to do; we go outside into the broad ocean and plunge along over the blue waves with the bluest sky in the world overhead. Or land on the north beach and stroll along for miles with the great waves rolling at our feet. You know the ocean is new to me and I am so fond of it already that I feel as if I never cared to go inland any more. The little town is almost too lazy to breathe. The people apparently have no curiosity in their organization and you might stand on your head in the middle of their little plaza all day, and they would hardly turn to look at you, much less take the trouble to ask "why." You go and come at your own pleasure, nobody knows or cares how or with whom. This, to me, is charming . . . The society is peculiar but pleasant in its peculiarity. It consists, for us in the U.S. officers and their families. Then, in addition there are about thirty people who seem congenial spirits, and being here for the winter, like ourselves they have nothing whatever to do but "have a good time." From one week-end to the other, it is nothing but go, go, go; always in a sociable, easy way, with no preparation or forethought. For instance, last Saturday the Commandant had a large sail boat and invited the whole forty to go over to North Beach for the day. As the thirty guests and ten officers' wives are from all the points of the compass, you may imagine there is no danger of monotony. We stayed all day; it was so warm that we reclined on the beach, basking in the sun; the soldiers put up a tent, made a splendid chowder, and did all the work. We sailed home in the evening and the gentlemen sang all the way. That is a specimen. Of course I do not represent much in all this gaiety. But they are always kind enough to ask me and when I do go, which is not always by any means, I always have a pleasant time.

. . . . . When I said "the society consists, for us of" &c, I meant that because we are church people it is so. The line is strictly drawn here—it is really absurd. There is a stiff Presbyterian element which never dances, or sings or goes sailing, or anything else except go to prayer meeting. It comprises "the oldest and most respectable" citizens, and they gaze with scorn upon our light amusements and hold themselves sternly aloof. As usual, most of the winter visitors are church people. The Rector here is a very pleasant man . . . and he always goes on all the excursions . . . The Rector has only been in the ministry a few years, having fought all through the war as a Colonel in the Rebel Army.[2] We have struck up quite a friendship and he tells me all kinds of stories of the war; you know I am <u>really</u> interested in the subject. He was with Lee at the time of the Surrender. The little church is very pretty, with several Memorial windows. We trimmed it up finely for Christmas. The Bishop came and one funny thing happened. We had, of course, no acquaintance with his Lordship, but the evening before he left, he sent up our hostess to say he would be pleased to call upon us at eight o'clock. I, at first, begged off, but Clara and Mother promised that they would do the talking if I would only go down. At eight he came, and how did it end? The Bishop and I were left entirely alone by ourselves in one corner of the room—for an hour! In my embarrassment I am conscious that I talked to him just like the immortal Mrs Proudie![3]

Notes

1. The letter appears to have been written from St. Augustine when Woolson first arrived there.
2. Woolson is probably referring the Rector of St Augustine's Trinity Episcopal Parish, founded in 1821 with its church building completed in 1831.
3. A character in Anthony Trollope's *Barchester Towers* (1857).

To Arabella Carter Washburn [1874?] (Benedict/CFW, 21–22)

Why did not the Dr send on that criticism on "Solomon"?[1] I was really curious to see it. It is not too late, now. Don't keep it back for fear of my feelings. I never supposed <u>he</u> would like it, for he likes not that style. I have taken (within the last year) a new departure in my writing. I have gone back to nature and exact reality. I have such a horror of "pretty," "sweet" writing that I should almost prefer a style that was ugly and bitter, provided it was also <u>strong</u>. Please say to your husband that he could not please me more than by sending me a review of "Solomon" or anything else of mine he is pleased to select. There is no one I know whose opinion is worth more, or whose opinion I should value more. I do not say I should always agree with it—but at least it would be a real help to me to see it. There is a sketch called "Wilhelmine" coming out this year some time in the "Atlantic" and another called "Jeannette" in "Scribner's," which I should be glad to have you both read and criticize.

Notes

1. The doctor is Washburn's husband.

To R. R. Bowker (LOC)[1]

St Augustine. Florida
Jan. 19th [1875?]
Mr R. R. Bowker.

Dear Sir.

As I cannot use my eyes after dark, and as the short days have been more than occupied for the past three months, I have not been able to answer your note until now. It requires no answer; still, I wish to express my appreciation of the kindness that prompted it, and the advice it gave,—advice which I have followed: the poem is laid aside, "for a year," and I "read Shelley, Keats, and Morris."—Robert Browning has long been my favorite poet; I think I like no one, living or dead, so well as Browning.—But that may be because I owned his works, and formed the habit of poring over them daily, just as I pore over George Eliot.—. You are right about "Two Women."—When it was finished I knew that its merit, if any it had, lay in the interest of the story and that alone. I shall, sometime, go over it again; and act according to the impression it then makes upon me.—But verses will never interfere with my prose; the former, such as they are, I write, in next to no time and cannot for the life of me alter,—they must go as they are; the latter I write very slowly, sometimes spending days on one page, and altering a dozen times before satisfaction comes.—I did not mean that I despised short stories; I agree with you in thinking the "opportunity in that field, splendid." Still, it has occurred to me that they are excessively ephemeral, and the necessarily condensed style injured a longer narrative; the merit of the one is the death of the other.—No one admires Bret Harte more than I do; but could he write a novel?—Is his ~~fame~~ work not like that of the journalist, brilliant but vanishing too soon?—And I cannot agree with you as to Hawthorne, for I love his "Blithedale Romance" and "House of the Seven Gables," so, so much better than his short stories.—Which, however, I shall continue to write; and I thank you for the pleasant notices in the "Mail"—I am really attached to that paper, and the day seems incomplete without it; I have read it, daily, since its birth.[2]—Our copy went from hand to hand up in those far-away North Carolina mountains where we spent the summer; and here it is the same.—I should like to know which editorials are yours.—

Truly yours,
Constance Fenimore Woolson.

Notes

1. Woolson published her long poem "Two Women. 1862" in *Appletons' Journal,* January 1877; therefore, the Library of Congress's date of 1878 is incorrect.

2. The New York *Evening Mail.*

To Edmund Clarence Stedman (Columbia)

St Augustine
Jan. 20th, [1875]

Dear Mr Stedman.

Yes; I received your letter of October 31st. I saw your Tribune article on Miss Field.[1] But,—what is of more consequence, if you will allow me to say so,—I have read your Browning; the "consequence," of course, being the essay, and not the reading thereof. I have never confessed it,—but for eight years Browning has been my favorite; of all poets living or dead I think I like him the best. I am not familiar with all his poems; but those I own I read and re-read, preferring, of the longer ones, "Pippa Passes," and "The Ring and the Book."—But in my circle of acquaintances I have found so few persons who know more than his name, and but one or two who like him. Therefore I have kept silence. Judge, then, with how much interest I began your essay. I believe I have read it ten times; and I know myself well enough to know that there is no limit to the number of times I shall go over it; for when I like a thing once I like it forever, whether it be tune, friend, or book.—On the other hand there are not many things that I care for at all, the vast majority of tunes, friends, and books, being nothing to me; as I am to them.—But, setting aside my love for Browning, the article seems to me superb in itself. I think I have never read, in English, (I say that because there is so exquisite a delicacy in some French reviews I have seen) anything in the way of criticism that equaled it; indeed it is more than criticism,—it is a study,—trenchant, profound, scintillating,—strong and clear as a lighthouse, which I am sure we need when sailing through the wild labyrinth of deeps and hidden rocks and storms which Browning's genius has created, a tempestuous ocean of poetry.—As a rule the critics annoy me by ignoring the greatness of an author and falling in a body upon some fault, comparatively trivial. But you understand the very breath of Browning's massive poetry;—even I, no critic, no poet,—can see that you entirely comprehend him, to begin with.—To go on with—has anyone ever seen a more powerful grasping of a great subject? To end with—, certainly there never was a more delicate touch in the lighter details, more keen analysis, more felicitous phrasing.—Well, I can not half express in a letter all I feel, and it would weary you; but let me say that I am charmed,—and picture to yourself, as the French say, that copy of Scribner lying on my toilette-table where I do my most prized reading, and myself poring over your pages the first thing in the morning, and the last at night. When the volume appears, I shall have it in better shape. I shall go over Landor, then; but someway, I do not believe I can get excited over Landor.—That may come, however. I know next to nothing about him.

Yes; your letter came just before I left Asheville. We had a wild and charming journey in a carriage down the beautiful French Broad River, and through the Great Smoky Mountains into Tennessee; there we struck the railroad, passed through Knoxville, stopped at Chattanooga and went up to the top of Lookout Mountain on a lovely Indian summer day, Missionary Ridge lying opposite us, going down towards Chickamauga ten miles distant where "the creek ran red all day." Then on we journeyed to Atlanta, and the name of every station called in at the car door was a battlefield we all remember, many of us with tears; we of the West, I mean.—It was a memorable and beautiful journey, and impressed me more than the route through Virginia, for the scenery was grander and the crowd of memorable names greater.—Everything is the same in the ancient city; this winter we are at the Magnolia Hotel, your old quarters. Mother continues well, and we shall probably remain until May or June. Your friend Mr Pell goes out in his little boat as usual; but it is now water tight, and he has at last procured a stick to push down the centre board, so that we can save one or two of our parasols.—The force of uniforms at the Barracks has been augmented by three new officers, and the Coast Survey steamer adds four naval men; so the sea-wall is well peopled at sunset and on moonlight nights.

Please remember me to Mrs Stedman with a sincere regard; but say to her that the Xmas bell was a sudden fancy, ordered by letter to Tiffany the week before Xmas. I was thinking of the season, and how much it used to be to me with its evergreens, church trimming, Xmas tree at home, gifts, songs, and general gayety for all the children,—a charmed time, which, I suppose can never come again; for care <u>will</u> creep in as we grow older.—And I thought, "how dull I am,—how dull is this Xmas. Is there no one from whom I can steal a little Xmas pleasure,—a breath of the old feeling?"—And then it came to me suddenly how bright your home would probably be, and I thought I would just steal in and get at least a few moments of remembrances from you, and from your wife, for whom I have a warm fancy which only needs a little more acquaintance to turn and deepen into true regard.—That was the whole story; but of course I was obliged to trust the choice of the bell to the Tiffany people.—I hope it was not ugly. Your defence of Miss Field was chivalrous. I have never seen the lady, neither have I been able to fix her, in a literary way, in my mind. I know what I think, for instance, of Mrs R. H. Davis,—of Miss Phelps,—of Mrs Spofford; but Miss Field prefers, or has preferred, the newspapers, has she not? At any rate I have seen little of her work knowing that it was hers. It seems to me that she has been very hardly used. But is it not next to always so with American actresses? Or rather, actresses?—It is a terrible ordeal, for it involves all a woman, personality as well as her genius; in the other arts one can escape that.—what do you think of Clara Morris?—I used to fancy she had the "divine fire," though hidden under a mass of faults, the result of want of education in youth.—

I am much pleased with Prosper Merimee's "Lettres à une Inconnue," Mr

Stoddard's Bric a Brac arrangement; it is a charming book,—the whole of it.[2] Please give my regards to Mrs Stoddard. She would smile if she knew the search I have kept up, ever since I met her, for her novels. It seems impossible to get hold of them; my last clue has just failed,—a friend who once owned them, but who has lost them,—borrowed and never returned. I shall not give up the chase however. I remember them,—but wish to re-read them.—

Yesterday I wrote a note to Mr Bowker, in answer, at last, to a long letter he sent to me in October after my New York visit, a letter of cordial advice which he wrote of his own accord; at least there was no need of it as far as politeness went. The long poem is laid aside, for the present.

I do not know whether you will approve of my volume, or rather, of any volume at all from me at present. But it seemed to me best to make a beginning, and it is a modest one, the best of my stories led by a new and longer one which gives the name to the collection. Please keep this entirely secret at present, as I have told no one.—I tried to make the new story more "ideal," (to use your own word) but I find I cannot go far out of my natural style; it makes me feel as though I was telling a thousand lies. The whole collection belongs to the lake-country.

I have been disappointed in not getting the Cooper autograph; they have had a grand wedding up there and the ripples have not yet subsided. In time, however, it will come. Do not answer this until the easy moment comes; I shall be here all winter and delighted to hear from you, but I know you are busy now, and I do not believe in keeping a debit and credit account with one's friends.—

Truly Yours
C.F.W.

I forgot to say that Miss Phelps is here, at our hotel; she faces me at table. Have you ever seen her? A pale silent woman, with fine dark eyes, a pleasant smile, and pensive expression. But it is next to impossible to get acquainted with her; she always seems to be lost in a far off dream. She is a "Dress-reformer," you know. There is not much beauty in the costume; the point seems to be, to look as man-ish as possible. Of her lady friend, a "doctor," our Plum remarked, "Mamma sometimes he wears a skirt, just like a lady." But, Plum, it <u>is</u> a lady."—"Is it? Why does it wear a coat, then?" demanded Plum eying the nondescript costume in perplexity. Whereupon Mamma,—not knowing, responded "Hush," in that comprehensive and finishing way mammas have.—I have (of course) thought of another thing. Please say to Mrs Stedman.—or rather, let her read it for it is outside your sphere,—that her ideas about that silk gown of mine have been carried out, and the result is fine!—I array myself in it often, and always think of her, and of Mrs Dodge.

Notes

1. Miss Field is American journalist Kate Field.

2. Mérimee's (1803–70) letters to Jenny Dacquin, his friend and perhaps lover, were published posthumously under the title *Lettres à Une Inconnue* (1874). Richard Stoddard edited the ten-volume Bric-a-Brac series from 1874 to 1876.

To Mr. Fay (Virginia)[1]

St Augustine. Florida
Feb. 26th, [1875]

Dear Mr Fay.

Of course I have not forgotten you. Do you still carry around photographs in your pockets, and have you as many charming books as ever?—Think of Georgia Gordon's marrying the count! Cleveland is so large now that it has forgotten all about those days. I have not been there for more than a year and a half, nor do I expect to return. My dear father's death broke up our home, and now I am traveling with my Mother; this is our second winter here,—last summer we spent among the wild mountains of North Carolina, and this summer we shall go to the Virginia Springs,—next winter Key West and Cuba, and then, I hope, abroad. The variety is pleasant after so many years on the monotonous shores of Lake Erie.

Miss Benedict wrote some time ago that she had heard "ever so much about Mr Fay," but she gave no particulars; which was aggravating.[2] However, do you not think that you can tell the "ever so much" better than she? I do. A lady here, who was formerly Miss Stevens of New Jersey, mentioned you the other day in connection with a little Memorial church, built, I believe, by their family. You were present with some friends, and attended some services did'nt you?—Well,—what do you think of—of—of—to pin it down to something definite we will say—Dr De Koven's election.[3] For my part, I am reading for the fifth time, Buckle's "History of Civilization."[4]

Please present my regards to Mrs Fay.

Truly yours,
Constance F. Woolson.

Notes

1. Fay was an acquaintance from Cleveland.

2. Probably Hattie Benedict Sherman, Clara Woolson's sister-in-law.

3. James DeKoven (1831–79) was elected Bishop of Wisconsin.

4. Henry Thomas Buckle's (1821–62) first volume of *History of Civilization* appeared in 1857; the second, in 1861.

To Daniel C. Eaton (Beinecke)

"Mills House"
Charleston. S.C.
April 10th, [1875]
Prof. D. C. Eaton.

Dear Sir.

The kind tone of your notes encourages me to come to you for some more information about ferns. I hunted all around St Augustine, finding in addition to the two Woodwardias, splendid specimens of the Osmunda regalis, and O. cinnamomea, with the fertile fronds, the Aspidium Floridanum, and Aspidium patens. I enclose a fern (the small one without a name) which showed no seeds all the time I was in Florida,—from December to April. It grew in groves on Anastasia island. It seemed to me to answer generally to the description of Aspidium Thelypteris; but I am so ignorant I prefer to refer it to you. The other small fern I found in North Carolina last summer, and placed it in my collection labelled "Cystopteris bulbifera." But I have been feeling doubtful about it lately; what is it? And will you be so kind as to return it when named.—The large faded leaf I obtained in the Ocklawaha river last week. Several persons on the little steamer insisted that this plant, growing away up like a parasite at the top of the tall palmettoes alongshore, was a fern, of the same habit as the Polypodium incanum, which also grew on the tree trunks, but lower down, and not confined to palms. It grows (this specimen) luxuriantly, and its leaves or fronds are often larger than this one I send; but although its shape is like Woodwardia angustifolia, I cannot feel sure it is a fern; neither can I find anything like it in Chapman. Please tell me what it is.

I regret that I have not been able to send you any sea weeds; we looked for them all winter, but could find only two kinds, both common. They do not seem to come ashore at St Augustine; perhaps because there is a sand bar all along the beach, outside. But if you have collections from the Indian River, you probably have all there is along that shore.

I shall be very much obliged if you will answer; we shall be here about three weeks.

Truly yours
Constance Fenimore Woolson.

To Miss Farnian[1]

"Mills House"
Charleston. S.C.
April 17th, 1875

Dear Miss Farnian.

Your letter has reached me at last having been sent from Cleveland to St Augustine, Florida, where I've spent the winter, and then, after some delay, forwarded to this proud battered old city where we shall linger some weeks.—I do not think I have any talent for pleasing children; writing for children I consider an especial gift,—which I have not. I made one attempt two or three years ago, and said, when I saw the printed result, that I would not try again.[2] I would like to write for your little people; but, simply, cannot.—I am pleased, all the same, to make the acquaintance of "Dolly"; I read every word of the "Two Girls," with interest. The sketch seemed to me both vigorous and fresh, two adjectives which, I am sorry to say, I can apply but rarely to the writings of our own sex. Do you not think we women are prone to run off into the beautiful at the expense of strength?—And, I think it will be a comfort for me to express my wonder over the change in children's literature which fifteen years has made. When I was a child we cared only for fairy-tales, real fairy-tales, the more wild and fantastic the better; now-a-days the stores are full of stories about how they got up in the morning, put on their stockings and shoes, what they had for breakfast, what everybody said, how they went out to walk, what they saw, how they came home, what they had for dinner, and so on ad infinitum in the most deadly practical manner. My own nieces will sit for hours listening to these details; but they do not care at all for the Arabian Nights, or Undine.—.[3] I hope you will be successful in your new enterprise, and I think you will be; the country needs more than the one children's magazine.

Truly yours,
Constance Fenimore Woolson.

Notes

1. This letter was archived at Stuart House Museum, City of Mackinac Island Museums, Mackinac Island, Mich. Its current location is unknown. Miss Farnian is an unidentified editor of a children's magazine.

2. Woolson is referring to *The Old Stone House,* published by D. Lathrop in 1873 under the pseudonym Anne March. She won a thousand-dollar prize for the novel; her sister Clara also entered the contest.

3. *Undine,* a popular novella about a water spirit, was published in 1811 by Friedrich de la Motte Fouqué.

To Samuel Mather (Anderson)

Charleston
April 25th, [1875][1]

Dear Sam.

Your letter came yesterday, and I was very much pleased to receive it. We are all feeling relieved and happy over Kate's improvement under her loving Mother's devoted care, and we turn to our everyday occupations with cheerfulness.—It is charming here,—the most picturesque city *I* have ever seen; but of course nothing like foreign towns. To a dweller in Cleveland the old Colonial tombs with their long inscriptions dating back to 1730–40, seem ancient indeed; and the calling of the hours all night from the tower of St Michael's Church by a watchman stationed there—"ten and three-e quarters! a—alls well," is like Old German stories. I went to the top of St Michael's the other evening to see the city and the bay by moonlight; for some unexplained reason, the historic harbour was much more distinct than it ever is by daylight, every outline of Sumter clearly visible; Moultrie standing out on the north point of the mainland (they call it an *island* because a little creek runs around it), and, opposite, the long low spit of Cummings Point, Morris Island, where the remains of Battery Wagner could be distinguished. Turning the other way, there lay the city between its two rivers, silvery ribbons in the moonlight, shining with lights from side to side. Battered, ruined, poverty-stricken as it is, it impresses me as the most aristocratic city I have ever seen. The old houses with these great walls and shut-in gardens are prouder even in ruin than anything we can show at the north. You see they had kept up the old manorial,—almost feudal,—ideas and customs, living with their slaves around them. Of course such things are as effete as moated castles now-a-days; but they are picturesque.—

It is said, Sam, that if you do the best you can, and then *wait*, things will come right at last. I have all along cherished a special regard for "St Clair Flats," and have felt troubled because no one else seemed to care for the poor thing. Now here comes along a young man, for whose literary taste I have a sincere respect, and this delightful young man picks out my poor neglected sketch for especial commendation!—2^{d}. Under the abuse which has been showered upon me for my "brutal" killing of "Peter the Parson," I have steadily maintained to myself that both in an artistic and truthful-to-life point of view, my ending of the story was better than the conversion of the miners, the plenty to eat and the happy marriage proposed by my critics. Now here comes along this same delightful young man and plants as it were his strong young flag beside mine—which has been flying forlornly on a deserted field all this time with never a helping hand. But, nephew Sam, where are your own productions? I have nourished a fancy that you were going to enter the field too. Have you ever thought upon the subject, or tried your hand at it? You might take it up in a small way as an amusement for leisure hours. It seems to me that you have every qualification; the interest attached to it is certainly great, and the compensation fair.—Think of it, or rather think it over; you are young, and have plenty of time before you.

Yes; I agree with you in thinking that Mother writes charming letters; she is very well, and is planning to spend a few weeks in Cleveland early in the fall, as soon as the mountains become too cool for her. Must tell you as a joke that I have just received through our St Augustine rector, a Virginia man, a written invitation to spend the summer at one of the fashionable Virginia Springs as the guest of the proprietor! Of course there is, as Mr Benedict would say, a colored individual in the woodpile—namely Harper articles describing the beauties &c&c.[2] Not liking to be fettered in that way I shall decline, preferring to pay my board out of the price of the articles, and be at liberty to find fault like a free American citizen. What! shall I not be able to abuse the biscuit, and scold the chambermaid at my pleasure! Take away the privilege of saying the eggs are cold, and what, oh what, is left!—We shall linger here as long as possible.—Give much love to your dear Mother and Father, and to Kate also. I am always really glad to hear from you; wish you would write much oftener.

Affectionately,
C.F.W.

Notes

1. Portions of this letter are in Benedict/CFW, 22–23; Benedict/Voices, 249; Benedict/Abroad, 746–47.
2. Woolson never wrote a travel sketch about a fashionable resort.

To Paul Hamilton Hayne (Duke)

Charleston. S.C.
Mr Paul H. Hayne
May day. 1875

Dear Sir.

Your note sent from Augusta to New York, from New York to St Augustine, Florida, and thence here, has overtaken me at last; I answer immediately, en route for Virginia. Your kind words so unexpected, so pleasant in many ways, give me a charming encouragement. I consider myself still a beginner, and as I had lived in the Lake-country I wrote of what I knew; the descriptions are all from reality, written down as exactly as possible. I love my Lakes, their scenery and associations, very dearly.—Your notice of "Castle Nowhere" was especially pleasant; the other stories all ran the gauntlet of the magazines, but this was new, written in St Augustine last winter,—and when I had finished it I said "it is my best." But as no one else said so, I began to doubt my own judgement; a very unsettling state of mind, do'nt you think? Now comes your letter, the clouds part, and I take courage again. As to Waring, he is all you say. But do you not think they are so, now-a-days,—lovers, I mean? I do. Waring came straight from real life.—I thank you sincerely for any notices you may write of my little volume, and feel especially pleased that your words may be read in the south and southwest, where I am entirely unknown.—And now, sir, will you let me express to you something which has puzzled me ever since I came over the border? I have been at the South almost two years now, and again and again have I been brought up against a stone-wall, as it were, in literary matters. I supposed I knew who were the writers of the day; it seems I do not. Names that to me are the brightest stars in the horizon, are known not at all; names that I have never heard, take their place. Often have I asked myself during these two years "have I lost my senses? Or have they? Which is the right?"—For instance, (to make clear my meaning), last summer in North Carolina we made many acquaintances, among them persons of culture and taste. In no case had they read "George Eliot"; in almost no case had they more than heard the name of Bret Harte; in no case ever heard at all of "Joaquin" Miller. (The last I could have pardoned; but not the others.) On their side, then, they spoke with the utmost enthusiasm of poets whose names were unknown to me, (one, I remember, was "Flash") and, with even more warmth, of a cloud of women, novelists, poets, &c&c, who are, or rather each one <u>is</u> "the greatest genius of the day."—It is pleasant, now, to think that the only person upon whom we united was yourself. "Paul Hayne," I exclaimed, glad at last to touch bottom in the (to me) unknown sea of enthusiasm around me. "I <u>do</u> know Paul Hayne! I have often read and admired his poems in the magazines; and I have known of him a long time. In fact he is to my eyes <u>the</u> Southern writer." So we often talked of you, and they told me of a shrine you have where reposes a letter from the Laureate; and other pleasant things.—But, Sir, the perplexity still remains. Only the other day I was referred to a "Mrs Jordan," as "the gifted poetess of Virginia."[1]—And the person who spoke,—a gentleman of more than ordinary culture, had never heard, apparently, of Jean Ingelow or the Rosettis.

I saw some time ago the announcement of your volume of poems, and said to myself, "<u>that</u> I should like." I wish to read much poetry this summer, up in those Virginia mountains, and shall no doubt pore over your pages with great interest. The melody of your verses is always perfect to my ear; and my fault is roughness, I think. I have the idea that women run too much into mere beauty at the expense of power; and the result is, I fear, that I have gone too far the other way; too rude; too abrupt.—So if you send me your volume, I shall probably know most of it by heart before the summer is over, and your verses will be studied as well as enjoyed during many a solitary walk. For southerners do not walk, apparently.—I find I must always go alone; four or five miles seem unearthly to southern women.—Thanks for the enclosures. I saw "Preexistence" and it struck me particularly, not only for its beauty but also for its clear picture of a phenomenon which has haunted me often; although not so much now as formerly,—probably because I am farther away from my last world! I hope it will be in the volume that I may carry it with me in my wandering life. I take a few friendly books; but alas! can have no library in trunks.—I think it will be safe to address me in the care of "H. M. Alden, Harper & Brothers. N.Y."—They will know where I am because I am writing some articles for them now.[2] And I do not myself know at present where I shall be, for we are to try several Springs before we decide.—With sincere thanks for your cordial kindness, I am, sir, yours truly,

Constance Fenimore Woolson.

Notes

1. Probably Cornelia Jordan of Lynchburg, Virginia.
2. In 1875, Woolson was writing travel narratives for Harper's.

To Daniel C. Eaton (Beinecke)

Mills House
Charleston. S.C.
June 4th, [1875]
Prof. D. C. Eaton.

Dear Sir.

At the risk of making you laugh at my ignorance, I again come to you with a fern to be named.—Some weeks ago while hunting up the old Colonial church at Goose Creek, some seventeen miles from Charleston, I found growing on one of the terraces of the ancient garden of "Newington," the enclosed plant.[1] I seized upon it at once as "a fern," but on going back to the rest of the party, I was covered with ridicule; it was not a fern at all; who ever saw a fern like that? &c&c. I held on to my conviction until we reached the boarding house, when the landlady pronounced my specimen "the old man's soap-plant!"[2]—All the way back in the cars my mistake was the subject of much merriment, and to this day there is a great deal said about "Miss Woolson's soap-plant fern."—I pressed the three specimens I had found, and silently laid them away. But this morning comes a letter from another amateur fern-gatherer, sending ~~the~~ a small specimen which he calls "Botrychium Virginicum"; and it is so much like my poor "soap-plant" that again I take it out and compare them. "Botrychium Virginicum," is the one *I* made out *mine* to be; but what confused me was the description of "Botrychium" saying positively "frond with an anterior fertile and posterior sterile segment"; whereas my plant seemed to have *three* sterile segments. The "B. Virginicum," being "ternate" gave me a little hope; which however was crushed out by the word "soap plant." Now then what *is* the thing enclosed? If it is a fern after all, with what joy I shall come down on my merry friends! If it is after all "the soap-plant,"—why,—at least I shall be sure of it.—Do not trouble yourself to return the specimen, as I have several others here.

Major Haskin showed me your note. I was very sorry we failed to find the sea-weed; but he will take pleasure in obtaining it next winter, if it is to be found.—A friend has just sent me a Bulletin of the Torrey Club, containing four "little-known ferns,"—by yourself.[3] But they are not in Gray or Chapman, and a beginner must have a bound somewhere, or become hopelessly confused. I stop with Gray & Chapman; for the present!—Even within that narrow limit I am all in a maze over "Ophioglossum," "Schizaea," "Struthiopteris," and "Cystopteres," having seen or found them not, with all my searching and studying.

I feel, Sir, sincerely grateful to you for your kindness under so many questions, which often seem stupid to you, no doubt. But I have never been so fortunate as to study botany, and, indeed, have time only for the walks and the gathering of specimens, the exercise being necessary for my health.

Very Truly Yours
Constance Fenimore Woolson.

Notes

1. Settlements at Newington, Goose Creek, South Carolina began to be established in the late seventeenth century by the English aristocracy.

2. The soap plant, or *Chlorogalum pomeridianum,* is a relative of the fern.

3. The Torrey Club, named after botanist John Torrey (1796–1873), was a botanical club that emphasized the study of ferns.

To Paul Hamilton Hayne (Duke)

Charleston
June 15th, [1875]

Dear Mr Hayne.

I received your charming letter; also the poems; and yesterday, the little note. You must let me tell you why I have not written before: After receiving the letter I waited for the poems, which were longer in coming than I thought they would be; and since then my eyes have been behaving badly, and two long Mss. due in New York before this date, lying on my table unfinished!! I am obliged always to defer to my eyes, and even in their best state I never use them at all after dark; then, it is absolutely necessary to my health and well being generally to walk at least two hours of each day for the pure exercise of the thing. Do you see, now, how curtailed my time is? But I did enjoy your letter so much! I can not write a good letter my-self,—never could; but there is scarcely any pleasure greater to me than receiving one. And the few correspondents I have, are generally kind enough to write two letters to my one, knowing how hard it is for me at times to force my eyes to write. I was much interested in what you wrote of the southern ideas upon the literature of the day; then I have not lost my senses, after all! I sometimes feared I had.—I have not seen Mrs Preston's collected poems but I have seen a number of her fugitive pieces, and never one that did not strike me as especially strong and sweet. Yes; she is a power in the southern land. If we go to Lexington this summer,—and we may, I am anxious to do so,—I shall with pleasure write to you for the promised note of introduction.—

You just allude to your own life, and then pass on. Now, Mr Hayne, it is your own life which, of all the things you can tell me, I should most like to hear about. You have lived through stirring times, and I, having spent two years in the south, can go as far as this: I begin to <u>understand</u> now, the ideas, the life, the training &c&c which brought about the differences between the two sections. Before, I did not.—

You ask me if I know literary people. Hardly one. My mother's uncle was Fenimore Cooper, so we have literary traditions in the family, but I have spent my life so far at the west where there are no literary people. I met Mr Stedman in Florida two seasons ago, and was charmed with him; he was very kind to me. On making a flying visit to New York last September, he made me come to dinner and there I met Mr and Mrs Stoddard, and Mrs M. M. Dodge of the "St Nicholas." I took a great fancy to Mrs Stoddard. I had always admired her odd strong novels. You speak of Stedman's Victorian Poets; they are, they certainly are, superb! <u>I</u> have seen nothing approaching them anywhere, in any language, in all my life. I cannot express what an impression they made upon me. How delicate! How strong!—Poor Stedman, how sad that he should lose his strength just when at his best;—so full of plans, so glowing with ambition and energy the last time I saw him. I see he has returned to New York. If you know, do tell me how he is; and if you write to him, do call me to his remembrance with warm regard.

I do not know anything of Miss Lazarus—(I told you I knew nobody of literary fame) but I shall get her "Admetus" and read it, since you like it so much.[1]—

So you saw Mr Howell's criticism on my Castle Nowhere.[2] Judge after reading <u>that</u>, how pleasant it is for me to have your first letter to fall back upon!—But the criticism, as a whole, was very high praise, I thought; of course I am smarting a little about the "Castle," which, to tell the truth, <u>was</u> something of an ideal, instead of a <u>real</u> tale,—like the others. But then I had been abused so for writing such deadly "real" stories that I did branch out, in that one, into the realm of imagination. Still, Mr Howells is mistaken in thinking the situation fantastic; the islands, the fogs, the false lights, the wreckers, the Mormons are all exactly from <u>real</u> <u>life</u>, true descriptions.—I am curious to know what you have read of my verses. I have not yet decided whether I can write verses or not. Perhaps you can help me to a decision. Such as they are they come by themselves without the slightest effort; whereas my prose is always the result of long and careful thought.—

I have not seen your "Lyrics and Legends," nor can I find it here. But I did find your "Avolio" in the Charleston library, and it now lies on my table by the side of your exquisite volume, the "Mountain of the Lovers." In "Avolio" I selected many bits to copy; I wrote them on the blank leaves at the beginning and end of other volumes of poetry,—a way I have. For instance I put your "Life" and "Death" sonnets in H. H.'s Verses; and your "Now While the Rear Guard of the flying Year," in Shelley. I trust you are satisfied with your company. I read and enjoyed "Avolio" the first; but when the "Vengeance" came I saw how much finer it was, at once. I have read once or twice your beautiful "Mountain of the Lovers," but have not had time to study it, as I intend to do when I reach the mountains. It will bear close study I see. Of the shorter poems I greatly admire "The Visit of the Wrens." "Midsummer in the South." ["]My Daughter.["] And my old favorite "Pre Existence." You can think of me carrying the dainty little volume out on my long afternoon walks, and reading it at the resting place, a log by a brook, probably; or else the breezy top of some high hill. I have a few worn little books that go with me in my wandering life, and are as dear friends; a few, because one cannot carry a library in a trunk; and a trunk is all the home I have had for five years, and all I expect to have for twice that time in the future. For I am outward bound;—for the old world, before very long, I hope. In this small company of books I place your little volume. By fall it will be well known and every line will be familiar. Do write again, Mr Hayne. Your letters are most charming. We have lingered here much longer than we intended, for we like the old city; but we are off now in a few days. Address me as usual [through?] Mr Alden, please.

Truly yours
C. F. Woolson.

Please return this I wanted you to see what Miss W—thought of our Mrs Preston.

Notes

1. The correct title of Emma Lazarus's poem is "Ametus" (1871).
2. See letter to Howells dated June 28, 1875. The apostrophe error is Woolson's.

To Samuel Livingston Mather (Benedict/Voices, 243; Benedict/Abroad, 742)

. . . The thermometer here has several times stood at 86, and 88, in the shade. Mother enjoys it; the well ones find it rather warm. This year the plan is to try some of the quieter resorts among the mountains of Virginia . . . Mother does enjoy travelling so very much; she is far fresher and more excited about it than her daughters . . . She is planning now to drive "up the Ashley" while we are staying in Charleston, and see the ruins of those fine old mansions that once belonged to the very people we met at Asheville last summer—old Charleston grandees, impoverished by the war. . . .

To Samuel Mather (Anderson)[1]

[1875]

Dear Sam.

So you went to Zoar? Did'nt you hear any "mad" remarks about my "Wilhelmina"? Since I have been here [some one sent me a New Philadelphia paper containing a savage article on "Wilhelmina" based upon the idea that my characters were all from life, and consequently "the leathery woman" was the good Mrs Beiter, the gardiner's wife, &c&c. Of course the article in the country paper was of no consequence; but I was distressed to think that perhaps the Beiters, always good friends of mine, thought so, too. I therefore wrote to Mr B. telling him it was but a fancy sketch &c, and this is his answer. Most of it I have made out, but not all; and as I have no grammar, no dictionary, and what is worse no time, I send it along to you. When you have leisure, make me out a translation, please.[2] But there is no sort of haste—take your own time,—all summer if you like. I happened to think of it to-day while clearing out some papers.—Mother is charmingly well here; I never saw her so pleased with any place as she is with Charleston. We shall not hurry away. The weather is lovely—warm summer air, the band plays in the Battery. Ice cream. White dresses, &c&c. Love to your dear mother, and father—In haste

C.F.W.

Notes

1. A portion of the letter is also in Benedict/CFW, 22.

2. The gardener [Woolson's spelling is *gardiner*] at Zoar, Simon Beiter (1819–?), sent Woolson a letter dated April 23, 1875, which is archived in Anderson. The first three sentences are in English. The remainder of the letter has been translated by Bill Weißker and Silke Weißker-Vorgias. Given the tone of his letter, Woolson must have known Beiter well and he may at least informally have been her teacher. The manager of Zoar's extensive gardens, Beiter was also a Trustee of Lawrence Township for twenty-four years and a Justice of the Peace.

> Esteemed friend, yours of 10th is just recd although it reached Zoar a week ago but during my absence from home—, hence I could not reply any sooner—. Your story "Wilhelmina" was the cause of a great stir up, not only here at Zoar but in the whole neighborhood—. O now, I remember you said in your story you studied the German Language carefully—therefore I will set forth my apistle in that Language—"
>
> I myself took the novel with philosophical coolness—but not the others over here, because they do not understand enough about what novels are—. Then you gave the names of the people too exactly—you say for example Wilhelmina was the

adoptive daughter of the gardener—and, the leathery woman was the gardener's wife, who certainly doesn't like to be called "leathery" . . . Also, you contradict yourself in reference to Wilhelmina . . . , because she had to collect strawberries, guard the cows, to churn and to milk, and to talk with you simultaneously, nearly everything at the same time. In some parts, Wilhelmina speaks in a very broken English and at another place you say that she spoke English very well; in general, it is wished, that if you furthermore use the name Zoar, or make use of the names of people who live here, the stories or novels, as they may be called, may be more related to the truth, in order not to generate bad blood and hostility, which, as you claim education, should not be indifferent to you.

What excitement this article caused amongst us neighbours you can easily see in the "short angry article"—many people asked me, if this or that were true in "Wilhelmina" and when I said no, the people wondered and said—: such lies should not be published in public about people one knows so well.

Also I have to tell you as one of my scholars, that you should study grammar a little better—for you said "der Regiment" it is "das Regiment"—, well never mind.

In Zoar have happened great changes since you hadn't been here—To enumerate everything would be too circumstantial—. My son is professor for music—my daughter Emily is still at home with us, she is big and strong and my wife still looks as healthy and fresh as if she were only 30 years old and her face doesn't show any sign of leathery constitution.

Would like to hear from you every now and then to tell you off afterwards.

Respectfully

Simon Beiter.

To William Dean Howells (Houghton)

Cleveland Springs
Shelby. North Carolina
June 28th, [1875]

Dear Mr Howells.

I give you above, as desired, my address for the next two months, or so; "Shelby" is our post-office; the nearest town,—about two miles from the Springs. We came up from Charleston last week, and finding here a shady retreat, a primitive hotel in the heart of the woods with sulphur springs and baths, with utter quiet, not even the country turnpike in sight, with a circle of blue mountain-peaks on the horizon-line, we decided to remain for the present, leaving Virginia for September, and perhaps another season. It is not like last summer at Asheville where we were in the mountains' arms;—I miss my sunsets, and my crowd of peaks over toward Tennessee. But one cannot have every thing, and this year it was sulphur water we were seeking.—Your note accepting "Rodman the Keeper," reached me at Charleston where we passed two delightful months; I think Charleston the most picturesque city I have ever seen. But I have not been abroad.—Yes; I think "Rodman" is good. It is an exact picture of local reality; as I saw it. I hope to send you one more story this summer; but it is not yet written. If there were only forty eight hours in a day!

I do not know whether you wrote the review of "Castle Nowhere" in the "Atlantic" for June, or not; but I assume that you at least read it, as it was under your own covers.[1]—Now I care so much about standing right in your eyes, that I want you to let me tell you how the title-tale came to be written; saying at first, however, that this is for you, personally, and not for the editor of the "Atlantic;" for Mr Howells the writer (whom we claim for the Western Reserve, you know), who, as I believe I told you before, has been with Geo. Eliot and Bret Harte, one of my classics.—After this "Lady of Little Fishing," "Solomon," "Peter the Parson," "St Clair Flats," and the rest, had appeared in the magazines, some praise came to me; but it was mixed with this suggestion, from various quarters. "You are too realistic; you have gone after false gods. Give us something ideal, something purely imaginative;—like Undine, for instance."[2] This, in various forms, was repeated again and again, I all the time opposing it, and maintaining at least to myself that the stories were not too realistic; and that even if they were, I could not write otherwise. But, at last, the same opinion came to me from such high authority that I began to question my own faith, and ask whether, after all, I was as good a judge as the public, the all-reading, impartial, indifferent public. So, when a new story was needed, unwillingly, and a little cross-ly, I penned "Castle Nowhere." But even then I could not let go reality entirely; the fogs, the islands, the Mormons, the false lights and the wreckers are all from real life. We had a cottage at Mackinac for two summers when I was a young girl, and I knew all about the islands just west of the Straits, and their lawless inhabitants. I think it was the next year that the Mormons over there were finally dispersed.[3] "Old Fog" was deliberately intended for just what you read; "Silver" is a pretty shadow; and "Waring" is, alas! my young-man character. Whenever I want a lover (not a hero, but simply a lover), this same fellow always persistently appears; I suppose because that is the kind of young man I have always known; and the only kind.—Well, I finished the tale with care; and it appeared. Will you believe that I have received letter after letter saying that it was so much, much, the best! So much more "beautiful" than the others! But all the while, in my own heart, I still held on to my original opinion. Judge then whether it was ~~not~~ a comfort or not to read the review in the "Atlantic."—I had become confused, and a little irritated by this clashing of my opinion and everybody else's. The "Atlantic" speaks; and with that to back me, I shall go back to my own, relieved.

The rest of the review was high praise, very high praise; it made me happy, and proud. I feel like telling the writer, whoever he is, how much pleasure it gave me; and also how much delightful encouragement for the future. I am, shall I say unfortunately, excessively sensitive to praise and to blame; these critics seem to hold my very life in their hands. I am sleepless, often, after reading what they say, whether for good or for ill. Your friend Miss Phelps is above all that. I think I never saw any woman so absolutely removed far away from any personal sympathy with those around her; she seems to live in a dream. I bought her poems in Charleston, as soon as they appeared, because you spoke so highly of them (Paul Hayne says you are the most fastidious and difficult critic in America. I do not know Mr Hayne; he wrote to me, however, not long since, and that was in the letter), and they are here now on my table. I like them. But they are very personal, are they not? This reminds me that I was charmed with "Spring in New England," by Aldrich, in the "Atlantic" for June. He has voiced at last those feelings which have lain deep in our hearts all these years; not forgotten; but unspoken. You see, I have been down here in the South, among those poor graves, for two long years.

You will pardon this personal letter, Mr Howells; I have never regarded you exactly in the light of a stranger,—I hardly know why; unless it was because I also tried my hand at "Rondinella Pellegrina," away back in Cleveland those early days. You remember I sent you Mr Case's translation. Did you see that Kate Hillard was out with one, too?[4]—That makes six. They ought to be published together.

Very truly yours,
C. F. Woolson.

Notes

1. Cheryl Torsney names Howells as the reviewer in her reprint of the June 1875 *Atlantic Monthly* article; see *Critical Essays on Constance Fenimore Woolson* (New York: G. K. Hall, 1992). In his review, Howells criticizes "Castle Nowhere" for its "disagreeable fantasticality," preferring her more realistic stories in the *Castle Nowhere* (1875) collection (Torsney 17).

2. See letter to Miss Farnian dated Apr. 17, 1875.

3. A group of Mormons under the leadership of James Jesse Strang (1813–56) settled on Beaver Island, Michigan, where Strang declared himself king and the heir of Joseph Smith (1805–44). In 1856, Strang was murdered.

4. Woolson is referring to a musical score by Tommaso Grossi (1791–1853). Kate Hillard, a friend of William and Alice Gibbens James, frequently published in *Harper's New Monthly Magazine.*

To Daniel C. Eaton (Virginia)

Cleveland Springs
Shelby. North Carolina
July 3^{d}, [1875]
Mr D. C. Eaton.

Dear Sir.

I write to thank you for the ferns. You can have no idea how much pleasure and satisfaction they gave me. The "Cyslopterus" has been a standing enigma to me always; and also the "Struthiopteris,."—I never shall know that ugly little "Adder's Tongue," however, no matter if it grows under my very feet. It is not like a Fern.— We are here for a few weeks, and then we go to Virginia. I have found only one new fern, the "Aspidium Noveboracense." But I am afraid to wander in the woods as I did last summer on the mountains farther west, for they tell me there is here a minute creature "no larger than the point of a pin," who "burrows in the flesh," and, "the woods are full of them"! His minuteness strikes me as appalling; if he was only as large as the head of a pin, I might meet him on his own ground,—but the point—! With many thanks, I am,

Truly Yours,
Constance Fenimore Woolson.

To Scribner's Monthly (Virginia)

Cleveland Springs
Shelby. North Carolina
July 3^{d}, [1875]
Ed. Scribner's Monthly.

Dear Sir.

I write to ask about the Ms. I sent you in May,—called, "Eight-Mile Swamp."[1] If you have come to any decision, please send word, to the address given above. I shall remain here about two weeks, and then go to Virginia; please do not send here after that date, as they will not know at the post office where to reach me; we do not know ourselves where we shall be; somewhere in the mountains,—where things look pleasant.

And I should like, when writing to you, if you have no objection, to write to some name beside "Ed. S's M." I do not know whether to address Mr Gilder; Mr Johnstone;—or whom.—Can you kindly tell me how Mr E. C. Stedman is? I have heard nothing about his health since he returned from the West Indies.

Very Truly Yours,
Constance F. Woolson.

"Shelby" is not the name of the county; but the town two miles from here, our post office.

Notes

1. No record exists of a Woolson piece titled "Eight-Mile Swamp."

To Paul Hamilton Hayne (Duke)

Goshen
Rockbridge Co. Virginia
July 23^d^, [1875]
Paul H. Hayne E^sq^.

Dear Sir.

Your letter of June 28th reached me at Cleveland Springs, North Carolina, where, after leaving Charleston, we stayed three weeks. The sulphur water and baths were excellent, and the place secluded enough to suit even me; but rain fell daily in the little valley, and rheumatic pains attacked Mother with their old northern ferocity; now we did not come south to enjoy rheumatisim; so we left. I must confess, too, that I missed my mountains of last year, the magnificent purple peaks around Asheville that I used to watch at sunset from the height back of the town. I shall never forget the far look towards Tennessee, the sunset gap with "the golden mountain" beyond, and near me in the foreground, gaunt [smoky?] Pisgah. At Cleveland Springs, by walking a mile, and then climbing up a six-railed fence and sitting on top, one could just see the blue line of the peaks in the west! But that grew monotonous after a while. We traveled in our slow way through Charlotte, Danville, and Lynchburg to Charlottesville; I say "slow way" because as we never ride at night, but always stop over somewhere and sleep in a bed we constantly find ourselves considered very slow, in every way. The crowd, you know, rushes through by sleeping car. At Charlottesville we stayed two days, driving out or rather up to "Monticello," and also to the "University of Virginia." My mother has had from childhood a strong desire to see "Monticello"; now, late in life, it is gratified. Her grandfather, Judge Cooper of Cooperstown, N.Y. was a strong Jefferson man, and taught all his descendents to revere the name. Judge Cooper was one of the members of Congress at the time of the exciting "tie" between Jefferson and Aaron Burr.[1] It was at Charlottesville, too, that my dear Father,—who died five years ago,—made his first venture in life, as editor of a paper. A northern man was desired, and he sailed from Boston when only twenty-two years old, and filled the place for a year; something of an adventure for a Yankee boy! From Charlottesville we came out here,—in the "Valley of Virginia." On Mother's account we do not stay at any of the "Springs," which must all necessarily be in ravines or low places, I suppose. We are at a little wayside cottage, <u>with</u> a post office, <u>with</u> a telegraph, <u>with</u> an express office, <u>with</u> ice,—things we have come to the conclusion we cannot do without. At Cleveland Springs, they sent for the mail whenever they pleased! And several times forgot it entirely!—We shall go next month to the Greenbriar White Sulpher for a few days; I suppose if we see the White, we see <u>the</u> Virginia Spring. We are also within a morning's drive of Lexington. I think we shall go over there before long. And if you will send me the letter of introduction to Mrs Preston, and give me the privilege of presenting it or not, as I please,—I shall like it. For, Mr Hayne, if there is anything I dread it is a new acquaintance. I evade, and avoid, and back away from everybody. It is, unfortunately, my nature to do so. I am sorry. It is a great fault. But I cannot change it now, I fear, after so many years' indulgence. Early in September we shall go up the lovely Shenandoah Valley to Harper's Ferry.—You say we travel constantly. Yes, we do. But it is for my Mother's health. It is pleasant; and yet it has its drawbacks. Sometimes we sigh for our own household gods; our own easychairs, our pet pictures, our favorite books. And sometimes, arriving in a strange place, after a contest over our trunks, and a mistake about rooms perhaps, or something of the kind, I cannot help a tired sigh, and something very like moisture in the eyes, when I remember how my dear Father used to take care of us.—However, that is only when I am tired. I will say, for America generally, that the amount of kindness and attention we receive, as ladies traveling alone, is quite remarkable. But I find it is not so common a custom at the south as it is with us at the north.—Ladies traveling alone,—I mean. By the way,—you speak of means. Ours are not large at all. But we see the world very pleasantly in our quiet fashion. It seems to me, Mr Hayne, that it takes less money to travel than it does to stay at home!—You say you have exhausted the resources of the scenery around you. True, I can see much of it in your late volume of poems; some of the verses are like pictures. I can imagine just how your favorite nooks and walks look. But,—do'nt laugh,—did you ever study ferns? Now I am on my hobby! I feel sure I could find the most lovely ferns by the "Solitary Lake," or in "Golden Dell." Only a year ago I took up the study, and oh! what fresh new interest and pleasure I have found in it! There is quite a band of fern lovers in the country, and we correspond, exchange specimens, quarrel over a new one, &c&c, although we do not know each other at all save by letter. But you will not care about this. Yet I must tell you before stopping, that yesterday I went out between showers and found on the rocks behind the cottage five kinds, and one new one! That last one gladdened all the day, and sent me to bed happy as a child.—You see, my hobby rides well!—I was so very much interested, my dear Sir, in what you wrote of yourself.—Do you know, I had mixed you with a relative of the same name, Arthur Hayne, I think, who had quite a gay career.[2] That is not you, after all, I am told. Does that make you smile? Oh, you South Carolinians,—how proud you are! I never understood it at all until I came down among you. Why, you seem to me the proudest people on the face of the globe! The blue blooded Castillians can be nothing to you. There is a height, and a breadth; and a depth, to your pride, which actually goes beyond even the comprehension of a plain Yankee woman like myself.—And (another thing I did not understand until I came down South myself) there is cause and reason for your pride. You do bear the marks of your old Cavalier descent, and in spite of my unwillingness, I am forced to acknowledge it. I have never seen such courtly manners as those of the elderly Charlestonians; I mean rather, those whose manners were formed in ante bellum days. Forgive me if I say that the boys and girls of today are not like their fathers and mothers.—So you were at Sumter.—And I (lately) was on Morris Island! What days they were! After all, we lived then. It is in vain for our generation to hope to be any other than "people who remember." Sometimes even now, I wake early, and think I hear the distant call of the newsboy far down the street, "Extra! Extra! All about the last battle!"—And then how we rushed out to get it, how we devoured it, and then hurried down to the "Soldier's Aid" rooms to do the little that was open to us faraway ones to do,—prepare boxes of supplies for the soldiers.

I wonder where your house was, "overlooking the Cooper River." Out of town? I should have been so glad to have mentioned it in my forthcoming article (now in the printer's hands I suppose) on "the Ashley & Cooper." I searched out many old houses in the "Drayton Hall" & "Goose Creek," neighborhood. I asked, particularly, too, if there was not a "Hayne" house somewhere.—Then, you went to Augusta. Did you ever know a school mate of mine, Kate Milledge? I believe she lived there. I was at school at Madame Chegaray's, New York, with a number of Southern girls; Julie Gordon, Penie Wragg, and Madgie Reid of Savannah were among them. It is just possible you may know some of them.—While at Cleveland Springs I saw a number of the "Southern Review," containing a criticism of your poetry by "Sydney Lanier,"—I think that was the name. It began by saying, that immediately after the war, Paul Hayne shut himself up in the pine woods of Georgia and gave all his thought, time, and life to poetry. That sentence would have attracted my attention even if I had not known you. Who is Sydney Lanier? I did not agree with the review, by the way.—What you say of your wife makes me admire her so much! But after all, what is there more in life than what she has,—home, child, and husband.

I am going to send to Lippincott for your "Legends and Lyrics."—I am so glad to know that Mr Stoddard has a government appointment. When I was in N.Y., it seemed to be the fashion to talk about "poor Stoddard." For my part, I could not see why he should be especially "poor"; (We were none of us rich!) His Bric à Brac Series has prospered wonderfully, his writings meet you in almost every magazine; he has only the one little child. I confess I did not quite understand it. I grieve to hear that Mr Stedman is no better.

I am especially pleased to know that you, a Southerner, liked "At the Smithy."[3] Yes; what there is of me, I fear, tends to the dramatic. It is a dangerous tendency. I love Charles Reade's novels; also the elder Dumas', and Victor Hugo's. And a recent novel called "Young Brown." Have you seen it? Please tell me what novels you like.

I fancy I can judge people by the novels they like. Really like,—not the pretense of liking. Now to me, Hawthorne seems intensely dramatic. Look at the "Scarlet Letter," and the "Blithedale Romance," the latter my favorite of all.

Sometime when you are writing, please give me your definition of "a sonnet." Also tell me what is "subjective," and "objective" poetry. I do not comprehend the terms. But I always was an outside barbarian.

You speak of Howells.—Have you ever seen his poetry? Mr Stedman told me it was fearfully criticised and abused by everybody when the volume came out, and that Howells felt very sore about it. Perhaps that will explain some things! I do not know Mr H.—His family have lived always in Ohio, not far from my old home, Cleveland. Thus, we reckon him "a Western Man."—But I must stop scribbling. This is a poor return, Mr Hayne, for your charming, interesting and exquisitely written letter. But you will excuse the faulty work of poor tired eyes. I shall be here in Goshen some weeks. With regards to Mrs Hayne, I am Truly Your friend

C. F. Woolson.

Notes

1. James Fenimore Cooper's father, Judge William Cooper (1754–1809). In the 1800 election, members of the Electoral College could cast two votes for president, with the person receiving the most votes becoming president and the runner-up becoming vice president. The vote resulted in a tie between Thomas Jefferson (1743–1826) and Aaron Burr (1756–1836). Alexander Hamilton (1755?57?–1804) wielded his influence to have Jefferson elected president, with Burr becoming his vice president. The dispute prompted the 12th Amendment, which separated the two positions.

2. Hayne's cousin.

3. Woolson published this poem in *Appletons' Journal* (Sept. 5, 1874).

To Paul Hamilton Hayne (Duke)

Goshen
Rockbridge Co. Virginia
Aug. 26th, [1875]

Dear Mr Hayne.

I must send a line to tell you that I have seen your friend Mrs Preston, and that I feel much indebted to you for the opportunity of making so delightful an acquaintance. We went over to Lexington last week for a day; I rode on top of the stage in order to see the scenery through Goshen Pass, and a chance made me say to a gentleman by my side, that I had expected a note of introduction to Mrs Preston, but as it had not arrived, of course I should not call upon her, as she would not care to meet a stranger. "Why.—I am going to visit Mrs Preston myself," he said. I said nothing more; but, most kindly, Mrs Preston came immediately to the Hotel, and our short stay was made charming by her attentions.—She took me in her carriage to the Military Institute where her husband is Professor, and also to her own delightful home, where I had the pleasure of seeing a photograph of yourself, finding it much younger than I had fancied you to be.[1] In these days of haste and carelessness, the exquisite style of your letters had led me to suppose you at least forty five, if not older; but this picture does not look more than thirty.—

Mrs Preston is a charming woman; quiet, gentle, and the reverse of the common idea of a "literary woman." Colonel Preston is a very fine looking gentleman, much older than his wife, I should say. Their home in that quaint little academic town, with those superb mountain views in every direction, seemed to me very charming.

I saw the Lee Chapel, of course; and I stood for a long time by the grave of Stonewall Jackson; it was for that I went over to Lexington; I have always had a strong admiration for that plain earnest man and brilliant soldier.

At Lexington, too, I found your volume of Timrod's poetry. What a sad sad life!—I think I shall like the poems; some of them very much. I have never seen them before. It is a little singular that several of them express almost the same ideas that several of my own poems express! We fell upon the same train of thought, it seemed.

I have also been over to the Springs; of course I mean the Greenbriar White Sulphur. There I saw a thousand guests, several celebrities, a number of pretty faces, and some diamonds.—But I must confess, of the two places, I prefer Saratoga.

Tomorrow I take my Mother up the beautiful Shenandoah Valley to Harper's Ferry, there to meet my sister and her little daughter. The three will then go North, and the one (myself) return South again. I cannot go visiting this fall, I have too much to do. I shall return to this quiet place, and write very hard for five or six weeks. I never was in a better place for writing; mountain air, and absolutely no interruptions. Then, when November comes, I shall be ready for Richmond, Norfolk, the Dismal Swamp and Key West,—our fall and winter programme. But Goshen will be my post office for the present, and I hope to hear from you while here. Did you receive the letter I wrote you some weeks ago?—

Very Truly Yours,
C. F. Woolson.

P.S.

I do not think Mrs Preston has any idea who am, save that I know you.

Notes

1. Margaret Preston's husband, Confederate Col. John Preston, taught at Virginia Military Institute. Woolson never met Hayne in person.

To Samuel Mather (WRHS/Mather)[1]

[Goshen, Virginia.
August 1875]

Dear Sam.

Much as I should love to see you, I think you would enjoy Cooperstown so much that I ought to say "go there." It is the loveliest place I ever saw and the society is so charming. You will love the "Fenimore Coopers" dearly, I know; just as I do.—And the Lake is as lovely as a Swiss Lake.

C.F.W.

—They will pet you, all of them; they are so kind and cordial.

Notes

1. This note appears across the top of a letter written by Hannah Woolson to her grandson Samuel Mather. Hannah has been advising him whether to visit Virginia or Cooperstown.

To Paul Hamilton Hayne (Duke)

Goshen
Rockbridge Co. Virginia
Sept. 12th, [1875]

Dear Mr Hayne.

I am relieved to know that you did write, in answer to mine of the early summer and that the fault is in the mails, only.—I had feared that something in my letter might have offended you. I write and speak, always, too rashly,—too thoughtlessly.—May the last letter appear soon. Did I not ask you about what is called subjective and objective poetry? And did you answer that? If so, and the letter does not appear, please do repeat what you wrote. I have asked the question more than once; but nobody ever will answer it.—

I have just returned from Harper's Ferry. How beautiful is the historic Shenandoah Valley, where my favorite Southern general, Stonewall Jackson, fought. At the ferry we met my sister and her little daughter, and then having exhausted "Maryland" and "Bolivar Heights" and the memory of John Brown, and having still a few days to pass together, we went up to Harrisburg, Penn., and thence by a roundabout way, the only one, to Gettysburg. I have always wished to go there. Friends of mine died there. It was a heavenly day, and standing under the great monument among the thousands of low green mounds, we could scarcely realize that the beautiful scene was ever one of agony and horror.

I always go to see the soldiers' graves. I cannot bear to think that they are so soon forgotten; as they are, at the North,—and indeed the War itself is already a thing of the past up there.—My Mother and sister then went westward to Cleveland and Chicago, and I, resisting everybody's wish and advice, returned here for four weeks of uninterrupted quiet work.—I find it all that I hoped it would be. But the weather is cold and rainy.

Nothing you write ever "strikes" me "as feeble or mediocre," where ever I see or find your poems; so do not apologise. I like both the sonnets; but I like the last one "Day follows day," much the best. It seems to me exquisite in its grace and meaning; I do not know when I have seen anything more beautiful than the last six lines.—But, Mr Hayne, do you not know that I am only an outside barbarian? I assure you I often feel myself so when with literary people. I have such strong likes & dislikes. And for what I care, nobody else seems to care.

I am reading Robert Buchanan's poems carefully. But,—Well, I do'nt care much about his gods and ~~and~~ goddesses; still less about his Scotch people. So much the worse for me, do you say?—I can tell you one thing;—I very often put down my task, and go and get your volume to refresh myself with.—

When you are writing, tell me, sometime, what works you like. I always wish to know that; I fancy I can judge character by the novels a person really likes; provided he tells the truth.—

I hope you will write while I am "in retreat" here. My evenings are long, and still as a desert. The mail comes at seven, p.m., and what it brings gives me my evening amusement, and thought. I read my letters slowly, and do them full justice. But, from me, on the other hand, you can never hope to receive any adequate return, Mr Hayne. The Fates have not gifted me in that way. I never could write a good letter. And now that my eyes trouble me, I find myself cutting off every additional word. Will you excuse these defects.—And still write to me?—

Do you know I am charmed with that sonnet; (it always takes me some time to get acquainted with anything I am going to really like).

—"Something sweet Even in a weed's heart,—the carved leaves of corn, The spear-like grass,—the silvery rime of morn,"—It is most beautiful,—yes, I do think so. Thank you for sending it.[1]

I shall be here, probably, several weeks longer.

Very Truly Yours,
C. F. Woolson.

Notes

1. Woolson quotes Hayne's "Freshness of Poetic Perception" from his "Sonnets On Various Themes."

To Paul Hamilton Hayne (Duke)

Society Hall
Darlington Co. South Carolina
All-Saints Day
[1875] 1876[1]

Dear Mr Hayne.

Saturday afternoon, at the window of the little post-office here, I received your note of inquiry, which had been forwarded home from New York. The delay is not the fault of Mr Alden, but my own; I postponed writing to him until I had finished something I was preparing for his magazine, and, in the meantime, he had no idea where we were.[2]—Yes; I received your former letter while at Goshen, and it was doubly welcome in my great isolation and loneliness there. Five weeks I spent in my little cottage-room at some distance from the hotel, entirely alone. The fall of leaves came early this year you know, and there was rain and much dismal weather up there in the mountains. Writing over for the day, I used to sit at the window and watch for the evening trains that brought the mail; by and by I saw its red light down the valley, then over the bridge, and then past my low door it rushed, and in five minutes I would be at the post office waiting for my share of evening amusement and good cheer. It was on one of these dismal evenings that your letter came and I enjoyed it very much. Enjoyed also the beautiful "Vision by the Sea," that came with it. It is a lovely poem and it impresses the reader with its reality. I should have known, even if you had not said it, that you really saw just such a vision. "Standing between the blue sky and the sea,"—that is an exquisite line to me; it brings out the picture clearly, as a human form is brought out on the level beach against the sky. Do you know that all this time I have gone lazily along asking for your Lippincott Volume, everywhere, but have not yet sent to Philadelphia for it.[3] Is not that very shiftless, to use a New England word? But, if I may say so, I never give up anything I really wish for, and all the time I have known that I should certainly send for the book sooner or later, and have it for my own. But in the meantime I have asked for it in Charleston, Charlotte, Charlottesville, Baltimore and Norfolk without finding it, and in the larger places I have remarked with censorious accent "I should think you would keep a stock of Mr Hayne's books on hand always! Are you aware that he is the representative Southern poet? Where else should we northerners expect to find his books if not in Southern book stores." At Charleston and at ~~Norf~~ Baltimore they really were ashamed of themselves.—When I go into Charleston a little later, I intend boxing up the volumes that have accumulated on my hands during these two years, and then I can begin on a fresh supply. My poor trunks have grown fuller and fuller; you know how heavy books are. And I have quite ruined myself in paying for extra baggage. Mother and I, two very plain persons as far as dress is concerned, travel with eight trunks! Is'nt it dreadful? And my books, botanies, and fern-herbariums have made most of the bulk.—In addition to your lyrics I shall then send for Henry James' volumes which I am anxious to see; also a complete set of my beloved Thoreau. If you have any pet books, now would be a friendly time to tell me their names.—I am delighted that you like Charles Reade. I am devoted to him. "Geo. Eliot," "Geo. Sand," and Charles Reade are my favorite living novelists. Of the dead I prefer Charlotte Brontë and Dumas père; but I ought to say, in connection with the latter, that all my admiration of him is founded upon one novel, or rather one series, viz. "Les Trois Mousquetaires." The stirring adventures of Messieures Athos, Porthos and Aramis, together with d'Artagnan are the only ones in literature that ever kept me up all night! To be sure that was a number of years ago. Still, I shall never forget the pleasure or rather stirring interest that novel gave me. Of course you read French? I know no difference between it and English.—Then too there is Victor Hugo.—Let me mention however that I never should have had the courage to confess my liking for the "Mousquetaires," if I had not seen last year in an article on Thackaray by Mr Stoddard that the great author of "Vanity Fair" preferred the "Mousquetaires" to any novel he had ever read; And said too that of all the characters ever drawn in literature, "Athos" came the nearest to his idea of a grand hero for a romance. Since then I have felt emboldened to speak out my opinion.—I am pleased to know that you, too, love Dickens; now that it is so fashionable to call him "low."—St Augustine in the winter is full of grandees you know; by grandees I mean scions of those old New York City families who come down from the Dutch times and have "Van" in their names somewhere; people who have been rich for generations and absolutely know nothing of their own country outside of the "City," although very familiar of course with Europe! Several of these gentlemen I know quite well. This is what one said: "Dickens: Yes,—I know; some people like his works, but I do not; they are very 'low.' I never care to read about the lower classes." And then he offered to lend me the last novel by the author of "Guy Livingstone!!"—[4] These are the people who make it a point to travel with "portable baths" always, in the charge of their valets. They have only two adjectives, "nice," and "beastly."—I am always getting into quarrels with them. And yet, they have spoiled me for any other kind of society almost.—They are so (to use their own word) nice, in a great many ways, after all. My favorite novel, though, now, is "The Mill on the Floss;" and I was therefore glad to see you too liked it. It is the favorite of my mature years. And this reminds me, Mr Hayne, that you are quite mistaken in supposing I am young; I am young in literary life; but not in years.—I take up your letter:—What was it that made me think I might have annoyed you? Well,—because I write so hastily and so carelessly, and because I am by nature so abrupt. I have learned not to be surprised when people show displeasure, and I always know it is owing to something I have said or written. In your case I did not know what it was, for I never can remember exactly what I have written. But I thought it might be perhaps my having mistaken you for your Cousin. There was a Miss Elmore (I did not like her at all) at Cleveland Springs (a dreadful place) who seemed to think my mistake was something fearful.—However, let it go. You are not offended, and that is the only thing of consequence. But I wonder why it never recurs to the "Miss Elmores" of the South how utterly and hopelessly adrift <u>they</u> would be if they went up among the aristocratic old families of New York and the Hudson River, or among the equally cultivated and proud circles in Mass. and Conn. They might think themselves fortunate if they escaped with no greater mistake than the mingling of two cousins of the same well known and distinguished name.—Your definition of subjective and objective poetry is clear. <u>At last</u> I understand the terms, and I am really thankful to you for telling me. I hate Wordsworth. Yes, I really think I hate him. And the reason is because people keep flinging him at your head all the time. And I am afraid you cannot make me like Robert Buchanan either. And also, in spite of all the nice things you say, I know only too well that I cannot and never could write a good letter. Every other member of my family wields a graceful pen save myself. In the old times I used to try to do better; now, I no longer try. And, as I have said before, my poor eyes must often excuse delays. When the Ms. work is done for the day, and the four mile walk taken, there is no light left often save candle-light, when I can do nothing at all.—Do you know where we are? I do'nt.—We had planned to spend a month or two in Norfolk, with excursions to all the interesting localities thereabouts. I went up to Baltimore the first of October to meet my Mother, and after some days there we sailed down Chesapeake Bay and landed at our destined abiding place. But oh! how cold it was. I shall always maintain that Norfolk, Virginia, is the coldest place I was ever in, in all my life! We stood it a week, and then fled southward. In Wilmington it was freezing, so on we came, not knowing where to go, not daring to be in Charleston so early, and not wishing to go far from our route to Florida. We heard of this place and came out to look at it, finding a very pretty little village, with "Hills"!!! of South Carolina height,—say sixty feet or so,—and ever so many old-fashioned places scattered around among beautiful trees. We knew no one of course, and expected to know no one. But the whole town has called upon us in the most sociable and hospitable way. The pleasantest person we have met is a Major Lucas.—We shall not stay long, but it will be long enough for me to receive an answer to this, if you care to write so soon. Otherwise, wait,—and I will send you my Florida address as soon as we are settled for the winter, which will be about the first of December. I presume we shall go to Key West, with Havana (and the Opera!) for an outlying attraction.—By the way, at Wilmington I chanced upon the paper containing your notice of Miss Fisher's latest story; which I have not read, by the way. Now then,—I shall have to come right out and confess that I too have criticised (in my own mind) not only Miss Fisher's stories, but those of other southern women, for the very thing you defend!! They have seemed to me exaggerated in style, and too full of a certain spirit, which I can best describe perhaps by saying that their heroes are always "Knightly,"—for the real life of to-day. Now I was at Madame Chegaray's School in New York City just before the breaking out of the war, and my school mates were all Southern girls, of fine old families too; their mothers and their grandmothers had been to the same school before them; for "Tante," as we called Madam C was a very old lady.[5] These girls were charming to me for the very simplicity of their manners; they were delightfully and naturally well-bred, from the ends of their curls down to their pretty little high-arched feet. But, Mr Hayne, they were very simple in their manners and notably so in their talk. They used to talk to me by the hour of their homes, their parents, brothers, <u>and</u> lovers,—and—well, it was not at all like "The Daughter of Bohemia," "St Elmo," "The Household of Bouverie," and other novels I have read since.[6]—You see, I must have my say. Just as yesterday, when I sat down to write a friendly letter, and before I knew it I had filled the sheet with that great "school question" we have up North, and which <u>I</u> think, is to be the next great national trouble. But, I suppose (to go back,) you were especially trying to show some of the northern critics that there <u>was</u> a grand old way of living down here before the war. It is true. There was. The patriarchal system of your households with their retinues of servants, gave a way, a manner, to your style of living that we never had at the north no matter how rich we were. This I saw at "Chegaray."—We would be up in our 3[d] story room perhaps, and one of the girls would begin calling "Elisabeth," "Elisabeth." Now Elisabeth, the Irish chambermaid[,] would be down in the lower hall perhaps at work on the panelling of the front door. "Elisabeth"! "Elisabeth," the voice would call from time to time. At last, unable to study I would say "Kate, what do you want of Elisabeth? She wo'nt come away up those two pair of stairs for you; she is busy." "I want her to shut the door," Kate would reply placidly looking up from her Italian. "Now Kate, why not get up and shut it yourself?"—And then Kate would laugh and do it, saying what was no doubt perfectly true, "do you know, Constance, I never thought of it."—And all this reminds me of something else: Do you see the Charleston "Courier and News." If so, did you notice the gallant way in which the editor took up the cudgels for me recently as against some interior paper? I do not know whether you have or have not seen anything of the affair, or how many newspapers you read. Generally speaking I care very little about the opinion of the southern press, which can neither make nor mar me; but for your opinion, Mr Hayne, I <u>do</u> care, and as you may have seen something of it, I prefer <u>you</u> to know the whole.—To begin with then: if there is anything I detest (for myself) it is the writing of a newspaper letter. I have no talent that way, and I do not like to approach so near the public. It is too "personal" a place for a lady, I think. But my only sister's father in law is the proprieter of the Cleveland (Ohio) Herald, and to him I am warmly attached. He likes a letter for his paper very much, and once or twice a year I try to send him something as a pure personal tribute to my regard for him. Last July from Goshen I sent him a letter, and oh! how I have rued the day! It was copied all over the country, beginning with the N.Y. Times, and of course I appreciated the compliment although hating to have my name given out as a "newspaper correspondent," all the same.[7] But when the southern papers fell on to it, there began trouble. There was a harmless little paragraph at the end of the letter about "Southern girls." I wish I had kept a copy of the letter that I might send it to you, so that you could see for yourself how harmless it was. But "A Southern girl," answered it in a furious vein in a Memphis paper, and that set the whole thing going again. It seems as though I was never to hear the last of it. A letter from Boston the other day said "are'nt you afraid to go in to Charleston after that letter of yours."—Afraid to go into Charleston! A city I admire and like more than any other save New York,—and a city I thought I had praised enthusiastically. Why—I do'nt know what I shall do if people are so thin-skinned as that. However the Courier & News gallantly came to my defence, and I was much pleased. Although angry at myself none the less that I had ever, (even to please a dear old friend) allowed myself to step down into the place where certain kinds of pens think they have a right to assail you. Mea culpa.—From this annoying little experience I begin to think that I shall have more of the same kind when my little "Charleston" article comes out in the next number of the Harper.[8] And yet I wrote it with the pleasantest feelings of interest in the subject, and treated it with much more care and courtesy than I should have done had I been writing of the vicinity of Boston. I believe I made a little fun of the high sounding title "High Hills of the Santee." Do you suppose I had better get out of South Carolina before the 15th? Oh Mr Hayne, Mr Hayne,—the trouble is all with the women. Major Lucas says "we are trying hard to get northern farmers to settle in our county. It is a great mistake to suppose we shall not receive them well."—"Yes," I answer; "but will their wives and daughters be received? You can not expect, of course, that gentlemen will come down here, when they are comfortably settled for life. But you might get the class below, the well to do small farmers and mechanics. Now will the wives and daughters of the class below you, Major Lucas, receive the wives and daughters of our small farmers and mechanics, who are generally quite well educated persons?" O women's tongues! From Eden down ye have made all the trouble.—I send you a little poem, or rather two. What do you say to them? I am excessively tired this fall, and rather depressed owing to isolation I suppose, and over work. I must hurry down among the grandees and hear some good music again. I shall come fresh from the desert into the ring again, and hear that "flounces are worn very flat now," and "that "Miss Rhinelander is not enjoyed after all," and that "Mr Aspinnall's yacht is expected," and that "Mrs Van-Something is as silly as ever with her five poodle dogs." Wo'nt it be refreshing? And then when the wind blows, they will say "it is a nasty day." And they will all take immensely long walks English fashion, and growl because they cannot have their beef rare. And really, Mr Hayne, what is the reason we never can have our beef rare down here? When I asked that question of a southern gentleman last year, he replied "because we have no fondness for dishes that remind us of the slaughter-house, Miss W."—That was crushing, was'nt it.—When are you going abroad, Mr Hayne? I am going just as soon as I can, and I intend to stay. "It may be for years, and it may be forever," as the song says.[9]—What a long letter I have written to you! I seldom do such a thing. Burn it, please. I think all letters should be burned within the year. A letter (at least mine) is not intended for a permanent thing. I see Mr Stedman's book is out.[10] Good luck to it. I shall get it in Charleston.

Truly yours,
C. F. Woolson.

Notes

1. The date in Woolson's handwriting appears to be 1876, but internal details suggest 1875 shortly after she had left Goshen, Virginia.

2. The piece Woolson is preparing for editor Henry Mills Alden at *Harper's New Monthly Magazine* is most likely the travel narrative "Up the Ashley and Cooper" (Dec. 1875).

3. Hayne's Lippincott volume was *Legends and Lyrics*, 1872.

4. The 1857 novel *Guy Livingstone* is by Guy Alfred Lawrence.

5. In her novel *Anne* (1882), Woolson calls the title character's mentor "Tante."

6. *A Daughter of Bohemia* (1874) is by Christian Reid (Frances Christine Fisher Tiernan); *St. Elmo* (1867), by Augusta Jane Evans; and *The Household of Bouverie* (1860), by Catherine Anne Warfield.

7. Woolson wrote a series of "Letters from Gotham" for George Benedict's *Daily Cleveland Herald* between Jan. and Feb. 1871. Portions of the letter about Southern women that she mentions were reprinted in the *New York Times*, July 31, 1875. Her depiction is hardly flattering: she describes Southern women as "rounder than her Northern sisters" with movements that are "slow and indolent." Further, she describes their accents, their "picturesque" clothing, and their curls. Her description of Southern men of whom "she cannot speak so highly" also reveal her regional bias: "They are either swept down, bewildered by the stream, or else, having drifted ashore in some little bay, they sit on the bank, and talk about their ancestors." She does conclude, however, that a "younger race" of men is developing "ideas more adapted to the times."

8. "Up the Ashley and Cooper" (Dec. 1875).

9. Lyrics from a popular Irish ballad.

10. *Victorian Poets*, 1875.

To James R. Osgood[1]

Mills House
Charleston. S.C.
Dec. 1st, [1875?]
Mr James R. Osgood.

Dear Sir.

I have just received your letter of November the twenty second which was forwarded from Society Hill, and I am glad to know that the Ms. volume reached you.

I could write several pages about the volume, and should like to do so; but, after all was said, the question would still be, or ought still to be, upon its bare merit solely,—So I will write nothing. But I am very curious to know what your opinion will be, and I am glad that until "immediately after January 1st" is not a very long time to wait.

I should be quite as well satisfied if only the new poems were published, and the volume an anonymous one.[2] It would then be a fair test; and that is what I want.

We leave Charleston in a day or two, and next week we shall be settled in St Augustine, Florida, for the winter. The account of "Castle Nowhere" can go there as soon as you please.

Very truly yours,
Constance Fenimore Woolson.

Notes

1. This letter was archived at Stuart House Museum, City of Mackinac Island Museums, Mackinac Island, Mich. Its current location is unknown.

2. Woolson seems to be referring to a possible collection of poems. No anonymous volume has been credited to her.

To Daniel C. Eaton (Beinecke)

Charleston. S.C.
Dec. 2^{d}, [1875]
Prof. D. C. Eaton.

Dear Sir.

Major Haskin and I have been disputing over these ferns. The most complicated and powerful microscopes have only increased our perplexities. We now refer them to you; what are they?—I gathered some of them in North Carolina, and some in Virginia last summer.

Will you be so kind as to write the names on the half-sheets, as I send them. For I have persuaded the Major to let me have the first look, and (I hope) the first triumph; and if I do not send him these same half-sheets just as they are, he will be fancying I have changed the specimens to prop up my failing cause! Please direct to "St Augustine, Florida"; I leave Monday next for a third long winter in that ancient city.

I wish there was something I could do for you, Sir, in return for your kindness in answering so many fern-questions. I was much pleased to learn that Major Haskin found the sea-weed for which we searched last spring. We may possibly make one more excursion to the Island for a better specimen before I leave; but the weather is very unfavorable at present.

Yours Truly,
Miss {Constance Fenimore Woolson.

To William Dean Howells (Houghton)

St Augustine. Florida
Dec. 11th, [1875]
Mr W. D. Howells.

Dear Sir.

I wrote to you from South Carolina, enclosing a sketch. We are settled in our old quarters for a third long winter; my address will be as above until April.—When I reached civilization, i.e. Charleston—I found two numbers of your new story already out.[1] I had been six weeks away from newspapers and magazines, or I should not have made such a mistake.—I bought the two numbers, and, if you will allow me to criticise—, I think them better than anything you have published yet. The little touches in the second number, where a woman describes a woman are delightfully real, and I suspect Mrs Howells aided you there; for no man, unaided, knows such things.

Truly yours,
Constance F. Woolson.

Notes

1. *Private Theatrical,* published in *Atlantic Monthly,* Nov. 1875–May 1876.

To Elizabeth Gwinn Mather (Benedict/Voices, 101; Benedict/Abroad, 690)

St Augustine
1875

My dear father—as I read Mr Mather's letter, I could not keep the tears from my eyes. Nothing has even been quite the same without him.

To Paul Hamilton Hayne (Duke)

St Augustine. Florida
Jan 16th, [1876]

Dear Mr Hayne.

I return your poem with my ideas about it written along the margin; I took it verse by verse. As a whole, I think it is very expressive and real; (I am very fond of "the real" you know,—almost too much so, I fear,) and equal to your best work. In truth the last two verses strike me as rising on high wings, the wings of soul-felt aspiration. They are the real Soul cry of a dying poet. They have a divine pathos too which only the yearning artist-heart can understand.

So now I have told you honestly what I think, and you ought to be very much obliged, because to do so has seemed to me both absurd and impertinent; and I am not one who enjoys doing either absurd or impertinent things. That a person so ignorant of poetical art as I am should sit down to pass opinion upon the work of one of the most melodious poets of the day is absurd. And that a person so bluntly incapable of seeing either sense or beauty in fully half of the most admired poetry of the age, should act as a judge of verses, is impertinent absurdity. That is my candid opinion.

However, I have done it,—because you asked it. And on the whole, perhaps I may do very well as a representative of a certain class of outside Philistines who form part of every audience; and it will do no harm, although it may make you smile, to know their opinions. Like a dear good aunt of mine who always, unconsciously to herself, represents to me the immense general class of ordinary readers, below the region of the critics and the few really cultivated people we have in this new country of ours. She confounds "Christian Reid" with the great Charles of the same name; she is devoted to Mrs Southworth; and her latest joy is "Infelice." I send her "The Princess of Thule"; "Lorna Doone"; "Put Yourself in His Place"; and "Middlemarch"; and wait for her opinions.[1] She pronounces the first two "countryfied." The third "pretty good, but queer." And the last, "stupid"!—These opinions I regard attentively,—as the opinions of "the Mass." As a side remark,—have you, O, have you read "Infelice"? What in the world can any cultivated reader see in that mass of words, words, words,?—

Yes; I received your former letter, and should have answered it before this, if I could have found the time. In the first place, as I have told you before, I dislike writing letters, although I love to receive them. I suppose the dislike began in the consciousness that I could not write a good letter, being always too hasty, or too abrupt; but now the feeling has become a part of me. Then, I can use my eyes only by daylight, and as I never fail, rain or shine, to walk my three or four miles, also by daylight,—do you not see how my time flies,—my daylight time? All this is my excuse. A person who writes such letters as you can, and with such ease, ought to excuse the friend who cannot do anything of the kind. Come now,—can you skate? Can you walk? Can you row twenty miles in a boat? I can.

I am sincerely sorry, Mr Hayne, for all I write so lightly, to know that you are ill and suffering. I have thought of you many times "confined to a chamber of 18 feet by 11, surly as a bear, and despairing as—," and wished that I could do something that would cheer you, even if ever so little. Would you like some oranges? Or have you plenty? I suppose you have all the new books. I think I will send you one of my unanswered letters to read; it is just possible that the pleasant little description of Concord and Emerson may while away a weary hour. The lady who wrote it is not a literary person at all; but she likes literary people. When you have finished, please return; but there is no hurry. I shall not be able to answer it at present.

I like your idea of Centennial ballads. I think a stirring Revolutionary Song or Ballad would be received with enthusiasm at this time. Especially as coming from you, the representative poet of the South. This place is everywhere accorded to you by common consent. I suppose you are aware of this.

I beg you to fight against "Depression," that evil spirit that haunts all creative minds. Do not let him conquer you. Think of yourself highly, persist in thinking of yourself, as well as you can; be just as "conceited" as possible. It will buoy you up; and, my word for it, even then you will probably estimate yourself lower than you ought to. Think of all you have accomplished in the face of obstacles which you alone know fully, and take glory in the thought. You may laugh at my preaching self conceit as a virtue; but I have long thought that a good strong dose of self conceit was the best medicine for the creative mind. And I think you will find that the great artists are nerved to their greatest works by a sublime consciousness of and a belief in their own great powers. And if a creative mind can only be surrounded and buoyed up by the close appreciative warm belief & praise of his own family, then he has reached the highest place this world can give him; he is inspired to do great things. Alas; few, few are so surrounded.

All this is brought out by the tone of depression in your last letter.

I now turn to the former epistle. I never heard of such a dreadful thing as writing while "standing at a tall desk"! Heavens! Do have a chair.

You make me tremble when you tell me that your fastidious eyes have rested upon this or that article of mine. Do you not see that I am putting out all kinds of work? A little uncertain myself as to which is my best field? If I ever see my way out of the mass of "short stories," discipline articles, and "dialect verses" in which I am entangled, my intention is to write a novel. But there is one fact that appals me: I generally throw half across the room all the new novels of the day. Now these novels the Public like! Moral: will they not be likely to throw mine entirely across the room? I fear so.

I have not a fault to find with your poem "The Shadow of Death." It is beautiful. The versification is exquisite. I have just read it over and am again struck with the beautiful wish to be close to the warm breast of the earth when the great hour comes.

And, by the way, if you have no objection, I should like to see your photograph again; Mrs Preston showed me one. Have you a better? My photograph has never been taken; so there is no use in asking for one in return.

I must stop; they are calling for me. I wish you could see the miles of blue ocean I see from my windows.

Very Truly Yours,
C. F. Woolson.

Notes

1. Christian Reid was the pen name of Frances Christine Fisher Tiernan; William Black wrote *The Princess of Thule* (1874); Richard Blackwell, *Lorna Doone* (1869); Charles Reade, *Put Yourself in His Place* (1870); and George Eliot, the classic *Middlemarch* (1871–72).

To Paul Hamilton Hayne (Duke)

St Augustine. Fla.
Feb. 13th, [1876]

Dear Mr Hayne.

I return the Mss. as requested, with a few pencil notes on them. I spoke of myself as a "Philistine," because I do not seem to belong to anybody, or any class. The Boston writers, young and old, hang together; the New York journalists and magazine people have ~~the same~~ their own creed; and the Southern, ditto. Whenever I hear any of those people talk, or receive letters from them, I perceive this.—Then, much of the praised literature of to day, and all days, I do not like; another "Philistine" trait!—Of course I understand that the fault is mine,—that something is lacking; just as some persons have no ear for music, &c—And it still strikes me as absurd, in spite of all the pleasant things you say, that I should attempt to give opinion on your Verses! I hope you will always bear in mind that you asked me to do it, and that I only did it to oblige you.

I have no prejudice against Miss Fisher, I hope. I have heard high praise both of herself and her novels many times. I think I saw her once, in Asheville, N.C., but am not quite sure. I have read "Valerie Aylmer," and "A Daughter of Bohemia." But the truth is, Mr Hayne, I am too old to enjoy her stories. (Does'nt that sound blasée?) I go back to my Geo. Eliot, Chas. Reade, & Co, and read over and over the splendid strong pages I like. (I tell you I am a "Philistine"!)—Yes; I am going to write a novel—sometime. But if I like so few myself, it is probable that few will like mine!! A dark prospect.

"Howells of the Atlantic," you say? Yes; he is a "trying" person. Mr Hurd, of Hurd & Houghton, is here. A pleasant gentleman, not especially literary; rather, a business man I should say. He has let out that Howells has "favorites." Chief among them at present, Henry James, Jr. I suspect there is a strong current of favoritism up there. As to poetry, I have been told several times that Howells was exceedingly difficult, and a little bitter, owing to the ill success of his own volume of verse. He lets in the Piatts, because of his early friendship and copartnership.[1] As to Bayard Taylor, he does not succeed as well as you think. I happen to know something about that. He is many times among the "rejected." Ditto of Stoddard, who used to go the rounds with his verses patiently.—As to what you say about various famous short poems, such as "The Psalm of Life," and "Marco Bozzaris," I have long ago decided that it was a matter of school "Readers" entirely.[2] We have all of us been brought upon those poems from babyhood. Get out a new series of "Readers," put in new poems equally concise, and the next generation will rank them with "Marco" & Co. For instance, I do not think much of my "Kentucky Belle." But Charlotte Cushman's reading made it, and now that one little ballad is better known than anything I have written.[3]

By the way, do you know a Mrs Westmoreland, of Georgia? She is here; said to be, an authoress. What has she written? And have'nt I heard something about her having given "Readings" somewhere? She is a fine looking woman.

What do I think of Emerson's "Boston"? I could see neither beauty nor greatness in it. His poetry is often rugged, but there is generally strength; but in this I find nothing to like.[4]

Certainly; keep the letter a while longer; I shall not answer it for some weeks yet. I write to my friends, ordinarily, about twice a year!—

The winter has been divine; such moon-light!—By way of contrast I am reading Carlyle,—30 volumes!, all over again. Miss Phelps is coming here after all, and the "natives" are threatening to scalp her on account of her satirical sketch in the Atlantic.[5]

I trust you are better; but do have a chair and a low desk. I am not surprised that you break down under such severe training. We shall stay here two months longer, I suppose.

With Regard,
Yours Truly
C.F.W.

Notes

1. John James Piatt (1835–1917) and his wife Sarah Morgan Bryan Piatt.

2. "The Psalm of Life" (1839) is by Longfellow; "Marco Bozzaris," by Fitz-Greene Halleck (1790–1867).

3. Emma Stebbins (*Charlotte Cushman: Her Letters and Memories of Her Life,* Houghton, Osgood, and Co., 1878: 227) quotes a letter that Woolson wrote to Cushman:

> Last spring, while at St Augustine, I received from New York the programme of your Reading at the Academy of Music, and was equally surprised and pleased to find among the announcements 'Kentucky Belle.' Ever since, I have wished to thank you for the honor, to tell you how much real pleasure it gave me.
>
> It was little to you, Miss Cushman, but a great deal to me, and I thank you. It is not quite four years since I began to write, and in that time nothing connected with the work has given me so much pleasure as this.

Woolson's name does not appear on the Library of Congress Web site of the Cushman papers.

4. Emerson read this poem from the steps of Faneuil Hall, Boston, in 1873, on the anniversary of the Boston Tea Party.

5. Woolson is referring to Elizabeth Stuart Phelps's "Going South," *Atlantic Monthly,* Jan. 1876.

To Paul Hamilton Hayne (Duke)

Savannah. Ga.
April 7th [1876]

Dear Mr Hayne.

I send to you to day, by Express, a small wooden box containing a few St Augustine oranges which have come with me so far en route northward. I have directed them simply to you, "Augusta, Georgia."—I hope they will reach you in good condition; I have just finished packing them.—We leave in a day or two for Charleston, and may stop in Summerville for a week or two. I think a letter sent to the latter place would reach me. We shall be in Cooperstown, Otsego Co. New York, from the first of June until October. It is my mother's native place, and I look forward to many a delightful row on the lovely mountain lake there.—Will you excuse this hurried letter? I am feeling far from well today, and have much to do.—I look over your last letter; I do not know Mrs Westmoreland at all, personally. She was pointed out to me as "a distinguished Southern writer"; that was why I asked you about her novels.—Yes; Mr Howell's notice of Mrs Preston's book is too bad.[1] If ever there was "faint Praise," there it is. Mr Harper of Harper Bros. was in St Augustine when I left; he said to me "The Atlantic is but the reflection of Mr Howell's own peculiar tastes & ideas." I think that is true. At present Mr Howells is much engrossed with Miss Phelps. He thinks she is "a true poet."—I have a delightful letter from Mrs

Preston which I shall answer soon.—I do'nt know when I have been more entertained than I was with your account of "country visitors." I know them of old!

You ask me to ask Miss Phelps a question about ghosts. She was not in St A. this winter; expected, but failed to come.—Your "First Mock Bird" seems to me a remarkably beautiful poem. No one has, so far, done justice to the subject in my opinion. I like this of yours better than anything yet. I make no exceptions.—It is rich and fresh; sweet and also <u>originally</u> treated. "Spring," is good, too. Pardon this scrawl.

In haste
Yours Truly
C. F. Woolson.

Notes

1. Howells's comments on Margaret Preston's poems appear in *Atlantic Monthly,* March 1876. The apostrophe errors are Woolson's.

To Paul Hamilton Hayne (Duke)

Summerville. South Carolina
Easter Monday
[April 17th, 1876]

Dear Mr Hayne.

We shall probably remain here "among the pines["] until the middle of May. We shall then go in to Charleston and sail for New York from that port. After the first of June we shall be in Cooperstown; Otsego County; New York,—until November. I mention this, because one of the disadvantages of our wandering life is the constant change of address. This year, however, we know, more accurately than usual, where we shall be.—As to Mr Howells—, I have long ceased to waste any time upon conjectures as to the why and wherefore of his ideas and actions. If I please him, I am glad; if I do not please him, I am not in the least dismayed. He is a man of strong and peculiar tastes, and (I fancy) subject to caprices. I mean that he "takes fancies," as they say; and likes novelties. He is a Western man, coming from my own Lake Erie neighborhood, and therefore I think I understand him better than I do some of the other editors. He never goes by the rule, for instance; we never do "out west." Now if he was a <u>born</u> Boston man he would be "set in his ways." Whereas, he is the reverse. You never know what he is going to do or say.—"The Mocking Bird" <u>was</u> good; in spite of Howells. It may be that he is crowded just now. I know (do'nt repeat this, please) that Mr Hurd (Hurd & Houghton) already objects to the amount of poetry he (Howells) puts into the Atlantic. Why not try "Scribner"?—That magazine has not the regular circle of contributing poets that the Boston maga. has. At any rate, as you ask my opinion, here it is. Mr Howells' rejection of the poem proves nothing, and you need not feel in the least depressed about it in a <u>literary</u> way. It was a very charming poem, and the best thing yet on the mocking bird.—

I am glad you liked the St Augustine oranges. They are certainly much better than any I found in Savannah and Charleston. I myself am very fond of oranges, and you would be astonished to see how many we eat down there among the groves. Eight a day for each person is a moderate allowance. I miss them here very much.

We came to this little pine-woods place for absolute quiet. I am exceedingly busy this year, and wished much for a month of solitude just at this time to start me off well in my summer's work. I can do nothing if I am in the least interrupted. Is it so with you?—But I do not like your Southern woods in spring as much as ours, because you have such vast amounts of insect life. Why,—the caterpillars alone are enough to appal the stoutest heart! The truth is Mr Hayne, that, at last, I am a little home sick. Three long winters and two long summers have I been down here in Dixie without intermission, and I want to hear northern voices again, and have stewed potatoes for breakfast! Now then <u>do</u> you say gyar-den for garden? And if you do, <u>why</u> do you? I asked that question of Gen. Martin of N.C.—an officer of the Confederate army, a West Pointer and a pleasant man,—and what do you think he said?[1] "Why do you northerners say <u>Bar</u>, for Bear?"—Now I never heard "Bar" used for "Bear" in my life! And yet he maintained that that was the common pronunciation at the North.—Well,—I am homesick; and I [am] going up to hear "guess" again. I am tired of "reckon." Do'nt you think that for a red hot abolitionist, Republican and hard-money advocate, I have behaved well down here in Dixie during these last three long years? I think I ought to have a word of commendation when you consider that the pen has been in my hands all the time, and that the beaten track was all the other way. I have tried to "put myself in their place," and at least be fair. Finis! The page is turned. I shall write no more about the South.—The South will not miss it.—The wind sighs through the pine trees here, and the air is spicy. I walk alone for miles, and come home laden with new flowers to analyze. There is a beautiful white lily growing wild here; the little church was decorated with them yesterday.—Do you write to Edgar Fawcett? If yes, I wish you would convey to him my good wishes and tell him I am following his career with much interest; I always read everything that bears his name. Someway, I like him. But I could not give a reason for it. In the same way I seem to have picked out the "Alfred <u>Albert</u> Webster, Jr." who writes for Appleton's.[2]—I must stop.

With Regards,
C. F. Woolson.

Notes

1. After the Civil War, Gen. James Green Martin (1819–78), the adjutant general of North Carolina, practiced law in Asheville.
2. Woolson wrote the correct name, Albert, underneath her line.

To Paul Hamilton Hayne

Summerville
May 14th ~~April 7th~~, [1876]
I don't know how
I made that mistake

Dear Mr Hayne.

I cannot make much out of Mr Lanier's "Centennial Meditation," sent in your last letter. But it is always a difficult task, I suppose, to write the words for music already composed—to make the words fit the music, and not the music the words. I like "Hate is not hopeless"; and I return it, as it may be the handwriting of a friend.—We leave tomorrow for Charleston, and shall probably sail for New York sometime during the week. Exactly how many days we shall stay in New York, I do not know; but not many. It will be safer, I think, to address me hereafter and through the summer at "Cooperstown. Otsego Co. New York." It is my Mother's native place. We shall remain there until November. I shall be delighted if you send my book to Charles Reade; nothing could please me more. Shall I not send you a copy for the purpose? I have only one with me, and that is not in good order, but I can easily obtain one. Please let me know.—You speak again of Mr Howells. I could see plainly that Mr Hurd (Hurd & Houghton) had enormous confidence in his (Howell's) judgement. Everything concerning the "Atlantic" is left, I think, entirely in Mr Howells' hands. Mr Hurd said, "Oh Howells is very much taken up with Henry James, just now. He thinks there is no one like Henry James, Henry James." From this, and from the letter Mr Howells wrote to me concerning Miss Phelps' poetry, I have taken the fancy that he is led by his personal likings more than some other editors, perhaps. I have not seen the later numbers of "Private Theatricals." I am more and more inclined to the opinion, however, that the editor of a magazine should not be a writer of magazine articles; the two pursuits interfere.—I am so eager to go north that I can scarcely wait; an "exile longing for home." I like the South; no Yankee-born northerner ever liked it better; but, three years away from home! I have no real home, however. I shall never return to Cleveland, save for a visit. The death of my dear Father six years ago broke up my home there, and for the town itself I care nothing. My father was a New Hampshire man, my Mother a New Yorker; I myself was born in New Hampshire. I prefer New York City as a residence; but for my dear Mother's health we must have warmer air.—Have you seen the accounts of Miss Anna Dickinson's deplorable failure on the stage?[1] What could have induced her to attempt it? She failed, as Kate Field failed, because she had neither beauty nor youth. All the genius in the world will not compensate for the lack of those two qualities in a debutante on the stage. Now that our western girl, Clara Morris, who went to New York and won the highest Laurels (American) in the profession, is ill and forced to retire, I am looking for the new coming star. There are rumors about a Southern debutante, Miss Anderson;—a Kentucky girl I think.—Wo'nt I go to the opera, the theatres, picture galleries, & concerts while in New York!! I am starving for some music. The spirit of this letter has its face turned northward, as you see. You must excuse it. I long to see a certain rocky spring I remember and taste its water. Now then, I have been thinking this, lately: at the north the summer is delightful, and when the winter comes, you can warm the house. But at the south although the winter is delightful, when the summer comes you can <u>not</u> cool your house. Moral.—I leave you to imagine it. Do you respond, "<u>Go</u> north, then!"—I am going,—yes I am going at last. If only the steamer is not lost at sea the days will not be many before I enter my favorite "Westminster." Do you ever stay there,—corner of Irving Place & 16th St? It is a charming quiet little hotel, on the European plan. Chas. Dickens stayed there; and Wilkie Collins.—If you see any interesting novels, please remember me, and send the names. I shall look for Mr Fawcett's with interest; I never happened to see his first one. The critics fell upon it tooth & nail, I remember. Excuse this scrawled letter, and believe me very truly your friend

C. F. Woolson.

Notes

1. Anna Dickinson (1842–1932) was an abolitionist and suffragette as well as an actress and the author of the failed play *Crown of Thorns* (1877).

To Mrs. Markland (Ohio)[1]

June 12th, [1876?]

Dear Mrs Markland.

Thank you for your charming letter. I cannot answer as I would like, for my eyes have given out. I am forbidden to use them, and really ought not to scrawl these lines; but I could not resist it.

I have much to say to both of you, but you must imagine it until I am better. I only need rest.

I send some portions of Hattie's letters.[2] She would be annoyed to know they had been put into the paper, as she intended them strictly for the family. You may be interested in them.—

I send a story too; because you said you liked stories. This was reprinted from Appleton. I write any number of stories,—such as they are! I should be glad to hear from both of you. Will answer when I get back my eyes! Have been for days in a dark room. Shall be here until July 1st. After that, "Cooper House, Cooperstown, Otsego Co. New York." Do write.

With love for both of you
Constance F. Woolson.

Notes

1. Mrs. Markland is an unidentified acquaintance.
2. Hattie Benedict Sherman, Clara Woolson Benedict's sister-in-law.

To Edmund Clarence Stedman (Columbia)

Cooperstown
Otsego County. New York
July 23d, [1876]

Dear Mr Stedman.

I have received your letter, sent to me from Harper's. I have not written before for several reasons, but principally, because you are so—,—so, shall we say sarcastic? that I am afraid of you. I never could write a letter. I never could talk. I have always known it, because the other members of my family fly by me on the swiftest wings, and laugh at my slow progress. Still, I get along tolerably well, and with sufficient content, unless some person undertakes to praise me for what I have not; that confuses me, and, after a while, frightens me to dumbness, because I know sarcasm is there. Come now,—do not say I write a good letter. You have not a correspondent so devoid of the light graces of letter-writing as I am. I am keenly aware of this, but do not cry about it since, fortunately, there are other things one can do in the world besides letter-writing. We shall be excellent friends if you will only be impartial about this, because I have such an enormous admiration for your "Victorian Poets" that, whether I knew you personally or not, I should be inclined to make a great deal of you. Indeed, I put you above all critical writers of whom I have any knowledge. Your book stands by itself in my regard, at the top of its own vista. You will be obliged to behave yourself extremely well to come up to your own work, and you will tell if you please no more delightful fibs, even to "the ladies." There! have I given it to you well?

We came northward in May, northward at last after three winters and two summers at the South, broken only by those few days in New York one September when

I had the pleasure of first meeting Mrs Stedman;—nearly two years ago, I think was it not? Think of the long years among people who say "gee-arden" and "street-ce-arr," who talk about Addison and the "Spectator," and who mix up "Christian Reid" and her feeble stories with the great English Charles of the same name! I like the Southerners; but it depresses one to live too long among them.—Well—, we are here, in my Mother's old home, surrounded by her relatives and old friends. Otsego Lake is lovely; I have a little row-boat, and can now substitute a row for the long afternoon walks I generally take. Ferns grow here, and some rare varieties of orchids, so that I have the excitement of going after them, and, so far, never finding them; I shall be almost sorry when they do turn up, it is such a pleasure to hunt for them ardently every day. There are a great many people here,—it is quite a resort, you know,—but we see little of them being caught in the whirlpool of relatives; we go round with the circle, do the things they do, and go where they go. Some of the relatives are very pleasant, however, especially so the daughters of Fenimore Cooper,—who, by the way, are almost as old as Mother. We hope to be able to stay here through all the coloring of the leaves, say until November; but of course it will depend upon Mother's health; she is very comfortable at present. Then, I suppose, we must return to Florida, I having to give up my plan for going abroad. So much for myself.

I thought a little of sending you word when I was in the City this spring; but I was out of spirits and concluded to be a hermit. I was there only a short time. I hoped you would be in St Augustine again during those two long winters. At any rate, wherever you are or are to be, I trust we shall meet in some way before long. There are any number of dreadful people in the world,—do'nt you think so? And we have to keep meeting them all the time. Why can we not be with the people we like? Emerson says "never read any book you do not wish to read." And why would it not be a good rule to add, "never be with people you do not wish to be with"?

My niece, Kate Mather, is with us at present; she lives in Cleveland, near the Stones, and is very intimate with Flora Stone, the sister of Mrs John Hay. She has much to say about Colonel Hay himself, who is esteemed very agreeable in society there although out of health and far from strong; the trouble whatever it is, seems to be with the head. Did you know this? Mr Stone has built for his daughter a pretty "Stone" cottage on his ground, and there the Hays live, with their adored baby. I always thought they would return to Cleveland; you did not agree with me, I remember.—They have had Clarence King there, and also Whitelaw Reid; and both names have been mentioned in connection with Flora Stone, the younger sister. Does this make you smile?—Mr Stone has a great deal of money, you know. As my nephew is also an admirer of Miss Flora, of course I take his part, against these literary men. Mr Harte also goes out there a good deal; reads "Gabriel Conroy" aloud to a select few.[1]—Just as I left, Cleveland began to grow literary!—You too have your close readers there. A club of young ladies and young married ladies read your "Victorian" aloud "with discussions and comments" last winter and spring. And, as I was much interested in the book, and what they thought of it, they used to send me a report of progress now and then. Their admiration grew and grew as they went on; they could not find words to express their opinion of your words. In short, their estimation of the book rose almost to the level of mine, which is saying a good deal. Not quite to the same height, because they are not up to Pre-Raphaelitism yet; they stop at the 342ᵈ page.—What a book it is! (You see I keep going back to it!) Of course you are tired of hearing about it, and, as you said yourself, you know all about it already, and do not want to be told. But perhaps you do not know all about how much people think of it, and how much they read it, over and over, now when it is no longer new. I could not count how many times I have read it. I often read it for the style alone, so felicitous is it, so full of points, so apt, so clear. You dipped your pen in diamond dust, I think. Of course I do not always agree with you; so much the better. I like to be sharply convinced, against my will, and in one or two cases it has only needed a careful re-perusal of the books in question by the light of your candle to bring me to the truth. In the case of Landor, I still hang back; but that is because I cannot find his books. Apparently nobody has them. Of course I cannot buy all sorts of volumes; they cost money, and besides I live in trunks and have not even a shelf to call my own; so I am still trying to borrow Landor. I do'nt mind waiting at all; I rather like to have something ahead; I shall come across them by and by. But, just answer me one question; if I cannot find Landor in any household or library among the many where I have sought of him, what does it show? You must not answer that those people and library-owners were illiterate;—because they are not. They have all sorts of odd and rare books; but not Landor.—I smile a little every time I turn over the "Victorian" pages to see how nicely you have veiled your entire disbelief in the possibility of true fiery genius in woman. I consider your essay on Mrs Browning an absolute triumph of art. You have no objection to a woman's soaring to lofty heights in the realm of space allotted to her; the only thing you wish understood is that it is in her allotted space, and nobody else's. The lovely Peris had a beautiful life in the clear blue air; but they never entered, or even reached, the gate of Heaven.[2] Well,—I do not quarrel with you about this; and the reason is—that I fully agree with you! But, you might have put my sweet singing Jean Ingelow a little higher, I think.—By the way, I read your "Custer" first in the Tribune, which I am taking this summer, (and find it not so brilliant as I expected), and since then it has been sent to me by Mrs [Haskin?] of Navesink; you know her, do you not? We met her first in St Augustine, and our acquaintance has grown into a warm friendship. She it was who kept me informed as to your health all that time you did not write to me and did write to Paul Hayne; you remember? (That was a good thing you said about it in your last; viz; that it was just "those tasks imposed upon us by thoughtless acquaintances which prevented us from satisfying those whom we really courted as friends.") To go back to your Custer,—how fine it is! The best thing yet about the poor gallant-hearted fellow who won a great fame before he was twenty-six by sheer merit and bravery, while hundreds of others who now decry him, never rose above mediocrity. And I see by this that in spite of that grave business card you sent to me, you do occasionally take up your pew-of-poetry for a while? I always want to see everything you write. Come; go to work and write a novel. By the way is it worth while to buy Edgar Fawcett's two romances? Some of his little verses are nice. I was very much disappointed in Henry James "Roderick Hudson." Did you like it?

I am grieved to hear that Mrs Stoddard is ill; why do literary women break down so much, and—I do not allude to Mrs Stoddard here of course,—act so? It almost seems as though only the unhappy women took to writing. The happiest women I have known belonged to two classes; the devoted wives and mothers, and the successful flirts, whether married or single; such women never write.—Do you think Miss Phelps much of a poet? Mr Howells does; I think he ranks her above any American poet-ess. (I hate that word; but it was needed there.)

My long "poem" is withdrawn; I am rather sorry on the whole, because I thought it would be a success, of its kind. A low down kind. For it only was a plain narrative of our bald everyday American life; if it belonged to any school, it was the school of "Lucille." I shall never bring it out now; neither shall I write any more verses; save "dialect" now and then perhaps. They are only prose, you know. As to the novel about which you inquire,—I do not know when it will ever be finished. I grow disheartened over it when I see the sort of novel and the style of writing people like, for then I know they will not like mine. However, I am at work on it, and perhaps five or six years will see it finished![3] I could see that the Hurds (Hurd and Houghton) thought I was making a mistake to give up short stories. And that is what your man, Mr Bowker, wrote. (By the way, what has become of him?) But heavens! Can one go on writing "short stories" forever?—Why did you find fault with the love-making in "Old Gardiston," I wonder; such a small bit of it as there was, too! I always steer clear of it if possible; I am afraid of betraying my ignorance; fancy-sketches, you know, are usually unreal! My idea of love is, unfortunately, so high, that like my idea of the office of minister, nothing or nobody ever comes up to it. Result—I have an especial dislike for ministers!—Ah well, Mr Stedman,—about the writing, I am much obliged to you for the interest you take in it. (I have a tremendous need of encouragement,) and I shall do the best I can, the very best. But I am overweighted with a sort of depression that comes unexpectedly, and makes everything black. My grandfather gave up to it and was a dreary useless man; my father battled against it all his life, and again and again warned me about it; but I was young then, and only half believed in it. Now, he is gone, and it has come to me. I try to conquer it and sometimes I succeed, sometimes—I do'nt. Give me your good wishes, and kind thoughts now and then, and wish me God speed. I would not have put this in, but, upon re-reading your letter of last March, I was struck by the sincere kindness of its tone, and the interest evinced in what I was doing, little as it is.

I am glad that you have entirely recovered your health; for you must be quite well, I think, to engage in such a business as yours. I have but a vague idea of it, having been brought up among iron-men and manufacturers, principally; but, I suppose it to be something which requires the brightest and quickest of brains.—. I am so glad you did not write any Centennial Ode; I am quite exhausted reading them. I have not yet been able to get up any enthusiasm about the year, excepting as to the man who wrote the description of the opening day for the "New York Times," and described Mr Corliss' climbing through the underground passage in his white kid gloves![4] And, by the way, I suppose you saw "Jean Ingelow" in "The New Century," did'nt you? What sort of paper is it? They wrote to me through the Harpers, and I only sent them two small bits of verse, having no prose on hand. Thereupon my brother wrote to me from Chicago, warning me to "fight shy of that paper and its editors, the whole lot of them." But then you know what a horror young men have of anything in the least approaching the suffrage question.

I have just finished the whole of Boswell's "Life of Johnson"; it is somewhat long! I have always known that I ought to read the old thing. But what an atmosphere of loving admiration for a man to have lived in! No wonder he was dogmatic.

Mr Pell is at Milford as usual. St Augustine in the winter, Milford in the summer; he desired no change. We tried to play chess last season but did not do much; we made it up however in botany. Did I tell you I had become a devoted botanist? It is like a new world opening before me to walk in the woods now. As my circle of human friends grows narrower, I take the lovely blossoms instead.—I have always felt ashamed at not having sent, long before this, that autograph of Fenimore Cooper to your son. I have applied for one everywhere, but the relatives declare that the last one has gone. I myself own several; but they are in the bottom of a large box out in Cleveland. Someday, however, I can fulfill my promise; and shall.

Give my love to Mrs Stedman; I hope to see her again sometime. I do not know where Bergen Point is; but I think all the places near New York must be nice,—with people coming in and going out every day.—What paper do you suppose they read, up here? The Evening Post!—By the way, do tell Mrs Stedman that the only dress I have bought in New York since the black-silk which she draped for me, was a black grenadine which was made for me this spring at a swell place, and for which, without the silk underskirt, I paid one hundred dollars. Since I have been here, the long bones down the back (I do'nt mean my own exactly) have come out, and the sleeves have come apart! Miss Phelps is "Dress Reform"; I am thinking of joining; it means, one black alpaca.

Who in the world is this dogmatic John Burroughs? How old is he, and what does he represent? You speak of Mr Harper. I saw him for about half an hour. He was very pleasant, but he told me of all things to "avoid the subject of the war in connection with the South"; "Gardiston" was just out.[5] I thought he meant that and was abashed accordingly. I am glad to hear he did not entirely cross off my name from his list. I should think it would be a very comfortable lot to be a Harper.

You have observed, perhaps, that Ohio again gives the country a great man, I do not allude to Custer this time, but to our next President.[6] I am no longer afraid to mention my native air. A lady said to me last winter, in St Augustine, "do you not think we have a very different class of persons here this season than ever before?" "I have not observed it especially." "Have'nt you? I have. There seem to be a great many people here this winter who wear green merinoes and come from the West."

This is rather a disconnected letter, I fear; excuse it. I was obliged to go to a dinner party in the middle of it, and I am finishing it by the light of one forlorn candle. But the Lake is not forty feet from my window, and day or night I can look out on its lovely expanse and watch the hills, the clouds and the shadows. It is so cool to night that we forget we were ever too warm. Tomorrow I am going to row ten miles,—up to the Dugway and back again. There is a small Unknown River up there which I wish to explore for ferns. I should like to take you as a passenger. I never allow any one to row save myself, so you would have a nice lazy time, better than you had when we walked to "Ponce de Leon Spring" through the deep sand. I am always delighted to hear from you, as you know. Write when you can.

Sincerely your Friend,
Constance F. Woolson.

Apropos again of the "Victorian,"—I rejected with scorn and disbelief your friend Mr Pell's assertion that "Stedman was at heart a man of no convictions; brilliant quick,—he could write just what he wanted to, and make it seem real." If this is true, I don't want to know it.

Notes

1. Harte published his novel *Gabriel Conroy* in 1876.
2. The Peris are fallen angels who must do penance before entering Heaven.
3. Woolson may be referring to "Two Women," published in *Appletons'* in Jan. and Feb. 1877. Harper and Brothers published both the magazine (Dec. 1880–May 1882) and book version (1882) of *Anne.*

4. Perhaps Ira Moore Courlis (d. 1903), minister of New York's Fraternity of Soul Communion, a spiritualist church.

5. Cloaked in a love story, "Old Gardiston" portrays a reconciliation between North and South (*Harper's New Monthly Magazine*, Apr. 1876).

6. Rutherford B. Hayes was president from 1877 to 1881.

To Paul Hamilton Hayne (Duke)

Cooperstown
Otsego Co. N.Y.
Sept 10th, [1876]

Dear Mr Hayne.

I received your two interesting letters as well as the postal card, and should have answered them before this if my eyes had allowed it; they have been giving me trouble this summer. In addition to this I am by nature (as I have often told you) a wretched correspondent. Those who are kind enough to write to me,—and I dearly love to receive letters,—must have large charity for a fault which will never be mended.—O no; you are not in earnest about beginning to believe in the old Hindoo theology,—that the summit of all good is "unconsciousness." I cannot credit it. I think we may safely trust our creator as to the next life. Neither, have I ever been able to see the black side of this. I think it is a very beautiful and generally speaking a very good sort of a world; all we want is a little improvement in man. But although I do not approve of your wish for a century's "rest,"—still I think your "Underground" a very beautiful poem.—You speak of New York. I did not last spring nor do I ever, go out much in literary society there. I am not in the least fond of society; never was fond of it in my best days. To enjoy society a woman must be either personally attractive, gifted with conversational powers, or else must think herself one or both, whether she is in reality or not. I do not come under any of those heads. Result; do'nt care for society at all. When I am in the city I like to go to the Theatres, the Opera if there is any, to the Picture Galleries, the book stores, and the Park. I enjoy also a well-appointed city hotel. I keep away from all chance callers and flee all invitations. If I am invited to dinner I put on a sackcloth and ashes. But you warm hearted hospitable clan-gathering southerners do not understand this reserve of the north, particularly the New England north. I am very strongly "New Hampshire" in all my ways. I have a row of tall solemn Aunts up there,—silent, reserved, solitary, thin, and a little grim; I am as much like them as the kind of life I lead will allow.—

I bought "Ellen Story" some time ago, and read it with interest and constantly growing pleasure. I consider it by far the best story of the kind since Curtis's "Trumps." In some respects it is better than Trumps because more natural. Its charm to me consisted especially in the absolutely natural conversations between the young people. That is exactly the way they talk at the northern watering places today. Hardly any writer has ever hit it so exactly. "Ellen" herself is an interesting character. Is Mr Fawcett a young man? I am glad you told him what I said. I love to express,—or have expressed for me,—a real liking. I have never seen a copy of his first novel. "Atonement" is certainly extremely striking.[1] It is like a picture by Doré. I have an inner fondness, I think, for the "striking." I am obliged to keep the balance straight by reading quantities of such writings as Lamb's &c&c.

I quite agree with your criticisms of Deronda. Of course it is not natural for him to feel so jubilant over his Hebrew birth. It is against the realities of today's life in England. But Geo. Eliot set out to write a Jewish novel, just as in Romola she set herself the task of writing an Italian one. Of course she has succeeded; but she was obliged to shut her eyes to some prosaic English facts, and turn them into the atmosphere of Isaiah and the old Hebrew prophets. Grandcourt is a far more telling character (to women, at least) than Deronda. I have found this out by asking. Every woman I have asked has said so with emphasis. And I myself have thought so all the time. "The Mill on the Floss," still continues my favorite.

All you say of country callers amuses me particularly. I know so well the reality and wearing qualities of the annoyance. It is precisely for all these reasons, (given in your letter) that I so dislike boarding houses, no matter how good they may be. Heavens! Shall we not choose our friends? Are we to be at the bid and call of any chance passer-by whose only claim is propinquity. Imagine a person venturing to speak to another at a New York Hotel! But at Summerville—! And in spite of enormous efforts at amiability on my part, I am quite sure I left a very disagreeable impression behind me.—This is a lovely place; I suppose you know all about it as it has been described so often. My windows look directly up the Lake which is ten miles long, surrounded on all sides by high rocky heights,—almost mountains. I have a little boat, and go out rowing every day; I row five or six miles always; when the wind blows hard I walk about the same distance through the woods. There have been four or five hundred people here this summer; most of them gone now. The trees are beginning to color. We shall probably remain until the last of ~~November~~ October, and then go to the Centennial for a day or two; then southward again. Of course we are in the midst of our Cooper relatives; and deriving much pleasure from their society. Fenimore Cooper's daughters, are to my idea, the most charming ladies I have ever met. This is a meagre answer to your delightful letters, Mr Hayne; but you will forgive the blind, wo'nt you? I follow you in the magazines with much interest. I think you write better and better as time goes on. You may not like that. But surely it is a natural result of cultured time. How savage are the critics over Bret Harte's play![2] But they all hate him. He is not a nice person, I am told. I return the

Ms. poems with written comments. But you might as well rely upon a canal boat's opinion of a yacht! The idea of my attempting to comment on your verses! But as you ask it, I willingly try to say what I think; although I am quite conscious that I am out of my sphere when I do so. Very Truly your friend

C. F. Woolson.

Notes

1. Edgar Fawcett published his novel *Ellen Story* in 1876 and his poem "The Atonement" in an 1878 collection; George William Curtis serialized his novel *Trumps* (1862) in *Harper's Weekly*, 1859–60.
2. Harte's play was *Two Men of Sandy Bar*, 1876.

To Edmund Clarence Stedman (Beinecke)

Cooperstown
Ohio Election Day!
Oct. 10th, [1876]

Dear Mr Stedman.

At last I have succeeded in obtaining some of the Ms. of Cooper, for your son. The family have no autographs left; Uncle Fenimore had a habit of signing initials, merely. This is part of the original Ms. of one of his novels.

Very likely the young gentleman has forgotten about my promise of two years ago; but I have not. I only regret that I could not keep it sooner.

I wrote to you some days ago, directing to what I suppose is your Broadway address. But I do not think much of your way of making the figure eight.

With regards to Mrs Stedman, I am as ever, your friend,
Constance F. Woolson.

To Daniel C. Eaton (Beinecke)

Lock Box 537
Wilmington. North Carolina
Nov. 27th, [1876]
Prof. D. C. Eaton.

Dear Sir.

Can you name the enclosed fern for me? The person who gave it to me,—out of her greenhouse,—insists that she found it in the woods, near this place; that it is abundant. I may be very stupid, but I cannot imagine what it is. There is no fruit to solve the puzzle. It looks a little like some of the "Pellaea" I found on the Smoky Mountains, Tennessee; but certainly is not leathery as that was.

Although I do not send you so many letters full of questions as formerly, I am as much interested in ferns as ever. Last winter I found "Vittaria lineata," Chapman; "Blechnum serrulatum"; in a swamp near St Augustine; or rather they were found by a boy, and I went to see them. And this summer at Cooperstown, New York, I found the Walking Leaf,—"Camptosorus."—But I cannot find any where, north or south, the Ruta-muraria; the Asplenium montanum; the Pteris cretica;.[1] I do not wish specimens obtained by exchange; I want to gather them with my own hands. Where on the (United States) earth do they grow?

I suppose you have the "Venus' Fly Trap." I shall be happy to send you some fresh specimens if you care for them. A friend has just brought in a quantity for me.

I have recently branched off from Ferns, or rather gone on, to general Botany; but am only at the alphabet as yet. I spent two weeks this last spring, while in South Carolina, over—what do you suppose? "Lord Flax," Linaria canadensis!—

We are here for a few weeks en route southward. I have been told that the flora about here is unusually rich. Of course it is too late now to see much. Not a copy of Dr Curtis' "Plants of Wilmington," can I find in the town![2] Not even in the city library.

I hope Major Haskin's Charleston deputy succeeded, at last, in finding for you the sea-weed you wanted.

Very Truly Yours,
Miss {Constance F. Woolson.

No need to return the fern.

Notes

1. The double punctuation is Woolson's, suggesting that she may have intended to list more ferns.

2. Woolson is probably referring to an article by Moses Curtis (1808–1872) that appeared in *Boston Journal of Natural History*, vol. 1, 1834.

To Daniel C. Eaton (Beinecke)

Wilmington. North Carolina
Dec. 10th, [1876]
Prof. D. C. Eaton.

Dear Sir.

I have received your very kind letter, enclosing the ferns. I am very much obliged to you, and I must add, that I was not able to resist the temptation of putting the specimens into my book of Ferns, although my intention is to have nothing there which I have not gathered with my own hands. I am going to confront the green-house woman with your letter as soon as I can walk out again, and see what she says.

She declared, with solemnity, that she gathered that identical plant in the woods! The specimens of the "Fly Trap," brought in for me before the frost, are being kept in this greenhouse until I can see to them. I shall send them to you by express; but it will be safer to wait until the extreme cold moderates. It is colder here, to day, than it has been for fifteen years.

Yes; I am related to the Coopers,—the grand-niece of the author. My Mother, for whose health we are living at the South, was his niece; my grandmother was his sister, the only daughter of Judge Cooper of Cooperstown. My grand-mother was much older than her brother James. We go back to Cooperstown often, because it was Mother's home, and we have still a number of relatives there, among them our cousins, the daughters of the author, who are, I think, the most entirely charming ladies I ever knew. I am very fond of rowing, and when there I row on the Lake every day. It is a lovely little highland Lake. My dear father, who died seven years ago, was a New Hampshire man; while I was still a child he removed westward to Cleveland, Ohio, where we lived until his death. Every summer we went "up the Lakes," and the whole lake-country is engraved on my memory as no other country can ever be, because I saw it all at the most impressionable age. Do you know Fort Gratiot?[1] I am quite devoted to the little Fort, and used to wish I could live there. It was such a wild lonely little port, on the edge of the great Lake. I remember that the steamer always passed it just at twilight, hurrying to get through the river before dark. Fort Gratiot and the St Clair Flats were my favorite points on the way to Mackinac. Mackinac is the only spot on earth for which I have what is called "local attachment." I often dream of its outline, as one sees it coming around Bois Blanc point; and I always think of it when I am sick. As now. I am laid up with erysipelas;—it is on the [ancle?]. I do not know what to make of it. Never had anything of the kind before in my life. The cramped position in which I am writing must be my excuse for such a crabbed looking letter.

Major Haskin told me that you were of "the old Army." I think you are delightfully placed in life, with that background, a wife, and three little [pets?], the grandparents on both sides still with you, and Yale College as a habitat. I should say there was nothing nicer in America than that!

I am sorry about the sea weed. We are afraid to go in to Charleston, as we are only three women alone, without escort. The blacks there are insolent, and the whites bitter. We shall probably go directly to Florida when we leave this place.

I shall probably send all sorts of things to you this winter asking if they are not "Pteris cretica" and the two "Trichomanes" of Chapman's Flora.

With thanks, very truly yours,
Constance F. Woolson.

Notes

1. Woolson is referring to the summers she spent on the Great Lakes, especially on Mackinac Island on Lake Michigan. Fort Gratiot is on Lake Huron.

To Edmund Clarence Stedman (American Antiquarian)

St Augustine
Florida
Dec. 12th, [1876]

Dear Mr Stedman.

I was glad to see your handwriting again. I feared you had forgotten me. And I feared you were vexed about something; although what it was, I could not imagine. I knew you were ill; but I knew, too, that you were writing to all kinds of people. Paul Hayne for instance, and a whole year has passed without my having a line from you. I do not ask people to write often; I dislike letter-writing so much myself that I cannot hope for much in return. But once in six months or so, I should like a hail from your quarter of the sky,—just "how are you? We are well. God speed you,"—and I will answer in kind.—I want your book; if you will send it, well and good; if not, I will send for it. Indeed, it is only ill luck that I have not had it ere this. I counted upon the bookstores of Charleston, and I was much disappointed when I found they did not have it. They had nothing but countless copies of "Infelice"?[1] The South is only half-civilized.—Then, I waited until I was settled for the winter before sending for books from Boston, as my trunks were already hopelessly crowded. So you see how it has happened that I have not the "Victorian" already. But I think you are very disagreeable to shut the door in advance upon my comments. Of course I have seen the high praise of the critics everywhere all over the country, and of course you really are tired of their remarks; and of course I can add nothing that would be new or striking to the chorus of praise. At the same time there is not in the United States one person who has a more deep and thoroughly sincere, impartial admiration for your book than I have. I mean of course the essays I have seen,—those that have appeared in Scribner. In all [my life?] nothing that I have ever read in the way of critical writing has begun to please me so much as your essays; nothing approaches them, in my opinion, in the English language. And by that I do not mean that there is anything in the French or German language either; I was only trying (and with poor success as usual) to express what I feel. There is one book in the English language to which I am devoted; I read it over and over for the pure pleasure of the thing. This book is,—now do'nt laugh,—Buckle's History of Civilization; it is my big "classic."—With this book goes the "Victorian Poets." As I have read the essays one by one I have said to myself, "now <u>here</u> is another 'classic' for you; a companion for your dearly beloved Buckle." Three novels go on the same shelf, and only three: George Eliot's "Mill on the Floss"; Dumas père's "Trois Mousquetaires"; and a recent romance, "Young Brown" by Grenville Murray.[2] Do you object to the company you are in? But, mind you, I put you right alongside of Buckle, and above all the others.—Seriously, Mr Stedman, I wish I could worthily express the great admiration I feel for the work you have done in these essays; not merely what you have said, but also how you have said it. It is beyond anything I know for incisive vigor and for exquisite delicacy. Why,—compared to your style, the style of all the other critics is like mush and milk!—I do not always agree with your opinions; for instance, as to Landor. But that is not the point. Any body, agreeing or not, must become fascinated as he reads, in spite of himself. I am not in very good spirits this winter; but I think your book will cheer many a lonely hour. Send it down. I presume I shall read it through over and over again; and still again. That is the way I do with a book I really like. And alas! I like so few.—You cannot answer letters [I?] know; yet if sometime you would only tell me about Wordsworth. I have always felt only a cold dislike for his productions; and yet I know he is considered one of the great poets. Therefore, what a great ignoramus am I!—Recently, while spending six weeks in South Carolina, I obtained the key of the little village library, and went prowling among the old books; there, face to face, I came upon a ponderous "Wordsworth," and I said "the time has come," and carried the thing home, and read every word, the "Excursion" and all. With the exception of the "Ode to Immortality" I found nothing to like. What in the world or out of it does anyone see in "The Wagoner" for instance? And what in the world or out of it does "Peter Bell" mean? And again, what in the world did Shelly mean by writing "Peter Bell the Third"?[3]—But of course you have not the time to answer all this by letter. If I ever see you again, face to face, wo'nt I ask you though!

We are down here again for a third long winter, as you have seen by the heading. We did not wish to come,—did not intend to come; we had our hearts fixed upon Key West, with the chance of Havana on the horizon. But Fate, in the shape of Plum's grandpapa, interfered, and here we are. Plum is my little niece, my only sister's only child; and when grandpapa said she should not go so far south, of course we yielded; for we all revolve around her ladyship. She is a beautiful little girl; her father was killed in that awful accident at New Hamburg on the Hudson River railroad four years ago, and, as he was an only son, the "Baby" has a vast amount of love lavished upon her by all the relations.—My sister is with us, and we are all established in one of the old coquina houses overlooking the water; we have an upper piazza of our own; oranges are abundant; and the "fashionables" are beginning to crowd in. I am a little tired of them, myself. I think one is apt to become tired of people who have a hundred thousand or so a year! The atmosphere ~~becomes~~ grows oppressive when so many magnates are around. If I live, I will not come here again. And yet—so I said last year!—The inlet is just as blue as ever, and the pine-barrens as green. Your friend of the "Argo" is here, and with him his friend "the Governor." Mr Hurd of "Hurd and Houghton," came a day or two ago with his family; and Miss Phelps will be here in a few days. I wonder what you think of her poems. But I suppose you would not tell.——We spent two months in Charleston last spring, and then went up into Virginia among the mountains. We visited the Springs, went over to Lexington-in-the-Valley, where I saw Mrs Margaret J. Preston,—and spent some days at Harper's Ferry. We also made an excursion to Gettysburg; and went three times through the entire length of the beautiful Shenandoah Valley. A week in Baltimore followed, and then down the Bay to Norfolk for a time, and so, on into South Carolina again. I have not been in New York at all; is it not too bad? I begin to fear I shall never be able to live there; Rome is far more likely; or Cairo.—My dear Mother's health continues comfortable, I am glad to say.—

It is good-natured to say "I have followed you in the text of Harper,"—when you disapproved so utterly of those descriptive sketches. And you advised me not to publish "Castle Nowhere" too. Do'nt you remember? Well, Mr Stedman, we must all do what we think is best for our own selves. I have tried to do what seemed to me best; and I could do no other way with any contentment. If I make mistakes, I must bear the consequences; but at any rate, all is right between Conscience and me. I shall (I think) write no more short stories after this month. And the novel is under consideration,—is fairly begun. But oh! how dare I write it when everybody disapproves of everything!—And were you not greatly disappointed in Henry James's novel just finished? "Roderick Hudson"? The idea of throwing the hero down a cliff just to get rid of him.—And if you could see the number of letters I have received both from friends and from strangers seriously attacking me for the theology of old Fog in "Castle Nowhere," as though his theology must necessarily be mine, you would understand how the novel appalls me. For I wo'nt write it at all unless I write it as I please.—And I poured that "stream of ice-water down Osgood's back,"—you said that you remember,—by offering him a volume of Ms. poetry! He has it under consideration.[4] Now then, all my evil deeds are out. This last is a secret, of course. You will not betray me, I am sure.——I believe I have told you "all about myself," at some length. It is one of your delightful habits to show real interest in other people's work. I remember how steadily and yet how quietly you kept the conversation on my affairs and myself that day on the sea-wall, and that evening on the shell-road! And I am so accustomed to the eternal "I" of all my male friends that I forgot how to talk when I was with you those times. The usual "indeed!" "Did you really say that!" "How strange!" "How very remarkable!" "That is just like you!" were not necessary in that case at all. And I did not know where I was exactly. You see I have played the part of "listener" all my life. There is a sort of compensation in things after all; at this late hour I have gotten hold of the pen, and now people must listen to me, occasionally.

You must not make game of my letters. I never could write a letter, and I only write to persons I really like, knowing well that I must trust to friendship to excuse the heavy style. My Mother and my sister write charming letters, so easy, and so amusing. But the gift has not been granted to me.

We have seventy wild Indians here for the winter; they occupy the old Fort. They are prisoners for life for the small crimes of murder, scalping &c, and yet some of the ladies here have taken them for pets; they all go to church, and they are now without guard of any kind. They are horrible wretches, and some of [these?] fine days they will do something dreadful, I fear. I should not like to pass them on the wall at high tide! They are quite "high church" in their religious tendencies, and bow devoutly in the Creed. As they are in the charge of a Cavalry officer, they are all dressed in full Cavalry uniform, and they generally carry their shoes in their hands. Once in a while they go over to the Island and have a War Dance. I suspect this is when the church catechism is too much for them.—Seriously, is it not singular that the United States Government should have selected this crowded fashionable resort for such a dangerous set of prisoners? Why not send them farther down the coast away from everybody?——. What do you think of Mr Gilder's "New Day"?[5] But I suppose you will not say. I have only seen selections so far; my sister will have the volume in a few days, however. There was a review of it in Appleton's Journal, Mr Burlingame's I suppose,—that made me laugh until the tears came; the review said the book seemed to be principally about "a [wan?] man," and a remarkably "[wan?]" kind of love. The same idea came to me while reading the selections. Good Heavens! Love is love,—and not a shadow.—.—. And how are your friends the Stoddards, the Bayard Taylors, Mrs Dodge, Miss Kate Field, and the rest? Please give my regards to Mrs Stoddard. I have never relaxed my search for the "Morgesons" and "Two Men." I had them from Case Library, Cleveland, years ago; but am anxious to read them again. For a year I have been trying to borrow or buy them, without success. But I know I shall find them some time. For for years I have been trying to get Mrs Shelley's "Frankenstein"; and at Charleston last week it turned up.—.—.[6] Shall we see you here this winter? Why not come down with Mrs Stedman for the whole season? It is just the place for rest; the very atmosphere is lazy. The Mr Van [Alew?], with whom you came originally I believe, is to be here again with his yacht. And crowds of other people,—if you like "people." And we have three cases of California wine which you might help us drink, as a penance. As for young ladies,—I do not count myself in these of course,—there are scores, all with the very latest fashions. They walk on the sea wall like so many silk-cased umbrellas, and I think they look very prettily; much better than they did in the days of hoops.

I hope Mrs Stedman is well. Please remember me to her with warm regard. If I come to New York next spring I shall hope to see you both; we shall not try southern mountain life another summer. Possibly we may go to Cooperstown.

I am very glad to hear that you are so much better. All you need, I think, is rest for a certain time. You have overworked yourself mentally by being writer banker, and society-man at the same time. That last made the trouble. Why,—do you know I think "society" is a profession by itself; and a hard one too.

Think of John Hay's living in Cleveland! I thought he was "on" the Tribune. My sister tells me that Mr Stone has built a beautiful stone cottage (no pun intended) for them on a corner of his own lot. Sic transit.—[7]

With sincere regard, I am your friend,
Constance F. Woolson.

Notes

1. Stedman published *Victorian Poets* in 1876. *Infelice* is a novel by Augusta Evans (1835–1909).

2. Henry Thomas Buckle's (1821–62) first volume of *History of Civilization* appeared in 1857; the second, in 1861. Eustace Clare Grenville Murray (1824–81) published *Young Brown* in 1874. *The Mill on the Floss* appeared in 1860 and *The Three Musketeers* in 1844.

3. Wordsworth published his long narrative poem *Peter Bell* in 1819; Shelley published his the same year. The misspelling of Shelley's name is Woolson's.

4. Woolson never published a volume of poetry.

5. Richard Watson Gilder's collection of poems, *A New Day,* appeared in 1876.

6. Elizabeth Stoddard published *The Morgesons* in 1862 and *Two Men* in 1865. Mary Shelley published *Frankenstein* anonymously in 1818; her name appears on the second edition in 1823. Woolson added the second "for" above the line, perhaps intending it to read "four."

7. Literally, "Thus it passes over"; here, a comment on how close Hay's home is to his father-in-law's.

To Samuel Livingston Mather (Benedict/Voices, 249; Benedict/Abroad, 747)

[1876]

. . We are back in our old quarters, and very pleasant they seem to me after six months of country board; there come times when one longs for a chair that fits one's back and something to eat besides bacon and hominy! . . . It has been very warm here—too warm to exercise much; foggy, but I like the sea-fog. It seemed so pleasant to catch the smell of salt marshes as the cars neared the city. Two long winters at St Augustine have given me a great liking for salt air . . . The sixty wild Apache Indians who have been confined in the old castle since last spring, will make things very different for us, I fear.[1] I had supposed that they were kept closely confined, but one of the army officers told me yesterday that "since Col. H. had brought them all into the church, it was understood that they were completely Christianized, and would require no guard this winter." I could scarcely believe it, for these Indians are condemned by the U.S. government to imprisonment for life for all sorts of crimes. Most of them are murderers.

But another officer told me yesterday that the last Sunday he attended church at St Augustine, he happened to peep out from behind his hands during prayers, and there, in a pew across the aisle, he caught the eye of a big Indian who was doing the same thing. The Chief gazed at him for a moment, and then without a change of countenance he winked gravely with one eye at the young officer, and bowed his head again in the most devout manner.

Col. H__ is to leave St Augustine this month; I wish he would take his Christianized Indians with him. . . .

Notes

1. A group of Apaches was imprisoned at Fort San Marcos.

To Arabella Carter Washburn (Benedict/Voices, 242; Benedict/Abroad, 741–42)

[1876?]

. . . . I cannot quite make out what you mean when you say; "I have heard something and would like to enquire." Is it anything about us? It sounds as though something particular was intended. There is nothing "particular" any more in the world save engagements, and the only person in our party who might be a candidate for such honours is Clara. She receives a great deal of attention both here and in New York City . . . but . . . I do not think she will ever marry again. She is satisfied to live as she is. As for me, I go fern hunting, take long walks, and go to bed promptly at ten every night. . . . Nobody is "at my feet" at all, do'nt be satirical. . . . I am as truly out of that kind of talk as a nun. I go about a great deal, but always as an "observer," "a very superior person," and that sort of thing. I should have put on glasses long ago, but Gram. would not let me. Glasses will give the finishing touch! I must tell you a joke. I went to the expense of ordering an elegant navy blue silk suit from New York, this fall, colour very dark and everything in the latest. Price $150.00. I did not want the thing at all, but there are so many grand people here, and Clara does not like it unless I am respectable. I could ill afford the gown, and hated paying for it dreadfully. Well—I wore it with hat, gloves and parasol to match. And what remark do you suppose was made about that time by two ladies staying in the same house who did not know me at all? "Is not that lady opposite us at table a literary person? We have felt sure she was an authoress, and not only that, but there is something about her which makes us think that she was the daughter of a clergyman!" Now then, they had on short, black alpaca gowns, their noses were sharp and red at the tips, and they wore glasses and had gristly hands. Ages 40 and 50 perhaps. Wasn't it disgusting? After all my trouble and spent money! Elizabeth Stuart Phelps is here again this winter and she is "Dress Reform." I am going to be "Dress Reform" hereafter, in spite of Clara. Dress Reform means two dresses, "et praeterea nihil."[1] At least, that is the outward manifestation of it so far as I can see.

Notes

1. et praeterea nihil: and nothing further.

To Arabella Carter Washburn (Benedict/CFW, 20–21)

[1876?]

Now just hold your peace about my "want of morality." At least twenty awful letters have I received because I made "Old Fog" say he did not believe in eternal punishment.[1] Is it possible that I am to be held personally responsible for the theology and morality of all my characters? I want you to think of me not as your old friend, when you read my writings, but as a "writer," like anyone else. For instance, take "Adam Bede" . . . Would you like to have a friend of yours the author of such a story? Dealing with such subjects? And yet it was a great book . . . The truth is, Belle, whatever one does must be done with one's might and I would rather be strong than beautiful, or even good, provided the "good" must be dull. All this applies more to what I hope to do in the future, of course, than to the slight sketches I have already brought out. But there must always be prentice work—"stepping stones." I have had to get used to my pen, and to "speaking in public" as it were. You are mistaken, I have but little ability of the kind you mention; all I have is immense perseverance and determination. "It's dogged that does it." Do you remember how Pete used to set his teeth and hold on to a mat when the boys pulled it away from him, or tried to?[2] The mat might be torn in two, or Pete himself, but let go he would not. I wish you were here, I think you would be amused by some of the letters on the table. They vary as widely as this: "How can you ever write poetry? It is an utter mistake. You are only fitted for prose. Excuse plain speaking, but, &c." "How can you ever touch prose? Why, your few poems are so far above your poor little stories that I wonder, &c." Then comes this: "I wish you would not write those sketchy, descriptive articles in "Harper's"; they only do you harm." Then, right alongside this: "Do you know, I really think 'Up the Ashley and Cooper' the very best thing you have ever done!" I must confess that last opinion, just received, has a depressing effect. If your "compilations" are better than your original work, you had better hang up your harp and tie it with crape. One grand reply I would like to make to all my unliterary critics; Try it Yourself! This is not meant for you. I like to know what you think. And you are honest and tell the truth.

Notes

1. "Old Fog" is a character in "Castle Nowhere," which came out in book form in 1875.
2. Woolson's childhood dog was named Pete Trone.

To Samuel Mather (Anderson)

St Augustine. Fla.
Jan. 30th, [1877?]

Dear Sam.

This is a private letter to you; by that I mean that, if possible, Charly is not to know I have been writing to you. Clara and I are extremely anxious about Charly; we cannot understand, from what he writes himself, how he really is. I wish you to sit down and send me a few lines telling the exact truth. Of course we do not allow Mother to see our anxiety at all; she is anxious enough as it is, with what she already knows. As she never goes to the Post Office, and we do, it will be easy to keep your letter from her knowledge. What I want to know about is his health. As to all the rest he has already written me his own account. In a letter received by Clara today, he speaks as though he was completely broken down. What is the matter with him? I know he has had much pain in his head, but even that has never had a medical name. I do not at all understand his case. I think you will see how important it is that we should know the full truth. If he is in any danger, Mother must of course be told. If he is not, she must be spared, if possible. Her whole happiness, even her life I might almost say, depends, and always has depended upon how Charley is, and how he feels. I spend my whole time trying to keep her well and comfortable; but all is of no use if she thinks Charly is in trouble. It is a great comfort to her now to know that he is in Cleveland where you are, and that you have all been so kind to him. We shall never forget it, Sam. We are so very far off! And it seems almost impossible to go North at this season; certainly it would be extremely dangerous for Mother to go.

I sent Charly money by telegraph just before he left Chicago; and Clara is sending some more to day. He must have what he needs, of course. We expect and are glad to lend him all he wants while he is sick. I have not much; but all I have I willingly share with my only brother. I have told him so, more than once. Keep an eye to him; you are near, and we are so far away.

It is all very distressing. I try to keep cheerful. But it is hard work.

Write me just what you think, and all you know. Why not persuade Charly to see

Dr Weber? I will pay the bill. And if he consents, be sure and write me all Dr Weber says.

This is a hurried scratch. I am sick to day myself, so you must excuse it. Have never been quite strong since the erysipelas at Wilmington.

Mother keeps pretty well, considering anxiety. Be careful what you write to her.

I do not think it best to have Charly come here, unless he is anxious to do so; for the journey is so very long & hard, and the climate so very warm & debilitating. Besides it is an extremely expensive place, and I am forced to think of that also. Clara expects to go north in March & look up a small house somewhere near New York; say Yonkers. Charly can go right there as soon as it is ready. Mother and I will come up in May. That is the present plan.

Love to all; you can show them this letter or not, just as you please; but keep it from Charly. And I will never betray to him what you write to me.

I shall wait for your answer with anxiety.

Affectionately
Constance F. W.

To Samuel Mather (Anderson)[1]

St Augustine
Feb. 24th, [1877?]

Dear Sam.

I have received both of your letters, and am very much obliged to you for writing so promptly and so fully. You have relieved my anxiety very much. Mother now knows the general condition of affairs, and writes to Charly herself concerning his health; she feels hopeful and cheerful now; that is since Dr Weber's opinion has been given. She has, as I have, the greatest confidence in Dr Weber. What you write shows me that underneath all lies the one thing that I have known and preached to Charly for years; he has now learned it himself by a hard experience, the only way I suppose that such things are ever learned. May the lesson last! This thing is that we as a family can not do what many other people can, without breaking down. We cannot go without sleep; we cannot overtax ourselves; we cannot "overdo" in any way. If we persist either from ignorance or obstinacy, we break down. But on the other hand if we will only take good care of ourselves, we are able to do as much as most people each day, and have, too, better health than most people; that is, fewer illnesses in the course of the year. But we cannot, must not, transgress. Charly has smoked, according to his own confession last summer, almost incessantly, day and evening, for several years. That was no doubt the beginning of his trouble with the head. Then he has never been particular about a good long night's sleep; a fatal neglect in our family.

Well—, we are all thankful it is no worse; that he is on the road to recovery. His own letters to me were simply appalling. He seemed to be completely broken both in mind and body. Beginning with his sudden telegrams at New Years, so unexpected, so terrifying, and continuing with these dreadful letters, I have been in a state of constant trouble and dread which has worn upon me heavily. Now that Mother knows, the hardest part, which was the concealment, and the being cheerful to her all the time, is over. Charly himself seems to be regaining courage and hope; his last letters are more cheerful. His mind seems however to be fixed upon this plan of going to Penn; it seems a wild idea to me. But I do not see what I can do to influence him since he positively refuses to come and spend the summer with us for a change and rest. This is what we all hoped he would be willing to do. I beg you to do all you can to keep him in Cleveland until safe spring weather has begun.

Your idea that these feelings he has after pain, are the result of morphine, is my own exactly. I am <u>sure</u> it is owing to that. We all know the effect and strange power the drug has on some constitutions. I am intensely glad and relieved that wise Dr Weber has at once struck at the root of the matter.

I am much interested in your plan of going to the North Carolina Mts. The scenery is far finer than any <u>I</u> have ever seen; but of course it is nothing to the Alps. You must be careful, however, not to go too early. Although so far south by the map, the region is elevated, and very cold; the spring comes late. They had six feet of snow at Asheville in January; the cars were snowed in for several days between Old Fort and Salisbury. The roads are very rough all through the mountains; the clay washes out badly, and there are sudden freshets in the spring. In fact the bad roads and the miserable stages have kept us from ever going back there; although there is no region in the South I like so well. I think you will enjoy the trip provided you do not go too early. The accommodations are primitive. I <u>suppose</u> the best hotel now is at "Warm Springs," on the French Broad, west of Asheville. I send you two letters of introduction to friends; very pleasant people. Rev. Mr Buel was once the rector of the church at Cooperstown; his wife is a daughter of Bishop Atkinson of N.C. One of Mr Buel's brothers is a Prof. in the N.Y. Theological Seminary.—Gen. Martin is an old West Point officer; he joined the confederate service. Lost his arm in Mexico. His present wife is a New York lady of excellent family,—the Kings. They are very agreeable people, all of them. There are young sons and daughters of your age.

Very much love to your mother and father and Kate.

As I think you are interested in the subject, I will mention how much gratification I have had over the reception of "Rodman the Keeper," in the last Atlantic. The Tribune (semi-weekly) copied it entire; the Times gave it a flattering notice; and from many quarters I have received letters full of praise. Last but not least it called out a letter from a well known firm asking whether it would not be possible for me to send all I wrote to their house? That they would gladly take every line, and pay as much as any other house had ever paid; & in fact I could set my own price.[2] Of course I shall not do this, as I have never thought it best to be bound to any one magazine or publisher. But in such depressed times as these, I thought the proposal very flattering. Do not mention this outside the family, please. Mother is well today; Clara & Plum at church.

I forgot to say that the Buels lost this last summer their only daughter, Josie, a beautiful girl of 16. She used to be a great friend of mine when I was there; took long walks with me. I was very fond of her.

Affectionately,
C.F.W.

Please be sure and burn these last 2 or 3 letters of mine.

Notes

1. Portions of this letter that do not involve Charly also appear in Benedict/CFW, 23–24; 36–37.

2. Woolson's story appeared in the March 1877 issue of *Atlantic Monthly,* which, typical of the monthly magazines, would have come out a month earlier than the cover date. The firm asking for Woolson material is likely Osgood's.

To James R. Osgood (McGill)

Yonkers. N.Y.
May 19th, [1877]
Mr James R. Osgood.

Dear Sir.

I have received your letter of the fourteenth.—I did not suppose you would wish to bring out another collection of short stories at present. Two of the sketches are still to appear—in "Scribner" and the "Galaxy"; and I have nothing written or imagined to lead the volume. I should want something very good and dramatic for that. If you wish to bring out the book, I can think it over, and perhaps be able to satisfy myself in a longer story.[1]

Yes; I did mean that I would like to have you publish my novel when it was ready, and I am glad you are willing to take it. But there is much to be done upon it still.

I enclose what I consider the best criticism yet upon "Two Women." It takes in the "Lake Country" Sketches too, you perceive.

Very Truly Yours
Constance F. Woolson.

Notes

1. Osgood published Woolson's first collection of stories, *Castle Nowhere* (1875), but did not publish her second collection or her novels.

To Edmund Clarence Stedman (Columbia)

(Box 772)
Yonkers. N.Y.
May 27th, [1877]

Dear Mr Stedman.

While in the city yesterday, I went to your former abiding place to see Mrs Stedman; and was told that she was no longer there. Where is she? I go in often, and should like to call upon her.

My sister has taken a small furnished house here, for the season, and Mother and I are happy in something like a home after so many years of wandering. We shall probably remain until November.

How are you? I earnestly hope, better and stronger.

I am better; in better spirits. I told you I should come out of the shadows in time.

Always very sincerely your friend,
Constance F. Woolson.

To Edmund Clarence Stedman (McGill)

P.O. Box 772
Yonkers. New York
June 10th, [1877]

Dear Mr Stedman.

I was glad to see your hand-writing again; but sorry, on my own account, that you are out of the city. I do not go in often, now that the weather is so warm; but, if it is cooler, (it <u>must</u> be,) I shall ask Mrs Stedman to meet me some day; so that we may at least lunch together. I am going down to Navesink, to spend a few days with Mrs Washington, between now and September; is Navesink near Summit? I am sorry you are not well; very sorry. I should so much enjoy being near you this summer, so that I could see you, and hear you talk. You know everything; and everybody. And I am more isolated than ever. It is good of you to refrain from speaking severely of "Two Women"; for I know,—and have always known,—how it is,—would be—like the sharpening of slate pencils to your ears. Let me say, as part explanation, that I distinctly proposed to myself to make it all "loquitur," and not only that, but plain loquitur of to-day. In fact, it was as much written to be spoken, as "Miss Multon."[1]

And, by the way, "Miss Multon" is just below us; at Mount St Vincent. I saw her the other day, trying to stop her horse, who at last ran away entirely, and left her alone on the lawn. As she advanced to the fence to meet her husband, I had a good view of her face, and the impulse came over me to step out of the train and shake hands with her, both as a former townswoman of hers, and also, an admirer. I used to go and see her when she first acted in New York, at the old "Fifth Avenue," and, with her awkwardness, her few dresses, and her genius, was such a contrast to the other actresses. I liked very much your sonnet to her.

I care a great deal about Hawthorne, as, possibly, you may remember; therefore, I am especially interested in the new poem you mention. Where will it appear, after it is delivered?[2] I have kept track of you all through the winter and spring, in the magazines. But you do not do half enough. I want to ask you, frankly,—do you think Osgood as energetic a publisher as some others? And what are we to think of the success of such a book as "Helen's Babies," where even the "babies" are not, (to me) in the least natural.[3] And, is it true that the "Tribune" will not "notice" the Messrs. Appletons' books? And why do you not write a play? And ever so many more questions, which I spare you—for the present! Hoping we may meet before long, I am, with regards to Mrs Stedman, always sincerely your friend,

Constance F. Woolson.

Notes

1. Clara Morris starred at the Union Square Theater in *Miss Multon,* a play based on *East Lynne* (1861), a sensational novel by Ellen Wood (1814–87).

2. Stedman read his commemorative ode on Hawthorne at the Phi Beta Kappa Society in 1877.

3. John Habberton's (1842–1921) *Helen's Babies* was intended as a humorous novel for adults, but became popular with adolescents.

To Edmund Clarence Stedman (Columbia)

P.O. Box 772
Yonkers
July 8th, [1877]

Dear Mr Stedman.

I am charmed with your "Hawthorne"; (I have the "Tribune" copy,) it seems to me worthy of the man. Nothing higher can be said by me, since Hawthorne is one of my gods. Has always been. I am always, you know, a little afraid of your keen words,—still, I am going to say, anyway, that I like best the seventh, twelfth, thirteenth, fifteenth, nineteenth, and last verses. I am like a tune played on one string, because, if I like anything, I like it very much and always; I never tire or change.

And, I have not forgotten how weary you were of my great liking for your "Victorian Poets." But, it does not make any difference; I am just as devoted to it today as ever, and just as fond of quoting it, and talking about it.—I am at last hard at work on Landor, having found his "Complete Works" at the library; Moxon edition. I am going to read the whole, twice through, at least, and copy out whatever strikes me. It will take all summer! So far, I find it heavy work; impossible to skip one word. And you are a nice man! Here you have twice told me I was like the women in Landor's "Pericles and Aspasia," and all this time I have supposed it was something delightful. Good heavens! I have just finished "P. & A." and, which of the two long-winded, pragmatical, intolerable conceited creatures did you mean?[1] I do not know when I have had such a blow!

We like it very well here; but have had a series of visitors; relatives who look upon us as persons returning from exile, and hasten to see us before we disappear again. It is not my house you know; it is my sister's. I am visiting her. Some of these days, if I should give you twenty four hours' warning, I wonder if you would drive with me in the Park for two hours or so? It would be a pleasant way of seeing you, and would put you, I hope, to no trouble; after dropping me, the carriage could take you to your ferry. I should like so very much to see you and hear you talk. How are you really? Do not stand on the least ceremony; if you are not strong enough for any such performance, say so, and I shall understand it. But I do not want all the summer to pass without seeing you. With my very sincere regard to Mrs Stedman, I am always your friend,

Constance F. Woolson.

I find I have two things more to say. One: after I have read the whole of Landor faithfully, I am going to read your "Cameos," a book I have not yet seen.[2] But I go first to the fountain-head.—Second: I have a letter from Hawthorne, written to me when I was postmistress at a Sanitary Fair in reply to our asking for autographs. I have it among my treasures; it is quite a long letter. I am going to put your "Hawthorne" with it. I have a flower, too, that was on his coffin.

It is a heavenly day up here on the river; I have a north view from my window which is an unending source of comfort.

I have found out that your "Summit" is a fashionable place among the Orange Mountains.

C.F.W.

Notes

1. Landor's 1836 poem is in the form of a letter to Cleone about the development of Pericles and Aspasia's love.

2. *Cameos* (1874), which Stedman coedited with Thomas Bailey Aldrich, was an anthology of Landor's poetry.

To Daniel C. Eaton (Princeton)

P. O. Box 772
Yonkers. N.Y.
Aug. 15th, [1877]
Prof. D. C. Eaton.

Dear Sir.

A friend has sent to me from Cattskill the ferns I forward to you by the same mail. She cannot remember whether all the smaller ones grew together, or not; but I think they did, and that they are the sterile and fertile of "Pellaea gracilis." Am I right? It is a fern I have never seen. I am almost afraid to hope the other is "Aspidium aculeatum"; perhaps it is one of the varieties of "Aspidium spinulosum." You see what slow progress I make in my botanical studies! But they can be, at present, merely a recreation; I have only little straggling ends of odd hours to give them, after more pressing work is done.

I use the "Gray's Microscope," price $2.50. Can you tell me where I can buy a more powerful glass of the same construction; I mean not an elaborate mounted instrument. The only "Coddington lens" I know, is so small that it tires the eyes.

I proved very deficient about that Charleston sea-weed; and about mosses last winter. But can I not make up for it by doing something for you here? I did not send mosses, because I hardly know what a moss is; I looked through the books, found that my old spring-friend "Liverwort," and one of the mosses[,] were both called "Hepatica"; and gave it up.

Very Truly Yours,
Constance Fenimore Woolson.

To Daniel C. Eaton (Beinecke)

(P.O. Box 772)
Yonkers. N.Y.
Sept. 8th, [1877]
Prof. D. C. Eaton.

Dear Sir.

Excuse my delay in answering your kind letter; I have been absent from home.—Thanks for the lens; it is just what I need. I enclose the price,—three dollars; and I am very much obliged to you for the attention.—I am so much pleased to know that the fern was the "aculeatum"; it was one I have been rather despairing about, because I am almost continuously at the South, where it does not grow—A recent letter from Major Haskin (the Sullivan's Island seaweed is still heavy on his conscience) doubts whether I ever found the "Aspidium Floridanum" at St Augustine, as something he found near Tallahassee "is so much more like the description.[”] I think I did not send my "Floridanum" to you, because I was so sure of it; it is a dark colored fern, dark green. And rather leathery. Major Haskin may have found the "A. Ludovicianum," which, apparently no one has seen.—No; I did not sketch the "Adiantum." It was done by a lady who has remarkable talent in drawing, painting, music, poetry, botany, fancywork, and conversation, and only one fault, viz: she never finishes ~~ever~~ anything! Her work, good as it is, is always "a fragment." The Adiantum[,] the drawing of it[,] was sent to me as a present, and was less than half completed. Having, on my side, just as strong a tendency towards exact completion, our intercourse is comical! She knows a great deal about ferns; but mixes American and foreign specimens indiscriminately, and is never quite sure which is which. Now my collection is exclusively American, and not only that, but takes in only the ferns "east of the Rocky Mountains," following exactly your arrangement in Gray and Chapman. I would not have a foreign fern in it for the weight in diamonds, and I gave her that very Jamaica fern, pretty as it was, in order to be rid of it! Then she sent back the drawing, half-finished of course. And I cut it up!—I am going next to take up orchids; they are so odd.—I have, you see, fifty-six out of the seventy-seven ferns you give, and a new one is now a rarity. But, how trifling this amateur ~~trifling~~ study must seem to the real botanist! When your textbook on "seaweeds" is published, then I will begin upon those fairylike flowers of the sea. I suppose you do not care about Thoreau; and John Burroughs; and that charming book so little known, "Rural Hours," by my cousin, Miss Cooper. I liked Burroughs especially, until lately; his last book is "too much so," I think.

Very Truly Yours
Constance Fenimore Woolson.

To Edmund Clarence Stedman (Columbia)

(P.O. Box 772)
Yonkers. N.Y.
Sept. 11th, [1877]

Dear Mr Stedman.

I have been wishing to answer your long and delightful letter for some time; but I have been away—to Lake George and Saratoga; and we have had a house full of company. I now write to ask when I can see you? Can it not be next week? How would it please you to come out here on the "Tally Ho," Colonel Kane's coach, with us, (my sister and myself) on Wednesday, Thursday, or Friday of next week,—the 19th, 20th, or 21st, and spend the night at our house?[1] There are plenty of early morning trains to take you back the next day. My sister (Mrs Benedict) presents her compliments to you, and would be very glad to meet you. She has a small furnished house here for the season and we have a sort of home. The coach leaves the "Brunswick" at half past four in the afternoon; we would be there to meet you. Will you please answer, as, if you come, we must secure the three seats some time in advance; they are, I hear, in demand. Let me know also, please, whether you can come on any one of those three days, so that we can have some latitude about the seats.

If this plan does not accord with your pleasure, I fall back upon my old one,—that you would take an afternoon drive with me any day next week that you select,—say from two, or three, to five o'clock; or at any other hours you prefer. I should probably ask you to meet me at the "Westminster."

Now which will you do? Do just which you like; but do one. I cannot have any more time slipping by without seeing you in some way. Thanks for the photograph. It is fairly good. I like the "Hawthorne" all the time more and more; it lies on my table and I take it up and read it over very often. That is the way to know a poem. At least with me.

I forgot to say that we are all women here, Mother, Clara and her little daughter, and myself comprising our family. With very sincere regards to Mrs Stedman, I am your attached friend,

Constance F. Woolson.

Notes

1. The Pelham or "Tally-Ho" coach operated by Col. DeLancy Astor Kane.

To Edmund Clarence Stedman (Columbia)

(P.O. Box 772)
Yonkers. N.Y.
Sept. 16th, [1877]

Dear Mr Stedman.

I am very glad that you really will come out here. I consider it a compliment worth having, because we have nothing to offer you save ourselves, as we are in "a furnished house," in the centre of a dusty bustling little town. It has been a pleasant change for us, after so many years of wandering, to have even this kind of a home; but, city people need not suppose it is a rural dervy locality.[1] One young lady came out here in June, and the first thing she asked for was a bunch of lilacs!—I enclose the list of trains. The train I have marked,—leaving the forty-second street depot at four, fifteen, (quarter past four) in the afternoon, is a fast train which does not stop at all the numerous stations between here and New York. If you will take that train, it will bring you to Yonkers at about a quarter to five, or a little later. If I hear nothing to the contrary, I will be at the station on Friday afternoon to meet ~~up~~ you, upon the arrival of that train. We dine at six, and of course you must come out in time to break bread with us. I am very glad that at last I shall have a glimpse of you.

Thanks for the vest pocket "Browning." I wish they would bring out your essay on "Robert B." in the same form. That was one of my favorites, you remember. *Especial* favorites, I mean; they were all "favorites." I am glad to see that the poem on Hawthorne is also coming out. It is indeed a noble poem; that is the exact adjective for it, in my opinion. Always looking at the ideas and feelings of a poem more than at the measure, it is only lately that the remarkable metre has forced itself upon my attention. It is so melodious and so perfectly sustained throughout, that, only upon examination, does one see how extremely difficult a measure it is. How could you do it? But I have always said that you are the only American writer I know who absolutely *commands* the language. Words walk right into their places at a glance! It is a marvelous power to me; I never cease wondering at it.—Yes, I like the "eighth verse" too; but I will not give up "my twelfth"; "the few and rude plantations," & the "Massachusetts Path," are so fine. "The one New Englander" is perfect. If I had known that Emerson was going to hear your poem, I would have—but no; I would'nt either. What I mean is that I would have liked to look at him. But I would not have liked even that, if it had taken me into a crowd. I suppose it would have been almost impossible to have obtained an invitation, also. Emerson has been thrown at me all life; out in Cleveland he has a few ardent disciples, and I have often heard them talk. But only within the last few years has he dawned upon *me*, and words can hardly express ~~my admiration~~ for—no, belief in *some* of his Essays. The sum of all earthly wisdom seems to me embodied in his "Nature"; "*Essays*"; "*Second Series*." (There are several "Natures.") I have two sentences of his copied and hung up on my wall at this moment. They help me when I feel disheartend, as nothing else does. And this wonderful man came to hear you! What an event. Not that I consider him in the least a judge of poetry, in spite of his rhymes; but he is as great a man in his own sphere.

I am disgusted with John Burroughs (whom I have heretofore liked) because in his last book, he presumes to place Whitman Whitman! before Emerson. The man is mad. I have never been able to find any of Whitman's work anywhere, save a very fine "Ode to the Ocean," once published in the "Atlantic"; another, to a locomotive in winter, which I liked very much; and an extraordinary "thing," on the "Fair of the American Institute" I believe, with pages of lists of all the articles exhibited, divided off into an irregular broken-winded sort of meter! But, even supposing Whitman is the poet some persons think he is, to compare him with Emerson is, in my opinion, like comparing Byron with the Bible.—

Of course Mrs Stedman "looked handsome"; she always does. She has one of the loveliest faces I know. I do not suppose you confine yourselves to "literary society," exclusively when in the city during the winter; still, you must see a good deal of it, and I have often thought how Mrs Stedman must enjoy herself among the crowd of "literary women," who, as far as my experience goes, have a remarkable facility for looking like scarecrows! I have seen—just seen but not known,—a good many of them.

"Why" do I "bother" you "about Landor"? Well,—because your praise of him was something tremendous. And as I believe in you, of course I knew it would end in my believing in him. You may always know that when I make a hard fight of it, I am coming over. Well; I went through every word of those immense volumes, and became deeply dejected over such things as the "Emperor of China and King-something," as well as Landor's own conversations with Southey and others. Having finished the last word, I took a list of those I really liked, and here it is. Now if these were in a little volume by themselves, I should like them. "Cardinal Legate & the Picture Dealers." "Maid of Orleans & Agnes Sorel." "Princess Mary & Princess Elisabeth." "Dante and Beatrice." "Queen Elisabeth, & Duke of Argon." "Mary & Bothwell." "Louis the 18th or Tallyrand." "La Fontaine & De la Rochefoucault." "Vittoria Colonna & Angelo." "Tallyrand & Arch-bishop of Paris." "Gen. Kleber & French officers." "Hume & Home." "Henry the 8th and Anne Boleyn." "Marcellus and Hannibal." "Bossnet & La Fontanges." "Alexander & the Priest." "Walton, Cotton, & Oldways." And, of the Hellenics, "the Hamadryad," "Drinacos," "Theron & Zoe," "Iphigenia," and, most of all "Artemidora," the version given in "Pericles & Aspasia." You say he is great "in range & variety." He is; I acknowledge that. Still, I am not yet enthusiastic. I have just brought out from the library another immense volume (Landor seems to inspire size) the "Life," by Forster.[2] I am now going to wade through that! You will never dare say much before me again about any writer, will you? I bother you with the subject for years after! I am so glad you stand up to your expressed opinions however, whether I agree with them or not. I hate people who veer. You have "convictions" of the most decided kind about Landor; as you have about the Kane coach, too, apparently! I am curious to know what it is about the coach. My sister Clara has rather a liking for the colonel and his drag; the horn and the prancing horses light up our commonplace street. She has driven ridden out here on the box seat, and found "the gentleman driver" agreeable.[3] As I am not fond of prancing horses, I have not made the journey.—By the way, Col. Kane always has the guard sound his horn as the coach passes the residence of Clara Morris, on the outskirts of our town. A salute to genius! "Why did," I "not speak to Clara Morris"? Well, not for the reason you suppose; no fancied superiority of birth or education kept me back; I am not so absurd as that. Genius is genius. I should be proud to know her. But do you now know how strong a feeling I have about making new acquaintances? I would go twenty miles any day to avoid it. It was always somewhat so with me; it is now much increased. I have not, personally, a particle of self-confidence. Persons have to like me, and show they like me, before I can get up my courage to talk naturally to them. Now who is going to take this trouble for a woman like me? Hardly anyone. I know this, and no longer expect it; or place myself where I look as though I expected it.—"A prophet is not without honor" &c;[4] and I am well aware of the early life of Clara Morris; all the same I admire and appreciate her wonderful powers,—although, so far, I have not seen her "Miss Multon." My sister was carried away with it, and she insists that I must go over to Brooklyn next week, to see her in it. Do you know whether she will play at the matinée? I go to matinées; but hardly ever to evening performances. But I admired Clara Morris as long ago as "Man and Wife" at the old Fifth Avenue theatre. Do not tempt me about writing "a play." I have such a strong taste that way already! And I suppose that, knowing nothing practically of the requisites, I should make a complete failure. Very likely I shall write one some day; and then—not print it.

I am sorry you have been ill; do you still sit up until two a.m. as you used to do?! I am afraid you are not prudent. And that handsome boy "Arty" has gone to Yale! How time flys. That is not spelled correctly, I see; never mind. I have been reading Landor!

So Mr Burlingame is your neighbor? I have long had a great liking for his book-reviews in Appleton's Journal, preferring these to all others. Having had for years this quiet admiration for his work, it seemed funny enough to hear my blooming niece, Kate Mather of Cleveland, speak the other day of "Ned Burlingame" as a charming "young gentleman," a friend of her intimate friends, Molly Payne, the Sherman girls, and (I think but am not sure in this case) Flora Stone. "O!" I said. But it was a surprised and somewhat down-dropping inflection. Is it possible Mr Burlingame is only twenty two or three? He must have begun work in earliest boyhood, then. Henry Sherman, the brother of the "Sherman girls," has just left us, having spent a week here on his way home from England, with his wife, Hattie Benedict, my sister Clara's sister in law.

I spoke of the Osgoods because it seems to me that they do not push their books enough. They merely announce them from their literary throne, and then sit down again. I do not precisely know what to do with "my novel," when it is finished (I have lost a whole year and more, owing to the depressed state of my mind, of which I spoke to you some time ago),—that may not happen for six months yet. Mr Osgood will take it if I please. But I want to have it pushed a little. Hurd & Houghton offered to take the short stories the week after Osgood did. Osgood will bring out a volume of southern stories (Rodman the Keeper et al) this fall if I say so; but I do not think it will be any especial advantage to me; do you? It might come out after the novel.

But I must stop. I shall look for you on Friday, rain or shine.—Do not disappoint me.

Yours sincerely
C. F. Woolson.

Notes

1. dervy: laborious or weak.
2. John Forster published *The Life of Walter Savage Landor* in 1869.
3. Woolson uses both words, with "driven" written above "ridden." Since this is a rare instance where she does not strike through a word, she may have been unsure of the correct form.
4. Mark 6:4.

To Edmund Clarence Stedman (Columbia)

Yonkers
Sept. 30th, [1877]

Dear Mr Stedman.

Your sparkling letter was like a continuation of your sparkling talk on the one memorable evening when our little household enjoyed your presence. It was kind to come; I knew it would give you some trouble, but I wished much to see you, and also to make you acquainted with my Mother and sister. They enjoyed your visit extremely, and hope to see you again; my sister would like to make the acquaintance of Mrs Stedman this winter if possible, when you are in the city.

I thought you would like Clara. But you did not see her at her best. She is a favorite wherever she goes, and when she feels well, she can be charming. I hope you will meet her again; she would like to know you better.

Thanks for your attention about the Osgood affair. It was odd that Mr Ticknor should happen to come in on that very day. His judgment is mine also, regarding the Southern stories.[1]

By the way,—did you not say to me while you were here, "You have had other advisers"? I have not. If you think so, you are entirely mistaken. Whether for good or for ill, the fact remains that I am entirely alone. You are the only adviser I have had. And how often do I see you?

Why do you care about the trifles in the "Contributor's Club"? Yes; I did write that about the "Lass O' Lowrie's" in the September Atlantic; but you must not tell.[2] The pleasure of it is the incognito; trammeled at once if names are known.

It is too bad I cannot see you oftener. Give my sincere regards to Mrs Stedman; if you move into town before December, will you not send me word? Clara is urging us to spend the winter; but I dare not.

Very Cordially your friend
Constance F. Woolson.

The shell necklace is much admired.—See how I have condensed this letter!

Notes

1. Woolson is referring to her hesitation over publishing with Osgood. See letter to Stedman dated Sept. 16, 1877.

2. Woolson's comments on Frances Hodgson Burnett's "That Lass o' Lowrie's" appeared in the Sept. 1887 "Contributors' Club," a regular column in *Atlantic Monthly*.

To Edmund Clarence Stedman (Princeton, Archives of Charles Scribner's Sons)

Yonkers. N.Y.
Oct. 28th, [1877]

Dear Mr Stedman.

Thanks for "favorite poems." "Pan in Wall street," and "Harper's Ferry" are especial favorites of mine; but more than almost anything else do I like,—have I always liked,—"Bohemia." How many times in my own writings,—both letters and magazine sketches,—have I quoted, or stolen, snatches of its melody.—It is a charming poem.—

Mother and I must depart before long; I wish I might spend the winter at the North; but of course her comfort is my first object in life, now.

My sister Clara still talks of your visit. I hope you will send us Mrs Stedman's winter address.

I shall look for your poem on "The Last Token," with the greatest interest.—I see Mr Stoddard has you in the "Wide Awake"; shall get a copy the next time I go into the city.[1]

No more long letters from me! But probably not infrequent short ones.

Very Sincerely Your Friend
Constance F. Woolson.

No; cannot bring myself to ask Osgood to put me into the "Verse Packets." Too much like "pushing."

Notes

1. Richard Stoddard's magazine *Wide Awake* eventually merged with *St. Nicholas* magazine. All the title references are to poems by Stedman.

To William Dean Howells (Houghton)

Yonkers. N.Y.
Nov. 5th, [1877]

Dear Mr Howells.

I congratulate you on the success of your play.[1] Letters that I have received recently from Cleveland, speak of it with enthusiasm; it was greatly admired by the best people they have out there. "I do'nt know when I have seen anything better or brighter," writes a lady whom I consider an excellent, and fastidious, judge. I want to say too, that for five or six years I have had on the list I keep of books to be obtained sometime, and read, the two following: "Memoires de Wilhelmina, Soeur de Frederic le Grand"; and "Lord Herbert de Cherbury's Memoirs."[2] The two were together; and now you have brought them out together! I send something for the "Club." I am much pleased to be put into the Atlantic announcements for 1878. It is a little thing which gives me always particular satisfaction; I could hardly explain why. But it does.

The poem "November" by "C. L. Cleaveland" in the November number is, to my mind, the best little poem I have seen for a long time. There is a reality about it that comes home to an autumn walker like myself.

Very Truly Yours
Constance F. Woolson.

Notes

1. Either *A Day's Pleasure* (1876) or *A Counterfeit Presentment* (1877).

2. The memoirs of Wilhelmine (1709–58), wife of Prince Frederick of Bayreuth, and the favorite sister of Frederick II (the Great) of Prussia (1740–86). Edward Herbert (1583–1648) was a British philosopher, poet, and diplomat.

To Paul Hamilton Hayne (Duke)

Hibernia
Clay County. Florida
Feb. 24th, [1878]

Dear Mr Hayne.

Thanks for the "Simms" Poem.[1] It is excellent in its allusions; and beautiful in itself.—I received no letter from you last summer; so the one you sent must have been lost. I was at Yonkers-on-the-Hudson until the middle of December, when we migrated as usual; this is an island in the St John river, a quiet pleasant place, neither so gay nor so delightful as St Augustine; but still an epitome of peace. I have a row boat and row daily on the broad still, chocolate-colored river. The spring flowers and young leaves make the shores very lovely at present;—I did not send Mr Alden my address until we had been here a month, so my delay also unfortunately delayed your letter; the one of December the fifteenth. You will, I hope, kindly excuse me for not having answered before this time, when I tell you that I am still a slave to eyes that require the strictest rules, eyes that will allow me to do nothing whatever after sunset. As I must be out two or three hours every afternoon, my day is a very short one.—I merely write a few lines to explain matters, and to thank you for having remembered me; I dearly love to receive letters, although I write so few myself. I do not even write to my own and only sister! She understands what an effort it is, and excuses me.—I follow you in all the magazines; and particularly liked the "Unveiled"; and very particularly your Whittier tribute. It seemed to me one of the very best. I hope we shall have your new volume soon. I shall watch for it.

"Ouida"; yes; I have always admired certain powers she possesses greatly. If she had chosen she might have occupied a noble place. She has undoubted power and originality. The story called "A Dog of Flanders," I always carry around with me. With some other favorites, also "bits." But Ouida has horrible taste. I have heard a good deal about her. She has been spoiled by her own inordinate vanity as regards the attentions of gentlemen, they say; although fifty and over, she expects to have half a dozen lovers about her all the time. Did I not hear she had married a Russian lately?—Yes; I also greatly like "That Lass o' Lowrie's." But I have never seen the other story you mention, "Old Martin Boscawen's Jest." I have written down the name of "Wearithorne," & shall try to find it when I return to the world again.—Clarence Gordon, author of "The Gentle Fire Eater," is a real ~~name~~ man of that name.[2] I know a lady who knows him well. I liked his story all but the tobacco. It is the one thing which I never have and never can pardon; of course I allude to the "chewing." The fragrance of a cigar or a pipe is delightful to me. Who the Atlantic "South Carolinian" is, I do not know; have heard the name of "Eggleston" mentioned as that of the author. But not from good authority.—You ask what I am doing. Well—I am on a novel. But it is not sufficiently far advanced yet to be spoken of, so please keep it a secret. No one can be more doubtful about it than the woman now writing it! Still, I shall persevere and bring it out anyway. If it fails, I shall at least have made the attempt honestly. And that will be the end of the matter.—What a terrible review of "Avis" by Gail Hamilton in the Tribune! Now let someone review Gail Hamilton.[3]

If you are writing to Mrs Preston, I wish you would be as kind as to give to her my sincere regards and remembrances. I often think of her, and of my short but charming visit to Lexington. We shall be here probably until May. I shall be much pleased to hear from you when you feel like writing. Your letters are unique. Charles

Lamb was not a poet, to be sure; but your "prose" is certainly like his in its charm. With good wishes I am yours sincerely

Constance F. Woolson.

Notes

1. Presumably a poem by William Gilmore Simms (1806–70) with whom Hayne worked to found *Russell's Magazine*.

2. *That Lass o' Lowrie's* (1877) was by Frances Hodgson Burnett; Marion Calhoun Legare Reeves's *Wearithorne* was published by Lippincott in 1872 and her *Old Martin Boscawen's Jest* was published by Appletons' in 1878; Clarence Gordon's "The Gentle Fire-Eater" was published in *Atlantic Monthly*, Jan. 1878.

3. Woolson alludes to *The Story of Avis* (1877) by Elizabeth Stuart Phelps.

To Edmund Clarence Stedman (Columbia)

Hibernia
St John River. Florida
May 5th, [1878]

Dear Mr Stedman.

I was glad to hear from you; in spite of the tidings of trouble and bitter disappointment your letter brought. Life is hard. But you have that great gift, and indomitable spirit. You will take heart; and you will succeed a second time. The fact that you accomplished what you did in two years, fills me with astonishment and admiration. It is the only story of success I have heard, among hundreds of those of failure.[1] No one I know has in that time done anything more than just keep his head above water. Whereas, if it had not been for the guilt of other people, you would have had this extraordinary record of success to show. Take four years this time; and do not work so killingly hard. At the end of four years you will only be forty-eight; and can go to England with as much enjoyment as now. A man is young until sixty. (How I wish a woman was!) But, do not suppose that I have not appreciated the great disappointment and discouragement you have had to bear. I do appreciate it. I have heard too much of care and anxiety myself, not to know what the words mean. But by this time perhaps you have recovered all your old spirit, and are wondering why I am "talking blue"! I hope so!

We move northward soon. We shall spend the summer either in Cooperstown, or at some quiet seashore place. Clara has given up housekeeping. She never liked the house she was in, and, when it came to buying, or renting for a term of years, Mother & I opposed it decidedly. If we could be with her all the time, it would be very nice; but we cannot. And Clara is lonely without us. Clara says that she waited all winter for Mrs Stedman's address; and that she is much disappointed that you did not send it. She particularly wished to call upon Mrs Stedman; and she still hopes you will give her an opportunity to do so sometime.

I am glad you have met Mrs Boardman. A very pleasant person, I think. I never knew her at all intimately. "A little patronizing"? Oh yes. Of course. "A prophet is not without honor," you know, &c.[2] When Charlotte Cushman read my "Kentucky Belle" in Cleveland on her farewell tour, there was less applause, she told Clara, than in any other town! But I like Mrs Boardman. Thanks, especially, for what you said to her about me. It is particularly gratifying to me that you should have said it to her.

The novel is finished. Think of that! To me it seems unbelievable. Nine hours a day for the last month. I frankly add that I am "finished" too!—As to whether it is good or not, I am entirely uncertain. But at any rate it is an honest attempt. Not a word of it is copied yet; I am wondering whether the phonograph could not be utilized. I suppose it will not appear until autumn. God prosper it.

From whom do you think I had an unexpected call this winter? Stopped here to see me. Col. Higginson. I wonder if you know him. And what you think of him. I had never met him. And what do you suppose brought him? "Two Women." But when the third came in with her glasses on, tired, pale, prim, and sober, his face fairly fell! I don't know what he expected. But evidently I was not it.

I see everything you publish in the magas. Do you suppose I would miss a line with your name on it? "The Rose and the Jasmine," I especially liked. But I did not like at all, in any way, shape, or manner, the Pratt review of your poetry generally. I wish I could have written it! It was not true. And it was not heart-felt. Jealousy showed through every line. Those Pratts, never having obtained any real following themselves, are, I suppose jealous of everybody else. But I'm glad that the At. had a review.

You speak of Daudet. I had one of the first copies of "Fromeut Jeune et Risler Ainé,[''] (Sidonie) sent over from Paris.[3] I admired it, & admired it, when no one else did; I mean ordinary American readers. I have always read all the French novels I could afford to buy. They are very expensive; & useless after they are read because no one ever wants to borrow them. I have boxes of them. "Christern's" is my one great temptation when I am in New York.

Give my love to Mrs Stedman. I hope I shall meet her again before long.

Why ~~What~~ does the Tribune allow Gail Hamilton to assault people so, in its columns? Why does not someone assault "Gail" in return? Col. Higginson answered that "le jeu ne vaut pas la chandelle."[4] But Gail is clever. That is the trouble of it.

You say you are "going to answer no letters." That is right. And I give you therefore no address. When the novel comes out, will you write then and tell me what you think of it? But you do not care much for novels, do you, after all. Mother sends her regards. She likes this place very much. Hundreds of snakes, here. I saw last

Thursday one, just killed in the road. 5 feet 5 inches long, 13 rattles! Moccasin snakes numerous.

I have'nt said half I would like to say; but do'nt you remember I said I should write no more long letters?

Always your friend,
C. F. Woolson.

Notes

1. Woolson may be referring to Stedman's role on the New York Stock Exchange during the protracted economic downturn of the 1870s.

2. Mark 6:4.

3. The full, correct title of Daudet's 1874 novel is *Sidonie: Fromont Jeune et Risler Ainé* (*Fromont Junior and Risler Senior*).

4. le jeu ne vaut pas la chandelle: it's not worth one's while.

To Katharine H. Johnson[1]

1878

How did I prepare myself for literary work? you ask. Not at all—that is, any more than having had an excellent education, which I kept up all the years after I left school, and before I began to write, by always having masters and taking lessons in something or other to amuse myself. There are no 'avenues to success' in literature, save the commonplace one of sending a manuscript to an editor with a line or two, offering it, without explanation or comment, to his magazine, and inclosing return stamps. There is no favoritism, no 'ring.' I used to fancy there was, but I know better now. I have sat in the editorial offices of magazines for hours and watched how the business went on. An editor told me this: 'I always open a manuscript from a new quarter with hope; I am always on the lookout for new stars.' And that is exactly true. My first manuscript I sent to ______ without asking a question; it was accepted, and that inspired me with courage to go on. They knew nothing whatever about me; I even had an assumed name.[2]

You ask about profit from literary work. It varies. There is no regularity in it. When you first begin the magazines pay you about five dollars per page (I mean, of course, five dollars for what fills one of their pages—not yours). After a time they pay you more—if they choose. But you cannot demand it. They pay me now much more, but that is entirely at their option. I get from seventy-five to one hundred dollars for a story; for the pictorial articles more. I received three hundred dollars for those two on St Augustine, and more for the two on Charleston and the Oklahoma River.[3] There is a difference in the method of payment adopted by the different magazines.[4] Messrs. Harper and Appleton pay on acceptance; all the others on publication. As they may have to delay publication it follows that authors of accepted manuscripts have sometimes to wait months and months for their pay. One thing is fixed; they won't have the same contributor appear too often; it is against their policy. Supposing you get into 'Harper's,' 'The Galaxy,' 'The Atlantic,' 'Scribner's,' 'Lippincott's' and 'Appletons' ' once each year; you will then have, supposing your article to be of good length, four hundred and fifty dollars. If you are fortunate enough to get in twice you then have nine hundred dollars. But, you see, there is no certainty about it. Some years I have run up to two thousand dollars. But I have been particularly fortunate. As I have property enough to live in a quiet way without the writing you see I can afford to let things take their course, and not press my manuscripts on the editors.

But there is another side! You cannot achieve success in literature, even of a small kind, without being bitterly attacked by the malicious and envious. And I have had my share of biting criticism. I do'nt mind it now, and you must not either when you begin, as I am sure you will.

"All you say of your education is very well. But it is not knowledge which will give you success so much as ease, humor and originality of style. . . . If I were you I should not give up my position as teacher, but I would take my leisure time for writing and commence to send out manuscripts. At first, do'nt send out long ones: about five magazine pages is a tempting length to the editors, who are over-burdened with long manuscripts. Do'nt be discouraged if one comes back declined; send it right out to some one else. And keep doing it. The editors do'nt know who you are, and they do'nt care. If you could only see the reams of manuscript they get every day. It is all a pure matter of business. Write on paper no larger than this (regular note size), and on one side of the sheet only. Never roll your manuscript; in fact, it is much better to send it unfolded, the sheets held together by a thread at the top and numbered. A large square envelope will take such a sheet without folding. Put your name and address not only on the note to the editor, but on the first page of the manuscript. . . .

Sincerely ever,
Constance F. W.

Notes

1. Katharine H. Johnson sent this letter to *The Ladies' Home Journal.* The magazine published this excerpt under the title "A Successful Author's Advice" in its Aug. 1896 issue. I have made changes to be consistent with Woolson's style: underlining rather than italics, no period with *St,* her spelling of "do'nt." Apparently Johnson did not become a successful writer because I have been unable to identify her.

2. Probably *The Old Stone House,* published in 1873 by D. Lothrop and Co. under the pseudonym Anne March.

3. "The Oklahoma River" must be the magazine's error. The travel narrative would be "The Oklawaha," published in *Harper's* in Jan. 1876.

4. *The Ladies' Home Journal* adds a note here that payment methods have changed by 1896.

To Edmund Clarence Stedman (Columbia)

Yonkers. N.Y.
Tuesday
Jan. 15th, [1879]

Dear Mr Stedman.

Good by; we sail tomorrow on the "City of Columbus."—I received your November card with the World's scolding about the Atlantic's "C.C."—I like the Club; naturally; because I am generally in it! My brother was with us here, ill, until Dec. 1st. Since then, I have surprised my family with a serious illness. I am still hardly able to stand. My sister went west to spend Xmas; was forty eight hours in a snow bank near Buffalo; and their train was run into! Meantime poor Mother, here, alone, found herself confronted with me, helpless, and out of my head; and the coldest weather for twenty years besieging the house. We have survived; and, after several postponings, we now hope to start tomorrow.

I was much interested in your aerial article in "Scribner."[1] As I have always expected air-navigation, I read it in a serious light; and I am sure you were serious when you wrote it, although people persist in calling it "fun." Are you going to write a volume of "American" Victorian Poets? Do.

How much you must miss Bayard Taylor. Shall you not write something on the subject?

I have not read the "Masque of Poets"; and shall not, unless you plainly say you are in it.[2]

Do you wonder what has become of my novel? I think you will see it in print during the year. I say no more; although I would like to. ~~It has~~ You can have no idea how fond I am now of Mr Osgood.[3] I fairly dream of him at night.

I am always delighted to hear from you; I wish you would write a line occasionally. We are not quite sure where we shall spend the winter; but Clara will forward any letters sent to me, here; p.o. box 772.—Your Bryant is remarkably fine.

It seems so strange to be weak and ill.

Very Truly Yours,
C. F. Woolson.

Notes

1. Woolson may be referring to anonymous comments in the "Culture and Progress" column of *Scribner's*.

2. *A Masque of Poets* was a collection of poems published as part of the No Name Series by Roberts Brothers in 1878.

3. Woolson did not trust Osgood's and is being sarcastic.

To Edmund Clarence Stedman (Columbia)

1342 New York Avenue
Washington. D.C.
March 14th, [1879]

Dear Mr Stedman.

Your letter was forwarded to me from Yonkers; thanks for the sincere sympathy it expressed.

I am so very desolate without my Mother that I cannot speak of it. The whole world is changed to me. The one person who loved me dearly has gone. Nothing,—nobody,—can ever fill her empty place. She was "glad["] to go. But I miss her,—miss her.

We are spending the spring here on my account, the cold being considered dangerous. My sister, little Clare, and my niece Kate Mather, are here with me. We shall not return to Yonkers at present. I have no especial plans; shall probably go with my sister to some summer-place, later. I have got to learn how to live, over again.

In the meantime I have taken refuge in my writing. That Mother did not see in print the long story in which she felt so great an interest, is, and always will be, in my mind, a very bitter memory. The book will come out later; but it will not be the same to me. Mr Osgood's course was strange from the beginning.[1] But I must leave the question to time; if I cannot conquer my place myself, then I do not deserve one.—I say this to you because you have always been in my confidence; and I know also that you will not betray it.

While in Cleveland, Col. Hay called upon me; I enjoyed his visit very much; and I feel sure I owe it to you. My niece says it was "Kate" Mather you met; and not Mrs Hay's friend "Nellie" Mather. Kate desires to be remembered to you; as does also my sister.

I see that you are now engaged in the last rites over all that remains of your friend of many years, Bayard Taylor. I have not yet seen your poem; Col. Hay admired it greatly; deeply.

You will excuse this letter; I feel so very badly all the time that I make mistakes.

Very Sincerely Yours
C. F. Woolson.

Notes

1. See letters to Stedman dated Sept. 16, 1877 and Jan. 15, 1879, for Woolson's hesitation about publishing with Osgood.

To John Hay (Brown)

1342 New York Avenue
[Washington]
March 14th [1879?]

Dear Colonel Hay.

I was much pleased by your kindness in sending me "Castilian Days." I read it when it first came out; but, as my own copy has been hopelessly packed away for some time—one of the deprivations of a wandering life—I have been re-reading it; and with double interest now that I have met the author. It is certainly a vigorous, vivid, and, in addition, very charming book.

I shall scan the "Club" for your hand; and I am glad you said what you did about "Daisy Miller"; it was needed.[1] I have been surprised to see how many sensible people persist in misunderstanding that natural little sketch. As the "Daisies" are what they are through pure ignorance, Mr James' work—, and yours also in calling attention to it—, is a sort of "Tract for the Times" which will do good.

Sincerely yours,
Constance Fenimore Woolson.

I find here two letters from Mr Stedman; one speaking of my dear Mother, whom he met one evening at Yonkers, a year or two ago; the other enclosing his "Musae Americanae."[2] I presume you have seen it.

Notes

1. Hay published his travel narrative, *Castilian Days,* in 1871. He discusses James's *Daisy Miller* in a March 1879 review for *Atlantic Monthly's* "Contributors' Club" titled "Girlhood on the American Plan."

2. Stedman's poem, published in *The Independent* (March 6, 1879), honored American women writers.

To H. K. Armstrong (McGill)[1]

Cleveland. Ohio
Oct. 16th, [1879]

Dear Sir.

Excuse the delay in answering your note, received some time ago. The photograph "Miss Vedder" had was an imaginary one; but the picture was not. I had in my mind one of Boughton's paintings—I think (but am not sure) that I saw it at the "Centennial Loan Exhibition" in New York, in 1876.[2] What it was called I do not know; but I have never forgotten the girl's face and expression. I have a vague idea that it was either the "Summer of Life," or "Winter of Life." It was owned in New York, of course. When I saw it, the verse you quote came instantly to my memory.

Yours Truly
C. F. Woolson.

Notes

1. The letter is to H. K. Armstrong, whom I have been unable to identify. Its date from one of the few letter envelopes that survive confirms that Woolson visited Cleveland in 1879 just before sailing for Europe.

2. "Miss Vedder" appears in *Harper's New Monthly Magazine* in March 1879. The painter Woolson names is George Henry Boughton (1833–1905).

To Samuel Livingston Mather (WRHS/Mather)[1]

Steamship Gallia
November 24th, 1879

My dear Brother.

. . . Sunday dawned clear and bright, with but little sea. There was an English Church service in the cabin at 10:30, with an English clergyman, and English Prayer-book. There was a large attendance; crowded; singing in which all joined. During the sermon our first ship came by, very near us, under full sail; it was a splendid sight. In the evening we had sacred music. It was quite interesting to see how many of the passengers let their books fall to join, from all parts of the large cabin, in "Abide with me," "Sun of my soul," and "Jerusalem the Golden." To-day it is rougher, but bright; none of us in the least sea-sick. Clara and I walk miles on the broad deck. A Scotch gentleman, who has crossed many times told me this morning that our storm of last Thursday was very severe; and that we might cross twenty times without seeing another like it. Every wave swept over us; I could see the water rushing across the little thick glass light let into the deck, which lights my room, and in Clara's room the shock of the waves as they struck the side was terrific. So after all, we have seen a storm at sea. . . .

Evening. Head winds and rough sea. They say now we shall not reach Liverpool until the tenth day. I am eager to reach the warmth of Southern France.

Thursday evening.

We hope to reach Queenstown tomorrow, Thanksgiving Day,—how many of them we have spent with you, no notice taken of the day on this English vessel. It has been steadily rough all the way, but we are quite well.

Affectionately,
C. F. Woolson.

Notes

1. The letter is in a typed transcription at WRHS. Portions also appear in Benedict/CFW, 151–52.

To Samuel Mather (Anderson)[1]

Clarges Street
Piccadilly. London
Dec. 8th, [1879]

My dear Sam.

I wrote a few hasty lines to your Mother from Liverpool; and will now take up the hasty narrative of our adventures, not because anything remarkable has happened, but because I think you may be interested in us and our impressions of "old England."

We left Liverpool on Tuesday morning, December second, having had a good rest there of two days. Dr Porter and Mr Shaw arranged our departure for us; bought our tickets; secured a queer little compartment with seats for three, and accompanied us (sitting on the little shelf), as far as Edgehill, one of the suburban stations. Then, having presented us with fruit, a flask, filled! and a map of London, they said "good-bye"—and away we went across England, for the first time all alone. We have happened upon what the English call "very severe weather"; the papers speak of it as remarkable,—the coldest winter known for twenty years. It is cold, but nothing like our cold. This day, from Liverpool to London, was like a picture; the whole country, trees, hedges, houses, grass, everything sheeted in clear ice, although the people here call it "frost." Occasionally in America, after a sudden thaw, we have such fairy-like effects for a few hours; but here it lasted all day. We had long flat tin-boxes filled with hot water, renewed at the stopping-places, upon which our feet rested, and we were really quite comfortable in our little "clarence"; although I think we should not have been, if obliged to ride a longer time. At Rugby, we had coffee and "buns" at the station described by Dickens; then on again, swiftly and noiselessly, across the white country. At London our "guard" procured a "four-wheeled cab," and in this ridiculous vehicle, we three, with our luggage piled in a mountain on top, drove at a harum-scarum speed through streets upon streets until we reached "Half Moon," where we found that Mrs Searle had not a free corner, her house being crowded. But she directed us here, the next street; and, finding good rooms, we installed ourselves in them, thus plunging for the first time into thorough "English" life,—that is, "lodgings." We were told, both on the steamer and in Liverpool, that the neighbourhood to which we were going was the most "swell" part of London—what is popularly known as "Mayfair." Since we have been here, we have been told the same; and our guidebooks reflect it; so it is probably true. Yet Half-Moon, Clarges, Bolton, and the rest are all narrow dark little streets, and the houses are small and by no means elegant. Yet, O! the comfort of it! If I am never to have a real "home," then the next thing is certainly English "lodgings." We have a large, pleasant front parlor up one small flight of stairs, with a generous open fire; from this room open two bedrooms, each with open fire. No gas, moderator lamp and wax candles. Our meals are served in our own parlor by two excellent waiters in dress-coat and very white ties, precisely like our young men at home when in ball-costume! We order what we like, and are charged accordingly; that is generally—, I do not mean that each thing has a price, like the "European plan" at home. But, we say, for instance, "a soup, joint, salad, and simple dessert," and they provide as they please within this limit. We have breakfast at nine, lunch (if we are at home) at one, dinner at half past five. The cooking is wonderfully good, and the table service dainty. It is quite true, however, that the English coffee is wretched; at least, that has been our experience both at Liverpool and here. They like tea themselves so much better than coffee, that the latter has no chance. As Clara does not like tea, we continue drinking the coffee, and make it up in abuse. The "comfort" I spoke of is in the way things are done. In the morning, before we are up, the maid comes softly into my room, makes the fire carefully and slowly, as though time was a thing of no consequence, and does not leave it until it is burning finely. Then, softly, she draws aside the heavy chintz curtains, hung on wooden rings, fastens them back, puts down by the hearth one can of hot water, another on the wash-stand, takes the towels and spreads them before the blazing fire, gets my slippers, warms them, and then, approaching the bed, gently says: "Will you rise, now, Miss? Everything is in order." She goes out, taking with her my boots and dress, which she returns cleaned and brushed. At evening, just before dinner, the same process reversed. Fire replenished, curtains drawn closely, wax candles lit, more hot water, warm towels, hot slippers, arm-chair rolled up, and everything you leave out, brushed. Also bed turned down, and pillows warmed. This is the habitual custom, it seems; no unusual attention. As I dislike very much the constant dress-parade of a hotel-table, and the "home-circle" of a boarding-house, this "lodging" plan, with your meals in your own parlor, seems very pleasant to me. We are not living cheaply, of course; but Clara bears the heavier share of the expense, which amounts to something over three dollars a day, each. We could not have half the comfort or space at a hotel, and the price would be more.—

We made up our minds to see a few of the most interesting places, but also determined not to wear ourselves out with sight-seeing. We have attended service at Westminster Abbey; have been there more than once. To me it is the most interesting spot in London. The music is delightful; I presume you have all heard it, also.

I must say that my enthusiasm rose high, and remained away up, as I wandered through the aisles and chapels, and read the old and new inscriptions. It was to me a deep and great pleasure; one of the deepest of my life. We have also been to the Tower, where I was more interested in the chamber with the prisoner's inscriptions, and the poor little burial-ground and chapel where so many lie undistinguished together, who suffered death there, than in the tiresome armor and arms, and the disappointing crown jewels. On the day we were at the Tower, we had lunch at a real English down-town chop-house; we did it on purpose to see what it was like, and found it very odd. Beer, beer, beer! We were obliged to pay extra for our napkins! But what we had was clean and good; pea-soup, &c. There were about two hundred men lunching in the lower room; we went upstairs. I spent also a whole day at the National Gallery, hard at work among the pictures. I had Baedeker and all the catalogues, and became simply "steeped" in paint. This is only the beginning. I am going to try if possible to acquire some of that great and real pleasure which is to be obtained from pictures. There is no doubt but that to some persons a fine picture gives as much actual pleasure as music does to me; or as a fine wine, or a delicate dish; or anything else which is delightful. May-be it cannot be learned in this way, but I am going to try. I suppose you have all visited this Gallery; how much I should like to talk over the pictures with you. I will only say here that I was disappointed in the two Raphaels (both Madonnas) and also in the Claude Lorraines and Salvator Rosas. But much pleased with some others. To be disappointed in Raphael sounds heathenish, I know. But I am not going to lie about it. I was disappointed. Perhaps after more study, I shall appreciate them better. Tell Kate that the two "Turners" whose photographs I had in Washington, are here, and both very beautiful, I think. Did she see them while here? They are "The 'Fighting Temeraire' tugged to her last berth to be broken up," and "Dido building Carthage." [2] In this gallery, as elsewhere, we were interested in noting the great difference in the dress of English and American women. The English girls are so much more robust, and have so much more color; but this pink hue extends over the nose as well as the cheeks, and their feet and boots are very broad and large. Their bonnets, round hats, furs, cloaks, and dresses are all unlike ours; not totally, but enough so to make heads turn on Broadway, for instance. To our eyes, the English girls look heavy and awkward; I suppose they think Americans altogether too thin. The older ladies who drive by in their carriages, remind us of the pictures of the Queen; I suppose they imitate her old-fashioned way of wearing her hair. We admire, however, the English men; in their Ulsters, with their fine height and glowing complexions, they look well. We have seen St. Paul's; the Bank of England; Houses of Parliament; the Palaces (we are near Buckingham, St James, and Marlborough House) the Embankment and Cleopatra's Needle; the Temple; any number of statues and monuments with the foggy result of never remembering which is Nelson and which Wellington,—the Parks, Stafford House, and, on Clare's account, Madame Tussaud's Wax-works. We have still (that is I have) a long day for Kensington Museum and its "decorative art," and many other places. Besides the shops. My shopping consists first and last and all included, of one umbrella; and that is already purchased, and is a beauty. One shilling over five dollars was the price. The English money we have learned, all save that sly half-crown, or "'arf-crown." That there is the difference of a sixpence between them, we know; ~~but~~ (by "them" I mean the two shilling piece and half-crown); but we generally pay it the wrong way! I began my performances in England by paying the Liverpool cabman just double fare! The truth is, however, that to get any sort of a carriage for four persons for thirty-seven cents, seems to us too ridiculous.

We have not quite decided on what day we shall start for Mentone. The papers warn travelers bound for Italy to "wait until the snow has been cleared from the tracks" in France! No communication between Paris and Lyons, for instance. Trains out all night in the snow. It sounds familiarly to ears accustomed to the drifts of western New York and the Lake-shore, but I must confess I did not expect to find such a state of things here.

Please give our warmest love to Kate, and tell her how delighted we were to get her letter. We shall both answer it soon. We took the trouble to go away down to the Alliance Bank in a hansom expecting to find treasures (although why I expected to find anything, I am sure I do'nt know, as I asked everybody to write to Mentone), and if Kate's letter had not been there, we should have come back with only a shabby little note from Mrs Palmer which was almost worse than nothing. But Kate's letter was charming; we read it aloud in the flying cab, and enjoyed every word. How these cabs go! It is fearful. I was not at all surprised to see in the papers to-day that a humane society had been instructed to "provide ambulances to remove to hospitals persons run-over in the streets!" It is certainly as much as one life is worth to cross the great thoroughfares, and (what amuses me, as I am apt to run myself) everybody runs. Men, women & children. So I am in good company. Since Kate's letter, others have come. But hers was the best of all, as well as the first. I have written to Mentone, telling them to take care of our letters there until we come. I must tell you one of my entertainments. All my life, saturated as I am with Dickens, I have wanted to see an English "Punch and Judy." The other day, one came through the street; I seized my chance, signalled the man, the stage was set up opposite our windows, and Clare and I wrapped in shawls on the little balcony, watched the whole of the exciting drama from where Punch beats the baby to his own final extinction by the Evil One. With the audiphone I heard all the dialogue, recognizing it piecemeal as it went along. They had some novelties, a negro who has "just arrived from America"; Punch demolishes him and then sings: "Stop that knocking at the door" as a delicate compliment, I suppose, to his nationality! Everywhere we see "American apples," advertised and offered for sale as great dainties. Likewise, I am sorry, to say "American Drinks."

Henry James is in Paris, and will not be here before Xmas. So we shall not see him after all unless it is on our way to Mentone. His lodgings are in the next street, and his landlady sent us his Paris address. I am sorry it has happened so. I suppose he prefers to be in London in "the season." I see that our lodgings are just double price during those months.

We are all well. Clara has suffered from dizziness,—the roll of the steamer. I have heard that those persons who are not at all sea-sick, are apt to be dizzy afterwards. Personally, I am anxious to get to Mentone. I am afraid of the cold, and want to be at work again. I hope we shall start soon.

I wish you would let me know if I am not still in your debt? Did the money cover what you paid for me,—my hotel bill, I mean? Please let me know just how it was. I am sure you also paid for a dinner of mine,—did you not? The one I asked you to pay Mr Hanna for. Tell me about Charly, too. It was a very happy little visit in New York, did'nt you think so? I enjoyed it <u>very</u> much, although at times I felt tired. Mary Crowell writes enthusiastically of you, and of Kate. I am so glad you saw so much of her, and she of you, because I have always wished you to become better acquainted. Next to your family, in Cleveland, come the Benedicts in my heart. And I have always felt that if you knew them better, you would love them too.

Will you tell Mr Willey that I received his letter, and that I shall write to him before long. And give my regards to Dr & Mrs Brown. I suppose Col. Hay is in Washington;—is he?

I have sent three letters before this, one to your father and two to your mother; I hope they arrived safely. As it is "vacation" for me now, I have time to write; I shall not have so much time, later.—I hope you will all write to me; I am quite homesick for letters and anxious to reach Mentone in order to find some. Dearest love to all.—O—please do not forget if you (or any of you) see Tom Walton, to tell him that I find his "Dictionary of London," of the greatest use, and better than anything else.

Good-by. Take care of yourself.

Affectionately,
C.F.W.

Notes

1. Portions of this letter also appear in Benedict/CFW, 152–57.

2. The paintings were by J.M.W. Turner, done in 1838 and 1815, respectively. The Raphael Madonnas were *Madonna and Child* (before 1520) and *Madonna and Child with the Infant Baptist* (1509–10). Most of the paintings by Claude Lorrain and Salvator Rosa have only

tentative composition dates. The National Gallery owned the following in 1879: Lorrain's *A Seaport, Landscape with Goatherd and Goats, Landscape with Aeneas at Delos, Landscape with Cephalus and Procris Reunited by Diana, Landscape with David at the Cave of Adullam, Landscape with Hagar and the Angel, Landscape with Narcissus and Echo, Landscape with the Death of Procris, Landscape with the Marriage of Isaac and Rebecca, Seaport with the Embarkation of Saint Ursula, Seaport with the Embarkation of the Queen of Sheba*; Rosa's *Landscape with Mercury and the Dishonest Woodman, A Coastal Scene, The Philosophers' Wood, Tobias and the Angel.*

To Katharine Livingston Mather (WRHS/Mather)[1]

Menton. France
December 22^{d}, 1879

My dear Kate.

. . . It was very cold in London, but nothing like the bitter cold in France. In crossing the Channel, we were nearly frozen, and we continued frozen all the way to Marseilles. If we happened to hit in London, "the severest winter known in twenty years" we found in France the "coldest season in the present century!" Paris was fairly blockaded with ice and snow; passage-ways cut for the carts and carriages, but great heaps left on each side, of four or five feet in height; and this even in such streets as the Rue de Rivoli, and Avenue de l'Opera. Some of the theatres gave up, and closed their doors; also many shops. Great scarcity of milk, butter, and eggs. Under such circumstances, as you may imagine, Paris was hardly Paris. We only remained one day, and were so uncomfortable that we were glad to hurry southward; but with no idea that the cold would still be with us. We went as far as Lyons the first day, and we really suffered. Shut into a coupé, with the windows frosted thickly up to the top so that we could see nothing, and only a tin foot-warmer as a heater, we became chilled through and through. The same state of snow blockade at Lyons as at Paris. The snow continued nearly to Marseilles, where we passed the next night; and again we suffered. As we approached Marseilles, however, we saw the fields stretching out on each side covered with vines; saw chateaux; castles on cliffs; ruined towers,—and I began to grow excited. The next morning we struck the sea, and from there to Menton it was as beautiful, and more beautiful, than I ever imagined anything in this world could be. To begin with, it was warm. Gradually we threw aside cloaks, and wraps, and the "chauffe-pied," which had been more precious than diamonds, was pushed contemptuously aside. Cannes, Nice, Monte Carlo, were all passed, and each place more beautiful than the last. I suppose a woman more thoroughly tired out with cold, fatigue, and journeying, never entered Menton; and yet even she (that is I) was perfectly charmed. The Mediterranean is bluer than any water I have ever imagined; the sunshine is brighter; the great mountains behind us are higher, and the old Italian towns more picturesque than I thought they would be. Mentone is composed of two Bays, the East (where we are), and the West. Between the two Bays, is the old town, as picturesque and dirty as possible, full of priests, pretty girls in red handkerchiefs, and swarms of children . . . We have had one or two lovely walks up the mountain through the orange and olive groves. Pink and white roses in bloom in the gardens; heliotrope in bushes six feet high. Two English churches, one quite near us; they are preparing for Christmas now. I bought a French botany and am going out this afternoon for wild flowers. Oh! The South Kensington Museum. Weren't you fascinated with it? I was; spent two whole days there. That, and the thrilled feeling one has at Westminster Abbey, were the best things I had in England.

To give you an idea of the fog there, when twenty feet out on the Westminster Bridge, we could not see even the outline of the Houses of Parliament . . . The climate is not as warm as Florida; scenery much more beautiful. Quantities of grandees here with horses, carriages, and servants; Russians, English, and French. Love to all who inquire after me.

Affectionately,
C. F. Woolson.

Notes

1. The letter is in a typed transcription at WRHS. Portions also appear in Benedict/CFW, 156n, 158–59.

To Edmund Clarence Stedman (Columbia)

Menton
Alpes Maritimes. France
Dec. 28th, [1879]

Dear Mr Stedman.

I am now established, as above, for the winter. Do you want to know what it is like? I will tell you truthfully, with no more colors than nature herself has used. I am sitting in an open window, with the hot sunshine flooding the room; below, roses, orange blossoms, heliotrope trained in bushes ten feet high; behind, within one minute's walk the Alpes Maritimes or Apennines, covered half-way up with groves of olives, but their peaks gray and bare; on one side, the beautiful point of Bordighera, with its palms; on the other, the old town of Menton built on a crag from fear of pirates! its streets six feet wide, houses six stories high, dominated with a cathedral and slender square tower full of girls in red head-dresses, priests, and donkeys; and now, best of all, in front, with only the road between, the expanse of the Mediterranean, more blue and soft than any water I have ever seen, the dear sea of Florida included. There; is'nt that a picture? I will confess that I had feared I should be homesick for Florida; I hardly appreciated myself, until I was separated from it, how much I loved that warm hazy peninsula where I spent five long happy winters with my dear Mother. I still love it dearly; but it is so new and beautiful here, that I shall not have time to be homesick. Do you think the very idea absurd? It comes no doubt from loneliness and also from want of physical strength. I am not as strong as I was.

We had a stormy passage on the Gallia; but tossed and pitched in distinguished company, as you may have seen by the passenger list. Fortunately, we were not seasick, either on the ocean or the dreaded channel. But we *were* very cold. Ten days in London, in delightful lodgings in "Mayfair"; a few sights, of course. But *I* spent all my leisure time at the National Gallery, and South Kensington Museum. A terrible journey through France; the "severest cold known during this century!"—perhaps you have seen the account of it? Paris blockaded with ice and snow, heaps four and five feet high in the streets. Some of the theatres closed, and many shops. Scarcity of milk and vegetables. Under these circumstances, as you may imagine, Paris was not Paris; and we fled away. But the cold went with us! Lyons was Arctic; Marseilles frozen. However "let us forget what it is not pleasant to remember," (*your* Landor), and say no more. Menton is perfect. That is enough.

And now let me tell you something amusing about that evening at the Grand Hotel; I do not know when a more complete and ridiculous misunderstanding has ~~occurred to~~ befallen me. I went down to the parlor, by appointment, to meet a lady; she was not there, but you were. An agreeable surprise. I let the lady go to —— say oblivion, and sat down delighted with the chance of seeing Mrs Stedman and yourself, even although you were busy with your friends, strangers to me; and I dread all strangers. I thought perhaps I could have a little chat with you between times and at the fringes of the call, as it were; and should have patiently waited there all evening if you had not asked for, and indeed rather insisted upon seeing, Clara. As I knew Clara had long wished to make Mrs Stedman's acquaintance, I went up to her parlor, where I found her, however, very tired and depressed, (we both had altogether too much to do during that last week in New York), having a quiet talk with her friend, Mrs Palmer, who had come from Hartford to see me off.[1] When Clara heard that you were not alone, but with a party of strangers, she did not wish to go down; her hair was not arranged as becomingly as usual, and she did not feel herself. I said, "Go down with me; and I promise to stay only a few minutes. *I* will make the move." This sentence, it seems, she did not hear. And when, after my "few minutes" had passed, I rose, I was stupefied with astonishment to see her *sit down* again, leaving me to make my exit alone! Mrs Palmer was as much astonished as I was; so she said afterwards. Now my sister is a person who always knows just what she wants to do; and does it. I never interfere with her. I therefore suppose that some new idea had come to her, which made her wish to have a longer conversation with Mrs Stedman, and I left her accordingly. The lady I was to see, came to our parlor, made her call, and went away; and I was wondering what it could be that detained Clara, when Mrs Palmer and herself returned, and Clara covered me with reproaches for my calm desertion! Now, the truth was that I really wished to see both yourself and Mrs Stedman; that I had ever so much both to ask and to say; that I was disappointed at having to leave you so early, and that it was a pure piece of self-sacrifice on my part although it turned out so badly. It is not uncommon for me to make just such failures, because a thing once decided upon, I know no other way than to carry it out as agreed upon. I am afraid I am rather dense, as I find I do not modify, as other people do, but go straight at a thing, whether large or small, without turning. Do not suppose Clara was not pleased to have the opportunity of becoming acquainted with Mrs Stedman. She was. She has long desired it. But she was vexed ~~at~~ with me at what she considered my calm way of walking off! She hardly believes, even now the real truth of the case!—I am truly sorry that I saw so little of you. I never have half enough of you; I do'nt know any one I like to listen to and talk to so much as yourself. I congratulate you upon your new house; how delightful it will be for you. And I shall watch with the greatest interest for your American Poets. How glad I am that I am a "novelist"! I should tremble under your diamond pointed lance. Of course I shall read the Scribners when "Mary Annerley" (Blackmore) is finished.[2] My story begins—in Harper. Did I tell you that I have seen a good deal of John Hay during the past year, when I have been in Cleveland, and that I like him sincerely. I sent your message to your friend Capt. Mason (whom I do not know although you insisted I did) through my niece, Kate Mather.[3] Kate was with us in New York, by the way; but at the Opera the night you were at our hotel. She regretted that she had not been at home that she too might have had a look at you.—I keep thinking about your new house (tell Mrs Stedman) and how charming it will be. I am beginning to feel the "little miseries" of this wandering life I have led for ten years; to sigh for a pleasant room with books and easy chairs, and the right kind of a lamp! Therefore, I envy you. I hope you are quite well this winter, and without the cough that tires me. Clara, whose life is now donkey riding and excursions up the mountain,—sends her regards. As this letter is to you, and not to "Laura," it will not be too bold to say that she thinks (as I do) that your wife is one of the prettiest and sweetest women she has met. So she is. You are a fortunate man.—I hope you will write. I shall be here all winter. I know you are busy, so a line or two will do. With all good wishes for the New Year, I am always your attached friend,

C.F.W.

Notes

1. Possibly a relative of George Palmer (1818–1916), a U.S. Republican representative from New York, who, like Woolson's Mather in-laws, was connected to iron manufacturing.
2. R. D. Blackmore (1825–1900) published his novel *Mary Anerley* in 1880.
3. Perhaps Capt. Henry W. Mason who served in New York's 9th Cavalry.

To Clara Stone Hay (Brown)

Monday
[1879?]

Dear Mrs Hay.

I return the book—the best album I have ever seen—with a few unimportant lines added; Kate's ink played me false, and I was obliged to retrace the lines.[1] I am very proud to be in such fine company, although I have so little to say.

Thanks for the "Advance Guard"—which I like extremely.[2] I must confess that I also read everything else in the book.

Please give my regards to Colonel Hay; I am sorry not to see him again.

With all good wishes, and good-by, I am

Yours sincerely,
Constance Fenimore Woolson.

Notes

1. Petry (20) identifies this as a possible reference to a "Mental Photograph Album," a genre where a person would answer a series of standardized questions or more likely a reference to Clara Hay's or Katharine Livingston Mather's autograph album.
2. A poem by John Hay.

To Samuel Mather (Anderson)[1]

Menton
Alpes Maritimes. France
January 25th, [1880]

My dear Sam.

The above is our address without the name of bankers; or hotel. We receive the letters safely in either case; but when the letters go to the Banker's office, it makes a little delay. I think we have received all your letters, so far; the last were from Kate, and the next day one from your mother and from yourself. From Menton, I have written to Kate and to Will; I think Clara has also written. It seems the most unearthly length of time before we can receive answers to our first letters from here. They should begin to come by tomorrow or next day. I shall not feel comfortable until they do. I take up your first letter to look it over and again notice what you say about mailing me a letter (which came after I left) to the "Alliance Bank, London." Do'nt you mean Clara! I received a letter while in London; and if one was sent, I wish to make inquiries. Also, I am still ignorant whether Mrs Willey received the books I borrowed from her—the ones I so carelessly left in Kate's room, without telling your Mother anything about them.

—All goes on pleasantly here without anything new save the constantly renewed surprise each morning over the wonderful, never-changing blue of the sea, and the tints of the sky, both over the water and mountains. Last Wednesday, St Agnes' day, we went on an excursion to "Sainted Agnese," an antique little village perched up on the side of a high mountain, over-topped by a ruined castle, which owing to its position on the extreme point of the gray peak, is a noticeable object for miles. It is the best and most "thorough-going" ruin I have yet seen and must have been impregnable in old times. It dates back to the tenth century, I believe. We were a party of ten, all on donkeys. I wish you could have seen us! To my mind a donkey is the most ridiculous animal in the world; and the man who rides him the next. We women look better; but by no means romantic. Two donkey-men on foot were with us, carrying our lunch baskets. Clara and I only rode up the steepest ascents; we preferred walking when we could.

The path led directly up through the lemon groves, vineyards, olive groves, and finally, bald rock, hot in the sunshine. It was the day of the village fête, and we reached the little plateau where the nest of stone houses hangs on the mountain side, in time to see the procession. An image of the Virgin, carried by the priests; an image of "St Agnes" carried by girls dressed in white; then boys with bouquets and long streamers of colored ribbon on their hats; then all the population of this town, two and two, in gay costumes. They marched around singing hymns, and at stated points stopped to pray. In the meantime, the little chapel bell pealed, and, on the small square little heaps of gunpowder were exploded; their nearest approach to cannon, I suppose. We all bought some of the "blessed" flowers, and then we went to take breakfast in the inn, a small house with a veritable "bush" over the door,—a little evergreen branch studded with cones. "Good wine needs no bush"; but still the wine we had there, "vin du pays,"[2] was excellent. It looked very innocent and countryfied; but that was one of its "little ways!" I think we were all quite merry (without knowing it) when we issued forth under the primitive "bush" again, on the way to the old castle above. As soon as we reached it, I, for one, sought a sunny spot under its old walls, and sat there watching the blue sea and the exquisite landscape spread out below for at least an hour. I think I shall never forget that delicious sun-bath, high, high up in the blue heavens.

After that, we went down to the village again, and watched the dancing on the green. They had a rustic-band of five performers, and danced in the merriest way.

Clare was invited, and danced with much delight. A number of young English girls, belonging to another party, danced with the young men of the village, to the intense pride and joy of the youths, who, nevertheless, wore their hats all the time! I suppose they thought them too fine to cast aside—adorned as they were with long gay ribbons, several yards. We reached home at sunset, having had a most delightful day. This is the only time I have been out for all day; but almost every afternoon we have a small excursion somewhere. I wrote, I think, that we had been invited to visit one of the English families here, next summer. Yesterday I received a second invitation; namely to visit at another house on the borders of Wales,—the house of one of our two artists. I was much pleased; although, as you know, I seldom visit, I love to be <u>invited</u>. It is quite unexpected to us, and very pleasant to get on so well with the English. The people in the house are delightful, and we are fortunate, I think, in finding agreeable companions so soon. French progresses. I talk it almost constantly, and Clara really progresses.

Please tell your Mother, with my dearest love, that I received her most welcome letter, and was much gratified by it. I hope she will write again; as I certainly shall to her. I am so glad she wrote to Charlie, as her letter must have reached him when he was much depressed. Last evening I received my first letter from him; I have written him six. He wrote from St Luke's Hospital, San Jose Avenue, San Francisco, where he had been for a week, after a week's illness at his boarding house. He says it is the same old trouble in his head; but that the Doctor there says he will cure him in less than a month. He writes that he has good care and attention, paying thirteen dollars per week for it. He adds that he has not told anybody where he is, and does not intend to. But I think you ought to know, as you represent us. Of course I am much troubled and distressed by this tiding, as it was unexpected. I thought him much better. The doctor at the hospital is named "Jenks." Poor Charlie—he never seems to prosper. Although it may be his own fault, partly, that does not make it any the less hard and painful for him. I am very anxious and much troubled; but will try to hope that it is no worse now than the anxieties we have had before. If he was only happy with us, we could arrange something. But for years he has not been. He likes better to be by himself. No doubt we may be to blame. But I really have done my best to try to please him, poor fellow. And failed. He thinks I have a bad temper. And perhaps I have. I know myself that I am often impatient. You have all along been so kind to Charlie that I have written freely.

I am hard at work again every morning from half-past eight until one. It is not half long enough; but Clara looks so tragic if I attempt anything more, that I do'nt dare to. I am on my second novel and have work before me for a full year. Clara takes "Galignani's Messenger"; but there is not much American news, I am sorry to say. I read the London Times lent by our English friends. It seems to think we are going to destruction! My neighbour at table, a Swiss lady, showed me the other day a letter from a friend in Geneva, just received. It was in French, and as follows: "How delightful it must be for you to know these intelligent Americans! So new and interesting! They will be able, no doubt, to tell you all about the habits and manners of the American Indians." Isn't that good! Dearest love to all, in which Clara and Clare join. I am writing in haste. Excuse [?].

Affectionately,
C.F.W.

Notes

1. The letter is in a typed transcription at WRHS. Portions also appear in Benedict/CFW, 160–61.
2. vin du pays: wine of the country.

To Paul Hamilton Hayne (Duke)

Menton
Alpes Maritimes. France
Feb. 16th, [1880]

Dear Mr Hayne.

I was glad to receive your letter, which has been forwarded to me by Mr Bunce. You will see that I am in Europe. This is quite unexpected to myself as well as to my friends. It is a sort of effort on my part to break up the depression which took possession of me after the death of my dearest Mother in Florida, just one year ago. She had been my all for many years. I did not know how to live without her. After spending the summer in Cooperstown, her girlhood home,—my sister and myself decided to come abroad. We sailed in the Cunard Steamer "Gallia" on the nineteenth of November, and, after some weeks in London, came here; the "St Augustine" of France. My windows overlook the blue blue Mediterranean, our hotel standing on the beach, almost. Behind the house rise the mountains, four thousand feet high, which protect Menton on the north, and give it its exceptional climate. When I say "behind the house," I mean that the mountains begin in the garden itself, and, standing in our doorway, we have to throw our heads back to see their tops. Of the lemon-groves, the olives, the flowers; of the quaint villages high on crags, the ruined castles and Saracen towers; of the Roman roads, arches, acqueducts, and tombs; of the Corniche road; of the walks and drives, I have not time to speak. Please imagine them. We go on from here (where we have been two months) to Florence, in April. The summer, I suppose, in Switzerland. Beyond this, we have not planned. But it is probable that I shall remain over here some time. I shall be glad to hear from you.

Please address me according to the heading of this letter. If I am gone, the post master will forward.

I can sympathize with you very sincerely in your loss, since my own tears are still very near the surface, and well over at the slightest remembrance of her.

I trust, too, that the improvement in your health of which you speak has been a real and decided one. Did I not see that a complete edition of your poems was soon to appear? A new one? I hope it is so. I am now so far from the magazines that I shall not see many of them. If you have newspaper copies of some of your later poems, I should like much to see them.—Yes; the Appletons are to bring out the Southern stories. One of them has a motto by you, and another by Timrod. The mottoes are all by our younger poets.[1] John Hay's was written for the story it heads; and I think it charming. Do'nt you? My novel, "Anne," is to appear in Harper's Magazine as a serial at the conclusion of Blackmore's "Mary Anerley" now running. The three English serials, Black's, Blackmore's and Miss Mulock's have kept "Anne" waiting nearly a year![2] But I considered that the advantages of appearing in that magazine, more than made up for the delay. It will be illustrated. I cannot guess whether you will like it. It is very "American" and very "realistic."

Dear Mr Hayne, I trust you will excuse this hastily written letter. If you were here, you would see what a crowded day mine is, now. So much to do; see; and feel. Such a constant procession of new impressions. And I myself not so strong as formerly and obliged to exercise the greatest care, lest I break down again, as I did last spring. My eyes are still far from strong; which must be my excuse for scrawling. Have you ever been here? We are on the Italian border, you know, the last town in France. We have the "Italian sky." With the best good wishes, I am, yours sincerely,

C. F. Woolson.

Notes

1. Epigraphs were added to the book versions of Woolson's fiction.

2. *Anne* began serialization in Dec. 1880. The serialized novels Woolson alludes to are William Black's *White Wings: A Yachting Romance*, R. D. Blackmore's *Mary Anerley*, and Dinah Mulock Craik's *Young Mrs. Jardin* (1879). James's *Washington Square* was also serialized in *Harper's* in 1880.

To Katharine Livingston Mather (WRHS/Mather)[1]

Mentone. France
February 23^{d}, 1880

Dear Kate.

. . . We have been on another charming excursion. We took carriages up a valley as far as the road went, and then went on foot up the mountain to a quaint little walled village on a peak, with an old castle and church. The violets are out! That is easy to say; but it is not easy to describe their number and hue; they fairly make the fields and roadsides blue. The large white anemones are also in bloom, English daisies and cowslips. We visited the Castle and church, and then had our lunch in the little plaza under an elm, with a bottle of the "wine of the country," which was very good, although looking just like cider. We then started away and walked across the mountain to another valley, with another village and castle (I am gorged with castles and full of Roman remains!) where we had donkeys waiting for us, and came triumphantly home on their backs. They have an impressive way here of putting up lofty iron crosses on the mountains wherever there is an especially fine view. At first I supposed they commemorated something, but I am told it is not so; it seems to be simply a way of calling to our remembrance the Creator when gazing upon His works. . . .

Affectionately yours
C. F. Woolson.

Notes

1. The letter is in a typed transcription at WRHS. Portions also appear in Benedict/CFW, 162.

To Samuel Mather (Anderson)[1]

Care Madame Barbensi
N° 13 Lung' Arno Guicciardini
Florence. Italy
March 20th, [1880]

Dear Sam.

Here we are on the bank of the Arno, with the Duomo and Giotto's beautiful Campanile, opposite. I feel more foreign, more far away in the old world, in Florence, than I have felt since leaving New York. London I seemed to have learned from books so thoroughly that it was not novel; Paris was New York over again; Menton was a country place; but Florence! I foresee that I am going to be quite roused up here. To begin with—we shall carefully watch our health; that is of the first consequence. If that does well, we hope to stay two long months, or perhaps three, if the heat does not become too great. For my part, it is so long since I have felt any really warm air, like that of Florida, that I could willingly take a few days of August weather and be thankful! No high Swiss mountain will tempt me this summer; no resort noted for "cool air." Give me the warmest, widest, sun-bathed valley I can find.

It has not been cold at Menton; but here is the trouble—they do not know how to heat their rooms, and their ideas of heat are not ours. The sun may be shining brilliantly out of doors, and flowers may be in bloom, but if you are sitting still in your own room without stirring all morning, and the temperature of that room is only fifty-four or so, I maintain that you are as cold as though there was snow outside. And this is what these people cannot comprehend. I find it quite true that no people are accustomed to so much heat as ourselves; our English friends at Menton considered "sixty" the proper temperature for their rooms. Now I like seventy. But dear me! look at the amount of blood the English have! At Menton, and here as well, dinner is not more than half over, when every Englishman and Englishwoman, even the young girls, have what we would call a deep red face; over the cheeks, forehead, and nose, extends a broad crimson flush!

As we only arrived night before last, we have not, as you may imagine, seen much, we hope we have time enough before us to see it all "quietly" (as the English say) and at our leisure. I glance now and then at the list of pictures, with a sort of awe. At last I am going to see some of the great pictures of the world. We have been to the Duomo; but that is all. What did you like best here among both pictures and buildings?

We are at the old and well-known "pension" of Madame Barbensi on the Lung' Arno, near the Carraja bridge. We had a card of introduction to Madame B. from Miss Campbell of Cherry Valley, who spent two winters here. It is one of the old palaces of the Medici, surrounded by statues and built around a court also adorned with a number of gods and goddesses much the worse for wear. The interior is the most rambling, odd, up-and-down-stairs sort of labyrinth I ever was in; did you get into any such barrack when you were here? Old battered furniture, rags of carpets and a generally slip-shod air, very different from the Swiss cleanliness of Menton! But, a very good table, with wine included, (whereas at Menton we had to pay for it), and about sixty nice-looking people, almost all English, some of them with titles. No Americans. For this we pay less than at Menton! But at Menton, you have to pay for the sunshine.

We saw the Peter Whites before leaving. I was in a book store one day when a gentleman came up and said smilingly, "Is'nt this Miss Woolson?" I answered that it was, but of course had no idea who he was, as I have never seen Mr White. What follows will be hard for Kate to bear; but tell her to brace up. He then said "I knew you at once from your resemblance to Kate Mather!" I met him again a day later, this time with Mrs Senter, who had just arrived. So Clara and I went over to call upon them, because of their being friends of yours. They were staying in the West Bay two miles and more from our Bay. We saw Mrs White, all the others having gone on some excursion. She looked very delicate and said she was not able to walk at all. She had just received a letter from her sister Mary, and was rejoicing over it. She seemed to us a little homesick, but perhaps that was temporary. She was very pleasant; I have not seen her since I was Clare's age; I see she has the same fine eyes, and gentle voice she had as a child. They drove over to return our call, but we were unfortunately out, and so did not see them again.—The Webers came to Menton for a week, and hunted us up immediately; they called three times, and were very kind and polite; very much so, considering our slight acquaintance.[2] The Doctor urged us to come to Bonn this summer; they are to be there, and he offered to introduce us to agreeable people; and go with us on excursions &c. Clara is much impressed with the remarkable improvement in his health. But as I have not seen him for eight years or so, he simply looks to me just as he always did, only, as he has shaved his beard, he seems younger. He is brown, stout, full of life and spirits. Mrs Weber looks very pretty. They left Menton before us; but we met them at Genoa, and traveled as far as Pisa with them. They have gone on to Rome.—We left Menton on Wednesday, two of our English friends going with us as far as Ventimiglia, the first Italian town, to give us a "send-off" and see us through the Italian custom-house there; a scene which beggars description! But we succeeded in checking our trunks through to Florence, and so started for Genoa light handed. The route along the Riviera is beautiful, as well as that from Genoa to Pisa; but we only saw brilliant glimpses, as we plunged into and out of tunnels; one hundred in five hours! We went to the Hotel de Gênes at Genoa, and had no trouble about anything. We had of course, only a glance at the "superb" city; and no glance at all at Pisa save its railway station. Do not fancy that I do not quite appreciate how much I lost in not seeing both these cities. But the only way I can manage "Europe," and my own life here, is to settle down for a number of months in each place. The hotel bills are too much for me; at a "pension" we make it much less. Besides, I feel it's necessary to write always in the mornings, and this I can only do when established somewhere with all my belongings about me. So I shall see Europe slowly and by no means extensively; but I shall see and enjoy thoroughly the places I do see.—We left careful directions at Menton about our letters, and some have already been forwarded. I received yours of February 20th before leaving, and was very glad to get it. In the meantime, since writing to you, I have had two letters from Charlie at Riverside.[3] He speaks with much feeling of the kind cordial letter you sent him upon receipt of his; and says it was the pleasantest he ever received in his life. I feel as grateful to you for it as he does; it must have reached him at a time of great depression. He seems to like his present employment, and I think it is the best for him. If he had only been willing to take to out-door life long ago, it would have been much better for him. He said he would do it when he left Omaha; but this is the first time he has really tried it. He writes to me in fair sprits; but is anxious to cultivate for himself later, when he understands the business. I think Clara would help, and I will, all I possibly can,—if he will only keep to this idea. I have been constantly anxious about him since his letter from the hospital until these later ones came. I hope you will continue to write to him; you represent us, you know, and [you?] must do whatever is necessary in our name, for him. He seems to like the life out there. I give a sigh as I write, thinking how little after all I know of or about him! He has led his own life entirely since Father's death, ten years ago. I have been so anxious about him at times since that hospital letter, that I have thought I would give up Europe, and come home—perhaps go out and join him. I could not sleep, and kept thinking of Mother, and her long devotion to him. But the trouble with that; or any such plan is, that Charlie would rather be by himself. He has very plainly told me so. I find that the old Latin saying holds good with me too—that the skies change when we cross the sea, but not our own minds; they remain the same. And if we were anxious there, we are anxious here. Pictures and Campanile cannot change that!—

What a very great sorrow the death of Mrs Mansfield must have been to your Father, and to all of you.[4] The first break in that circle of brothers and sisters—; all must have felt it deeply. Give my dearest love to your Father, and tell him that I thought of him with much sympathy and affection when the first tidings of her illness came. For her, it was a release; but that will not lighten the sorrow or keep down the tears of those left desolate here. I remember her as such a sweet gentle lovable person. But all your Father's sisters are unusually charming women, I have always thought.

Did I mention that I received your letter from Ishpeming? The cold mentioned made me shudder. It made me "creep" a great deal more than ever the moccasins did in Florida. I wo'nt say I am fond of snakes; but I like to look at them from a safe distance. I used to row up the creeks, especially to find them.—I hope we shall hear from you all while here. The "Guicciardini" added to "Lung' Arno" is the quarter,—as perhaps you remember. How long were you here? Give my dearest love to your Mother and tell her I shall be thinking of her constantly now that I am among the pictures; I wish she was here to go with me to see them, day after day.

I shall not be able to write much while here; but Clara will, I presume. If I do not write, remember that I am thinking of you all with as much love as ever. The truth is that I have been trying to do too much; trying to keep on with all my Mss. regularly, see Europe, and write letters, all at the same time. Result: I do nothing really well, and become very tired. I must make some change. Much love to Kate & Will. Kate's letter to Clara received. Good-by.

Yours affectionately,
C.F.W.

Notes

1. Portions of this letter also appear in Benedict/CFW, 23, 179–81.

2. Dr. Weber cared for Woolson's brother Charly when he was likely addicted to morphine. See letters to Samuel Mather dated Jan. 30 and Feb. 24, 1877.

3. Riverside, California.

4. The reference may be to Maria Mather Mansfield, Samuel Livingston Mather's aunt, who married General J.F.K. Mansfield of Middleton, Connecticut.

To Samuel Mather (Anderson)

Casa Molini
13 Lung' Arno Guicciardini
Florence. Italy
April 13th, [1880]

My dear Sam.

I must snatch a few moments this morning to send you a few lines about Charlie. Another letter came from him yesterday, this time to Clara. I have not known how she felt about investing in some land out there for him, until yesterday afternoon, when, as we were walking to Fiesole, she broached the subject.[1] I could see that she felt unwilling to do it. She did not say positively she would not, and perhaps she may still decide to do it. I never speak about business affairs, hers or mine, to her, unless she begins the subject, and therefore I seldom know what she intends to do. I can quite well understand how she feels, and should perhaps feel the same in her place. She has Clare to think for, you know. Besides she has already assisted Charlie by buying from him for cash his share of the Milwaukee land, property she did not want, of course losing the interest she might have obtained from the sum if otherwise invested. In addition to this she has lent him other sums. Whereas what I lent him was repaid by Mother's will. But while I quite understand her feelings, I still feel extremely anxious that Charlie should be assisted, and therefore I think I shall try to buy the rest of the land he wants myself. I send you one of his letters as guide, because I am so busy just now that I have not time to write much. What I want to ask you is—do you really think of buying that amount of land out there, as he supposes? If you do then I wish you would advise me. He seems to have his heart set on the other plot of land, beside[s?] yours. Now as my income is only six hundred a year I am really giving away nearly one year's worth of it. I cannot afford to give the sum outright; besides it would be a bad way to do it for Charlie as well as myself. What I ask you therefore is—if you are going to buy, buy for me at the same time and on precisely the same terms, having all the papers made out for me too, as well as for yourself, and guarding my interests as carefully as you can. Will you do this for me? I am sorry to have to ask you to take all this trouble for me; but I do not know any other way to arrange it. If I hear from you in the affirmation on all these points, I shall enclose you an order on the Savings Bank for the money, and at the same time write to Charlie that all the business part of the arrangement will be attended to by you.

—Do excuse this unsightly scrawl. What with my own writing & all there is to see & to do here, I am quite distracted, sometimes. Florence is enchanting. We are all well. Tell me about my beloved N.C. mountains. The scene of "Up in the Blue Ridge," in "Rodman" is at Asheville, you know.

—Dearest love to all. We shall stay here until, and perhaps into, June.

In great haste
Yours always most affectionately,
C.F.W.

Shall write to Kate soon.

Of course if Clara should decide to buy, I should withdraw.[2]

Notes

1. This is likely California land near Riverside where Charly had been living.
2. This last sentence is written across the top of the page.

To Katharine Livingston Mather (WRHS/Mather)[1]

Casa Molini
Florence. Italy
[April 27th, 1880]

My dear Kate.

. . . Florence is charming. I have begun visiting the galleries in the mornings, and so very much enjoy it. I am looking at the pictures very slowly. I sit down in front of those I like, and let them "grow" into my memory. I shall spend every morning among the pictures now, for the next month. For the past month, I have spent part of every afternoon in one of the churches. The grandest thing I have seen so far is Michael Angelo's statue of the Medici in the helmet, at San Lorenzo. In addition to the pictures and churches, the very streets of Florence are full of interest to me. And certainly the country is a never ending pleasure for my eyes—the snow-capped mountains in the north-east, and the lovely valley of the Arno going down towards the west. I am up to my head in Florentine history, books on art, &c. But although very busy, it is an occupation crowded full of enjoyment. I am getting quite thin with all I am attempting. It is warm, but not too warm; pleasant summer weather, the windows all open; and such masses of superb flowers for sale everywhere, on almost every corner; all kinds of wild flowers; tea roses, in great bunches, both hands full, for ten cents; wild flowers by the bushel for half that; it makes the streets lovely to have so many of them . . . With much love, I am,

Yours affectionately,
C. F. Woolson.

Notes

1. The letter is in a typed transcription at WRHS. Portions also appear in Benedict/CFW, 182–83. Benedict footnoted this letter with extracts from Woolson's Florentine Catalogues that record impressions on various works of art.

To Samuel Livingston Mather (WRHS/Mather)[1]

Casa Molini
Florence. Italy
May 7th, 1880

My dear Brother.

. . . Florence is delightful, and I am quite fascinated with it, I cannot bear to think of going away. The pictures interest me deeply; the old churches charm me. Best of all, the scenery round-about is a never-ending source of pleasure. The high blue mountains, and the Valley of the Arno delight my eyes every day. . . . Yesterday, "Ascension Day," was a great Florentine festa. It began at sunrise, when all the common people of the town, went out to the "Cascine," or park, and caught crickets, one for each family. These they put into little fancy cages made of straw, and then they all had a picnic breakfast there. When we went out, about ten o'clock with Mr James, we saw the remains of these festivities, especially the piles of straw covered flasks of wine, <u>empty</u>. The crickets are taken home, and fed as carefully as a pet-bird; they are for luck; the longer they live, the luckier the house will be. Clare has four now, hanging in the window in cages. She feeds them to that extent that they will soon be gorged. In the afternoon there were races. The "races" were not worth much, but the toilettes of the ladies were worth a great deal . . .

My dearest love to you all.

Affectionately,
C. F. Woolson.

Notes

1. The letter is in a typed transcription at WRHS. Portions also appear in Benedict/CFW, 189–90.

To Mary Crowell (Basel)[1]

[Spring 1880]

Florence is enchanting. All that I have dreamed and more. Mentone was lovely; but as much "country" and primitive as parts of America, unless you made yourself hunt up that old Roman tomb on Cap Martin, or made a point of remembering that all that blue water was the old, old "Mediterranean." But Florence! here I have attained that old-world feeling I used to dream about, a sort of enthusiasm made up of history, mythology, old churches, pictures, statues, vineyards, the Italian sky, dark-eyed peasants, opera-music, Raphael and old Michael, "Childe Harold," the "Marble Faun," "Romola," and ever so many more ingredients,—the whole having I think taken me pretty well off my feet! Perhaps I ought to add Henry James. He has been perfectly charming to me for the last three weeks. But of him, later.

I am fascinated with the old palaces here; with one of them, the Strozzi—I have fallen in love. . . . But O! I cannot tell you half. The remains of the old nobles' towers everywhere, the della Robbia Madonnas looking down upon you from street corner shrines; the six bridges, the wonderful flowers for sale everywhere in great stacks and sheafs; the beautiful soft violet hills and mountains rising all around—this is a little of it . . . It is now pouring again and all the twenty-five old statues on the terrace below my window look very mournful. The window opposite, which some one keeps screened with a "Madonna" turned upside down, is as mysterious as ever.

I have been perfectly honest and even to myself would not pretend to admire what I did not admire. The only way was to "begin at the beginning" and this I did. I commenced with the hideous wooden Byzantine style and then I took Cimabue, Giotto and the rest, one by one, and in due order . . . Giotto has nearly extinguished me. I took Ruskin as my guide and patiently went at it. The hours I spent in those chapels at Santa Croce and in the Spanish Chapel will, I hope, some day be of use. At present, I confess, Giotto remains beyond me. And H. J. says calmly, "Some day, you will see it." May be.[2]

One of the most interesting places we went to was the old convent of San Marco—it contains the best of Fra Angelico's frescoes, just as he left them; he adorned the whole convent with his lovely little angels. . . . [3] I don't think I have mentioned how fascinated I am with the cloisters here. I get into them whenever I can and wish I had one of my own to walk in daily. . . .

The churches in Florence, with the exception of the Duomo and its beautiful bell-tower, are, as buildings, very disappointing. To any one who is used to and fond of Gothic, these long, rather low buildings of common yellow broken stone roughly mortared, with the façade (if there is one) of marble and richly-ornamented, looking as if it was stuck on, like the front of a child's toy house, are very ugly . . . The truth is, the Italian idea was to treat the front as a screen to be as richly ornamented as possible, but to our ideas having nothing in common with the body of the church. The beautiful Gothic completeness, sweeping around the whole with pointed arches, porches and spire or tower, they know nothing about. But then, when you come to the interiors and the rich and wonderful and lavish ornament everywhere within, you are astonished and delighted. . . . The interior of Santa Maria Novella is to me very beautiful. The Duomo (interior) is too vast and cold. I went there one rainy afternoon alone, and had the weirdest time! It was almost dark inside, and I was the only person in all the great gloomy space. I went there again with H. J. who admires it, and tried to make me admire it too.

The statue of "Lorenzo" in the new Sacristy of San Lorenzo, is the finest statue, a thousand times ~~I~~ over, <u>I</u> have ever seen; and at once completely satisfied my expectations of Michael Angelo, which were extremely great. What I have said is very strong when you consider that in the Uffizi stand the <u>antiques</u>—the Venus de Medici, Dancing Faun, the young Apollo and the Niobe group. But I confess frankly that it is going to take some time for me to appreciate "the nude." I have no objections to it; I look at it calmly; but I am not sufficiently <u>acquainted</u> with torsos, flanks, and the lines of anatomy, to know when they are "supremely beautiful" and when not. Now "Lorenzo" is clothed; and therefore comes within my comprehension and O! Mary—he is superb. The whole expression of the figure is musing and sad, but it is the sadness of the strongest kind of a human mind,—almost the sadness of a God. He seems omniscient. To my idea, he seems to represent the whole human race; remembering all the past; conscious of all the future; and <u>waiting</u>. Nothing in the way of marble has ever impressed me so much, and I only wish it was where I could step in and look at it every day. But this you cannot do, without going at the especial time, and under the guardianship of the custode,—the whole thing quite troublesome. It is not the franc you pay; you pay that at the galleries; but it is the bother. The strange half-reclining figures at the base of the two statues, called somewhat arbitrarily, "Day," "Night," "Evening" and "Dawn," are rather beyond me—as yet.[4] They are gigantic (nude of course), and seem very weary. The one called "Day," which is only half finished, is striking; although I believe "Night" (a woman) is most admired. In speaking of these statues, Henry James said—"Of course you admired those grand reclining figures?" "No," I replied "honestly, I did not. They looked so distracted." "Ah yes," he said, "<u>distracted</u>. But <u>then!</u>" Here words failed him, and he walked off to look at a fresco (we were in Michael-Angelo's house) and (probably) to recover from my horrible ignorance. The second Medici statue is fine of course; but to me has nothing of the strange charm of "Lorenzo."—We walked through the crypt (so-called) to reach the sacristy and ~~the whole~~ most of the floor was made of

Medici grave-stones. Just their names and dates. The real crypt is below; and there they lie, fifty or so of them, not under their grave-stones at all but piled up one above the other like a cord of wood! The last Medici was put there about a hundred and fifty years ago. About that time (I believe) the pile was overhauled; they were all there—"Eleonora" with her still golden hair, "Giovanni" with his one leg, and so on.[5] Then they were piled up again and the door sealed. I always think of them lying there when I go by. How much better if they had been placed quietly to mingle with their mother earth.—The richest piece of work in the way of the mosaic, colored marbles, inlaid woods, &c. I have ever seen is in the "Chapel of the Princes" attached to the same church, another mortuary chapel of the Medici family. It is one solid mass of the richest materials; not large—only one spacious vaulted room, ~~and~~ costing nearly five millions of dollars; so you may imagine!

Notes

1. The original of this letter is pasted into *Constance Fenimore Woolson* at the Cooper Library, University of Basel, Switzerland. Portions are also in Benedict/CFW, 184–89.

2. This paragraph and the following two appear in Benedict, but not in the cut-up original letter. Benedict (185) adds a footnote excerpted from an unidentified Woolson letter about James. James's age indicates that it was written in 1880.

> About H. James, Jr. . . . He is not in the least like John Hay in his appearance, but his manner to me is very much like that of J. H. . . . Mr James is 36; rather taller than John Hay, and with a larger frame, a beautiful regular profile, brown beard and hair, large light grey eyes from which he banishes all expression, and a very quiet, almost cold, manner. . . . His "style" is extremely unpretending and unobtrusive in every way, yet I wouldn't like to be the person who should think from his unpretending quietness that he could not be incisive when he chose. . . . He was very kind to me. He has many acquaintances in Florence and he was constantly invited out to lunch and dinner parties; yet with all this, he found time to come in the mornings and take me out; sometimes to the galleries or churches, and sometimes just for a walk in the beautiful green Cascine. . . . His criticisms were new and remarkable, at least to me. I mean that he chose such remarkable things to admire! You will find some of his Florentine opinions in his "Transatlantic Sketches," although he says, rather contemptuously—"O that was written when I was a boy."

3. Fra Angelico worked on these frescoes from 1436 to 1445.

4. Michelangelo sculpted several de Medici statues, including *Day, Night, Evening, Dawn*; the other sculptures Woolson mentions are ancient ones cast by unknown artists.

5. The wealthy and powerful de Medici family dominated Florentine life and politics from the fourteenth to the eighteenth century. Lorenzo the Magnificent (1449–92) was particularly known for his patronage of the arts; Woolson wrote Eleonora (1567–1611), but it was her daughter Eleonore (1598–1655) who became a Roman Empress; Giovanni (1475–1521) became Pope Leo X.

To Samuel Livingston Mather (WRHS/Benedict)[1]

13 Lung'Arno Guicciardini
Casa Molini
Florence. Italy
May 12th, 1880

My dear Brother.

We are all well and enjoying ourselves. The only trouble, at least as far as I personally am concerned, is that there is so much to see and do, and so little time for it. Now and then there comes a day when I am forced to give up my writing, and be out both in the morning and afternoon,—a thing which goes against my conscience! Yesterday Mr James came to take me to one of the galleries, and; as he is a delightful companion because he knows all about pictures, I went,—although I knew we were going in the afternoon to Fiesole with Dr and Mrs Weber, who are now here on their way back from Rome. It is one of the loveliest drives around Florence,—this to Fiesole, which is an ancient Etruscan village, much older than Florence, on a high hill some miles distant. There is the most beautiful view there from the little plateau, in front of the old convent. Some friends of the Webers, with whom they are travelling, were in a second carriage, and, after viewing the old Roman amphitheatre, and Etruscan wall, we sat down under the rose covered arbor, and had some modern wine,—which was very good. Dr Weber looks the picture of health and good spirits, and this journey seems to have effected a complete cure. We hope to stay here,—that is, I do,—until June, then, after a few days in Venice, I think I shall go straight to some quiet place in Switzerland and establish myself for three or four months; while Clara and Clare, making that their head-quarters, can take excursions wherever they choose.

April 10th

I am enchanted with Florence, it is even more beautiful than I expected; and I think that is saying a good deal, because I have been "expecting" so long! The Duomo, Campanile, Bronze Gates, the Palaces and bridges, are even more beautiful and interesting than I imagined, and I feel as though I ought to spend months here, in order to take them fully in. Every afternoon, I give an hour or two to one of the churches, generally managing to go by the Campanile and "Gates of Heaven," and then off I go for a long walk outside the city, often up one of the hills in order to get the beautiful views which open in every direction. It is useless to attempt describing a view on paper; but one I had this afternoon from Bellos Guardo, was so exquisitely lovely, that I wish I could do it. I will only say that the Apennines were snow-capped, while in the valley of the Arno below me, all the leaves were out, and everything in the freshest lightest green. Fifty years ago, at this season, the Coopers were here with their father. They remained ten months, living first in an old palace in the city, and then in a Villa outside of the walls, which I have been trying to find. I have discovered, I think, the little country church, which was near it. We have been much interested in finding at a library here, a book of Uncle Fenimore's which we had never seen—"Excursions in Italy." It was published in Paris in 1838, and gives an account of their Italian journeyings.

Our old Palace, which is now one of your favorite "pensions," is treating us very well. We have a good table, and sometimes a taste of Italian cooking, by way of variety. One of the luncheon dishes is a sort of cake made of ground chestnuts, and fried with bacon! Then we have meat, dressed with raisins and vinegar!

Lovingly,
C. F. Woolson.

Notes

1. The typed transcription at WRHS is not in chronological order. Portions of the letter dated April 10th appear in Benedict/CFW, 181–82, and those dated May 12 appear under the date May 7 in Benedict/CFW, 189–90.

To Samuel Mather (Anderson)[1]

Venice
June 8th, [1880]

My dear Sam.

I received your letter written with your poor disabled wrist, while in Florence, and answer it from this enchanting place, with a disabled thumb! I was stupid enough to put your letter in my trunk instead of my bag, and therefore, as all our luggage has gone on to Switzerland, I shall have to write a sort of solo, and not answer any of your questions,—if there were any. As no luggage is allowed free in Italy, save such small articles as you can take into the railway carriages with you, we decided to send the trunks through to Lucerne by "petite vitesse,"[2] as it would not only be cheaper, but also save us some trouble in the roundabout route by which we proposed to travel. It is something of a joke on us, since we have done nothing but laugh at the English for taking such quantities of small articles into the railway carriages with them, everywhere. But now behold us joining the army ourselves, with valises! great rolls of wraps in shawl-straps, and umbrellas! I am happy to state that we have not yet descended to bonnet-boxes. Florence continued enchanting to the last. I could not bear to come away; and I think, if Clara had not driven me into naming a day for departure, I should have stayed on there all summer! You know I like the warmth, and I was fascinated with studying the pictures. I think this is going to be my greatest pleasure over here. No one is more fond of natural scenery than I am; it makes a part of my life. But it seems to me, so far at least, that the natural scenery of my own country is as fine as anything there is here. But what we have not at home, is the Art, and the associations. So these make my pleasure here. I wrote to your Father, sending back the Milwaukee deed; I hope it arrived safely. We met in Florence, or rather Clara did, an American lady, the wife of an artist; they have lived there for twenty years. The lady is by birth a relative of Mrs G. A. Benedict, through the "Browns of Brownville," and Clara discovered her through another of the "Brown" descendents, a Mrs Palmer of South Carolina, who happened to be at the "pension" where Clara went to call upon some Louisville people she knows. This is rather a mixed-up story, and I have a suspicion I have mentioned the Florentine lady before, in one of my letters to your house. But the point is, that, through her, we had a glimpse of the artistic society of Florence, & could have had more if we were going out. She invited us to dine, but we declined. Clara went out with her however several times, and her children came to take Clare to the Boboli gardens to which they have private admission. It was amusing and novel to hear her talk; she has not been in America since she was a child. In addition to this we saw another American lady who has lived in Florence since childhood, having married a Florentine of noble family, who was for some time the Syndic or Mayor. The old lady (seventy-five) was quite a curiosity. She lives alone in a suite of apartments at the top of an old palace, and goes to the theatre every evening regularly. So she told us. She invited us to spend the evening (I suppose on that night she would deprive herself of the play) and said she would give us some music. But we excused ourselves. She is a great musician even now, playing, I was told, very finely. She used to know Chopin and play duets with him. As we came away, we saw her lonely little dinner-table with one plate, one wine glass, &c. But the table was placed near a little balcony full of ferns in pots, and roses; and on the whole, I presume the old lady enjoys her dinner, her solitary glass of wine, her little balcony, and her theatre in the evening. But it was a curious life to lead, according to our ideas.

I wo'nt bore you with long accounts of all I learned, thought, and fancied about the pictures & statues in Florence. I will only say that I was intensely absorbed and interested, and that I could see I made some progress in appreciating. I knew it would require study; and it does. But already beauties I did not see at first are unfolding themselves, or rather, revealing themselves. In this connection I enjoyed very much being with Henry James, who was a delightful companion, and, in addition, very kind to me. He has been so much in Italy that he knows the pictures as well as I know Florida. He is a very quiet fellow; and very (although in an unobtrusive way) English. I put in the correction, because I have seen so many Americans in the last ten years who were "English" obtrusively.—Well—we had to come away at last, and the day was last Thursday. We decided, after two months and a half of Florentine life, that we knew enough to attempt the "second class." You know the proverb—"only fools & Americans travel first class." We knew it too; but heretofore we have not felt enough at home to attempt it. This time we did; and it was a great success. Our companions in the carriage were all nice persons, especially a young English clergyman and his sister. At Bologna I got out, and had lunch in the lunch room; Clara and Clare preferred to eat what they had brought with them from Florence. But I like to get out and see all the novelty; besides, when no one is near, I like to air my rusty Italian! We reached Venice at four in the afternoon; the day was lovely, warm and hazy, and we went the entire length of the Grand Canal in a gondola to reach our hotel, which is near the harbor. We had written in advance for rooms. It is one of the smaller houses, a "pension" (tell your Father), but well situated on the Grand Canal, opposite the imposing church of "Santa Maria della Salute"; you may remember the locality. We allowed ourselves one week here, and expect to leave on Friday morning for Milan; and, after, spending Sunday there, we go to the Lakes, and over the St Gotthard to Lucerne. Our plan is to find some quiet spot on that lake, and there I shall stay quietly for three months, or longer. But I hope Clara and Clare will make excursions. I was so taken up with the pictures in Florence that I could not write much. I am very anxious to have a summer of uninterrupted quiet; in fact I must have it. We are enchanted with Venice. After having read of it and dreamed of it and looked at pictures of it all my life,—I find the reality even more picturesque and wonderful than my expectations. This, I think, is quite remarkable. Remember how many long years I have been imagining! The motion of a gondola is, to me, the most perfect in the world,—a combination of row-boat, sail-boat with a soft breeze, and hammock. As the fares are very low (like carriage-hire in Florence) we go out continually; and when we are not in one, we are sitting in our little balcony on the Grand Canal, looking at them, as they glide by. We have also spent a great deal of time in the Piazza of San Marco, where the fine band plays every evening, beginning before dark. As it is so early, we go over (it is but a step) take one of the little tables outside the Caffé, have an ice or coffee, & sit there listening to the music and watching the wonderfully beautiful line of the domes of San Marco & Campanile against the sky. We ran into the Weber party again, here; they have just gone on to Vienna. We spent one evening with them in the Piazza, and the Doctor was as charming & agreeable as he was in Florence. He has a great deal to say about two or three of the pictures which have made a great impression upon him. The "Aurora" of Guercino (not Guido) at Rome. And the "Concert" by Giorgione at the "Pitti,"—Florence.[3] The latter I saw; and admired as much as he did. The Dr was good enough to look at my thumb both at Florence & here. It has been quite serious, but his remedies subdued the pain. It was an inflammation of the matrix of the nail, and now the nail is coming off, and the new one growing. It is a great bother, & keeps me quite crippled. But the pain is over. Of course we have been through the Doge' Palace, and into all the churches where there is anything to be seen. We have also visited one of the private palaces, which was most gorgeous with red leather hangings, chandeliers and mirrors of Venetian glass, wonderful vases, inlaid floors, &c.[4] Perhaps you saw this one; it is the property of the Duke of Bordeaux. We have been in gondolas all over the city, and always insist upon going under the Bridge of Sighs. To day, we got out and went on foot over the "Rialto." This morning I spent before Titian's "Assumption" I presume you remember that glorious picture.[5] I shall be at that gallery all day tomorrow. I also admire greatly Titian's "Presentation in the Temple"—do you remember it, with the little Virgin in a blue dress, going up the steps, alone? The city seems to be very full of strangers. Parties are constantly going by, in gondolas, armed with "Baedakers."

We shall not get any more letters until we reach Lucerne, which will be, I hope, in a week's time. The Florence people will forward whatever came after we left. If you will direct to us, "Care Sebastian Crivelli & Co. Lucerne. Switzerland," we shall get the letters. They are the Bankers there. I have heard from Charlie twice lately. Of course you know he is at Los Angeles, and that he has something to do. He does not tell me what it is, but says he likes the place, & that he is well.

June 9th

I have been all the morning at the "Belle Arte," and feel quite gorged with rich colors. The Venetian pictures are certainly most sumptuous. I am charmed with <u>the Bellini</u> Madonnas.[6] Do you remember them? We have decided to go <u>tomorrow</u> to Milan, and give the extra day to Como instead of Venice. So the plan is to go out in gondolas <u>all</u> the remainder of the day & evening too! Having seen everything, we can now afford to go out and lazily <u>rock</u>. To go back to Charlie. He says he is still anxious to have land at Riverside, and I am desirous to help him all I can, if that <u>is</u> his wish. I think Clara feels the same. The point is—does he <u>really</u> wish it, & will he be likely to stay there long enough to make it an object? I wish you would keep watch of this point as well as you can, through his letters. Has he told you <u>what</u> position he has at Los Angeles?

You must excuse this scrawling letter,—of which I am quite ashamed when I remember how clearly your own letters are always written. But my right hand also is a little lame with a mass of copying I did that last week in Florence. It seems a <u>very</u> long time since I have heard from Kate. I hope she is not ill. Cleveland must be looking its prettiest now. Dr Weber says he would rather be "Dr Weber of Cleveland" than the grandest Lord over here. Mrs Weber talks of spending the winter in Paris on account of Ida's going to school there, & Clara talks of doing the same thing. My own heart rather turns towards old Rome. But that is too far ahead to plan.

Remembering your taking milk, I will mention that I too am on milk. I drink it regularly & intend going on with it. And it seems to agree with me finely. I take it instead of wine, which I do not like. Dearest love to your Mother & Father, Kate & Will. Shall I include my new (future) niece? And now good-by—We are going out to rock.

Affectionately yours
C.F.W.

Notes

1. The letter is also in a typed transcription at WRHS. Portions appear in Benedict/CFW, 190–92; 216–18.
2. petite vitesse: low speed.
3. Guercino painted his fresco of *Aurora* in 1621; the reference to Giorgione's painting is to *Concert*, which still hangs in the Pitti Palace.
4. Benedict identifies this as the Vendramin Palace.
5. *The Assumption* (1516–18) is at the Basilica of Santa Maria Gloriosa dei Frari, Venice, and *The Presentation in the Temple* (1537–40) is at the Accademia, Venice.
6. Benedict (218) identifies the Bellini Madonnas at the Accademia with Woolson's notes on each: *Madonna of S. Giobbe* (1487), "Very beautiful Madonna with commanding face"; *Madonna with Two Trees* (1487), "Very beautiful Madonna who looks like a Cleopatra"; *Madonna with St. Paul and St. George*, "This is the most beautiful. The Madonna's face is unlike those of Raphael, Botticelli or any other artist."

To Jane Averell Carter (Benedict/CFW, 273)

[1880?]

Sometimes we go off on the lagoon; sometimes we float down the Grand Canal. I have seen something of Venetian society, and like it. I think it more picturesque than the society of Florence.

To Katharine Livingston Mather (WRHS/Mather)[1]

Beckenried
[Lake Lucerne. Switzerland
June 21st, 1880]

My dear Kate.

. . . We have been two weeks coming from Florence. The "Water City" Venice, continued enchanting up to the moment of departure. If I never go back there, the memory of that week will remain like a lovely dream in my mind, for ever. I shall always say the perfection of earthly motion is a gondola. But—never go to Venice unless you have some pleasant escort, who can take you out in gondolas in the evening; remember that piece of advice. To your two aunts, who are old ladies, it was not so important; but even they sighed for some one, in spite of having been in gondolas all day. There was the greatest amount of music in Venice, bands of singers with guitars came by the Hotel every evening in large barges, and often we would hear one voice and a guitar from some gondola floating by. Well, all lovely things have an end, and we left Venice, and went to Milan, where we spent a day, or rather two, looking at the beautiful Cathedral, and "The Last Supper," as well as the pictures at the Brera Gallery.[2] We were fortunate enough to see some sort of a grand service at the Cathedral; the effect of the organ rolling through the immense body of the church, was grand; it is the finest interior, viewed architecturally, which I have yet seen. I do not know how St Peter's will strike me. The exterior was like a great mass of white marble lace-work, with its pinnacles, tracery, and two thousand statues. "The Last Supper," although much faded and discolored, made a great impression upon all of us. Next, we went up to Como, and spent a day and two nights. We went up to Bellagio to lunch, and sat for several hours looking at the loveliness there. It was surpassingly beautiful. Then we went to Lugano, which I admired even more than I did Como. Then, by diligence and railway, to a little town called Biasca, which is, at present, the last station on the St Gotthard railway. Here we remained over night, much entertained by the quaintness and novelty of all we saw; especially by the English families there preparing to go over the Alps by "private diligence." One party of four ladies had four large trunks, two large tin bathing tubs, and twenty-four small pieces, like old-fashioned carpet sacks, great rolls of things, that looked like bedding; hat boxes; band-boxes; medicine chests; easels, valises; air-cushions, &c, &c. It was a funny sight to see <u>that</u> carriage unloaded. Early next morning we started, in the coupé of the regular diligence, and <u>up</u> we went. First we had four horses, then five, then six, and finally seven; they were all great broad-backed strong creatures, and were very frequently changed, so that we passed everything on the road, even the carriages that had started hours before. The scenery on the St Gotthard road is wonderfully grand. I believe it is considered finer than that on any other. Of course I <u>saw</u> it; whether I admired it properly when all my attention was devoted to the horses' ears, I leave you to judge. Why "ears"? Because I always judge a horse by his ears, you know! We had dinner at a little high-up place, where it began to be cold (it had been August weather at Como), and then they put on some <u>giants</u> of horses, and we went <u>up</u> to the <u>top</u>. That last three hours of road before reaching the Hospice, was, to me, terrific. The road, a model of engineering, was perfectly smooth, but so winding and dizzy, going in long zig-zags on the edge of the most frightful precipice that I was completely tired out with watching it when we reached the bleak top. Here we had hot coffee, and ran round to get warm; everything covered with snow, and the strangest, wildest desolation was all around us. It was unlike anything I ever imagined. Then they put in four little chunky horses, and after rolling by the frozen lakes, we began to race <u>down</u>. I say "race," for we never stopped tearing along, as fast as the horses could run, from the top of the Alps to the Lake of Lucerne! Of course the horses were frequently changed; but when once in, they ran all the way to the next relay. The road was superb, and of course all of the way down-hill, but oh, how we spun round curves! I was dizzy with the flying motion. We reached Fluellen, at the foot of Lake Lucerne, at ten o'clock in the evening, and spent the night there. The next morning we took the steam-boat, and came up the whole length of the beautiful Lake to Lucerne, when we rushed first of all, for our letters! We stayed at the "Swan" two days, taking the little steamer and going to points on the Lake. Of course we saw the "Lion," the monument to the Swiss Guard, and we were much impressed with its grandeur.[3] We heard the great organ also, but were disappointed; the organist played nothing but trifling "variations." We have now come to this place "Beckenreid," and here I shall stay all summer. It is a very quiet, small, rural village on the south shore of the Lake, about an hour by boat, from Lucerne. It is opposite the Rigi, and the scenery all round is magnificent. We have the whole from our windows, as the house stands directly upon the water. It is a German village, and reminds me of Zoar. I mean the people, not the situation. We have extraordinary things to eat; but although new, they are generally good. We breakfast in an arbor on the little terrace before the house, overlooking the Lake. Here a maid, in Swiss dress, brings us our café-au-lait, fresh butter, rolls and eggs. Here we sit, and eat and drink, our eyes resting on the grand mountains. If this is not "rural," what is? . . .

Much love.

Affectionately,
C. F. Woolson.

Notes

1. The letter is in a typed transcription at WRHS. Portions also appear in Benedict/CFW, 218–21.

2. Da Vinci's fifteenth-century painting is in the Church of Santa Maria delle Grazie in Milan.

3. The lion monument is in memory of Swiss Guards who were massacred during the French Revolution.

To Samuel Mather (Anderson)[1]

Care Sebastian Crivelli & Co.
Lucerne. Switzerland
July 6th, [1880]

My dear Sam.

When I arrived at Lucerne, I found your letter of May 24th waiting for me, and was glad to see from your handwriting that you were quite well, again. I write a few lines to tell you that we have moved to Lucerne, and that the above is now the address. We remained two weeks at the little Zoar-like village of Beckenreid, but the hotel became too "German." The situation is wonderfully lovely, and the table was good; but there was nothing but sprechen Deutsche[2] (that may not be correct; I have forgotten my German); and Clara and Clare found it wearisome. So we are established in Lucerne, and I think we shall like it better. We shall have, of course, more society, for everybody comes to Lucerne. Already there have been a number there whom we knew. That was another trouble; politeness required them to come down and call upon us at Beckenried, which they proceeded to do; and found it a great bore! It took pretty much all day, and we could do nothing especial for them when they came. It was not as though we had a house in which to receive them. At Lucerne, civilities will be more natural and easy.

—The scenery here continues to charm me, more and more. I am never tired of watching the lights and shadows, the rain and sunshine on the mountains. But the milk of Switzerland is a deception! In Florence they gave me all I wanted without charging for it. Here I have to pay a good price for every drop. However, I am living for a dollar a day. To be quite accurate—a dollar and ten cents. It is another "pension,"—tell your Father.

A letter from Mary Crowell mentions having seen Kate, and that Kate had said her mother had not been at all well. I am afraid that attack of faintness has had some bad results. I shall be anxious until I hear. Give her my dearest love, and tell her how earnestly I hope it is nothing serious, and that she is by this time well again. When there is any illness, it seems <u>so</u> long before we can hear.—You asked about Dr Brown. He has sent me but that one "Hearth and Home," which I keep as a memento! However, it does not make any difference in my liking for him. He is a charming man. I am glad he is well again.—I have heard quite regularly from Charlie. He writes that he still continues anxious to have land at Riverside, as he feels that he may break down again under the confining work in an office. I am desirous to do what is best for him, as far as I can. I suppose I could advance five 5. hundred dollars towards buying what he wants. Or rather I would do it anyway. What does he say to you?—

I suppose we shall remain here two months. I shall stay longer, probably. Clara will go to Paris in September and Clare will go to school. The plan is to go to Rome afterwards.

Were you in Lucerne? Did you not admire the Lion? I do; very much. Did you go up the Rigi? I detest that little railway. In the old days there must have been much more "adventure" about it. It is like the tunnel under the St Gotthard,—very prosaic.

Mr James has just sent me from London a recent number of the Spectator which contains a cordial notice of "Rodman." It is the first time I have received attention in a paper of that stamp. What is the news, and what are you doing with yourself? Let me know. Clara and Clare send their love to all of you. The latter can speak French quite nicely now. Not that I consider, or ever have considered—that it was such a heavenly acquisition as some people think. Still, it is well to be able to do it. German is a finer language. I suppose your Father will immediately break into Spanish! My love to him, and to Kate. I don't suppose Will needs any!

Affectionately yours
C.F.W.

Notes

1. Portions of this letter also appear in Benedict/CFW, 32–33, 223.
2. sprechen Deutsche: German spoken.

To Samuel Livingston Mather (WRHS/Mather)[1]

Lucerne. Switzerland
August 28th, [1880]

My dear Brother.

. . . My life here has been so quiet as regards incident, that I have little to write. There are always the beautiful mountains, and the lights and shadows and clouds to watch, but they do not make incidents for a letter. I came here for quiet, so I am having what I wanted. The town is crammed with the usual crowd of tourists, arriving and departing. They go down the lake, and back, in the little steamer; they go up the Rigi, and back; a few go up Pilatus,—then away they go, their places filled the next hour by another crowd. But all this does not reach us in our quiet Swiss pension where, if you will believe it! I am really beginning to grow fat; as this has been for years the wish of my heart, I am much delighted. Our German Baron, (who has the first floor, and a private table,) continues as mysterious as ever. It is really a curious existence for a good looking man of not more than forty-five. He never has a visitor, or a letter, or a newspaper, and he speaks to <u>no</u> one. He takes a furtive walk early in the morning, and again after dark, and he has lived in this way for years. There are but few rooms in this house beside his and ours. . . . I am so charmed and interested and fascinated with all I see here, from these great snow-capped peaks to the gondolas of Venice, and the pictures of Florence, that when I am not actually at work writing, I am quite absorbed by them. I presume that is one reason why I am not homesick . . . Colonel Hay has sent me a pamphlet copy of his Cleveland speech,—I think it very fine, it quite stirred me up. I had been thinking there were no special issues this campaign, but reading that speech was like a trumpet call to arms, and I felt like going over to America to be present at the encounter.[2]

I wish the family, generally, would give an opinion on my first "foreign" sketch, which will, I think, come out in the "Atlantic" before long; it is called "A Florentine Experiment," and the reason I speak of it is that Mr Howells has written me that he considers it "an immense advance in manner and arrangement over anything you have hitherto written." It is more of a "Society" sketch than my others. . . .

Yours affectionately,
C. F. Woolson.

Notes

1. The letter is in a typed transcription at WRHS. Portions also appear in Benedict/CFW, 222–23.

2. The differences in the 1880 election between Republican James Garfield and Democrat Winfield Hancock (1824–86) were small. One issue concerned tariffs, which the Republicans supported raising. Hay became Garfield's Assistant Secretary of State.

To Jane Averell Carter (Benedict/CFW, 24–25)

[1880]

When we arrived in Lucerne last week, we found a letter awaiting us, with the sad tidings of Marcia's death . . . [1] It seems so short a time since I saw you all together in Cooperstown, looking so well and so happy. . . . Marcia was a child full of promise. I thought, last summer that she would be remarkably beautiful; I saw that she was very bright. She was unusual in many ways. Her short life here is ended, and she is safe; but your heart must be aching over another broken tie. How strange it is that she should have died in Cleveland and be buried there . . . I like to think of them all there so near the graves that are dear to me. I wonder if <u>I</u> shall go back and die in Cleveland too!

I write, not because I can say anything of worth to you, but because I want you to know I am thinking of you, and sympathizing with you in your trouble. But you <u>did</u> say something of worth to me when I was suffering . . . I have never forgotten it; you wrote that you believed that, by my care, I had prolonged Mother's life for years. No one else had said this to me; I had not thought of it in that way myself. But it comforted me more than once, when I was tormented by the thought that if I had only done this, or that,—perhaps I might have saved her. . . .

Notes

1. George Pomeroy Keese helped to fund the Saint Agnes Chapel at Christ Episcopal Church, Cooperstown, in memory of the Carters' daughter Marcia.

To Katharine Livingston Mather (WRHS/Mather)[1]

Geneva. Switzerland
October 2^{d}, 1880

My dear Kate.

. . . My first summer in Switzerland may be said to be over, although it is still warm. The scenery of the Lake of Lucerne, that around Interlaken, and Mont Blanc from here, will always remain in my memory as long as I live. But I shall not come back to Switzerland, I think, until I can come with people who want to walk; want to go up to the high valleys; and until I, myself, have leisure to do the same. I was continually tantalized by the impossibility of doing what I wanted to do. We left Lucerne at 7 a.m. on the 15th of September; went by steamer down the south arm of the lake, and there took the diligence (coupé) over the Brunig Pass. But before long it began to pour, so we lost much, much of the scenery. The days at Interlaken, however, were superb. To my eyes the Jungfrau, as seen from Interlaken, is the finest single view, (limited view,—not an extensive one) I have ever seen. Of course we saw the Giessbach, and the Staubbach. But our grand expedition was "Mürren," which is an Alpine village, three thousand feet higher than Lauterbrunnen, where you are right in among the Bernese Alps. You go first to Lauterbrunnen in a carriage; there, after seeing the Staubbach, we had the horses taken out, saddles put on them, Clara and Clare mounted, the latter's horse led by the guide, and then, I safely on my own two feet, off we started. The path goes in zig-zags up the cliff and there are only two spots on the whole ascent where the foot rests upon a level, and these spots are not more than five feet long. We were three hours going up, as of course the horse women had to wait for me now and then. But who cared for cold, fatigue, or rarified air, when that superb panorama of the Jungfrau, the Moňch, the Eiger, and the rest, burst into view after a while, and then accompanied us all the rest of the way? I am sure I didn't. We spent the night at Mürren. It was very cold, but the moonlight on the snow peaks was most beautiful. You are very near the mountains, snow all around you; five glaciers in sight. It was a scene never to forget in its wild white, cold desolation, with the brilliant moonlight shining upon it. The next morning opened still colder, and we started down, Clara on foot this time also; but few ride down from Mürren; the constant jerk, jerk, of the horses going down the steep descent, is very tiresome. All the way down, the feet were at the "down" angle; and the next day I was very lame. Still I enjoyed the excursion greatly, my only "pedestrian" attempt.

From beautiful Interlaken we went to Berne, and then came here, where we found some friends awaiting us. With these people we went up the Lake to Vevey and Chillon. Oh, how much I enjoyed that! It was a lovely day, and the young people spouted all the proper poetry, and spouted it very well too. I want to spend a month at Vevey sometime. Then, having settled me here, Clara and Clare took their departure for Paris, where Clare is attending school. My "pension" here is just like the places you read about in French books; it is very interesting and funny. No one can speak English at all. But I find that I have not now the least difficulty and talk as rapidly,—though probably by no means as accurately, in French as I can in English. It is a satisfaction to feel that all those long years of study in America are of use, after all . . .

I like Geneva very much. Its blue lake, with the lateen sails; the view of the Jura and of Mont Blanc. The grapes are almost ripe, and the miles of vineyards are gay scenes. I am going to Coppet soon, to see the house of Madame de Stael, or rather, to stand there just for its associations with her and Madame Récamier. And to "Ferney" where Voltaire lived. I have found a delightful French library here, and am deep in the literature of Lac Leman not only all the poetry, philosophy, &c., but any number of the books of those French women of the 18th century, who wrote such voluminous "Memoirs." Indeed for the last week I have hardly been in the 19th century at all! . . .

Affectionately yours,
C. F. Woolson.

Notes

1. The letter is in a typed transcription at WRHS. Portions also appear in Benedict/CFW, 223–25.

To Samuel Mather (Anderson)[1]

Care Lombard, Odier, & Co.
Geneva. Switzerland
Oct. [1880]

My dear Sam.

I received this cheque a few day ago. Will you please deposit it in the Savings bank to my account. I was wondering what Mr Howells would do about an address, this time; whether he would repeat his exploit of sending a cheque to me, in the care of Mrs Hay![2] But he decided to let it come across the ocean. And now it goes back again! There does not seem to be any other way to arrange it. The last cheque I had from Harper's however, was in the shape of a draft on London, which I could use here.

I heard from you towards the last of August. Since then I have had a letter from your Father; and Clara sent me, from Paris the other day, a long and interesting letter from Kate, which I enjoyed greatly. I wrote to Kate soon after our arrival in Geneva. I supposed I should be here only a few weeks; but it will [be] two months. I think there is now no doubt but that Miss Clark will go with me to Rome, for the winter. Do you know who she is? She is the lady who talked quite seriously of going abroad with us in the beginning. She came over herself in June, with her sister, and some nieces and nephews, and waited here in Geneva to see me, after I left Lucerne. She wanted to go to Italy for the winter, but her sister was opposed to it, and I have not had much confidence in the plan until a day or two since. But now I think she will go, unless some one is ill between now and Nov. fifteenth. Her sister has withdrawn her opposition, on condition that Emily (my friend) takes an experienced maid, so that if either of us should be ill, there would be help at hand. The maid, however, is Emily's not mine; as you may well suppose. I am much pleased at this plan for the winter. Emily Clark is a cultivated, congenial, easy-going person; she is fond of the things I am fond of; she likes to discuss a book threadbare, for instance,—as I do! I first met her in St Augustine, where I met so many agreeable people; then I used to see her in Yonkers, where one of her sisters has a house. They are New York City people. Emily is somewhat older than I am, and has an easy fortune. My only fear is that she will not like the "pensions" where I always take up my abode. So you can think of me, going over to Chambery (near your Mother's "Aix-les-Bains") on, ~~the~~ or about the fifteenth, and there waiting for Miss Clark and her "experienced" maid ("experienced" in what, I wonder?) and then going on through the great tunnel to Turin, Genoa, Pisa, stopping over night at each place; then to lovely Florence for some weeks; and finally, before Xmas, to old Rome.—It has been a hard decision for me, whether to go to Rome; or to give up Italy and go to Paris, in order to be with Clara and Clare. But I do dread the cold of Paris, very much; and besides the city does not attract me. I should like to be there for a few weeks in the Spring, some time. But not the winter. In addition I have no heavy clothes. But the principal reason is my throat, which already troubles me whenever it is cold, even ~~here~~ now! It fills up almost in a minute as soon as a cold change comes. I remember what Dr Rossa said about the advisability of living in a warm climate. I certainly am much more comfortable where it is warm. Clara has probably written to some of you since she has been in Paris, so I will not repeat what she writes me. She has very pleasant rooms, and it seems to me that she has enjoyed Paris more than any other place, so far. She ~~has~~ made all the "excursions" during the lovely October weather,—to St Denis, St Cloud, Sevres, Versailles, Fontainebleau &c&c; and she has been several times to the opera. There have been a number of persons whom she knew in Paris, and she has enjoyed being with them. Mrs Weber is to be there all winter; Ida Weber attends the same school that Clare attends. Clare is much interested in the school; and I think that both "Mamma" and "little girl" are now much less homesick than they were in Lucerne, and are likely to enjoy their winter. It is probable that Clara and Clare will come to Rome for the Carnival, and then we shall all come north together. Dr Weber, I hear, is to sail for America very soon. The other afternoon I met Mrs Tod, Lizzie, and Mrs Earle in the street. They had come over from Neuchatel to see the lake; Vevey; Clarens; and Chillon. The death of Anna Morse was a great grief to Mrs Tod; she could not speak of it without tears. I pity deeply the poor Mother. Mrs Tod is to be several months in Paris; so Clara will see her.

I have had or rather have *led*, such a curious sort of existence here in Geneva. I have been all alone you know, and have managed to keep away from the people in the house in a great measure; not that they are not agreeable—they are remarkably so; but I wanted my time. All the morning I keep busy; then about three, out I sally, and go rambling through the old part of the town—the historic "Geneva," or else miles up the shore of the lake, now on one side, now on the other, always planning it so as to see the sunset light on superb Mont Blanc, as the *last* thing. Then in the evening (when not writing letters) I read, and read, and read. I do'nt know when I have read so much. I began with those writers who have lived on the shores of this lake—there are a great many of them—from Goethe and Byron down to D'Aubigné and *Calvin*!—but I soon became so interested in the "eighteenth century" that I plunged in over my head, and have not come to the surface yet! It is very likely I mentioned this in my letter to Kate. Well, it is just the same now, only *more so*! I am fascinated, and keep reading on and on through more and more "Memoirs," "Letters," "Journals," "Biographies," &c, until I feel as if I had been the intimate friend of Mesdames Récamier and de Staël, and of all those witty people of that letter-writing day. I get all these old books from a fine French library they have here. I took a subscription for two months; ~~at~~ a dollar. And I have already drawn out forty-eight volumes! They are worn out with the sight of me! I go every day except Sunday. Almost all of these "eighteenth century" people came to the shores of this lake.—Its water seems to me very blue; and the lateen sails are a wonderfully picturesque feature. But I do not think it approaches the Lake of Lucerne. However, there is always magnificent Mont Blanc! Tell your Mother that it has been such a very great pleasure and comfort to me, to have it to look at every day; I am sure she will appreciate the feeling.

In the house have been several Americans; now gone to Italy. Among them, the Misses Vermilye, from Hartford. They knew Mr & Mrs Burnham; and had often been to Long Meadow. Now we have only Germans—very accomplished ladies;—and French. Among them an old French countess, who is so droll. She picks *me* out for her attacks. I think it amuses her to hear my American-French! The other evening in the parlour they were talking about the marriage of the Baroness

Burdett-Coutts to "that young American," &c.[3] "Ah well," said the old lady, looking at me over her spectacles, "I have always understood that the Americans were extraordinarily fond of antiquities!"

I have been honoured with two invitations since I have been in Geneva;—think of that! The Geneva family I met at Menton invited me to dinner; and a very nice English family who ~~hav~~ are here for four years for the purpose of educating their children, invited me to "five o'clock tea." They have taken a house here. Geneva is full of English and American girls and boys, attending schools,—which are said to be excellent. The Geneva family are friends of the Countess Gasparin, who has a villa near Geneva, and they sent me all her books to read! I have never seen them, but I had read in America, the book of her husband, Count Gasparin, which came out during our war, and was considered so fine—"The Uprising of a Great People."[4] But very likely you are more familiar with the Gasparins than I am. This Geneva lady (the one who invited me to dinner) is the one about whom Clara tells one of her stories; and, for a wonder, it is not in the least exaggerated,—I can vouch for that. She had written to her brother about us (from Menton) and she read me his answer. It was in French of course; none of them can speak a word of English. He said he "had been much interested in her account of these American ladies, and he had envied her her opportunities of conversing with them. It must be so extremely entertaining, and instructive as well because they of course conversed much about the manners, customs, and history of the American Indians!!"

The English "five o'clock tea" family saw one of my cards, by chance. Immediately the mother asked me if I was "related to the distinguished American author, Fenimore Cooper." And upon my confessing the same, she said that her father and all her brothers were devoted to Cooper's novels, and she immediately invited me to tea! Now I want to know whether you obtained invitations over here on account of the celebrated Cotton who burned the witches?[5] And on account of the Indians?

I laughed until the tears came to think of Paul Carter's coming abroad to cultivate his voice! The Carter boys have no other idea of music than a low deep roar. But it is sad, too, to see them amounting to so little as the years glide on. They were a very bright, prosperous, happy family, in the old days before Mrs Purdy was married, when they were all together at the "rectory." I have had a letter recently from Mrs Washburn; but little in it. Is Annie Carter (Bingham) still visiting her?—I am afraid, Sam, that you will not praise my handwriting again! I am learning to write with a quill-pen; and you see the results! The quill makes a blacker broader mark. Besides costing but a penny! My last gold-pen shows signs of old age. Your handwriting is a remarkably fine one; I have always thought so.—I continue to weigh one hundred and twenty nine pounds. I think I put it in Kate's letter; but I like to repeat it!—Soon after this letter reaches you, you will see the first number of my long-delayed "Anne." If the Harpers make any "announcements" about it, and the new volume, will you please send what you happen to see to me. Perhaps the preceding number, that is the "Nov." No., may contain them. Or they may be published in the newspapers with the regular advertisement of the "Dec." number. The firm send me the magazine itself, through the publication of the story. I cannot remember, as I write, whether I have told any of you the secret about the long delay in the publication of "Anne," or not! Now this is annoying, because if I have, it will seem very self-important to repeat it. Yet still, if I have not, I want you to know. So pray forgive—if it is a repetition. With the opening of the new volume, that is the "Dec." number, the Harpers begin the publication of an English edition, which is to be published in London. This is quite a "large" enterprise, I believe; and they have kept "Anne" for that. I suppose because it is a purely "American" story. This—the Ed. of the magazine—considered quite a feather in my cap; and I could see that he thought the honor to me compensated for all the delay. But as I could not tell this, the delay has been to me, annoying. There is no secret about it now of course.[6]

Now, Sam, I have written you a "long" letter; whether it be interesting or not, I have my doubts. But at least it carries a great deal of love to you all. What I wish especially to say is that I expect an answer. I have now been away a year; and I wish you to tell me, like a dutiful nephew, what you have been doing, generally and particularly, since my departure. Especially

Particularly.

My dearest love to your Mother and Father. I hope they are both feeling well, now. And I want to hear about the Convention. Did your Mother go too?—You really must elect Garfield because if you do not, all the nice American ministers and consuls over here will be changed for terrible democrats. My especial wish is that Col. Hay should take a foreign appointment; not in too cold a climate. Not Sweden or Russia for instance!

—Love to Kate and to Will. I suppose those fine silk-lined overcoats are going to last through this winter also, of course. I must now go on with "Mme de Rémusat."[7] Goodnight.

Affectionately Yours,
C.F.W.

I wish your Father would write me an account of the conversation.

Notes

1. Portions of this letter appear in Benedict/CFW, 225–27.

2. Woolson is probably referring to a check for either or both stories published in *Atlantic Monthly*: "The South Devil" (Feb. 1880); "A Florentine Experiment" (Oct. 1880).

3. Reputedly the richest woman in England, philanthropist Baroness Burdett-Coutts

(1814–1906) at age sixty-seven married her thirty-year-old secretary William Lehman Ashmead Bartlett (1851–1921), an American-born member of Parliament.

4. Countess Valerie de Gasparin wrote many books on religion and morality in addition to fiction. Her husband, Count Agenor de Gasparin (1810–71) was an experimenter in telekinesis. His book *The Uprising of a Great People* (1862) is subtitled *The U.S. in 1861*.

5. Mather was an indirect descendent of Increase and Cotton Mather.

6. *Harper's New Monthly Magazine* serialized *Anne* from Dec. 1880 to May 1882 and published the book version 1882; Sampson & Low published the English version in 1883.

7. Paul de Rémusat published the memoirs of his grandmother Claire de Rémusat (1780–1824), a friend of Napoleon's Court, in 1879–80.

To Katharine Livingston Mather (WRHS/Mather)[1]

Florence. Italy
December 10th, 1880

Dear Kate.

Your October letter reached me in Paris, where I spent a month in a quiet little place, where I had a pretty parlor to myself, and my meals served in it, on a little round table with spotless cloth, and excellent French cooking; such a delightful change after the tasteless English fare. You know, it was my first view of Paris—and I enjoyed it very much; the weather was bad, but I went about just the same. At last I grew restless, and anxious to be "settled" for the winter. So I departed, taking the long journey back to Italy,—which is not, and cannot be, easy, unless one travels at night (which I never can do, you know), and arrived here, tired, but well, and oh, so fat. I don't mean that I gained especially on the journey! but only that when I come to speak of myself, I am continually amazed at my own expansion. You see I am not used to it, I have been thin all my life until now. I am at last established for the winter. I have taken a nice little parlor with open fire-place, and bedroom opening from it, also with fire-place. This old place, "Casa Molini," is on the Arno, and I have two windows on the river, and two on another street, with a very pretty little glimpse of the Apennines on the north, and the Carrara mountains on the south, and the beautiful singular tower of the Palazzo Vecchio, and Giotto's lovely Campanile, beside the Duomo, and several other picturesque towers against the blue sky. One of my favorite entertainments is hearing all these numerous bells in the high campaniles ring out the Ave Maria. They are not very powerful bells,—but clear and sweet, and the Italian way of ringing is to send them swinging far out of the campaniles into the air, back and forth; as the pictures of bells on the Christmas cards at home are represented as doing; here it is a reality. As I always walk in the afternoon, I always hear the Ave Maria.

Well, to go back to my arrangements for the winter. My breakfast and lunch are served in my own parlor. I appear only at the dinner table, at six o'clock, which I do not so much object to. It is the breaking up of the day, by lunch, that I so much dislike. I write until about three o'clock, then go out for a long walk, generally up one of the hills to get the beautiful views in all directions that abound here. I receive such visitors as come, in my own parlor, and so, you see, that though in a "pension" I am quite independent. I feel at home here, and the servants are excellent, they have been in the house twenty years . . . Yes, I meet quite a good many people I know, and I have made a number of new acquaintances. But I am, after all, a solitary sort of an old bird, and as poor Sothern used to say "flock by myself"![2] I am all the time busy, and I am not strong enough to take much part in Society, or go out much, and do writing-work at the same time. The best of me goes into my writing. I get tired very easily, and so, on the whole prefer to write quietly for the freshest part of the day, take a good walk, and then curl up in an easy chair with an entertaining book, and go to bed early. If people will be so kind as to seek me out in my <u>leisure</u>-times, or come and go to walk with me, I am delighted; but that is all the time I have for them. I find I know a good many people here this winter, and have even been invited out several times to dinner, to evening companies, and to lunch parties. I have declined everything except one or two afternoon teas, which come in nicely with my afternoon walk. One of these teas was with Mrs Launt Thompson, wife of the sculptor; she is the daughter of Bishop Potter, and sister of Dr Potter of Grace Church . . .

I make the best of the bells of Florence, the Arno and its bridges, (all of which I see from my windows,) and when it is cold, and that horrid wind sweeps down from the Apennines, I call up Angelo to make a bright fire, and sit before it dreaming of Florida air. The servants in the house are named Rafaello, Angelo, Bartolo, Giuseppe, Catarina, Beppa, and Gemma. Isn't that Italian?. . . .

"For the Major" of which you speak, is quite short, not a long novel like "Anne." I consider it the most (to <u>me</u>) satisfactory piece of work I have done, viewed from the literary point of view. . . .

Lovingly,
C. F. Woolson.

Notes

1. The letter is in a typed transcription at WRHS. Portions also appear in Benedict/CFW, 32, 236–38.

2. Benedict identifies Sothern as "E. A. Sothern, senior, famous as Lord Dundreary." Sothern (1826–81) played Lord Dundreary in Tom Taylor's (1817–80) farce, *Our American Cousin* (1858), the play Lincoln was attending when he was assassinated.

To Samuel Mather (Anderson)[1]

Florence
Dec. 19th, [1880]

My dear Sam.

Your letter of November twenty third was, as you may imagine, a very interesting one to me. I send you my warmest good wishes, and my dearest love; and please give the same to Flora from me. I like her and admire her very sincerely; and I look forward with pleasure to seeing more of her when I come home; or, when you (you two) come abroad. How much I should like to be in Cleveland for the Xmas holidays, and give you my congratulations in person. Then I should slip over, secretly, to see Flora, and give her the sage "Aunt's" opinion of the nephew.—Then I should have a look at the Xmas evergreens; at the snow, and the sleighs; one kiss all around, and back to Italy again.

This letter poorly takes the place of all that;—but it is sent with much love. It will reach you early in the New Year, which will I hope be a very happy one to you, my dear Sam, in all ways.

Not long ago I received a delightful note from Colonel Hay, enclosing an "Evening Post" notice of "Anne." And this reminds me to ask whether his proximity—that is, the associations called up by it—had anything to do with your silence, while we were at tea together, the evening your Mother invited Mr & Mrs Philip Brown? There is no doubt but that you were very silent upon that occasion, since I noticed it even when talking with so agreeable a companion as Colonel Hay. Confess now that, even then—![2]

As you see, I am still in Florence. Miss Clark's sister and two nieces are here, so that we are now a party of five; and four of the five are so afraid of the Roman fever that they have persuaded me to wait here until January first. But then I shall insist upon going. I must have my three months in Rome; although I know they will be hardly more than an introduction. My address there will be "Care Macquay, Hooker, & Co. Piazza di Spagna." Florence is as enchanting as ever; I can never have too much of it. So far, fires have been necessary but a few times. To-day it is like September, and stacks of roses and narcissus are for sale on every corner. Meanwhile we hear that it is "winter" in America; and we feel quite gay and tropical in consequence.

I was much interested in what you wrote about the "Florentine Experiment." Your opinion of it agrees with my own. You may tell Miss Jessie (if you choose) that I think men like "Trafford" generally are conceited. But that is not the worst of it; the worst is that they are generally, also, so charming (in other ways) that one has to accept the "conceit" to get the rest! As "Margaret" did.

As to "Anne," I can form no idea whether you—or anyone—will like it; or not. I am much interested in the career of the "English edition." The English monthly magazines are so entirely inferior to ours in every way, that I think "Harper's" and "Scribner's" together, will "sweep the board,"—as the good old Mackinac chaplain used to say, when he played whist by sitting behind me, and directing me in a whisper.—"Play your Queen, Miss Conny, and ye'll sweep the board!"[3]

Give my love to Kate, and tell her that I think her pictures excellent; they adorn my wall at the present moment. I sent Clara and Clare theirs; and they write they are delighted with them. The "Parisians," as I call them, are pretty well. Clare learning French and music rapidly; but Clara not well satisfied with the other studies. So I think when this winter is over, and Clare speaks the language with fair fluency, a Paris School will not again be selected. The "Parisians" have seen a good deal, I believe, of the Tods. Give my love to Will; I received his letter, and will write to him later, from Rome.

A year ago we were in Mentone; and how cold I was! I am hoping that my one hundred and thirty pounds are going to keep me warmer, this winter! The next time you have a good photograph taken, wo'nt you send one to me? And, later, perhaps a certain young lady will let me have one of hers. I hope so.

Charlie writes that he carried a torch miles in the mire for Garfield; and that Los Angeles and its county went Republican (owing to this, of course!) for the first time in the history of the State.

My dearest love to your Mother, and Father. I wish I might be favored with a glimpse of the "Bishop's Trot."

Good-by, my dear boy. I have heard nothing for a very long time which has given me so much pleasure as the tidings in your letter.

Always affectionately yours,
C. F. Woolson.

I will be careful not to betray your secret.

Notes

1. Portions of this letter also appear in Benedict/CFW, 32, 199n.
2. Woolson is alluding to Mather's impending engagement to Hay's sister-in-law, Flora Stone.
3. The Mackinac chaplain was the Episcopal minister, Rev. John O'Brien.

To Jane Averell Carter (Benedict/CFW, 190)

[1880?]

I spent all my spare time over the pictures. I think I told you I intended to study them, with the hope that they would, in time, give me a part of the pleasure they give in such high measure to other people. My idea is that as one must have some musical education in order to appreciate the best music, so also one must have some art education in order to appreciate the best pictures. Of course I could not go into it deeply, but I did what I could in Florence, and before I left, I could see that I was gaining. I found myself liking pictures which I had not at first understood, and getting real enjoyment them.

To Katharine Livingston Mather (Benedict/CFW, 192n)

[1880][1]

I wish the family, generally, would give an opinion on my first "foreign" sketch, which will, I think, come out in the Atlantic before long. It is called "A Florentine Experiment." It is more of a "society" sketch than any of my others.

Notes

1. Because Woolson's "A Florentine Experiment" was published in *Atlantic Monthly*, Oct. 1880, this letter was probably composed in that year.

To Katharine Livingston Mather (WRHS/Mather)[1]

Sienna
January 13th, 1881

Dear Kate.

I am writing in Sienna, "that old city of the middle ages" with its beautiful slim tower, its old walls, and wonderful Cathedral, which we shall see more fully tomorrow. We left beloved Florence this morning, and rolled westward down the valley of the Arno toward Pisa, as far as Empoli, where we changed cars, and came southward. It is warm, I am thankful to say, but raining hard. However, I have already been out to see the front of the Cathedral, and the tower, and admire them greatly. . . .

Friday afternoon. This morning opened lowering, but fortunately with no rain. Out we went, and with the exception of a half hour for lunch, have been at it all day. It is now nearly dark and snowing! yes, real flakes, although they melt as they touch the ground. Sienna is high up in the mountains, therefore the air is much colder than in Florence. It is the most medieval place I have yet visited, with walls, towers, and a supremely beautiful Cathedral; by that I mean beautiful in the Italian way, which is very different from the magnificent Gothic architecture of the North. The tower of the Palazzo Publico made the deepest impression upon me. We have also seen some beautiful old pictures, and, for the first time, I have come close to the life of a real "Saint," Sainte Catherine of Sienna. We have been to her house, have seen her clothes, lantern, and the block of wood she used for her pillow, &c. There is nothing mystical about this Saint Catherine, because she lived as lately as 1360, and the incidents of her life are all historical and authentic. I am not referring to her visions, and that part of it, but to the real events, and her work among the poor. The most extraordinary part of it to me, was a facsimile of her head and face which were embalmed immediately after death, and which are kept in a shrine, and exhibited to the people on her Feast Day once a year.[2] You would suppose that it would be repulsive, but it was not; it was calm and quiet, and even sweet. It seemed all wrong of course, to keep the poor mask of former life from its rightful return to dust; still, it was curiously impressive to see the quiet, still sleeping face, and think how long ago it lived. Altogether, Sienna has been very interesting, although I see, of course, how much more beautiful it would be in Spring. . . .

Rome
January 16th

We left Sienna, its old walls all white with snow, yesterday morning, and rolled down hill towards Rome. The road really descended so constantly that it seemed as if we were merely going down by our own impetus. The snow turned into rain, and such rain! sheets of dark grey water; I think I never saw such heavy rain before. We rolled by Orvieto, where [there] is another marvelous Cathedral, towards which we looked with longing eyes. We reached Rome at four in the afternoon. The rain still fell in sheets; we could see nothing of the city. We hurried under umbrellas, to the omnibus and rolled through wet streets to this small hotel, thankful to be under cover, somewhere. In spite of all this, I was a good deal stirred in a quiet way, by the thought that I was really and actually in "Rome!" the city I have dreamed about since childhood with a real, and sometimes, very intense longing.[3] I was a good deal stirred all the evening, it was a sort of surprised content, to be really within the old walls at last! I hope to be here two months and a half. . . . My first pilgrimage, after arranging my quarters, will be of course to St Peter's and the Vatican art treasures. I think I shall spend all my leisure time there for several weeks! . . .

Yours affectionately
C. F. Woolson.

Notes

1. The letter is in a typed transcription at WRHS. Portions also appear in Benedict/CFW, 238–39.

2. The Dominican St. Catherine of Siena (1347–80), whose feast day is on April 30, not only worked among the poor but also worked for church reform and peace among the Italian city states. After her death by a stroke, her head was smuggled out of Rome. More than three hundred of her letters survive.

3. Woolson's comment that this is her first time in Rome explains why her story "'Miss Grief'" (*Lippincott's*, May 1880) has an uncharacteristic lack of setting.

To Henry Mills Alden (WRHS/Benedict)[1]

Care Macquay, Hooker, & Co.
20 Piazza di Spagna. Rome
Feb. 5th, [1881]

Dear Mr Alden.

I have wished to write to you ever since I received your delightful and most satisfying letter of December tenth. I have literally had no time. Since I left Geneva on Nov. 15th, I have scarcely been my own mistress. And I do not like the new state of things at all! My sister has not been with me, you know; and I have been for the first time, one of "a party," and could not follow my own way, unimpeded and unnoticed, as I am accustomed to do! The result has been that the one or two carefully saved hours of the evening, which I have hitherto had for letter-writing, or any other little personal pleasure, have been interfered with, and indeed literally taken from me. This state of things, however, is nearly over. My sister comes down from Paris soon,—for the Carnival. And I shall never put myself into "a party" again.

You do'nt know how much interest I felt—and still feel—in your letter. And how much satisfaction it gave me. I will tell you (this is for you alone) that I completely and heartily agree with your criticism of the "Florentine Experiment." I did not say, I think, what I thought of the story myself when I wrote to ask your opinion. But, secretly, I was not a little vexed, ~~almost~~ troubled,—and not a little bewildered, by what Mr Howells had written; and by praise of the same sort from many other quarters, which had come to me. If you knew the amount of advice I have had, both outspoken and hinted, to follow that sort of writing,—you would be surprised, I am sure. The tone is that it is much the most "refined," "superior," "cultivated" style. And that my own needs just what that style excels in.—I have been told,—not always of course openly, but implied-ly—that there should be next to no "plot"; that the "manner" should be more than the "matter"; and that the best "art" left a certain vagueness over all the details. I have been especially warned against anything that looked "dramatic." And, in fact, the point seemed to be to have nothing that came either conversationally or in action, to any definite end.—As I have said, this has not always been offered as direct advice; but has been "suggested" by high praise of books that followed these rules.—It has been going on, now, for at least two years, and has depressed me sometimes not a little, because I began to fear that my own judgment (which remained through all, obstinately set in the other direction) might be a mistaken one. Yet I knew, even then, that I could not change it, any more than I could change the color of my complexion.—Well, then, when the "Florentine Experiment" came out, all these people overwhelmed me with applause. Now at last I was on the right path!

I wrote that story simply as an experiment. I thought I would ~~try to~~ see if that "conversation" style was difficult. It had never seemed to me that it would be; but I had simply never cared for it, myself.

I am so glad you have said what you did. It entirely sustains my own beliefs and "convictions," that I feel quite strengthened, & comforted. And, since your letter, I am glad to add, others have slowly come along, from persons not literary yet of excellent general judgment, who say, briefly, pretty much the same thing.—And so now I shall go on in my own way again, & not be shaken by these "admirers" who have troubled me. "Troubled," is the very word. That is all they did; they did not change me. But it is depressing to be "troubled"; and I am enough inclined that way even at my best, without any additions. A thousand thanks to you for your letter, & your help.

Rome is fascinating. Most of all the antique marbles.—Next, the Campagna, with its long blue sweep. Next, the ruins. I could stay here for years, & never be weary! The weather is very fine. I gathered spring anemones at the "Palace of the Caesars" the other day; and yesterday wild violets in the lovely Borghese Gardens. I may remain through April and May; I am anxious to. And I may go to England in April. My sister sails for home April 16th, and returns in the autumn.—I have received only the first number of "Anne,"—the "December" magazine. Were the others sent? It may be that they have been lost.—The illustrations are excellent.[2] I have seen (but not bought,) the English "Jan" number. I hear they are pronouncing it "Annie" in America. It is Ann,—"Queen Anne": English people I meet, (who have no idea "Anne" is my story) speak of the magazine as a "marvel," in every way. It seems to be exciting much comment. This is but a short letter. I will do better later, when this crowded life is over.

I felt as if I had lost a dear friend when I saw that "George Eliot" was gone.

Best of good wishes for you all. The address given at the head of this letter will serve for three or four months. Tell Mrs Alden I see the Queen out driving every day, & she looks very sweet and amiable!

Yours sincerely,
C. F. Woolson.

Notes

1. The letter is pasted into Woolson's *Dorothy*, New York: Harper's, 1896.

2. *Anne* was serialized in *Harper's New Monthly Magazine* from Dec. 1880 to May 1882. The illustrations were by C. S. Reinhart (1844–96).

To Henry Mills Alden (Non-Catholic in Rome)[1]

(Care Macquay, Hooker, & Co.
20 Piazza di Spagna)
Rome
April 8th, [1881]

Dear Mr Alden.

There is nothing of importance in this letter, so you can keep it—if you are busy—for a leisure moment. I thought I would write you one "Roman" sheet, although I have not heard from you since I last wrote.

Well,—I have now had fulfilled one of the strong wishes of my imagination: to spend a winter in Rome. And I can truthfully say that not only have I not been disappointed in any of the many things I have pictured to myself, but that the reality is even more wonderful and enchanting than I had imagined. The lady who has been with me, and my sister and little Clare who came down from Paris for the Carnival, have gone; and left me behind. I would not go! My sister is, I suppose, in London to-night; she sails April 16th for home. She will, I hope, return in the autumn. And, meanwhile, I am trying "housekeeping" in Rome! That is, after a fashion. I have taken a little "apartment" very high up under the sky; you must go high up in Rome to get good air. I have a bright little parlor, bed-room, and dinner-room, and balcony with pots of flowers. I go along this balcony (which is very narrow, and so far above the street that it would make many people dizzy to look down and see the ~~people~~ carriages passing so far below), and, at the end, is a door. This opens upon the queerest little flight of stone steps leading up a steep gray roof, as though it was a hill. The stairs are under cover, and have a hand-rail. They lead to a "loggia," on top of *our* house, the stairs going up the roof of another. This loggia is a little square room, with windows towards all points of the compass, and an arbor outside, made of lemon-trees, plants in pots, and climbing vines. The walls are hung with pretty hangings, and it is prettily furnished. Here among the roofs and campaniles, and under the deep blue sky of Rome, I can sit and write in perfect solitude when tired of my little parlor below. It all seems so wonderful and strange,—the being here at all! I think of Ohio and the Zoar farm where I used to spend so much time; of Mackinac and the peculiar color of Lake Huron; and of Florida, and the pine-barrens. And, all the while, I am in "*Rome*"!

Do you care to know what has impressed me the most? The antique statues. This rather surprises me. I have not heretofore cared much for statues,—the few I have seen. But there is something extremely beautiful in these old Greek marbles. And nothing in Europe has impressed me so much as the stretch of the grand halls of the Vatican, with these shining silent forms on each side. The "Capitol," in itself, is not impressive as the Vatican is; but it contains as you know, the "Dying Gladiator" and the lovely "Marble Faun."[2] I could easily write you a dozen pages about my favorite statues, and all I think about them. I am full of the subject. But my remarks would of course have no value as criticisms. And, as you have not been here yet, I cannot have the pleasure (a great one) of simply saying "O do you remember" such an expression? Or "can you ever forget"—such a group or face; the sort of delightful but invaluable talk which enthusiastic returned-travelers delight in.

The pictures of Rome do not seem to me as beautiful as those of Florence.

Next to the statues, I think the Campagna still fascinates me more than anything else. I am never tired of climbing up to the top of the Coliseum to look at it, or walking over to the open space in front of St John Lateran, for the same purpose. If I go to the "Palace of the Caesars," the best part of it is not the gloomy halls of Caligula; the frescoes of the house of Livia—or whoever it was;—or even the basilica of Augustus where St Paul ~~was~~ is supposed to have been tried; instead of these it is the ruined end of the palace of Septimus Severus, from whence there is a wide view of that soft blue expanse like a sea, stretching toward the south.[3] For it is the level part of the Campagna that charms me most. The other day I had a drive down the Appian way, with the old tombs on each side. About five miles down, we stopped, and climbed up to the top of a massive old tomb to get a view. On top is a farm-house and small olive-grove!—I often go to the Roman Forum, select some old column for a seat, and remain there for an hour, looking about me, and thinking. Having now been here three months, of course I have "seen" almost everything, at least once. I mean, gazed at it after the fashion of "tourists." But now I am "seeing" in a much better way. I am feeling the spirit and the meaning of all these old ruins; the spirit and the meaning of "Rome."—I shall stay until early in May, perhaps longer. It is not quite

Notes

1. Pasted into Clare Benedict's personal copy of *Constance Fenimore Woolson*. In the past, scholars have referred to this cemetery as the Protestant Cemetery in Rome, Woolson's burial site.

2. *The Dying Gladiator* and *The Marble Faun* are the most famous Roman sculptures in the collections of the Capitoline Museums. Hawthorne used the latter as inspiration for his novel *The Marble Faun* (1850).

3. All of the places Woolson mentions are on Palatine, one of the Seven Hills of Rome and the site of the Palaces of the Caesars. At the time of Woolson's visit, they were under excavation. Other references are to the Criptoporticus of the Emperor Nero (54–68 AD), the House of Livia, the wife of Emperor Augustus (27 BCE–14 AD), Augustus's own palace and the palace of Septimus Severus (193–211 AD). The third Roman Emperor, Caligula (12–41 AD) was assassinated; St. Paul, whose conversion is documented in the *Bible*'s "Book of Acts" and whose evangelizing for Christianity is reflected in many of his "letters" in the New

Testament, was tried in the Augustan basilica in Rome and buried in St. Paul-without-the Walls. Although the view from the Palace of Septimus Severus is now blocked, from there Woolson would have been able to see the expanse of the Campagna. I am grateful to Nicholas Stanley-Price, volunteer at the Non-Catholic Cemetery, for this information.

To Katharine Livingston Mather (WRHS/Mather)[1]

Rome
Easter Even, 1881

My dearest Kate.

I cannot write to you a long letter tonight, because I am extremely tired, having written about seven hours during the day. But I want to send my love and "Easter" good wishes for you all. . . .

I am living in an "apartment," it is on the fourth story. A little parlor, prettily furnished, bed-room, dining-room, and up on the roof, reached by the queerest little flight of stairs, a "loggia,"—a little room with windows on all sides, and a sort of arbor outside, made by plants in pots, and climbing vines. The whole high-up "apartment" always makes me think of the rooms of the "Old Mam'selle," if you remember the novel of that name.[2] I have been wanting to try apartment life all winter; now I am at it. Indeed it is the only way to be comfortable in Rome, where the Hotels are crowded and noisy, and very high priced. I rent my rooms of an English lady, a governess, whose scholars are of the best Roman families, I am told. She is a widow and keeps an Italian servant. I make my own breakfast, coffee and boiled eggs, with a little coffee pot and spirit lamp. Bread, butter, eggs and milk are sent in every day. At noon, the Italian servant serves a hot chop. At seven in the evening a very good, but simple, little dinner. Then I make my own "five o'clock tea," to which, by the way, I have become quite devoted. You can't imagine how I enjoy the space, the quiet, the ease, after the two months and a half of that Hotel! I hate the "table d'hote" system. The long array of courses, half of which I never touch, tires me out. I have only taken the apartment for a month; it was a "Roman experiment"; and so far, a great success. Rome continues perfectly enchanting, I could write for long hours about all the fascination if I was not so tired. The singing of the "Miserere" yesterday, at St John Lateran, was wonderfully fine. On Thursday going into the Pantheon, I met the Queen there, praying at the Altar near which Victor Emmanuel is buried.[3] It was quite an impressive sight to see her come out under that grand dome, the people making a lane for her, and all bowing and "blessing" her. The Italians seem very fond of her. She is a graceful sweet-looking woman. The statues & the Campagna continue to hold me bound fast; I love them deeply, but I do'nt desert the ruins. The other day I spent several hours in the "Roman Forum," walking with my own feet on the "Sacra Via," sitting down at the base of all the old "temples," visiting everything. I take immense walks, and very little escapes me. I come home so excited with it all, that I fairly glow! For it is so interesting, so wonderful, so beautiful! You see I have "gone over" body and soul, to Rome! Not in a religious sense however. I heard, by the way, the other day, that James Kent Stone, once President of Kenyon College, was here, in the Passionist Monastery.[4] I often walk by them, and have seen some of the Brothers, dressed in black with a heart embroidered on the breast. I should like to see him. . . .

I am going to the Hon. George Marsh's next week; their reception.[5] He is our minister, you know. I should think Roman society might be very entertaining, but I am not a "society" person. . . . The Coliseum is lighted up tonight; but I have no taste for artificial shows of that sort, I prefer the moonlight. Clara and Clare were presented to the Pope; I was not curious enough to go. . . . Goodbye, with much love,

Affectionately,
C. F. Woolson.

Notes

1. The letter is in a typed transcription at WRHS. Portions also appear in Benedict/CFW, 241–42.

2. Benedict identifies the book as *The Old Mam'selle's Secret* (1869) by Eugenia Marlitt. The translation of this novel was by Mrs. A. L. Wister.

3. See appendix for Italian royalty.

4. Stone (1840–1921), a renowned theologian, converted from Episcopalianism to Catholicism.

5. Diplomat and environmentalist, the Vermont-born George Perkins Marsh (1801–82) is, like Woolson, buried in the Non-Catholic Cemetery in Rome.

To William Dean Howells (Houghton)

Rome
May 4th, 1881

Dear Mr Howells.

I have been seeking an excuse to write to you; and now, fortunately, I have one; you will find it further down the page.

I have been wishing to say how glad I am that you have left the editorial chair of the "Atlantic." It took too much of your time, time we want you to give to your own work, and not to that of five hundred miscellaneous and weakly people. You are now free. And we are all glad of it.

As a contributor, I heartily regret your departure. You have been, from the first, most cordially kind to me. Several times you have said the right word at a time when it was especially needed; when perhaps if you had not said it, I should have lost heart and stopped. I have always written in a lonely sort of way, as regards anyone to consult; and therefore what you have said, now and then, has been particularly helpful.—Let me thank you now, from Rome, for many past kindnesses; and offer you, in this lovely Italian spring, my very best wishes for your American year. I wish you were coming abroad, and that it might be an "Italian" one.

And this brings me to my "excuse." My sister and her little daughter, after a year and a half of it, have gone home; for six months, possibly longer. I, left alone, and obstinately refusing to leave Rome, have been enjoying the most delightful and odd little "apartment" here, for a month. It is on the fourth floor of an old Roman house, three bright pretty rooms and a loggia above, covered with vines. Here I have been very content and happy after a winter of the "table d'hote" of hotels! I am still lingering, because the weather is so charming, and Rome so enchanting, that I cannot go. But later, I shall be in Florence. And now for my plan. It is as yet vague; but still it persistently haunts me. It is this: to spend the summer in Venice. I write to you for your opinion, because you were there so long, and because I fancy you are not so carried away with Italy as most (not "<u>most</u>," after all; but "<u>some</u>"; and I am of the "some"!) people, and will give me a truthful account of its pleasures and drawbacks. I must tell you, in the first place, that I am so changed by my years in the South with my dear Mother, that I can only be comfortable in a warm climate or summer weather. It is no affectation; I adore the heat. When everyone else is languid, I feel at my best. Also I am in much better health when the weather is warm. The least cold affects my throat. So dismiss any thought of Venice being too warm, merely as a matter of comfort. I was there ten days in June last year; and was completely fascinated with its beauty. It now occurs to me that instead of going down to the Baths of Lucca, or up to Perugia, why not try that enchanting spot again? Do you really think it an unhealthy place? And what part of the city would be best for a summer stay? I should prefer a small "apartment" such as I have now. I am heartily sick of hotels. Do you know of any small apartments, & can you give me the addresses? I should be very much obliged. And do you know the present consul; could you give me an introduction to him?—This is all a little private plan of mine, and I may not be able to carry it out. My sister supposes I am going to England; and, in one way, I wish I was! I should dearly like three months in great dusky old London. But England is far far away, and London is an expensive place. And Venice is near and very enchanting. If my sister does not return next winter, I shall spend it in Italy. And, by remaining in Venice, I escape two long journeys. Will you be so very kind as to tell me what you think, remembering that I love the heat, and consider a gondola the next thing to a

Beethoven symphony. Could I take any walks there, of any fair length? I am a great walker and should miss it, if deprived of it. I cannot get your "Venetian Life" here, or I should go to that for information.

I wished so much to send you another story, as you suggested. But Rome was so bewildering at first,—a pleasant bewilderment—that I could settle to nothing. I have given my heart entirely to the statues of the Vatican and Capitol. And every other sentiment I have, has gone into the Campagna. So there is not much left for mss! However, I am now beginning to recall the wandering thoughts; I have been nearly four months, and must go to work again. Sometimes I can scarcely believe it is I, & not some one else, enjoying all this beauty.—I sent to Mr Aldrich the story I intended for you.[1] But it may be that he will not be to me as you have been.—Will you send me an answer to Florence. "Care Macquay, Hooker, & Co. Via Tornabuoni."—I should not go to Venice before the middle, or last, of June. My regards to Mrs Howells.

Yours sincerely,
C. F. Woolson.

I make a guess at an address. I do'nt know the number, or street.

Notes

1. Thomas Bailey Aldrich took over the editorship of *Atlantic Monthly* in 1881; therefore, the story Woolson references must be "In Venice," published in that magazine in Apr. 1882.

To John Eliot Bowen (Barnard)

Geneva. Switzerland
July 9th, [1881?]
John Eliot Bowen, Esqre.

Dear Sir.

I have two letters to acknowledge, from your office. The long delay in my reply is owing to my having been bothered, for the past year, by something resembling "writer's cramp." It is now cured, I trust. I am much obliged for your offer; I like & value the "Independent." But, much as I should like to write for its columns, one can only do what one can, you know; &, all that I can possibly write, for the present, is already promised. I am sorry; but so it is. I regret, on my own account, that I am not a more rapid writer; I lose much.

With thanks for your kind attention, I am,

Yours truly,
C. F. Woolson.

To Oscar Fay Adams (Phillips Exeter)

Geneva. Switzerland
July 10th, [1881?]
Mr O. F. Adams.

Dear Sir,

I beg you to excuse my long delay in answering your letter—a delay caused not by negligence, but by a little difficulty resembling "writer's cramp" which has bothered me for the past year. I trust it is now cured. But, in the meanwhile, my letters have had to wait.

I presume you have already brought out the volume on "March," and that therefore my answer comes quite too late.[1] It is, or it would have been, "yes"; though, at the same time, I must say that I do not think much of the verses myself, nor should I include them, were I gathering together the few verses I have written. There is a little poem called "Cornfields" (for August), which was published in Harper's Magazine for August, 1872,—which I should include. But probably your "August" volume is already prepared. With all good wishes for the success of your collection, I am,

Yours truly,
C. F. Woolson.

Notes

1. Adams must have been asking to reprint Woolson's poem "March," which she published in the March 1873 *Harper's New Monthly Magazine*.

To Samuel Mather (Anderson)[1]

Engelberg
July 18th [1881]

My dear Sam.

I understand that the secret is out, and that we can offer congratulations, publicly. I offer mine with the warmest love, and most confident good wishes to you and to Flora whom I especially like for herself, and admire; and whom I shall now begin to doubly like and admire as my future niece. I have not so many nieces and nephews, you know, that they seem an ordinary affair; only four. And you ~~are~~ were the first. I can remember perfectly the tremendous importance you had in my eyes, and my own increased dignity in consequence.

My dear boy—I am far away; and being alone, I have many musing hours. Since your engagement, I have thought so often of your Mother, whom you do not remember, but I do—and the deep and warm interest she would have taken in it.

And also of the one who went later—more than two years ago, now, although it still seems to me like a month or two only—who also loved you so deeply, and would have sent to you and to Flora such earnestly-affectionate good wishes. But I am sure they bear you in mind—the "son" and "grandson."[2]

As you may already know, I have come up among the Alps; this green valley is three thousand five hundred feet up, and surrounded by mountains ten and eleven thousand feet high, whose tops are covered with snow. A glacier descends into the valley, and all together, it is very Alpine and delicious to a person who spent "Fourth of July" in Florence! I did not intend to be there so late; but was caught by "circumstances." Circumstances over here, generally mean "people." I was going to Venice; but so many people I knew turned up, who were going there too, people with the most voluminous plans for "sight-seeing," in which I was positively to join, that it ended in my not going at all. I have seen the sights; and detest sight-seeing in any case. <u>My</u> idea of Venice was a balcony over the Grand Canal; the beautiful lights, colors, and shadows; long quiet hours of writing; and then, out in a gondola for the sunset and twilight. I may be able to carry it out later; in October perhaps. That Fourth of July in Florence was a terrible day. The news had just come that the President was dead, and flags were out at the Consulate, and the houses of American residents, draped in black.[3] The streets were deathly languid in the heat and blaze; I went out in it all, read the dispatches, and felt heart-sick! I felt as though I ought to be at home. That night I could not sleep. The comet was shining splendidly in the sky; but it seemed like a portrait. I was homesick enough! But I made up my mind that something must be done, immediately, and that the best thing was to flee to cooler air, and the Alps. So I did; the journey being cheered by better news from home, and hopes that, after all, the President might live. Curiously enough, I have not seen one account of it yet in English; all the dispatches I have seen have been in Italian, French, and German, and you do'nt know how oddly the familiar names look; "Casa Bianca"; "Maison Blanche" &c.[4]

I do'nt know how long I shall stay here; but probably until September, if all goes well. The snow peaks, Alpine flowers, delicious milk, and quiet, please me much. A great Benedictine Abbey, founded in the twelfth century, makes rather an unusual feature in the Swiss landscape. The present building is only two hundred years old. (That "only" will show you [how] pampered with "antiquity" I have become!). There are said to be several thousand mss. in the Abbey library. I have not been to see them, having a surfeit of mss. at home! There are plenty of people here, but I think no Americans; the feet and round-hats are all English and German, I should say. I have my meals served in my own room, and so make no acquaintances. The hearty fraus and frauleins see me issuing forth for my solitary walk, and look at me curiously; I suppose they wonder what I represent! <u>Their</u> idea of entertainment seems to be to play at bowls. But there is another class, and one that interests me much—the pedestrians. Engelberg being one of the "high" places, is a point of departure for several of the favorite Passes; and early in the morning, I see the young men going by, dressed for Alpine walking, and in the evening, see others come in, their straw hats decked with Edelweiss and Alpenrosen. I envy them! If I had any one here, I would at least go over the Joch Pass to Meiringen and Interlaken. But, as it is, I have to imagine it! But I ought to be content. I can climb up to the real snow and ice every day, if I choose. Another nice feature—the artists. I find them in the most unexpected places making sketches of this magnificent scenery. An English clergyman was franticly trying to catch the afterglow with water colours, the other night! I mean the "Alpenglühen,"—that is the word, isn't it? I have had to make a terrible jump from Italian to German in three days!

Give my love to your Mother, and Father; and to Will. Tell Kate I received her letter, and shall write to her before very long. But I am not writing many letters this summer. Although I am at Engelberg, my address is,

"Care Sebastian Crivelli & Co.
Lucerne. Switzerland."

They are the bankers, and they forward.

I have one rather hard blow, in connection with your engagement; it puts me back on the line of an aunt of Colonel Hay![5] That is something of a cross, but I shall bear it with dignity! I wish you would send me a "Tribune" now and then, while Colonel Hay is editor.

—Clara writes that you are looking remarkably well. Send me the next good picture you have taken; and one of Flora, when she will permit it. And now, with much love to you both, I will mail this; and go up to the "snow" for some Alpine flowers.

Always affectionately yours,
C. F. Woolson.

Notes

1. Portions also appear in Benedict/Voices, 86 and Benedict/CFW, 259–60.

2. Woolson is referring to Mather's mother, Georgiana Woolson Mather, and her own mother.

3. President James Garfield was shot on July 2, 1881; he died on Sept. 19, 1881. Woolson may also be referring to an 1880 photo of Halley's Comet taken by French astronomer Nicolas Camille Flammarion (1842–1925) that showed the Comet's pointing away from the sun.

4. Casa Bianca, Maison Blanche: White House.

5. Flora Stone Mather's sister was John Hay's wife, Clara. Woolson often mocks her own role as an aunt.

To Hjalmar Hjorth Boyesen (Virginia)

Care Sebastian Crivelli & Co.
Lucerne. Switzerland
August 9th, [1881?]

Dear Sir.

I have just received the notice of my "Southern Sketches" (in the Midsummer number of "Scribner's") and it has given me so much pleasure that I feel like writing a little private letter to say so.[1]

I am especially pleased that "Miss Elizabetha" and "Felipa" were commended, because they are favorites of mine. The little word of censure about "Felipa" was quite deserved; I yielded, there, to temptation. You are right, too, as to the over-touch in "Rodman." As to the way my southern girls talk, I do not think it is over-drawn. They do—or did—talk in that way, when excited. Not all southern girls, of course; but the daughters, for instance, of those old Virginia and Carolina families who ruled their own neighborhoods and their own State in the old days. Just before the breaking out of the rebellion, I was sent from Cleveland to an old-fashioned French school in New York,—that of Madame Chegaray. At that period, almost all her boarding-pupils were southern girls, and they were so entirely new to me.—I was so fascinated by their ways and grandiloquent style of talking, that I spent most of my time listening to, and looking at, them. Later, when I went south myself I met some of these girls again, and I noticed in what they said (as well as in the stories other southern ladies told me), that the same old grandiloquence had survived through all their sorrows and sufferings. I do not deny that there was absurdity in much of this old-time rhetoric. I have given it as it was, intentionally. But, they lived up to it in one way. The very girls who, at school, had grandly called themselves "The Daughters of Carolina," (to the astonishment of the new western pupil, who had never thought of styling herself "The Daughter of Ohio"), proved themselves her daughters indeed, when the time came, suffering with her—although mistakenly—every privation.

That you call the book "convincing," gives me much gratification, because I tried hard to be accurate. It is much easier, I think, to imagine than to simply describe, and I called myself back many times, when at work on those sketches, from tempting exaggerations and fancies, to plain fact.

I do not know to whom I am writing; but the cordial and appreciative tone of the notice has made me feel like sending a letter immediately across the ocean to say "Thank You."

Yours very Truly,
C. F. Woolson.

Notes

1. The notice of Woolson's *Rodman the Keeper: Southern Sketches* (1880) appeared in the "Culture and Progress" section of *Scribner's* in Aug. 1880. Boyesen, who reviewed the book anonymously, criticized the title character of "Felipa" when she claims that she wears boy's trousers because she does not want to be despised by refusing to wear what had belonged to a dead friend.

To Edmund Clarence Stedman (Columbia)

Engelberg. Switzerland
[Aug. 11, 1881][1]

Dear Mr Stedman.

Your letter, written at sea, was a most delightful one. It reached me at Rome, where I stayed, very obstinately, until the 4th of June, reducing everybody at home to serious preparations for my funeral. Never believe anyone who tells you that winter is the best time in Rome, or early spring. May is the best time. Enchanted and fascinated as I was all winter, I felt, in May, as if I was for the first time seeing the real beauty of everything, from the Palace of the Caesars down to the Claude Lorrain in the Doria gallery. You do'nt get the right atmosphere on the Campagna, the ruins, or even the city itself, until then. Well—I might go raving on through pages, and yet not say the tenth part; so I will stop. Descriptions are stupid unless you have seen the places yourself, and do'nt need them. Then, they are enchanting. I believe you have not been in Rome; all I can say is—Go.

My sister, who came down from Paris for the Carnival, and Miss Clark who spent the winter with me, went northward the first day of April. I then left the hotel, and tried a little "Roman housekeeping" for two months. I took a small "apartment" high up in an old Roman house, and set up my "household gods,"—principally photographs (unmounted) of all the pictures and statues which have especially impressed me, put up with four pins! I must not forget a little kettle for five o'clock tea, of which (both tea & kettle), I have become very fond. It was all so funny and so Roman! My landlady, who attended to the meals, was an English governess of middle age, employed by all Italian grandees of Rome; but as she was out all day, I was left mistress of the operatic black-eyed maid, with a boddice & flower in her hair, who could not speak a word of English. The result was that I had to brush up my old "Chegaray" Italian, which, however, did not concern itself with such matter as "more butter,"—"make the coffee," "bring the lamp." In addition to my little parlor, I had a vine-covered loggia on the roof, from which I could see the Campagna, & Soracte.—Well—I had to come away at last, & did so with a real pain at the heart. Before leaving the subject however, let me say that I saw a good deal of the Danas, of Boston, who had an apartment in Rome this winter, and that Mrs Dana was much interested in hearing of you. When your letter came, she asked many questions about it, and came to see the picture you sent. She knew you when a baby, I believe, and once made for you a blue silk net, at your Mother's request. She has always wanted to see you, since; and keeps watch of your work. It is the R. H. Dana family. They are ever so nice, all of them. I hope you will be more interested in the net than Dr Dix was in the flannel bag of his infancy.[2] We met him at the White Sulphur Springs one summer, & Mother told him that she carried him all the way from Cooperstown to New York in a green flannel bag,—which his mother had made for him on account of the great cold,—when he was six months old. He was not impressed with the incident.—At Florence I was at last able to get your "Poe," & the "Whitman" again, and the Gifford poems, and "Ye of ye Poet Chaucer."[3] Florence has the only modern library worth anything, in Italy. I enjoyed reading the "Whitman" again, although I really know nothing of his work. The "Poe" is admirable. The best thing I have ever read on that erratic genius, without exception. You know what I think of your critical writings. I am an enthusiastic admirer of them all. I see, in a late newspaper, that you are announced for some articles on "American Poetry." What does that mean? Are they introductory? Or has your spirit failed when it came to writing of the young Moderns, in single articles? I hope not. I want to see what you will say.—In some respect, I have to bear a good many privations over here; one is the not being able to see our magazines, save now & then. It is quite impossible in the life I lead. As it is, my mail matter is still coming from Rome—the envelopes black with crossed-out addresses; four, before they reach Engelberg. The Gifford poems I liked greatly. But what charmed me most of all was the "Chaucer." It seems to me as perfect a thing in its way as you have ever written. I have no copy; but its melody rings in my memory still. It ought to be brought out in a little book—(with a few others if you please), with one perfect little illustration. I see—also in the newspapers—that you have had a Concord poem. I shall write Kate Mather to send it to me. Did you know, by the way, that my nephew Sam, Kate's brother, ~~is~~ was engaged to Miss Stone, the sister of Mrs Hay? Clara and I, Sam's only maternal aunts, are much pleased. I have always liked Miss Stone especially. The only objection I have is, that it puts me back upon the line of an aunt of Colonel Hay! Now as you & Colonel Hay are on the same line, and you are a grandfather, that makes me a relative of the fourth generation back! There is something essentially comical to me, by the way, in your attempting to be a grandfather.

Clara writes from Cleveland (she went home in April) that meeting Mrs Hay at a reception, that lady told her that she had sat next you at a dinner given to Barret (that eminently meritorious but ungifted-by-genius actor, whom you literary men, for some mysterious reason, persist in admiring), and that you had said some very nice things about "Mrs Benedict." Clara wishes me to "tell Mr Stedman," when I write, that she thinks it is "lovely" of him to remember her, and "say nice things" about her, as he has done "more than once." I obey. She is very well, now that she is at home again. I presume she will spend the winter in New York, so that Clare can attend school there; she was not pleased with the Paris school. They promise me to come over in the Spring for an English summer.

I left Florence late,—the 7th of July; I had expected to spend the summer in Venice; but the great heat that came down upon Italy suddenly, and the effect of the news from home, drove me away—to higher air. For two days in Florence we believed that the President was dead; and I could not describe to you, in a letter, the strange feeling of those days in the languid heat, with the dispatches, and the flags draped in black, and the sleepless nights with the great comet blazing over-head. Better news came, & I started, rushing northward as fast as trains could carry me, buying papers all along the route, & reading the latest word, in Italian, French, and German, as I rushed through Turin, Geneva, & Lucerne. The familiar names, like "White House," looked so strangely! "Casa Bianca." "Maison Blanche."—Thank God, the news grows better & better each day.—Do you know where Engelberg is? It is about six hours from Lucerne, high in the Alps. The picture I send does not show how thick & white the snow is. The valley is 3500 feet up, to begin with. It is only six miles long, & surrounded entirely by these grand mountains. The Benedictine Abbey, founded in the 12th century, is the feature of the valley. We have glaciers, Alpine water falls, Alpine flowers, Alpine milk. I am comfortably settled & have my meals served in my own room, so I escape the usual acquaintances of mere propinquity. The air, coming from all this snow, is delicious. I gather flowers on the edge of snowbanks ten feet deep! I am extremely well here, and shall probably stay into September. Then, back to Italy.

I was quite excited by the intelligence in a recent letter from my cousin Charlotte Cooper, that you were expected in Cooperstown. I wish I could have flown over for a few days! Did you like it, & whom did you see? Is'nt it a ~~deal~~ dear little place? I sometimes think I shall come home & end my days there. Mother always wanted to go back there to live, & even Father, although a pronounced New Hampshire man, had a great love for the village. "We," of the old inhabitants, do'nt like its being turned into a summer resort. "We" used to be important. Now we are only "the villagers." I wonder if you saw my cousins, the Coopers? Three quiet old ladies they are now (four, including Mrs Phinney), but to me the dearest people in the world. They are all in grief now, over the death of young Sutherland Irving, the husband of my young cousin, Susie Phinney. Possibly you knew of him.—he was an Insurance Broker in New York. I suppose you visited the John Worthingtons, &, in that case, you were upon part of the old garden of "Deacon Place," my grandfather's house. The old stone house on the corner; the gardens are back to the next street.[4]—I am glad you liked the Worthingtons. John has a great deal of humor; but as he has lived there quietly in Cooperstown, it has not been appreciated as it might have been in a larger society. I do not know them well. Clara was extremely fond of Jennie Cooper, John's first wife, & can scarcely speak of her, even now, without tears.—How many many hours I have spent, rowing my dear Mother up & down the lake! She was never tired of it; she loved the outline of each hill. We often went off for the day, and then I would have a little picnic dinner for her, & make coffee, on one of the points—

Your letter was a treat. Why did we never go to Nassau? Because Mother always wanted to be within railway reach of my brother. You know I have one brother, & Mother was devotedly fond of her "boy," & never would go where she could not be "within reach" of him. In the meanwhile, Mr Charly went twice to Europe & twice to California! But that made no difference,—Mother, on her side, would always be "within reach." My dearest Mother—what a loving heart she had! It is the greatest comfort to me to think that she is freed from all pain, and care, & trouble, forever. Charly is now in Southern California. His health is not strong, & the climate there, he says, is very delicious. I really think he is the brightest of all our family. That is saying something, as I consider my sister Clara ~~something~~ rather remarkable in that direction. I wish you knew her better. She has the most delicate flashing sort of wit, sometimes.—

Your descriptions made me a little homesick for my Florida beach. I must go down to those islands some day.—It was a wise thing for you to do. Do it again when winter comes round. How are you? I hope better.—"A little girl-baby"—. Dear me! Mrs Stedman looks about as much like a "grandmother" as a rose does! Give her my love.

Thanks for your very kind offer of a letter to Mr Lowell. But my courage has failed me. I should never present it. I hope to spend next summer in London; but, much as I should like to know Mr Lowell, I do not think I could send him a letter. If I could meet him "by chance," I should be delighted. I am not making any efforts towards people & society, over here. The little I have seen of "society" (in Rome) frightens me somewhat. I do'nt know how to "hold my own" with people of that sort. And yet it seems very necessary to "hold" it; otherwise they bite you in small pieces! They are so quick; & heartless; & clever!—Now you would find Roman Society amusing, I feel sure.—You would take the best of it, & let the rest go.—

I do not expect any answer to this letter, as you especially said you should be too closely occupied, for a long time, to write again. I quite understand this. My letters are the bane of my life; I love to get letters, & enjoy writing them (some of them) but literally cannot find the time. To show you that I am sincere, I give you no address. One of these days, when your book is out, I will send one.—

I have recently a letter from Mr Mabie, in answer to a sketch I sent to the "Christian Union,"—which paper they have sent me, as a compliment, for more than a year. He spoke of you, & so I know you know him. Will you therefore tell him, the next time you see him, that his cordial words gave me great gratification, and are very encouraging to a person completely cut off from all home literary news, all home emulation & companionship of that kind. And they are a great deal, after all. It is difficult to get on without them.—I have not heard, or spoken, a word of English, since the first of July. And shall not hear, or speak it, for weeks to come.

"Anne," I suppose, is to appear in England. The Harpers have written that Messrs. Low & Co. London, have requested permission to bring it out in book form if I was willing. I was! When it is within covers, & you can read it all together, I really should like to know what you think of it. But, probably, you would not tell me. Come to think of it—do you care for novels? At this moment, I cannot recall your ever having spoken, with real interest, of a single one!

Well—I must say good-by. Best wishes of all kinds. I predict that you are immensely fond of that "little girl."

Yours Always Most Sincerely,
C. F. Woolson.

You don't know how much I have enjoyed the "Emerson" over here. And <u>every body</u> borrows it & reads it eagerly.

Notes

1. The dating is Columbia's.
2. Probably Dr. Morgan Dix (1827–1908), rector of Trinity Church, New York City. His father, John Adams Dix (1798–1879), was born in New Hampshire and relocated to Cooperstown.
3. Stedman eventually published his essays on American poets in *The Poets of America* (1885). Gifford is British poet William Gifford (1726–1856).
4. Woolson based her novel, *The Old Stone House,* published under the name Anne March in 1872, on this residence.

To Barnett Phillips (NYPL)

Care Sebastian Crivelli & Co.
Lucerne. Switzerland
August 16th, [1881?]

Dear Sir.

I have received from Messrs. D. Appleton and Co., the New York Times notice of my "Southern Sketches," with your line written on the margin; both have given me much pleasure.[1]

I am especially pleased by what you say of the appreciation of southern women which the stories show, because I have felt for them not only a deep sympathy, but also much personal liking. They charmed me in my school-days; and, later, when I went south myself, the interest increased. Their quick warm-hearted impulsiveness, their pride, their generosity, the grand ways and lofty phrases which were quite natural to them, their soft unhurrying voices, and sweet southern pronunciation—all these were new, and made a strong impression upon me, an impression no doubt strengthened, or rather deepened, by the bitter sufferings they had—many of them—gone through.

Northerners have complained that they have not been well received at the south, that they have met only hostility and coldness. I must then have been especially fortunate, for throughout the years I spent there, (northerner and republican as I am,) I met nothing in the way of hostility, and, very often, my Mother and myself were the recipients of a hospitality which seemed to us,—strangers as we were—remarkable.

I see you know the South. You have divined the scene of "Bro." And also of "Old Gardiston." I used to linger in Charleston every spring and autumn, on my way to and from Florida; I became fond of the little old city, with its jealous high walls shutting in the gardens, its two rivers, its beautiful harbor, its ruins and its undying pride. The old Charleston library, where there are so many fine old books and no new ones, was one of my haunts; a complete contrast to the libraries to which I had been accustomed. But I liked even better the little country-libraries, like the one mentioned in "Up in the Blue Ridge." I should have enjoyed saying more about the old-time literary taste of the South, to which your review alludes. My knowledge of it—such as it is—comes from an acquaintance with some of the old gentlemen of South Carolina and Virginia,—the most courtly and charming old gentlemen, when talking with ladies, that I have ever met. They quoted as you describe— Pope and Addison. I had to read all those old books over, secretly, in order to be able to breathe their atmosphere! I ended in feeling a sort of affection for it, however.

I attempted, in those Sketches, merely a few outlines from the South of to-day. But that "To-Day" is already departing. In another twenty years, I think the war of 1861 will be more a thing of the past than that of 1776; because we shall not want to remember it.

I am much attached to the South, its scenery, and its climate; the latter I am homesick for, even here. When I come home, I shall go down there again, to see if the beaches and pine-barrens have as much charm for me, after Florence and Rome, as they had before. I think they will. I spent three months in Florence this spring; and I hope to pass this coming winter in Rome.

I have written at greater length than I intended; but it is because I feel sure that you know the South, and are attached to its old-time atmosphere (the pleasant parts of it) now almost gone. In addition, the author of the sketches was very much pleased by the kind words of the Times about her ~~book~~ work in other respects; and sends her thanks for them.

Yours Truly,
C. F. Woolson.

Notes

1. The review of *Rodman the Keeper: Southern Sketches* appeared in the *New York Times,* June 11, 1880: 3. The stories Woolson names were collected in this volume.

To Henry Mills Alden (WRHS/Benedict)[1]

(The address continues "Care Sebastian Crivelli & Co.
Lucerne. Switzerland")
Engelberg
Aug. 23^{d}, [1881?]

Dear Mr Alden.

I have received your letter of July 30th, and enclose the "Coppet" story.[2] I have two things to say about it. First—as to its origin, &c. I spent two months in Geneva last year, and found there a library especially rich in French literature of the last century,—the memoirs, letters, &c of that gay witty much-writing society that preceded the Revolution. I read a mass of it. Later, the whole forty volumes of Sainte-Beuve. Then I went out to Coppet and spent an afternoon in Corinne's old chateau and garden. This may seem an elaborate explanation of so slight an affair as the story enclosed; but I want you to know the "atmosphere" that produced it.—I finished my 18th century studies with a series of articles on Madame de Stael and the Neckers, contributed, year before last, to the "Revue des deux Mondes" by M. d'Haussonville; this gentleman has access to the archives of Coppet, as he is a grand-nephew (I think) of Madame de Stael.[3] He writes well (although he is not the "Sainte-Beuve" he aspires to be), and one of his articles ends with the little apostrophe which I have put, as a quotation, into the mouth of my poet. Who wrote the little verse d'Haussonville quotes, I do not know. It sounds like de Musset. (Or is it "Musset"? There has been so much said lately about the use of the "De." As in "De Tocqueville.") In my Geneva reading, I came across a good deal of Ronsard,—the minstrel poetry in old-time French. The two lines "Ford" quotes, are from the following verse, which seemed to me very nice and quaint: "Le temps s'en va, le temps s'en va, ma Dame Las! le temps, non; mais nous en allons, et tôt serons étendus sou la lame; et des amours desquelles non parlons. Quand serons morts, n'en sera plus nouvelle; Pour aimez-moi pendent qu'êtes belle."

Ronsard 1552

One more item: I have quoted from you. Once you wrote "Nothing ever happens any more." The phrase struck me as very expressive. I have ~~often~~ used it often since, in conversation; and now have put it into the mouth of my "Mrs Winthrop."[4]

The second thing I have to say is that the story may be too long for your purposes; I suppose it will fill sixteen or eighteen pages of the maga. Of course you must not give yourself the slightest trouble about it. Send it back, if unavailable. I presume I can get it in elsewhere, especially if I divide it. I have sent to America for some American stamps, but they have not yet come. If you find the story too long, or do'nt like it, will you kindly return the Ms. in a closed envelope, & I will send you the postage you use as soon as I[5]

how much pressure has been brought to bear upon—what shall I call it?—society,—about this light delicate highly-finished style of writing that holds itself far above subject, incident, and plot. It is the worship of manner; not matter. As it happens, almost all my friends,—I do'nt mean writers, but simply the readers,—greatly and strongly admire it. The funny part is (to me) that I admire it too! I really believe I admire it and appreciate it as much as any of them, if not more. I enjoy the skill displayed, with a real intensity. Only—it seems to me that there are other ways of writing. And that the matter is more than the manner, though the skies fall!

And the magazine is a triumph and marvel of perfection. A number of English people I have met have spoken of it with astonished enthusiasm. I like the English. They are so honest. Fifty times slower than we [are?] And perhaps fifty times more "solid!"

Notes

1. The letter is pasted in Woolson's *Dorothy*, New York: Harper's, 1896.

2. Woolson is referring to "At the Château of Corrine," which was published in *Harper's New Monthly Magazine* in Oct. 1887. Although this suggests that the letter was written in 1887, Woolson's time in Geneva was in 1880 and would make an 1881 date more likely. This would establish a long time between her first composition of the story and its publication.

3. Madame de Staël's parents were Jacques (1732–1804) and Suzanne Necker (1737–94). Jacques Necker was the finance minister for the French King Louis XVI. Count Joseph d'Haussonville (1809–84) published *Revue des deux Mondes* (*Review of Both Worlds*) in 1867.

4. Ford and Mrs. Winthrop are characters from "At the Château of Corinne." The French from Pierre de Ronsard translates as follows: "Time is fleeting, time is fleeting, Madam. Alas! Time, no, but we are passing away, and soon shall be laid out upon the sword the loves of which we speak. When we shall be dead, nothing more shall be new. Therefore, love me while you are beautiful."

5. The rest of this passage is illegible because of the paste in *Dorothy*. The order in the remaining excerpts is unclear.

To Boston *Traveller*, Editor (McGill)

Sorrento. Italy
Dec. 3^{d}, [1881]
Editor "Boston Traveller"

Dear Sir.

Your letter has been forwarded from place to place, and has finally reached me, here; I have been coming slowly Southward, stopping in Turin, Milan, Padua, Venice, Florence, & Rome,—Naples. As you will see, it is too late to write anything for the "Series Supplement." And it would, in any case, be rather hard to get up the home Xmas feeling, which is connected with snow, ice, evergreens, & cheery fires—on this sunny shore, with the air of our June, miles of oranges and roses, and not even a remembrance of winter.

With thanks for the invitation, and best wishes for the "Supplement," I am,

Yours Truly,
C. F. Woolson.

To Harriet Benedict Sherman (WRHS/Benedict)[1]

[1881?]

I am afraid to think how tall Clare will be when I see her. Have you ever thought that Clare is like me; mentally, I mean. I have always noticed it, &, now that she is older, the resemblance is marked. She has my reticence, at least I had it at her age outwardly, as she has. And at present, I have it inwardly, just the same,[2] but have covered it outwardly with a sort of manner, which I have learned gradually as the years have passed. I never could bear to hurt any one's feelings. Acutely sensitive myself, I have always been silent rather than say anything that I thought might hurt any one. Or at least I have said something else—not anything sharp or blunt. Clare has the same trait. I repeat, it is extraordinary how much she is like me! I see myself right over again as I was at thirteen (I mean mentally). I shall never care to have her study as hard as I did. I am longing to see her. She and I are great "cronies" and talk long hours together with the greatest mental satisfaction. We are thoroughly "simpatica," as the Italians say, Clare and I.

Notes

1. Fragment pasted in *European Backgrounds,* Edinburg: Andrew Elliot, 1922.

2. This opening portion of the letter survives only in Benedict/Abroad, 12. The remainder of the letter is also in Benedict.

To George Pomeroy Keese (WRHS/Benedict)[1]

January 1882

I am glad you called upon Mr Stedman, & was much amused with your description of the visit.

He ~~generally~~ often calls me "Parthenia." I never knew why. But it is true that he knows all the literary people, ladies as well as men, & takes an interest in them which is so real & generous, & above everything like small jealousy, that they all like him. I only know him in a "literary" way. But, in that way, we are great friends. I met him first in Florida, when I was scarcely known at all as a beginner at writing, even;—& he immediately took the kindest interest in all I was doing, or, rather, attempting to do. He is the most loyal of friends, as well as a very outspoken one. At least so he seems to me. I never forget the people who were interested & helpful in those days of beginning; & never shall. I have now a good many literary friends. But, agreeable as they are, they will never oust those who came forward first.

[Mr R. H. Dana ("Two Years Before the Mast," you know) died this month in Rome. I was much attached to him. He was the finest conversationist for his age, I have ever met. I see he was not an old man—not seventy—but he seemed old. I do'nt mean feeble; but majestically old; old of the "old school." . . .]

[Sorrento
January 1882[2]

I am very well here. The weather is divine. All the fruit trees are in blossom, and the woods are full of wild violets and anemones. It is just the weather we had in Mentone in March, so this climate is about six weeks earlier. As the winter did not begin until the first of January, you will see that the season has not been severe. It consisted in the necessity for a little fire in the evenings now and then—more for the cheer than for absolute need; as one has it at home sometimes in October.] The sun shines all day long, & never stops. But it is not the clear strong sunshine of the South of France. It is a softer kind. There is a mild moisture in the air. At Mentone the sunshine was like steel. I like this better. It suits my throat perfectly; & I have forgotten here that I have a throat. The scene spread out before my eyes, whether at home or when I am out of doors, is, as you know, so beautiful that the adjectives of all languages have been exhausted upon it. So I will not try to picture it with mine. I have been fortunate enough to see an eruption of Vesuvius; not one of the grand ones; still, a fine sight. Now the old mountain seems to have gone to sleep again.

[I take long walks here, in the afternoon.] Yesterday I went up the mountain behind the town, in the high rocky hill, rather—hill-ridge—which forms the backbone of this long point stretching out into the sea. The little path wound up through two gray old stone villages, each with its big church, of course! (priests-power) although the peasants' homes are very poor; I went through meadows that were fairly abloom with violets, large purple anemones & little lilac lilies, millions of them. At last at the top, perched on the higher point, I came to the "Deserto," an old monestery, now turned into an orphan asylum. (How furious the priests are over these changes!) The view from there was the most beautiful water-view I ever saw. Capri has an outline which is beyond anything in loveliness. The whole Bay, of course, & the South Coast of Italy towards Sicily. I came down another way, through two more villages.—Well—good by. Love to all. I hope you are in good health this month.

Yours always,
C. F. Woolson.

Notes

1. Portions of this letter are pasted into Edmund Clarence Stedman, *Victorian Poets*, Boston: Osgood, 1876, and reprinted in Benedict/CFW, 30. Bracketed passages appear only in CFW.

2. These last paragraphs, also written to Keese, are in WRHS/Benedict, pasted into Woolson's *The Front Yard and Other Italian Stories* (New York: Harper's, 1895) and in Benedict/CFW, 261–62. Bracketed passages appear only in CFW.

To Henry James (Houghton)

Hotel Bristol
Sorrento
Feb. 12th, [1882]

Dear Mr James.

I was much mystified by those two letters of yours. The solution, which slowly presented itself—that you had forgotten on the 21st that you had written me two weeks earlier—was rather mortifying. But I know how full your life is of all sorts of things—engagements, enjoyments, society, duties, traveling, "people," the plans for, &, more than all, the constant accomplishment of work like yours—it is a marvel to me how you can carry them all on together as you do. "If we will take the good we find, asking no questions, we shall have heaping measure"—you know; so I took my "good," & made it as "heaping as possible.[1] Two letters and a photograph heap quite well.

But the real truth is—I simply forgave you. It does'nt make much difference what you do as an individual—one has to forgive the author of "Hawthorne" and the "Portrait." In the same way you might have said the most horrible things in Florence & Rome, & I am afraid I should have forgiven them on account of the voice. I have always been critical about voices (of late years there is of course a second reason), &, when I find one to my mind, my temper becomes beatific.[2]—If you did'nt say any very horrible things in Florence & Rome, you are mentioning a few from Washington—when you tell me my letter was full of "amiable elements"! I do'nt think a letter could be described in a more depressing way.

The motive of that second letter of yours, I have of course divined. When you wrote on the 6th you had been only a week at home, & had not been seized by homesickness (that anomaly of words is your fault, not mine); but on the 21st you were full in its deadly clutches, & you wrote, I have no doubt, to every foreign friend you have in the world, so that the long snowy winter of exile might be broken by the arrival of the answers, one by one. I presume the very postage-stamps have been like old-masters to you. The head of Victoria is dearest, probably. Then, the mythological figures of Paris. The moustache of Umberto is, I hope, third on the list, because you ought not to care for people who are so thick-skinned as to spend winters in Switzerland & Germany.[3] But I fancy that first homesickness has abated, somewhat. And you are so Americanized already—oh yes, you are; you address this ~~le~~ last letter with my first and last name & a middle initial!

Your being in Washington interests me. I should have said that you would have preferred Boston or New York. Washington society is more national; it is not the limited (your word) or local (my word) circle of Cambridge-Harvard & Westchester county tradition & antecedents. I do not say that limited is your word; but the Boston ladies do, it seems. In Florence I heard a part of a Boston lady's letter read aloud, & in it was this: "I am afraid she is awfully 'limited'—to use Harry James' word." Day before yesterday, by the way, I heard a portion of a Washington letter read aloud (a young lady's letter), & in it was this: "It has been extremely quiet here—more quiet than it has been for years. But we have got Henry James,—who has just arrived." I wanted to say—"And now of course it will immediately become hilarious—he is such a turbulently gay, eager, excitable person." But I hope you are finding something to like over there. I note that tepid little line in your letter—about seeing "plenty of people" in New York,—but "no one in particular." But there are a number of very particular people indeed in Boston—so I have always been given to understand—& perhaps they have branches in Washington. Perhaps too that New York line was a "subterfuge." I might go on & say that I shall always be looking out for subterfuges after this. But it would'nt be true, & I could never live up to it. So I had better not pretend. I am not clever—as you must have seen for yourself before this,—& I have given up trying to learn the manner of it. It was of no use.

Washington is very pretty in the Spring. They have wonderful flowering trees there, like no others I ever saw. Arlington too at that season is something to remember. But you won't remember it. In this connection let me say that I did not fully express myself about that southern beach & "inspirational" headland—to which you refer. I said that you would not believe in them. But what I meant was—not that you would not, or did not, believe in their existence, or even in their beauty—for you have shown in your writings that you appreciate both. But that you did not believe that they could ever be more to you than so much horizontal sand, well smoothed, & so much perpendicular limestone, well set-up; whereas *I* believe that, if you could see them under the right conditions, they would be more. I did not fully express myself, but cut off my thread—as I have done before—for fear you would think it "unimportant"—that terrible word of yours! I do'nt deny, you know, that generally it *is* unimportant.

No—you do not love your native land. It is plainly evident. One of Cherbuliez' cleverest divinations—perhaps you remember it?—is "Quand les femmes aiment quelque chose, cherchez bien, vous trouverez que sous la chose qu'elles aiment, il y a *quelqu'un*" & it has occurred to me that this may not be an exclusively feminine trait, &, that under your dislike for America, there may be—*quelqu'un*.[4] Or perhaps it is the converse. But, do you know, though I am an American of the interior of New Hampshire (my birthplace), an American of the Western Reserve of Ohio, I quite understand why you feel as you do. It is owing to personal characteristics more than to the accident of the sort of life you have led,—although the latter has of course intensified the former. But if you had never left the banks of the Maumee, you would still have been, dumbly, an "alienated American" (I suppose you have no idea where the Maumee is!)[5]

I see the "Century" announces a biographical notice of you, with portrait. A "biographical notice"—if only the biographer of Hawthorne could write it, we should see some fine things.[6] I should be sorry for the biographed! I have often noticed your keen judgment of your own work. I do not always agree with it; it is sometimes too keen. I mean by that that you do not always come down fully into the place of the reader—we will say the best reader, for you would'nt accept the ordinary ones. The portrait will show the pretty American girl of seventeen, whom I met at Engelberg, how correct is her idea of you. She had asked if I knew this & that literary personage, & came after a while to you. "How does he look?" she inquired. "I have always fancied that he was very slender, very fastidious & aristocratic-looking, that he spoke in a very low voice, & had those cool sarcastic eyes, & a lovely straight nose, you know." I told her that was precisely you. You ask about Engelberg; I arrived there July 10th, & remained until Sept. 16th. I did not know of course that you were within a thousand miles. But, even if you were, our missing each other was not remarkable. Our meeting would have been that. I have never had such a sense of being hidden, merged, lost, as in this crowded compact little Europe.

I am wondering if you have seen Mr G. W. Curtis—the champion who used his graceful lance for you in Harper's so many times, during the Hawthorne tournament. And I am wondering if the rumor of a play you are said to have written for Willie Edouin is true. And I am resigned in advance to the tidings that you have written one for Lawrence Barrett—that eminently respectable actor whom all our American literary men persist in admiring.[7] I never could understand why. (If you see any subjunctives wrong here or anywhere, please remember how little they ~~knew~~ cared for subjunctives on the Western Reserve! I have always been awe-struck by your use of them—it is so infallible.)

My kind friend Mr R. H. Dana has passed away. They have made his grave in the beautiful cemetery at Rome. During my last stay in Florence—in October—he was so good as to talk to me quite often in the evenings. He told me of the old Transcendental days,—of Emerson as he was at that time; of Thoreau, whom he ridiculed highly; of Margaret Fuller, whom he called "Mag"! & many others. I had known the times and the people only from books. More than once—while listening to him—I caught myself smiling over a remembrance of your group, gather round "Flaxman's attenuated outlines."[8]—Your poor serious soul-to-soul enemy, Miss Phelps—I wonder if you saw her. I have recently listened to a rather intimate description of the Miss Howard ("One Summer") of whom you spoke in Rome as the writer-ess who wished to make your acquaintance; & I am sure you would not like her. However, I had better be careful; you like that Miss Fletcher![9] But you do not want to know the little literary women. Only the great ones—like George Eliot. I am not barring myself out here, because I do not come in as a literary woman at all, but as a sort of—of admiring aunt. I think that expresses it.

Thanks for the "Portrait." I have seen quite a number of the criticisms that have appeared, & have been interested in them because of one point.

But first—what a splendid success for a book of that grade—a book of such delicately fine workmanship—to have every journal, from the London dailies down through all the magazines to the newspapers of Ohio, bringing out a notice of it as an important event of the day. No other novelist has this but you. (It is true that you do not appreciate the newspapers of Ohio.) You know what I think of the rank of your work; it entertains me much to watch the careless public advancing toward my opinion.

The point I note is—that, over the "Portrait," our American critics have come to an entirely new, & this time I think permanent, tone about you. Their first tone was unmitigated praise. I don't think you appreciated, over there among the chimney-pots, the laudation your books received in America, as they came out one by one. (We little fish did! We little fish became worn to skeletons owing to the constant admonitions we received to regard the beauty, the grace, the incomparable perfections of all sorts & kinds of the proud salmon of the pond; we ended by hating that salmon.) It was but human, however, that this laudation should not go on forever. In addition—as you were all the time advancing—it began to occur to these critics that you were going by even their encouragement; that possibly too you did not estimate at its true worth the importance of their help and sympathy. They began, in short, to be jealous. Your "Hawthorne" gave them their opportunity; your "Washington Square" did not decrease it. That was their second tone.—The "Portrait" has now brought them to a third. The first—, flattering as it was, was never without the accompanying chord that you were a young fellow; your talent your style, your this & that, were marvelous in a young fellow &c. They looked forward "confidently" to your "future." But, after all, they would have preferred to continue looking forward. It gave a pleasant sense of patronage. But—in the "Portrait"—this future is more than suspected to have become the present. They see it & cannot deny it. They do'nt like it. The whole tone is different. With ill-humor here & there according to their tempers,—with more or less clearness according to their powers of perception, they are virtually acknowledging, one and all, in these criticisms, that you are no longer the coming man, but that (whether for good or for ill) you have "arrived." To acknowledge this has been for some of them like little Rosier's selling his bibelots, or rather as that sacrifice of his struck Isabel—"as if he had had all his teeth drawn." One or two remark, gloomily, that you have founded a new school of novel-writing, and get out of it in that way; because they are free, of course, to not admire the school.—I notice that they have all brought out their very best language for the occasion; there has been a great display of theory & choice of epithet.—I have'nt yet seen the review in parallel—whatever that may mean—of you and Mr Howells, in the "Atlantic"; it is on the way over.[10] But, as I have never been able to comprehend how anyone could possibly compare you two, I shall probably not care for it when it comes. I like to think that you like Mr Howells,—he has such a warm generous feeling for you. Men, as a general thing, are not nice to each other. I told you that once before, & you laughed it to scorn. But it is true.

And now I am going on. On the subject of your book, I do'nt have my usual remembrance that you will think what I say "unimportant." It is'nt that I think it in the least important, but that I don't care whether it is or not; I am amusing myself—if you like. Your books are one of the entertainments of my life, & I cannot give up talking about them just to please the author. But he can always evade hearing what I have to say by not writing to me. And I shall not quarrel with you, if he does so evade. I shall go on amusing myself;—I shall talk them over with someone else.

I have come slowly to the conclusion that the "Portrait" is the finest novel you have written. "Slowly," because I so much like the others, & hate to desert old friends. I did'nt completely yield until I had read the last two chapters. Then I had to. The scene between Goodwood & Isabel at the end is, in my opinion, by far the strongest scene of the kind you have given to the public. It has the naturalness which all you write possesses, but it has in addition a force (which real life does contain, I think)—a force which you have rather held back—at least the expression of it—in your other books; purposely—as I have always supposed. I wanted to see it let out a trifle. And here it is let out. I did'nt want much. But that little I did want. Now, I am satisfied.

Goodwood is a marked figure. It suits him that you have not described him minutely; he has no minuteness to describe. But you have made us feel his strength, his narrow strength, his unwasted concentrated strength. We feel him on the page as we feel the living Goodwoods—we women, I mean. We do'nt always like them, or at first prefer them; but, as we grow older, & the great insincerity of life widens out all round—then we appreciate the Goodwoods. And come back to them. Only—it is generally too late.

Most men are so stupid about some women—if you know what that means! I will restate. Most men, although clear-sighted enough about many women, remain dense about the women of Isabel's temperament. A nice man, a lawyer of more than middle-age, fond of books and society in a quiet way, wrote me not long ago—"I was vexed enough when Isabel refused Warburton. He was of course preeminently the man for her,—the man with whom she would have been happy. But James, for his own purposes, preferred—" &c&c. Now see that for denseness—Warburton! Save that he was a manly man, she might as well have married Rosier.

Warburton, by the way, is capital throughout. Is it possible the English do not see how you show them up?—I know a Warburton or two—without the title & setting—& I am never weary of noticing the narrowness, yet extreme & hopeless depth, of the chasm which separates them from the almost ideally delightful man.

Nothing could be better than the Touchetts, Henrietta & her Bantling, the Countess Gemini—whose face I perfectly see—, little Rosier, & those enchanting Misses Molyneux. (Only, did they, could they, wear seal-skin jackets in summer? Because if they did, I can never stay long in England, much as I wish to. Life would'nt be to me "a vast old English garden," if that is the weather; nor could I even enjoy pulling "down the stream to Iffley, & to the slanting woods on Nuneham" if seal-skin jackets were required!)—Ralph is very touching.[11] We love Ralph. Pansy is an exquisite little creature from beginning to end. I have plenty more to say about each & all of these people. But, as one envelope wo'nt carry it all, I reserve my space for the things I most wish to mention.

I think you were mistaken in the judgment of the story you gave me, briefly, in Rome—mistaken in two points. One is Madame Merle. You thought that in the beginning she was too much described—that it gave the impression that she was to be more prominent than she really becomes. I do not agree with you. She looms up in the latter part of the story so darkly and powerfully—powerfully although always in a sort of haze—that for the time being she overshadows Isabel, & one cares more for her than for the younger woman. The touch that does it is given when the Countess says—"And the end of it is that he is tired of her. And what is more, to-day she knows it." Life holds no deeper tragedy than that. I have never believed that bad people suffered any the less because they were bad.—And, beside Osmond, Mme Merle is almost good! Who can help feeling for her when she buries her face in her hands after Osmond's horrible—"You seem to me quite good enough," &—"Good enough to be always charming." (49th chapter). It is tragic. Yet Mme Merle herself is not tragic. The combination marks your skill.

The other point is Osmond. You said you saw him distinctly yourself, but that you doubted whether he would be distinct to your readers. Rest easy (only you are always easy!); he is. He is a more finished creation even than Grandcourt ("Daniel Deronda"); as distinct; more finely detestable; & haunting, & suffocating than George Eliot's Englishman, & overtopping him by not being emphasized by a violent death. It is real life in all its unavenging cold monotony that Osmond should go on living; & that point shows by how much you are the finer artist. But George Eliot could'nt stand it; she had to kill off her Englishman. A woman, after all, can never be a complete artist.

Such a character as Osmond's is an entirely new one in literature. Yet one sees at once, that he is completely possible. What a combination to be fine, & fastidious, & without heart! I have known one or two persons who were cultivated, & fastidious, & without heart; but they also had a brutal side—which Osmond has not. Save in the thought, which underlies his words. The whole of the 42^{d} chapter is a masterpiece.

I have a good deal to say about Isabel (I wo'nt say it all). With no character of yours have I ever felt myself so much in sympathy. I watched with much curiosity your Christina, Mme de Cintré, the Baroness, Mme de Mauves, & others,—I looked on with interest as Gertrude & Charlotte, Mary Garland, Bessie Alden, Angela, Catherine, poor Daisy & the rest, came & went. But with Isabel it has been quite different. I found myself judging her & thinking of her with a perfect sympathy, & comprehension, & a complete acquaintance as it were; everything she did & said I judged from a personal standpoint. I never said to myself as I did about Christina, for instance—"I do'nt know,—it may be so." I always knew exactly all about Isabel. (Of course I only mean that it has seemed so. Very likely you will say that my fancied knowledge is not correct.)[12]

Poor Isabel! poor idealizing imaginative girls the world over—sure, absolutely sure to be terribly unhappy. And the worst of it is that it cannot be prevented. One would suppose that a father & mother might do something. But, strangely enough, a mother is often the last person to understand her daughter; she understands her as her child, but not as the woman. And the father, if he really loves his child, ~~cannot~~ does not welcome the thought that she may ~~will~~ love someone else; he puts it as far from him as possible, & only accepts it, when it must be accepted, as a dose to be swallowed with as good a grace as he can summon. He never wants to talk about it beforehand! And thus the poor Isabels go believingly to their ruin. One gets hopeless enough sometimes (while watching them) to think that a duller mind, a more commonplace character, is the better gift. Simple goodness, & a gentle affectionate unjudging nature, seem the high prizes for a woman to gain in this lottery of life.

The Isabels—your Isabel—are ~~is~~ always so sure! She knows she is right. She cannot say so openly, because it pre-supposes the superior fineness of her own comprehension & intelligence over that of her friends & relatives. And this is the fatal pitfall; because, if she could talk it over frankly with someone, she might be saved. But she never can. She sees her Osmond in a certain light; the different light in which others see him, is only their own coarser vision. And being always self-conceited,—poor Isabel!—she at heart rather prefers this state of things. And so she moves onward proudly, securely, and often nobly according to her light—to the miserable end.

How you know her! In chapter 14, for instance, where she begins a half-explanation, saying that she can't escape—escape by separating herself,—& the rest of it—that is a wonderful & true bit of portraiture. Again in the latter part of the 21st chapter, where she sees that she might even like the limitations of Goodwood, some day far in the future—that they might then be like "a clear & quiet harbor, enclosed by a fine granite breakwater"—that is also a perfect divination. Because that is the peculiarity of such a temperament—there is no end to the visions, the imaginations. It is like the spirit which the fisherman let out of the vial, it grows into a great mist & fills the whole sky.

Poor Isabel!—(I am afraid I shall be beginning every paragraph with that)—what a cameo-like picture of her, & her sure mistake, is that visit with Mme Merle to Osmond's villa on Bellos Guardo. His method of beginning to interest her; his assumed half-embarrassment yet desire to please; his asking her how she likes his sister; his leading with him his little daughter, in her short white frock—everything so exquisitely designed & carried out to produce a certain impression,—nothing underscored, all so delicately moderate.

And then the impression, summed up in chapter 26—page 242—how perfectly one understands the effect,—sees what she saw, feels what she felt. It was precisely the sort of picture to win an Isabel. And it almost seemed to me as if you were the only man who has ever divined it.

I have some criticisms to make. Small ones. In the 21st chapter, page 196,—from the 8th line to the 20th. I do'nt altogether agree with your portraiture there. It is true that an Isabel has a great capacity for enjoying the present & the future; but it seems to me also true that the past is always safely stored in her memory. The lower floors of her tower are firm ~~although~~ & well filled, although ~~while~~ she enjoys life in an upper story.

Again, in chapter 27, page 255—I do'nt think she should say—"Poor Lord Warburton!" It seems to me that a girl of her age, & of her delicate feeling, would not say it. A woman of the world might; but even ~~for it a~~ a woman of the world ~~it~~ would feel it to be dangerous, or at least a false note—unless she intended to yield to him sometimes.[13] Women do'nt pity men (who amount to anything) to their faces! They often do it behind their backs.

(And I must be allowed to put in here my great satisfaction in the enchanting naturalness of Isabel's using the word—"Incommoded," & thinking it "a ridiculous word" even then, but being unable to change it—on page 272, chapter 29. I put it in here so as not to forget it. So long as you give us such morsels, you may behave as badly as you please otherwise. I do'nt know that you do. But you could.)

My last criticism is that you do not let us see, with any distinctness, whether Isabel really loved Osmond. She tells Mrs Touchett that she does'nt love Lord Warburton; but she does'nt tell her or anybody (if my memory serves me) that she does love~~s~~ Gilbert Osmond. You do'nt let her even tell Osmond himself—at least with the public en tiers.[14] We are therefore left to a choice between two beliefs. One is that she never really loved Osmond; it is her imagination, not her love, which has been led captive. He fills ~~her~~ an ideal. No one else did that. She thinks she loves him; but as she does not, the absence of heart-breaking, insupportable, killing grief in her heart & life, after she finds out what he really is,—is explained, & quite natural.

The other hypothesis is that she did love him. But that a distinct expression of it, & of the following agony, is left to the imagination of the reader, as things easily to be supplied,—according to the time-honored method of Mr Henry James.

Personally, you know, I would rather not have it "left." But I add, with willingness, that probably you know best.

How did you ever dare write a portrait of a lady? Fancy any woman's attempting a portrait of a gentleman! Would'nt there be a storm of ridicule! Every clerk on the Maumee river would know more about it than a George Eliot. For my own part, in my small writings, I never dare put down what men are thinking, but confine myself simply to what they do & say. For, long experience has taught me that whatever I suppose them to be thinking at any especial time, that is sure to be exactly what they are not thinking. What they are thinking, however, nobody but a ghost could know.

Feb. 23^{d}

I have been to Pompeii, Salerno, & Paestum. We drove from Salerno to Paestum on a divinely beautiful day, the air as soft as that of June at home, the sea & sky marvelously blue, & the landscape veiled in that soft haze you know. We had lunch in the cella of the Temple of Neptune. We gathered acanthus leaves. After gazing & gazing & gazing at everything—all so beautiful—I confess that I secretly purchased some very ancient coins, proffered by a very ancient man. If they turn out treasures, I will send you one, & you must pretend to believe it was not made in Naples, & buried by that mariner.

I look over my letter, & it seems very "unimportant!" But what can I do? I am not important, you know, & my letter is naturally like its writer. I shall probably stay here some time longer, although I am homesick for Rome. The violets will soon be out in the Villa Borghese! Of course you find the women over there "sympathetic." They are more sympathetic as well as more ~~sympathetic~~ intelligent than any other women in all the world. Did you see a Miss Palmer? I don't know her in the least, but I am told that several persons have picked her out for you. The one I picked out you met in New York; & then you write me "no one in particular"! Remember the crooked-stick proverb.[15]

Later

A letter from Miss Dana, at Rome, mentions that a great sorrow has come to you—that your Mother is dead. At first I thought I would not send this letter at all—but merely a few lines of sympathy. I will, however, let it go, as it will come to you long afterwards. A tie is broken in your life that can never be replaced, & I know you will feel it greatly. I sympathize with you the more, because I have never been my old self since my Father died, but have always felt desolate and oppressed with care without him; & then when, three years ago, my Mother too was taken, there seemed nothing left to live for. A daughter feels it more than a son of course, because her life is so limited, bounded by home-love; but the son feels it in his own way, & I want you to believe that I am very sorry for your sorrow.—It must be a comfort to you that you were at home; & not far away in London.—Death is not terrible to me; I don't know what it is to you—you have never spoken of it, or alluded to it in your writings. To me it is only a release; & if, at any time, you should hear that I had died, always be sure that I was quite willing, & even glad, to go. I don't think this is a morbid feeling, because it is accompanied by a very strong belief, that, while we are here, we should do our very best, & be as courageous, & work as hard, as we possibly can.—I feel sure there are no uncertainties in your belief—whatever it may be—; you are much too calm for a person who is swayed by uncertainties.

I hope you are well; & I send you my best wishes. Take care of yourself; & be as determinedly good, in all this splendid success, as though you were a "failure." Failures often fall back on their "goodness"; let us see a man of genius who is "good" as well.

Always sincerely your friend,
C. F. Woolson.

Notes

1. The quote is from Emerson's "Contentment."
2. Woolson was becoming increasingly deaf.
3. Woolson is referring to postage stamps of Queen Victoria and Italy's King Umberto I.
4. "When women like [or love] something, look well, and you will that find beneath the something they like there is a someone they like."
5. The Maumee is in Ohio.
6. The notice is "Henry James, Jr." by Howells and the pencil portrait by Timothy Cole (*Century*, Nov. 1882).
7. George W. Curtis defended James's portrait of Hawthorne against many other critics who faulted him for finding Hawthorne parochial. Willie Edouin (1841–82) was an English comedian and Lawrence Barrett an Irish-American actor.
8. British sculptor John Flaxman (1755–1826).
9. Blanche Willis Howard (1847–98) published *One Summer* in 1875. Constance Fletcher, aka George Fleming, (1858–1938) wrote *Kismet* (1877).
10. Horace Scudder's (1838–1902) review of *The Portrait of a Lady* and *Dr. Breen's Practice* appeared in the Jan. 1882 *Atlantic Monthly*.
11. The first quotation is from James's *A Passionate Pilgrim* (1871); the second from *Madame de Mauve* (1874).
12. The characters are from James's *Portrait of a Lady* (1881, Isabel Archer), *Roderick Hudson* (1875, Christina; Mary Garland), *The American* (1877, Mme de Cintré), "Mme de Mauve" (1874, Mme de Mauve), *The Europeans* (1878, Gertrude, Charlotte, the Baroness), "An International Episode" (1879, Bessie Alden), *Confidence* (1879, Angela), *Washington Square* (1880, Catherine), and *Daisy Miller* (1878, Daisy).
13. Several illegible strikethroughs in this passage suggest that Woolson was carefully considering her words.
14. en tiers: wholly.
15. The women are unidentified. According to Leon Edel, the proverb is likely one about dying a "sour old maid" or taking a "crooked stick" for a husband; see *Henry James: Letters*, 4 vols. (Cambridge: Harvard University Press, 1980): 3:537.

To Katharine Livingston Mather (WRHS/Mather)[1]

Hotel Bristol
Sorrento. Italy
March 2^{d}, 1882

My dear Kate.

It is a long long time since I have written to you. But all last summer I knew Clara could report the little there was to tell of my quiet life at Engelberg, &, as she seems, to me, to have scarcely stopped going to Cleveland about once a week since, I have felt that you knew all that was important. There is'nt much that is "important," except that I am very well. (I consider that important not for itself so much as the other side of it, namely, how dreadful it would be to be ill over here alone!) My health amuses me quite a good deal, because it is so absurd. Every year proves to me more & more decidedly that it is entirely a matter of warmth; so long as it is warm, really warm & not any make-believe of it—I am well, & remarkably well. The instant it becomes cold, I am wretched. Sometimes the wretchedness takes one form; sometimes another. Sometimes a doctor would give it this name; sometimes that. But the point is that the moment it is warm, all the wretchedness; no matter what serious & dignified name it may have borne, vanishes into nothing & never comes back until the weather is cold again.—The Sorrento winter, now over, has been much warmer than the Mentone one was. And of course much warmer than the Roman one last year. None of them approach however the climate of Florida.

It happened quite provokingly that during the two weeks Sam & Flora were here, we had our coldest weather for Sorrento. I suppose they will never believe that it was summer up to about the time they came (with two or three times when the "tramontana," or north-wind, blew, for a day or two) & that it grew immediately warmer after they left. To-day is like warm June at home. No—they will never believe it, but will always maintain that Cannes has the best climate. When they were at Cannes, people were fairly fanning themselves here! But I am quite well, aware there is no use trying to convince them. We were at Mentone during the coldest winter known on the Riviera for 20 years. Everybody told me so, & even showed me tables of the average temperature for 19 seasons. But I still am perfectly sure that it is never really warm at Mentone; that its glittering sunshine has always an east wind concealed in it; & that one's hands always chap there; & that the chimneys always smoke. I shall think this as long as I live!

Sam & Flora's visit was perfectly delightful to me. I have been so much by myself since Clara went home that to see dear & familiar faces, & hear home-talk, was the greatest possible pleasure. They were both so kind & agreeable & charming to their "Aunt Connie," that she felt quite brightened up by their visit. I am only afraid that what was so delightful to me, may have been rather dull for them—for there really is nothing to entertain people in Sorrento. There is always the beautiful Bay to look at; but that is all. However, Sam & Flora are so congenial, & so perfectly happy in each other, that perhaps the dullness of Sorrento did not trouble them. I think Sam is quite a good deal changed since I said good-by to him at New York. He has broadened out generally, looks a good deal older. He was the same dear good nephew to me that he has always been, & while he was here, I quite stopped taking care of myself, & rested in the very fact he was here—if you know what that means! I have taken care of myself so long, & for so many years also was the one who had the direction & responsibility of the journeys South & back with Mother, that I have the habit of feeling always the weight of more or less care—like the people who go about with always a frown between their eyebrows. Well—while Sam & Flora were here, I let the care go, leaned back in an easy chair, & laughed & enjoyed everything.

They took a parlor with me, & had their meals served there—in which I joined. I think it possible they did this on my account, as they knew I was not going to the table d'hote. I meant to have told them in advance that it was not at all necessary to do this, as my objections to a table d'hôte are principally contained in the fact that when I am alone, it is not agreeable. All last winter, when I had Miss Clark with me, we went to the public table. But Sam had made his arrangements before I knew of his intention; &, to tell the truth, it was so much pleasanter that I was very glad to have it so. One of the results of having lived about the world in hotels & boarding houses for so many years, is, that I have'nt a particle of curiosity left about "people," & never want to see them if I can help it. I want to see my friends. I do'nt want to see strangers. I shall never forget my surprise—& how I then realized that this was my own peculiarity, in which all others did not share—when Miss Dana said to me in Florence last spring—"O, do you know Father & Mother have taken a fancy to have ~~their~~ our morning-coffee upstairs—as you do. I am so sorry." I looked at her in wonder. "Why?" I said. [“]Why are you sorry?" "O—because I like to see the people," she answered frankly.

You do'nt know how charmed I am with my new niece. I have always thought her very agreeable—as I presume you remember. But now that I have seen more of her, I think her brilliant, & not only that, but very lovable & winning too. I do'nt know when I have heard anyone talk so well—& all without the least attempt,—just in an easy natural way. She told a number of the best sort of stories, & in the way that is so delightful to me—I mean leaving out the unimportant details with which so many people will persist in clogging a story, & thus tiring you out before the point comes. For a person who does'nt talk well herself, & who ought to be grateful when people try to entertain her, Constance Woolson is certainly a most obstinate & ungrateful woman—in that she is so easily tired, & hates so deeply to be bored! She ought to go out & live somewhere in sack-clothes & ashes! Her only excuse is that she does try extremely hard to conceal her ingratitude; I do'nt know whether she succeeds!—The point of this is that Flora—in addition to my natural interest in her as Sam's wife—was perfectly delightful to me in herself. I have met no lady so agreeable in many years. (I was going to say "girl"—for so she seems to me; but you young people are always so indignant when I let you see how youthful you are in my estimation.)

I quite reveled too in all Flora's pretty things—beginning with her "Princess Dagmar" cloak, & ending with the little sewing case you gave her. That cloak is superb—is'nt it? Also the velvet dress. I quite insisted upon seeing everything, & she read me the list of her presents, & described them, so that on the whole I at last feel as though I knew something about my nephew's wedding. The ring Sam gave her, I greatly admire; it is a beautiful gem. Of course the bracelet I still only know from description. I have a great taste for nice things, although I do'nt know much about fashions, shopping, & dressmakers; & I enjoyed all Flora's things almost as much as though they had been my own. Sam showed me, by the way, the very nice dressing-gown you gave him. It is a beautiful piece of cloth, I think.

We had a delightful excursion together. I did not go with them to Capri, but I was very glad of the opportunity to go to Paestum with them, as that is something I could never accomplish alone, & I never join "parties." Sam arranged it all in the most charming & easy way, so that the excursion generally considered the most fatiguing in the vicinity of Naples, was not the least so to us, but on the contrary without flaw. We left here, in a comfortable carriage, & drove along the beautiful road, overhanging the Bay, to Pompeii. It was a lovely bright day, &, taking a guide who spoke English, we went through the wonders of the uncovered city, my first visit; Sam & Flora had seen it before. As everybody knows all about Pompeii from pictures & descriptions, I will only say that the reality exceeded my anticipations. I had no idea the walls of the houses were so high or so well-preserved; that it was so little like a ruin, & so much like a modern Italian town. In fact, take off the roofs & upper-stories of any one of the closely built Italian towns of to day, empty the houses of everything, & banish all the people, &, you have Pompeii. There is also another & important difference: Pompeii is scrupulously clean;—while all the Italian towns are—well, come over & see! The narrow streets, well-paved, stretch away in all directions, with their lines of silent houses; overhead in the blue sky smokes old Vesuvius. But it is almost impossible to realize how so large a town could have been so deeply buried.—I said it was like any modern Italian city, but I mean only in its general aspect, viewed from a distance, or as a whole. When you enter the houses, you see at once the well-known peculiarities of Pompeian building & decoration.—Leaving Pompeii, we took the train to Salerno, a picturesque old place on the Gulf of Salerno, south of here. Here we spent the night comfortably, & the next morning started on our grand day's excursion to Paestum, to see the Greek temples—the one thing in Italy, south of Rome, in which I have felt the deepest interest. Beside these temples, even the Coliseum is modern. They were built by a colony of Greeks 2400 years ago, & are considered the finest specimens of Greek architecture in the world, save those at Athens itself. The Coliseum was built 1800 years ago. (Very likely you know all this, are smiling at my putting it in!) We left Salerno in a carriage drawn by 3 horses abreast, Italian-fashion, at a pleasant hour in the morning; no getting up at dawn if you please—as the people have to do who make the excursion from Naples. The day was divine—in fact the only absolutely perfect day we had while Sam & Flora were here. Warm, with the sky & sea oh! so blue (the road runs along the shore) & that soft haze over the purple mountains which is to me the feature of an Italian landscape. It was a drive altogether of 52 miles—there & back. We passed through a number of small villages, & as it was Carnival-time, the whole population was enjoying itself, with masks & processions, & much dancing of the Tarantella. This road has been always a favorite haunt of Brigands. Only lately has it been considered safe for travelers. Ten years ago, Taine, who was visiting Naples, could not go to Paestum at all, although he waited a month for a safe time, & would have taken an escort. The thought that we were passing along the road where real Brigands so recently hovered, quite added to the enjoyment of our drive. We looked up toward the near mountains, & imagined them sallying down from their strongholds, & retreating thither with booty & prisoners! No one assailed us, however. We even met two armed patrol men. "United Italy" has been very determined with her Brigands. Those who are not hanged are sent to one or two desolate islands, far out in the Mediterranean, where they have a fine opportunity to meditate, & earn their living in Adam's way!—After a while the great columns of the temples began to loom up against the blue; we rolled through an old gateway between the crumbling town-walls, &, passing the few houses of the modern village, drove directly to the "ruins." But "ruins" they can hardly be called, so perfectly are they preserved. Roofless of course,—but the great solid yellow-brown stone pillars standing as evenly & firmly as ever. I do'nt know whether you care about architecture—but will say that the Temples are Doric.—I was not in the least disappointed in my first sight of Greek columns. Indeed—the temple of Neptune seemed to me the most perfect building I have ever seen. I mean in pure simple beauty.—We had our lunch in the "cella" of the Temple, looking out on the soft sea on one side, on the hazy mountains on the other. Sam invested in two little vases, supposed to be "antique," & formed "in tombs," & in a collection of coins, also supposed to be antique—the cleaning of which I am now attending to here with breathless interest. I am sorry to say that, so far, they seem to be entirely copper, & that I greatly fear no inscriptions will come out distinct. But no one is to be allowed to say they are not at least "antique," & when I am home with one set as a scarf-pin, you are to pretend you have never heard that such things are made by the thousand in Naples, & buried by deceitful Italians in order to take in credulous pilgrims from a western world. Some of the coins one sees are undoubtedly genuine; thus why not these? After, gazing & gazing at the beautiful proportions of the temples from various standpoints, we went to a tower on the old-wall, to get a general view, & here Sam got up a sort of platonic flirtation with a very handsome peasant girl who opened the door for us. She tried to sell Sam a ring, whose stone she said she herself had found near the old-wall; but Sam preferred to admire her bright eyes & blooming cheeks. (Flora has not these!) We reached Salerno again at dusk, having had a most enchanting day. The next day Sam had planned to go to Amalfi, & on donkeys to Ravello; but a wind came up so we did not do that part, but came home.[2]—Just here comes a letter from Flora—at Rome. The first I have had from them since they left. (They were here two weeks & 4 days) So—I see it was written at Rome & mailed at Assisi—where I too so much want to go! Are they having a good time, though!

I am not going to be much alone after this—shall I say, I "fear"? That does'nt sound very nicely, so I'll change it & say that I do like to see people if they will only understand things & not keep me all the time "apologizing" but I am so busy.[3]

a pretty one in Rome—palest pink & quantities of white lace; slippers & little cap to match. The lady was supposed, of course, to have slipped it on hastily, upon coming in from her drive—just to drink her tea in,—before beginning to dress for dinner; but I know she took a solid hour to arrange it!

I get such numbers of letters about "Anne,"—I wish I could show them to you. I am sure they would amuse you. Every mail brings them, & some are quite remarkable. One of the latest is from Judge Tourgee (who wrote "A Fool's Errand," you know) & he not only says nice things about the novel, but quotes Whittier as saying the same. I ought to explain that Judge T. is writing to me about contributing to his new periodical, "Our Continent"; probably he would not have written to me about "Anne," alone.[4] This is in confidence, of course. I [was] much distressed to hear such bad news about Mr Howells. Is it true? I mean that his health is so broken? What do you hear?

Well—I must stop. Tell your Mother, with my dearest love, that I never notice the Bay—or an Italian landscape anywhere—looking especially fair, without thinking of her, & of the time when we took Italian lessons at Farilla. I am extremely fond of Italy—I cannot deny that. I must not forget to put in that Sam gave me my Paestum excursion. I—who count so carefully all my outings—would have hesitated a long time over the expense of it, I fear.

From what you & others write, I think Cleveland must be a gay place nowadays; something going on all the time. Enjoy it all. Take all the good of it. I am so glad that you are so well.

Tell your Father that I use his present, the audiphone, a great deal now, for conversation. I have learned all its "ways," & found it very useful back in Florence & here. When I am the least tired, it rests me to take it; then I do'nt have to "listen" so much,—but the words come to me. By the way—why did no one ever tell me Flora sang? I think she has a remarkably sweet voice; not powerful, but very agreeable. She sang some of the "Patience" songs for me.[5] She wo'nt like it that I am speaking of her voice. Her own idea seems to be that she can't sing at all.

Give my love to Will. His handwriting is growing so like his Father's that before long I shall hesitate over them! I think I have thanked him for his photograph before this; if not, I do so now. It is good; but does not flatter—to say the least. He must try again. I want the very best looks of my friends in their photographs. Did Sam write you, by the way, that when Mr Goodrich was here, he saw a photograph of your Father & one of Garfield on an etagère in Sam's parlor, & said "Ah—Blaine & Garfield, I see."[6] Mr Goodrich, Lieut. Com. in the Navy—came over to see me one day, the Flagship the "Lancaster," having stopped at Naples for a week. He is a "Roman" friend of mine, a nephew-in-law of the Mrs Washington of whom you have heard me speak. The Goodriches had an apartment in Rome last winter.

This Xmas I was quite proud—I had 20 Xmas cards. Will's "cherub" is the centre-piece. Two Birthday ones have just come; so I do'nt feel "forgotten" any more.

I feel that I know a great deal more about you all, now that I have had so many long talks with Sam & Flora; sometimes all three together; sometimes with one of them alone. Talking tells more than letters can.

The next one I expect to see is <u>you</u>—on a similar tour!! Then I shall hardly have returned to my usual quiet when along will come Will! I'll welcome you all; I only wish I had an Italian villa in which to receive you. Good-by. Love to all.

Yours affectionately,
C.F.W.

Notes

1. Both an original and a typed version of this letter survive; therefore, it provides a good example of variations from original to typed version to Benedict's CFW (263–65). See Addendum of Letters for documentation on the changes. In the case of this letter, the typed version omits a great deal. Pages of the original letter that Woolson numbered 10 to 13 are missing. The above transcription is from the original letter.

2. The typed version of the letter ends here with "Lovingly C. F. Woolson."

3. Missing pages 10–13.

4. Albion Tourgee's 1879 *A Fool's Errand,* set in the Reconstruction South, was enormously popular. The weekly magazine *Our Continent* ran only from 1881 to 1884.

5. Songs from Gilbert and Sullivan's 1881 opera *Patience.*

6. Secretary of State James Blaine (1830–93), who had run against Grover Cleveland in the 1876 election, delivered the eulogy at the assassinated President Garfield's funeral.

To Little Readers (Knox College)

Sorrento. Italy
March 18th, [1882?]

Dear little Readers.

Jimmie, Grace, & Margaret.

If you are not "little," you must remember how young the oldest age you give—fifteen—seems to me. Your letter has been forwarded to me by Messrs. Harper & Brothers, & I am glad to know you like my story. As to Anne's marriage—do girls always marry as their friends would have chosen for them? Let us see what you will do. It will be easy for you to go to Mackinac.—You are so near. Not even this beautiful Bay of Naples has made me forget the island that was so dear to me when I was about your age.

Very truly yours,
C. F. Woolson.

To Thomas Bailey Aldrich (Houghton)

(Care Meuricoffre & Co.
52 Piazza del Municipio. Naples)
Sorrento
April 10th, [1882]
Mr T. B. Aldrich.

Dear Sir.

Several times during the past month I have reminded myself that I ought to write & ask you whether you had received a sketch I sent you in December, or whether it had been lost. This morning comes the magazine itself—"April" number—containing it—[1] Now after I had finished that sketch, a sort of uncertainty stole over me regarding the exact title of the implement I could so distinctly remember, among others, in the drawer of my sister's sewing machine, & whose shape I had compared, in the sketch, to that of a gondola's prow. I therefore noted down the page on which the word occurred (I had called it a "hemmer"), and, after starting the Ms. on its long journey to you, wrote to her for instructions.

She replied, from New York, "What you are thinking of is not the hemmer at all, but the gauge. I hope you are not going to buy more machines & break more needles." (This allusion of hers has reference to the singular persistence with which all the machines I have ever approached immediately set to work & dislocate everything.) I made a memorandum of her correction, intending to send it to you if I should hear, from your office, that the sketch was to appear. When the magazine came therefore, I turned at once with fear & trembling to my unlucky word—which I found on the 493^{d} page—and, behold, you had given it an extra turn of mysteriousness by calling it a "hammer."

What the hammer of a sewing-machine is, I have no idea. But the instant recognition of its existence and appropriateness, by the five personages of my story, adds a fine final inscrutableness to the whole affair.

The unimportance of the matter would give me small hope, amid the microscopically clear knowledge of the Atlantic circle. But another hope I do cherish, namely, that no one who knows & loves a gondola, could possibly know & love a sewing machine; & vice versa. This hope I share with you.

But should the worst come, do'nt retract. Say, darkly, that it was a western sewing-machine, & that they have a wild & prairie-like construction, which includes not only hammers, but axes. No one in the neighborhood of Boston, will be able to contradict you.

Yours truly,
C. F. Woolson.

Notes

1. "In Venice," the last piece Woolson published in *Atlantic Monthly* (Apr. 1882).

To Ethel ? (McGill)

Sorrento. Italy
April 14th, [1882]

My dear Ethel.

As you are only fourteen, and as I have a little cousin who has the same name, perhaps you will let me call you so. Your nice little letter has been forwarded to me by Messrs. Harper & Brothers, and my autograph I will write out in full at the end of this note, although generally I content myself with initials. By tomorrow you will know, in America, I suppose, that "Anne" does end happily. I am glad you like the Southern Sketches; they are dear to me because they are, in one way, records of the years I spent at the south with my dear mother, who is now gone from earth forever. I think no one has liked "Miss Elisabetha"—"best" but you. But, do you know I like it myself, ever so much.

Yours Very truly,
Constance Fenimore Woolson.

To Flora Stone Mather (WRHS/Mather)

(Care Macquay, Hooker, & Co.
Via Tornabuoni)
Florence
May 6th, [1882?]

My dear Flora.

I reached Florence on the evening of the 4th, & the next morning I received Sam's letter from Paris, which had been sent up from Rome. My first impulse—& it was a very strong one—was to send you a dispatch, & start as soon as possible for Paris, for I can think of nothing I should enjoy more than being with you there for a while. It would be delightful in every way. I could stay somewhere near by;—see you & hear you talk (you will excuse the laziness of that when you read on), both of you; you could initiate me a little as regards Paris attractions; &, altogether, it is one of the most tempting plans that could possibly be offered to me. But I suppose I ought not to go. What do you say to my having been quite ill! (It is more of a surprise to me than to any one else. I have forgotten whether I mentioned my health in my last letter, or not. But, generally speaking, I have not mentioned it when writing letters, because each day I expected to be well. At last however I had to give up, & acknowledge that I was ill. I fled northward just as soon as my cousin returned from Rome, & came here to consult Dr Wilson, the good old English physician of Florence, in whom I have great confidence.[1] He says I have had intermittent fever,—though but slightly, for three weeks, & he very carefully examined my lungs! I have never had them examined before, though I have always wanted to have it done for curiosity's sake. It was his own idea after hearing me cough—for a most harassing cough has been the feature of this case—so much so that I did'nt appreciate there was any fever, though I knew I was eating nothing, & living on inordinate quantities of lemonade. He says the left lung is not so strong as the right, but that the present trouble there has come down, he thinks, from the throat. He says the fever was virtually over by the time I reached Florence, & he is now giving me tonics, & I am "inhaling" things with steam. So you see the trouble is past. I asked him if I could not go to Paris, as I was so tired, & cast down, & I knew that seeing you & Sam would do more to "build me up" than medicine. But he thinks the sudden change from Sorrento to Paris would be too much; I mean that Paris might be too cool. I do'nt think so; but suppose I had better obey. All my life, when run down, change of scene has always revived me at once, & Paris with you & Sam would be so fresh new & bright.—However Florence is very beautiful now, & I have a nice room at Casa Molini—my old pension. I suppose I shall stay here until I feel better, & then go over the Brenner to Munich & wait for Clara there. What an ignominious ending to all my hopes. No "England" at all. No clothes! No tailor-made cheviot. Clara & Clare will be ashamed of me & my ribs, swathed in the same old rusty black! For all the flesh of which I was so proud at Sorrento has gone—16 lbs!—I presume however that I shall now gain rapidly.

I stopped at Assisi to sleep, but had to give up Perugia as I was too tired. Forlorn as I was, Assisi quite soothed me—not only the old church, but especially that wide soft Umbrian landscape which one sees in all Perugino pictures & Raphael's early ones; the same thinly foliaged trees. I found your dear little Virgin & thought her lovely. It was a great fiesta, & the church was crowded with kneeling people.

When you have time, do tell me about Seville, Burgos, & especially the Madrid gallery. I hope you are well. Take care of yourself. Give my love to all the pretty costumes, & bonnets, & lace &c which I cannot come to see, with you. Tell Sam that anything left addressed to Clara, "Care Cunningham & Shaw. Water Street. Liverpool." will reach her.

Should you have a dress maker who turned out to be especially satisfactory (Paris), will you sometime send me the address? But I do'nt include Worth!

Love to Sam. You do'nt know how much I want to come!

Yours affectionately,
C.F.W.

This is a poor return for your delightful letter from Grenada.

Notes

1. The cousin is probably Julia Smith. Dr. Wilson is possibly Dr. Erasmus Wilson (1809–84), who was particularly known for his treatment of skin diseases.

To Young Ladies (McGill)

Florence. Italy
May 9th, [1882]

Dear Young Ladies.

Your letter has been forwarded to me from Sorrento, and I comply with your request with pleasure; the more so because I myself once had a great fancy for collecting autographs. I thought I could read character in them. But I hope you will not see mine in these very poor strokes I am making now; I have been ill, and my hand is not steady. You will find the signature on the second page.

I have always wanted to see that part of Pennsylvania from which you write; it must be very beautiful.

I am glad you like "Anne."[1] My own school-girl life was a very happy one, and I like to please school-girls.

Very Truly Yours,
C. F. Woolson.

Notes

1. At this period of time, Woolson seems to have been receiving many requests for autographs, prompted by the 1882 publication of *Anne* in book form.

To Miss Richards (Virginia)

Baden-Baden
June 24th, [1882?]

Dear Miss Richards.

Your note of May 16th has been forwarded to me by Messrs. Harper & Brothers. I send my autograph with pleasure, though it seems comical enough to sit down and gravely write it! It ought to come from Rome,—I see you love Rome too; but, after two attempts, I have given up trying to spend the summer south of the Alps. So it comes from this green nook in the Black Forest, with my regards.

Very Truly Yours,
Constance Fenimore Woolson.

To Thomas Bailey Aldrich (Houghton)

Baden-Baden
June 30th, [1882]

Dear Mr Aldrich.

I should have answered your letter sooner, had I not been quite ill; I have been through a fever, which I do not acknowledge as "Roman," simply because I do not acknowledge that there is anything unpleasant in Rome.

It gratified me much to be asked, by you, to write a serial; and in the "Atlantic." I have always had an especial regard for the magazine,—in fact I have never outgrown the reverential respect with which I used to read it when I lived in Ohio. And those of my sketches which have come out in its pages since then, have always had the air to me of having been presented at court.

And so I am sorry that I cannot send a story in answer to your suggestions—or rather—offer one for you to look over. But, at present, all I can do is promised. I am not a rapid writer. It would be much better for me if I were!

The papers say that you are "in Europe for the summer." If this should be true, and this letter follow you over here, I hope you may take in Baden-Baden, and that I may have the pleasure of seeing you. My sister and I are spending the summer here, and the Bankers, "Meyer & Diss," will always know where we are. Baden is lovely—but probably you know all about it.

I want to tell you that I have carried round with me, ever since it came out in the "Atlantic," your "Spring in New England"; for its exquisite beauty of form, and expression, its pathos, and depth of feeling, it is, to my mind, unparalleled. I have stood in many of those southern cemeteries—"National" they call them—poor lonely unvisited spots, the very perfection of their order only increasing their solitariness. I used to go out of my way to visit them as I came and went, to & from, Florida.

If Mr Howells is still at home & you are, will you please give him my regards. The rumor over here is that he is to spend next winter in Florence. That is what I am thinking of doing, and I hope I may see him.

With kind regards, Yours very truly,
C. F. Woolson.

To Edmund Clarence Stedman (Columbia)

Baden-Baden
Aug. 4th [1882]

Dear Mr Stedman.

I have been hoping to find the time for a letter to you; not merely a note—like this. But the time is not found yet, & so I will wait no longer, but send at least a note; & the letter later. I am very busy; & as I have not yet recovered my strength since my illness of last May, every little extra thing tells—no matter how pleasant it may be.

I was so very sorry that you had to go back. I felt a real regret that you should lose your summer of freedom from business. It seemed cruel. And to have to go back from Venice too—of all places in the world! (Your note did'nt say that you liked Venice; but I am sure you did.) Then, I was sorry on my own account. I had counted upon seeing you, & had ever so many things to ask you. You know I always asked you questions!—And now—when will you come again? I have just made up my mind to stay a while longer. It seems on the whole the wisest thing to do. If I should go home with my sister, I should probably be afraid of a New York winter, & go to Florida. And so I should be as far from her as I am here. And there is much to interest a person like me on this side—a person who does not go into society much; there is always a beautiful picture, or statue, a ruined castle, or some old majolica jug. (I suppose of course that you care for jugs.)—I wonder if you went as far as Rome? I fancy not—it was so late. You would be a Rome-lover, I know. It is the only place. As, once in a while (a great one) one meets a person so congenial (though that is not quite the word) that one immediately feels—"Oh, here is my true home!"—meaning that person's presence, friendship, sympathy,—so in Rome one feels it physically. You would. You would never go away.—I read with the greatest pleasure & interest your essay on Lowell. And I am waiting for some more. But work like yours takes time. I am now very familiar with your Poe, Whitman, &

Lowell (for I read each one (in my slow way) over several times), and I am curious to see what you will say about Bryant, Longfellow, & Whittier. Now & then I ~~see~~ hear you have something in the "Critic," & now & then I do get a hold of a poem in one of the magazines. But it is one of the privations of living over here that one is separated from all the current literature of the world at home; I mean if one moved about as I do. I met Mr Lowell in Florence last October; he was calling upon Mr R. H. Dana, & I was in the room about half an hour. He was not talking with me (save for a few minutes—) but I got quite a good idea of him. I like very much the Boston people who are extremely "Boston." Not the halfway ones. I am never tired of hearing them talk. Mr Lowell did not know ~~Mr~~ who Mr Vanderbilt was, for instance. I said he was only the richest man in the world; that was all. I expatiate on "Boston People" a little because, for the first time in my life, I have been with them familiarly since I have been over here.—I should be so glad if you would now & then send me (cut out) the little poems of yours that come out. I specify the "little" ones—meaning the short ones; I do not want you to take the trouble to send anything long. I will get those myself.

Kate Mather has recently written that she saw in Mrs Hay's album a lovely poem of yours on the same page as my signature. I wish you would send it to me. Never fancy that anybody ever sends me anything! (I put in all the "anys" I can to make it strong.) Nobody ever does. Months afterwards they say—"Oh—I supposed of course you saw that!"—I have not seen for instance, one single notice of my own story, not even the Cleveland ones. About that, however, perhaps it is as well. I do not think ~~I shall~~ it a good place to be all the time reading "notices." Still—about one's first long story, one naturally feels some curiosity. I see what you say about the "Street of the Hyacinth." But why do you again accuse me of putting real persons into my pages? Real persons are seldom usable, in a novel. They can only serve, I think, as—something of which one says—remember not to have it like so & so.

My sister has had a great deal to say about Mrs Stedman & yourself. She is hoping to see much of you next winter. And I am hoping it for her. I am the more willing to say so, because I think you will find her unusually agreeable. She is the bright one of our family.—I must stop for my eyes are extremely tired. This letter is really to say how sorry I was not to see you, & that is all. May you come over soon again.—We go from here to Dresden, then to England. I return to Italy for the winter. Should you write me, you can always, hereafter, reach me by addressing, care of

"Knauth, Nachod, & Kühne.
Leipzig. Germany."

They are the Bankers upon whom I have my letter of credit, & only the jawbreaking quality of the names has prevented me from using this address as my general one, before. But I have at last been driven to it.—I hope at least that your 2 ocean voyages did you good. My love to Mrs Stedman. And the very best wishes for yourself. Believe that I am speaking literally when I say that I want to write a better letter, but am unable to do so at least for the present. I cannot use my eyes at all after dark. Good-by. Come over again soon.

Always your sincere friend,
C. F. Woolson.

P.S. I hope you made millions by going home. I am convinced that was what you went for!

To Henry James (Houghton)

("Care Knauth, Nachod, & Kühne
Leipzig. Germany")
Dresden
Aug. 30th, [1882]

Dear Mr James.

School is out. And now I am going to amuse myself writing to you. As a beginning let me say that the above Leipzig address will be hereafter my general address, while I remain abroad. You may feel that instead of a beginning, it is an ending;—three such names are enough to end any acquaintance. I acknowledge it. But, tired of asking so many favors of Macquay, Hooker, & Co., I have been driven at last to use these Leipzig bankers because, as my Letter of Credit is upon them, I have a right to their services. Why I have a Letter of Credit upon them instead of upon Brown Brothers, or Munroe, would take too long to explain; it dates back to a period before my birth! As I write, I seem to remember, or half remember, that I sent you this Leipzig address in my last. If I did, ascribe the repetition to the curious state of fatigue in which I find myself. In Baden-Baden, for six consecutive weeks, I worked ten hours a day, and for two more (making eight in all), thirteen. I then started immediately for this place, & have not really rested at all save for a sort of serenity that came over my spirit after I had seen the Sistine Madonna and that beautiful little picture of Van Eyck's in the Holbein room—I am sure you remember it? It is the first Van Eyck I have seen, & comes fully up to my high expectations.[1]

Do'nt suppose that I approve of such hard work as that of this summer, or of traveling when one is tired out. I do'nt. You, master of all the situations in which you find yourself, would never have been caught in any such position. But I am constantly doing the things I do'nt want to do. The hard work came from a misunderstanding. I had agreed to have ready a little thing for Harper's Magazine this autumn; as I supposed, October. But in May I heard that August, not October, was the time. I had then to make a choice between disappointing the magazine-people, & throwing their winter arrangements into confusion, or working very hard myself.[2] It seemed best to do the latter. Mind you—no one else, probably, would have taken anything like the time I do for so small a piece of work. That is my own slowness. I always write very slowly, & when there is any pressure, I write more slowly than ever! It is unfortunate for me. But cannot be helped. The work of those last two weeks—from five in the morning to six at night—was the copying—always with me a painful task. I do'nt hold a pen easily, & my hand soon becomes cramped. The arm often aches to the shoulder. And this brings back to my mind an occasion (which I have no hesitation in ~~mentioning~~ describing because of course you have forgotten it; you forget everything) when, seated upon a bench at the end of the pretty little Cascine, surrounded by Italian children, you said, in answer to a remark of mine, "Oh I never copy." And upon a mute gesture from me, you added, "Do you think, then, that my work has the air of having been copied, & perhaps more than once?" I think I made no direct reply, then. But I will now. The gesture was despair,—despair, that, added to your other perfections, was the gift of writing as you do, at the first draft!

I finished my Ms. at last, & came here as fast as I could. As you may imagine, my sister has not enjoyed my being shut up in my own rooms, invisible until evening. She wanted me to go with her to various places, among them Baireuth, to hear "Parsifal."[3] But I could'nt. So she & Clare had to go without me. We met here, & have still some weeks together, as she does not sail until September 21st. She greatly detests all my mss. & has already presented me with a new dress and round-hat, so that I shall not look too "literary."

As I believe I told you, I have decided to stay on over here, for a while longer. I came very near going home. To be ill alone in a foreign land is a dreary experience. And it seemed to me as I lay feverish & coughing, that I must go home; go home, get my precious books, & little household gods together, a dog or two, & never stir again. This is the thirteenth year I have spent without a home. After the death of my father, in 1869, I took my mother south for her health, and we led a wandering life, after that, for many years, in search of climates. It was a happy life in one way, for we were together, & one's mother cares for one. But, in other ways, there is nothing like a home. My sister, however, has represented to me that probably I should not be contented (in America) without two homes—one in Florida for the winter, and in Cooperstown or Mackinac for the summers. And that all three localities she hates! In addition, she wishes to bring Clare over, now & then, during her school days, & if I am here,—why, that is an anchor out. Meanwhile, as I regained my strength, I also regained my courage or some of it; & I remembered how beautiful was Italy. So here I am for an indefinite time longer. Indefinite does not necessarily mean long;

it means only "indefinite." But I suppose there never was a woman so ill-fitted to do without a home as I am. I am constantly trying to make temporary homes out of the impossible rooms at hotels & pensions. I never give it up, though I know it cannot be done; I keep on trying. Like a poor old bird shut up in a cage, who tries to make a nest out of two wisps of straw. Or the beaver I saw in the Zoological Gardens here, who had constructed a most pathetic little dam out of a few poor fragments of old boughs. I stood & looked at that beaver a long time. He is an American—as I am! But I suppose you know nothing of beavers, but hats. You do'nt know beavers, or prairies; you only know—Mme de Katkoff.[4]

It was good of you to speak so sympathetically of my illness. You say you knew, in former years, what it was to be ill over here, alone. I have heard that you were not strong,—that it was your health which kept you living on over here. (I do'nt believe the latter; you stay for your pleasure.) But you are such a picture of blooming composure, that I can never realize, when with you, that you have ever been ill in your life. You see I associate illness with nervousness & bones. My illness was fever, & a bad cough. The English doctor said the two had no connection with each other. I think they had. I think I had the American "lung-fever,"—a fever the English have outgrown, with their avoirdupois.[5] I presume the ancient Saxons had it,—when they took cold. As I am not strong, the cough pulled me down. But I am well now, or shall be when rested. I sometimes think I was enervated by the densely sweet perfume of the miles of orange-blossoms at Sorrento. I lived in a cloud of it, day & night. It was—the air—so warm, & thick with fragrance, that it was a sort of lethargic intoxication. Or an opiate. It is so hard to leave Italy early. Yet that is what one should do—I suppose.

In your letter you say—alluding to the illness—"Pray do me the ~~favor~~ favour not to recommence." That brought back instantly to my mind poor little Desirée & her hummingbirds, in Daudet's "Fromont,"—do you remember the place? Where she has tried to drown herself, & has been rescued, & they tell her (at the police-station) that she must promise "not to recommence." She does so, & goes home. Not to recommence. By delightful good luck (once in awhile there is some good luck) I fell upon that very copy of the "Atlantic" which contains your article on Daudet, in the reading room of this hotel. I have been anxious to read it ever since I saw it announced, & vexed enough with you because you would not send it to me! Now that I have read it, & know that you like Daudet, I dare mention Desirée. I should not have done so if I had not fallen upon this "Atlantic"; I should have thought, without it, that probably you considered him sensational. He is French; but, in some things, he captivates me, & always has. Desirée, for instance. And I don't know when I have enjoyed a little thing more than I did his "Tarascon," which I chanced upon at Mentone, three years ago.[6] I am now enchanted to know that you like him too. And I am so much obliged to you for writing that article & saying so. Your essay converted me to Tourguénieff; but I had to study him for some time before it was accomplished. Daudet I like of my own accord. By nature; not by grace. Did I tell you, by the way, that I at last got hold of that "Dominique" you admire so much, & that there I am not yet converted.[7] I suppose however it is only the different point of view.

At Bamberg, where I was wearily waiting for a train (the Crown Prince was there reviewing troops, so that the crowd was dense; & at Nuremburg, where there is a great Exposition, I could'nt get a room, tired as I was), what do you suppose I found among the news-dealer's wares? Your "Eugene Pickering" done into French under the title of "Une Femme Philosophe."[8] Of course I instantly bought it. Have you seen it? But I should not have asked that question—there's no use. A question of any sort you never answer! If, however, you would make one exception & tell me—sometime when you are writing,—there is no hurry—where in London I can get some really delicious tea, its name, & the price I should pay per pound, I should be deeply grateful. I want the address for future use—as I have at present a quantity on hand,—just sent to me from America.

I am writing on in the most inconsequent inartistic way. But you know I never wrote to you half so much for your entertainment as for my own. At present it rests me to write to you. But the letter itself wo'nt be, can't be, good.—If I were clever, I should always bear in mind the fact, that, when I have written to you many sheets, I have received a short note in reply, beginning with some such sentence as this: "Dear Miss Woolson. One does'nt answer your letters; one can't. One only reads them & is grateful"; & this followed up by three very small pages (in a very big hand) in which no allusion is made to anything I have said, the "faithfully" of the signature occupying the room of several of my sentences. Then, when I have written you a short note myself, I have received from you a charming letter in reply, eight pages long, & not such a very big hand either, & the "faithfully" even put across the top or side of the first page, instead of being relied upon to fill the half of the last! But I am not clever. And then I am always thinking that perhaps you will improve. I hope right in the face of facts. It does'nt do any harm; & it amuses me. My idea is that we shall make a George Washington of you, yet.

I sent you back that article ~~notice~~ written by Mrs Rollins, because I supposed myself obliged to. You did not say—as you have said at other times—"destroy it"; or "you need not return it." So I thought that possibly you might wish to keep it. It was certainly nice enough to keep. I continue to be jealous of her; the very fact that she did not answer your note will make you think her more important—make you like her better. Ah—do'nt suppose I do'nt know that—though I have conducted myself so differently. You see I was enjoying the pleasure of a very real & deep admiration, &, if I had to choose between that & your having, perhaps, a higher idea of me, personally—why, the first was of the most consequence to me. Especially as the second was so doubtful in any case! Mrs Rollins can take another stand. She has, perhaps, a Greek nose.

I will now tell you that American story. Not that it has any connection with the above; I am too tired to be connected. A young lady, whom I have mentioned to you, wrote it to me just after you had left America. She said that she had met you at a dinner-party at her brother's, in New York, but, after that, she saw no more of you, to her disappointment. (You see I had written to her how nice you were. Evidently you did not take a fancy to her. I suppose because she is not tall & thin, with grey eyes! She is one of the most sympathetic girls I know. If you had cared for her, she would have adored you.) When you came back to Boston, she said to herself, "Now I shall see him." For she knew you were intimate with some intimate friends of hers, & she thought they would be having you to lunch & dinner, & that she would be included. "All of which" (I quote) "came to pass but the last part. They had him, but they did not have me! I did my best; I asked at what hours he generally came, & said frankly that I should like to happen in at the same time. But nothing definite could I get out of them. At last, after he had finally gone, I asked my friend—a most lovely girl—why I had been let so severely alone. 'It was because you were so horrid about him in London,' she replied. I, having a perfectly clear conscience, exclaimed at this. 'You said,' said my friend with heat, 'that he would not care for simple pleasures. That nothing would induce him to go, for instance, to a simple picnic!'—And all this time she has been treasuring that poor little speech of mine up against me! What do you think of a man capable of inspiring such partisanship as that?"—I wrote back that I was as bad as the Boston friend; that if anyone so much as dared to allude to you in anything less than superlatives of liking, I instantly brought out my biggest guns & blew them into mid-air in a minute. I have done it; several of my friends are floating there still! Do we spoil you, telling you such stories? But I think not. The best part of you is your incorruptible, & dignified, & reasonable modesty; & your perfectly-balanced common sense. It is such a comfort that you have them!—Besides, there are always, I suppose, people enough who do'nt like you, to keep the scales ~~balance~~ straight. At least I hope there are.

Baden-Baden was the prettiest little place I have ever seen. I felt so sorry that I could not spend all the time in those pretty forests all about,—forests so queer to me because they are all "preserved,"—each tree known, & guarded. Still, they are lovely. It is the most restful landscape I have seen. Sometimes I must go back, & walk every day for miles; in all directions. Of course I brought another copy of "Confidence" (my third) to read over on the spot. I fell in love with the little Oos, & was never tired of walking in the Lichtenthaler Allée—all I had time for; though I did walk up to Hohen Baden twice, & get in some sunset hours in the dear old garden of Schloss. We were in lodgings near the Trinkhalle. They were not "over a confectioner's," however. I could'nt find any confectioner who had rooms to let. It did'nt strike me as in the least a gay place. Plenty of stout common-looking Germans, & English girls in shirred dresses, big boots, & two-button kid gloves. But the music was very good, & I spent every evening listening to it, with closed eyes. I suppose it was gay in the gaming days. At present Newport, Saratoga, & Long Branch far outshine it in dress, carriages, jewels, & that sort of thing.—I thought of you writing "Roderick Hudson" there. Would that I had been there at the same time! I should like to see you when you are actually engaged, for part of the day, upon some piece of work. I want to see if you would be cross. I am very fond of "Roderick Hudson"—as you know. Did you see the notice the "Nation" (N.Y.) had of your "Portrait of a Lady"?[9] In some respects it was very good, &, if by any chance, you have not seen it, you must let me send it to you. I kept it. It spoke of the excellence of "Roderick Hudson," and the deliberate change you made in your writings, after it.

I am sorry that I said anything to you of my small success in "Anne," at home. When your answer came, I was vexed that I had. At the time I was writing you, I was in a state of surprise over a letter from the Messrs. Harper voluntarily doubling the sum they had already paid me for the story, & also proposing to give me a liberal per-cent on the sale in book-form,—a thing expressly denied me in the original sale of the Ms.[10] This struck me as so remarkable that I mentioned it to you. But of course you understood that what is a great success to me, would be nothing to you. All the money that I have received, or shall receive, from my long novel, does not equal probably the half of the sum you received for your first, or shortest. It is quite right that it should be so. And, even if a story of mine should have a large "popular" sale (which I do not expect), that could not alter the fact that the utmost best of my work cannot touch the hem of your first or poorest. My work is coarse beside yours. Of entirely another grade. The two should not be mentioned on the same day. Do pray believe how acutely I know this. If I feel anything in the world with earnestness it is the beauty of your writings, & any little thing I may say about my own comes from entirely another stratum; & is said because I live so alone, as regards to my writing, that sometimes when writing to you, or speaking to you—out it comes before I know it. You see,—I like so few people! Though I pass for a constantly-smiling, ever-pleased person! My smile is the basest hypocrisy.

I suppose you did not go to Cooperstown at all. Mrs Leslie told Clara that you declined her invitation to visit her in the snows of winter.[11] You did wisely. But in summer Cooperstown is very pretty, & when I have made my fortune, & built that cottage on the little lake there, you must come & stay with me, bringing with you that sweet young American wife I want you to have—whom you <u>must</u> have,—even if only (as you horribly write) as "a last resort." And then you must come down to Florida, & I will show you a beautiful swamp.

Cologne
Sept. 3[d]

I have seen the Rhine. And the Cathedral. Beautiful. But Italy is better.—All this while, even in the midst of my hard work at Baden, I have been reading "Daisy," with the greatest delight. Each time I take it up, I like it better. I should never have believed that you could make an actable play of it, without the positive evidence of the book in my own hand; the conception seemed to me too delicate for the stage. But you have succeeded.[12] I have always thought Daisy a masterpiece. No one but you would have dared select the subject; but some of us can at least appreciate the exquisite quality of the workmanship you have put into it. Not only that, but I have always been so proud that you were capable of the conception! Its beauty is of such a fine quality that it escapes the common observer. It was this that made it seem impossible to me, for a play. But you have arranged that difficulty by bringing out more distinctly M[me] de Katkoff. Against her, as a background, Daisy shines out in the way the common observer can understand. (Here opens out in my mind a long parenthesis. But I will postpone it until later.) The humor all through is delicious. And the minor characters strike me as excellent for the stage: Mrs Costello; the camp-stool youth & Miss Durant just "getting" in their proposal & acceptance; Mrs Walker; & the always incomparable Randolf. The Italian & Eugenio are now much more distinct, & strike me as capital for acting purposes. As a whole, it reminds me more of some of the perfect little French comedies I have read, than of anything we have in English. Still—I may be mistaken. I do not know much of plays. The difficulty would be, I think, to find an actress who could play Daisy. I cannot imagine an English woman in the part. A French woman would make an ingenue of it, & Daisy is not that; no American girl is—though they are as innocent as wild flowers in the woods. I hope you will let me keep the book longer. It is under lock & key, and no one has seen it or heard of it; or shall ever see it, or hear of it. I am a very faithful sort of person in such respects. I want to read it more, & when I am not so tired. I will return it to you sometime during the winter. I am so desirous to know whether you are going on in this new field? And everything you are doing.

I now come back to my parenthesis. You do'nt like the "personal note" I know (poor Henrietta!), but, after admiring the play as a whole, I return to what struck me instantly upon the first reading.[13] You may say, or not say, what you choose, but I am sure I know now, beyond a doubt, the sort of woman you care for, or rather the sort that interests you—though one side of you is against her. Probably that has been your trouble—, you could'nt unreservedly admire. Yet you do'nt care for the other kind. You touched upon the same subject in the Baroness (Europeans); but you felt it a sort of duty, there, to show her up; & you did it. Here, as Mme de Katkoff is a side-character, you have not felt it so necessary to point a moral. Oh, of course, for the ordinary observer, the moral is there; Daisy conquers, &c. I only mean that you have'nt put your incomparable skill to work to make us despise her, in spite of her charm; as you make us despise the Baroness before we get through with her. You leave her as she is probably, in real life. You have'nt dissected her as a public warning.

You know I have found fault with you for not making it more evident that your heroes were in love with the heroines; really in love. There is no trouble about that here! Winterbourne is more in love with Mme de Katkoff—or has been—than any of your other men have been in love before. It has the true ring.—True,—there is equally no doubt of Goodwood's love for Isabel; but Goodwood was an exceptional fellow and his love is exceptional too; not a type. Winterbourne comes more within the range of one's daily life. He will love Daisy—yes. He will be a good husband. All the same, Mme de Katkoff interested him in a way far beyond Daisy's charm.

Do you suppose in the next world you will find a person who combines the two characters? That is what you want.

I must stop; it is late. I hope you are well, & happy. I send you my best wishes.

Always sincerely your friend,
C. F. Woolson.

Notes

1. Raphael's *Sistine Madonna* (1513–14) is in Dresden's Gemäldegalerie. The Jan Van Eyck may be his *Virgin and Child in a Church* (1437) in Dresden's Alte Meister Gallerie.

2. Woolson must have been working on *For the Major* (1883), which was not serialized in *Harper's New Monthly Magazine* until Nov. 1882 to Apr. 1883.

3. Richard Wagner's opera premiered in Bayreuth on July 26, 1882.

4. A minor character in the playscript of James's *Daisy Miller* (1882).

5. avoirdupois: heaviness.

6. Alphonse Daudet published *Fromont Jeune et Risler Aîné* in 1874 and *Tartarin de Tarascon* in 1872. James's review of Ernest Daudet's *Mon Frère et Moi* (*My Brother and I*) appeared in *Atlantic Monthly*, June 1882.

7. James's review of Tourguenieff appeared in *French Poets and Novelists* (1878). *Dominique* (1863) was the only novel by painter Eugene Fromentin.

8. The Crown Prince was probably Frederick III of Prussia, the husband of Queen Victoria's daughter Victoria. Woolson quotes James's novel *Eugene Pickering* (1879) later in this paragraph.

9. The Feb. 2, 1882, review was anonymous. James published *Roderick Hudson* in 1875.

10. See letter to John Hay dated March 16, 1883, for Woolson's difficulties with the Appletons.

11. Mrs. Leslie (Henrietta) Pell-Clark.

12. James published the script for *Daisy Miller,* subtitled *A Comedy,* with Macmillan in 1882. Although it appeared in *Atlantic Monthly,* May 1883, the play was never produced.

13. Henrietta Pell-Clark.

To Samuel and Flora Mather (WRHS/Mather)

(Care Knauth, Nachod, & Kühne
Leipzig. Germany)
London
Sept. 18th, [1882?]

My dear Sam & Flora.

My dearest love & congratulations to you both, and many kisses to the little boy, in whom I take the profoundest interest. If I were in Cleveland, I should arrive, probably, daily to inspect his funny little hands & feet, the color of his eyes, touch his soft little arms very respectfully, once in a while, and discuss his various expressions. For I know he has a great many. And if, later, he would come to me without being afraid, I should probably become his faithful slave, permanently. I do not care for all children by any means;—care for them simply because they are children, as many women do. But for a few, here & there, I have cared a great deal, & I find it growing upon me to care the most for a little baby,—they are so sweet, helpless, & endearing. I am sure your little boy is one I shall greatly love, & I am extremely sorry I cannot come over & have a look at him before he is put into "short clothes." You must send me a picture of him when you succeed in getting a good one; & don't forget to add one of yourself, here I mean Sam as you (or Flora) promised.

We have your letter; & Kate has written; &, a day or two ago, we met Mrs Hay on Bond Street & had a little conversation under an arcade; and the result of all is to give me a very complete impression of Flora's bravery & unselfishness. It seems to me very remarkable.—I have often thought of you since you left this side, & wished to write. It has been impossible. I did not get my strength back for a long time after that illness, so that I was quite discouraged. I was able to be about, but felt so tired & weak. Then, when I began to feel better, I discovered that I had misunderstood the date when they wanted the short serial in New York; it was Aug. 1st, instead of Oct. so I had either to throw their winter arrangements into confusion—(for, as you know, perhaps, all their arrangements—magazine arrangements—are laid out months in advance) or work very hard myself. As it was my fault—the misunderstanding—I thought I ought to try not to disappoint them; hence the two months, & over, of very steady work. The "Tribune" you sent, containing the title announcement of the story, showed me that they were really waiting. ~~As they~~ For the Harpers had sent me a Cable dispatch two days before the date of the paper, & I had answered the next day, saying it was done, though not copied. Upon that they brought out the notice. For, with my best efforts, I could'nt get the story copied & all ready before the last of August. If it had not been, therefore, for all this, I should have written to you both long ago. I enjoyed so much the letters you wrote me, just before sailing, Flora's from London partly, yours from Liverpool. They reached me in Munich. I spent a little while at Innsbruck; then Munich. Baden-Baden for about nine weeks; Dresden; the Rhine from Mayence to Cologne. Brussels; Antwerp. Over the channel without the least sea-sickness—a very unusual passage everybody said; no one was sick of all the crowd on board. Here I am at last in this pleasant interesting smoky old city, & we have been very busy going about on various excursions as the weather has been lovely. I greatly enjoyed "Harryston Court," & can think of nothing in the world so delightful ~~than~~ as being one of the old ladies who live there, pensioners of the queen. It is so peaceful and lovely & "historic." But, as I understand it, the old ladies are all of rank; so there is no hope for me! Clara & Clare go over to Liverpool on Wednesday, and sail Thursday. Mrs N. C. Winslow and Mr Chamberlain sail on the same steamer.[1] For myself I have'nt quite decided whether I shall spend a month or two here—now that I am on the spot, or go over to Paris for the same time, or hurry back to my beloved Italy & establish myself for the winter in a small apartment. I shall probably try Florence, as Clara objects so strongly to Rome. I am very well now, though still tired. The other day I was weighed, & was astounded to find that, in spite of all, I weighed over 141 pounds! Certainly I can no longer pose as an invalid.—Let me put in here that the address at the head of the letter will be mine for the future—as long as I remain abroad. I was ever so much obliged for the "Century"; & the criticism of "Anne" I thought wonderfully, kind & cordial note. And the two "Tribunes" too I enjoyed, as I always do. The "Patience" Flora was thoughtful enough to send me, never came. It was too bad. But now now I have heard it "upon its native heath," & laughed over every scene. An odd fact to me is that I have always supposed that no one was in London in September. That they might linger on after the "season" far into August; but "September" was tabooed. Everybody I knew, or have ever heard of, seems to be here now! The evening after we saw "Patience," Mr Gladstone & several prominent "lords," were there,—so the papers said. Mrs Hay (who looked remarkably well) said that ever so many distinguished people (whom she named) were here; &, calling upon Mrs N. C. Winslow (your friend) at the "Laugham" yesterday, we met Mr & Mrs W. I. Chamberlain. Mr C. goes home on the same steamer with Clara; Mrs C. & the beautiful daughter remain, & they are going into our old lodgings in Clarges Street. Mrs C. said that Jennie had had these "delightful invitations" to various country houses, & that they were going to accept them. Jennie seems to have made one of the great successes as an "American beauty." At Hombourg they were with (traveling with) the Prince of Wales & his party. I think it should be mentioned too that the Princess of Wales has also showed her attention (so I am told) as that is quite another matter.[2] All this I get from Mrs N.C.W.(your friend.) Clara & I are so proud to think that the lodgings where we stayed should be the ones selected by the "American beauty," & that royalty's carriage has stopped at the door where our modest hansom used to wait! We no longer go to Clarges Street, (I never went but once), but are here in South Kensington, near the Museum, in comfortable lodgings at reasonable rates. The Howells are near us somewhere; but just where I have not learned. Col. & Mrs Hay have gone into the country now, I believe.—Flora, I am taking the advice in your last letter; I am going to hear "Romeo & Juliet" to-night. Irving & Ellen Terry. They too are here, & playing "in September." Clara, you see, is stirring me up, & making me go about a little, while she can!—England is very fascinating to me, & I long to stay. But it is not the season for me, & I know it will soon be cold & damp. I have already had a bad cold, & don't want to take another. I must come back in the spring, & stay a long summer. Baden-Baden is the prettiest little nook I have ever seen. But not in the least gay—as I had supposed it was. Charming music every evening.

If I go over to Paris, I shall use Flora's letter as a guide when I buy my few things. Everybody seems to be going to Italy; but I fancy it will be Rome; not Florence. And Rome is by far the most fascinating, I think. I wish I could go there. Give a great deal of love to your father & ~~father~~ mother (this to you, Sam,) Kate & Will. Tell Kate I shall write to her soon. My letters are fearfully behind; but I know Kate, at least, will understand & excuse.

I have never in the least forgotten our faultless days at Paestum. How beautiful & delightful it was! But I suppose there is a little gentleman in Cleveland who now seems to you & Flora far better than Greek temples! Well—I think he would seem the same to me.

Good-by. Yours affectionately,
Grand-Aunt Connie.

It seems, Flora, that Mr King has been in London lately,—so Mrs Hay said. I would go round a corner to see him—after your descriptions. I would go round two corners to see that Mr Adams who said he wanted a little calf.[3] If he should ever come over here, let me know, please.

Notes

1. Woolson is speaking of the W. I. Chamberlain family of Hudson, Ohio, and their daughter Jennie; the N. C. Winslow family was from Cleveland.

2. The Prince of Wales was Edward Albert, Queen Victoria's oldest son, later King Edward VII. He was married to Princess Alexandra of Denmark.

3. Possibly Henry Adams, whose friendship with Clarence King and John Hay has been well documented.

To Katharine Livingston Mather (WRHS/Mather)[1]

London
October 2^{d}, 1882

My dear Kate.

. . . I have been exceedingly busy, through every hour of daylight, and in the evening could only stroll or sit in the pleasant grounds of the Kur-Saal (at Baden-Baden), and listen to the lovely music,—most of the time without talking at all. Baden-Baden is the sweetest, loveliest place I have ever seen. I don't mean the little town, (though that is pretty too), but the green gardens and slopes, and the enchanting forest walks all about. It is in the "Black Forest" you know. I should like nothing better than to spend another summer there, when not so busy, and drive or walk every day in different directions over the shady roads. The orchestra too, in the evenings, was a great pleasure to me. I missed "Parsifal,"—too busy to go.[2] But I saw Dresden to great advantage, and was greatly charmed with the gallery, which is the most splendid one (of paintings) I have ever seen. I mean "splendid" in its size, light and comfort; there are seats; oh! there are seats! You can not only see the beautiful pictures, but you can see them without that terrible insidious gallery-fatigue, which comes, I think, from the poor body's getting so very tired, while the mind is taken up with its own pleasure. Then we came to the Rhine, and down it to Cologne, and the Cathedral. Then Brussels, its old City Hall, Cathedral, and pictures. Antwerp, <u>its</u> Cathedral and more pictures. The Channel, and London. Of course, I am seeing everything here. In fact, I have seen so much since I left Baden the last of August, and I shall go on "seeing" so much for another month probably, that I shall arrive in Florence again, gorged with impressions! There won't be room left in my mind or memory for a feather's weight more; and I shall be glad to settle down for six months, and live monotonously, so as to sort over and classify my remembrances.

I am enjoying London very much. I go to see the things I especially wish to see, get the books I especially wish to read, take long walks, see as much lovely scenery as I can find; and fence my days round with a great deal of quiet peacefulness. Yesterday, I went down to the "Inner Temple," to attend service in the beautiful old "Temple Church," within the walls of the "Temple." I have always had a great interest in the "Temple," and was much disgusted when I heard that old "Temple Bar" had been taken down. "Murray" says that strangers are only admitted to the round part of the church; to get into the Choir, where service is conducted, you must have an order from a "bencher," that is, one of the barristers who belong to the "Temple."[3] But the Verger invited me into the Choir, and I greatly enjoyed everything. The exquisite roof, the solemn old bronze effigies of the Knights Templar, full length and life size, each with his sword and shield, so old that their names are lost,—lying on slabs in the floor; the beautiful choral service; the eminently "English" congregation, composed in a large measure of law students and barristers. After service I took the liberty of roaming all about the enclosure, stepping very gently, and pretending every time I met anybody that I was on my way out! I wasn't! I saw everything. The house where Dr Johnson had his rooms; and Charles Lamb, and Goldsmith. The old churchyard where Goldsmith is buried. Also the "Temple Garden," where Shakespeare makes the roses plucked, the beginning of the "Wars of the Roses." "No person admitted to this garden without an order," read the notice at the entrance. So I gently walked in, with the countenance of one who has an order! The garden is a broad green lawn sloping down to the Thames. I ought to say, in half explanation of my boldness, that I knew it was the "Long Vacation," when rules are relaxed, as a large majority of the students and lawyers are away for some weeks in the country. The "Knights Templars" were old heroes of mine, so I made an especial journey to their old church. It is in this way that I am "seeing" London. I am now going to Westminster Abbey; a fourth visit. I like to take it in slowly, sit there and "meditate"; stroll about and look at the inscriptions at my leisure. . . .

Yours, always affectionately
C. F. Woolson.

Notes

1. The letter is in a typed transcription at WRHS. Portions also appear in Benedict/CFW, 267–69.

2. Wagner opera that premiered at the Bayreuth Festival in 1882.

3. John Murray's travel guide. Woolson is discussing her views on Britain's Knights Templar, originally a monastic order that traces its origins as far back as the Crusades. In London, its property eventually was rented by lawyers.

To Edward F. Strictland? (Schlesinger)[1]

London
October 3[d], [1882?]

Dear Sir.

Your letter has been forwarded to me by the Messrs. Harper & Brothers. I comply with your request with pleasure, and the more so because I once formed quite a collection of autographs myself. But, after the rare collection in the British Museum here, it makes me feel ashamed to gravely write down my own unimportant name.

Yours truly,
Constance Fenimore Woolson.

Notes

1. This note is in the Edward F. Strictland Autograph Collection at the Schlesinger

Library. It is impossible to know if the recipient was Strictland. The autograph is attached to an advertisement for *Anne* and other recent Harper's novels (1883) that reads as follows:

> Miss Woolson adds to her observation of scenes and localities an unusual insight into the human heart. Sometimes one is ready to say that a fragment, and not an inferior fragment, of the mantle of George Eliot is resting on her capable shoulders.
>
> *Century*
>
> It proves the author's right to stand without question at the head of American women novelists.
>
> New York *Tribune*
>
> Clearly a work of genius.
>
> Boston *Traveller*
>
> It is one of the most remarkable combinations of feminine delicacy and acuteness since "Uncle Tom's Cabin" was given to the public.
>
> *Christian Advocate*, Pittsburg

To Elinor Howells (Houghton)

Xmas. Eve
1882

Dear Mrs Howells.

Will you accept a small Xmas remembrance from a fellow exile. The books are for your daughter; she said that she has not had them. They are full of information about Florence; though I remember thinking, when I read the work myself, that I had never seen a poetical subject so prosaically treated.—I hope to see you soon; but please do not include me among the people whose calls "must be" returned within a given time; come when just the right evening happens to arrive. For that, I will willingly wait a month. The lion-hunt has begun, I fancy![1]

Yours very sincerely,
C. F. Woolson.

I suppose you all go down to Rome, to spend Xmas with your dear friends, the [Veddues?].

Notes

1. Woolson is referring to those who seek out famous writers.

To Clara Stone Hay (Brown)

Florence
Jan. 8th, [1883]

My dear Mrs Hay.

I am very sorry to hear of your father's illness, and also the possible necessity of a winter voyage for Col. Hay, and the consequent loneliness for yourself. I shall hope—and should be glad to know—that your despatch of inquiry brought better news. But, in case Col. Hay would think it best to go back, should you stay all winter where you are?[1] We should be very glad to see you here; when I say "we," I refer to the Howells and myself; and, very probably, you have other friends here besides.

So you are at Cannes? From Sam's and Flora's account of the place, it was the nearest thing to Paradise our poor earth affords. The sunshine at Cannes was said to be continuous; it "never stopped." It was peculiarly "golden"; yet never "glaring." It was "very warm"; yet at the same time "very bracing"; very "strengthening"; yet also "dreamy." One could be "out all day at Cannes, and never want to come in"; and yet it was just the sort of weather, too, that made it "so cosy round one's own bright little fire." As I understand it, they wore their "nice warm American wraps," and felt "invigorated"; yet, at the same time, "lounged," in summer clothes, under "the olive trees." And then how they felt! How inspired, how well! There was certainly nothing like it. All this, repeated to me while the tramontana shook the shutters and whistled down the old chimneys at Sorrento, gave me a chastened humility of spirit, which still continues. For I have never been at Cannes.

As for weather here, I cannot say much that is favorable, so far—except that it is better than it was at Paris! We have had some superb days—one of them Xmas day—which I spent at Pisa. I have had some delightful walks over these lovely hills, and am contented as far as I can be—away from Rome! When I remember the Campagna, a lump always rises in my throat. So I try to "remember to forget" it, as much as possible. I shall probably stay quietly where I am until some time in May.

Your friends the Howells are here, not far from me; they are well, and, I fancy they like Florence—though of course I may be mistaken. The last time I saw Mr Howells, he was starting for a dancing-party. This sounds rather gay. And my idea is that he is leading a gay life. The lion-hunt is well organized, and, as the Piazza Santa Maria Novella (where he is staying) is not large, they run him down in spite of his efforts to escape. But I imagine that he finds something to amuse him in the mixed society here. I should, I know, were I going out more. But as I very seldom accept an invitation, I miss the amusement; and I fear also that I shall miss the Howells (I mean miss seeing as much of them as I should like to see), for their time will be all engrossed. I dined with them at their hotel on New Year's day; and, on the preceding Saturday, I met them at another dinner, where, as Mr Howells was placed beside me, I had a very pleasant hour or two. I have been re-reading Mr King's "Mountaineering," and find it delightful.[2] After meeting him in Paris, I sent to America for the volume, curious to see if it would seem like him, now that he was a personality to me, and not a name merely. What a pity for us readers that he will not write more. And the same remark applies equally to Col. Hay.

I have made up my mind that they did write "Democracy."[3] They wrote it together. In this way they escape direct falsehood. They wrote it during that first winter of Col. Hay's residence in Washington when you were not with him. Voilà.

So the Chamberlains are at Cannes. I am sure all sorts of amusing things are happening; do remember them and tell me.—Various Clevelanders are here, and more are coming. My sister writes from Cleveland, December eighteenth—that she was expecting to dine with Hattie Sherman—the next day I think—to meet Flora and Sam.

Please give my regards to Col. Hay; and a kiss from me to the children. Please believe me always, very sincerely your friend,

C. F. Woolson.

Notes

1. Clara Hay's father was Ohio railroad magnate Amasa Stone (1818–83). According to Petry (24), the often-ailing John Hay may have been returning to Paris or to Cleveland.

2. Clarence King's *Mountaineering in the Sierra Nevada* (1872).

3. The anonymously published novel *Democracy* (1880) was eventually identified as being written by Henry Adams.

To Samuel Mather (WRHS/Mather)

Care Macquay, Hooker, & Co.
Via Tornabuoni
Florence. Italy
Jan. 10th, [1883]

My dear Sam.

A happy new year to you all. I feel quite near to you to day. In the first place, I have your nice long letter of November 12th before me, & have been re-reading it. Then I have Clara's letter from Cleveland of Dec. 18th; and, yesterday, came your father's of Dec. 22d. Give my love to your father, & tell him how delightful his letter was to me, in every way. But, tell him, also, that he is quite in error when he supposes me "wedded to Europe." No, no; it is nothing of the kind. And, for the last few days, I have really thought of almost nothing else than "home." It has been cold here; you know Florence is a cold place, & makes no pretensions to warmth. It declares itself "healthy"; & stops there. The cold I can not, and do not, and will not stand. I hate it, and despise it, and anathematize it with all my heart. It is certainly the most diabolical thing on this earth. Though I weigh 145 lbs., I find the cold nips me as cruelly as ever; in fact I am in some way more sensitive to it than formerly. I have made great efforts to be comfortable here; I have had all the windows & doors of my parlor & bed-room carefully "listed," & portières & heavy curtains put up.

Jan. 31st

My letter was interrupted by calls. And it really seems as if the "cards,"—either receiving or returning them—had been continuous ever since! It sounds ungracious to say so (so do'nt say so) but I shall not try another winter in Florence until I have one of perfect leisure, because "society" here is too kind, and too hospitable for people who want their time undisturbed. I have made some delightful acquaintances, & it is extremely pleasant to be so kindly treated; still, it is quite impossible for me to be going out to lunches, & dinners, and evening-companies, & go on with my writing at the same time. I decline almost all the invitations,—but still merely to make the "party-calls"—or rather invitation-calls, takes far too many of my hours to please me. The Howells, who have been here since Xmas, are going to run away soon,—though they had intended to spend the winter. Mr Howells simply has'nt a moment, he is so called upon & invited. If *I* complain (to you, safe in America) of the too great attention, you can imagine what the condition of a real "lion"—like poor Mr Howells—has been! How different this winter from the Sorrento one last year,—so quiet, so still; I ~~should~~ could'nt have had a twentieth part of the pleasure from yours & Flora's visit had it been made in Florence. In Sorrento I had you both all to myself. And this reminds me to ask you what you are about, dropping the title "Aunt" from my name? I have been "Aunt" to you all my life, &, now that my hair is turning gray, I see no reason for becoming suddenly so juvenile. Besides Flora's "Aunt Connie" I am quite devoted to, & I have no intention of allowing for her to drop it after having so bravely learned it in Sorrento.—I have just had a letter from Mrs Hay, announcing their arrival here in a few days. She says your "boy" is a fine little fellow, and its Grandmother (she refers to Mrs Stone) *very* proud of it. Clara, here I mean your *Aunt* C, writes in *high* praise of the young man. As also does your father. I do'nt know the child's name yet! Do tell me. I am to be godmother at Easter to the little son of Comm. Goodrich, U.S.A. and Lord Wolseley is Godfather! Comm. G. was the American officer detailed to accompany Gen. Wolseley in the Egyptian campaign & the child is to be called "Wolseley." Lord W. has sent a gorgeous gold spoon as a christening gift,—a full-rigged ship at the end of the handle. Of course he will be godfather by proxy.—Little Wolseley is a nice child; but I am sure Flora's boy is a great deal nicer. I wish I had him here this moment! Why should I be wandering about the world, standing godmother to strange children, when I have grandnephews of my own waiting for me over there?—I am now going back to your November letter, before taking up the photographs.—I must say—more especially to Flora—that I saw no more of Mr King after that pleasant evening at the theatre,—though I was in Paris some time longer. My feelings about him are therefore divided between liking and ~~vexation~~ disappointment. For he was to have taken me to the Louvre; yet did'nt. I have heard, since I left Paris, that he is "enormously rich"; "has made a tremendous fortune." This I did not know when I was seeing him in the gay city. Mr Howells told me of it at a dinner-party here; &, when I said, "Are you sure?" (for I was rather surprised by the story) he answered—"Why he thinks nothing of ordering fifteen pairs of trousers at one time. Did it in London." So I suppose that is a proof. Mrs Hay says that his cousin & sister will probably not come to Florence, after all; so I suppose that means that Mr King will not come either. I am sorry. (There is a period after "sorry.") I sent to America for his book—"Mountaineering in the Sierra Nevada," & I find it charming.

I think it very clever of Robert Chamberlain to divine a feminine influence against me in the "Nation" office. Give him my regards, & tell him that I should like to talk over some literary matters with him,—theories & methods. I am so entirely alone—~~shup~~ shut up within myself—as regards literary work, that it would do me ever so much good. I have always had a confidence in his opinion; & have felt sorry that I could see so little of him. I am especially pleased that he perceived that my "climax" (in "Anne") was the court room scene. Of course, it was; & everything else led up to it. It was the supreme test of the girl's brave pure fidelity; or rather the most perfect example of it that ~~which~~ I could imagine.—

You object to my going to the Italian Mts. What do you say to a summer in divine Venice? The Italians go there as we go to Newport. Sea-bathing on the Lido. If Clara does not come over, I want to go to Venice & establish myself in some old historic rooms on the Grand Canal, with gothic windows, & a little high balcony. I shall employ an aged and highly respectable gondolier, &, hidden in my gondola, float about every evening for lovely quiet meditative hours. There will be no "calls" there, thank Fortune. No "society." But I shall not be quite alone because I know some people who live there. One of our walking-party here (such magnificent walks as we have over these Tuscan hills in all directions, 6 and 8 miles 3 times a week; 3 ladies & 3 gentlemen.) Mr Felton of Cambridge—son of the former President of Harvard—spent all last summer in Venice with his wife, & found it "an ideal existence." He goes to Athens this week to spend a year or two;—what do you think of that? A "year or two" in Athens! By the way, Mr Felton wears a Greek coin (set as a pin) 2,000 years old! And an exquisitely beautiful one it is, too. He is extremely tall, or I should have made a jump & stolen it before this. Our Paestum coins repose in their box, rather sadly. A few came out of the "cleaning" with vague traces of heads on them. But the others are without any traces of anything. They are all copper. One of them, a very small one—really looks as if it might be genuine. And everybody thinks so too. But it is not silver, & one person, somewhat skilled in such things, said it was not an especially rare one. But I do not give up about them yet. And I still mean to submit them all to a coin-dealer of experience & we may find that we have treasures unbeknown.—Yes indeed, poor little rosy-cheeked Fiorentino,—what has become of him, I wonder. Mrs Calvin Goddard & her family, & Mrs Cutter (Carrie Pease) & hers, have just gone to Sorrento, after a month or two here. But they were to stay at the "Tramontano." Mrs Henry Clark has just come to Florence. I met her on Via Tornabuoni the other day. The Carter girls, & my beautiful young cousin Julia Smith, are much admired in Rome, I hear. They will be here next month.—

I sent out immediately about your photographs, & have purchased as good an assortment as I could find. By that I mean that sometimes the most characteristic pictures of a painter are those which blur badly when photographed. So I had to take examples that were clear. They go by mail, registered. I have numbered them, & the numbers correspond with those on the paper enclosed. The large Fra Angelico is my Xmas present to you. I had spent all your money, yet felt disappointed that you had'nt a good example of his style. So I added this "Paradise." With the "Angel" I gave Flora, it will do fairly well as an illustration of your essay. I presume you were not in earnest when you suggested (in your first letter) some notes from me on these early artists. I have only a very little knowledge of them; & you probably have all the authorities at hand. I will add a few quotations,—though I presume you are already familiar with them. I grow fonder of these early painters every day. Only the Venetian masters compete with them in my heart.

Thank you very much for the "Life of Cooper."[1] I especially wanted to see it. I am still sailing on my middle name—as I have done ever since I came abroad. A beautiful old villa here (which I think is the one described as Osmond's, in "Portrait of a Lady,") is occupied by a beautiful old lady, Miss Greenough, sister of the sculptor of that name, who was an intimate friend of Cooper when he was over here. Miss Greenough has invited me three times, the last time to the most elegant lunch party I ever attended. Wonderful old china, & old wines. On the walls two Velasquez, a Van Dyke, Guido, & Paul Potter! Well,—the point I am making is that she invites me because I am the grand-niece of my uncle. And she takes me out to the table, & puts me on her right hand, for the same reason.

My dear Sam, I am writing in the evening because it is the only time I have. Please therefore excuse scrawling.—I have had several "Tribunes" from you, & one, I thought, from Flora; her handwriting. All the marked items were just what I wanted to see. I have only the N. Y. Herald! Do you wonder how I come by it? Because Clara's friend, Mr Prince of Yonkers, insists upon sending it to me, probably on her account. It is'nt the paper I dote on! But I appreciate the motive, & kindness. Charlie writes quite often. How anxious I am that he should do well with his farm this next season. The winter seems to depress him.

You never sent me that photograph of yourself. Kate Targer owes me a letter.

Dearest love to your Mother & Father. Also to Will. Jane Carter offers me a charming little lot in Cooperstown for a cottage, with view of lake. I mean at a low price. Shall I go there to live? I have just signed & sent off contract for "For the Major" in book-form. Have not yet received report of sales of "Anne." It is customary, I am now told, to wait until one year has expired. Good-by, with a great deal of love to Flora, & a thousand kisses to the dear little boy.

Yours affectionately,
C. F. Woolson.

Notes

1. Probably Thomas Lounsbury's (1838–1915) *Life of James Fenimore Cooper* (1883).

To Clara Stone Hay (Brown)

[Florence]
Monday morning
[February 1883]

Dear Mrs Hay.

If you have not seen this, would'nt you like it for the not very interesting journey to Sienna? If you have already read it, my messenger can bring it back. I have been trying to get the number for you ever since I heard you say you wanted it; but it is not easy to get the late magazines in Florence. Will you please return it by mail from Sienna, as it is a library-book.

I see that you reach the mediaeval city before dark. My impression of the hour of arrival was a dismal snowy December one; from the looks of things, it might have been midnight. Give my love to the beautiful tall tower (only that sounds like the N. Y. Tribune!) & the superb cathedral; &, with love & best wishes for you both, I am, yours always,

C. F. Woolson.

As I call the servant to take this to you, your beautiful flowers appear. They give me great pleasure. Good-by.

To Clara Stone Hay (Brown)

Florence
March 16th, [1883]

Dear Mrs Hay.

What do you suppose I have before me, as I write? The photograph of a certain bright-eyed little boy. Your nephew Livingstone has politely sent his likeness to his grand-aunt. I am very proud of him, and consider him a bright and handsome boy. Flora writes in good spirits, and says she gets her ideas of Cleveland gayeties from Sam, and of society elsewhere from the "fashionable news" of the Tribune. She is for the first time discovering the enjoyment of sending a charming little note of regret, going to bed early, and hearing all about it the next day—which has long been my favorite pastime.—I am glad she is taking care of herself.—Plans and walks and even life itself have been at a stand-still here. "No such weather has been known in Italy for thirty five years"—they say. But "they" are always saying that, & wherever I go, it is the worst weather of the century. Two weeks ago it began, with a fierce north wind and dust-storm; after that, for eight days it snowed every day, so that all the roofs remained thickly covered with it, and not only were all the mountains white, but even the slopes of the low hills, like Bello Sguardo. One might have thought one's self in Canada; out on the country roads, boys were rolling up great snow-balls three feet high. It has been bitterly cold, too. Today the sun is shining; but the snow on the mountains is not melted.—I hear vague rumors that the Howells have come down from their Sienna mountain; but I have not seen them, or heard from them. It must have been arctic there.—I was almost tempted, by your description of your visit, to go to Sienna myself for a month when I leave here, before going to Venice. But I think now I shall adhere to my original plan, giving myself the treat of a day or two in Ravenna, en route. But one does'nt want to think of "Venice" in all this snow!—I am sure, in that provincial quiet city where you are now, you must be longing for news from this gay Florence. Miss Paget & Miss "A. Mary F." I have seen several times; but have invariably found them—as Colonel Hay did at the Stillmans—distrait. It is rather a distrait household; they are always getting up and going out of the room, and coming back through some other door; they are very processional. It seems that Mr Paget-Robinson-Hamilton has written "three books of poetry."[1] This does'nt prevent him from calling Miss Robinson "The Young Hag." I do'nt know why. I made one attempt to follow up our country man, Pennel; I asked Miss Paget if she knew him. She said "Oh yes"; & immediately got up and went out of the room. I was afraid to ask her anything more when she came back—of course through another door.—The large blonde man at Miss Greenough's, with Mrs Ibbertson, was Mr Ibbertson; two of the young girls were their daughters.[2]—I have seen Mrs Barstow several times. But the J. J. Jarvis' ladies have not carried out their good intention.—Mrs Launt Thompson is a disappointed woman. She wanted very much to see you. That mysterious door she was trying to get into led to the terrace of the villa, where she had left her children; she was on her way to give an order to the nurse, but hastened back immediately, hoping that she should find us in the lower hall; but we had already gone up stairs. She then delayed her call on you to the last possible moment, hoping that you would have reached home. Her next hope was that you would come back via Florence; "they must do so" she said; "there is no other way." I mentioned "Empoli;" and she had to give it up.—The Goodriches (U.S.N.) have got the Chadwicks staying with them for a few days. I fancy you know who the Chadwicks are; he is attaché—in some way—in London; a Navy man, and Mr Goodrich's especial friend. They have come down to Italy to see the launch of that fine Italian ship at Leghorn.—In the midst of the worst weather last week, arrived the Masons & Mabel Boardman. In the evening, in a driving snow storm, Capt. M. came over to see me, from the Hotel d'Italie. I do'nt know whether he intended to be funny; but he was so. They had put off their Italian journey all winter so as to be sure to have fine weather; they had waited until "all the almond trees would be in bloom," &c, &c. he had dreamed all his life of "Italy," &c&c. All he could say was that during the entire winter in Basle they had had no weather approaching this! They were almost frozen. Neither of the chimneys "drew" in their rooms, and the rooms were full of smoke. They had been out to drive "on a road some where up there on the hills, where you stop at a church" (San Miniato, I presume) and "the wind blew so that we could scarcely make each other hear a word." The horse had fallen down on a sharp descent, and broken things generally, besides frightening the ladies so that they were reduced to tears. Armed with all the rugs, guidebooks, &c, they had been obliged to walk almost all the way home, before the mended carriage overtook them. The ladies had now gone to bed, in their smoky rooms, in order to get warm. They were to leave on the first train in the morning.—Mrs Henry Clark; Miss Smith & her nieces; & Mrs Custer are here; also Miss Hurlburt. Mrs Goddard & Mrs Cutter are coming. The city is full of frozen surprised depressed tourists. They talk to me in the most injured tones.—I must tell you that ~~the~~ Mrs Chamberlains~~s have~~ has been, & gone, & I did not see ~~them~~ her. I regret this very much—for several reasons, which you wd. not be especially interested in; they date back to our school-days together. Will you be so good therefore as to send me the name of their Bankers—in case you happen to know it as I may write.—I supposed they were to stay two weeks—they told Capt. Mason so; and, in addition, I waited for them to send me word, as they knew I was here, Mr Chamberlain having written down my address when we met in London. Four days passed—extremely stormy all of them; & then I wrote a note to Mrs C., asking her to come & see me the next afternoon. A note wd. not be like a call. It wd. leave her free to come or not as she chose. My note came back to me; they had left the city. They were only here five days.—In the mean while Mr Chamberlain is telling my sister in New York that one of "Mollie's principal pleasures in the plan of going to Italy is that Miss Connie is there"! I hear that they went to Paris, and from there are to go to London for the season. I also hear that Gord—I forget his name—, the one you know, is painting Jennie's portrait. It seems he requires but three sittings. Has Cabanel begun to paint you?

Do not forget—by the way—that you half promised to send me a photograph of yourself. I have a great desire to have one.—

Will you ask Col. Hay who wrote "Carcasonne," that little ballad about the old peasant, dying, who "never had seen Carcasonne." We have had a great discussion about it here. I feel almost sure that the version I saw was a translation from the French. But they are all against me.—I am reading "John Inglesant;" & am disappointed in it. I shall next get through "Mr Isaacs."[3] Perhaps you are shocked at my daring to "not care for" Inglesant. But if a novel pretends to be a real story from life, I like it real-er; & if it is a romance dealing with the weird, I like it weird-er. "John Inglesant" tries to be both.

I see by the papers that they have been so good as to amuse you with a few riots, and émeutes, up there on the Seine.[4] When the streets are safe, I wish you would find out the whereabouts of that picture of Regnault's, which ought to have been in the Luxembourg, but was'nt; at least I could'nt find it; I mean the "Exécution sans Jugement."[5] I must put in a little "shop," which I want Col. Hay to hear. "Rodman the Keeper" was brought out by the Appletons, on the terms that they should first pay themselves for the expence, & then, on further sales (if there should be any), they were to pay me the usual ten per cent. They reported, at the end of the first year, that they had by no means paid themselves back, & were much out of pocket &c; &c; a doleful tale. Last summer my sister wrote me that they had brought out another edition (a cheap one), on the tide of "Anne," I suppose. So not long ago I wrote to them, inquiring about this new edition &c&c. I never expected any money from the first edition—as that is not the Appleton's way! I wanted to have the book brought out at just that time, &, as my connection with Osgood had been broken, & the Appletons were urgently desirous to have it, I allowed them to publish it. My object now is—& has been for some time—to get it back into my own hands,—before making arrangements for English publication.—Well, I received recently the Appletons' reply. The first edition I think—1500 copies, in cloth—has been sold out.[6] The new edition, cheaper, (about which they never consulted me) a thousand copies—is also ~~almost~~ sold—or almost. But they have still not paid themselves for their expenses, & have therefore nothing due me! As to the sale of the book to me—they now "do not wish to part with it"; they consider it "valuable." They intimate that if I insist upon buying it back, they ~~will~~ shall feel obliged to charge a good deal for it; in justice, I suppose, to themselves! "Perhaps"—they continue—they may be able to begin paying me copyright next year. And then they close with a most earnest request for other books from my pen "on the same terms"! Is'nt that good?—I think I shall persist, & get the book back.—Please tell this to Col. Hay; & also that I have been dreadfully haunted by that "Stirrup Cup!"[7] It keeps sounding through my mind. But, though it haunts me so, I have grown very fond of it. He must not forget his promise.

If you are seeing Mrs Mac Kaye, & Miss Howland, please give them my regards.—And, with love to the children, and all good wishes for yourselves, I am always, very sincerely your friend,

C. F. Woolson.

Notes

1. Petry (33) tentatively identifies Hamilton as Eugene Lee-Hamilton, Violet Paget's (Vernon Lee) half-brother. A. Mary F. is Paget's close friend Agnes Mary Robinson.

2. As thorough as Petry's research has been, she has been unable to identify all of the people Woolson mentions in the remainder of this letter. See appendix for identified individuals that Woolson names more than once. Others whom Petry has tentatively identified are Frank Holcomb Mason (1840–1916), editor of the Cleveland *Leader* and U.S. Consul in Basle, Switzerland; writer Elizabeth Bacon Custer, widow of George Armstrong Custer; and Marian Howland, half-sister of Clarence King. This expansive catalogue of names indicates just how well connected Woolson was in Florence as well as why she found the society there overbearing.

3. "Carcassonne" was a French ballad translated by Gustave Nadaud; Woolson varies its spelling in her letters. *John Inglesant* (1881) was an historical novel by Joseph Henry Shorthouse (1834–1903); *Mr. Isaacs* (1882) was by Frances Marion Crawford.

4. Unemployed artisans rioted in Paris on March 9, 1883.

5. A painting by Alexandre-Georges-Henri Regnault, eventually hung in the Louvre.

6. Appleton's published *Rodman the Keeper: Southern Sketches* in 1880. They did not bring out a second edition, so Woolson is probably referencing a second printing. Harper's published the book version of *Anne* in 1882 and the second edition of *Rodman* in 1886.

7. Poem by John Hay, published in *Scribner's*, May, 1881.

To Flora Stone Mather (Basel)[1]

Florence 1883

The winter is about over here, and it has been to me in some respects pleasant; in others, vexatious. I have met some delightful people; but on the whole, the demands that Florentine society makes upon one's time are too great for any person who has other things to do. It is a very hurried, breathless sort of existence. Every family has its day for "receiving" and if one calls on any other day, it is considered to mean that one does not care to get in. Result: one has to take all the precious afternoon hours—my only ones for walking and visits to the galleries—for these tiresome receptions, and one cannot even walk at that time, because there is not time for it! One has to go in a cab. Even I—a stranger—have been driven to a "day." In my case, however, it does not mean so much the "day," as the saving of the other six; no one gets in save on Saturday! I mustn't complain too much, though, for I have had some enchanting walks; we have been in all directions within a circle of eight miles, and nothing can surpass the beauty of the views and the soft purple of the mountains. . . . You ask about the Howells. They were here two months, and I saw a good deal of them. . . . He is not in the least like those of his friends whom I happen to know, and with whom I have unconsciously classed him all this time—Colonel Hay, Mr King and Mr James. . . .

Did Mrs Hay write you of the party at the Stillman's? You know who Mrs Stillman is, I presume; the beautiful Greek lady, the original of the Greek lady in Disraeli's "Lothair."[2] The party consisted of such aesthetic ladies as London has sent to enlighten Florence; in pale blues and wan greens, with the most extraordinary arrangement of hair; they stood about, their distrait eyes fixed on space, having nothing to say on any of the usual topics—scorning them. Ever and anon through the rooms glided the tall thin figure of the dreamy hostess, also with extraordinary hair, and, on the walls hung the still more extraordinary pictures of the aesthetic painters, Rossetti, Burne-Jones, Madox Brown—all wan, and mystic and mysterious—so much so that one was afraid to ask what they meant lest it should be too unusual, let us call it, for poor, plain, uninitiated Americans. . . .

But on the whole, Flora, I think your present way of enjoying society by far the best: to go comfortably to bed and hear all about it the next day! I do'nt think that I shall go to any more "companies" large or small, and I am going to run away to Venice pretty soon. . . . I have the opportunity for making the acquaintance of Mr Symonds in Venice. Miss Poynter, one of my especial friends here, sister of Sir E. Poynter of the Royal Academy, wants to bring it about. Shall I embrace it? The opportunity, not Symonds. . . . I fancy I shall not. . . .

I wondered last night in the pauses of the "Musicale" how it was that "Society" had grown so ineffably stupid! Of course it wasn't any change in myself! Oh, no! . . .

I was glad to hear of the appreciative H.'s. I am as devoted to compliments as Henry James is not. I am always delighted to get one. This is really true. I think it likely that I may stay in Italy a full year, going up into the Apennines somewhere for the summer. It seems to me but a little while since we were drinking tea over the fire at Sorrento. I shall not see those shores this year, as I have decided upon Florence. Of course I prefer Rome, but my sister dreads the fever so sincerely that I have given it up. It seems to me now as if I should be the only American in Florence this year. Every other one is going to Spain. Nobody cares for anything but Velasquez and Spanish draperies. And I shall be left alone with my young man in black ("Rascal") and Botticelli.[3]

Notes

1. A fragment of the original of this letter is at the Cooper Library, University of Basel, Switzerland, pasted into Benedict's *Constance Fenimore Woolson*. A fuller transcription is in Benedict/CFW, 269–72.

2. Benjamin Disraeli's novel *Lothair* was published in 1870.

3. Benedict identifies the "young man in black" as a Titian painting, *Young Englishman* (1540–45).

To William Dean Howells (Houghton)

13 Lung 'Arno Guicciardini
Tuesday morning
[1883?]

Dear Mr Howells.

I wrote to Mr Mead, telling him how I felt about a portrait medallion. I have just received his reply.

I do'nt quite know what to do. I do'nt want to seem absurd, or unreasonable. Yet, at the same time, there is no doubt about my personal preference; it is most decidedly against the idea.

Now if you will be so good as to advise me in this little dilemma, I shall be very grateful; and I will gladly do as you think best. You know I have no one to go to; supposing therefore that I were your sister, should you tell me to consent?

Yours sincerely,
C. F. Woolson.

To John Hay (Brown)

Venice
April 24th, [1883]

Dear Colonel Hay.

I cannot write you a perfectly delightful letter—like yours to me. But I can thank you for it; & also for "Carcassonne"; I can remind you of a promise you made me, a promise which was to be fulfilled in London; & I can let you see that I am in Venice.[1]

Yes—I am here at last, & propose to stay. Though I have been here several times, I have never had half enough of the beautiful water-city, & so my intention is to live here a while. When I say "live," I mean that I have got out of the hotel. I have taken some rooms at the top of an old Venetian palace, on the Grand Canal near the great domes of "Santa Maria della Salute" & I'm going in for local color with all my might.[2] A rather dark & very winding stairway, with mysterious doors & unexpected landings, leads up to these rooms, &, when you get to them at last, you find them large, with low vaulted ceilings, & five windows on the Grand Canal. These windows are adorned with ancient little balconies, over which I propose to "lean" (let us hope they are strong!), & look, & look, & look, at all the beauty far & near. I can see old palaces, the sunset, the great rose-colored campanile of San Giorgio Maggiore, with the tall gold angel on the top, the tints of water & sky, and all the fishing-boats coming up the harbor with their red & orange sails. This strikes me as very enchanting. In addition, there is a courtyard down below, which most happily contains everything it should; an old carved marble well in the centre, armorial bearings on the walls, & an adorable crumbling outside marble staircase, that leads to the second-story apartment (under mine), inhabited at present by whom do you think? Nobody less than Symonds, the English writer on Italian art. It is the climax of my lucky chance here that I can always imagine Symonds looking from the windows below, as I look from mine above. For of all the modern writers on Italian subjects, he seems to me the most deeply imbued with the 15th century spirit; & I have never yet got any further down the ages than that. I mean in my amateurish art-studies. I do not like all he writes; far from it. But, as it happens, I have read it all. I like his shorter sketches better than I do his elaborate work on the Renaissance. I knew he was to be here, since both Miss "A. Mary F." Robinson, & Miss Poynter, are to visit him (them; he has a wife & family) here in May. But I had no idea that he was installed below me until I took up the landlady's book just now.

I got these rooms through the sad fate of Newman.[3] I believe I described that fate in my letter to Mrs Hay—did'nt I? Miss Willis had engaged them for May & June, no doubt expecting that she should be "Miss Willis" no longer. She is Miss Willis still, & intends now to go down to Lerici, instead of Venice; so I have stepped into her Venetian place. At Lerici the sad Newman is at present painting a picture. I do'nt know the subject, but presume it contains some more blighted flowers.

Your "Carcassonne" gave me great pleasure. It was such a kindly thing to do—sending it. I triumphed over the disputers, as to its French origin. Not only that, but we had it sung, & Nadaud's music is infinitely more original & sweeter than the other arrangement by Mr Edmund Potter (Mrs Thompson's brother), which Mrs Clymer had unearthed from some where, & with which she expected to "sweep the board"—as the old Chaplain used to whisper to me at Mackinac, sitting behind my chair, & directing all my playing eagerly, & supposing himself not to be playing whist—Oh no! "Play your queen, Miss Connie, & you'll sweep the board!"[4] The old red tower on the hill beyond the Val d'Ema, which gave rise to the discussion (I had called it "Carcassonne") I never reached—of course!—though we started out to find it many a time. "Tout le monde a sa Carcassonne!"[5]

The Howells are here, but I have not yet hunted them up. Nor Mr Noyes either. Shall do so later—as your letter to Mr Noyes is too nice a one to be wasted. But "hunting up" applies to me rather than to them, as I am up so many stairs. No doubt the Howells are in some fine apartment lower down; while as to Mr Noyes—I hear his abode is "sumptuous." There are plenty of Clevelanders here, of course; where are there not?

Mr Mead has made a medallion portrait of me, like yours & Mr Howells'. I hardly know what to say about this, lest I should say too much. I tell you about it, because

I can't help hoping that you will sympathize with the very strong objection I had—and have—to anything of the kind. I am not a subject for a sculptor; in addition, I do not at all think that because a woman happens to write a little, her face, or her personality in any way, becomes the property of the public. Do'nt you agree with me? You do'nt know how I long for some sympathy; &, better still, some comprehension.—Mr Howells asked me to sit. That was the beginning. I declined—in what I thought a very kindly & sensible note, a note I sent to Mr Mead himself. Mr Mead did not accept my decision; he spoke of making the portrait from photographs, if he could get any. There was some note-writing & discussion after this, &, finally, I became convinced that the Howells considered my declining pure affectation & foolishness. I say the Howells; I am sure Mrs Howells thought so; and I fancy her husband sees all other women, & their motives, through her eyes. The fact that Mr Mead was Mrs Howells' brother, made, of course, the difficulty of my position.

Well—the thing is done. And I regret it more deeply every moment. I have made what is to me a very great sacrifice (for one's personal feelings are sacred to one, no matter how unimportant one may be); and they will never in the least appreciate it. I do'nt know that I care now that they should; it is much better to let it all drop; & I shall. But I do care that Mrs Hay & you should understand how I felt, & feel, in the matter. "Think" said Mrs Howells, the last evening I spent there,—"think how nice it will be! When the Harpers want your portrait, to put in the magazine—as of course they will—it will be all ready."—In the magazine!

Mr Mead said to me that he thought it would be a good idea to have a relief of "American authors" on the Washington Monument. Do you want to go on the Washington Monument? but could'nt you—if it should come in your way—suggest that it is, at least, not the place for likenesses of women—especially living ones. I do'nt think there are any living personages on the Albert Memorial. The whole thing has become to me a sort of night-mare.

Now that I have made my wail, I will turn to a more amusing subject—(though, after all I do'nt know that anything could be more amusing than Mr Howells, Mr J. J. Jarvis, yourself, & myself on the Washington Monument.) It is, at present, but a legend; that is, I cannot swear positively that it is true, until later. But it is probably a fact. Violet Paget, "A. Mary F.," & our countryman Pennell (the young man sent over by the "Century" to etch the illustrations for Mr Howells' Tuscan articles), have gone off on a ten days' excursion into Umbria. To Assisi, Montepulciano, & such places. Miss Poynter told me of this expedition; she thought they had gone, as she had seen nothing of them; they were to go if Pennell could get the time. "O, I am delighted!" I exclaimed. "Why?" said quiet Miss Poynter, surprised at my emphasis. I explained to her that ever since I came abroad, I had been brought to book sharply by English people about the way our American girls go about unchaperoned &c.

The utmost, however, that I had been obliged to defend had been such things as afternoon walks, or drives, or some hour or two of loitering on beaches or in gardens. No American girls I knew had ever gone off for ten days, or longer, with young gentlemen, without a sign of a chaperon, as Miss Paget & Miss Robinson had now (probably) done.

Poor Miss Poynter tried to explain that it was purely a business excursion; the young ladies were writing articles which the young gentleman was to illustrate, &c.—"All that is undoubtedly true," I replied. "But the fact remains that they are 25, & 26, respectively; while Pennell is under 30; which is all I claim for my comparison." Between you & me and—the window curtain, is'nt it singular that the English seem always to prefer our roughest specimens to our really agreeable people. Pennell is—but perhaps you have seen him?

By the time I get to Paris again, the "Execution sans Jugement" will be unrolled, & in a fine place at the Louvre.[6] In all my vague plans for the next few years, no "Paris" appears. Spain is nearer. And even Florida. If I could have a little coquina cottage by the southern sea at St Augustine, I would come home; & stay forever.

I did'nt write to Mary Chamberlain after all. I remain very sorry that she should not have sent me word that she was in Florence.

For a man who is of course going to keep his promise, I mention that "Care Messrs. S. & A. Blumenthal. Bankers. Grand Canal. Venice" will be my address for some time.—Mr Stedman sent me advance sheets of his "Emerson" essay. What did you think of it, I wonder?

You & Mrs Hay will soon be at home again. Of course they want you back, & of course you want to go. My love to Mrs Hay, & a kiss for the children. Did Mr James see the children? I was talking to him about them, in Paris one day, & fancied he had not. He cares more for a child than for a grown person, any day! When there is a child (a nice one) in the room, he can't keep up a conversation. Just try it. I suppose you are seeing Mr King; give him all good wishes from me. And remember me too to the Chadwicks.—Did you write the article in the "Tribune," called "The Case of Mr Howells."[7]

Miss Greenough wanted me to come up & take the apartment under hers, on Bellosguardo, for the summer. I wonder if I have made a mistake in refusing. And I have found a young artist in Florence who paints the most remarkable Rossetti-ish pictures, without eve r having heard of Rossetti![8] For 50 francs I got a little sketch called "The Garden of the Hesperides" which you wd. give all your old shoes to possess.—Good-by—I am so sorry to say it to you—you both—when it means the ocean between us.

Yours most sincerely,
C. F. Woolson.

Notes

1. In addition to asking for a copy of "Carcassonne," a French ballad translated by Gustave Nadaud, Woolson had asked Hay for a photograph.

2. Alice Hall Petry (43) identifies these as rooms in the Gritti Palace.

3. Petry (43) identifies Newman as the painter of architecture and flowers Henry Roderick Newman.

4. Petry (43) identifies Mrs. Clymer as possibly the wife of George Clymer, a Navy surgeon. Mrs. Launt Thompson was the daughter of an Episcopal bishop, Alonzo Potter (1800–65). The Mackinac chaplain was John O'Brien.

5. All the world has their Carcassonne.

6. Painting by Alexandre-Georges-Henri Regnault.

7. Hay did not write the article published in the March 18, 1883, New York *Tribune.*

8. Petry (44) identifies the artist as Ricciardo Meacci.

To Elizabeth Gwinn Mather (WRHS/Mather)[1]

Venice
April 25th, 1883

My dear Libbie.

. . . You see where I am. I ran away from Florence the other day. I knew too many people there, and had to spend too much time paying visits. Here I hope to know no one, and have already met twenty-three acquaintances! However, they are tourists, and tourists never stay long,—even in this enchanting water-city. I have never had half enough of Venice, though I have been here several times. I have stepped into some quaint old rooms at the top of a dilapidated palace on the Grand Canal. They had been engaged by an English lady I know in Florence, but she was obliged to change her plans, so I gladly took her place. I have five windows on the Grand Canal, with ancient little balconies, and the view is delicious. My dinner is sent in from a restaurant, and the German landlady supplies my breakfast and luncheon. I am up a good many stairs, but I have the view, and I am in Venice. How long I shall stay, I don't know,—as long, probably, as I enjoy it. It is a sort of Italian Newport, you know; people come here for the sea bathing. But, probably, when it grows warm, I shall go up into the mountains somewhere. I am so extremely well that it is comical. When I see a great sturdy, broad-shouldered woman coming along by my side, I find I am looking at myself in some deceptive mirror in a shop window. . . . I had a pleasant winter in Florence, I went out quite a good deal—for me. If there is any improvement to be derived from mixing in "society," I must be immensely polished! But I only <u>feel</u> "mixed." I couldn't write much because they left me no time, so I have come here to make up the lost hours. I could tell you some remarkable and amusing stories of Florentine society. For one thing, it is no place for <u>young</u> ladies;

they have no liberty, and can hardly speak unless spoken to, can go nowhere alone, and flirtation is for them unknown; if they indulge in it, they lose their reputation; the only thing they can do is to marry; and they generally do that at once. The question of "dot" is a very important one, and if it is not known exactly how much a young girl is to have, she has no offers. They do not call this "mercenary"—as we should do at home; they say it is only proper prudence, to provide for the future. But if the young unmarried girls have a much better time in America than they can possible have here,—I mean if they go into "society" here—, the married women, and in fact, all older women, married or not, have a much better time. They are not "shelved" as they are at home, they are important, considered. I have not become used to it yet,—to hear the chances of this or that woman, of more than middle age, gravely discussed,—as to whether she is likely to accept this, or that, man, whom she really likes, &c&c. Even poor, quiet old ladies, over sixty, with white hair, are not secure from this sort of remark. If they have a little money especially, they are never secure, but are considered proper subjects of discussion as long as they live. These, of course, are the widows, or old maids, they who are free. As to the married ladies, there is a great deal of flirtation going on. What our young ladies amuse themselves with at home, the married ladies amuse themselves with here. It is all very curious, and to a looker-on like me, amusing. But for purity, and the sweet fresh air of real home life,—give me my own country! . . . [2]

Yours most affectionately,
C. F. Woolson.

Notes

1. The letter is in a typed transcription at WRHS. Portions also appear in Benedict, CFW, 272–73; 26–27.
2. CFW (27) adds a line at the end of the letter: "There is no doubt, Libbie, that one keeps younger longer over here."

To Edmund Clarence Stedman (Columbia)

(Care Knauth, Nachod, & Kühne
Leipzig. Germany.)
Venice
April 30th, [1883]

Dear Mr Stedman.

Do you see where I am? It seems very appropriate to be writing to you from Venice,—where, a short year ago, you yourself were established, with the expectation of spending some enchanted weeks in the beautiful water-city. I have just established myself here, with the same expectation. Now let us see whether I too shall be disappointed.

But I think not. There are many disadvantages in my isolated position in life,—many disadvantages, & much loneliness; but there is also one advantage—such as it is:—liberty. If I were to take a fancy to go to China, or the North Cape, tomorrow morning at ten precisely—there is absolutely nothing in the world to prevent it! Fortunately, my tastes are conservative, & growing more so every year, so that I shall never be heard of doing anything unusual. The utmost that I want to do now is to stay here in Venice, serenely and luxuriously, through May & June; & this I shall probably do. Let me hasten to add, however, that "luxuriously" does not apply to my actual surroundings, which are of the simplest kind; I mean it to apply only to the mental condition which seems to belong to Venice—which constitutes (to me) its chief charm. (Oh—the hurry—the breathless ~~social~~ "society" life of Florence!) I have been so long in Italy that I have taken my degree, & therefore I am not in a hotel or pension. I have a small apartment, on the third floor of an old dilapidated Venetian palace, on the Grand Canal, with plenty of windows & ancient little balconies, & a beautiful view of all the beautiful things that abound here,—tints of sky & sea—stately old façades,—the lateen yards along the Riva,—the rosy Campanile of San Giorgio Maggiore,—the fishing-boats coming up the harbor with the sunshine on their red & orange sails. My surroundings are deeply "Italian";—though, fortunately, my padrona has had many English & American lodgers, & is accustomed to their (to her no doubt mysterious) "ways." In the large apartment below me, for instance, is Mr J. A. Symonds, with his family. I have just discovered it. When Miss Poynter comes ~~over~~ from Florence to visit him, later, she will be amused to find me over her head. Miss Poynter was one of my especial friends in Florence. Do you know who she is? The author of a novel called "My Little Lady," which was much liked by some people—many people I should say—in England & America; & the sister of Mr Poynter of the Royal Academy. I must tell you, too, that I have met your Miss Robinson. She spent the winter in Florence with her friend, Miss Paget, who writes under the name of "Vernon Lee." I thought "Miss A. Mary F." very pretty. And I got her two volumes of poems from Miss Poynter (who is an intimate friend of hers), & read them—on your account; I mean, because you admire them so much. I shall also read, with much interest, her forthcoming novel.—These two young ladies—Miss Robinson & Miss Paget—took afternoon-tea with me one day in February—to meet the Hays. But, on the whole, I did not see much of them. Florentine society does not leave one time to see much of any especial person. Or much, even, of one's self! You spend all your days driving about leaving cards. It is a most unsatisfactory existence; I mean for a person who cares nothing for "society," nor for invitations to dinner—which is my case. "Society" there fairly drove the Howells out of the city. They stood it two months, & then fled. They were left without a moment to themselves.—They are here now—by the way—& will stay through May; perhaps longer. I see them often. The young etcher, Mr Pennell, who came over to illustrate Mr Howells' Tuscan articles has been a great ~~friend~~ admirer of Miss Paget and Miss Robinson in Florence, I hear. Perhaps you know Mr Pennell? I only met him once,—at the Howells' one evening.

I have just had a letter from my sister, describing the beautiful dinner she went to at your house. She greatly enjoyed it, & sent me a long account of much ~~all~~ that was said—knowing I should be interested in it all. It must have been very brilliant; & I am so glad Mrs Stedman asked her. I hope, sometime, to meet Mr Hawthorne; I have always wanted to know him. It is rather presuming in me to wish to know such men; but a very sincere & faithful—by faithful I mean unchanging—admiration is not, after all, so common a thing; and that, in my case, must make up for the lack of the various other attractions.

I did get your letter; it reached me early in December in Florence. It was a delightful one, & I enjoyed every word of it. But, about writing letters, I have undergone a change. I write fewer & fewer. I might give you a long explanation of this, &—as you are so appreciative of the delicate things of life—I am sure you would enter into it, & comprehend me. But, after all, it is unimportant. Suffice it to say (& I do'nt mean it in the least—the very least degree of bitterness or disappointment) that I have learned, in the slow course of the slow years, that my long letters—like many other things about me—are unnecessary. I take (not always; but often) more time & pains than other people take. And that, too, is unnecessary. The best wisdom is to touch life, in every way, with a lighter grasp. And this I have been trying to learn. I can say this freely to you, because it does not apply to you; I am inclined to think that you, too, take trouble; that you, too, take time & pains. Certainly, as far as letters are concerned, you have—even in the midst of your busy life—written me some, which must have taken as much time & pains as any I have written. You have the generous nature—

Your "Emerson" seems to me a splendid piece of work. It was a most difficult subject—Emerson as a poet. I do'nt know a more difficult one. As I think of it, it seems to me that nothing—(in the way of prose)—you have every written shows so much skill. It is eloquent. Of course perfectly & wonderfully appreciative (one of your greatest gifts); & beautiful in itself with splendor of stately sentences, which accord with the man himself. Yes—I think it is a triumph in every way.

And I applaud it more because I do'nt believe he has been your Bible as he has been some people's; mine for instance—(in a measure, of course). I don't believe you have clung to him as some of us have. You have'nt needed it. Yet you appreciate fully what his often rough-edged sayings (in verse, or prose,) have been to other people—though, poet yourself, I am sure it must have been extremely difficult for you to pass over the defective form in which he often chose to express himself—you—such a master of perfect melody.

You speak of the cry that went up when Longfellow passed away. True. But I have never cared at all for Longfellow (until—you will smile at this—I met his daughter Edith—Mrs Dana—over here last year, &, becoming fond of her, grew to love the memory of her father because she loved him so), while for Emerson I have cared very very deeply.[1] I should add that it was a thing of some years back, when I was younger. I no longer keep certain sentences & verses of his, copied in large hand, & pinned up on my wall, to "hearten" myself under the daily burden of existence. But his aid—the aid given by his strong assertiveness has been a great deal to me. There was a time when Emerson, & Emerson alone, put me on my feet again; a time when I greatly needed such help.

That is a beautiful, & most true sentence of yours—that he was "an optimist with reverent intent."

And I greatly admire, too, the closing sentence of the essay—"He chose the part of forerunner & inspirer" &c&c. It is noble.

How good is your image of Mosaic: "Speech is not song; the rarest mosaic lacks the soul of the canvass swept by the brush." How many times have I thought the same thing as I sat drinking in the splendor of the mosaics here—the rich dimly-glowing domes of San Marco. I always sit there a while at sunset—until the custode jangles his keys as a signal that we must go—as a close to my day. What a sumptuous light it is! I know nothing like it. Beside it, the light that prevails in St Peter's at Rome, is garish & thin.

But there is no finer thing in the whole essay—finer to me—than "I am not sure but one must be of the poet's own country & breeding to look quite down his vistas & by-paths." "Every American has something of Emerson in him, & the secret of the land was in the poet." That is perfect. And perfectly said.

And there is where I too feel a fellow feeling with the great thinker. For I am so American! I did'nt know it until I came over here. I see, now, that, though I should stay in Italy ten years longer, I should never be anything but American; should never write any but the most "American" prose. The reason is—not that I do not appreciate all the beauty here; I do. I adore it. But because I lived my life there before I came over. All the deep feelings of my existence are inseparably associated with home-scenes,—"scenes," too, having always been in themselves a great deal to me.—I do'nt know why. The Lake-country & Mackinac, the beautiful South, the farming-country of Ohio—these are the scenes that I belong to, that I can never separate myself from,—though I should live years in Venice and Rome.

I do'nt feel that this rambling and egotistical string of remarks on your superb essay has any right to be sent. But you must remember that I am not pretending to criticize, or do anything more than chat a little. I should never attempt to criticize Stedman on Emerson; the combination is quite beyond me.

You speak of Miss Hutchinson; once I think I saw her,—down at the Harpers, Franklin Square.[2] We were not introduced; but I remember how pretty she was. I have seen two or three exquisite little bits of verse from her pen, in the magazines.

Yes—"Anne" (of which you speak) seems to have ~~made~~ been a popular success. I saw very few of the notices; the publishers did not send them; but I did see the one in the "Century," which gave me great pleasure; I should like to know who wrote it. "For the Major" is not a novel; though I see it is so announced. It is a little genre picture of village life, with strong local color. I have tried to paint it well. And I consider it a better piece of work, artistically viewed, than "Anne,"—though its motif will not, I suppose, attract the "average reader" as that of "Anne" did. I hope you will read it in the book-form. It was too short for serial publication. You advise me not to be one of the rapid writers. Alas, I could not if I would. I shall never produce much.

This does not mean that I am not well; I was never so well in all my life as I am here. I am outrageously well; there is no end to my health; I think neither you nor Mrs Stedman would know me!, unannounced. But I mean, that, in actual written pages, I produce little; though my brain teems with material of all sorts, whose end I feel I never could reach though I should live a thousand years. I do'nt say it is good material, you notice.

Ah—what a pity you are not here. As I lift my eyes, & see the lights & tints on the water, & on San Giorgio Maggiore, it seems so cruel that you should have been swept away from them, as you were last year. However—perhaps you do not care for them so much as I do. Many people I see do not. Yes, yes, I care for them. But the blue outline of Mackinac has always a place in my heart. And, do you remember the pine-barrens of Florida, starred with those little flowers? There were "lagoons" there too; & shimmering inlets; & channels; & beaches. Some day I shall come back; & live in St Augustine—perhaps!—Give my love to Mrs Stedman. And my thanks to Arthur for his letter.[3] I hope he will go & see my sister sometimes; she likes him so much. Take care of yourself. The Leipzig address is always safe.

Yours always most sincerely
C. F. Woolson.

Isn't it needless to say how glad I am always when I get one of your letters?

Notes

1. Richard Henry Dana's son Richard Dana III married Longfellow's daughter Edith.
2. Ellen Mary Hutchinson was coeditor with Stedman of *An American Anthology, 1787–1900*.
3. Stedman's son.

To John Hay (Brown)

Venice
May 5th, [1883]

Dear Colonel Hay.

Your beautiful verses have given me much pleasure.—I have read them over every evening when the busy day is done, and I am alone here for the tranquil hour before going to bed.[1] I always keep the best things for then,—the few books I like (I read them over & over); or a nice letter—if I have one, or some especial article in a magazine or paper which I have thought might be interesting. But it is a long time since I have enjoyed any thing so much as these few poems of yours (I am sure you have others which you did not send); they were just the things for the first nights in Venice—at the top of a lonely old palazzo. I presume you know the two I like the best:

"Roll on, O shining Sun,
To the far seas!"

and,

"I strove like Israel with my youth."

These seem to me very beautiful; & I thank you for letting me see them. They are not only exquisitely melodious as poems, but they have, also, that indescribable touch of sincerity which is everything;—that touch without which the most perfect poem leaves us cold. These do not leave us cold at all; I am afraid they would come near to bringing moisture to the eyes of lonely people—if they should be published.

"Miles Keogh" seems—on re-reading—even better than it did at first. It reads like the sound of trumpets for a cavalry charge. I shall take the liberty of copying this (as it has been published); I want it myself; & I also want to send it to Comm. Goodrich (who has joined his ship)—your especial admirer, you know. I wish I might send him also "Golyer," as I know he would appreciate it so much. But, as I do not know whether you would be willing, I refrain. I think it very fine. Do'nt tell me you did'nt enjoy writing it;—such lines as

"He wa'n't the best man that ever you seen,
And he wa'n't so ungodly pizen mean,"

—; I know you did.

As a whole, it seems to me to have the strong striking human undertone which belongs to all your poems in dialect; & then, as usual, in the last verse, with the simplest phrase you carry us up to the realm of our purest & highest feelings,—& leave us there.

I think the translations excellent. But a man who can write as you can, should write originals. Is'nt "Asra" one of Rubenstein's songs? I wonder—did you ever see any of the translations of Leonard Case?[2] They were so wonderfully well done. But he could not write originals. He could think them,—& perhaps feel them; but he had not the gift of expression, I mean expression of his best. If you did not know him, you have missed knowing a remarkable man. I do'nt say attractive; only talented, & singular.

I copy nothing but "Miles Keogh"—because I do'nt think I have the right. Oh—I will copy, if you will allow it, the last verse of "I strove like Israel." It is but one. And I greatly like it.

I envy you the English Spring. And the prim roses. I have no idea where Knole Park is; nor the other place you mention; but I have made a note of it for future use. For that long summer I hope to spend in England, in the happy time of "sometime."

Why have bronchitis?

I was glad to see Mr Stedman's lines. He has combined Mrs Hay, & Cleveland, & the Bosphorus, and "Anne," & myself, and advice to me (en passant) to improve in my writings, and a word for you, in a very skillful & kaleidoscopic manner.[3] I am glad he has covered the page which I had spoiled (with my stupid four lines), in Mrs Hay's beautiful album. This reminds me to say that my sister dined with the Stedmans, recently, to meet Mr & Mrs Julian Hawthorne, & Mr & Mrs Whitelaw Reid. She writes that the talk of the three gentlemen was very brilliant. Mr Hawthorne was assigned to her, & she liked him greatly. Mrs Whitelaw Reid announced herself as a particular admirer of yours, (—I do'nt know what Mrs Hay will say to this).

I have seen a good deal of the Howells. And I do'nt care so much about the medallion. Or rather, I care just as much about the thing itself,—must always do so, but the slight feeling I had against them in the matter has faded; for they never dreamed, probably, that I "took it so hard"; & I am glad, now, that they will never know. Winifred is better, & enjoys Venice beyond any thing she has yet seen; of course this makes her father & mother happy. They have a perfect view from their windows; they know remarkable Armenian priests; they talk of pictures that "may be" Veroneses, & that may be bought "for a song." There is nothing better than this. I mean the life—, not the Veroneses.

I should like to see the sketch of Mrs Hay. My little "Garden of the Hesperides" stands on the table as I write.[4] I think the young Italian, who painted it, is to be here soon; he has always longed to see Venice, but has never had money enough to take the journey. Now that people are beginning to buy his little things, he has laid up enough for a few weeks here. How he will enjoy it! I expect to see him sketching everywhere all day long. The point of my story is, that, should he have with him some of the pictures that struck me as so interesting, I will get him to send you one—if it can be done. But it is uncertain whether he will have them. And you must remember, too, that what struck me was (perhaps rather a literary view of a picture) the fact that he had drawn from the original source of the modern "Pre-Raphaelite" painters, without ever having heard of them or their work. He has derived his inspirations from the real pre-Raphaelites,—the Lippis, Botticelli, & the rest.

I envy you the Grosvenor.

And, as to coming home—I do'nt know. It wo'nt be just now, at any rate. You should see how Mr Howells longs for his own land, and people. It is quite pathetic.—The trouble is with me that I love Italy so much that I never have time to see the other countries. Yet how can I come home without having had about three long, soft, green, misty, delightful Summers in England. And ever so many months in the romance & color of Spain,—the color especially. What do you say to my trying Algiers next winter? Would'nt that be a bold move!—I should, perhaps, find there the climate of St Augustine. And here, by the way, let me say—do not make light of that old dreamy Florida town, until you have seen it. There are lagoons there too, as well as here. And all sorts of wonderful beauty. I grant that few of the usual "tourists" ever see it.

I hope the children are well; & of course they are "assez sages."[5]—I am writing on through many pages, because this is my last appearance as a letter-writer, for the present. I hope to be busy this Venetian summer—after the petty vexations of Florence. You will receive this just before sailing away from beautiful England. I send you my best wishes for the voyage. And my love to my own country, as well as to yourselves. I am so very glad to have seen you,—In Paris, & Florence. Come over again & you will find me either in Rome; London; or here. Oh yes, Venice is enchanting.

Yours always, very sincerely,
C. F. Woolson.

P. S. Evening.

I have just finished copying Miles Keogh. It is a splendid thing. It stirs the blood,—that

"Shall parade with the regiment!"

The Howells came to see me just as I had finished this letter, & I made them some tea. They say my quarters are more "Venetian" than any thing they have seen! My wee balcony with its red cushion they admire. But I fancy they object to the stairs, & general inaccessibility. They had just heard, they said, from Mrs Hay.—Well, good-by to you both, again. I do'nt know why, but I feel a little downhearted to-night, even if I am in Venice. I should say I was a trifle homesick—only how can one be home-sick who has'nt a "home[”]? Be thankful that you have one; & keep kindly thoughts for the less fortunate.

Yours C.F.W.

Notes

1. Woolson quotes or refers to the following poems from those Hay eventually collected in *Poems* (1890): "Expectation," "Quand Même," "Miles Keogh's Horse," and "Golyer." She also refers to his Spanish, German, and French translations, including Heinrich Heine's "The Azra," which was set to music by Anton Rubinstein (1829–94). She often wrote out copies of poems she liked and was hesitant to copy what Hay had not yet published.

2. Petry (49) tentatively identifies Case as Cleveland lawyer and real estate broker Leonard Case (1820–80), who gave up his career in favor of travel and writing.

3. en passant: in passing.

4. Painting by Ricciardo Meacci.

5. assez sages: wise enough.

To Henry James (Houghton)

(My general address is always:
"Care Knauth, Nachod, and Kühne
Leipzig. Germany")
Venice
May 7th, [1883]

Dear Mr James.

I have been wishing to write to you ever since I reached Venice (about two weeks ago), because I know how fond you are of the beautiful old water-city, & I thought that perhaps the sight of a "Venezia" postmark might please your expatriated eyes. I do'nt know how long I should have held out—against the wish to give you this faint little pleasure; fortunately I am not called upon to solve the question, because, at Blumental's, the other day (my gondola waiting at "the wave-washed steps"), I found your letter of April 17th—which had been forwarded from Florence. I was very glad to get it.[1]

You asked for "a picture"—to keep you "going." But it wo'nt be Florentine—or even Bellosguardo—as you imagined. Do you know the Palazzo Gritti-Swift? Probably not—by that name. Well, then, do you know the dilapidated old yellow palace, not quite opposite Santa Maria della Salute—below it—which is decorated with the signs of "Salviati?" I presume you do—because you are so fond of signs. In this old palace—on the top floor (3d), are two large low-ceiling-ed rooms, with round-arched windows, and small—very small—balconies, on the Grand Canal. In addition, there are two side-windows, one of which is the treasure of the abode because it faces the east (jutting out beyond the next palace), commanding the harbor, the Riva with its masts, the fresh green of the Public Gardens, & best of all, San Giorgio Maggiore, its pink campanile tipped with your tall gold angel.—The other side-window—by greatest good-fortune—looks directly down into one of the narrowest & darkest emerald-green canals in the city; so narrow that the gondolas can pass only by closely hugging the walls. You may be sure that I immediately demanded cushions of the padrona, for my little balconies (they are so small—the balconies—that you use them as sofas), & that these cushions are freshly covered with red. And that I also have red ledges for my two side-windows. Nothing but red would do.

Now should'nt all this make me happy? If you will only stop treating me as you did about the "Salvini" article, it will.[2]

To my top-floor, a very winding stone stairway leads—like a stairway in a lighthouse—though it is'nt by any means a light stairway. And, when at last you reach the top floor, you find the entrance-door guarded by a little loophole, with a grating over it; & through this aperture the handsome Italian maid, Pietra, will inspect you, before she lets you in. And when at last you are in, you can't imagine where to go, so involuted is the hall, with all sorts of inscrutable doors, & curtains, & even steps (though you know you are at the very top of the house), leading out of it.

And, down below, the water-story ("sea-story" of Ruskin) is the lowest and darkest I have seen,—empty, save for high-backed seats, with a coat of arms painted on them, fixed against the walls.[3] And then, suddenly, out of this low vast hall, opens an ideal courtyard, with a round well, armorial bearings set on the pink facade, a willow tree, & an outside stairway of ancient white marble, which leads up to the second story, at present most happily occupied by no less a personage than Mr Symonds, the English writer on Italian Art. I do'nt know him; but he leans from his balcony below, as I lean from mine above; & I wonder if he is writing any more of those articles of his,—so rich in some aspect, so fatally defective in others. He little knows that he has an American, who criticizes him, over his head! And he would'nt care if he did know;—~~that~~ which is the advantage of an English temperament ~~constitution~~. When Miss Poynter comes over from Florence to visit the Symonds, she will be astonished to find me above her. Miss Poynter I met in Florence; & liked. She is a sister of Mr Poynter, the artist, whom perhaps you know, A writer herself, very quiet, & typically "English" in appearance & dress—I thought her at heart more—more appreciative—than some of the English ladies I met at the same time.—

Behold me, then, established. Nothing could possibly be more deeply Venetian than my surroundings. How long do I expect to stay? I do'nt know. I am here at last. Here at the perfect season of the year;—and I have no plan or date for departing. I suppose sometime I must go away; if it should become too hot, for instance.

Through May & June I shall remain; & possibly July. Then I shall seek the mountains somewhere—on the general principle that a whole summer in Italy is not the best thing for an American woman. Though I do'nt know that it makes much difference now—I am so shamefully well. I am well all the time—every minute. And ~~my~~ the back view of me as I depart from you, is like that of a Veronese woman! One of the elderly ones, not very clearly seen.

Do you want to know what I am doing here? I get up very early; look out of the arched windows; have my coffee; look out of the arched windows; see to the flowers (for of course I have ever so many, all in pots, all in bloom); and more looking out of the windows. Then I write, for a good part of the day (diversified by occasional looking), until it gets to be, say, four o'clock. Then—having had a bowl of bread & milk meanwhile—I put on my straw hat, & go down my lighthouse stairs, & either take a gondola & float luxuriously through all the color until six; or else I go, on foot, to all sorts of enchanting places—like Santa Maria dell'Orto,—over myriad bridges, losing my way all the time and enjoying it, & wondering only now & then how I shall ever be able to get away from Venice; whether the end of the riddle of my existence may not be, after all, to live here, & die here, & be buried on that plateau in the lagoon. This prospect does'nt make me sad at all, & I come home,—having dined on color—to my tangible dinner—first, of course, stopping in at St Mark's for a few minutes, as a fit close for the beautiful day. Then, immediately after dinner, out I go again in another gondola. And when respectability requires that I should come within at last, I come. And then I sit in my red-cushioned balcony, & watch the lights on the gliding gondolas, & the colored lanterns of the music-barges, & listen for something of the music—& make out Schubert's "Serenade." Is'nt this being as happy as Fate allows us—no I mean allows me—to be?

But what can I say to you,—in reality—of all the enchantment,—all the delicious, rich, lovable beauty of this sweet place, when you know it all so well,—when you have written out your feeling about it in ~~that so~~ those exquisite pages I love so much myself—whose every word I know, almost by heart. The magazine containing them lies on this table as I write,—the copy you sent me in Paris. And I care so very much for it that—like the old Indulgences—you may sin a good deal, on the strength of it; let letters lie forever unanswered, not answer them even when you do write; stay continually over there in America; &c&c. Of course I have all Ruskin, & read it. And of course I go to see Tintorettos. And Carpaccios. And Bellinis. And I stand in front of the "Europa" picture, & fail to "ache with envy";—yet comprehend that you may feel differently about it; though still I think you like a Memling better.[4] I wander everywhere. I shall never come to the end of it. I can't begin to tell you. And why should I try, when you know it all so much better than I do? In the same way; but better. I wonder if you will understand me if I should tell you that this is the deepest charm of your writings to me—; they voice for me—as nothing else ever has—my own feelings; those that are so deep—so a part of me, that I can not express them, & do not try to; never think of trying to. Once, at a dinner-party in Florence this last winter—a small one—, the conversation had turned upon Clarence King (that remarkable man); &, as it veered from the subject again, John Hay, who sat next me, could not let it go without a few words more; so he said to me—under cover of much talking among the others—"When I heard, the other day at Cannes, that King was in Paris again, I felt like taking the next train there! I said to myself—'Ah, where *he* is, there is my true country, my real home.'" I think I have got the words—or very nearly—for they made an impression upon my memory; John Hay was so much in earnest as he said it,—though he spoke, too, with a half-laugh. Well—that is my feeling with regard to your writings: they are my true country, my real home. ~~Do~~ And nothing else ever is fully—try as I may to think so. Do you think this is quite an assumption,—or presumption? But one may be as quiet as possible, yet comprehend. One may be a bad workman one's self, yet appreciate perfect work. One may admire the path (as Mr Wentworth said to Felix—with variations) which one is at the same time, unable to follow.[5] If you will only bear all this in mind, it will—or should—excuse me to you; for your writings have been to me like a new, & beautiful, & unexpected land.

Do you know, by the way, how much John Hay is your friend? I did not, until one day in the Boboli Gardens, when he said—among other things—(I omit the context): "If anyone speaks against James' writings in my presence, I consign that person to contempt. And if anyone speaks against James himself, I immediately *hate* him" (The speaker). "He cares nothing for me; I have always known it, & it came out again, plainly, in Paris. But I care a great deal for him." You will be glad to know that John Hay is better. I have just had a letter from him, describing with enthusiasm the "carpets of primroses" they had seen, on some of their English excursions. They sail for home, May tenth.

You once remarked to me that Mrs Hay occasionally expressed herself with a singular lack of cultivation. What, then, do you say of Mrs Howells? (I have not known her until this past winter.) It seems to me that Mrs Hay has at least a large, & even noble, nature; that she is above the petty things of life. Small feminine malice, & everlasting little jealousies.—I am afraid I fail to please Mrs Howells. Yet I have tried—; because she is Mr Howells' wife; I have tried a good deal. And failed. I do'nt in the least mean, however, that we have had any difficulty. Far from it. She wd. probably tell you (at least I *think* she would; I never feel sure what she will do!) that we—she & I—were "great friends." Certainly, I have seen her often.—Ah, well—why should I care? Probably because Mr Howells is your friend—an especial one, I mean. For herself, she is happy—(or should be; though she never seems to be *very* happy about anything), because Mr Howells is entirely devoted to her, markedly so; & he thinks everything she says, & does, most admirable. I like Mr Howells. He strikes me as having strong convictions, & even principles (the old-fashioned ones which have rather gone out of fashion); and ~~that~~ as standing by them honestly, & as closely as he can. He has never had a millionth part of your experience in the world—the world of society. And he is as unlike you as it is possible to be. Perhaps I do'nt do him justice; I have seen—known—<u>so</u> many men of his manner & experience. They were all (no; almost all) I knew, when I lived, in the old days, in Cleveland ("Cleveland, <u>Ohio</u>," <u>you</u> would say in your amusing foreign way). I have to put in "the old days," because even Cleveland—<u>Ohio</u>—has gone ahead, & become cultured; I am told there is now no end to their cultivation, out there.

I might as well say, here, that my regard for Mr Howells (a regard he cares nothing for)—made me at last consent (it is a long story; I will tell it you, if we ever meet again on this earth; on the next, I prefer to forget it) to a horrible suggestion for a portrait-medallion, to be made by Mr Mead, Mrs Howells' brother. The whole thing was, & is, acutely disagreeable to me. I made a great sacrifice; which they did not in the least—& never will—appreciate. Comfort me a little by appreciating it yourself. I am not a subject for a sculptor; as far as possible from it. In addition, I do not think that because a woman happens to write a little, herself, or her personality in any way, becomes the property of the public. Mr Mead has done Mr Howells, & admirably. John Hay,—not so well. He wishes to do you. For a man, that sort of thing is quite in order, & I beg you to consent when next you find yourself in Florence. It is the only thing that can console me, in a measure, for my own sufferings in the matter. You have just the profile for it. And be sure & have the exact profile. I ~~did~~ do not like the picture in the "Century," nor the photograph I have (should you ever feel generous, you would send me another), because they are not exact profiles. I am rather devoted to profiles; it is the profile-view of a face that I notice first; & remember longest.

I have something for you,—if you will have it. Two Greek coins. I had them set, by Accorisi of Florence, as scarf-pins. It is quite probable that the settings are not at all right; but they could easily be changed. I have a weakness for old coins, & have bought several—in Paestum, Sorrento, Rome—only to find that they were not "old." Mr Felton—who belonged to our Florentine walking-parties until he went off to Athens—wore a beauty, &, upon my speaking of it one day, he said, that, if I had a fancy for such things, perhaps I could get one from Mr Stillman (whom perhaps you know), as he had a few fine ones. It ended in my getting three. One—an owl—I have kept for myself. The others are first: "Drachm of Thebes." Obverse: head of Bacchus, bearded, crowned with ivy. Reverse: Shield of Boeotia." Second—& much smaller,—"Drachm of Thebes. Obverse: wine-jar. Reverse: Shield of Boeotia." Date of both, 350 B.C." I should say that the coins are not especially beautiful, in themselves. The head of Bacchus was the rarest Mr Stillman had. Was'nt it Benvolio who wore a Syracusan coin?[6] I asked Mr Stillman if he had any "Syracusan coins." And he was rather scornful about them; said his Greek ones were better. Such as they are, they await you here, in a little satin case—if you will have them. I confess I am going on general principles merely—having seen you wearing six rings on one hand, you know. Perhaps you will say that rings are not scarf-pins, and that scarf-pins you detest, & never wear. In that case you must wait until I can dig up an antique intaglio for you on the Campagna; & then you will have seven. Rings, I mean. If I had not dug it up myself, I should never believe—nor you either—that it was authentic. Nobody knows of my coins—the ones destined for you. So, will you have them, & shall I send them to America, & by whom? Or, will you have them, & shall I keep them, & send them to your London lodgings—should you ever arrive there during this life? Or, do you really not care for scarf-pins at all, &, in that case, ~~I~~ shall I wear them myself—all in a row,—the owl, the head of Bacchus, and the Shield of Boeotia—astonishing newly arrived American ladies, who wear only diamonds, & mosaics? John Hay says (I seem to be all the time quoting him! But wait—I have a Julian Hawthorne still in reserve ~~on hand~~) that you have "extraordinary candor." So be candid now; I only want to do what you like best.

You ask what the winter gave me. Not much—save such advantage as may be derived from constantly seeing a "lot of people," and caring not in the least for it, or them. (Let me put in, though, that I did have a great many most delightful walks, over the Tuscan hills in all directions—walks of six & eight miles in length.) Florentine society—as I saw it,—seemed to me like that picture of wraiths & shades being swept round in a great, misty, crowded circle, by some bewildering & never-ceasing wind; I do'nt know whether it is Flaxman's with "attenuated outlines," or Blake's. Have'nt you heard that Mr Howells was left without a moment to himself, & that his wife could not begin to keep up with their invitations, engagements, & calls? The same fate that befell the great masculine Lion, befell the very little feminine one—though on a much smaller scale. We happened to be the only Americans in a crowd of English—I mean American writers. Nobody knew of me, of course, as they knew of him; but because I was there, & an American, & the only one, they sometimes included me, when they were inviting him. The English invitations came, I think, from their usual half-patronising, half interested curiosity. And the Americans, of course—residents & tourists—rallied round their national productions.—I do'nt know how the Howells liked it. I did not like it at all. And never again, if I can possibly help it, shall I be drawn into anything of the "society" over here. It does'nt amuse me. Nor do I amuse it. Did we see the best, you ask? I doubt it. And here let me whisper to you, in all confidence, that this was the Howells'—I wo'nt say mistake,—for perhaps they did it on purpose; preferred it. One day, you would hear of them, dining with very nice people. The next, they would be at a reception given by persons of whom the first people—those of the dinner—had probably never heard. They made no distinctions. Perhaps they would say they could not.

For my own part, I met a few people I liked; saw hosts I cared nothing for; & a few I greatly disliked. Let me see if I met any one you may perhaps know. Mme Villari—who says she knows Mrs Kemble; and Mr Cross. Mme Rahe—who lives in the Via del Mandorlo, & entertains a good deal, & had to visit her a Mr ______ Synge or some such name, whom I was given to understand was a London literary man. But I did not see him. Mrs Launt Thompson (I saw a great deal of her), who is clever, but perchée—as you said of Mrs McKaye—on her "family."[7] I saw Miss Greenough often. She was very kind to me,—asking me ~~to a~~ a number of times to come up to the villa and lunch with her. She had a lovely plan, towards the last; nothing less than that I should take Mrs Bracken's apartment, under her winter one, & spend the summer in Bellosguardo. She made terms with Mrs Bracken for me, & was so good as to do everything she could in the matter. I hesitated some time over this; it was a temptation; the greatest I have had in Italy. You know how I adore that view,—down the valley of the Arno towards the west. And I should have had that old garden—with the parapet. But I have the conviction that a whole summer in Italy is not the best thing for me (I do'nt in the least mind dying, you know, if one could be sure to die, & have it over; but I have a horror of being ill—ill a long time, over here all alone). In addition, Mrs Bracken's furniture is all "choice"; each article has been "collected," with affection & care—as I understand it; every table is a "treasure," & every chair "cinque-cento."[8] And I did'nt want to spend the summer thinking of chairs. Also, she wished me to keep her two servants; & thus it wd. have ended, probably, in my living as they wished, because I should not have had the power to discharge them. Do'nt betray me, I know Mr Boott corresponds with Miss G. but I was a little afraid, too, of Miss Greenough herself; the dear old lady had plans for our taking "excursions" together, & "drives"; & all sorts of things. These were delightful in themselves, & I like Miss Greenough much. But I cannot give the time for that sort of life this summer. I am such an absurd individual that, if I know that "at four o'clock" I must go somewhere, with somebody, I cannot write at ten, or at two. If I have not promised to go, beforehand, if there is no engagement, it is very probable that "at four o'clock," I shall find myself delighted to do the very thing. But, I must not know it beforehand. I must have the day serenely free. I go into these details because the villa is yours, you know; Osmond and you have known, perhaps, how I have wished to live on Bellosguardo.—Mrs Bracken's rooms are a terreno, & just a trifle gloomy. Miss Greenough herself has all the best rooms in that house.

I am most sorry to hear that you have had "care, and anxiety." It is difficult for me to think of you with anything of that sort to bear. I have thought of you as a little spoiled; yet have rather enjoyed it—in you. Perhaps a little "care" will be good for you. I hear you are staying on in America to be with your sister, who is now, save for you, left alone. That you are doing this only confirmed my idea of you—that you are, really, the kindest hearted man I know,—though this is not, perhaps, the outside opinion about you.

Oh—such a quantity as I have heard about you, lately! I mean, since I last wrote. Names—dates—or rather times; all sorts of gossip. Nothing against you, though. I would tell you, if I supposed it would amuse you. But you have never responded when I have put in such things. So I leave it out.

You could not possibly have pleased me more than by telling me—as you do in this letter—of your plans for work. I have often thought of the motif you told me about, in Rome; now I shall see it completed. You have undertaken a great deal. But I am very glad you have undertaken it. You will do it all; & superbly. There is no one like you; & pretty much everyone—(who amounts to anything)—knows it now. Tourguénieff is dying, I hear. You are now our Tourguénieff. (I do'nt mean that you are like him; but that you have his importance.) The other day, in New York, my sister dined with the Stedmans, to meet the Julian Hawthornes & Whitelaw Reids. Mr Hawthorne was assigned to her, & she liked him so much. She writes me that the conversation turned principally upon yourself, & Mr Howells, & that a great many bright things were said. Then she goes on to add "Mr Hawthorne, in his slow deliberate way (such a contrast to the quickness of the other two men), said this: "I like, I greatly admire, every word James ever wrote in his life."—Do you smile at my putting these little things in? I do it because they please me so much, myself.

I shall be delighted to get the criticisms in the "Century," if you will be so good as to send them. That you did not send the "Salvini" (I have it, however), gave me a quite little ache of disappointment. I had not expected you to write; I never want you to do that, until just the right time & mood come to you,—though you should wait ~~for~~ months for them; but I did think that perhaps you would send the magazine. When you did not, I drew the conclusion that you were tired of sending. It must come, of course—, I mean that you should be tired. But—stretch it a little longer. When I go home, I cut the thread of everything over here. And then you need send no more. I wonder if you have seen Clara Morris with Salvini, & what you think of her. And I remember that—but I wo'nt go on; it was only about someone who was such an admirer of Salvini.

I speak of going home. It will not be this next winter, probably. I am thinking of trying Algiers. What do you say to that plan, for me? I should at least have the climate I like—the climate of Florida. It is all very well to hold out the prospect of "talking it over" (the going home) "against an Italian church-wall." Your letters are better than you are. You are never in Italy, but always in America; just going; or there; or just returned. And as to a "church-wall," there has never been but that one short time (three years ago—in Florence) when you seem disposed for that sort of thing. How many times have I seen you, in the long months that make up three long years? I do'nt complain, for there is no reason in the world why I should expect to see you; only, do'nt put in these decorative sentences about "Italian church-walls."

There is a very nice sofa here, placed at just the angle that commands the beautiful eastern view. And there is a tea-table, with the same sputtering little kettle you saw in my sky-parlor at Rome (I have left my nicer one, packed, at Florence). If you could come in now, & rest a while (till time to go to the next dinner-party), I would make you some of the water-bewitched you consider "tea." And you would find at least the atmosphere of a very perfect kindness. You say you "fall back" upon my "charity," feeling that it is "infinite." You can safely fall back; for infinite it is. Only charity is not precisely the word. Call it, rather, gratitude. This is'nt for you, personally—though of course you have to be included; it is for your books. You may be what you please, so long as you write as you do.

I have scribbled a very long letter. It is because I am in Venice. I do not ask you to answer at present; I give you six months to do it in. I am entirely in earnest when I say this; and I should be glad if, once in a while, you wd. believe me. I expect to be very busy all summer; & you will be the same. So, send me, as they come out, the "Century" articles; & answer this next year.[9] Oh—I forgot the coins. If you would like them sent to America, you will have to write a line—wo'nt you.

I send my Venetian blessing to you. I am now going to San Giorgio Schiavoni, & then, on foot, to the far Fondamente Nuova, for a breezy walk; then home by gondola, on the Grand Canal. If there is anything in the world I can do for you here, command me. The Howellses are at the "Citta di Monaco," & Winifred is better, & enjoys Venice—which makes her father & mother happy.—Your lodgings (at least those belonging to the number I remember) are to let; white papers are pasted on the shutters. I go by, on my way to the Gardens; but I do'nt see the young lady, with one little white button on her black gloves.[10] Good-by. I hope you keep well. Be quite sure that you have added much to the pleasure of my summer by writing as you have; & that I shall often think of you, as I grow fonder and fonder of all this beauty you love so well.

Yours sincerely,
C. F. Woolson.

Mr Howells seems very much attached to you.

Perhaps you will go to Cooperstown this summer. If you do, please go & see my dear cousins, the Coopers. They are old ladies now. I have plenty of relatives in Cooperstown; but these are the ones I love best. Only, you needn't say I said so!

Notes

1. James uses this phrase in one of his essays on Venice (*Century*, Nov. 1882) that he later collected in *Portraits of Places* (1883) and *Italian Hours* (1909).

2. James wrote on the actor Tommaso Salvini in the March 1883 *Atlantic Monthly*.

3. *The Sea Stories* is the second of Ruskin's three-volume *The Stones of Venice* (1851–53).

4. Titian's *The Rape of Europa* (1562), housed at the Galleria dell' Accademia, Venice.

5. Characters in James's *The Europeans* (1878).

6. Woolson describes both sides of these drachm or ancient Greek coins: Bacchus is the Greek god of wine and Boetia a region in ancient Greece. She refers to a Greek Syracusan coin that she gave to James, who, Leon Edel believes, had it made into a tie-pin; see *The Letters of Henry James*, 4 vols., (Cambridge: Harvard University Press, 1974–84) 3:558. She also alludes to James's story "Benvolio" (*Galaxy*, Aug. 1875).

7. Perchée: perched—by which Woolson suggests that Mrs. McKaye is fixated only on family.

8. Cenque-cento: the 1500s (i.e., the sixteenth century).

9. James's articles on Trollope (July 1883) and on Daudet (Aug. 1883).

10. Edel (559) identifies this as a reference to James's article on Venice in *Century*, Nov. 1882.

To Winifred Howells (Houghton)[1]

Venice
May 11th, 1883

In this beautiful old water-city, where you were born, my dear Winnie, I must now take leave of you. For you are going back to our own land. You are young; it is right that you should go; I send with you my warm good-wishes. But, as for me—I will stay a while longer. As was once well written, in Venice "Repose takes you to her inmost heart, and you learn her secrets. Old lines of lazy rhyme win new color and meaning. The old mystical poems now reveal themselves to you, and now at last you know why 'It was an Abyssinian maid' who played upon the dulcimer. And 'Xanadu'?—It was the land in which you were born."[2] That Abyssinian maid is now my friend; and this is my "Xanadu."—But not for always; Xanadu never lasts, you know! I shall see you again; and at home.

Notes

1. This note is in Winnie Howells's autograph book.

2. The quotation is from Samuel Taylor Coleridge's "Kubla Khan" (1816).

To Elizabeth Gwinn Mather (WRHS/Mather)[1]

Venice
May 20th, [1883]

My dear Libbie.

. . . Venice is enchanting. I hope to stay through June, but may find my rooms too hot. Last night, in the full moon, the Canal was dotted with gondolas, and music filled the air. It was beautiful as a dream. I went with Mr Howells and his daughter to a reception on board of an Egyptian Steamship this past week, afternoon tea,—. It was a pretty sight with awnings and flags. Ever so many titles, three Princesses, and plenty of Countesses, with the gentlemen belonging to them. Lady Layard, and Sir Henry Layard. Ever so many young people who played "nautical" games on the deck. Of course I only got this invitation through the Howells, who as usual, are much sought for.

I have now been over three years and a half, and it is certainly and quite unprejudiced-ly true that our country women, young and old, are on all ordinary occasions—such as travelling, in galleries, shopping, in streets of cities, &c&c, by far the best looking and best-dressed ladies one sees. I believe the French in full toilette, and the English girls when dressed for balls, with their beautiful complexions and plump necks and arms, shine out splendidly. But, on ordinary occasions, the American ladies are so much more attractive that there is simply no comparison. In all this time I have never seen an English lady who had a nice neatly fitting shoe, or a dainty glove. The French are better; but they are seldom really pretty, as our girls are. No, for the beauty of women, give me America. For comfort, and even luxury in living, give me America. But there is no doubt, Libbie, that one keeps young longer over here; there's a niche for such elderly persons as I am, which doesn't exist at home! I do'nt care much about it, however,—that niche, and shall come home before long, quite content to do without it.

Yours affectionately
C. F. Woolson.

Notes

1. The letter is in a typed transcription at WRHS. Portions also appear in Benedict/CFW, 273.

To Henry James (Houghton)

Venice
May 24th, [1883]

Dear Mr James.

I have been thinking about all this work you have undertaken; & I have wished that I could send you a message across the ocean—a spoken one. I will write it instead; you will believe, I hope, that it is said with the utmost sincerity, though you may not care for it ~~for~~ in itself.—In one of the three novels—or if that is impossible, in one of the shorter stories, why not give us a woman for whom we can feel a real love? There are such surely in the world. I am certain you have known some, for you bear the traces—among thicker traces of another sort.—I do not plead that she should be happy; or even fortunate; but let her be distinctly lovable; perhaps, let some one love her very much; but, at any rate, let her love, and let us see that she does; do not leave it merely implied. In brief, let us care for her, & even greatly. If you will only care for her yourself as you describe her, the thing is done.

We pitied Mme de Cintré, & we pitied Daisy. One step more & we should have loved them. To my idea, all that was needed—and the same applies to Isabel—was that we should have been sure that they themselves loved,—really loved; that Mme de Cintré felt for Newman the first love of a repressed, until then unopened, heart; &, that, fluttering in poor Daisy's primitive soul, was the beginning of a real love for Winterbourne.[1]

If you answer that the reason you did not make a love of this sort clear was simply because it was not clear—was not clear to themselves; that Mme de Cintré's feeling for Newman was a mixture of gratitude, tremulous suspense, & sweet surprise; and that Daisy hardly knew herself whether she loved Winterbourne or not; & that Isabel was led more by her imagination than by simple love—if you say all this, then I reply, take the one further step, & use your perfect art in delineating a real love as it really is. For you will never deny that it exists—though it may be rare.

There was Mary Garland—but I never liked her; and you yourself confessed that you did not like her, either—; that is, not very much; (which of course, en passant,[2] is the reason I—representing here the public—did not care for her.) and Gertrude is but a sketch; though in the right direction.

You have described some men who really love. Now give us a ~~who~~ woman who loves.

Believe me, it is the touchstone to sympathy. Why—I even cared (for a few moments) for Mme Merle, as she ~~sits~~ sat with her face buried in her hands before the man she had once loved, while he ~~says~~ said "Good enough to be always charming." One feels, there, that she had loved him. But with Isabel one is not so sure—you do not allow one to be; one is not certain whether, added to her dread & horror, is a tortured love—or not. On the whole, I think I fancied that her love for Osmond (if she ever had really loved him) had died, early in her married life.

This is all commonplace enough no doubt; this desire in the reader to be stirred; to be worked upon; to care. But I only ask you to do it once. You can do, & have shown that you can do, everything else; now do that also. And silence those who say you cannot—when it is simply that you have not chosen to do it.

Last of all forgive me—if you dislike what I have said.

But no, that is not quite last. Quite last is that if your judgment pushes away all these suggestions of mine, I yield. You know best.

The Howells have gone. I am sorry. I went with Mr H. to a reception on board a steamship here, and met a Mrs Bronson. The Captain came to me & said a lady wished to be introduced. The introduction was made, & we sat down to talk a while. Of course it was "Anne" ("Anne" is a book I once wrote), & the lady paid me some very pretty compliments. I had no idea who she was (I never have, you know; never get a name right; Mr Howells had been carried off to see some English people, so I was vaguely looking on), & I think she may have thought that I received her compliments rather as though they were perfunctory, for she appealed to a friend near. "I want you to tell Miss Woolson how <u>few</u> novels I really like. How I <u>hate</u> most of them." The lady appealed to, confirmed this statement, & informed me that the other one, the first speaker, generally threw all the new novels on the floor, after the first few pages. They then abused Hardy's last,[3] & one or two others; & then the friend began "And as to James"—Here I woke up. "Oh," I said "<u>of course</u> you like James. I am sure you like all he has written—as I do." Upon this the lady who had asked to be introduced to me, began to look pleased, &—I hardly know what to call it—happier; less indifferent, less cold. "Mr James is one of my dearest friends," she said. "He is also a friend of mine," I answered. Upon this we both began to smile, & be content. She informed me (upon my speaking of that "Venice" article of which I am so fond) that it was <u>her</u> balcony where you used to end your Venetian day, with a cigarette.[4] I had'nt anything so nice to tell her in return; but it did quite as well for me to admire her advantage—which I most cordially did. She has asked me to come and see her. I do'nt know that I shall go—because I do not want to be making calls here. Yet perhaps I may go once, as she is sure to be charming if she is such a friend of yours. I mean that I shall be sure to like her if she likes you as much as she appeared to, on the steamer. Yesterday I saw a lovely Cinna in Santo Maria de Carmine; I wonder if you remember it? I have paid two visits to S. Giov. Crisostomo to see your two pictures.[5] Here is a piece of good fortune: they are repairing the Nun's Chapel in San Zaccaria, & the beautiful Bellini is out in the church, in an excellent light, & seeable position. The lagoons, the Piazzetta, & the little still canals all send their love to you. They wish you were here. And so do I. I could go by in a gondola, you know, and see you on Mrs B.'s balcony. That wd.—be something. Good-by.

C.F.W.

Notes

1. Characters in *The American* (1877), *Daisy Miller* (1878), and *Portrait of a Lady* (1881). In the next paragraphs, Woolson is discussing *Roderick Hudson* (1876) and, again, *Portrait*. The novels James published after this letter were *The Bostonians* and *The Princess Casamassima*, both in 1886.

2. en passant: in passing.

3. *Two on a Tower* (1882).

4. See Woolson's May 7, 1883, letter to James.

5. Leon Edel identifies the two pictures as Giovanni Bellini's *St. Gerome* and a painting above the church's altar by Sebastian del Piombo (1485–1547); see *The Letters of Henry James*, 4 vols. (Cambridge: Harvard Univ. Press, 1974–84) 3:562.

To Hamilton Mabie (Duke)

(Care Knauth, Nachod, & Kühne
Leipzig. Germany)
Venice
June 18th, [1883]

Dear Mr Mabie.

Thanks for your delightful letter, received some time ago. I have been thinking that I might have something to send you; but time passes, and I still have nothing. I have not written any short stories lately. I produce so little, in comparison with most of the other American writers of fiction, that sometimes I feel troubled; and sometimes ashamed. But we are as we are, and I can do no otherwise. I must be a very slow workman.

Yes; my copy of the "Union" comes regularly, and I always read it with much interest. Each number is sure to contain something which rouses thought. It is certainly edited in a very able way. The broad views are delightful. The ground it takes upon the Temperance question, for instance, gives me especial pleasure; it seems to me the only sensible ground among a crowd of untenable ones.

Will you kindly inquire when the subscription I took for

"Mr C. J. Woolson.

Los Angeles. California."

will expire. I have forgotten. I wish to renew it for another year; and if you will be so good as to order the bill sent to me, when due, I will return a p.o. money order for the amount.

Thanks for what you say of "Anne" and "For the Major." The latter makes no pretensions to the character of a "novel." It is but a short simple tale; a little picture of village life in a part of the country where I once spent a number of months. I shall be curious to see what the critics will say of it,—if they notice it at all.[1] It is so quiet that it will not, probably, strike the popular eye; but, to me, it is the best piece of work I have done. I am afraid I shall hardly be able to write upon a European background—as you suggest. The moment I take up my pen, the old home scenes are all I ever see; I see them so vividly that I can see nothing else. I have a theory, too, that those of us who remember the war,—who were old enough to be stirred by it, yet, at the same time, young enough to have it the first great event of our lives,—we, of that generation, are the most deeply-dyed "Americans" that exist. We cannot help it. Our "country," and all that means,—patriotism in its warmest form, was burned into us by a red-hot fire, and the results are ineffaceable. And so though I should stay years over here, I remain as I was when I first landed; and American scenes—at least in serious work—are all, I fear, that you will ever have from me.

Venice is enchanting. I have been here two months. I go soon to Switzerland. My regular address is at head of letter. With best wishes, I am, yours truly,

C. F. Woolson.

Notes

1. Some reviews of *Anne* (1882) and *For the Major* (1883) have been reprinted in Torsney, Cheryl B., ed., *Critical Essays on Constance Fenimore Woolson* (New York: G.K. Hall, 1992).

To Elinor Howells (Houghton)[1]

[1883?]

a correspondence when I give them to a confiding friend. They are the Bankers upon whom I have my Letter of Credit. Why I have one upon them, goes back to forty years ago; & longer. I must now hurry with this myself, through the twilight to the very post office, in the hope that I may reach you tomorrow.

Good by—with much love to you all.

Yours very sincerely,
C. F. Woolson.

I must tell you something amusing. When Mrs Symonds came up to see me, I meakly supposed it was on my own account, because I knew Miss Poynter. But after a few minutes' talk, Miss Poynter gave me the clue (unintentionally). She asked me where you were now, & your plans, &c. Then I saw! Mrs Symonds was calling on the friend of the people who had been distinguished by the Crown Princess, of course. That was the whole story! So we never once left you, after that. We talked of you for a whole half hour, & I'm so sorry you could'nt have heard the conversation. Nothing less

Notes

1. Only this fragment survives.

To W. H. Rideing (WRHS/Mather)

Engelberg, Switzerland
July 12th, 1883
Mr W. H. Rideing.

Dear Sir.

Owing to a mistake of the Banker at Lucerne, I have only just received your kind letter of April 29th, 1882. I am sorry about this, as it must have made me seem lacking in courtesy.

You have probably got, from some one else, long before this, the serial you were seeking. To write for children and young people is a talent by itself; and I do not think that I possess it. So many others have it, however, and to such a marked degree, that I should not think you would have any trouble—especially with the generous terms you offer—in securing all the good stories you need.

With best wishes for the "Companion," I am,

Yours very truly,
C. F. Woolson.

To Katharine Livingston Mather (WRHS/Mather)[1]

Engelberg, Switzerland
July 12th, 1883

My dear Kate.

. . . You see where I am? The same Alpine valley where I spent the summer two years ago. I hated to leave Venice,—it was so enchanting there. But I had a slight attack of illness, which showed me I needed higher air, so, a few days ago, off I started, and came over the new St Gotthard road,—of which I can speak in high praise. I like it better than the Mont Cenis route. The scenery is superb; cars much nicer; the tunnel is well ventilated and only twenty-five minutes long. I may stay here until September, and I may go higher, to the Engstlen Alps, 6000 feet up; I am now up 4000 feet. . . .

Goodby, I am very busy here; came up on purpose to write. There are plenty of people here, but so far I am the only American, the others are English and German;

it is not one of the American places, in fact, hardly known to Americans, as many other Swiss resorts are.

Yours affectionately,
C. F. Woolson.

Notes

1. The letter is in a typed transcription at WRHS. Portions also appear in Benedict/CFW, 280.

To John Hay (Brown)

Baden-Baden
August 9th, [1883]

Dear Colonel Hay.

I don't know whether you have as yet received the picture which Mr Noyes was to send. In thinking over what you said about wishing to have some little thing of Meacci's—my Florentine artist who paints Rossetti-ish pictures without ever having heard of Rossetti,—or rather, to give him an honester title—who is a bona-fide Pre-Raphaelite, and not a London one, loving and imitating the work of the Lippis, Botticelli, & the others, on its native heath, as one may say,—it seemed to me that the best thing to do was to order for you a replica of my own little picture, "The Garden of the Hesperides."[1] Not that he has not many others, & some of more weird design; but I was in Venice, & he in Florence, & I could not be sure that he would know what I meant, if I should try to describe to him, in my fantastic Italian, my own idea of any of the others. For my own idea & his might not agree at all! For instance, he had several little pictures which I once called scenes from the "Vita Nuova," because so exactly in the spirit of that "twilight land, no man's land" effusion.[2] But <u>he</u> seemed to have never heard of the "Vita Nuova." This is, really, what interested me in the man; he has absorbed the spirit of those early Florentines who came before Raphael, without knowing anything about it in a literary or historical way. He <u>is</u> it; & that is enough. Like those soldiers who <u>are</u> the battle; who are too much in it to know anything about it.—So Meacci did the "Garden" again, & sent it to me. And, when it came, believed it was not like mine. It was a garden, & a brook, & three nymphs, and the golden fruit growing from red roses on antique pedestals, while the dragon kept watch below. But the whole color was much brighter. It seemed to be in the morning, while mine is almost twilight; at any rate, much duller in hue throughout the whole. (Now Newman, if copying, would have produced an exact fac-simile. Not so Meacci.) I showed the two to several persons. Mr Noyes liked mine the best. But Mrs Goodrich, who is, as you know, something of an artist herself, preferred yours. As also did the American physician of Florence, Dr Baldwin, who happened to be in Venice at the time. And one or two others. I therefore decided not to send it back to Meacci to be "darkened," but to leave it with the coloring he himself liked; for he had sent me word that he liked this brighter one better than mine.—I am sorry to say that we are not the only ones who have this little picture. I foolishly talked about it (mine) in Florence, & that gave it some identity among Meacci's rather unintelligible & numerous designs, & several persons, I believe, bought it; i.e. ordered copies. For it began to be quite the fashion to "go to Meacci's," & "pick up" something. I think people have got a little tired of Newman, & his high prices. "The Garden" cost fifty francs, which I paid. Do'nt trouble yourself to send over the money now. Some one will be sure to be coming in person, before long; if no one else, there is my sister, who hopes to join me next Spring.—

Levorati I discovered, after some hunting. I think they are jealous of him in Venice, for at all the picture-shops, & shops for artists' materials, they pretended that they knew nothing of him. To which I responded that he was well known in London; &, when they thrust other pictures upon me, I said "Ah yes! very pretty. But these men have only a <u>local</u> reputation, you know." I do'nt think, however, that "vous savez" can ever have the real sound of the "you know"—or rather the "<u>do'nt</u> you know"—which is so fine, & which I am trying my best to acquire. It seems to be "Dun-tyer-kno'—,' <u>very</u> short. As you probably wrote the new serial just opening in the "Century," called the "Bread-Winners," you will understand that my difficulty is in my natural "flat monotone," I being one of the "Western people." Why do I think you wrote the new serial? Because you wanted to know why I did'nt lay the scene of "Anne" in Cleveland; & you did'nt seem to agree with my reply that there was no "background" there but the lights from the blast-furnaces at Newburgh on a dark night, and the lake. I see you have boldly taken Euclid Avenue for your "background." But I notice that you have been driven to "the lake" as well! And I am waiting to see how long it will be before the blast furnaces come in. The same number of the "Century" (August) also contains your experiences about "Democracy." (In Bric-à-brac).[3]

To go back to Levorati. When I had obtained his address, from a dealer in artists' materials who had no protégé of his own to protect, Mr Noyes offered to go to the place for me. He reported that Levorati had some lovely things, but unfinished. He was to finish up two or three, & bring them to the Consulate for me to look at. But, before the day came round, I had had a little attack of illness, & felt that I ought to get away as soon as possible to higher air. Mr Noyes, in the meanwhile, had asked me to allow him the pleasure of getting this picture for you, himself. He said it was just the opportunity he had been wishing for. That he had long been wanting to send you some little remembrance, & had been looking at bits of rare old Venetian glass, with that idea. But that glass was almost impossible to send. And he did'nt know, either, whether you would care for it. But to send you something that you had a fancy for, that would be delightful. He was so much in earnest that I consented.—As I left Venice before the pictures were finished, of course I did not see them. But Mr Noyes told me that the one he had selected for you was, he thought, "lovely."—He told me that Levorati had many English orders. His prices must have gone up since Mr King bought his picture, for there was nothing in Venice of his to be had for less than five or six guineas, I believe.

I do'nt know how Mr Noyes was to send the pictures to you. I left the "Garden" with him. I told him if he should send it in a package by itself, & pay the charges in advance, he was to let me know how much they were, so that I could repay him, & thus have but one bill for you. But I have not heard from him lately; so do'nt know how he arranged it.

My first rooms in Venice, in the old Gritti palace on the Grand Canal, were picturesque when you got to them! & very Venetian. But the stairs were terrible, & so I did not ask any one to come & see me. But, after the first month, I found my abode was going to be too warm, & then, I made use of your letter, & Mr Noyes most kindly responded, & did everything he could for me. It ended in my taking some nice rooms under his apartment, on the Riva, where the view down the harbor is beautiful. Here I stayed until the 7th of July; & every moment was more divinely fair than the last. Before Mrs Noyes went to America, they invited me twice to dine, but as I presumed they were to have other guests, I declined,—as you know I seldom go to dinner-parties. But after Mrs Noyes had gone, I did go there to dine once; Mrs Goodrich (wife of Lieut. Comm. G.) had come to Venice, and, as Mr Noyes' first parish had been the little church at the Highlands of Navesink which her father built, he (Mr Noyes) wished to invite her, & so I went too, on the condition that there should be no one else. The apartment is charming, & beautifully furnished with all sorts of lovely things; old carved chests, tapestries, Japanese hangings, & vases,—& some beautiful sketches on the walls.—I liked Mr Noyes very much. He struck me as one of the most unworldly of men, & one of the kindest. When I was ill, he was so good. He wanted me to take his wife's maid. And he put his beautiful gondola, one of the most beautiful in Venice—at my disposal. I went out in it several times in the evening, quite alone—far out on the lovely still lagoon. It was just what I needed; I was too ill to talk. The delicious motion & soft sea-air did me worlds of good. At other times I went out with him; & he was always agreeable. He has a very perfect sort of kindness as he is never in a hurry, & has no suggestions to make, one can lean back & rest; one knows that he is'nt going to suggest a single thing that one "ought," or "had better," do. He took me to the station early in the morning when I went away, &, all together, he did a great deal for me, & in the loveliest way. For all of which I thank you. For I owe it to your letter. He is very fond of you,—as I suppose you know. We had long conversations about you. He wanted a copy of my "Miles Keogh" (the "Stirrup Cup" he already knew) (the copy I told you I made from your "Atlantic" print), & I gave him one. (I also, by the way, sent one to Comm. Goodrich—& he admires it most warmly.) I think Mr Noyes was a little hurt that you did not let him know you were so near him in Florence, last winter. He said he would have gone there in a moment, if he had known you were there. He went back & told me about your college days. And he confided to me that, in his opinion ~~that~~, "John Hay had more literary ability in his little finger than Howells had in his whole organization!" Yet he likes Howells' writings, too. He struck me as on the watch, with jealous affection, to put down any one who should attempt to surpass "John Hay." He will let them know, at least, what "McWalter Bernard Noyes" thinks about it!

You started me wrong on that name, did'nt you? I am sure you put "Bernard" first. With great difficulty I got it right. And then, what did he do but come out with another name at the head of the "McWalter"; what it was, I do'nt know, but the initial was "C." He has dropped the "Rev^{d}" while he is "consuling."—The vice consul, his adopted nephew, is a nice boy. Mrs Launt Thompson & I delighted in him. He runs the Consulate, & drills the servants, & sails the yachts (a beauty, that yacht!), & knows everybody, & puts up the flag, & passes the plate in church, & wears half a dozen different suits of clothes in the course of a day, and, all together, is most refreshing. His name is Budd, & I used to spend a good deal of time at my window watching him come tearing in from the Lido in his yacht, sitting on its extreme tilted edge, & going far ahead of everything Italian, with the Stars & Stripes gallantly flying at the mast head. When he had nothing else to do, he wd. throw down flowers from their window into mine! I naturally liked him. I am told he calls me "that dear Miss Woolson";—so I flatter myself that he approved of me.

At this late day, of course you have heard the Crown Princess Story?[4] Have'nt you? You know, do'nt you, that when she heard that Mr Howells was in Venice, she expressed a wish to see him; and that the English Lords & Ladies who were circling round her, were therefore obliged to bestir themselves, & get hold of him as best they could. At last they succeeded, & he was begged to come to Lady Layard's, where the Crown Princess (Germany) was to pass the evening. He went. Was presented to her. And had quite a long conversation. And the Lords & Ladies stood round, & looked on.

I saw a little something of Venetian society. And fancied I should like it better than the hurrying crowds of Florence. It seemed to be a small circle. And a cozy one. No strangers; few Americans. But such picturesque persons as Don Carlos

& various dispossessed princesses of remote provinces like Montenegro (I believe), circling through it. I went to an afternoon-reception, & the ladies, many of them, smoked. I do'nt think any body ever "makes calls." And they all sit up half the night; & never have any "walking dresses" because they never walk. Lord Ronald Gower—who is, in my mind, a vague mixture of "Reminiscences" & the "Grosvenor Gallery"—has my rooms, under the Noyes', from the first of September.[5] Mr Noyes knows him a little; but Budd knows him "intimately," of course. Shall I go back to Venice, & take the rooms on the other side of the hall, & enter a little into this distinguished society this winter? I am mortally tired of Florence (though I like a few of the people there), and if I am again obliged to give up (with a big heartache) Rome,—where else can I go? For they are heaving up with earthquakes the Bay of Naples.

I left Venice at the last rather sadly. For my little god-child, Wolseley Goodrich, had died suddenly, after a short illness. His mother took him back to Florence, as it seemed less desolate to her than to leave him in that island-cemetery at Venice. The physicians say that it was a release for the poor little fellow; that he could not have lived to grow up. And so his mother tried to think it was for the best. As also did I.

After leaving Venice, I went first to Switzerland, & then came back to this pretty little nook in the Black Forest, which I liked so much last summer. I shall stay here for the present.

"Anne" & "For the Major" have both been brought out in London, by Sampson Low & Co. And another firm wants to bring out some of the short stories there. I would give a good deal to have you here to ask advice of! But, as you are not, I must e'en go along in the old way.

Give my love to Mrs Hay, and to Flora. I wish I could see my grand-nephew; and your lovely children as well. I should like to send my love also to Mrs Stone—if she remembers me. I remember her visit to Cooperstown, when I myself was in much sorrows.[6]

I hope you continue well; as well as you were in Florence. Shall I go down to Provence to spend the autumn? Your pictures of Aigues Mortes linger in my mind. I should like to see Daudet's "Provence." But I am perfectly sure that the wind across some of the wide "barrens" I know, with the low blue sea gleaming endlessly on the east side of them, is as "characteristic" as anything in Provence. The mind sings in Florida; & hums. But you tell me you have been there. I do'nt (in a poetical sense) believe it! Ruskin is funnier than ever, over Miss Frances Alexander—the maker of the book of sketches & translations which you saw in Florence.[7] He calls her a "girl." "This girl," &c. Did you see Miss Frances Alexander, when you saw the book? It reminds me of my dear cousins, the Coopers. When they all got to be sixty and over, they at last decided to say, in their mild way, "Dear Aunt Pomeroy" (my grandmother), "do'nt you think that perhaps it would be as well now, not to call us any longer 'the girls'"? But this is frivolous conversation for a Secretary of State. Good-by.

Yours sincerely,
C. F. Woolson.

P. S.

Aug. 10th

On taking up the "Century" a 2d time, I see the blast furnaces are already in your serial,—on the very first page.

Notes

1. See Woolson's letters to Hay dated Apr. 24, 1883, and May 5, 1883, for more discussion of artist Ricciardo Meacci.
2. Dante's *La Vita Nuova* (*The New Life*).
3. Hay's *The Bread Winners* (1884) was being serialized anonymously in *Century* from Aug. 1883 to Jan. 1884. Henry Adams's *Democracy* (1880) was also published anonymously.
4. Petry (60) reports the story of Howells's meeting with the Crown Princess of Germany, the consort of Frederick III and daughter of Britain's Queen Victoria: the Crown Princess had expressed a desire to meet Howells and when Howells reported about the meeting to his family, they heard nothing colorful about his ten-minute conversation with her.
5. Art writer and trustee of the National Portrait Gallery, Lord Ronald Sutherland Gower (1845–1916).
6. Woolson is referring to the death of her mother. Mrs. Stone would be Hay's mother-in-law.
7. Frances "Fanny" Alexander (1837–1917), illustrator and writer.

To Mary Gayle Carter Clarke (Cornell)

Baden-Baden
Sept. 5th, [1883]

My dear Mary.

I really feel that I must close up "the season"—in whose gayeties I took part with all of you. I am sure you will be interested; &, if you are not, you can pretend to be—on my account. For I have stayed behind, you know; I am not at Cologne; & Hamburg; & Ems; & the Engedine. I am still going up to the "old castle"; & still drinking milk at the dairy; & listening to the "cur-orchestra"—which, I am happy to say, has begun to play very well again, having recovered from the fatigue of being subdivided, & added to, & generally disintegrated during the Racing Season. It is'nt a horse,—that orchestra! But it has been made to work like one. It played a little like one, too, towards the last; your mother remarked upon the resemblance to an omnibus going down Broadway. However, last night, it played in the large hall of the

"Conservation House," & gave us the "Ride of the Walkürie," & Liszt' "Hungarian Rhapsodies,"—& it was fine.[1]—The Prince went off at 6.40 p. m. on Sunday. The Duke of Hamilton followed on the next train, at 7. And then, helter-skelter, all the little princelings & barons of German birth took flight, so as to be in the fashion.[2] By nine o'clock Monday morning there was not one left. Only that very ugly young man with a receding chin, who was talking to the Countess who had the Buffet, when we peeped in from the nook between the trees, behind;—& he, I think is only a plain American.—However it ended in a blaze of glory, for the fests on Saturday night at the "Old Castle" must have been one of the prettiest sights of all, & I wish I cd. have seen it. That is, if I had wings. Humanly speaking, the aid of "beasts" was required; & I should not have enjoyed it—or gone. The Prince started at 8. p. m. in the same "break" (I have found out the right name at last) in which he went to the last races,—belonging to the Duke of Hamilton. He was dressed as a medieval huntsman (he had probably brought the suit with him, & they had to get up the fête in consequence) & accompanied by friends. Behind him came all the other four-in-hands; & then all the private carriages, & then the other invited guests (it was an invitation affair) in such carriages as they cd. obtain. All the carriages were covered with white, & hung with sleighbells, & the guests dressed as huntsmen &c. I believe they were not in a procession going up. They came down all together, at break-neck speed! As the Prince's break reached a certain point, he was met by a Herald in medieval dress, who wished to know his name, & rank, before he cd. be admitted to the Castle. These were given, with due formalities. And then came a party of foresters down the road, & gave a salute with hunting-horses. The break went on & was met by Black Forest peasants, who sang their songs, & danced by an open fire. Then the castle-runners appeared, with torches, & the rest of the way was lighted by them. They were met at the closed Castle gate by the sentinel, & a parley was held. Then the bugle sounded, the gates were thrown open, & the "Count," "Countess" & all the "ball" sallied out to meet the royal guest, all in medieval costumes. These were the Club-men, & all those same ladies who have been taking part in all these things. They went with the "Knights' Hall" (you remember it?) & here a little peasants' play (medieval) was performed, the whole place being brilliantly lighted. As it was a little cooler, fires were burning. Then they had a supper, while the peasants sang above; & then a dance. That beautiful "Ritter-Saal" must have been very picturesque by the light of the fires & torches.[3]—A little after midnight they all came down together, to the music of the hunting-horns. The little Baden paper says, with pride, that a "reporter" who had seen "all Europe & half America" (I am so glad it was only half) "said, <u>with</u> <u>enthusiasm</u>, that he had never seen anything like it."—Of course if he had seen "all America"—he cd. never have said that; the medieval castles up & down the Ohio & on the Cuyahoga, wd. immediately have presented themselves to his mind.

That was the last. The season is closed. It has been rainy & cold. But I am very well; & I went to the lace-shop (tell your mother) & took my lace with me; & the man said it was "Point d'Angleterre." He did not impress me, however, as being a "specialist" in lace, because when I asked to see the "Brussels Platte" (of which I had heard) he showed me two kinds before he decided which was the right one! I asked if he had any handkerchiefs anything like my piece, & he had not. He said I could get a small one for about 35 or 40 dollars. So that gives me a clue to the value of mine. I have put it back in the box. And do'nt know when I shall ever wear it.—I hope your mother got my letter—though there was nothing important or interesting in it. I hope she will write, sometime,—& tell me how the Rhine impressed her. We had a beautiful day for it last year.—My old round-hat hangs on the peg. And I remember that it went to church on your head; & it still surprises me. I can bend it way down, like a shed-roof, when the lights are too bright. And I do. The only person here who seems to know anything about me—a woman—finds that hat in her way! I bend it down on her side always, whenever she is near me. I think she is a writer, with a ms. which she thinks I wd. greatly admire. There are a good many such persons. Much love to your mother, & to Grace, & Averell.[4] I have now "closed the season,"—the little Baden Season I had with all of you—; & so good-by.

Yours always,
C. F. Woolson.

Notes

1. The "Ride of the Valkyries" is the third act in Wagner's opera *The Valkyrie* (1856). The *Rhapsodies* are probably the ones Liszt composed in 1882.

2. This is likely the 12th Duke of Hamilton, William Douglas Hamilton (1845–95), whose mother was German.

3. A "rittersaal" is a hall of knights.

4. Mary's sister and brother.

To Jane Averell Carter (Benedict/Voices, 254; Benedict/Abroad, 750)

1883

I look back and see how wonderfully good to me Mother was when I was finishing "Anne." She was always pleasant and kind, never put me on the defensive, as one may say; never said "do'nt!" or tried to make me do anything I didn't want to! I get nervous mentally, when very hard at work, and little things wear on me.

To Unknown recipient (Benedict/Voices, 89)

1883

When you went to Hyde Hall, I am afraid you didn't see "the haunted room."[1] I suppose they no longer show it—if indeed it has not been repaired and put in order. It was the best and most complete "haunted room," I ever saw. I always admired Hyde Hall—tumbled down as it was; the long drive from the Porter's Lodge was so pretty. It only wanted a few deer to be as pretty as any of the smaller parks in Warwickshire—the Offchurch Bury, for example.

Notes

1. The George Clarke family owned Hyde Hall near Cooperstown.

To Jane Averell Carter (Benedict/CFW, 281)

[1883?]

I must tell you . . . what a great satisfaction it was to me to have you take the view you did of my remaining in London, or at least in England, all winter, in case the climate agrees with me <u>and I feel like it</u>. There is certainly no one with so clear, calm, sensible a way of looking at things as you! Of course it is the thing for me to do—if it will be any comfort and change for me. But every one else writes against it! Fortunately, I have learned to do what I think best and let the rest go. If I tried to follow all the advice I get, I should soon be in an asylum . . . So far, it has not been cold at all. Dark—yes, foggy, yes; but not cold; so, as it is only the cold that makes me uncomfortable, I do very well here. You will laugh—but it is warmer here than it was at either Mentone, Rome, Sorrento, or Florence! The air is less harsh outside, and the houses are infinitely warmer. But of course I quite understand that many people could not stand the fog and the dark days. I am now able to go to the picture exhibitions; I enjoy them greatly; a glimpse of contemporary English art about which I knew very little. Mrs Chadwick and I are contemplating a visit to the Christmas pantomimes.

To Samuel Mather (WRHS/Mather)

(Care Alliance Bank
High Street Kensington
London W.)
116 Sloane St. S.W.
Jan. 16th, [1884]

Dear Sam.

Very many times I have wished to write to you & to Flora in answer to your letters of last August. Flora's letter was such a delightful one, telling me so many things about that dear little boy whom I already love very much, although I have not yet seen him. And Flora told them, too, in such a delightful way (as indeed I think she always tells everything), that I wanted to go home at once, & see my little nephew, get some of those kisses he bestows upon the people he likes; I trust I shall be one of them.—He must be a great big boy, now. I do not altogether like that! His little picture, with his thumb in his mouth, has been a great delight to me; my eyes have often fallen on it, when ill & wretched, & it has always acted as a comfort. There is nothing like a little child as comforter. Everyone who comes to see me takes up the picture & smiles; the brave little man sitting there, with his fat little legs, & bright contented face, amuses everybody. Dear little fellow—give him 20 kisses from his Aunt Connie.

Just as I write these lines, the maid brings me the very beautiful Xmas card—(the most beautiful I have ever had)—from Flora & yourself, which has probably been making a month's voyage on the long & delayed "Celtic," which got in yesterday. The card was mailed in New York Dec. 14th. I am so much obliged to you both. And I again wish I had not been so long in replying to your letters. But the delay has really been inability. I have been ill three months. Three times during that period I rallied, & tried to call myself well; but only to sink back again. I have rather kept it to myself—this illness—as I did not wish to make Clara anxious; I knew there was no real danger, throughout the whole. But I have had a great deal of pain, & it has taken away my strength. It was not any one thing but a succession of ailments & difficulties. All is well now, I trust. The Dr has dismissed me.

I presume all came from the shock of Charlie's death,—which made me suffer more than I have ever suffered in my life.[1] I was so extremely unhappy for a number of weeks that I did not know where to turn. Charley left behind a letter, or rather two—a sort of diary—which he had written at different times during the summer. This diary showed suffering so piteous that it broke my heart. I cannot imagine any suffering greater than his was, at the last. I will say no more. I know you were sincerely attached to him; & to all your family, he was most grateful, for the kind acts which gave the only gleam of pleasure he had, during those last years. This diary of his only reached me, of course, after his death. ~~It was not written.~~ I have destroyed it, as he requested. Strange and mysterious are the ties of blood. I had seen so little of Charlie since he grew to be a man; we had been separated for so many years; & yet his death—out there in California—has made me perfectly desolate, &, for a time, it seemed to me that I cd. not rally from the depression it caused; & that it was hardly worth while to try. But I know that such feelings are wrong. I have long ago decided that simple courage—courage for the tasks of each day—is by far the greatest virtue. So I have tried to call up "courage" now. And have, in a measure (since I have got back my ~~strength~~ health) succeeded. I have just been sending some Xmas remembrances to Charlie's friend Mr O'Melveny, and to the Doctor who was so much with him in the Spring. Clara & I are having a stone put up in the Los Angeles cemetery. Charlie wrote me, that, if I so desired, I cd. remove him to Cleveland, later. But I do not care about such things; & neither did he; the resting-place of the body we both thought of small importance, I remember, when we once discussed the matter together. If I shd. die over here, here I am to be buried; that is my express desire.

I came up to London, in the beginning, on a vague sort of impulse. I did not want to go back to Florence, where I shd. have to see so many people; & Paris—(where Flora Whitney most kindly urged me to go with them) did not seem to me the place. I am most glad, now, that I did not go to Paris; I shd. have been such a cloud upon the Whitneys—ill & confined to my room; they too were in trouble, you know, over the case of their little daughter.

England has always greatly interested me. Next after Italy, I think I like England; and, if I were able to do as I pleased, I shd. divide my year between the two countries (as long as I remained abroad) & let everything else go! But the most surprising thing I have encountered since I left America, is the temperature of the English winter. I never wd. have believed it without seeing it myself. I assure you that so far—middle of January—it has been far far warmer than it was at Mentone; at Rome; at Florence; and at Sorrento. It is foggy. There is not much sunshine. Of "clear, cold, <u>bracing</u>[”]weather (how I hate that word!) there is none at all. But oh! how mild it is! How soft the air that goes down my easily-attacked throat! How exquisitely tranquil the soft English light—through which the bare trees—dotting the <u>green</u> stretches of Hyde Park—are actually as beautiful as when in leaf. The English light is to me the loveliest thing I know. The two things I cannot endure in weather are cold, and wind. Last Sunday it was 51 here, (I see it was below zero with you), &, as to wind—so far there has been none at all. There was a wind at Florence last winter that went to the marrow of one's bones. You may remember that there was <u>some</u> breeze, also, at Sorrento!

If a wind shd. rise here, after all, or real cold come, I shd. flee. Either back to Italy, or else to the Isle of Wight.—

I am comfortably lodged in the same house with the Chadwicks, whom Col. & Mrs Hay will remember. I went first to the place in South Kensington where the Howells once stayed. But this situation is pleasanter; &, during all these weeks of ill health & depression, the Chadwicks have been kindness itself. They have done everything they cd. think of to add to my comfort & keep me from too much loneliness. Mrs C. is a very sweet woman; she is a cousin of the Floyd-Jones of N.Y.; & the F.-J.s are cousins of the Coopers—so that makes a sort of link.[2] I am amusing myself—now that I am better—in looking at the pictures. Winter though it be, there are a number to be seen. The Grosvenor Gallery has the finest collection of portraits by Sir Joshua Reynolds <u>ever</u> made, &, wandering through the beautiful rooms is like being introduced to the England of a century ago. They were a splendid-looking set—the English "society" of that day; all the men are stately, & all the women handsome. But dear me! Who knows how we shd. look if we had such costumes to wear! Powdered hair, dressed high over a cushion, pink cheeks, parterres, a long laced corsage, & jewels & roses—all of us wd. undertake to be good-looking with such accessories. And I suspect that a crimson-velvet suit, lined with white satin, & trimmed with ermine wd. make you "stately" in spite of yourself. The "oil" & "water" exhibitions are giving me my first idea of the English school of painters of the present day.

Venice last summer was beautiful beyond words. And I <u>did</u> see Symonds; (Flora asks.). I spent part of an evening with them. He did not say much. I was sorry for that. But I believe his health is so wretched that he makes as little exertion as possible. The occasional lurid-ity that glows under his charming style, does not appear in his face. But perhaps he flames out when strangers are not by. He asked me to tell him about "the white spiders of Florida" (Miss Poynter put him up to that); & I distinctly declined to do so. However, in spite of this, he was so good as to speak well of my "manner" (I hear) after I had gone. He said I was not "shy." (The English consider that a compliment!) His daughters are shy however. One knocked over a chair & the other a table, while I was there. This may not strike you as "shyness." But it was. The man to whom you sent my address, wished me to write a "serial" for a certain wonderful paper wh. he is starting, & for which he has been "collecting material fifteen years." I was to answer "by cable!" But I did'nt. I thought a note by mail wd. do quite as well. And this brings me to the "Bread-Winners."

Jan. 20th

My letter has lagged; & I am glad, now, that it has, for last night there reached me a box—wh. I surveyed with astonishment, because I never get "boxes.["] I don't know whether you know that it is one of the little "peculiarities" of my life never to have had the luck of receiving presents. Such things seem to be governed by mysterious laws, wh. are not yet understood & analyzed. One person always has presents; another never has any, or scarcely any. It does'nt seem to depend upon merit, or even (always) upon attractiveness. Nor does it depend upon affection. It seems to be chance. But I suppose it is'nt, really. At any rate, I was astonished over my box. And opened it with the idea that it was some peculiar kind of dried flowers from Florida,—sent me by a botanical friend (I <u>do</u> occasionally get botanical flowers,). Imagine, then, my surprise & pleasure at finding the beautiful pin sent by you & Flora to the aunt who is over here alone, & not very happy. It touched me very much; I might as well confess that my eyes were full of tears as I looked at it. But they were not ~~the~~ tears of despondency this time. It was so good of you to have thought of me, & to have taken so much trouble—as you must have taken to send it all that distance. But it is fully appreciated; & I venture to say that neither you nor Flora ever gave a present that caused more pleasure. It is such a lovely pin, too, in itself. And something I needed, as I have nothing in black. Thank you a thousand times. My Xmas was lonely enough. But I did'nt care to see anybody. The Chadwicks went to Oxford for the week, & I was alone. This, however, is rather my preference for Xmas nowadays. Last year I went to Pisa, to escape invitations.

Clara writes that she has seen your mother, & finds her looking so well, though confined to her room again. I am so very sorry for this long & tedious siege; I can scarcely imagine how she bears it—active as she has always been. It must be very hard. Give her my dearest love, & tell her I think of her very often. And that I find England extremely beautiful, & interesting in more ways than I have time to express. In addition to everything else, it is certainly a most "comfortable" country. After 4 months in Italy, I enjoy very much the simple solid comfort of coal-fires; plenty of towels; muffins; general warmth & a "home-~~comfortable~~ like[”] feeling. All this will not prevent me from going back to "Rome," after the first frost next November! (Unless I shd. come home & go to Florida!) I had a nice letter from Will, & a pretty Xmas card. If he is at home again, give him my love, & tell him I shall answer his letter before long. I am so glad to hear that your father is improving. I think going to the Springs was an excellent idea, & I am so glad he went there instead of to the warm springs near Asheville; there are no comforts there. We need so many "comforts" as we get on in life, & I have "got on" so rapidly during the past three months that I feel like a very old person. I do'nt know any one so "old" as I am now! A few persons, a few little interests,—that is all I care for. But it is very fortunate for me that I have the same love for scenery that my Father had; that never fails me. Here it is the soft English light. Next winter it will be the Campagna. I don't say anything abt. the summer, you notice. That is because Clara has a plan for going to Vienna. I don't know anything about Vienna. I am quite willing, however, to go wherever she wants to. And, if only Kate can come with her, the summer will be sure to be delightful. I want to see Kate so much. I am now, & I expect to be for a long while, very busy. I have completely lost three months, & have also had to make a great effort to get back the interest I was full of last summer, & even to get back also the habit of daily work; I have been so broken up, mentally & physically, that it has been a struggle to resume anything regularly. But I am glad to be able to say that I have conquered, & got a firm hold of myself again at last.

What I was going to say abt. the "Bread-Winners," I will now reserve for a letter which I hope to find time to write to Col. Hay before long. Will you give my love to them, & say that, singularly enough, Col. Hay's letter from Colorado, & the one from Cleveland written recently, have just reached me, not 24 hours apart! I cannot imagine why Mr Noyes shd. have kept the first one all these months unless because he really had no idea where I was. How he has learned now, I do not know but he at last sends the letter & to the care of "Alliance Bank. London."

Henry James comes to see me now & then, & sends me books to read. Clarence King—I hear from his cousin Miss Vernon—is in London. But alas! he has not favored me with a visit. Tell Flora I have asked Henry James a thousand questions about that remarkable Mr Adams whom she described so well in Sorrento. And H. James has done his best to complete the picture. But his descriptions are not so good as Flora's! Good-by. I must stop. I still use Flora's shell pins every day for my hair, & cut all my leaves with your paper folder. Much love,

Yours affectionately
C.F.W.

P. S.

I hope Mrs Stone is feeling stronger this winter.

The Chadwicks have been in, & with much pride I showed them my pin. They admired it very much & Mrs C. is not a little envious.

Notes

1. Charly Woolson's death certificate reads suicide by poison. This letter suggests that he may have written Woolson a suicide note. The varied spelling in the letter is Woolson's. Charly's friend, mentioned later in the paragraph, may be Henry O'Melveny, founder of the Los Angeles law firm of O'Melveny and Myers.

2. Delancy Floyd-Jones (1826–1902).

To John Hay (Brown)

(Care Alliance Bank
High Street Kensington
London. W.)
116 Sloane St. S. W.
Jan. 27th, [1884]

Dear Colonel Hay.

Your two letters of September & December reached me almost at the same moment,—I don't know why. I was glad to hear from you again. But when are you coming over, coming over to this green England, to rest your soul, in its soft still light? I do'nt know that your soul needs resting. Mine did: & it feels now that it has found an atmosphere in which it can breathe in peace;—the others being Rome, & Venice; & Florida. That makes four; four atmospheres shd. content anyone. I think you know all the charm of London; so I need not try to send you my version of it. I go to see the remarkable collection of "Sir Joshuas" at the Grosvenor. To the Burlington House to see the "old Masters." And again & again to the Ex. of water-colors in Pall-Mall, & of oils in Piccadilly, in order to get some idea of the English school of to-day, of which I was very ignorant.[1] I can find nothing of your man, Solomons; & presume that his pictures are now all in private hands, as they are so fine. I am sorry.—I walk in the Parks, wh. are beautiful & green even now. It is not in the least cold; & I am amazed all the time to find it so warm. I make expeditions to all sorts of places; Turner's house on the river, where he went to live in order to see the sunsets; St Mary's Battersea, where Bolingbroke is buried, & his old manor-house near; a "Thackeray" walk, wh. takes in Becky Sharp's house in Mayfair, & ends at the Charterhouse, where old Col. Newcomb said "Adsum."[2] There is no end to the resources, & the interest. I have books from the Grosvenor Gallery Library, & have had some very entertaining ones;—principally French. Why is it that the French, of all times, write so well? I am sure we—I mean English & Americans—are far more solid in our knowledge, & are a better race in every respect; the French are so local, so "French" & nothing else! But how well they write!

I have been ill here three months. And very unhappy, besides. I am now better; & able to write again, wh. is a great gain in every way. And this reminds me of Mr Chadwick's recent letter to you, wh. he brought down for me to read.[3] I could'nt but smile over it, sadly enough—after he had gone. He has'nt the slightest conception of either grief, or illness. I really think that he believes I cd. have got better sooner, if I had only <u>tried</u>! He has never in his life had any real sorrows, or any illness—I mean the illness that hangs on, & baffles effort, & takes the heart out of a man. He is one of the best fellows in the world, & let us hope he never will have them. But perhaps, if they do come to him, sometime, he will remember his letter to you; & his kindly-meant but miles-away advice to me. I hope you are better. Having just come out of a condition that had some resemblance (as far as preventing all writing-work goes,) with yours, as you describe it, I can fully sympathize with you. The effort required for ~~the~~ my first attempts at writing again, was something wh. took every particle of will I possess. And I've got a good deal—on a certain line.

The "Bread-Winners."—I have twice been told that Mr Lowell is "sure" you wrote it. The Chadwicks are of the same opinion. I send you what the "Pall Mall" says. I myself am puzzled. I thought at first—during the first part—that I recognized Mr Howells' hand. Later on came touches (I cannot stand that quill pen any longer!) that were utterly unlike him.[4] My next idea was that you & he wrote it together. Now I am quite at sea. If you had ever written a short story before (that I knew about), I shd. have no difficulty in forming an opinion. But I do'nt think one ever knows how a man will write (in fiction) until one actually sees the work. Certainly "Mr Furrey" is much in one of your veins; & most delicious. Also some other things. But I confess that I am opinion-less on the subject—save, that, generally speaking, I am sure you can do, in the way of writing, whatever you choose to do. If it is you, how delightful to welcome you to the band, to which I, though ever so modestly, belong. And if it is you, I wish you would come over here, & & give me your ideas on novel writing in general. I shd. be so glad to have some talks with you, for I am sure you cd. give me a great deal of light. I am terribly alone in my literary work. There seems to be no one for me to turn to. It is true that there are only two or three to whom I wd. turn! But even if you wrote the "Breadwinners" (& "Democracy") I cannot let you off from poetry, wh. is so much the rarer gift. Lines from those exquisite verses you sent me from London last year, still linger in my memory. I wish I had not been so punctilious; I wish I had kept copies. I wanted to; but did not dare. I think the best way is to dare;—at least when one is as old as I am. And, henceforth, I shall. It would be ever so nice if you wd. send me some more verses to read—those you have written since you went home. It wd. please me much—both the reading & the remembrance.

Henry James, not having as yet read the "Breadwinners," ventures no opinion about your reported authorship of it. He confines himself to wishing that you wd. come back here, you & Mrs Hay; & stay. I hear, through Miss Vernon (his cousin), that Clarence King is in London. I wish he wd. come & see me; but have not much hope of it. You see that I have become exorbitant; I want to see the most agreeable people in the world, & only those! This is preposterous. I have nothing, absolutely nothing, to back it up with, alas! alas!

I have no "plans," I shall never have any, any more. They are tiresome, &, one of the few advantages of being alone in this world, is, that one can escape them.—Your letter from Colorado was very inspiring. Write me another; & send me some poems; & tell me whether you wrote the "B. W;" & give a pleasant half hour or two to the woman who is lonely, & not much entertained with the spectacle of daily life, as it exists for her. My love to Mrs Hay; & a kiss for the children. It makes me freeze to think of the cold you have had over there. I must live in Florida when I come back. I have just written to Sam—; last week. I hope he got the letter.

With best wishes, yours sincerely,
C. F. Woolson.

Notes

1. These are all art venues in London. The "Sir Joshuas" are paintings by Sir Joshua Reynolds (1723–92). According to Petry (66), Woolson could be referring to painter and illustrator Simeon Solomon (1840–1905) or to portrait and figure painter Solomon Solomon (1860–1927).

2. J.M.W. Turner's house is Twickenham; writer and statesman Henry St. John, Viscount Bolingbroke (1678–1751) is buried at Battersea, West London; Becky Sharp is a character

in Thackeray's *Vanity Fair* (1847–48) and Col. Newcomb (Woolson's spelling), whose last death-bed word is "Adsum," a character in his *The Newcomes* (1855).

3. The author of *Temperament, Disease, and Health* (1892), French Ensor Chadwick often gave health advice to John Hay.

4. Woolson had been advised to use a quill pen to avoid persistent writer's cramp. Her handwriting changed here as she discarded the quill.

To John Hay (Brown)

116 Sloane St
London. S.W.
Jan. 31st, [1884]

Dear Col. Hay.

I <u>have</u> an opinion, now. Either you, or Clarence King, wrote the B. W. Perhaps you did it together. All admire it here. I wish I cd. talk it over with you.

Yours,
C. F. Woolson.

To Charles Scribner's Sons (Princeton)

(Care Alliance Bank
High Street Kensington
London. W.)
London
Feb. 2d, [1884?]
Charles Scribner's Sons.

Gentlemen.

I have received your letter of Jan. 18th. I shall be very happy to have "Miss Grief" included in your collection on the terms proposed, and am pleased that you should wish to include it.[1]—From your having selected it, I supposed that you prefer it to any other story of mine which is not yet between bookcovers. There is one called "Miss Vedder"—published in Harper's Magazine for March, 1879 which I myself rather liked. The choice would be between that and "Miss Grief," as they are the only ones as yet uncollected, which I should care to have republished—save two or three I have written (on foreign backgrounds with marked local color) since I came abroad, which are to be placed in a volume by themselves.

With best wishes for your enterprise, I am,

Yours Very Truly,
C. F. Woolson.

Notes

1. Scribner's published "'Miss Grief'" in its 1884 collection *Stories by American Authors.*

To John Hay (Brown)[1]

116 Sloane St.
Feb. 4th, [1884]

You see? No use to deny farther. The book is a splendid success over here.

Yours,
C.F.W.

Mr Chadwick has just come in & says the Sat. Review has a fine notice also. Will get it tomorrow.

Notes

1. This letter to Hay, which has no salutation, is Woolson's final word on the authorship of Hay's *The Bread Winners* (1883). The novel was reviewed in *Saturday Review,* Feb. 2, 1884.

To Harriet Benedict Sherman (Benedict/CFW, 281–82)

London
March 29th, 1884

The most magical place in the world is Rome. The most divine place, Venice (in May, June and July). The most interesting, without the least beauty, London. . . . The winter has been the "mildest on record." It has been far warmer than it ever was (in winter) on the Riviera, in Florence, in Sorrento, in Rome. There has been no cold, not even frozen ground; no fog, no rain, no mud; best of all, no wind! All winter long the grass has been green in the parks, and the air has had that beautiful soft smoky look that I love. The flowers have been out for a month and over. I never imagined anything like it. I have grown very fond of London and have taken long walks in every direction. I am fond of walking in a city like Rome or London, because it is always safe. In the country, it is not safe for a lady alone, and half the time I prefer to be alone, when I prowl about this dear, dusky old town. I have hunted up all the Dickens and Thackeray sites. The other day I found the sunken stone passage in the grounds of Lansdowne House, the scene of the murder in Trollope's "Phineas Redux."[1]

But it is endless—I couldn't begin to tell you half . . . I cross the river; I go out to Hampstead and Highgate, the old "court suburb," Kensington, Chelsea, and down into "the city" to see Christ's Hospital and all sorts of places. Then there are always pictures to go and see—the Sir Joshua Reynolds collection at the Grosvenor is the finest ever made. . . . I have made almost no excursions. I did go down to Dulwich one beautiful day and see the college and excellent gallery there. The first warm—

I mean summer-warm—day, I am to go down the Thames to Greenwich, and then take the walk to Woolwich. But I am content with London itself. I couldn't finish the walks in it, in a year. . . .

I am always happy in England if for no other reason because the "lodging" system so exactly suits me. I abhor a public table! I have roast hare for dinner with bread (dreadful!) sauce; sometimes I have beefsteak pudding and then I think of Ruth Pinch. Five o'clock tea is my delight, and then I become French. I have "babas" to eat, and on very grand occasions, "petits-fours." . . . [2]

The whole city is in deep mourning to-day. I believe the Duke of Albany was very popular with the "people." I wanted to go down and hear the great bell of St Paul's tolled. It is only rung, I believe, when there has been a death in the Royal Family.[3]

Notes

1. *Phineas Redux* (1874) was the fourth of Trollope's six Palliser novels.
2. Ruth Pinch is a character from Dickens's *Martin Chuzzlewit* (1843–44). A baba is a rum cake named after the Arabian fictional character Ali Baba; a petit-four is a more delicate pastry.
3. On March 28, 1884, Queen Victoria's son Leopold, the Duke of Albany, died after morphine was administered to treat a knee injury.

To Charles Scribner's Sons (Princeton)

Care Alliance Bank
High Street Kensington
London. W.
May 14th, [1884?]
Charles Scribner's Sons.

Gentlemen.

I return the receipt with thanks for the draft. If not too much trouble, will you order a copy of the volume containing my story to be sent to me, whenever it comes out; my address is above. I do not now know the price you have put upon this series but I will send you the amount as soon as I receive the volume; I presume the price will be mentioned.

Very Truly yours,
C. F. Woolson.

To John Hay (Brown)

116 Sloane St
[May 1884?]

Dear Colonel Hay.

I am very sorry that I missed you yesterday. I can count, on the fingers of one hand, the people in London I really wish to see. You & Mr King are two of them.

So you can appreciate that I am bereaved. I hope you will come again soon. The evenings are my free time. But of course I know that you are probably dining out, &c. My people have any number of engagements for the opera & theatre, in which I never join. Kate arrives from Scotland tomorrow afternoon. They all go to the Continent June 30th. But I shall stay in England through July.

I have a thousand things to say to you. I am afraid they are not very important.

I am so glad Mr King has been to see me. One visit was all I required to revert comfortably to my old opinion of him,—which was superlative.

I hope you are feeling better all the time. Having been ill all winter myself, I can sympathize with you better than these brutally robust people can.

Yours sincerely,
C. F. Woolson.

To John Hay (Brown)

116 Sloane St
Wednesday
[June 1884?]

Dear Colonel Hay.

I am just beginning to realize that your going home is very near. From a selfish point of view, I do'nt like it at all! I was delighted—as I always am—to see you last evening. But should have been still more delighted if you had not been surrounded by outsiders. Now do'nt ask me what I mean by insiders. But come again as soon as you can, &, if possible, let me know by a line, by post or telegraph, beforehand. If you will come with Mr King to tea any afternoon, I shall be ever so much pleased. But, in addition, you must come by yourself another time. Of course this is all very exigeante[1] on my part. I can excuse it only by saying that however glad other London people may be to see you, they cannot be more glad than I am. And I doubt if they can be as glad. I don't intend at all to impugn them in this; I simply have in mind the amount of concentration there is in a gladness which comes to surface for so very few.

In addition, I want some advice from you. With regards to Mr King, I am, yours very sincerely,[2]

C. F. Woolson.

Notes

1. Woolson means "exigent."

2. Supposedly, Hay wanted King to marry Woolson and she may be alluding to her own interest in him. King had not yet met Ada Copeland, the black woman and former slave he secretly married, using the name James Todd.

To John Hay (Brown)

116 Sloane St
Tuesday
[June 1884?]

Dear Colonel Hay.

Thank you very much for the really beautiful letters of introduction; they are so nice that it is a pleasure to have them—even though I may never present them. But I thought I should'nt present the Venetian one!

As to your last word of advice—written—I shall ponder seriously over it, and decide within a day or two.[1] I can scarcely imagine myself having the audacity to do it. Still, your deliberate opinion, knowing the whole of the circumstances as you do, will have very great weight with me. As you say,—if they disapprove, they can make another proposition.

I am disgusted that you are going so soon. I have barely seen you. I have just had a note from Violet Paget, whom you may remember ("Vernon Lee"); she is here visiting Miss "A. Mary F. Robinson," & writes to ask when I shall be home, so that she can come and see me. I have named Saturday; but I am vexed that you won't be here to come too. You would come, I know; I remember how you admired Miss A. Mary F. in her little green gown embroidered with daffodils.

I am afraid you are not intending to come and see me again,—though I shall hope otherwise, up to train-time tomorrow. In case I do not see you, however, you must give much love from me to your wife; and to Flora and Sam; a kiss for my little grandnephew, and for your children as well. You'll not forget your promise about the photograph, I trust? A safe address will be "Alliance Bank. High Street Kensington. W."

I am extremely sorry you are going. From the full circle of your life, with so many ties, interests, "people," & everything else under the sun,—send word across the ocean, occasionally, to the very quiet person whose circle constantly narrows around her.

With the very best good wishes, I am, always, your attached friend,

C. F. Woolson.

Notes

1. Petry (74) surmises that the Venetian letter of introduction is to the U.S. Consul at Venice, Walter Noyes, and that the advice is about publishing. The advice, however, may have involved Clarence King, given Woolson's previous letter to Hay asking for advice about him. Who might "disapprove" about what remains unclear.

To Mary Gayle Carter Clarke (Cornell)

7 Holly Place
Hampstead. N. W.
July 5th, [1884]

Dear Mary.

Clara's address is "Care Sahler & Co. Bankers. Kreuznach. Germany." I send the book to your mother. I forgot to tell her that "Miss Grief" has recently had the honor of a translation into French under the title of "Mdlle Chagrin.""[1] I have'nt seen it myself. It was pirated.

I shall expect you on Monday & shall be very glad to have one more look at you. I hope Averell is better.[2] It's cooler here this morning. Yours in haste,

C.F.W.

Notes

1. The extra quotation mark is Woolson's.
2. Mary's brother.

To Mary Gayle Carter Clarke (Cornell)

Hampstead
July 8th, [1884]

My dear Mary.

It has come to me that I was probably mistaken when I told you, yesterday, that I was sure I had let you know, that day in Seymour Street, that your mother had asked me whether I knew anything on a certain subject;[1] I mean knew it from you. I have been thinking it all over; your sincere protest that you feared you must have lost your wits if what I said was true—led me to do so. At present I am inclined to think that what I said, that day, was simply to ask you what I should do, in case your mother should ask such a question? I put it before you that I should not like—(in case she did ask me)—to conceal anything. It was in answer to this that you looked away, as I described to you yesterday, & seemed to be so disturbed. And in answer to this that you said "Oh I should rather that you"—, [“]Oh, I wish—" &c, little phrases that you left unfinished, & from which I gathered that while you perceived my position, & acquiesced in the necessity I felt for speaking—(in case I should be asked—) you still felt very uncomfortable & regretful about it. So much so, that you never spoke on the subject to me again.

Does this coincide with your remembrance of the conversation?

I recalled the whole scene perfectly—what you said & how you looked. But I think, now, that I merely brought before you the necessity I felt for telling your mother, in case she should ask. And that the feeling I also distinctly remember in myself, afterwards, was simply a relief that I had spoken to you about it; & got your permission.

My memory of the matter now is that, at that time, your mother had not spoken. That she did so, later. And that there I again felt the same sense of gladness that I had brought the matter before you in time, & received your permission to speak; or at least told you that I must,—in case of certain things happening.

My idea was, I think, to have told you that your mother had spoken, upon the first good opportunity, afterward. But you will remember that there has been none; I have not seen you alone since.

I am quite ashamed to have mixed things up so, in my mind. But I see now that I simply felt that everything was right—; as I had told you what I shd. feel I must do, in case certain things happened; & that I rested on that, & let the details escape. I believe I told you, did'nt I? that I have been deliberately trying for the past few years to let things go,—not to charge my mind with remembering everything so exactly, as I have remembered all my life. But this incident of yesterday would seem to be a proof that I have succeeded better even than I intended! I wonder if it is the same about the dinner?

I am hoping to hear from you about Averell. I am afraid it must be rather sultry in town to-day. I enjoyed my hour for dining last evening greatly. I sat down at 9.15. Rose from the table at 10. Shd. like to do the same every night.

Tell your mother, with my love, that I want a good picture of her; of you; of Grace; & Averell, who is my godson.[2] I have nothing of him at all. With love,

Yours affectionately,
C.F.W.

Notes

1. The subject could possibly be Mary's impending engagement to George Hyde Clarke (1858).

2. Mary's sister and brother.

To Elinor Howells (Houghton)

(Care Alliance Bank
High Street Kensington
London. W.)
Hampstead Heath
July 15th, [1884]

Dear Mrs Howells.

I must write you again (though very busy) because I want to hear from you. I see, by the papers, that you have gone to Vermont. Do you see where I am? When one considers that it is still "London," the rurality is quite surprising. The view is completely so; every evening I see "daylight die" over the towers of Windsor and Harrow (spire of the latter), and fancy myself thousands of feet up instead of a few hundreds. I shall not stay here long, but go to the Rhine, where my sister and two nieces have preceded me. We had an apartment together in London for June & enjoyed it all greatly. There is no doubt about it,—I am going to break my heart over leaving England!

The only grain of comfort is that Venice is still down there, on the Adriatic.

John Hay was here some weeks, to my delight. He bought the most beautiful pearl necklace for his wife. He gave a charming breakfast at the "Bristol" for various nice people. He went over to Paris to see the Salon. Then he took flight again for home, leaving me missing him greatly. I mentioned to him that Clarence King had dropped me. He comforted me by the disclosure that he had dropped, in the same easy way, two Duchesses and the Prince of Wales.

I have a dreadful foreboding that you're not intending to come over here again. My sister intends to stay, this time. She is ordered not to expose herself again to a cold winter, &, as she is'nt fond of Florida—more's the pity!—she has come over to try, I presume, the Riviera. But though I shall be with her of course, I must get in a little of Rome.

Your friends Miss Paget and Miss Robinson, have both written me notes lately. They were to come to tea with me in Sloane Street; but the alarming illness of a friend of my sister's, prevented the small entertainment. I wish you would tell me what you know of Mrs Gordon Mac Kaye. I have never seen her, never expect to see her, & do'nt care in the least about her, one way or the other. But I have been applied to by a relative, who wishes to know if there is anything against her; of what her status is in Boston? Nothing that should be said in reply would ever, by the remotest possibility, reach the Mac Kays in any way. But it might be of service to some other people. Of course I should never mention that I had asked you. I was simply applied to, to find out, if possible, what was thought of her in Boston. And of course you will keep the secret of my asking. Most Americans over here do'nt know enough to go alone! I'm not referring to the Mac Kays, now. They seem to go alone very well!

I am greatly interested in Mr Howells' libretto. I see—in the Pall-Mall Gazette—that there is a possibility of its being brought out here. I shall come over from the continent on the opening night, take a box, fill it with my pretty nieces, and applaud.

Ask Mr Howells if it is possible he intends to be so cruel as to have his serial in "Harper's" run at the same time mine does![1]

I see Henry James quite often, and we talk of you. Did you know how much he admires your Minnie? Give my love to her; I am so glad she is getting strong. But tell her not to forget Venice.

I have got quite well again at last. How are you this summer? I am anxious to have a cabinet size of the photograph of Mr Howells' relief, by your brother. If you have'nt one to send me, I shall have my little one enlarged. Or has Mr Howells' a photograph from life that is good? If he has, I wish he would kindly send me one. John Hay has promised to send his. These, with Henry James', will make three. And a man has got to do something extremely distinguished, or make himself exorbitantly agreeable, before I shall allow him to be a fourth.

I go to Wiesbaden, Homburg, & all those places. Then, in the autumn, Italian lakes. Where are those Tuscan Sketches which Mr Howells thought of writing? I remember every word of the "notes" I read in the notebook he had kept—. And where is Pennel?

Oh come back, & let's all go & live in Venice. It's the only place. The swift boat "slid through old trouble of mine"—; I really forgot my troubles when I was there last year. I've done nothing but remember them since!

My love to all.

Yours affectionately,
C. F. Woolson.

Notes

1. Howells composed the libretto for *A Sea-Change* in 1883 and '84. Woolson's *East Angels* was serialized in Harper's from Jan. 1885 to May 1886; Howells's *Indian Summer* ran from July 1885 to Feb. 1886.

To Mary Gayle Carter Clarke (Cornell)

Hampstead
July 24th, [1884]

My dear Mary.

The beautiful pin gives me a great deal of pleasure; more perhaps than you know. It has been, I won't say a sore point, with me, but a source of a good deal of humility of feeling that, as the years have passed, I have almost never received any presents or mementoes, large or small, from anybody. It was'nt, of course, the actual gift so much as the remembrance that I should have prized. But all my friends had plenty, including my own sister, right by my side, who has always had & continues to have, a great many. And I had none at all. Of course I could not but feel that I must be very un-lovable, and very unattractive. I used to make myself quite unhappy, at times, over this! I have got over it now. Nonetheless I appreciate and prize very particularly your lovely gift. I've got it on at this moment; & shall probably wear it a great deal, as it is exactly the sort of pin I especially like and admire.

I was sorry not to see you yesterday. I was very far from well, & I fear Grace & Daisy found me dull enough.[1]

I have'nt much courage when ill. But I was very glad to see them,—Daisy is certainly very pretty & very bright. Grace, as you know, I am very fond of.—You will laugh when you hear that "the poor old thing" (that's what I generally call myself) is actually going to move again! I'm convinced that the trouble is the house; too small, ill-placed, *perhaps* ill-drained. At any rate I cannot run the risk of any more illness. I shall, most probably go down into town again. But *may* try some other country-place near. I feel a little better to-day. But not well. The truth is I want more room—space.

Poor Julia,[2]—I agree with you in thinking that the outlook is not bright for her. "Hard to be unhappy"—I should think it was! But I have met a good many people who really did not seem to have the capacity to be *very* unhappy. Fortunately for them—I suppose. People with plenty of capacity in other directions, too.

I think myself Mr Rutherford's call rather odd. Not his coming; but his insisting upon seeing you after he had been told you were at dinner. I wonder if you did not see him again; or if he wrote you?

When you write to your mother, please tell her that I received her letter, and shall answer it before long. Perhaps you will see Clara at Baireuth.—When you come back, possibly I may see you. "Alliance Bank. High Street, Kensington. W." is always my address. If you have any time, let me know.—I envy you Baireuth.—

Much love to Grace.
Affectionately yours,
C. F. Woolson.

P. S.[3]

I got your letter, my dear Mary, & the one you enclosed from Julia. Your letter gave me great pleasure; I think perhaps you wd. rather not have me answer it, or say anything more. My opinion of you & my regard for you are *greatly* heightened by this letter. Go on in the path you have marked out for yourself.—I do not know whether you have mentioned having written me, so I write the letter that accompanies this—as though you had not done so. You will know best what to do.—I am greatly troubled by Julia's letter. You see she has failed in her determination to go home,—as I feared she would. If Roy cd. only see that it wd. be better for them all to go! Perhaps he will. I will remember what you say about Julia's not knowing certain things. Good-by, my dear child; with a great deal of love I am & always shall be, most affectionately your friend

C.F.W.

You know where to go for Guidance in the little things—duties or pains—of each day.

Notes

1. Daisy is Juliette Gordon Low, founder of the Girl Scouts; Grace is Mary's sister.
2. Either Juliette Gordon Low or Julia Parsons, who was from Cooperstown.
3. This P. S. is filed with an 1888 letter written by Grace Carter, which seems to have no connection to it. I am speculating that it belongs with this letter to Mary. See appendix for Woolson's cousin Roy Keese.

To Samuel Mather (WRHS/Mather)

(Care Alliance Bank
High Street Kensington
London. W.)
Dover
Sept. 14th, [1884]

Dear Sam.

I write to send my love to Flora and the new little boy who has come to you. Kate brought the news when she arrived from Brussels, a week ago, and we were quite excited about it;—aunt and grand-aunt. I shall expect a photograph upon the earliest opportunity. Livingston's were so pretty. What, by the way, does Livingston say about his little brother?

It seems a long time since I have heard from you. But I am such a wretched correspondent myself that I ought not to say one word. But of course I have heard about you—first from Col. Hay, then from Kate. Kate's little visit here gave me great pleasure. In London there was so much going on, that I had but little opportunity to talk with her. Almost every evening (my time, you know,) they were out—opera & theatre. But in this ~~quite~~ quiet little place I had her all to myself, & enjoyed it greatly. I think her looking blooming; so much more color than she had when she first came from America. The baths have evidently done her good. I suppose she is well out on the ocean to-day; (not being fond of the North Atlantic, I say it with a grimace!). How much I wish she could have spent the winter. I would have taken her to Venice for at least two months in the spring, & I do'nt know anything better that that.—I came down here quite unexpectedly, driven away from London by the intense heat. I have never in my life suffered so as I did there—though my rooms were large & airy. My experience in English weather has been remarkable. It is lovely here as regards warmth & very "salty" air; the house stands on the beach. Clara is looking at Vienna. I suppose our winter rests between Vienna & London.

Write when you have time & tell me how Flora is, & all about the children & yourself. My love to Col. & Mrs Hay. Tell the Colonel I am waiting for the fulfilment of his promise.[1] Ask Kate if she received a letter I sent when at Queenstown? I got hers from Liverpool this morning. Love to all.

Yours most affectionately,
C. F. Woolson.

Especial love to your mother & father.

What is your number? I fancy I am directing this to the Hays!

Notes

1. Woolson is waiting for a photograph.

To Katharine Livingston Mather (WRHS/Mather)[1]

The Close!
Salisbury
October 21st, 1884

My dear Kate.

Nothing could be more ill-advised than my sitting down by gas-light, to write to you after writing all day,—therefore I proceed to do it! As I have always had a dream of spending a few weeks in an English Cathedral town, I selected Salisbury, as nearest to the coast,—after Canterbury. Here I am, and lodged, in the most enchanting way, in the Close itself. The house is immensely ancient, and very plain in its appointments. It is the home of one of the Cathedral Vergers,—the "pulpit verger," who makes a procession of himself before the Dean, when he, (the Dean) walks majestically from his stall in the choir to the pulpit outside. In all the Close, only two persons are allowed to take lodgers, my old verger, and the widow of another. You know, of course, the extreme beauty of the Cathedral; it is as different as possible from Canterbury, being all one style, early English Gothic. Perfect as it is,—with its beautiful spire,—I am perverse enough to prefer Canterbury! but as to the Close,—I give it up; this is more beautiful,—though it has not the charming ruins of Canterbury. But why make comparisons? It is the bane of travellers. If I could write pages I could not tell you how lovely the Close is; so I won't try. Imagine me, however, taking my daily afternoon walk there, (it is very large,) under the magnificent trees, now all colored a little, with the Cathedral forming the end of every vista,—different views of it,—and always that beautiful spire,—the highest in England,—far up in the blue. On Sunday I attend service in the afternoon, and owing to the verger being my landlord, I have the loveliest seat in a carved stall all by myself, with the most dignified Canon behind me, in his red hanging hood. The music is delightful, and the organ superb. I sit in my carved seat after service is over, as long as the organist plays,—sometimes twenty minutes, or so. My little rooms in this ancient house, are very bright and warm, with open fires in each. My sitting room looks out on an old garden, and on one side is a small old brick house, as old as Shakespeare's time I am sure, with leaden framed panes, and old beams outside, &c. I ask "Who lives there?" "The Bishop's bell-ringer, ma'am."—"Why the Bishop's, especially?" "Because he only rings the bell, ma'am, when the Bishop enters the Cathedral." "How does he know when the Bishop is going there? The Bishop might go on a week-day, or at any odd hour." "It is his duty, ma'am, to go every morning to the Palace, and inquire his Lordship's intentions!" That will show you how deep in I am! I am over my head in all sorts of ecclesiastical customs, and derive no end of entertainment from it all. My verger has a number of curious old books on Salisbury, the Cathedral, the town, &c, with old prints in them. I can tell you the whole history of "Old Sarum" now, as well as "New." I have been to Stonehenge; but the other excursions I have not time now to take.[2] "Wilton House" with the Vandycks, "Langford Castle" and Winchester.[3] I have been in England a year, and have only seen a little of Kent, that is, Dover and Canterbury; and now Salisbury, and that, with London itself (which I know well,) is all,—as I see very thoroughly the places I do see. My ecclesiastical lodging here is much more "characteristic" and "local to the soil" than it was at Dover. Being "Michaelmas time," I have goose and apple-sauce! Then I have partridge, pheasants, rabbits, and young hares! "Bread-sauce" of course with everything! I walk all over the neighbourhood in the late afternoon, always walking all round the beautiful Close the last thing before coming in. One day I walked out to the small ancient stone Church where George Herbert officiated so long. It stands open all the time, and I went in and sat down. It is no larger than your reception room, I should say, covered with ivy. I used to know a number of his poems by heart in the old days, but as I sat there I could only recall two lines:—

> "Who sweeps a room, if by Thy Will,
> Makes that, and the action, fine"[4]

What would your father say to a village, with forty inhabitants only, having a church, a nice rectory, and rector with $2500 a year? Endowment of course. There are literally, hundreds of villages, "parishes," with two or three hundred inhabitants only (often many of them Dissenters,) with handsome churches, a rectory, and yearly income of three or four thousand dollars a year. "My Lord Bishop" is very old and seldom goes out, but "the Very Rev. the Dean," a handsome dignified man, the three "Rev. and Venerable" Archdeacons, the "Canons," the "Minor Canons," the "Sub-Dean," the "Vicar's Choral" and the choristers, are always about the Close! besides an unknown number of young curates, who officiate at the three other Episcopal churches. I went into one of these the other day, a beautiful old stone church built in 1240, and a young curate was having afternoon service with the pew opener, an old woman, in a snuffy bonnet, down by the door. They both looked at me, so I had to stay. These beautiful old "Canonical" houses, where all the "Canons," &c live, all round the Close, are a constant delight to my eyes. Several of them,—more, fourteen or fifteen at least, are three or four hundred years old. As I walk around just before coming in, about 5:30, they are all having five o'clock tea; the fire-light shines out and I can see in; see the comfortable rooms and solid furniture, and very comfortable-looking clergymen, young and old, with their wives and female kind, all sitting about with teacups; then they will go and dress (the ladies will put on lace fichus and those dear caps), and be ready for a big dinner at eight, with a good deal of wine! However, I won't make sport of them; they are a handsome vigorous race as a whole. . . .

The 22[d]

My letter did not get off because I had no stamps. I must tell you,—or rather, your mother, for I always think of her over here, knowing how much she would enjoy some of the things,—of my walk this afternoon. Two miles through the English meadows, across stiles, over little streams, on rustic bridges, and finally I reach, first, the "Manor House" called the "Moat"; then a red brick Rectory covered with vines, where they are playing lawn tennis, and finally, the most picturesque little country church of grey stone, with a great Norman tower covered with ivy. It stands open, though no one is there. I go in, and look at the old carved tomb of the Duke of Buckingham who was beheaded in Salisbury, A.D. 1483; a curious piece of old sculpture. In one of the old houses in the Close (Salisbury) Richard the Third was staying when he gave the order for the execution of the Duke.[5] "Off with his head. So much for Buckingham." I prowl about the old churchyard,—which is most beautiful,—and then wander back through the green meadows home again, toward the soaring spire. I go about to all the country churches, and perhaps some one will want to know, like the Austrian student who wrote to me when I was at Innsbruck; "Why are you always so pale, and why do you visit three churchyards in one afternoon?"

Give a great deal of love to your father. Tell him to take a vacation and come over here; not try to see everything for that is so fatiguing. But spend a month or two among the English Cathedrals, and then go down to Venice!!

Affectionately,
C. F. Woolson.

Notes

1. The letter is in a typed transcription at WRHS. Portions also appear in Benedict/CFW, 283–87.

2. CFW (285) includes these comments by Woolson about her visit to Stonehenge with Henry James: "My own memorable visit to Stonehenge with Henry James, September 7th, 1884. It was so cold that we could scarcely speak, and finally we became silent. On Salisbury Plain, the wind blew so that I thought the carriage would be overturned. The driver turned out of the road down into a gully where we were somewhat protected and there we waited half an hour with the wind roaring overhead. At last we reached Salisbury, dined on a Michaelmas goose in my lodgings in the Close, and then we finished the day (and his visit) by going to see some strolling players in a hall not much better than a barn. They gave 'A School for Scandal'" [Richard Sheridan's 1777 play].

3. Wilton House in County Wiltshire has been in the Pembroke family for over four hundred years and boasts a large art collection, including many paintings by Van Dyck.

4. Poet George Herbert was rector at St. Andrew, Bemerton, near Salisbury. The lines are from "The Elixir" (1633).

5. Richard III (1452–85) had Henry Stafford (1455–83), the Duke of Buckingham, beheaded for treason when he supported Henry VII (1457–1509) in an attempt to overthrow Richard's kingship.

To Samuel Mather (WRHS/Mather)

(c/o Anglo-Austrian Bank
1 Strauchgasse
Vienna. Austria)
Vienna
Dec. 10th [1884]

My dear Sam.

I am so delighted with this excellent picture of little Livingston—; such a handsome, sweet, and intelligent little face is seldom seen. I wish I could see him myself—dear little fellow. But I am already fond of him, even without seeing. You and Flora must be fearfully proud by this time; I am afraid you will never return to the poor Hotel Bristol at Sorrento!

Dec. 21st

No—you will never go back there (I have been re-reading what I wrote ten days ago); you will always remember how the tramontana rattled the windows, and how we drew round the fire, & drank tea. Let me tell you here, by the way, that during the cholera epidemic at Naples this last season, Sorrento made its fortune. Half Naples took refuge there, & paid the highest prices; don't you hope poor Fiorentino got some of the money?—As I write, it is snowing hard here. Still, there has been nothing like sleighing, so far. Climate? Colder than any I have "experienced" for a good many years. But I have been remarkably well. I preserve my throat & temper by much sojourning in the house, not going out when it is very cold, or when there is a wind. The winds are as severe as those of Cleveland in March! Up to this time, it has been a peculiarly dry air. This suits Clara admirably. Fortunately our position

& rooms are delightful; on the broad Ring Strasse—with plenty of sunshine & a wide outlook. It strikes me—(Vienna)—as a very light place; blue sky, wide streets, & a wide light horizon. Plenty of space everywhere, both on the ground & in the air. I have forgotten whether you came here; but presume you did. To me, it seems by far the most brilliant city I have ever seen. The Hungarian element lifts it from the German heaviness. I have been through a good deal of surprise about it; I had no idea it was such a superb sort of place. The great Ring Strasse is wider and finer than the Paris Boulevards, &, to me, the buildings are the more magnificent than any modern ones I have ~~ever~~ seen. They are, to be sure, very modern; the whole "Ring," with all its palaces, only dates, I believe, back to 1858. Another feature is the wonderful beauty of the women. Generally they are dark; with the finest figures in the world. But I am forgetting that you have probably been here, & know all about it.

Do'nt imagine for one moment that all this brilliancy & sunshine make me forget my beloved foggy soft-aired England. It's that all this splendor keeps me from thinking (with a terrible longing sometimes!) of my dear down-at-the heels unimproved Italy!

I had such a pleasant journey, on here. I stopped over at Brussels, Cologne, Frankfort, & Munich. Tell Flora, that, stopping half an hour at Salzburg (I came that way from choice to see the scenery), I thought of her & her description of the place, at Sorrento. It was—even the little glimpse I had of it—wonderfully picturesque.

We stay here, I presume, all winter. Clare is hard at work at her music & German; also French; & a few English lessons. She has excellent masters, & is making good progress. She & her mother go to the opera, or some concert, five nights out of seven. It is early here; begins at seven; home at ten. They have just had all Wagner's operas, one after the other; & the two Claras have been in the 7th Heaven. When it is'nt Wagner, it's Brahms or Von Bulow. So you see what a treat they are having. They see a good deal of the U.S. Minister's wife, Mrs Francis; & of the Consul-general, Col. Weaver, & his family.[1] So you ~~see~~ observe that we are well under the protection of the Flag! Yesterday was the double-birthday of Clara & Clare, & they had many pretty ~~things~~ gifts finishing up with a gorgeously decorated thing—for dinner, in the evening; we hardly knew what to call it. It had a large rose (real one) in the centre, & was adorned with chequer-work of frosting & jelly. Within, it seemed to taste of all sorts of delicious things. Finally we learned the name. Translated it is "Hazel Nut Tart." T'was sent up by the housekeeper in honor of this birthday. (We are in furnished lodgings; or a sort of private hotel, rather.) It made me think of your description of the cake they got up for your birthday in Hanover.

I am very glad to hear, from several quarters, that Flora (Dec. 28th)—is better; & very much better. Give her my dearest love, & tell her I hope it won't be very long before I shall see her over here again. I still think, personally, that it is an immense thing to be in Europe. But I am aware that I am the only relic of antiquity that cherishes that opinion. A full half of Cleveland was over here last summer. It all went to Carlsbad, bought new clothes in Paris, & home again like nothing at all. But perhaps if I should visit Carlsbad & purchase new clothes in Paris,—it wd. seem "nothing" to me. Let me hold on to Italy & Salisbury, & old clothes, with a strong grip! Tell Flora I am still drinking tea, though the spurting little teakettle of Sorrento has departed this life! I began here, very recklessly, with "Vienna coffee" both in the morning & after dinner at night. It is so good! But I soon found that that amounted to "high living," so now I only have it in the morning, & tea in the afternoon before dinner, as in England. The tea here comes from Russia "on camel back," & they tie it up in parcels ~~the size of the~~ two inches square, "to make the load easier for the camel." This is the legend of the tea-shops. This appearance of the camel on the icy plains of Russia, is extremely new & interesting. But of course you have to believe it all, because the little packages of tea are "sealed with leaden seals"—which they show you! If I only had a "Samovar" I might really live, at tea-hour, in a Tourgnenieff atmosphere; & nothing cd. be more "remote" than that. Having no Samovars, I amuse myself with the ~~understandable~~ astonishing fact that I have arrived at the original habitat of "Vienna bread," & "Vienna coffee,"—without any "dairy" at all.

Give my love to Col. & Mrs Hay. I think Col. Hay might break his long silence & send me a letter full of American literary "news." Never was there a literaryish person so entirely cut off from every thing of that kind as I am here. Hawthorne says that it is a valuable experience for a literary worker to pass some weeks among persons—in an atmosphere—where the highest hopes he cd. possibly entertain wd. be considered of no interest, of no account. In that case, I shall certainly have accumulated a great heap of value by Spring! I shd. like to know what Col. Hay thinks of "The Story of a Country Town."?[2] Tell him he still has a solemn promise (to me) unfulfilled; & I hold him to it firmly. I'm so afraid, in the sweeping changes that are probably coming, that Mr Noyes will leave Venice. This will be a great loss to her; I had hoped so much to see him, & Budd, the beautiful yacht, & still more beautiful gondola, in situ again.[3]

This reminds me of your yacht on the Hudson. How delightful! Nothing cd. be better—(save a yacht in Florida!—). I see that an immense new lake has been discovered, north of Quebec. Is'nt that wonderful? And American? What other country keeps great lakes stowed away in odd corners to be discovered by accident. Another reflection & a very different one forces itself upon me just here & that is how much interest there can be after all in "clothing stores." The Cleveland Herald comes to me, & for long months I have been reading the mass of literature it contains concerning the "Excelsior," & Steinfeld "the old reliable."[4]—You will think I am becoming very frivolous. So I turn to weightier subjects. Do you know, or can you find out whether we still own the piece of property at Iron Ridge Wisconsin which we have always called the "20 acre lot"?[5] My impression is that we own it still; that it never was sold. But in looking over my accounts not long ago, I could not find any item concerning it. I know that the house we had at Iron Ridge has sold. By my idea is that this 20 acre lot was <u>not</u>. The absence of any mem. however, <u>may</u> mean that it was disposed of, & that I have simply forgotten it. I presume your father has some record of these things, &, when you have time (there is not the slightest hurry about it), I should be glad if you will look it up. Everything else my father had in Wisconsin (Milwaukee) was sold, I know.

I came the other day upon the mem. of my purchase from Charlie of the silver wh. was his, & which he left with your father. Is it still in your father's safe? I hope it is not in his way? I have more silver now than I know what to do with. People who have not houses, ought not to have silver! It's only in everybody's way.

You saw by my last date, that I had again been interrupted in my letter. I will send it off, bad as it is, if only to take my love to all four of you, & say that though often silent for long spaces of time, I am thinking of you just the same. My love to your father & mother, Kate & Will. Tell Kate we received her letter on Xmas eve, & it was very welcome. Nobody knows, who has not tried it, how dreary are such days as Xmas & birthdays over here. In spite of all one can do, old memories will creep in. When there are children, it is bright. But when there are none, (& Clare at 16! can be called so no longer—) I am afraid that one thinks more of the past than of the present. However, I am speaking for myself only. It was a pleasant day here, &, in the evening, Clara & Clare went to a small Xmas-Eve party at Mr Weaver's—(Counsul General), where besides the tree, they had music & charades.

I received your letter, & was glad to know you all thought "Targer" looking so well. To me, when she came to Dover, she looked really radiant. And I [we?] hear the Benedicts thought she has <u>never</u> looked so well as she did immediately after her return. Tell your dear mother & father that I quite understand their not writing. I shall soon come to that myself. So long as we know we are thinking of each other with the same old affection, it is all the same. What are words! The time will yet come when we shall call across the ocean to absent friends, "How are you today? I am well, & love you just the same." And they will call back their answer. And the mail-bags will go empty.—All the Cooperstown connections & relatives who were over here have now all gone back home. Jane Carter has taken a house in New York for the winter, & closed "Holt Averell." (That looks like "Hotel." It is meant for "Holt.") My 2^{d} cousin (& Jane's), Mrs Smith of Virginia, has taken her beautiful beautiful daughter home, & they are now in Petersburg (Va) & dreadfully homesick for Italy. <u>Their</u> cousin, Helen Campbell, <u>my</u> cousin's cousin's daughter!—is also in the U.S., at Castleton-on-Hudson, & dreadfully homesick, also. While Mrs [Anthon?], whose first husband, Campbell Turner; was my 2^{d} cousin,—has also gone home after 7 years here, & is broken hearted about it. I put this all in on purpose, because your ignorance of all your Cooperstown relatives is a great cross to me! If I cd. only stand that climate I shd. come home & live there; & then, Sir, you'd have to come & see me, & I'd have them all to meet you! By detachments. I am very much attached to the Fenimore Coopers—as I believe you know. You do know that much! They never fail, in their letters, to inquire all about you & Flora, & always wish me to tell everything. But they are growing old—dear old ladies. It makes me very sad to think how much of their delightful society I am missing. They are the most delightful ladies I have ever known.

On Thanksgiving, Mrs Francis (U.S. Minister) had an evening reception. We did not go. We stayed at home; & thought of old times at your house. At least I did.

I am quite scandalously well this winter. Have'nt had an ill moment; & am stout as can be. I am so much better—my health so much firmer—than it used to be that it is really quite remarkable. (I was ill last winter; but that was owing to mental depression.)—Mary Medlicott writes that Livingston's picture was greatly admired at Middletown. You must send one of the baby.—Much love to Flora; & regards to Mrs Stone.

Always yours affectionately,
C. F. Woolson.

Notes

1. John M. Francis was U.S. Minister to Austria in 1884 and '85.
2. An 1882 novel by Edgar Watson Howe (1853–1937).
3. in situ: in this place.
4. Excelsior and Steinfeld were clothing stores.
5. Woolson eventually sold this land and invested in the stock market.

To Jane Averell Carter (WRHS/Mather)[1]

[1884?]

I am deep in "The Complete Works of Walter Savage Landor," two large, closely printed volumes. Having been severely told that not to appreciate Landor was to sign oneself a dolt, I am now at work trying to "appreciate" him! "Imaginary Conversations"!—And I, who find it as much as I can do to take care of real ones! . . . [2]

I am, of course, tremendously busy. But I can be busy with more comfort in a pretty drawing-room! There's where my small money will go. Not in sapphire rings. This is a mere scratch—written between-times, while pages are drying.

Affectionately,
C. F. Woolson.

I must tell you that both "Anne" and "For the Major" have been brought out in England, and the English papers have had ever so many advertisements of them. I secured two to send the Coopers—I thought they would be amused—the London Times and Daily News. The latest style is—

The New American Novel
By a Niece of Fenimore Cooper.
"Anne."

Isn't that "Yankee" enterprise for an English firm? But that isn't all. In the advertisement of the second edition of "Anne" they have added a sentence from a contributed article in the "Century" for July, on "American Fiction," and signed it in large letters "The Century," as though it had been an editorial opinion. When you consider that both the books were in Harper's—the Century's great rival, I think you will see the cleverness of that stroke! . . .

Notes

1. Only the second paragraph of the original letter survives. The remainder appears in Benedict/CFW, 25–26. The signature mid-letter suggests that Benedict either changed the paragraph order or used two different letters.
2. Landor's *Complete Works,* including his *Imaginary Conversations* among Greek and Roman writers, were published in 1846.

To Elinor Howells (Houghton)

[1884?]

Dear Mrs Howells.

The dressmakers I employed, in Geneva, were,
"Mmes Giron et Nicolas
5 Rue du Commerce."

I found them obliging, and their things were pretty. They would not probably remember me, as they had a large establishment, and many customers. It is nearly three years since I was there.

I got a tailor-made ulster at "Old England." Place de la Fusterie. I think the same tailor also made jackets, and possibly walking-suits, for ladies.

The names of the two milliners I find I have not kept. But any one could tell you, as there are only two or three good ones in the town.

I must also say that the Pension Richardet was filled with Americans, when I was there. I think the Danas used to stay at the pension Picard, Quai des Eaux-Vives; and liked it. But I am not perfectly sure that was the place.

I am mournful, and lonely. Appreciate your good fortune in being all together, without one break; and have a kindly thought, sometimes, for others less fortunate.

Good-by,
C.F.W.

To John Hay (Brown)[1]

(Summer address)
c/o Alliance Bank
High Street Kensington
London. W. England
Vienna
April 29th, [1885]

Dear Colonel Hay.

Did you write "At the Red Glove?"[2]

Yours sincerely,
C. F. Woolson.

I confess that I have only read—that is read carefully—the first number. There were some sentences there which you might have written. If you are really coming round upon us on this entirely new tack, what in the world are we to do with you? I shouldn'nt mind it so much if you would only come over here where I could see you now & then. You have paid no attention to my appeals (in letters to Sam) that I was in great straits for friendly & congenial epistles, exiled as I was in this remote place, where the latest American author they have heard of is my own Grand-Uncle. These are the Austrians. The few Americans I know here are devoted admirers of the "Works" of E. P. Roe.[3]

With extreme joy I announce that we are going to England for the summer. And I hope also to go (it will be the first time) to Scotland. I have a fancy to drive up the "Deeside." But I begin "quietly" (as the English say), with the Isle of Wight. I presume I shall spend next winter in Italy, inordinately glad to be there again. Is Mr Noyes still in Venice—do you know? And who—who—is "KEILY"—the new minister to Rome?[4]—As I write, it comes over me how you have treated me! Comes over me freshly. I little dreamed, a year ago in London, that you would never write me even once, & never send me the picture—(cabinet sized photograph) you solemnly promised you would send. In the meanwhile, Mr Howells has sent me an excellent one of himself, ditto Henry James. And now the pretty case—which only holds three pictures—is waiting for yours. Those three are always to keep each other company; so if you do'nt send yours I shall know you are not satisfied with ~~such~~ your companions. But you must remember that I am not fortunate enough to know Mr Adams; or Mr King, pictorially. I suppose you have begun your house in Washington. I heard that you were there not long ago. Perhaps you saw Flora Whitney? I hear you Clevelanders have burned down the Stillman. Now go down to St Augustine & burn the "San Marco."[5] I asked the price you suggested for my story, & it was granted immediately.[6] This is nice for me; & I really owe it to your advice, & the strong expressions in your last note (before leaving London) to the same effect.

I hear there is another beautiful boy at your house, & I send my love to him & his mother. Tell <u>her</u> to make you keep your promises.

Very sincerely your friend,
C. F. Woolson.

(Love to Flora and Sam)

Notes

1. These two notes appear as one letter.
2. *At the Red Glove* (1885), first serialized in *Harper's New Monthly Magazine* from Jan. through June 1885, was written by Katherine Sarah Macquoid.
3. Edward Payson Roe (1838–88).
4. Controversial diplomat Anthony M. Keiley (1835–1905).
5. Woolson is referring to the Cleveland Stillman hotel and to St. Augustine's Castillo de San Marcos.
6. Probably *East Angels* (1886), which was serialized in *Harper's New Monthly Magazine* from Jan. 1885 through May 1886.

To Mary Gayle Carter Clarke (Cornell)

June 26th, [1885]
Ventnor
Isle of Wight

My dear Mary.

Your delightful letter would have been answered long ago, if the <u>desire</u> to answer could have given me time & eyes. It grows more & more impossible for me to write letters; and I regret this more than I can express, for it cuts me off from a great deal of comfort, & cheer, & pleasure, which I often stand in need of. But there is no use battling with fate. My eyes do not grow stronger, though my general health is so much improved; & they are used more than they should be, without including letters at all.—Do you see where I am? Inexpressibly glad to be in England again. I write from a very pleasant sitting-room on the cliff, directly over the Sea. The sitting-room windows open upon a piazza decked with vines & flowers, & here I sit & look across the blue water, dotted with many sail[s]. Clara & Clare are to be here in a day or two,—at least they say so. They are in London, supposed to be engaged in repacking their six or sixteen trunks; but from their letters, I fancy the Grosvenor & Burlington House exhibitions, the Lyceum, the Richter concerts & Handel festivals are taking more of their time than the "boxes."[1] We came from the continent together last week, after they had had a two weeks' tour in Germany; I came direct from Vienna. It is probable that I shall spend some time here; but they will see something of England—the cathedral towns, Lake district, Warwickshire; & perhaps Scotland, also. I hope to go to Scotland with them, later. I suppose (unless cholera should break out in New York) that they will go home in September, as Mrs Benedict is anxious to have them near her again. It was with the greatest reluctance that she consented to Clare's coming this last time; she feels the separation very much.

It is cold here, at least cold after Vienna, where we had had hot "American" summer weather for ten weeks. The English bread is so frightful after the delicious bread of Vienna, the English coffee so unspeakably bad after the Vienna coffee, & the general appearance of the Ventnor females so barbarous, compared with the exquisite dress & bearing of the Vienna women—whom I think the handsomest women I have ever seen—that one would suppose I should be homesick here. On the contrary I am supremely happy! I "stand" the coffee, & pretend not to see the bread, & go smiling about the streets from sheer content. I am very fond of England—there is no doubt of that. But I am fonder still of Italy. "Still-er" of Florida. And "stillest," perhaps of Cooperstown in June, and when the trees are colored in October.—I must add that I have a Vienna coffee-pot, or "machine" as they call them; & in a day or two, when I have got down some good coffee in the berry from Fortnum & Mason's, this severely English room will be redolent, I trust with ~~of~~ Vienna perfumes. I like tea at five o'clock. But not twice a day. The English bread, however, I shall have to endure. I think it is the worst bread in the world.—

I wonder—is everything so beautiful in Cooperstown now, that you regret nothing here? On a lovely warm day, just after I came, I drove to Carisbrooke Castle, & the drive was exquisitely beautiful all the way. (I cannot recall whether you came to the Isle of Wight, or not?) The hedges & flowers & "lanes" & cottages were all like a picture.

Leamington. Oct. 14th

A second beginning, my dear Mary. I have just heard the news—that you are to be married before Xmas! I send you my warmest love & warmest good wishes, & my very best regards to Mr Clark. I am so sorry now that I did not complete my letter sooner, & send it, for then perhaps you would have written to me again, & I should not have been left to hear by chance, through Clara, the announcement that interests me so very much. I have had a hard summer. Immediately after I began this letter, I was seized with a (slight in itself but) troublesome affection of the nerve of the spine, which prevents me while it lasts from using my hands at all. It is caused by too constant use of the pen! This has bothered me off & on all summer, & up to a week ago. Of course, with the necessary writing I had to do, it was impossible to do anything more. It is a nervous sort of feeling, & most depressing. You will be ashamed of your old friend, if she confesses that she gives way & cries. I am glad to say that the warm saline baths here seem to have broken it up. My Doctor tells me it is not at all serious; it comes from overwork; pen work. I never held a pen easily. It was the same with my father.—I only put this in to show you why I have not written before.

My dear Mary, I know you are very happy and I sympathize with you in it. Do not for a moment think that my long silence has been caused by the least lessening of interest; it has not. I forget the lapse of time. A few months seem to me a few weeks. It is because I am always busy. I should be so glad to hear from you if you have time to write; I should like to know what happened, after ~~that~~ the date of your letter. There had just been the interview. And I should much like to know, too, about your marriage.—Your letter was most interesting to me, in every way; the whole description of the winter. I am a bad correspondent, but I hope a good friend. My love to your mother, & Grace. I hear Averell is at Concord.[2] Tell your mother that, later, I hope to write to her. I am thinking of Venice for the winter. Warwickshire is to me an ideally beautiful country. The most beautiful part of England I have seen. But I am afraid you don't care for all this. I should'nt, at your age, within two months of my wedding-day!

Now Mary you must have a good photograph of yourself taken. I want one. Why not have a full view, & a profile, both with the hair simply arranged (but not straight back) & bare neck. There is no style of picture that lasts so well as that. In ten, in twenty years, it is still good, because there is no dress to look odd & old-fashioned. I've got one of Flora Payne (Whitney) now, taken twenty years ago, which looks just as well as it did at first, because no dress is visible, & the hair is so simple that it would pass in any fashion. Flora, too, was as far as possible from being a beauty. (And this reminds me of what your mother wrote about her. But I'll answer that when I write to your mother myself.) It is just six years since I was in Cooperstown last, shortly before Jennie's wedding. I saw Jennie try on all her beautiful gowns. I should like to see you try on yours.—Do write & tell me "all about it." Or, if you are really too busy, perhaps Grace will write. I do'nt want to be "out" of it, all just because I cannot write letters. Writing letters is something Fate has forbidden me to do. But I am sure you know, that, when I could speak, (not write), I was not uninterested, or unsympathetic. I have heard nothing of Maria or Julia.[3] How are they? To the Coopers I have written—as I was very much overcome by the death of Charlotte. She was always so good to me, & she was fond of my dear mother. Affectionately,

C. F. Woolson.
Care Alliance Bank
High Street. Kensington.
London. W.

I never heard you liked Florida.

Notes

1. On the margins of this page, Woolson wrote, "Do'nt I owe to you a very pretty blotting case received, without name, at Xmas? It was very acceptable. I use it every day."

2. Mary's mother was Jane Russell Averell Carter and her siblings were (Anna) Grace, (Lawson) Averell, and Jane (Jennie) Russell Averell Carter Brown.

3. Perhaps Julia Parsons; Maria is unidentified.

To Katharine Livingston Mather (WRHS/Mather)[1]

Leamington
Warwickshire
September 22^d^, 1885

My dear Kate.

. . . I did not come to Leamington for the warm saline baths, for which the place is famed; I came to see Warwickshire. But it fortunately happens that the baths seem to be just what I need. I am enchanted with Warwickshire, I like it better than any part of England I have yet seen, by far. Before Clara left, we took a number of excursions together; to Stratford-on-Avon; to Coventry; to Warwick Castle; Kenilworth; and Oxford.[2] My day at Stratford was so complete and perfect in every respect that its memory is like a beautiful little picture, all by itself, which will live in my recollection, distinctly, as long as I live. As a general thing, I hate "glimpses" of places, I hate "sight-seeing" just as I hate rapid travelling. But Stratford is so small, so rural; there is nothing to distract the attention. You wander from the house where he was born[3], down the rambling, quaint, old street to his school, the remains of his second home, and so, along the lovely river-walk to the old Church where he is buried; and it seems such a complete and natural sequence! Of course, to have the picture perfect, the day must be charming also. Our day was,—the perfection of the English September; warm, with the sun shining rather redly through haze. Before going back to Leamington for dinner, we had tea at the "Shakespeare Inn." Since I have been alone, I have walked all about the near surrounding country, more and more fascinated, more and more delighted every day. There are such picturesque, sleepy little villages of "half-timbered" houses, thatched, and covered with vines; and always a little ancient church, with gray Norman tower, and rooks soaring about it. But all this has been described far better than I can do it; in Hawthorne's "Our Old Home," there are some perfect descriptions of Leamington and Warwick.[4] I can go by train to Warwick or Kenilworth in a few minutes; then I have my "afternoon walk" either on the red battlements of Kenilworth, in the sunset light, or in the beautiful gardens of Warwick Castle. You must acknowledge that these are "resources" for a person like me. Yesterday I drove for an hour and a half in the Park of "Stoneleigh Abbey," about five miles from here. It was a perfect afternoon, and the magnificent old oaks and elms, the many deer, the Avon flowing through,—all was to me extremely restful and lovely. I don't know how long I shall stay here. I have a plan for spending a month in Oxford,—as I fell desperately in love with it during the day we spent there. I am so delighted to be "in love" with some of these English places. It makes a balance-weight for my love of Italy, so that I shall not grow one-sided! I have a half-idea of spending the winter and Spring in Venice. . . .

Affectionately,
C. F. Woolson.

Notes

1. The letter is in a typed transcription at WRHS. Portions also appear in Benedict/CFW, 287–89.

2. CFW (287) adds the following unidentified excerpt by Woolson, probably written to Clare Benedict:

> Do you remember our lovely drive to Coventry—with its three spires? And the marmalade and cresses with the tea? And "Mr Toots"—whom we surprised there talking to the barmaid?
>
> England is, to me, a lovely country, and if I were able I should like to spend all my remaining foreign summers there. I am afraid I shall never see "the beautiful Dee" (in Scotland). I grow less and less of a traveller each year. But you must certainly see it, and drive along the banks for me, and tell me all about it. I never want to "drive" along any banks, or anything else, you know! . . .
>
> That mysterious legend "By especial appointment to the Queen"—which one sees so often in England inscribed over the doors of little shops in provincial High Streets, where the inns have names which . . . are as fantastic as anything in "Tartarin": the "White Horse," the "Crab and Lobster"; the "Three Choughs" and the "Five Alls."

Mr Toots is a character from Dickens's *Dombey and Son* (1846–48); *Tartarin de Tarascon* is an 1872 novel by Alphonse Daudet.

3. Shakespeare.

4. Hawthorne's *Our Old Home: A Series of English Sketches* was published in 1863.

To Mrs. Nixon (Virginia)[1]

Leamington
Warwickshire
Dec. 5th, [1885]

Dear Mrs Nixon.

I have not been well; and have postponed answering your letters, on that account. I have written to the Messrs. Harper to send to you a copy of "Anne," & I enclose an autograph. This is the best I can do, as there is a new duty on books which prevents their being sent to America from here by mail; otherwise I could send you the English edition, with autograph on the first page. I wish you every success; & am sorry that I could not answer before.

Very truly yours,
C. F. Woolson.

Notes

1. Like many nineteenth-century writers, Woolson received requests for autographs. Mrs Nixon remains unidentified as does her access to Woolson's address.

To John Hay (Brown)

Leamington
Dec. 26th, [1885]

Dear Colonel Hay.

A note from Henry James, just received, tells me of the sudden death of your friend, Mrs Adams; I sit down immediately to send a few words of sympathy to you & Mrs Hay, for I know that it has been to you both a heavy sorrow to bear.[1]

I have never been able to think that a sudden death is to be deplored for the one who is taken,—I should like to die without warning myself; but for those who are left, it is very terrible. I suppose, too, that your two households were upon the point of taking possession of the two new homes side by side,—so that it will all be particularly desolate and sad. I send you much sympathy. You have had a melancholy Xmas this year.

A letter to you, half-written, has been lying in my portfolio a long time. I don't know whether anyone has told you how bothered I have been for months by something which I can only describe by saying that it is <u>not</u> "author's cramp." The half-finished letter thanked you for the photograph. As a likeness, I think it tolerably good—except that it does not do justice to the eyes. It stands before me now, in a three-divisioned velvet frame. I have tried the three pictures in every sort of combination. But, do what I will, you all stand with your backs to each other; or a least cold-shoulders. Mr Howells smiles & smiles; you look poetic; & Henry James cynical. It's odd how unlike a photograph can be, with all its close likeness! I've seen you look cynical; & Mr Howells furious—when he had to go to too many "teas" in Florence.

And this reminds me to ask—do you know who is the constructer of the article on "Cleveland," in a forthcoming "Harper," in which you & Mr Howells are to appear? And also (alas) my undecorative self? Who else will shine there? Mrs Garfield?[2] As you may imagine, it is a pang to every nerve in my body, to be produced in public in that way; they say that I should not be able to suppress a likeness altogether, since there is a fancy at present for bringing out "series" of "authors' likenesses;" & a photograph of some sort is sure to be obtained of everybody, somewhere; & the thing done whether the victim likes it or not. Therefore how much better to have a good likeness brought out in a proper place. Such is the argument. But there's no "proper place" for an ugly woman! To appear with you and Mr H., is some balm. About the "Red Glove"—that, of course, was a ruse de guerre, a pretext for a letter.[3] There was one description (short) of a woman's hand, in the first or second number, which might have come from you. And the hand might have been Mrs Hay's. I never finished the story. But when are we to have another B. W.? I suppose you are now working on the "Life"? The B. W. was magnificent.[4] I often think what a powerful thing it was. Must I still be so completely silent? Do let me just breathe it—(but not "by authority")—to one or two. I should enjoy so much telling it in Florence.—For I am going down to Italy next month. I have stayed here much longer than I expected to stay—taking the hot saline baths (which have done me so much good)—& seeing this exquisite Warwickshire from end to end. Such afternoons in Charlecote Park! And Stoneleigh! It certainly is the most intensely "English" part of England; &, to me, very beautiful. I am enraged to think of the summers I have wasted in that dreary Switzerland, with the ice-mountains above, & Germans & cuckoo clocks below.—I go to Warwick & Kenilworth as I used to go to Rocky River & Doan's Corners. But what do you know of Doan's Corners? I forget that there are depths in the ancient lore of Cleveland with which a poor late-comer like you is unacquainted. What do you know, for instance, of the wild romance of the original "Water Cure Woods?" Or "University Heights" when all the Flats were one broad green meadow?—Here a despatch from the Chadwicks interrupts me; they are at Oxford, & propose to come up by rail, & make me a call. No "petits fours" here; they will have to have stodgy British "plum cake" with their "five o'clock."—How is Winnie Howells? I hear—vaguely—that she is not well. As Mrs Howells has not written, I fear the report may have some truth in it. My love to Mrs Hay.

Yours very sincerely,
C. F. Woolson.

P. S.

After finishing my letter, I laid it aside, & began looking over a heap of papers that have been gathering in a corner of one of my trunks. There I came across two or three of your letters, & an enclosed notice of your father. I do not know whether I wrote to you in answer to the latter at the time. If I did not, I thought of you with sympathy. I have never recovered from the sense of desolation I felt when I lost my father; the world has never been the same to me since, for he made a pet of me. It is a loss different in its nature to a son; but a very very great one.

I looked over your delightful letters with a great regret that I cannot ~~sometime~~ oftener see you. If I come home & go down to Florida to live, will you & Mrs Hay come down there once in a while? Meantime alas! The rich men are all building things[,] houses, villas, hotels[,] in St Augustine. I shall have to go to the "Indian River." I think Florida strikes different people as Venice does; some people see in Venice only the unpleasant part—which certainly exists as well as the beauty. To me, Florida was a revelation. The climate, the flowers, &, best of all, the endless peaceful <u>leisure</u>—I had never seen any thing in the least like the leisure. It is true that we fell among as idle a set of people as can be imagined—idle New Yorkers of the yachting lounging class, & regular-Army people. I had fought against the Cleveland cold weather all my life, never even conceiving the idea that one could perhaps go somewhere where there was no cold. I had never seen people sitting about all day, doing nothing—but amuse themselves. Because at the northern watering-places I knew, even pleasure was pursued <u>actively</u>. I have no doubt I saw everything through a haze of enchantment. Yet there is not a twig, or flower, described in "East Angels" that is not literally "from life." I went into all the swamps, I walked all over the barrens & beaches, I sailed up & down the lagoons, & paddled myself up all the creeks. And if it was "a haze of enchantment," it lasted through six long winters, & was never dispelled.—All this is called out of your saying, in your letter, that Florida is more attractive in my descriptions than in your memory. I would come home tomorrow if I had a little house in St Augustine. And <u>this</u> last sentence is called out by another allusion of yours—to my supposed preference for foreign shores. If one is "wandering," there is more to see here. I shall never try to make a home here, however.—

I hear Mr Noyes has resigned. I am very sorry. Do you know the U.S. Minister in Rome?[5] From Cincinnati, I believe? Good-by again.

A 2^{d} Postscript

This letter was closed, & just going to the post office when a long one came from Sam. In it he mentions—knowing how much it would interest me—how rapidly you are coming on with the "Life," & how greatly he & Flora have been interested in the portions they have seen. I congratulate you with all my heart upon this nearness to completion of this great piece of work. It will be the important American book of the century, & I have not the slightest doubt but that it will be the best thing of the kind ever done. You see how I rank you.

But you must be so tired—are'nt you? You must feel the strain. For my own part, one novel takes my entire strength, & robs me of almost life itself! I am months-recovering. A man, however, is stronger.

Let me say here that the
"Alliance Bank
High Street Kensington
London. W."

is a safe address for me as long as I remain abroad; I keep an account there, & they forward my letters.

Notes

1. Petry (82) rightly charges Woolson with insensitivity for writing about photography in this letter if she knew that Clover Adams was a photographer and that she committed suicide by drinking photographic fluid. Since other letters suggest that Woolson never met Henry Adams, it seems unlikely that she knew of his wife's photography.

2. Edmund Kirke wrote the article "The City of Cleveland" for the March 1886 *Harper's New Monthly Magazine*. Among the illustrations is a photo of Woolson. Mrs. Garfield may be Lucretia Rudolph Garfield (1833–1918), the widow of President James Garfield.

3. Woolson wrote on Apr. 29, 1885, speculating that Hay had written Katherine Sarah Macquoid's *At the Red Glove* (1885). She is now calling that a ruse of war.

4. Woolson is referring to Hay's *The Bread Winners* (1883) and *Abraham Lincoln: A History* (1890). Apparently, Hay privately revealed his authorship of the anonymously published novel to Woolson.

5. John Bernard Stallo (1823–1900). He had been a university professor and lawyer.

To Samuel Livingston Mather (WRHS/Mather)[1]

Seymour Street
Portman Square. London
February 23th, 1886

My dear Brother.

I was extremely glad to hear from you; I could scarcely believe that it was really you yourself, and a real letter. . . . . I must tell you that I not only saw the great London mob,—but was in it![2] What do you say to that, for a nervous old maid? I was coming down one of the little streets of Mayfair that lead into Piccadilly, when I saw the great crowd pass along the latter street; as there were, of course, no windows across the mouth of my street, I did not see any stone-throwing. I noticed what a strange-looking tumultuous throng it appeared to be, and I wondered what they were about; it never occurred to me that it was a mob. I thought it was one of the numerous processions that are always going on in London about something or other. So I waited, about forty feet off, until the thickest part of the crowd had gone by, and then calmly pursued my way, and entered Piccadilly, turning eastward,—as I was going to the Strand to buy a trunk. Where I entered,—at Clarges Street—there are no shops,—only the high walls before the town residences of the Duke of Devonshire, and Lord Ashburton; so I passed on, seeing as yet no broken windows, but perceiving that the "procession," as I still supposed it to be, had banished the cabs and carriages that usually crowd Piccadilly. I noticed, also, that I was surrounded by workmen, all going in the opposite direction. They were in groups of eight and ten together, and while not in the least rude—as I made my way among them,—they had yet a sort of "larking" hilarious aspect. At length I noticed that I was the only woman in sight! Next, as I still went eastward, I began to come to the shops, and then I saw the traces of the "mob." All the shutters were up, or half up, and over the tops of some of them peered the white faces of the shop-people, looking, oh! so frightened. The pavement was covered with broken glass, and fragments of all sorts of things that had been broken. I was still surrounded by the workmen, but *now* I saw that it was something serious, so I tried every shop door (though I did it quietly so as not to attract attention) until I found one that opened, when without ceremony I went in. It was a picture store; the great plate glass windows all smashed, the pictures injured, the shutters up. I said to the proprietor "Can you tell me what is the matter?" "A mob, madam" he answered, "a *horrible* mob; they have been breaking all the windows and smashing everything all the way up from Trafalgar Square." I asked where they had gone now, and he said, "To Hyde Park!" My next remark was "Perhaps I had better go home." "*Decidedly*" was the impressive answer of the picture dealer. So I stepped out into the street again, and going through the first passage into Berkeley Square where all was quiet, I took refuge under the gateway of Lansdowne House and waited for a cab. Fortunately I saw one, and hailed it; then, not wishing to be taken through Bond Street, where is always danger of a block even on ordinary days, I said to the driver, "Cross Berkeley Square, to Grosvenor Square, and through North Audley Street to Oxford Street,"—the exact route,—as you may remember perhaps,—taken by the mob, who did *not* go to Hyde Park, or at least not until several hours later. As my cab crossed Grosvenor Square, the mob entered it, and as we flew along North Audley Street, they were just behind!—even I could hear the noise. I reached home safely, and not at all alarmed, I can truly say,—excepting as usual, over my cab horse. A horse at any time, seeming to me far worse than a mob. The next day I appreciated that I had had a most fortunate escape, as a number of ladies, not only in private carriages, but in cabs, were stopped, and very roughly treated. That day, the next, there was a black fog, so that I had to have my parlor lamp lighted all day. I cannot describe to you the strange sinister aspect of the huge town, filled with rumors of the mob, and all the street lamps lighted, in the middle of the day. The scare was not over for several days, and Oxford Street, on the third day after the mob, looked like a street in a besieged city. I presume you have read of the great damage done, but to see it with one's own eyes, makes a wonderful impression. I went over the mob's track on foot, as soon as possible, to see for myself. Many shops were perfect wrecks, and it was a sight to see all the superb windows of the magnificent residences on the west side of Grosvenor Square entirely gone, and boarded up temporarily, until new plate-glass could be obtained. The weather through all, has been the darkest I have ever seen in London, and you might imagine from the look of things, that the "last day" was near. "Babylon" seemed doomed. In my opinion, English "Society" is dreadfully corrupt. I do'nt say it is worse than that of Paris or Rome; but in Paris and Rome the corruption is not concealed, and in England there is always an outside surface of morality and respectability. Whether it is better to be wicked and cover it up, or to be wicked and proclaim it, I don't pretend to decide; I am merely a "looker-on," belonging myself to the one nation in the world which, in my opinion, is "good"; that is, has a large majority of well-behaved, moral people. The cold, dark weather, and the mobs, make me, this time, willing to leave England. Generally I leave with a deep pang, which lasts for weeks; as I am so very fond of the misty, green island. Fortunately, this time I am going to Italy,—the country I love best of all European ones; it comes next in my heart, after Florida.

. . . England is interesting to an American just now: "dis-establishment" is in the air, and sure to come; and the trouble over the Irish question reminds me of our own atmosphere at home, just before the Rebellion. I have,—for nine months,—read nothing but English books; the mass of "Memoirs," "Letters," "Biographies," and "Auto-biographies" with which the Circulating Libraries are filled. It has been very entertaining, and I have been amused and interested to see the wide difference there is between the way an English Bishop looks at life and its duties,—and the way an American Bishop looks at his. I have read half a dozen "Lives," (in three great volumes,) of eminent Bishops and Deans,—among the mass of other "English" literature I have been through.[3] I hope it is not un-American,—but it does seem to me that the fact that their living is secured, gives them (the English Clergyman) a better chance to study, and make the best of their talents. However,—the whole system seems to me sure to be swept away soon; so I must admire it while I can.

There are, of course, horrible abuses; "livings" with incomes of ten and fifteen thousand dollars, and perhaps one hundred souls, only, in the entire parish, of whom an underpaid curate takes charge. . . .

Lovingly,
C. F. Woolson.

Notes

1. The letter is in a typed transcription at WRHS. Portions also appear in Benedict/CFW, 38, 289–93.

2. In 1886, two rival groups, the Fair Trade League and the Social Democratic Federation, met separately in Trafalgar Square, both protesting labor conditions. At the close of the meetings, a riot between the two groups broke out. Lacking accurate information about where the groups would go, the police were unable to quell the riots.

3. Woolson is probably referring to Henry Wharton's (1664–95) books on church history, including a two-volume "Lives" of bishops and archbishops called *Anglia Sacra* (1691).

To Samuel Mather (WRHS/Mather)

Seymour Street
Portman Square
March 18th, [1886]

Dear Sam.

The deed has reached me safely, and I thank you & Kate most heartily and affectionately for this delightful present; delightful, in addition to everything else, because it shows you care for me. The aunt, you know, is lonely sometimes; and a little homesick!

My fancy had been—as I wrote your father—to keep the lot. I thought that it might increase in value, and, at the end of ten years (when I intend to stop writing!) bring me in enough to buy me a cottage in Florida. I should have taken a great satisfaction in doing this: seeing the last piece of my dear father's "western land" buy me a little home—which I should owe, also, to the other children, of whom he was so fond.

But dreams must give way to realities; & from the letters you have sent,—ie. that of Col. Bean; & the last of Mr Keenan—as well as from your father's advice and your own, I feel that it is much better to sell to this German, for the $1000—he offers.

I do not yet own but half the lot; yours & Kate's share, & my own. I have not yet received the deed from Clara. When I do, I will write again, accepting the German's offer. What else must I do? And do I write to Mr Keenan about it, or will you?

The money, when paid, I shall ask your father to invest for me. If there are any more investments left, like those delightful ones he obtained for me before—which still continue to bring in six and seven percent—I shall be very glad. Here, I only get one & a half, & two on the money I keep in the Bank, as "background."

I should have written to you, & Targer, long ago, if I had been well. I am miserable just now, & will defer writing a real letter until I am better, & "resting." I have been doing the Book-Revise of "East Angels," & am still hard at work. I cannot leave England until it is finished. My eyes, and right hand, & back, are all completely tired-out, & I long like a child for a "vacation." It will soon come, now. And then my spirits will bound up!—I sent you one of the artist's proofs of the Harper picture, because it is such a beautiful piece of work, artistically.[1] It does'nt look at all like me; but that is all the better.—When E. A. is out in book-form, & you have read it over as a whole I should like very much to know what you think of it. I have been very glad to get the little bits of comment on it that you & Flora have now & then put in your letters. I am tired—sometimes—of getting comments, & tokens of interest, from strangers only. I have had some such funny letters lately. The most satisfactory have been letters from southerners—about the truthfulness of the "southern" part. It is indeed exactly accurate; I have described nothing that is not a literal transcript from life.—I do not know when I shall get off. Soon, I hope.—The bank is always the safest address; they forward. It has been very cold here; gloomy; eastwind. To day is the first that has an indication of spring. I will write from "Italy," when I am better. The two dear little pictures of Livingston & Amasa are on my table in a folding-frame, & everybody notices them. The picture of Livingston in his sled, with Kate, is <u>excellent</u>. A really beautiful picture; I congratulate the amateur-taker of it. Much love to Flora.

Affectionately,
C.F.W.

Notes

1. Woolson's photo appeared in the March 1886 issue of *Harper's New Monthly Magazine* where *East Angels* (1886) was just finishing serialization.

To Mary Gayle Carter Clarke (Cornell)

30 Seymour St
Portman Square
Sunday [1886?][1]

My dear Mary.

I received your letter last evening, and write immediately to give you my address. You will see that it is the same old place. Only this time I have the drawing-room floor. I am very comfortable, and most glad that I persevered and made the change, for I was very far from well during the latter part of the time at Hampstead. I feel very well now, and take endless pleasure in walking in the Park at sunset time every afternoon.

I hope you and Grace will have time to come and see me.[2] Tomorrow will be Bank Holiday; possibly you will not care to be out? I have no engagement for the evening, if you could come then. If you would rather come on Tuesday, I shall be very glad to see you at six, when we can walk in the Park for a while (I do not dine until eight) or else in the evening; as suits you best. If I get no note from you by six tomorrow afternoon, I shall expect you in the evening. If it is more convenient for you to come on Tuesday, please let me know.

I want to hear all about Baireuth. I am glad you were not disappointed. Clara, I can see, is dreading lest it should not seem so absolutely perfect to her as it did before.

You do not say how long you are to be in town. Is it possible that you are to sail so soon as next Saturday! (I have just stopped to count). If you should have only tomorrow in town, & shd. be engaged for the evening, come at six in the afternoon. I fear we cannot walk abroad; but we can sit here & talk. Love to Grace.

Yours affectionately,
C.F.W.

Notes

1. Woolson lived a second time in Portman Square in Feb. and March of 1886 and wrote Sam Mather from there that she had not been well.
2. Grace Carter.

To Katharine Livingston Mather (WRHS/Mather)[1]

Florence
April 30th, 1886

My dear Kate.

. . . I left London nearly a month ago, and made a long slow journey southward. I stopped over along the route, among other places at Strassbourg to see the beautiful Cathedral. It is beautiful,—the exterior. As regards interiors, the Italian churches are to me always more interesting, because so crowded with marbles, and bas-reliefs, and carvings, and all sorts of exquisite things. But they have not, as a general rule, fine exteriors,—save the Duomo here;—the Cathedral at Milan, and St Mark's, Venice. I climbed up to the platform at the base of the spire, to see the valley of the Rhine, to see the same view that I used to see at Baden from the other side.

I had the most ridiculous adventure with a Frenchman, an elderly and irascible person. I met him first in the Cathedral, where he was trying to see the celebrated clock with moving figures. The sacristan told him it was out of order, and not exhibited. This enraged the Frenchman, "Since it is by far the most remarkable thing you have here,—in fact, what one comes to Strassbourg to see,—it is outrageous that you refuse to show it"—he cried, including me in his audience, as I too had gone to the south transept where the clock is supposed to be. I went off to another part of the building. Presently I heard, 'Puisque c'est la chose la plus remarquable, Madame," &c. He had followed me, to get a fellow-traveller's sympathy, I suppose. I went up to the top of the Cathedral. "Puisque c'est la chose,"—there he was again, and again he began. I went down to the sculptured porch. In a few moments "puisque" &c, and we had it all over again. I departed, and went to another street to look at some photographs. Over my shoulder I heard—"Ah, vous voilà encore." (But I thought it was he, not I, who was "voilà.") "puisque c'est la chose." So this time I answered him, and I suggested to him to go and mend it. He stared, and then burst into a laugh.[2] Twice after that I met him in the street, and each time he said "Mend it! Good!" I stayed two days in Lucerne to rest. But it rained one day steadily, and the next snowed! The snow was several inches deep when I left. The St Gotthard is as wonderful as ever; this is the third time I have been over the road. I will say, however, that this third time the great tunnel seemed to me shorter than it has seemed before. I do'nt think we were in it more than twenty minutes,—and the short tunnels much more numerous than I remembered them. It snowed tremendously up to the top of the Pass, and there I saw the winter drifts eight and ten feet high; it was so early that there was no sign of Spring. But about four in the afternoon, "Italy" began to announce herself,—as we slid down, down toward Lombardy. No more snow. Then the detached Campaniles; then the vines, the pink houses, the white oxen, and the blue, blue sky. At eight in the evening I reached Milan. The next day,—from Milan to Venice,—was all that I longed for, all that I have dreamed of during the three years of absence. Como and Lugano had been lovely as I passed them at sunset the day before; but it was still rather too early in the season to see their full beauty; they looked a little cold. But their sister, Lake of Garda, was enchanting as we skirted it for half an hour. Venice was unspeakably beautiful. It was moonlight, and warm as July at home, when my gondola left the railroad station, and shot out into the Grand Canal on its way to the Hotel, which I had chosen as far from the station as possible. I think I felt compensated for all my years of toil just in that one half hour! All the palaces were as beautiful as ever, and everything as dreamlike. I only stayed two days; but I hope to spend June there, provided there is no cholera. Then I came on to Florence. And here there met me a cable dispatch; a large portion of my revise for the book-form of "East Angels" had gone down on the Oregon!!![3] It was a most disheartening moment. I had so longed for complete rest from literary work for awhile, and I was so completely tired out,—hand and eyes. Then I hardly knew where my materials were, the duplicate proof sheets, and all the necessary things. In addition I was not sure what parts were lost, and in order to cover every possibility, I thought I should have to do over nearly half the book! I sat down, without even unpacking my bag, and for two whole weeks I worked fourteen hours a day. Two nights I worked all night. I kept sending off what I had finished, to the Harper's agent in London; and during all this time neither he nor I could find out exactly what Parts were missing in New York, because the head of the book department there, kept telegraphing by pages and chapters. And I had changed the arrangement of the chapters for the book-form, and had forgotten the new numbering! And the same with the paging. Well, I had sent off the last part which I supposed to be what they needed, when, an hour later, came another cable; all the original revise had reached them, and no second copy was required!! I was so glad to be free that it was not until the next day that I began to get strength (and temper) enough to make remarks upon my two weeks of terrible toil all quite un-necessary! The only way I could possibly account for the delay was that the missing sheets did go down on the Oregon, and, later, were fished up. I am sure you can imagine my first two weeks here were melancholy enough. . . .

Florence is lovely now, crowded to the last degree with English and Americans who spent Holy Week and Easter in Rome. I am such an old resident now that I no longer go about with a Baedeker at nine o'clock in the morning. But I anticipate the greatest pleasure in re-visiting, one by one, and at my leisure, all my favorite pictures, statues, churches, and places. . . . We are all reading Russian over here; the Russian novels in French translations. Have you read them? They are magnificent. I have long thought that Tourguenieff the greatest of novelists; now I am admiring several other Russians as well.

Goodby. Write soon.

Affectionately,
C. F. Woolson.

Notes

1. The letter is in a typed transcription at WRHS. Portions also appear in Benedict/CFW, 34–35, 293–95.

2. The man is saying, "since it is the most remarkable thing" and "Ah, there you are again." Woolson's reply is a joke about mending the clock.

3. The *Oregon* had made the Atlantic crossing from Liverpool to New York City in seven and a half days. Just outside of port, it was struck by the schooner *Charles R. Morse*. All on board the *Morse* drowned; all on the *Oregon*—nearly one thousand—were saved.

To John Hay (Brown)

Hotel National
Geneva
July 30th, [1886]

Dear Col. Hay.

Returning from Chamouni yesterday I found your letter. It gave me very great pleasure; praise from you is worth having indeed,—particularly sweet & exhilarating. The written words roused a glow, which completely banished, for the moment, the fatigue which has hung over me since my last attack of illness, in Florence.

I am so much pleased that you like the story; that you see in it what I strove so hard to put there. I think you see all I felt,—& I could not say more; whether the work as a whole is good or bad, my life, for three years, has all gone into it.

I thank you the more for expressing your liking, because to-day brings me Mr Howells' notice in his "Study."[1]

I could not expect Mr Howells to like "Margaret," for he does not believe in "Margarets,"—he has never perceived that they exist. But his writing as he has done, ex cathedra as it were,—from the literary chair of the magazine in which the story appeared,—strikes me as unfriendly; for the ordinary reader will not discriminate,—will not notice that it is Howells in his own person who is speaking; the ordinary reader will suppose that the magazine is coming out with a condemnation of its own contributor,—which is a course very unusual.

But your praise is more to me than Mr Howells' dispraise; I have not cared for his opinions (literary) since he came out so strongly against what I consider a masterpiece—"Le Père Goriot."[2] All I care for is the unfriendliness from one I had supposed a friend.

But what will it all matter a hundred years hence? or indeed less than that,—a hundred days. For, on Sept 1st I have a Tuscan villa! Do you remember going, with Mrs Hay & myself, to pay a visit to that dear old lady, Miss Greenough, in an old, oblong, yellow villa, on the lovely hill of "Bellosguardo," just outside of Florence? Well—I have, for four months (how I wish it were 8!) a small apartment under hers,—the one commanding the old garden, with the deep-plunging wall, and parapet,—the garden which seems to overlook half Italy. Miss Greenough still lives above; & across the court (in the same villa) lives Mr F. Boott, with his daughter, & her husband, Frank Duveneck, the artist. They, too, have a garden—in which they paint! And I shall write in mine! At least I shall write as much as is humanly possible—with that divine view spread out before my eyes.

I am resting, now; & you are at work; my interest & sympathy go with you, day by day, in this last long pull up the hill; the top will be very glorious, I know.

When this great work is done, the work of years,—you must give us another novel! And you must gather together your scattered poems—including those beautiful verses you once lent me—(which haunt me still), & bring them out in a volume.

I am glad your Washington house is such a satisfaction; Washington is the place to live in! Since they have spoiled St Augustine, I may have to come there. But it will probably be too costly; I shall end my days, I suppose, on the Indian River. Not a bad place.

I sail up & down this blue lake; Chillon, Vevey, Clarens. This hotel is outside of Geneva, & commands a splendid view of the Mont Blanc range. Chamouni was a horror.[3] I am, I hope completely cured at last of that tormenting trouble in back & arm; the cure has been effected by <u>electricity</u>. The trouble came from exhaustion, & electricity appeared to be just what I required. A clever American Doctor (in Florence) divined it. For two years, stupid English doctors have been making mistakes over it.[4]

Are you reading the Russians? In spite of all the outcry, I consider Tourgenieff far above either Tolstoi or Dostoievsky. They are all colossal.

Being "on the spot," I am trying to re-read the Lac Leman literature; but I yawn over it; yes, even over M$^{me.}$ de Stael, & "La N. Heloise," & "Childe Harold!" I have been to Coppet, Farney, & Villa Diodati (Byron's). There remains nothing left but to take up Calvin!—[5]

My love to Mrs Hay; & to Flora & Sam. A kiss for all the children.

Yours Cordially,
C. F. Woolson.

I must thank you especially for sending me the delightful "Tribune" notice, & Harper Advt.[6] As a general thing I see nothing; no one ever sends—but you.

Notes

1. Howells's review of *East Angels* (1886) appeared in *Harper's New Monthly Magazine,* Aug. 1886 (rpt. in Torsney, Cheryl B., ed. *Critical Essays on Constance Fenimore Woolson,* New York: G.K. Hall, 1992: 45–46). In the review, he objected to what he saw as the self-sacrificing nature of Woolson's character Margaret Harold.

2. Howells's criticism of Balzac's *Le Père Goriot* (1835) appeared in *Harper's New Monthly Magazine* in May 1886.

3. Petry (90) tentatively identifies Chamouni as Chamounix-Mont-Blanc, a resort near Geneva. Woolson's use of the word "horror" and her comment about St. Augustine being ruined illustrate her continued dislike of resorts.

4. Dr. William Wilberforce Baldwin or Dr. Eardley Wilmot.

5. Despite her yawning, Woolson borrowed de Staël's *Corinne* (1807) for the title of her story "At the Château of Corinne" (*Harper's New Monthly Magazine,* Oct. 1887). She omitted

the umlaut on de Staël's name. *Julie; ou la Nouvelle Héloïse* (1761) is by Rousseau and *Childe Harold* (1812–18) by Byron. Coppet was the home of Madame de Staël. Woolson is referring to John Calvin ((1509–64) because of his association with Geneva after he was banished from France.

6. The advertisement for *East Angels* in *Harper's Weekly*, June 5, 1886, quotes praise from both the New York *Tribune* and *Century*.

To Miss Ethel (McGill)

Geneva. Switzerland
Aug. 19th [1886?]

My dear Miss Ethel.

Your letter made me laugh,—it was so frank! It would indeed have been more agreeable for everyone, if Lansing Harold could have been (as you express it) "taken." But, in real life, such fortunate takings-off seldom occur, & it is real life I was endeavoring to picture. It is seldom indeed that I ask anyone to write to me, as I find it almost impossible to answer the letters I receive. But you are so honest that I propose that, after my next novel, you send a few lines more; what do you say? About "the happy ending" you ask for, we will see!

With best wishes,
C. F. Woolson.

To John Hay? (Brown)[1]

Hotel National
Geneva
Aug. 23d, [1886?]

From "Galignani" of last Thursday.—I chafe against my bonds!

C.F.W.

Notes

1. The letter, presumably to Hay, is unaddressed. The reference is cryptic, but could be to an English library in Paris opened by Giovanni Galignani (1757–1821) or to his newspaper, *Galignani's Messenger*, which his family continued to publish after his death.

To Katharine Loring (Beverly)

Villa Castellani
Bellosguardo
Oct. 9th, [1886?]

Dear Miss Loring.

Thank you so much for writing. I am grieved to hear that Miss James has been suffering. Tell her that an exclamation burst from me irresistibly, night before last,—namely—"I wish she were here this minute!" Mrs Duveneck was paying me a visit, & we were speaking of Miss James. The broad doors stood wide open; the moonlight outside lighted up my old garden, & the dark, rugged outline of Hawthorne's tower; perfume from a thousand flowers filled the room; & I was so happy to be here that it was almost wickedness! It seemed to me, then, that if Miss James' couch could be drawn across that door, she would enjoy it so much. And she would not be wicked. (I hear her exclaiming, "Yes, I should!").

But while I am grieved that she has been suffering, I feel a sort of jealous indignation that she sits up until after midnight, discussing points of theology with the curates of Leamington. I belong to their fold, & I was in Leamington six months; but they never came to discuss theology—or anything else—with me!

I am relieved to hear that Dr Eardley Wilmot has even a tolerable opinion of me.[1] He saw me when I was exhausted in both body & mind; I was either shedding tears, or very ill-tempered! I did promise to send him the book, which his skill enabled me to finish; but as he never came to see me after his professional visits had ceased, my courage failed.

Miss Litchfield (Grace Denio) has written again, this time from Aix-les-Bains. Her letter was dictated; I fear she is a great invalid. I have never seen her; but felt interested in her because her letters are so charming. She is returning to San Remo for the winter. Then back to the U.S.

I am going to look at a villa near by, to-day; with the hope of liking it well enough to engage rooms there for Jan. In Jan. I must leave the V. Castellani. Mr Boott & the Duvenecks go down to Florence on Nov. 1st. They are well, & happy. Mr D. has painted some magnificent pictures this summer.

This letter will, I hope, follow you to London; for I am supposing that you have left Leamington, & are now in Kensington, with Miss James. You will walk in Kensington Gardens,—lovely place!

I hope you will be able to read this blotted letter; I am struggling with a quill-pen; I must use it, they tell me, to save my hand & arm.

With love to Miss James,
Very truly yours,
C. F. Woolson.

Notes

1. The British Eardley-Wilmot lines boast many prominent politicians and physicians, the most famous being Sir Edward Wilmot who, in the eighteenth century, was physician to Kings George II and III.

To Gertrude Van Rensselaer Wickham (WRHS/Wickham)[1]

Florence
Oct. 13th, [1886?]

Dear Mrs Wickham.

I am afraid that this answer will reach you too late to be of any service. Your letter was forwarded to London by the Mssrs. Harper; from there it started on a wandering expedition after me, through Switzerland.

Yes, I have had a favorite. In our family history, he is celebrated, & his deeds & qualities have been chanted both in prose & verse (unpublished). His name was "Pete Trone, Esqre." He was a black & tan terrier. He was cultivated enough to be fond of grapes! Often have I seen him, after his dinner, walking slowly down the path beside the trellis, & selecting & biting off a particularly fine grape, here & there. He could fish. Once, in the country, when my brother had unexpectedly caught a large fish over the dam, & was puzzled to know how he should draw the fish up with his slender line, Pete Trone, Esqre, plunged into the water below the dam, & caught the fish in his mouth, in great excitement. He could carry a note, tied to his collar, a long distance, & take it to the person for whom it was intended; wait for the answer, & bring it safely back. In fact we never discovered the limits of his wonderful intelligence; he could do everything but speak.

Pete Trone (TRONE) Esqre had two intimate friends, old Turk, & little Grip (who were also dogs of ours). When old Turk at last ended his long life, we had a funeral for him. He was a magnificent old fellow, & well known in Cleveland. His grave was made in the garden, & all the dogs of the neighborhood were formally invited, by card, to the services. They commenced to arrive early in the morning; & were tied to different trees; there was a good deal of howling before the funeral began. At the appointed hour, our family, & the Carter family assembled, & walked in procession to the grave; old Turk was lowered to his last resting-place, his yellow paws folded, his breast covered with flowers; & ~~then~~ we sang a requiem, composed for the occasion, the tune being "Old Dog Tray."[2] All the dogs were then brought up to take a last look at the old patriarch; "Pete Trone Esqre" was chief mourner, & his expression was very solemn.

Pete Trone Esqre could walk a long distance on his little hind feet. We made him a pair of scarlet trousers, a little scarlet coat, & scarlet cap & feather; it was a funny spectacle to see him marching on his hind legs down Euclid Avenue, arrayed in these garments. He was very proud of them.

Yes, as you say, it seems appropriate to have the hospitable Carter homestead a "Home for the Aged & Infirm." They tell me that I should hardly know Cleveland, now; but I should always know that house; Grace Church; & the Lake.

With best wishes for your enterprise, I am, very truly yours,

C. F. Woolson.

If this should not be too late, & you make use of these few items, will you kindly let me know (through Harpers) the number of the magazine that contains your article.

C.F.W.

Notes

1. For information on Gertrude Van Rensselaer Wickham and her book on dogs, see Cheryl B. Torsney, "Mrs Wickham's *Dogs of Noted Americans*," *Biography: An Interdisciplinary Quarterly*, Summer 1993, 16 (3): 258–63. Wickham did include material from Woolson.

2. An 1853 tune by Stephen Foster (1826–64).

To Mrs. Houts (Vassar)

Florence. Italy
Oct. 15th, [1886]

Dear Mrs Houts.

Your letter gave me a great deal of pleasure & I should have answered it long ago, had I not been prevented by an affliction of the muscles of the right arm, resembling what is known as "writer's cramp"; it is caused by a too constant use of the pen. I trust it has now passed away.

Yes, I used to spend my summers at Mackinac; & I remember "Annie Glidden" perfectly; she was a very beautiful little girl.[1] You do not say whether you have ever been back to the lovely island? I went back a number of times. Then, after the death of my dear father, my mother & I spent a number of years in Florida, coming north only as far as the Virginia & North Carolina mountains for the hot months. When I lost my mother, eight years ago, I came abroad; I have been abroad ever since.

Soon, now, I shall be coming home "for good." And one of the first things I shall do will be to visit Mackinac again; they tell me it is very changed.

We are both far from the island now, you in Texas, & I in Italy. I hope some day to go to Texas; & if I do, I shall try to find you. Your kind letter wakened recollections that are very dear to me; I thank you for it, & send you my most cordial good wishes. Sincerely your friend,

C. F. Woolson.

Notes

1. Perhaps Annie Laurie Glidden (1865–1962), who was raised on a farm in DeKalb, Illinois, attended Cornell University's agricultural college, and returned to Illinois, where she ran the Glidden House Hotel and raised vegetables. A street in DeKalb is named after her.

To Emily Vernon Clark (Basel)[1]

[1886]

villa to the great tower of Hawthorne's villa, which is near! The tower was "the Keep," and they fled there when attacked. There is also somewhere, an underground chapel! And a ghost haunts my bedroom. I have heard him!! Miss Greenough (who has the apartment above me) began to explain "the ghost." But I begged her not to. I adore "the ghost" unexplained.

I wish I could send you an instantaneous glimpse of the view, as it looks this minute—with the "Arno wandering towards Pisa and the sea." But I can only send my love; & beg you to excuse a scrawly handwriting.—Miss Blagden, an English authoress, used to live in these rooms; she was the most intimate friend of E. B. Browning, and "every morning, Isa" (Blagden) "went down to Casa Guidi to see Lizzie, and every afternoon "Robert" came up here to see "Isa."[2]—Not far off is the villa where my uncle Fenimore spent two summers, sixty years ago. My cousins write that they were the happiest summers of his whole life.—The olives are bending the trees with their enormous crops this year, & the figs in my old garden are perfectly delicious. Come and get some!

Affectionately yours,
C. F. Woolson.

Notes

1. The fragment is pasted into Benedict's *Constance Fenimore Woolson*. Portions also appear in Benedict/CFW, 296–97.
2. For a time, Isa Blagdon lived with the sculptress Harriet Hosmer (1830–1903).

To Unknown recipient (Basel)[1]

[1886]

troubled feeling I had about the Maga's appearing to turn and rend me. All is well, therefore. Though I was a good deal startled by a recent letter from the gentleman who writes the personal column of "Harper's Weekly"; he wished to know the name & characteristics of my "next novel"! I, who have barely got my breath back, after the last.

But I shall get my breath back, here. I wish you could look in upon me this very moment. It is just eight years since I came over the ocean. And, for seven years out of that eight, I have longed to be on the top of this Tuscan hill. At last the dream has been realized. To be sure, it is only for three months. But one can get a great deal of happiness out of that time. Just outside the Roman Gate of Florence, rises this steep hill of "Bellosguardo." On the top are a number of old Tuscan villas, some of them with the massive square tower which is a Tuscan feature. The villa I am in overhangs the western brow of the hill, & commands what is to me the most beautiful view in all Italy: the valley of the Arno ("sweet Val d Arno" as Ruskin calls it),[2] with the mountains on each side rising clothed (apparently) in violet velvet; the broad plain below, dotted with villages; & the gleam of the river wandering westward "to Pisa & the Sea[”]; &, across the end the strange abrupt tops of the Carrara peaks, the loneliest-looking mts. I know. My apartment (the old stone villa has three apartments) belongs to a wealthy English lady, who has allowed me to occupy it while she makes a visit in London. And I <u>do</u> occupy it! I do'nt believe that, in all the centuries-long life of the old vaulted rooms, they have ever had in them anybody quite so glad to be there, before! There is the most enchanting old garden (with broad stone-parapet to lean upon) commanding the view. The roses & vines, figs, grapes & lemons make perfume & beauty. Below the parapet is an olive grove. Just beyond is Hawthorne's villa. A little farther, the villa where my cousins, the Fenimore Coopers, spent two summers, sixty years ago.

I am making an effort to find rooms in another villa not far from here, so that when my English lady comes back, I shall still not be driven from this lovely hill. But it is not easy; there are but few houses here, & they all belong to rich people who wo'nt take the trouble to bother themselves with "letting" the few rooms I require; they would rather, & do, close their houses entirely. But at present my life is "ideal." And I am appreciating every breath I draw.

Notes

1. The fragment is pasted into Benedict's *Constance Fenimore Woolson.* It does not seem to be from the same letter as the fragment above.

2. The quotation is from Ruskin's *Modern Painters* (1843–60).

To Samuel Mather (WRHS/Mather)

Villa Castellani
Bellosguardo. Florence
Nov. 14th, [1886]

Dear Sam.

It seems a long time since I have heard from you or Flora; & I suppose it is owing to my own silence, at least in part. But I am sure you both know how much pain I have had in my right arm & shoulder & how it has worn upon me. Since it was finally cured, in June, (by electricity), I have been trying to "rest," & recover my lost strength. The three months on Lake Leman were perfectly delightful, owing, principally, to my being able to row every day; the first time I have been where I could thoroughly enjoy rowing since I came abroad. By Oct. 1st, I had reached this old stone villa. And now I write to tell you an event which is, to me, quite miraculously important: I have taken the second floor of a villa near here for a year, beginning in December, with the privilege of renewing the lease for a second year at the same price, if I choose.

I do'nt know whether you & Flora remember Bellosguardo? At any rate, I fancy you know how warmly for years—ever since I first saw it—I have admired this view. To me it is the most beautiful view in Italy. Possibly when in Florence, you drove up here? Hawthorne's villa is here,—the "Villa Montanto." And almost all strangers drive up once to see the view. The villa I am in now—a delightful old oblong structure with a picturesque court—is occupied by people who prize its every inch, & wo'nt let anyone in (as tenant) unless he or she has been thoroughly inspected & approved by each & all of them. Judge then how careful I was last spring, when Mrs Bracken (one of them) took a fancy to go north & spend six months in her London house, & a chance appeared for me! How I wore my best clothes every day; spoke in a whisper; held myself in as "distinguished" a manner as I could; & pretended that I had 6 or 8 villas at home. I "passed," & got in! And, after six weeks here, I find the life, the air, the view, so exactly what I like best in the world (excepting Florida), that I have been searching for some sort of an abiding place near-by. It has been very difficult to find anything; there are but few villas here, & they are all owned, or tenanted (on long leases) by rich people, who when not living here themselves, prefer to close the doors entirely. But at last after long negotiation (very amusing in its way), I have got—so far at least as appearances go—exactly what I want; so exactly that it is quite ideal. A little nearer Florence than this Villa, at the top of the hill exactly (where the road comes up from town), is the Villa Brighieri-Colombi. It is not so old as this villa & Hawthorne's, & therefore not so picturesque; but it is old enough (200 years I suppose) & has been made modern by good drains & the introduction of water. I suppose I ought to prize these things; but I confess that our old court here, our "chapel," & the mysterious expanse of cellars underneath going nobody knows where—with, from one of them, a long underground passage to Hawthorne's tower—all these are more attractive to me than the "latest improvements." The position of the Villa Brighieri-Colombi is its great advantage; it commands the finest view from all Bellosguardo, the most extensive view I have ever seen from a private house. One can sometimes get as wide a view by climbing a steeple. My "terrace"—in reality an upper piazza—has the "Florence" view; the town with the Duomo, Giotto's Campanile, & the tower of the Pal. Vecchio; Fiesole on its hill; Monte Morello; & the range of the Apennines. Then my western windows command this view down the valley of the Arno, which I have loved so long. I have "an apartment,"—that is, the 2^{d} floor, which contains nine rooms, without counting kitchen & servants' quarters. It is all furnished, & I get it for a little over forty dollars a month, or exactly five hundred dollars a year. I shall "keep house" on a small scale—Italian housekeeping is very easy; & I hope to be happy & comfortable—more comfortable than I have been for many years. I move in Jan. 1st, & as soon as I am settled, & the little household wheels begin to move with tolerable steadiness, I shall go to work again. I hope to write another novel in "my" villa, & at the same time enjoy both health & peace. Bellosguardo is far enough from Florence to enable me to keep entirely aloof from "society" there; this hill is so high, & the road so steep & long, that only those persons who wish very much to see one, come out here. And of course such friends are always welcome. I am looking forward to a year of great tranquility, comfort, & hard work. Heretofore I have often had the last named, without the other two. I hope you & Flora approve of my plan, & send your benediction. It is not probable that I shall spend the entire year in Italy. Bellosguardo is really a summer place, & these villas are considered charming places to spend the summer in; but I have a fixed conviction that it is better for Americans to get a little high northern air in August; & so I shall probably lock my doors & seek a Swiss mountain, for six or eight weeks of the hottest weather.—For the present, it is safer to direct letters, as usual, to London.

I have heard of you & Flora as "well"; as "yachting;" as "at Lake Mohawk;" & I think of you always as very happy people. It is time for another & older picture of the baby. Now that I have a "home" (of a certain sort) for a year, I can give myself the pleasure of a standing frame on a table, with the faces I like to see looking at me with friendly kind glances, as I come & go. I must rigidly forbid myself buying things for a house which I shall live in so short a time—especially as I need all my savings for the Florida home which is my dream; but a standing frame for six or eight photographs I shall have. Also a dog, & a nightingale! There's an old cabinet in the villa, which I am hoping contains a secret drawer! Miss Greenough found five in a carved cabinet she bought. But the Villa Brighieri is a little too near Florence, & a little too modern, for me to discover great treasures in it.

Is Flora still riding? (This letter is as much to her as to you.) Her last letter described ~~how~~ her great enjoyment in careening round the circle to the music of the Mikado.[1] You don't know how much I have applauded your way—yours & hers—of going off somewhere every now & then to enjoy a little season of absolute rest. In my opinion, there is nothing like an absolute "rest," even if it only lasts a week; I think it preserves, cures, strengthens, cheers, improves and ~~generally~~ revises one more than anything else. More than tonics, whether of air, or food; more than traveling; more than medicine, or any kind of "treatment." And how few ever take it, I mean completely! One of Flora's letters from Lake Mohawk breathed the very atmosphere of rest; I mean—exhaled. I rested in this delicious way on the shores of Lake Leman this summer. And it did me untold good. Since I have been here, I have not been so completely idle; but I have had a great deal of happiness. All Saints Day, & All Souls Day, I shall always remember as ideal days. The weather was divine; though my garden was full of tea-roses in bloom (also white grapes & the delicious ripe figs), there came, about that time, the first slight feeling of autumn in the air. The sun shone softly, & the mountains were like violet-velvet in color; like the mts. on our left hand, the day we three had that delightful drive to Paestum—which I can never forget. I went out immediately after lunch, & walked westward over the hills until dark; did this both days, & I do'nt know when I've been happier. The views were so exquisite, & I was so glad to be here; & my mind was full of those who are no longer on earth, but who (as I believe) are in an even fairer world than this, the griefs & pains of this life forever at an end.

I suppose Col. & Mrs Hay are by this time in Washington? Everybody here is reading the great "Life," & talking about it. The opening is very fine, I think. I shall follow it with the most vivid interest. That it will be a magnificent piece of work, I am already convinced; for, in my estimation, Col. Hay stands at the very head of the literary men in the U.S. There is no limit to what he can do; his genius will carry him wherever he chooses to go. There is no one I admire more.

Poor Robert Chamberlain—my old friend; Clara writes that he has softening of the brain. I always liked him particularly, in the old days—though I think I felt, even then, that he had not much force. He was almost the only person in Cleveland at that day who had a fine library of foreign books; &, by twos & threes, at a time, they all passed through my eager hands.

I met, at Aix-les-Bains, on my way down here, a Mr & Mrs Hillyer of Hartford. Mrs Hillyer spoke of Mrs Burnham so affectionately & appreciatingly; I wonder if your father, or Kate, remembers her?[2] She went to Long-Meadow with them. She is a very pretty woman, & she & her husband have taken a furnished apartment in Florence for the winter.—

I suppose of course you know that Clara sent me her deed of the Iron Ridge lot from New York, not understanding that it was necessary to return it to Mr Keenan to be recorded. I think it strange that Fred Phinney did not tell her. It was not until she received the note you left with Henry Sherman, that she comprehended that anything was wrong. She then wrote immediately to me, & I sent the deed to Mr Keenan (from Geneva; in September I think); I asked him to have it recorded, & to communicate with me regarding the sale. I am still hoping that you & your father will be able to find some good investment for the money, (when paid), which will bring me in, like the others, seven percent. The more so since Mr Boott (whom I have been seeing every day, & who is a delightful man; a Bostonian who has lived thirty years in Italy) declares that such investments are "absolutely impossible." I replied that he was evidently not acquainted with "Samuel L." & "Samuel," Mather.—

Frank Duveneck, Mr Boott's son-in-law, has his studio in this villa. I have been allowed to enter several times, & have been greatly fascinated with his pictures; to my eyes they are both beautiful & powerful.

Give my dearest love to your father & mother. I received your mother's lovely note, congratulating me about the villa; tell her that I have taken a lease of the wonderful view for twelve long months! And tell Kate I shall answer her letter from my new "home."—If you care for one of those last photographs of me—the (one of two) Venice pictures, which Mr Washington had enlarged—(I think Clara gave one to your mother)—I will send you one. It seems to be considered the best ever taken of me.

I had a letter some time ago asking if I had "ever had a favorite dog"? I should think I had! Petie Trone, Esqre. Information was requested; an article in preparation; "Dogs of American Authors"—(What next?) I do'nt know whether you care for the poetry of Matthew Arnold? I have become a great admirer of it; &, among the minor poems, the one written on the death of his dog "Gheist," I am very fond of. I hope, Sam, you have'nt forgotten Pete Trone?—As I am writing to a boy of my own, as it were,—my own nephew—I will enclose a copy of a note I have just rec^{d}. I presume you know, or know of, Mrs James Brown Potter? Her aunt here (Mrs Launt Thompson—one of my intimate friends) "disapproves" of "Cora" highly. But I hardly think Cora cares!

My Paris morning paper announces the engagement of Miss Stager to an Irish lord.[3] I wonder if it is one of the girls I remember? or still a third & younger one? I have an idea it is the small, very fair one.

I am finishing the last of the Russian novels—I have read them all—a great many. They are magnificent. But I still prefer Tourgnenieff. When I say "all," I mean all that have been, so far, translated into French. I shall devote my (small) leisure to Italian from this time on; I wish to speak it more fluently, now that I shall be settled here for so long. It will be funny enough to plunge from the intensely modern realists ~~the~~ to the old-fashion sentimental Italians, with their flowers-of-speech, their "deh!s," & sighs. Mr Boott's dinner bell is ringing; it is a Medici cowbell! I have just discovered that this villa is 500 years old. There is a ghost; & his home is precisely my own bedroom! My window, it seems, is known to all the peasants roundabout as "the window of the Devil."—Ah well, Sam—I used to tell you stories; & now, in my old age, I have arrived at the land of stories. Nevertheless the St Clair Flats was (once) as beautiful & weird as anything here. My love to Will. A kiss for the little men.

Affectionately yours,
C. F. Woolson.

Notes

1. An 1885 comic opera by Gilbert and Sullivan.

2. The Hillyers may be the Charles Hillyers; Mr. Hillyer was a Connecticut politician and a founder of the Hartford and Connecticut Valley Railroad. Mrs. Burnham could be related to a Civil War officer from Longmeadow, Massachusetts, Howard Burnham, who was killed at Antietam.

3. The engagement of Ellen Sprague Stager to Lord Arthur Butler was announced in the Oct. 31, 1886, *New York Times*.

To Henry Mills Alden (WRHS/Benedict)[1]

Villa Castellani,
Bellosguardo. Florence
December 2^{d}, [1886]

Dear Mr Alden.

You will soon receive—if you have not already received—a little Xmas remembrance from me; it goes to you with the very best good wishes for all at the brown Cottage, & with my warmest & grateful regard. It is an etching by Frank Duveneck, & one of his Venetian scenes; I like his etchings so much myself, that I venture to send one to you. This one represents a bridge over one of the broader canals, on the outskirts of Venice—with the fishermen's great baskets.—

I am on the eve of going to housekeeping! For me, a great event. Finding the life at Bellosguardo exactly what I like, & the views more divine even than I had supposed, I have taken an appartement here for a year—with the privilege of a second year if I choose. My appartement is in a villa near here, & I have the 2^{d} floor; the views from my terrace & windows are (to me) the most beautiful in the world. I have the villa "furnished," so I have little to buy save linen. I have put in an Italian cook, & take possession soon—with an excitement I am willing to confess to <u>you</u>!; it will be "a home" (for a time), & my own. After 17 years of wandering, I shall at last have a perch which belongs entirely to me. I cannot express to you how much relief & <u>rest</u> this thought gives me. There is a little "writing room" at the end of the suite, with the most surpassingly beautiful view of the Val d'Arno; here I shall spend my time.

Yours as ever,
C.F.W.

Notes

1. The letter is pasted into Alden, Henry Mills, *God in His World*, New York: Harper's, 1890.

To James Osgood (Huntington)

Villa Brichieri
Bellosguardo 12. Florence
Dec. 30th, 1886

Dear Mr Osgood.

I have received a note from your office, asking where some copies of "Castle Nowhere" are to be sent. The address above will be mine for a year. I have taken an apartment in the "Villa Brichieri," & have begun to keep house, on a small scale, & in the simple Italian fashion. I hope you will see "Italy" sooner than you anticipate, & that you will come while I am living here. My villa commands magnificent views in two directions, & there is a cozy little "writing-room" where I hope to pass tranquil hours. The villa (near here) where I spent the autumn months, is five hundred years old; so the Villa Brichieri is considered "modern"—as it was built only two hundred & fifty years ago. Dr Holmes has recently written that a long sojourn in Italy "leaves after it a longing that can never be vanquished."[1] But I think he is mistaken; evidently his "long sojourn" was not long enough! I am very fond of Italy; but, as the years pass, a feeling is rising slowly, which will certainly end by carrying me home to my own land, never to return here again. This winter, my "six orange trees" are to be planted for me in Florida; for years I have been wishing for those trees.

I see you have had a great snowstorm in ~~Flo~~ London. It is cold here too—though, not ten days ago, there were twenty tea-roses in bloom in my old garden.

May I ask you to order sent to me, with bill, one copy of my story "For the Major"—(Sampson Low); I shall be greatly obliged.

With best wishes for the new year, I am, very truly yours,
C. F. Woolson.

Notes

1. Oliver Wendell Holmes never lived in Italy, but spent holidays there from 1833 to 1835 while he was studying in France. The quote may come from material he gathered during an 1886 trip to Europe that he eventually published as *One Hundred Days in Europe* (1887).

To William Wilberforce Baldwin (Morgan)

Sunday
[1886?]

Dear Dr Baldwin.

I fear that the maid you had in view has not returned, or else that she has some other engagement. Will you please let me know (a line will do), so that I may set about pulling the few wires that remain. If nothing responds, I shall have to start without one; but Swiss maids are excellent, & I may find one as soon as I have crossed the border.

I have the battery! And am greatly obliged to you for sending it. I keep well; but the heat has found us out this time, I think, & we shall all be glad to go.

With best wishes,
Yours sincerely,
C. F. Woolson.

To William Wilberforce Baldwin (Morgan)

~~Mond~~ Tuesday
[1886?]

Dear Dr Baldwin.

I enclose this note, which speaks for itself. I wrote to Miss S., declining to take Miss Lancushire—under the circumstances. She would cost me as much as a regular "companion," & it is a maid I need. I send the note so that you may fully understand the whole affair,—in case Miss Shuttleworth should speak of it. Will you please send the note back here some time before 6. p.m, as I wish to show it to Mrs Thompson. So, after all, I start alone! But I feel so very well I do not mind.

In haste, with best wishes, yours sincerely,

C. F. Woolson.

To William Wilberforce Baldwin (Morgan)

Monday. P.M.
[1886]

Dear Dr Baldwin.

I would have taken the capable German maid,—only she couldn't go. By that I mean that not only did she say it was impossible for her to start tomorrow, but she was not sure when she could start; she would have to give notice, first, at the place where she now is. When I said "It might be a week, then," she seemed to think it might be.—I cannot wait, so must start without her. I am sorry, as I am sure she would be very capable, & I like Germans. But I think it very possible that I may pick up some one in Geneva—where I have friends.—I can't tell you how much obliged I am to you for thinking of me in my perplexities; I am quite touched by it. I feel wonderfully well—better than I have felt for many months. I owe this to you.

With best wishes,
Yours sincerely,
C. F. Woolson.

Excuse pencil.
Inkstand packed.

To J. L. and J. B. Gilder (Rollins)[1]

Villa Brichieri
12 Bellosguardo
Florence. Italy
Jan. 28th, [1887?]

J. L. & J. B. Gilder.

I agree with Horace, with all my heart.

Thackeray's grief after he had killed Colonel Newcomb; the account of the way George Eliot's books "ploughed into her," she herself noting in her journal, "killed Tito in great excitement"; the description of Tourguenieff (in my estimation the greatest of modern novelists), as pale, feverish, so changed that he looked like a dying man, because the personages of one of his tales had taken such possession of him that he was unable to sleep, these, surely, are illustrious examples.[2]

Truly yours,
Constance Fenimore Woolson.

P. S.

I am overcome by your Italian postage stamps! When the answers to your question are published, do, pray, send me the number containing them. I intend to become a subscriber myself, before long.[3]

C.F.W.

Notes

1. All except the postscript of this letter also appears in Benedict/CFW, 31–32.
2. The characters are from Thackeray's *The Newcomes* (1855) and Eliot's *Romola* (1862–63). "Newcomb" is Woolson's spelling.
3. Woolson is probably referring to *The Critic,* which the Gilders edited.

To John Hay (Brown)

Villa Brichieri
Bellosguardo 12. Florence
Feb. 23d, [1887]

Dear Col. Hay.

I must send you a few lines, while the delight of having a home of my own (temporary though it be,) is still fresh; for I feel sure that you & Mrs Hay will comprehend my pleasure.

You have seen Bellosguardo; but probably you will not be able to recall this house. In the Villa Castellani near here, where I spent the autumn months, you once took tea, with Miss Greenough. The Villa Brichieri is a little nearer Florence,—directly at the top of the hill as one comes up from town. Though not in itself so picturesque as the Villa Castellani, it commands a more extensive view; I have not only the Val d'Arno, but all the spires & towers of Florence,—the mountains toward Vallombroso,—& range upon range of the Apennines piled up against the soft sky on the way to Rome. (For everything in that direction is "the way to Rome" in my mind; just as everything in the other direction, is "the way to Venice.") I have an apartment of nine rooms; an excellent cook, "Angelo," & maid, "Assunta" (I like to put in the Italian names); a little writing-room that overhangs all Tuscany; & peace & joy unlimited. Peace—being outside of busy Florence; & joy in the walks all about here, with these divine views stretching away on every side. It is a great event to me to have a home once more (though but for a brief space of time), after seventeen years of wandering. The immensity of the event accounts for this letter, partially.

But only partially. For the principal thing I have to say is that I have never seen anything, in the way of a "Life," which approaches your "Lincoln."[1] All biographies, of which I have knowledge, are poor, dull, & inadequate beside it;—I make no exceptions. Your treatment is so new, so living, that biography must be another thing hereafter, I should say.—I cannot find the proper words to express half I feel about it; I read each number five or six times, & my enthusiasm rises & rises until I hardly know how to control it. For the most part I do'nt control it, but say to everyone who comes in, "I have <u>never</u> read anything so good!" And they agree with me. The American residents here (not the travellers & tourists), have a habit of forgetting—in many cases have really in good faith forgotten—the plainness of our American life, as it is at home over three quarters of the continent; they remember & wish to remember only their own small circles in or near New York, or (more frequently) Boston. Upon these people your "Lincoln" comes swooping down, like a great draught of fresh strong air. I do'nt know whether they enjoy being seized by it, being carried along with it, rejuvenated & freshened as they go. But rejuvenated & freshened they certainly are. In talking of it, their coatings of Europeanisms, more or less numerous, drop from them, & they become (for the time) real—as Carlyle wd. have said. This of course is but a small & unimportant portion of the effect of the "Life." But I, being in the midst of this particular slice of atmosphere, naturally notice & chronicle it.

All you said, in your last letter, of Mr Howells' criticism of "East Angels" was true, encouraging, & very kind. I appreciated it; & thank you for it. And it comforted me greatly.[2] A really magnificent letter from Mr Joseph Harper—in fact two letters—removed long ago any pain I might have felt. For you know it was not the criticism, but its appearance in Harper's, that troubled me. Since then Mr Howells has said some generous things of "Castle Nowhere" & "Rodman." And perhaps you have seen the "Harper's Weekly" for Feb. 12th, with Henry James's article? I am told there was a frightfully severe notice of me in the last "Atlantic."[3] I have not seen it. But I am curious to know who wrote it. And if you can find out sometime, I wish you would tell me.

Henry James has gone to Venice, to visit Mrs Bronson; the Mrs Bronson who has been reported to be engaged to Robert Browning. I think he may stay two or three months in Venice; &, happy as I am at Bellosguardo, I envy him that. I have never known any one to be so run-after ~~by~~ as he was while in Florence. I think Mead's likeness of him (yours) the best thing Mead has ever done.

I must tell you how fond I have grown of a poem of yours, with music by Mr Francis Boott (who lives here, as you perhaps know, in the Villa Castellani)—"Through the Long Days."[4] Words & music are both supremely beautiful. I sing the song (under my breath), & play it, every morning of my life. I think Mr Boott's song exquisitely sweet—do'nt you? It would be very nice if you would send me a copy of that volume of your poems—which I have at home, but alas! not here. I have some shelves where I keep—or wish to keep—a few books I really love. I read a great deal, but always end my day by reading over some favorite of many years standing.—I am reading Italian just now; the modern novels—Verga & Matilda Serao.

I take the Sunday Tribune (N.Y.) & always scan the "society" letter from Washington to see if I can find your names. I know you gave "a tea." Likewise a dinner "for Col. and Mrs Harris." From Cleveland I hear that you entertained "Lord Butler." Is it "Lord Butler?" Is'nt it Lord Frederich, or John, or George Butler? This reminds me of an earnest note from Mrs Howells, which Mr H. brought me, secretly, at a dinner party here, three years ago. "Dear Miss W. Shall I say, in beging a note, 'Dear Lady Sarah Spencer—'or 'Dear Lady Sarah,' or 'Dear Lady Spencer'?"[5]

And I knew no more than she!

I walk often to the Certosa—where we went together. The wild flowers are coming out.

Spring in Washington is beautiful, too. I spent one spring there, which seems to me, as I recall it, as lovely as anything I remember; the early green, the blossoming trees, the soft air, the uncrowded spaces, the country round about, & Arlington.

Give my love to Mrs Hay.

Always sincerely your friend,
C. F. Woolson.

I thought Clarence King's "Helmet of Mambrino" delicious. I wish he would give us something more.—Did you recognize a deliberate theft of mine in "East Angels"? (I think the only one): I mean the allusion to the jester.[6]

Notes

1. Though not published in book form until 1890, Hay's *Abraham Lincoln: A History* had begun serialization in *Century* in Nov. 1886.

2. See letter to Hay dated July 30, 1886, for Woolson's reactions to Howells's review of *East Angels* in the Aug. 1886 issue of *Harper's New Monthly Magazine*. Later, in the Feb. 1887 issue of that magazine, Howells is more positive about Woolson's story collections *Castle Nowhere: Lake Country Sketches* (1875) and *Rodman the Keeper: Southern Sketches* (1880).

3. "Miss Constance Fenimore Woolson," an article James later collected in *Partial Portraits* (1888). The "frightfully severe notice" was part of an anonymous review called "Recent Novels by Women" (*Atlantic Monthly*, Feb. 1887).

4. Woolson uses this poem by Hay as a refrain in "Dorothy" (*Harper's New Monthly Magazine*, March 1892), a story set in a villa reminiscent of Bellosguardo's Villa Castellani where she lived prior to the Villa Brichieri.

5. Petry (96) speculates that the woman Woolson and Howells are joking about is the Lady Sarah Spencer, whom James met during an unpleasant weekend in Oxford. The error for "beginning" is Woolson's.

6. Petry (97) has identified this theft from *The Helmet of Mambrino* in Chapter 21 of *East Angels* where Dr. Kirby tells Garda Thorne that her ancestors would have used Lucian Spenser as a jester.

To Edmund Clarence Stedman (Columbia)

Villa Brichieri
Bellosguardo 12
Florence. Italy
Feb. 24th, [1887]

Dear Mr Stedman.

Do you observe that heading?

How many years is it since we first met on that lovely Florida shore? Do you remember the walk we took over the pine-barrens? Looked at from one point of view, it seems to me only a short time ago;—those Florida days. But, from another, I plainly see the years that lie between them & the present hour; years that, for me, have contained much sorrow; & pain; & toil. It has not, of course been all sorrow, & toil; I have had many exquisite weeks—; in Venice; in Rome; in Warwickshire; & other places. And now, for the moment, the wheel seems to have turned round completely.

"Time so complained of,
Who to no one man

Shows partiality,
Brings round to all men
<u>Some</u> undimmed hours,"

sings Matthew Arnold.[1] And I'm having mine now.

I have taken a villa (that is, a small apartment in a villa) at Bellosguardo, for a year; perhaps two. Bellosguardo is just outside the Roman Gate of Florence; it is the hill of Galileo; of Hawthorne (where he wrote "The Marble Faun"); of "Aurora Leigh." Take down that poem, turn to the Seventh Book, & look for the description beginning "I found a house at Florence on the hill of Bellosguardo—" &c—& you will comprehend the views I have from all my windows, & my terrace. It is useless for <u>me</u> to try to describe it after Mrs Browning; but I do believe it is the most beautiful view in the world. To me a view is everything; better than anything.

After seventeen years of wandering, I have at last a home of my own—(though but a temporary one). Such joy as I take in my own tables & chairs, tea-cups & cushions, I do'nt believe you can imagine; but perhaps Mrs Stedman can. I have a cook, "Angelo;" & a maid, "Assunta" (I write the Italian names for the pleasure of it!), &, altogether, I am supremely happy.—I felt like calling across the sky to you for a moment to ask ~~if you~~ you for your sympathy. For though years of silence lie between now and our last letters, I have never for an ~~moment~~ instant changed in my friendship for you both; & I have been always sure, too, that you remained unchanged towards me.

And now that I have sent forth so glowing a description of my new surroundings, I must hasten to add that there's no splendor about it; the old villa is shabby, & to the cheap Italian furniture, I have added only a few necessary articles. Everything is in the smallest scale, & all goes on as economically, as, even in economical Italy, it is <u>possible</u> to have it go. But the view, & the air, & the sun, & the flowers, & the sense of ownership (for a year)—the tranquility of spirit, the far-away-ness—these to me, just now, seem infinite riches.

Is there no hope of your coming abroad again, before long?

I have your "Poets of America," & often re-read it. A most difficult book to write (I should think), it seems to me extraordinarily good. Just; truthful; keenly discriminating; & brilliant as all your things are; & as you are; to a degree which always makes me (a person devoid of brilliancy) wonder & wonder. Wonder, (while I admire) how it must <u>feel</u> to have such intellectual radiance as that!

I know it is impossible for you to write letters, so I ask no reply. At this happy moment (which may not last), I wanted to send you word how it was with me,—by the memory of our pine-barren walks so long ago. I too cannot write letters; I have seriously injured muscles that move my right arm, by too constant pen-work. And all the rest of my life I shall have to be careful of them. Otherwise I am well; better than I have ever been! You would not know me; I weigh 150!

I always look for your name in the magazines; & do not like it that I see it so seldom. I beg you—do not remain silent (or so nearly so) longer. But perhaps you will say (contemptuously) that "the magazines" are not the poet's field—though they may be the field of the novelist. True. Then give us another volume—without the magazines at all.—I have the portrait of you, cut from "Harper's," pinned up in my writing room; the little writing room whose window overhangs "the street Val d'Arno."

Mr Pell—who was our companion on the barrens—had just sent me the first jessamine from the St Augustine hedges. I suppose you may have heard (from Clara) that I expect to live in Florida, when I come home? I am only waiting to store up a little more money ~~before I~~; then I shall return; buy a wee cottage down there; set up a crane & three orange-trees; & never stir again.

I have been enjoying, here, the songs of Mr Francis Boott. (He lives in a villa near mine). One of them is your—"I know not if moonlight or starlight—." It is beautiful—words & music.

I must send this to the "Century," as Clara has not given me your address—though she speaks, in her letters, of having seen Mrs Stedman. My niece, Kate Mather, wrote me how much she enjoyed her evening at your house, last year; & how much she liked your son Arthur.

Have you read the great Russians. I still think Tourguenieff the finest by far. Though one of Gogol's is as good. I am at present reading modern Italian—the novels. But this is for the sake of acquiring a greater fluency in speaking.

I suppose you are living, as usual, in the whirl of New York life? It is brilliant, I know;—that life. But all that sort of thing is denied to me. When I think of it (I do not often recall the subject,) I cannot express to you how grateful I am, that, in absolute reality, I do not suffer at all from the deprivation. I never had any taste for "society"; how thankful I am for this now!

Give my love to your wife. And accept my warmest good wishes. Always your attached friend,

C. F. Woolson.

Notes

1. Woolson quotes Arnold's "Consolation."

To Mary Gayle Carter Clarke (Cornell)

12 Bellosguardo
Florence
Feb. 25th, [1887]

My dear Mary.

I have long been wishing to write to you, to send you my love & warm congratulations on the arrival of the little daughter—(whose name I do not yet know). As soon as you have a photograph of her, do send me one. And do not forget how long I have wished for a really good likeness of you. This last desire has been quickened lately, by a glowing description, in one of Clara's letters, about you, in your "blue velvet & white lace," at a dinner she attended at Jennie's. Clara, you know, does not glow easily.—I am so very glad to know (from this) that you are perfectly well again.—

I have—as perhaps you have heard—gone to housekeeping here for a year. I was so delighted with my three months in the Villa Castellani (which you know, I believe; Miss Greenough lives there), that I have taken an apartment in another villa near it. I really think my windows & northern terrace command as lovely a view as the world contains.

All this is temporary. I fully expect to come home before very long. This morning, I received a letter from Mr Washington, our very kind friend; & in it he tells me that the men are at work clearing four acres of the six he has bought for me, below St Augustine, on the sea. He is going to plant a four-acre orange grove there. And leave the other two acres, "with their grand live-oaks & palmettoes as they are," so that, later, I can build my coquina cottage under them! I do not buy any of this now. But I am to have it at cost price whenever I feel able to take it; & in the meanwhile, "the orange-trees will be growing." Does'nt sound charming? But what I put this in for, is simply to show you that I am really coming home; & that I am not sure but that I like your suggestion of a little cottage at the "Hyde" and of the lake, better than a house in the village. Certainly—so far—this living in the country, as I am doing now, is delightful to me. I have almost all my time undisturbed. So please tell Mr Clark, with my regards, to remember me, in future plans about land.

My dear Mary, your letters have been very charming ones; I have enjoyed them particularly, & have read them over more than once. One you wrote in Feb., 1885—giving, as you said, "village details," was inimitable. I think I shall always have to keep that one. My long silences I hope you understand. I fear it must always be so. The Doctor seems to think that I have seriously weakened the muscles that move my right arm. As I must always use them for writing of one kind, you will see how little there can be of another. Save for this, I am extremely well. And more comfortable, & therefore happier, than I have been for years. I wish I could show you my terrace.

Give my love to Daisy, when you write;[1] love & good wishes. I red[d] her wedding cards.

Remember me, too, to Mr & Mrs Pell-Clark. I sub-let my apartment here to Henry James for December, as I was not to leave the Villa Castellani until Jan. So, during the month that he too was up on this hill, I saw him daily. He told me Henrietta was better.[2] Mrs Archie Pell has been in Florence; I heard of her, though I did not see her. I seldom go to town.

I was much touched by your speaking of the ray of light which sometimes comes, so unexpectedly, to cheer one at the darkest hour of gloom. You say—it must come from God. Surely it does. Such unexpected aid has several times been sent to me, when melancholy, like death itself, had me in its grasp.

But all such gloom has been taken from <u>your</u> life; I cannot tell you what pleasure it gives me to know how happy you are; & that all is well with you & Hyde.

Give much love to your mother. Tell her I am hoping to write to her before very long. She, of course, with you & Jennie & your children all on the other side, would never be contented in Europe—even though she should bring Grace & Averell with her.[3] But tell her that if contentment could be found anywhere over here, I am sure it would be in a Bellosguardo villa.

"I found a house in Florence on the hill of Bellosguardo"—(Aurora Leigh. 7th book.)[4]

My love to Grace, & a kiss for the baby,
Yours affectionately,
C. F. Woolson.

Give my love to Giulia.

Notes

1. Juliette Gordon Low.

2. Henrietta Pell-Clark gave Woolson a letter of introduction to James. Other records show that James lived at the Villa Brichieri in April and May 1887.

3. Her children (Mary's siblings).

4. Elizabeth Barrett Browning wrote *Aurora Leigh* (1856) when she live on Bellosguardo Hill.

To Linda Guilford[1]

March 1st, 1887

... I am so very glad, dear Miss Guilford, that you liked "East Angels." I have long wished for a word from you, since it was from you that I first learned how to write. Do you remember the wonderful and ceaseless pains you used to take with our compositions? As I look back upon it now, I wonder how you could have been so extraordinarily patient! But it was your conscience, I know; no slighter influence could have held you so firm through such an amount of what must have been to you intense boredom. . . . As I think of all this, a vision rises before me of the "Cleveland Seminary"—with its furnace-heated air; its crowds of girls, the woods behind with their early spring flowers, and you, and Prof. St John, and Miss Barstow taking charge of us all. I see the snow as it used to drive slantingly across the wide, empty fields outside my window on the north side of the house; I see the white road going towards town—a road whose principal interest for us lay in the fact that it led by "the Severance's," where dwelt "John" and his flute.[2] We cherished a romantic interest in John and were much offended that he did not marry Miss B.—I know very little of the Seminary girls, and should like to hear more. . . . The simple history of some of my schoolmates, truthfully told, would make, if printed, a tale of such sensational nature that everyone would say—"How absurdly improbable!" But writers of "fiction" (so called!) have to be very careful not to be as sensational as the truth.

Dear Miss Guilford, do you remember the time we stole the cherry pies?. . . . The pies were just from the oven—hot and fresh and tempting—and they had been incautiously placed on a window ledge (to cool) just within our reach! Nellie C.—(the boldest because the oldest of us), proposed it, and instantly we carried out her idea. When summoned before the Professor, how we trembled! But when he had us before him—with the door closed—he did nothing but laugh. . . . I am afraid I have forgotten most of my Latin—learned from you and from him; but it comes in play with Italian, which I now have to speak. . . . All that you said of my stories was gratefully received by your attached pupil. . . .

The long delay—which I regret so much—has been caused by a troublesome weakness of the muscles that move the right arm; these muscles have been overworked, and every now and then they tangle themselves with the nerves of the same locality and the two hold a witches' dance together that sends me to bed and keeps me there. At last I am hoping that a cure has been found in electricity. Twice, now, it has stopped the dance completely. But of course the best prescription is to abstain from using the pen! I should like to talk over with you—who first opened my mind to many of the deeper mysteries of life—the melancholy chance (if it is a chance) which causes a person, who never could hold a pen with ease and whose eyes were always excessively delicate, to set up precisely as a <u>writer!</u>

I wish I could show you my view here. Take down "Aurora Leigh," turn to the seventh Book, and find the passage beginning "I found a house at Florence on the hill of Bellosguardo," &c, and you have a good description, save that poor Mrs Browning—who almost never left her house down in the crowded town (Casa

Guidi)—seems not to have been familiar with our second view here, namely the view down "the sweet Val d'Arno" toward the west. From the north and east sides of my villa I have the view described in "Aurora Leigh." But from my little writing-room on the south side, and from my bedroom, I have the Arno view, which I think the loveliest on earth. The wide soft valley is so peaceful, with its myriad sleepy white towns, and the gleam of the westward-going river; then, on each side, rise the velvet Apennines, their sides dotted with old castles, and towers and campaniles; and across the western end stand the strange abrupt Carrara mountains, far in the blue sky.

Notes

1. Benedict/CFW, 39–41, 300. These two excerpts in Benedict could be from different letters.

2. Industrialist John Severance donated a million dollars toward the construction of Cleveland's music hall, Severance Hall.

To Samuel Mather (WRHS/Mather)

Villa Brichieri
Bellosguardo 12
Florence. Italy
March 24th, [1887]

Dear Sam.

The magnificent view of Niagara, after long delay & a good deal of trouble, has at last reached me; & forms the ornament of my Florentine drawingroom. It is far & away the finest picture of the Falls I have ever seen—paintings included; & I am very glad to have it; & grateful to you for sending it. It came (almost) in time for my lonely old birthday (which was otherwise unmarked); so that it did quite as well as Xmas. A little later, when it is warm, the plunge of the water—as I look up at the wall—will be very refreshing; the green hue of that immense stratum of water (at the real Falls) is the coolest thing I know.

I think I will spare you & Flora a repetition of my expressions of contentment at being a housekeeper again; & having my own spoons & forks; (plated.) It is delightful to me—& almost pathetic from one point of view—to see how intensely I enjoy "a home," even a temporary one. The apartment is rather rough; & it is but meagrely furnished—as Italians always furnish. I have added enough things to make it tolerably comfortable; & I have a view so superb & far-stretching that it is in itself great riches. I have taken the apartment for a year, with the privilege of a second year at the same terms. But perhaps I told you all this in my last letter? The one thing to add, at this date, is, that the experiment has proved (after three months' trial) a perfect success. I am very well here, & very happy. And it is going to be—already is—the best place I have ever had for working. My little writing room is already very dear to me.

I sent Clara's deed to [?] to Mr Keenan last August or September, asking him to record it, & return.[1] And I inquired at the same time about the sale. I have never rec^{d} the deed back, nor had any reply. Will you kindly look him up for me? I do'nt even feel that I own the lot, yet! I read with great care & interest your description of the Bond & Stock investment you propose making for me, with the proceeds of the sale of lot,—namely the [?] R. R. Company of Grand Rapids, Michigan. I shall be delighted if you will carry out this plan; it seems a wonderfully good thing. As I understand it, I get six percent interest (which I was told here I could not get;) & perhaps, later, I own stock! It seems like a little miracle. But I suspect <u>you</u> are the god behind the machine.

I have kept your letter, & enjoyed reading it to my skeptical friend, Mr Boott. I do'nt think he believes it yet! I mean the possibility of six percent.—

I had a letter yesterday from Julia Parsons, (at Rome); she speaks of being here later, so I shall probably see her. She has been in the thick of the "Pope's side" of Roman society; but (I should judge from her remarks) is in no danger of being converted.—

Let me know how your Scherer library resulted.[2]

Henry James has been in Venice for a month or so, & still lingers there.

About Russian novels—if you have read "Anna Karenine" & "Tarass Boulba," you have had (in my opinion) the best; always excepting the great Touregneniff. If you come across Dostoyevsky's "Crime et le Chatiment," try that. It is extraordinary. I am reading only Italian at present; the modern Italian novels of Verga & Matilda Serao; it is an easy way to acquire "talking-Italian."

Ouida (of whom you speak) has left Florence for good. She says she was not appreciated here. She is now in England—where, let us hope, appreciation surrounds her richly. She made a goose of herself here by falling in love with a young Italian 20 years younger than herself. She thought he wd. marry her (he is a Marchese); but he did not. While the affair was going on, Ouida (who is 55) wore her hair braided down her back in two long tails, tied with blue ribbon, & attired herself in short white frocks, with juvenile sashes. If he did not notice her sufficiently, (in company), she wd. sit down & pout, & swing her feet like a child. (N. B. her feet are her only beauty.)—

This is a scrawl, Sam. But I am hard at work again—after a long vacation; & my last attack (at Xmas) of pain in the shoulder-muscles, has made me an incurable sloven about handwriting; I save my arm as much as I possibly can. Dearest love to

Flora, & a kiss for the little boys. Col. Hay's "Lincoln" I think the finest biography I have ever read. It is greatly admired here.

Affectionately yours,
C.F.W.

Love to all at 544.

Notes

1. Clara Benedict's involvement in the sale of Wisconsin property is unclear.
2. Mather donated money toward (Case) Western University's purchase of a book collection belonging to Dr. Wilhelm Scherer of Berlin.

To Samuel Mather (WRHS/Benedict)

Villa Brichieri
Bellosguardo 12. Florence
March 31st, [1887]

Dear Sam.

I have just rec^d^ a note from Keenan, enclosing deed to [Henning?] for me to execute; namely sale of Iron Ridge lot to latter, for one thousand dollars.—I shall go to town tomorrow, & have it executed at the Consulate.—I shall write Keenan to pay the one thousand to you; & will you please invest it as you proposed? I was tempted to have the sum sent over here to lie at Macquay & Hooker's (where they pay three percent) as an anchor out, in case of emergencies. For it is a new thing, you know, for me to have a house on my hands—with rent, & all the steady expenses to provide for. But on looking over my accounts, I think I can get along without it; & I suppose such an investment as you propose, ~~as~~ is so extraordinarily good, that I had much better accept it. It will, as I understand it, pay me six per-cent, which will add itself to my income from the other bonds ($420^00^), so that I shall have $480^00^. This (with $20^00^ added) will pay my rent here-$500^00^.

Will you kindly write to Keenan (Northwestern Mutual Life Insurance Co. Milwaukee,) & conclude the business for me? I shall be ever so much obliged.

All goes well here, & I am very contented & happy. The villa is the greatest success of my life. For to be happy is a wonderful thing, when one is my age, & not very strong, & rather lonely. It is, of course, the feeling of being in a "home" which is such a warm comfort to me. I am so tired of a wandering life.

Florence is beautiful now, & full of people. There is to be a great fête in May, (when the new façade of the Duomo is to be unveiled,) & I presume I shall see hundreds of people. For everyone will rush to Florence, & Bellosguardo is enchanting in the Spring. I have a great many visits as it is, & have given up returning them, or trying to. They only get in on one day of the week—which is all I can afford to give up to that sort of thing. I do'nt think people care about the calls being returned; they come up for a drive, & to see the magnificent view.

Tell your mother that I was delighted to get her very kind letter. I could—if I only had the time—tell her many more details of Italian housekeeping which I am sure would amuse her. The cook is a marvel; there is absolutely nothing he cannot make, & everything is cooked & served to perfection. I mean his part of it; for my dishes are very ordinary; the common china that goes with the house. Assunta (my little old woman) always comes to kiss my hand the first thing in the morning, & the last thing at night before she goes to bed.—I am very busy now, & expect to continue busy for a long time. Lately I have been asked both by the Harpers & Appletons, to allow the collection of all my scattered verses in a volume next year. I have declined both proposals. "Cora" having stolen "K. Belle," I doubt whether a re-issue on my part would be wise.[1]—Everyone admires your "Niagara," which hangs over my little low book-case in the drawingroom. When are you & Flora coming over again? I suppose those Paestum temples are still looming up in the soft air, down there by the blue sea. For myself, travel is over for the present; I am enjoying staying at home.

I think it will be safe now to address (very clearly) as at the head of this letter. I say "very clearly" because the postman finds great difficulty in reading English & American writing. I will admit that the Italian writing is much clearer. It looks like engraving.

Love to Flora, & a kiss each for the dear little boys.

Affectionately yours,
C.F.W.

Notes

1. Actress Cora Urquhart Potter's readings of Woolson's "Kentucky Belle" (1873) made the poem famous.

To Samuel Mather (WRHS/Mather)

After this, direct here.
Villa Brichieri
Bellosguardo 12
Florence. Italy
April 23d, [1887]

Dear Sam.

I steal a moment to answer yours of April 6th, just received. A second letter from me probably reached you soon after the first; about Keenan, I mean. He sent the deed, & I had it executed at the Consulate, & returned it. Then I wrote you, asking you to make the investment you so kindly proposed—which, if I am any judge, is extraordinarily good.—The "Niagara" was very slow in coming; but now that it is here, it is the finest ornament of my drawingroom, & I am very proud of it (have resorted to a quill you see as my hand aches a little & a quill is softer). Every one who comes in, notices it; the English especially. The last, who stood a long time gazing at it, were Miss Rhoda Broughton & her sister; I mean Miss Broughton who wrote "Belinda," "Cometh up as a Flower," "Nancy," &c.[1] It arrived in perfect order as to glass & frame. I thought the charges from London rather high—66 francs—that is a little over thirteen dollars. I rec^d a note from the Alliance Bank, stating that they had rec^d the picture; I then wrote to a forwarding agent in London, who has sent my trunks twice, & it is he who makes this charge. I have written to complain, & they answer that they will investigate. So, very likely, they will take off some of the items (notably an absurd one of some man at Havre) & all will be well. Do'nt think of the matter again. I am delighted to have the picture & the pleasure of looking at it, & showing it as an "American" institution, has already far outbalanced the thirteen dollars. They are dollars well spent. As a general thing, it seems impossible, however, to send anything abroad, without unexpected charges at this end. Clara has just sent me some nice books—an edition of Emerson, & Lowell—&, though she supposed she had paid all the charges, I have had fifty or sixty francs to pay here—the charges of another man at Havre (which seems a piratical place!) The Vice Consul here is investigating that for me, as he was good enough to get the books through the Custom House, & so discovered how much I was charged.

I am so happy here, Sam, that (as I wrote before) it is pathetic—almost. The old Auntie enjoys, like a child, her own cups & saucers, & chairs & tables. The view is a constant Paradise to me. Florence is crowded—a great fete—; the uncovering of the new façade of the Duomo. King & Queen, & every kind of rejoicing. I am deluged with calls, for all the Americans in Italy are here. I am very curious to know how your father & Kate liked Florida. Do tell me. It's warm & lovely—thin clothes, & open windows. Love to Flora & little boys.

In great haste, affly,
C.F.W.

Notes

1. These are novels by Rhoda Broughton, published in 1883, 1867, and 1873, respectively.

To Samuel Mather (WRHS/Mather)

Villa Brichieri
12 Bellosguardo
Florence. Italy
May 16th, [1887]

Dear Sam.

The beautiful pictures of the children, gave me very great pleasure. The one of Livingston alone, is as sweet, & attractive, and intelligent a picture as I have ever seen of a little boy, in all my life. The one of the boys together is very picturesque. And I am amazed by the superb bigness, & health, & general hilarity of Amasa! I had no idea he was such a magnificent child.

Your letter makes me fully understand the new investment, which is certainly miraculously good. But of course ~~I owe it to you~~ you are the miracle worker. Please keep the bond & stock for me—as you suggest. The 75^{00}, remaining of the $1,000 Keenan will send you, & the 30^{00} interest you mention, I shall be glad to get; please send them to me here. And, henceforth, you might as well address as at head of this letter; or, if anything is to be sent, "Care Macquay & Hooker. Via Tornabuoni. Florence."

Please give best love to all at your Father's, & tell your mother & Kate that the most acceptable books have reached me in perfect condition, & that I prize them very much. I was extremely interested in what Kate wrote of Florida.

We are having great fêtes here. The façade of the Duomo is a last completed; & what with the unveiling, the processions, the fireworks & illuminations, regattas, tournaments, races, &c &c, we are all rather distracted. I thought I should be perfectly serene up here on my hill, no matter how enormous the crowd might be down in the town. But the arrival, five evenings in succession, of two English families "to see the fireworks" from my terrace, & the fact that no fire works have come off (on those particular evenings) has somewhat demoralized me. There are six ladies in all, & tea has to be made immediately, as the English always expect it. Then we sit on the Terrace from 8 to 11, & nothing to be seen! We talk about "The Prevention of Cruelty to Animals,"—a Society in which the six are interested. But I think I am the animal.—Julia Parsons passed through Florence without stopping—as she did when she went to Rome. I was sorry not to see her. Love to Flora. In haste, but most affectionately yours,

C.F.W.

To Samuel Mather (WRHS/Mather)

Villa Brichieri
Bellosguardo 12. Florence
June 7th, [1887]

Dear Sam.

This morning's mail brings me—out here in the country—your letter of May 24th; that is, fourteen days from Cleveland, which I think is expeditious. I am delighted to hear that I own, really own, that miraculous Bond, which is not only going to pay six per cent interest, but which makes me a present, in five years or so, of (perhaps) a thousand dollars more! It is like a fairy tale. Please keep the bond & stock for me, & let the interest be paid into the Savings Bank Cleveland, on my account there. But—as you kindly offer to do it—I will ask you to send to me, here the \$118.^{50}; that is the \$30^{00} of interest, & the \$88^{50} you have already deposited. I ask you to do it, instead of asking the Bank, because I have very recently asked the Bank to send some money; & I should rather not put them to the same trouble again, so soon. I enclose a line to the Bank.

I call for this money because I feel poor this summer. To put my apartment in order has cost a good deal; four carpets, 3 stoves, some curtains; a little good furniture for the drawingroom; & all the linen, bedding, blankets, silver (Christofle plate) knives, &c. And lately I have put up an awning over my divine terrace. All is now done; no matter how long I stay here, I shall have to spend no more. But just now I [am] (naturally) a little cramped. But if you could know, Sam, the intense pleasure & comfort this delightful home is to me—you would, I think, agree with me in feeling that it was a wise step. Every morning as I look at the beautiful view while dressing, I thank God for the delight of it. I have been in the house now five months; & every day I am more content than I was the day before.

We have had great fêtes here, the completion of the Duomo. Now almost every one has gone, or is on the point of going. I shall not stir until I feel the absolute necessity of it. Perhaps the necessity wo'nt come at all! Time was when people came up to Bellosguardo for the summer; the villas here are old summer villas. The Fenimore Coopers came up here from Florence for the summers, sixty years ago. There is always a breeze on this hill, & I have the whole house, with its large cool rooms, to myself.

I had the most delightful letter from Flora not long ago. It did me much good, & made the whole week bright,—it was so charming in itself, & also so cheering. Give Flora my best love, & tell her that I am going to give myself the pleasure of writing to her some day later in the summer, when the real summer-life here has begun; white dresses, stone floors, & the great shutters closed. As my apartment has rooms

& windows all round the sky, there will always be one room where I can write—I mean one room away from the sun. At present the sun is only warm enough for pleasure—(we have had a very cold May) & the long twilight & rising moon from my terrace—with the wide landscape—have been enchantingly beautiful.

I am much obliged for the payment of the exorbitant Express charges. It was an outrage that we should have been forced to pay them. I have just emerged from a long contest with the Express Agents respecting similar exorbitant charges on some books Clara sent me. The Vice Consul here took up that matter, & has written letter after letter about it; to Brentano (who sent the package); to the forwarding Agent at Havre; & to the man at Turin; & also to various R. R. Companies, & the Florentine authorities. He has worked hard, & has been determined that 30 or 40 francs at least should be returned to me. He had figured it all out, & was convinced that there was no justice in the charges. But this morning he writes me a despairing note (enclosing the last letters from the R. R. Companies & the Agents,) & says he fears "there is no hope." I could have told him that in the beginning!

I wrote to London about the "Niagara" charges. But could obtain no satisfaction. And Macquay & Hooker tell me I should never be able to get any reduction made "though I should write 100 letters." It seems impossible to send anything from the U.S. beyond London, without being over-charged. Let me put in here that the books sent by mail by your Mother & Kate, arrived safely, & with no extra charge demanded. Small packages can come by mail, apparently, without trouble.

I took cold during the fetes; so many people came up "to sit on the terrace," that I had, in common politeness, to sit there too. And it was much too cool for me. The great ceremony of the unveiling of the new façade of the Duomo was a beautiful sight from here. And the four evenings of fireworks, & the one evening of general illumination, ditto. The illumination was by far the finest one I have ever seen. All Florence, even the smallest houses, blazed with light; & the tower of the Palazzo Vecchio, the Dome of the Cathedral, & all the spires & campaniles were outlined in lines of glittering stars. Then all the villas & villages on all the hills roundabout, were also illuminated, including large bonfires on the tops of all the high mts.—However, beauty apart, I took a horrible cold. And at last had to go to bed, & send for the Dr. I have got well but slowly, & I have been taking short excursions & sitting lazily in the sun. Do you remember the high stone bench at Fiesole, above the town, near the old convent? I have spent hours there, in sunny silence, overlooking the world. For, the view is so vast, you remember, that it does seem as if one saw the whole world. I have also been out to Prato to see Donatello's outside pulpit; & to queer little Signa, with its old towers. My outings are about over as I am nearly well—thanks to the lovely weather. I am very busy again,—writing. The summer is always my busy time, as the cold weather destroys so much of my vitality.

I was greatly interested in Flora's mention of your essay on the "unification of Italy." It did me good, Sam, to feel that you care something for the lovely land; you would'nt have chosen the subject otherwise. The determined struggle & effort of the young nation to improve itself, & to take a place in the world is very interesting; & it is going on under my eyes all the time. The other day, when the Façade was unveiled, the Archbishop personally blessed the King & Queen; that is a step forward, for it betokens a chance of possible adjustment of the warfare between the government & the Pope. Yesterday all Italy went to Carrera—Garibaldi's tomb. I mean deputations from all Italy.—The majority of Americans care little for Italy; they come here for a tour of a few weeks, & that is all. It is true that those who do come to spend a longer time—a winter, say—always end by never going anywhere else! If you love Italy at all, you love it extremely. Clara, you know, cares little for Italy. Kate has (I believe) never seen it. Roy Keese came over last summer, & got no further than Como. And Belle Washburn writes that she is coming over in Oct.—to go to Dresden; not a word of Italy.

Sam, do'nt you think you could lend me your nose? Richard Greenough, the Sculptor, who has been here lately (he lives in Rome) has formally asked permission to "do" my head,—again reducing me to the embarrassed & vexed state of mind which the subject of "a likeness" always produces. Why have'nt I a nose? It would be such a pleasure to decline modestly; & then be forced into consenting; & then have a lovely bust in marble to send you. Your mother, now, might lend me her profile. I have declined Mr Greenough's proposal—with thanks. I shall never sit to anyone—painter, sculptor, or photographer, again.[1]

I have already written to you about the beautiful pictures of your little boys; everyone admires them; but I admire them most of all.—I am going to be Godmother, this week, to the little son of Frank Duveneck, the artist. His wife (who was Miss Boott) has asked me. They live in the Villa Castellani, near here. They are not church people at all, & the English Chaplain & I will probably be the only Episcopalians present! The American chaplain has become discouraged, & has gone home; to the U.S. I am not surprised.—Ouida has come back unexpectedly; there were threats of an execution in her house, for debts; & her mother was wildly writing notes to everyone she knew (in Florence) asking for the loan of 10 francs "to buy bread!" Ouida must be wildly reckless & improvident. Now that she is here, she says she has money enough; but that she forgot to send her mother any! She sighs for London "where they appreciate me. Here they do not." Her villa is not far from here; but down on the plain, in the hot dusty part, & with no view. I have written a long letter—though I ought not to have done it as I am using my eyes steadily now, many hours each day. Best love to all at 544. Continue to direct to the Villa. I am so sorry I shall not see the Hays. But I shall take no more long journeys, now that

I have this house. Kiss the dear little lads for Aunt Conny. And, with best love to Flora, believe me yours affectionately,

C.F.W.

Notes

1. Woolson did eventually consent to having Greenough cast a bust of her.

To J. B. Gilder (NYPL)

Villa Brichieri
Bellosguardo 12
Florence. Italy
June 10th, [1887?]
J. B. Gilder, Esqre.

Dear Sir.

I fear this letter will be of no use for your "little article"; it will arrive too late. Nevertheless I am going to answer, because I like the "Critic" so much. I do not see it regularly—alas! But every now & then some one sends me a number; & I always read them with pleasure.

I am happy to say that I am spending the summer in an old villa on a Tuscan hill; the hill called "Bellosguardo," near Florence. If you will take down "Aurora Leigh," turn to the Seventh Book, & look for the passage beginning "I found a house at Florence on the hill of Bellosguardo—" you will find a description of the view from my terrace. I do not think, however, that Mrs Browning has done full justice to the beauty of the scene; she was so much of an invalid that she was able to come but once to Bellosguardo; the evening lights & shadows over the vast landscape, she never saw.

I may go to the Engadine for a few weeks in August; but if I do, I shall return to Tuscany in time for the figs.

I have taken this villa for a year. My intention is to come home before long, and live in Florida.

With best wishes,
Yours very truly,
C. F. Woolson.

To William Wilberforce Baldwin (Morgan)

Villa Brichieri,
Bellosguardo 12
June 25th, [1887]

Dear Doctor.

The days are few, now, before your departure; please do not forget to send me the account of my indebtedness to you for your visits to me in December, & also lately. I am happy to say I am well again; warm summer weather, & absolute quiet, agree with me so perfectly, that if I could have a house twenty miles from everybody, & on the line of the equator, I have no doubt but that I should attain the health, & age, of the Pharaohs.

Cordially yours,
C. F. Woolson.

To John Hay (Brown)

Villa Brichieri
Bellosguardo 12
Florence. Italy
August 6th, [1887]

Dear Col. Hay.

All this while I have never thanked you for the beautiful copy of the beautiful poems.[1] The book has given me a great deal of pleasure. I venture to say it has seldom been more re-read, & closely studied, than here on this Italian hill, during this summer solitude.—Everyone went away immediately after the great fetes in May (completion of the Duomo); those who were residents (proud word for a homeless wanderer—to be "a resident" anywhere!), were left to themselves & such books as they had. For me, these have been a new edition of old Emerson—friend of my youth; always Tourguenieff; Matthew Arnold—poems, not prose. And you.—Imagine your beautiful book, then, read every evening, for a while, in the long bright twilight on my enchanting terrace which overlooks, I really believe, the most beautiful view in the world. I have a large Vienna rocking-chair, which is almost like a hammock; I swing in it, & read your book. Then, as night comes on, I put it aside & watch the great field of stars.—I have been particularly captivated by "In the Firelight."

Mr Boott—Francis—coming in one day this spring from his neighboring villa (where you paid a visit to Miss Greenough), saw the volume & instantly carried it off. He is a great admirer of yours. Bringing it back, he remarked that he should like to set one of the poems to music (he is a composer, you know,) if he could be sure that you "had not been carried off by the Germans!" Upon going further into the subject, I found that he, being a passionate admirer of Italian music, does not at all like the present rage for everything German. And he once set a poem of yours to music (I do not know whether it was "Through the Long Days"—a great favorite of mine; or "Violet"), & afterwards he saw that the same poem had been set by a German.[2] Why he fancies that you yourself preferred the German's arrangement, I do not know. But that has evidently been his idea. I told him I did not believe that you had anything to do with it; the German probably selected it himself. I went so far as to say that I did not believe you preferred the German arrangement, because nothing could be sweeter than the arrangement by Francis Boott.—I really think so—of both of those poems of yours which he has set to music; the "Long Days," & "Violet."

Mr Boott is now in the U.S. And I am to write to him whenever I have discovered whether or not "the Germans" have carried you off. Will you please reply, therefore, so that I may delay no longer to set him at ease. It is a subject—German & Italian music—to which he has given a good part of his life.

I am so sorry you & Mrs Hay are not coming to Italy. By Oct. 1st it will be lovely here; is it impossible? I want to show you my villa, or rather my apartment in a villa. The villa is ordinary; but the view extra-ordinary. At present it is hot, and I shall have to go to Switzerland for a few weeks. It is no hotter than we often have it at home; the difference is that here it is continuous, & goes right on, without change, for three months; & the nights are the same. It is like summer in Florida; "there's no outdoors." I get up at four every morning, & get my walk before half past five. At seven, we have to close up the house in the southern fashion, & so it remains until eight in the evening, when out-door life begins again under the splendid stars.

Meanwhile, I suppose you are at some cool green place in either Scotland or misty England. And I confess I envy you! To spend eight months of the year in Italy, & the other three in England, would be, I suppose, too much like heaven.

My best love to Mrs Hay. What can I say to waken in her a desire to see Italy again? Let me say, That old English lady, Miss Horner (author of "Walks in Florence") who devoted herself to Mrs Hay during a memorable evening when we visited the Stillmans, is now one of my particular friends, & as she lives near me, she would, I know, be delighted to come up every evening to see Mrs Hay again![3]—My pearl of a man-cook makes peculiarly delicious ice cream.—Also sirops of all sorts, which I imbibe daily.—All the pictures in the Pitti & Uffizi call you.—And the Italian sky.—And the view, the view!—Can't you decide to come?

Give my love to England. I love every inch of it.

The Lincoln is magnificent.

Always yours sincerely,
C. F. Woolson.

Please address as at head of letter. It is quite safe; if I am not here, they forward.

Notes

1. Hay did not publish *Poems* until 1890; Woolson could be referring to his earlier volumes, *Little Breeches* (1871) or *Pike County Ballads* (1871).

2. Another version of "Through the Long Days" had been composed by the Hungarian Francis Alexander Korbay (1846–1913). Woolson used this as a refrain throughout her story "Dorothy" (1892). Petry (100) surmises that "Violet" comes from Hay's poem "Words," which contains the phrase "When violets were springing."

3. Either Susan or Joanna Horner, authors of *Walks in Florence* (1873). See appendix for the Stillmans.

To Flora Stone Mather (Benedict/CFW, 47)

[1887?]

I have always wanted to stay at Fortress Monroe myself. Mother and I had a fine plan for seeing all that country—land and water—one October, on our way South. We began with Norfolk and it was so cold we had to leave and rush down to Charleston. The James, Yorktown, the Dismal Swamp, were all on our programme. I have an old schoolmate, Mrs Harrison (Gulie Gordon of Savannah) living in the old house at Harrison's Landing. Alas, le temps s'en va, le temps s'en va, ma belle, and I fear I shall never get there now. The quotation is from that new—old story of mine in the October Harper, which was written seven or eight years ago. I had forgotten all about it, and re-read it to see what was in it. I came upon "Le temp s'en va," and it has sung itself in my memory ever since.[1]

Notes

1. Benedict identifies the story as "At the Château of Corinne," which was published in *Harper's New Monthly Magazine* in Oct. 1887. The quotation from Pierre Ronsard translates as "time passes, time passes, my lady." "Gulie" is Benedict's spelling.

To Harriet Benedict Sherman (Benedict/CFW, 298–99)

Villa Brichieri
Bellosguardo
[1887]

I have now been house-keeping here since Jan. 1st, and it is an immense success in every way. . . . The villa has but two stories, and stands at the top of the steep hill of "Bellosguardo," as one comes up from Florence. The situation is unrivalled, for owing to its position it commands not only the "sweet Val d'Arno," as Ruskin calls it, but all Florence with its domes and towers, and range upon range of the Apennines beyond. Everywhere, when I raise my eyes from either drawing-room (there are two), dining-room, bedroom, dressing-room or writing-room, I see the most enchanting landscape spread out before me; mountains, hills, river, city, villages, old castles, towns, campaniles, olive groves, almond trees and all the thousand divine "bits" that make up Italian scenery.

My apartment has nine rooms besides kitchen and servants' quarters. I have the most excellent cook: a man. He is really a chef. Everything is served in the most tempting way. He learned his art in Paris. I pay him ten dollars a month, and am considered to pay a very high price. But I felt, living out here in the country, that it was important to have a good man-servant. He is over fifty, and as "handy" as a Yankee—mending everything that is broken or out of joint, and taking a great pride in having my house in perfect order.

Then I have an active little woman, Assunta; and the two form my force . . . All goes like clock-work, and I have no care at all. A few minutes in the evening I give to Angelo (the cook), and once a week I look over the accounts. Italian housekeeping is very easy—once you have learned it. . . . Once a week I am "at home"—as everyone is at Bellosguardo on that day. When it is pleasant, all of us here are overwhelmed with callers—for the view is one of the lions of Florence and every one drives up to see it. When it is not pleasant, we are let alone—or left alone. The other days I have to myself, and spend the morning in my little writing-room—which overhangs the Val d'Arno—and my afternoons rambling over these enchanting hills. You will see from all this that I am very happy here. I am indeed . . . happier than I have been for years—with this enchanting landscape and a home of my own.

To Jane Russell Averell Carter (Cornell)[1]

Villa Brichieri
12 Bellosguardo
Florence
Jan. 13th, [1888]

Dear Janie.

You perhaps have heard that I have been shut up for three months by a tedious lameness, brought on by the seated position at a writing table. This has thrown everything behind, and I am only just now beginning to take up the many broken threads of letters, visits, housekeeping duties,—to say nothing of literary engagements. This will explain my long delay in replying to your letter. I have now a standup desk, which is a great success. Hereafter I shall do all my writing standing. I am standing now—in my warm bright little writing-room, whose window commands the valley of the Arno for many miles, with the violet mountains all about. It is fortunate for me that I have always been able to stand. It never tires me as it tires so many. My lameness is now entirely gone, & I walk my five & six miles every day, with gratitude & renewed vitality.

I was very glad to hear from you again. I do not get as much Cooperstown news from Clara as you suppose. She says very little about Cooperstown at any time. She enjoyed her last summer's visit there; but her party was too large a one. I think it rather a pity she & Clare could not have been there by themselves. I was, however, delighted that Mrs G. A. Benedict—(Ma B.) saw the lake, & admired it so much. She is, & always was, one of the most charming women in the world, & I am greatly attached to her. Clara's letters now are describing the Xmas festivities at Cleveland; Clare & Kate Crowell are going to their first dances; & I am wondering how it seems to two such young persons as Clara & Mary Crowell to have daughters old enough to go out! Clare ~~writes~~ has written of Jennie's very pretty tea in New York the other day, & how very well Jennie & Grace looked. And how much she enjoyed her little visit with Grace in the tram.

I am very glad Mary is so well, & I wish I could see the little Anne Hyde. I ~~am~~ was relieved that you mentioned the baby's name. I feel defrauded & forgotten when I do'nt know the names of babies in whom I take an interest. Nobody has ever told me the name of Jennie's third child. Give my love to Mary.—What good news it is that Mrs Pell-Clark has recovered! Did Mrs Archie Pell come to Cooperstown after her return? I saw her several times last winter. I thought her heart was fixed upon spending this winter here. Her sister is to be here in a few days, & I dare say she will drive out here, as she is to visit a friend of mine. Of Mrs Gilliat I have heard nothing, so far. I asked Dr Baldwin (who hears of all the Americans) to look out for her. And the other day I asked Mrs McKibbin if she had met her. Mrs McK had her sisters from Dresden (whom you know, I believe) here for the holidays, & invited me to meet them. But I am only just getting well, &, so far, have declined all invitations. I take up your letter & see that it was the Consul at Munich, not Dresden, who married Miss Gilliat![2] And I—who assured Mrs McK that it was the Consul at Dresden! She was very much bewildered; she said he was such an old man!

About your pearls, I almost tremble, for I know nothing about pearls, &, for so large a sum, you ought to have something very nice. I literally never go into the shops here. All my clothes, &c, I buy when I go north, once a year. When I furnished my house, a year ago, I made the round of the linen & furniture stores; & bric-à-brac shops. But once done, that was the end. All the same, I will with pleasure do my best about the pearls, if you can give me until April or May. When does Mrs Major sail? If before that, you had better, ask Mrs Gilliat to buy them for you. If you can wait till then, let me know, please. I will ask some of my Italian friends to help me, &, before purchasing, I will have them valued by an expert. The weather has been abominable, & I seldom go to town. I take my long walks out here in the country. I have no carriage, you know. And I am such a coward that I send for a cab with fear & trembling. As the days grow longer, I shall be walking to town in the afternoons; then I could see about the pearls, if you like. My day is all laid out. I am not an early bird, you know; I always get up feeling a little tired. I breakfast at nine, & then, at ten, I begin to write, & write until two. Then a long walk, & home for tea at five. Dinner at 7½. Through all this horrible cold weather, my rooms have been delightfully warm; this is where my money goes! I keep ~~two~~ three fires (hearth) & the coke stoves going all the time, besides the kitchen-fire & the brasiers for the servants. It is the custom in Italy not to warm the houses, & I am considered either mad or idiotic. The great mistake about Italy is the idea that the climate is a warm one! In the winter Florence is frightfully cold. I remember you found it so, when you were here. The only good word I can say for it is that the cold does not last long; we have about two months of it. I am as much as ever in love with my magnificent views up here; & as much as ever amused with what I see of society. ~~here.~~ I do not see much, personally, as I do not go to dinners or evening receptions. But I hear a good deal. Once a week, I stay at home, & people drive out here; there are five other villas here besides mine, & they all receive on the same day. So now you have an abstract of my life. What you mean by saying you envy me, I cannot imagine. It almost seems as though you were indulging in satire. You have so much, in every way. And I so little. I do not allow myself to be sad, or lonely. But it is always an effort of firm will. I have quantities of acquaintances here. But if you think they are as dear to me as the old home friends, you are mistaken. I can live here for half the expense of a similar establishment at home. As soon as I can afford a cottage in Florida, I shall come flying back. I feel that I can no longer lead the wandering life I led for years before I came abroad; I must have a place of my own; my privacy; & good servants. Really—my writing depends upon it—because my health does. The servants here are treasures. So perfectly trained.

[Mescei?], I have heard nothing of. I will stop in there, later in the season, & inquire about Mary's casket. I have a commission for him also from Mary Smith; "Mary Ermina."[3]

Dr Baldwin says—yes—he did think Helen old. Or rather he thought her mind not properly balanced; she made much of unimportant things; & was apt to forget those of far more consequence. The Dr has a second son. And is well, & in greater demand than ever.—Clara says she hardy thinks Belle will come abroad at all. Belle never writes to me, so I do'nt know her plans. She would enjoy Italy if she could take it in the right way. But one can't import American, or even English, atmosphere here; if one is particular & strenuous about little things & details, one is soon exasperated half to death. You remember the Chadwicks? I have just had a letter from them, saying they are coming to Rome & should stop here. Gladstone is here, & lunched at the Villa Montanto (Hawthorne's villa,—the one he describes in the "Marble Faun") near here, the other day. The lady who was entertaining him, sent over wildly to borrow a Life of Hawthorne,—I suppose to read up about her own house before the Great Man arrived! Fortunately I had a "Life," & sent it to her with the leaf turned down at the place where the Villa Montanto is spoken of. Is'nt that English? It was Lady Hobart. The Miss Horners, who wrote "Walks in Florence," are so vexed that they never knew that Fenimore Cooper lived at Bellosguardo; they wd. have put it in their book. They—& all the English—call me always "Miss Fenimore Woolson," & I have at last ceased to explain that it is not my name! So if you ~~here~~ hear of me masquerading under that title, understand, please, that it is not my doing.

You do'nt know how haunted I am, sometimes, by the thought of poor Helen. Not that we were ever intimate; but we were together in Florence; & she was so fond of Florence. She would, I am sure, have been so happy here, if she could have taken a house & settled down—as I have done.

I watch the proceedings about the Clarke estate with great interest. (Freeman's Journal.)[4] To me Hyde Hall is the finest American country-place I know, save two or three I have seen at the South. It is quite as extensive—the grounds—& (with a few deer!) would be quite as pretty as many of the smaller estates in Warwickshire through whose parks I used to drive when I was staying in Leamington. It would be a melancholy thing for Cooperstown if that noble forest along the lake (Mt. Wellington) should be cut down. It is the feature of that end of the lake. If the land about the Hall is diminished, I shall almost feel~~s~~ like shedding a few tears! I do'nt know that there is the slightest talk of diminishing it. I am far away, & know only what I see in the paper. Give my love to Averell,—my godson. I have never sent him my books. But I shall do so some day. When the new editions of "Castle Nowhere" & "Rodman" come out (the late editions were brought out without my revision), I shall then send him the five volumes, bound in nice form. Perhaps by that time there will be a new volume!

Clara comes once before long—as you know. I am waiting to hear when she will be here so that I can take the ground-floor of this house. My apartment at present is only large enough for one. True—there are two large drawingrooms, & other vacant rooms. But they are not suited for bedrooms. Goodby—with much love to you all. My best love to the Coopers, Mrs Turner & Jennie R., & the Keeses. Write whenever you can & without waiting for me; it is a very great pleasure to hear from you, & now with so many dangers hanging over me about pen-work, my letters much to my regret, must be fewer than ever. But I myself am not at all changed—in spite of my long silences; I am always the same old friend & yours most affectionately,

C.F.W.

Notes

1. The name references in this letter are to Jane Russell Averell Carter's children: (Lawson) Averell, (Anna) Grace, Jane (Jennie) Carter Brown, and Mary Carter Clarke. Anne Hyde is Mary's daughter. Belle is probably Arabella Carter Washburn. Averell Carter's wife was named Helen, but it is unlikely that this is the Helen that Woolson names.

2. The American Consul in Munich was Edward W. Mealey.

3. The reference is confusing because it does not appear that anyone has died. These women may be pre-ordering coffins from an Italian coffin maker. The tone of this letter makes it unlikely that the coffin was for Jane Carter (Mary Clarke's mother), who died shortly thereafter (see letter to Mary Clarke dated Feb. 28, 1888).

4. *The Freeman's Journal* was a Cooperstown newspaper. It was reporting on the financial problems in the Clarke family and the purchase of Hyde Hall and 3,000 acres of surrounding property by George Hyde Clarke (1858) and his wife, Mary Gayle Carter Clarke.

To Samuel Mather (WRHS/Mather)

Villa Brichieri
12 Bellosguardo. Florence
Jan. 22^d^, [1888]

Dear Sam.

I received yesterday, your note with draft enclosed; for which, thanks. After I had written you, I got your letter saying that you had just put the G. Rapids's interest in the Savings Bank to my credit. I realized then, when too late, what a bother I was making you! I am very sorry about it. When a man makes Arabian Nights's investments for his aunt, he ought to be spared such small details. After this I will write directly to the Bank, at the dates when I think the interest has been paid in. This interest money from all the bonds—amounting now, thanks to you & Grand Rapids, to \$480.^{00}, I shall always spend; it is income. (I am awfully teased, by the way, that it is not \$500.^{00} exactly. I shall save up enough to add the lacking 20 dollars, & send it to you to invest in Eldorado for for me.[1] Now how much must I send to give me \$20.^{00} per annum interest?) You must attribute my thoughtlessness, dear Sam, to the state I was reduced to by my long three months of complete helplessness. Everything, of course, fell hopelessly behind—whether the housekeeping arrangements for the winter, my literary work, my letters, or whatever it might be. I was well taken care of, & comfortable in one way; but very unhappy in the forced idleness & lack of all exercise. Now I am well again, & take my long walks as of old. I do all my writing at a stand-up desk; & am hoping (& praying) that it is going to work ~~work~~ well.

I have had a little news about Cleveland, lately, from Clara. But not half as much as I want. I suppose she thinks she can tell me all, at length, when she sees me. I am wondering when you & Flora are coming over again? (You & Flora like Italy; I hold to that[)].

But Italy has been abominably cold this winter. My house is warm; but almost no other house is! Gladstone is here, & lunched at Hawthorne's villa, near here, the other day. The lady who was to entertain him, sent over wildly the evening before to see if I had a "Life" of Hawthorne. I suppose she wanted to read up about her own villa? before the Great Man came. Fortunately I had a Life; I sent it to her with the Bellosguardo leaf carefully turned down—to aid her in her studies. Of course she is English.

Tell Flora that Mrs Hodgson Burnett is here. I thought of Flora's description of her. It was a most true one. Mrs B. has been up to see me several times, & her manner to me is excellent. Friendly, & sensible, & companionable. But there is another side to her; she has a great desire, I fancy, to be thought young & handsome. In reality she cannot be far from my age, I suppose. But in her feelings about herself, she might be my daughter; or niece. This is all right, if it amuses her. She gives me a sad account of her health. My (comparatively) small trouble of lameness, sinks into nothingness beside the terrible nervous prostration she describes; she has to go to bed & stay there for six months; when she wishes to say one word, she says another; for instance if she means "tea," she may possibly say "chair." &c. This state comes on after each book. Did'nt you like her "Fauntleroy?" I thought it the prettiest little idyll I have seen for a long time. What does Burnett represent—do you know? I mean her husband.

What are you reading now? I have just finished Cabot's Life of Emerson.[2] Emerson, you know, is one of my gods. Tourgenieff is another, & I am very happy in at last obtaining a good photograph of him—which Mr Boott most kindly sent me from Paris the other day. This has enabled me to carry out a long cherished design of putting my pretty edition of his works (a present from Harry James) in a little shelf by themselves, with the photograph over them. You would not believe—without seeing it—the satisfaction this has given me! I think Howells is losing his mind about Tolstoi. If you read "The Study," (Harper's), you will understand what I mean. I do'nt know that Col. Hay ever said anything more delicious to me, than the closing sentence of his last letter (from London) "How wild our good Howells is growing in his Tolstoi mania! I like Tolstoi; but when I see a friend preferring him to Tourgenieff, I feel like ordering him measured for a straight jacket!"—All of which I echo. I have all of Tolstoi's books. But he cannot compare with Tourgneneiff. Then the funny thing is that Howells apparently believes that Tolstoi really practices what he preaches! The truth is—as I happen to know directly from Russia—that Tolstoi has never given up one penny of his large inherited fortune. It pleases him to dress in a peasant's clothes; to plough & reap; to make shoes in his drawing room in the evening. But his farm-work is so badly done that the farm-servants invariably do it all over after he has gone; & his shoes never hold together! His children either laugh at him, or become alienated from their home. "Les ideés de papa," are the despair of his sons, two of whom have left him, & vowed never to return. For my part, the fact that he he has held on to all his fortune stamps him—with his constant communistic preaching about "Give all; all!" as either a hypocrite, or a madman.[3] He is probably the latter.

The sun is setting as I write, & the whole valley of the Arno is the color of gold. Oh, Sam—it is so beautiful—this view! What a constant joy, & comfort it is to your rather lonely aunt, she cannot on paper express. You will have to come over—you & Flora & my two grandnephews—& see it for yourselves.

Our two Queens amuse themselves by calling upon each other, & having each other to dinner. The Queen of Wurtemberg, & the handsome Queen of Servia. Victoria is coming on Feb. 1st. She wishes to see the new façade of the Duomo, I am told. It is a great success—that façade. I take my long walks to town now, as the country roads are muddy—& generally manage to take in the Duomo. I like to pass under Giotto's campanile's when its deep musical bell is pealing out the Angelus. Then I ~~pass~~ go in one door of the Duomo, cross its vastness, & emerge under the new façade. This takes the common-ness from the day. Not that one's days are often "common" in Italy. But when I go to town—being a housekeeper—I sometimes have to buy buttons! (I hate shopping, you see, as much as ever.). My best love to Flora & the little boys. And to your Father & Mother, Kate & Will. My best regards to Mrs Stone. I am going to have a horribly busy year, & shall not be able to write to you often. But I shall hope you will understand the causes of my silence; I am pretty well now but I am not growing younger! Write as often as you can, & tell me all about you & yours. And all the news about everybody. What are the latest legends about Jennie Chamberlain? How is Bob, of that name? Is Ida Weber a great beauty? How is Julia Parsons? Did the Marquette Fay really discover a gold mine? Is your Father going to Florida? Where are you, politically? Blaine?[4] My complimentary copies of papers are all for Grover Cleveland! Just as my complimentary copies of Sunday papers are all Unitarian or Congregationalist! My own Church, & political party, leave me well alone![5]

Goodby.

Affec,
C.F.W.

Notes

1. Woolson is referring to mythical City of Gold, El Dorado, because of the investment returns Mather achieved with money from the sale of her Wisconsin property. The double "for" is Woolson's.

2. James Elliot Cabot (1821–1903), Emerson's literary executor and authorized biographer, published his *Life* in 1887.

3. les ideés de papa: papa's ideas. The double "he" is Woolson's.

4. Woolson is referring to various friends from Cleveland, and Grover Cleveland's Republican opponent, James G. Blaine (1830–93), in the 1884 election.

5. Woolson was Episcopal and Republican.

To Mary Gayle Carter Clarke (Cornell)[1]

Villa Brichieri
12 Bellosguardo
Florence
Feb. 28th, [1888]

Dear Mary.

A letter from Clara tells me of your great loss.

I know the grief you must be feeling. The loss of a mother is a sorrow quite by itself, I think; all the memories of childhood come back, and bring with them a peculiar desolation—a desolation in the thought that the mother, the "mamma," who has seemed such a fixed [part] of one's existence, has gone from this life forever.

In this grief of yours, I send you, my dear Mary, my heartfelt sympathy. It is sad that we can do no more for those we care for, in the hour of their suffering.

I had a letter from your mother not long ago. In it she spoke so cheerfully of you, as "looking better than she has looked for a very long time." And she gave me a description of your little [Ann] in words that showed [that] the child was very dear to her.[2] I heard of you, in a letter from Mrs Turner, as staying at Holt-Averell, with Mr Clark, during [the] holidays. Those last days with your mother must be precious memories to you now. Clara told me of your journey through the storm to New York. I too once made one of those dreadful journeys,—only I arrived too late.[3] I am thankful that you did not.

Her last letter seem[s] to me to breathe a happier spirit than any letter I have had from her since we parted in London. I noticed it when I read it; and I have thought of it many [times] since.

Personally I have lost one of my oldest and best friends; one who was associated with some of the pleasantest years of my life, as well as with some of the saddest. It makes me very melancholy—; for myself, not for her.

Write to me when you have leisure. You never sent me the photograph you promised. Give my best regards to Mr Clark, whom [I hope] some day to know.[4]

With love, yours affectionately,
C. F. Woolson.

Notes

1. Portions of the edges are torn from this letter. Words that are obscured are in brackets.
2. Mary's daughter Anne Hyde Clarke.
3. Woolson's father died before she reached him.
4. Mary's husband, George Hyde Clarke (1858).

To Samuel Mather (WRHS/Mather)

Villa Brichieri
12 Bellosguardo. Florence
Aug. 22^{d}, [1888?]

Dear Sam.

The cheque has reached me safely, & I am much obliged to you. May the day dawn, sometime, when I can invest more money, & draw more interest—as good as this!

I can write but a few lines. By & by, I shall gush out with letters. I want to write to your father, to whom I send my very best love; and to you—in answer to your delightful letter from Florida last Spring. In fact to all of you. Yours and Flora's letters I always enjoy so much.

I am spending the summer here—as you see. It is one of the consequences of having a house, that you must stay in it! In reality, however, I am staying because too busy to get away. It has been, fortunately for me, a cool summer. We get the edge of the cold & rains which have darkened England, Switzerland, & Germany this season, & the edge tempers our heat. Perhaps you will be interested in hearing how I arrange life! I am called at 4 $^{1/2}$ a.m. I take a cup of tea, & go out to walk at 5. Come in at 6, or soon after. Bath; breakfast; cool linen attire. Then my stand~~ing~~up-desk, where I remain until 7 p.m. with half an hour's rest at noon. The whole house, after having been thrown open at dawn, is hermetically closed about 8; windows, blinds, inside shutters. Only one little ray of light is allowed to enter, & this illumines my desk. In this way, while it may be 90° outside, we can keep it at 74–76 within. At seven, dinner; the house is thrown open again; & the evening is spent on my high-up terrace, under the splendid stars, & overlooking the wide view.

It is a regret not to be able to be with Clara & Clare—who, after an ecstatic ten days at Bayreuth, are now at green, pretty Baden-Baden. But I <u>must</u> finish my story, which is due in New York in October (I suppose it will begin in Harper's Maga. in Jan.); & the Claras have promised to spend part of the winter with me—to make up.[1]

Though I cannot write letters, I can read them. In my long warm solitude, they cheer me. I have'nt heard half enough, lately, about the 2 little boys. My love to Flora;

I hope she is well? If you—you & she—wish to do me a kindness, you will send me, now & then, an American novel; those that are talked about. After you have read them yourselves, charitably forward to me. I get—sent by various friends—all the English & French novels. But the American are hard to find here. I do'nt want to fall behind the literature of my own land,—especially as I expect to return there. All the magazines are sent to me.

If the Hays are in Cleveland, give them my love. I read the "Lincoln" with the most profound interest, every month. Everyone I know is reading it; &, as long as people remained in Florence, it was always a subject of conversation here on my "day"—after each fresh instalment. There are a good many Americans living in Florence; quiet people whose principal occupation is to read.

A blessed rain is sweeping up from Pisa. I watch its gradual darkening over the great valley.

"Paolina!—Angelo! chiudete le finestre!"[2] And the cook runs, in his long white apron, & fat, Paolina hurries—to close my 20 windows. For it is 7 a.m. & the house open.

Affectionately,
C.F.W.

Notes

1. *Harper's New Monthly Magazine* serialized *Jupiter Lights* (1889) from Jan. to Sept. 1889. If this letter were written in 1888, as internal evidence suggests, Woolson may be referring to "At the Château of Corinne" published in Oct. 1887 or one of three pieces published in 1888: "Neptune's Shore" (Oct.), "A Pink Villa" (Nov.), "The Front Yard" (Dec.).

2. chiudete le finestre: close the windows. Angelo, Woolson's cook, and Paolina, presumably another servant, who have come to close her windows against the heat of day.

To Mary Mapes Dodge (Princeton)

(Villa Brichieri
12 Bellosguardo
Florence. Italy)
Geneva
Sept. 13th, [1888?]

Dear Mrs Dodge.

I am very much pleased to be asked, by you, to write a tale for "St Nicholas." I think I have been a little jealous all these years of you, of Miss Alcott, of Sarah Woolsey, & now, lately, of Mrs Burnett,—because all of my life—long before I began to write—I have been a teller of stories to children.[1] Endless stories; stories that went on for months & years,—oral serials. One of my nephews, a man six feet high, with a black beard, re-told to me one of my serials (in outline) at Sorrento, some years ago, so that his young bride could also hear it! And now there is a little grand-nephew (who is also John Hay's nephew), waiting for me to come home, & begin again.

My feathers, therefore, are nicely smoothed down by your letter. And if I ever write a story for children (or young people), I shall certainly offer it to you.

I cannot at present write the tale you suggest—much as I should really like to because I have not a moment of time. I use the word "moment" literally; the slowest of writers,—forbidden to use my eyes at night,—& endlessly walking & loafing in the open air by day, you will see that I can only accomplish a small amount of work. And all I can accomplish (for the present) is promised. ~~Early~~ This summer, while still at Bellosguardo, I tried getting up very early & taking my long walk at four a.m. But it did not do. I am wedded to the afternoon lights, & the sunset hours—which are in Italy what you know,—do'nt you? Of course your Italy is to me extremely beautiful, & I have made a temporary home for myself in a villa (Aurora Leigh's) at Bellosguardo, near Florence. Are'nt you coming over soon? I invite you to dinner now; I have a wonderful cook,—"Angelo"—a real chef—& for ten dollars a month!—My dream is to come home & live in Florida in the winter; in dear little Cooperstown in the summer. But it would take four times the money that it takes to live here.

I wish you would give my best regards to Mr Gilder. He does not know how ~~I~~ greatly I love & enjoy the Century—which he is so good to send me. I feel almost ashamed to be so indebted;—but it is such a delight to me. And I wish there was something I could do for him—& for you—in Italy. Is'nt there something?—

I have just written Mr Drake. Pete Trone's name was never Peter; do correct it wo'nt you?[2]—My love to the Stedmans.

Cordially your friend,
C. F. Woolson.

Notes

1. See appendix for Frances Hodgson Burnett and Louisa May Alcott. Sarah Woolsey (1835?–1905) was the pseudonym of Sarah Coolidge, author of the Katy books for girls.

2. Pete Trone was Woolson's childhood dog. *St. Nicolas Magazine,* ed. by Mary Mapes Dodge, often featured articles on dogs.

To Mrs. McKibben (Virginia)[1]

Villa Brichieri
12 Bellosguardo
Thursday
[1888?]

Dear Mrs McKibbin.

I regret so much that I was not able to see you when you so kindly called. I came back from Switzerland ill; & am still very awkwardly lame. I hope soon to be better; & shall then come to see you. I suppose you are here for the winter, as you said you were coming the last time I saw you. Would that my sister were here also! But she is engrossed with German opera in New York just now, & her letters are Wagnerian. She sails, with Clare, in the early spring; & then, probably, will remain abroad several years. Pray come up whenever you can. With my regards to Mr McKibbin, I am yours, very truly,

C. Fenimore Woolson.

Notes

1. The McKibbens are unidentified.

To John Hay (Brown)

Villa Brichieri
12 Bellosguardo
Florence. Italy
Jan. 10th, [1889]

Dear Col. Hay.

Mr Boott is not sure that Ditson sent you "When the boys come home"; so he sends me a copy to forward to you.[1] (It goes by the same post as this.) You will see your words; his music; & my name!—

I suppose you have heard of his great loss and sorrow; his only child, Mrs Duveneck, died in Paris last March. She is buried here in Florence; but he & Duveneck have taken her little boy home to live with his aunt, Mrs Lyman of Boston. Mr Boott has broken up his Bellosguardo home of forty years. I miss them all very much.

I hope—and believe—that you are all well and happy. My best love to Mrs Hay. In haste—& wishing that I could see you instead of scratching these six lines—I am always, your attached friend,

F. Woolson.

Notes

1. Boston music publisher Oliver Ditson published Boott's musical score of Hay's poem "When the Boys Come Home" (1864).

To William Wilberforce Baldwin (Morgan)[1]

Dear Doctor.

Miss Greenough tells me that your lawyer is also the lawyer of Mrs Bracken the elder. Will you please send me his name & address, & tell me, also, whether he understands English. I am paying for a nurse for old Ansarro, Mrs Bracken's man-servant; but I think it probable that the Brackens would wish to do this themselves if they knew how ill the old man was. Mrs Bracken's affairs are, I believe, ~~now~~ in the charge of her sister, who lives in England; this lawyer will probably know the sister's address—which I do not know. If you will kindly reply, my man will call for your note early (very early) ~~tomorrow~~ Saturday morning, when he goes to town. I forgot to ask you this, (as I intended to do) last evening. I really think I am better; just as you said I should be!

With regards,
C. F. Woolson.

Notes

1. No date appears on this letter and no envelope survives. It and the Baldwin letters that follow were likely written in Feb. 1889 when Woolson was entertaining at Bellosguardo with her sister Clara.

To William Wilberforce Baldwin (Morgan)[1]

Villa Brichieri
12 Bellosguardo
Wednesday evening
[1889]

Dear Dr Baldwin.

I hope you will dine with us on Sunday, very informally; at seven. Mrs Thompson & Lanse are to be here; no one else. Will you please let me know? Thanks for the superb orange. Clara admires your house beyond any she has yet seen in Florence.

In haste, as ever, your friend,

C. F. Woolson.

Notes

1. Written on envelope: "This note has been delayed a day. My cook will now call for the reply on Sunday a.m. early."

To William Wilberforce Baldwin (Morgan)

Villa Brichieri
Friday evening
[1889?]

Dear Dr Baldwin.

As I do not know Mr Powers' address, may I ask you to say to him that I shall be very happy to see him on Sunday afternoon, at any time between half-past five and eight,—as I am dining late at present.

The lady who introduces him, is one of my oldest and best friends, and I shall be delighted to have news of her.

With regards, yours ever,
C. F. Woolson.

To William Wilberforce Baldwin (Morgan)

Villa Brichieri,
12 Bellosguardo
Saturday
[1889]

Dear Dr Baldwin.

I have just received Mrs Baldwin's regret. And I "regret" extremely that we cannot hope for her presence at our tea. She seemed so well, and she looked so very handsome, the day we called, that we have been counting upon her as one of our best ornaments. So many of one's friends, looked at artistically, are not ornaments!

But you must not fail us. I shall not forgive you if you do; What! The first time I open my house, my best friend in Florence stays away?

Though our cards say from "three to seven," we shall be delighted if people will stay longer; as long as they like. So find a moment among your engagements, and look in upon us even if but for half an hour. It is only an afternoon-tea; that is all. The dancing will be in bonnets & jackets;—it will be confined to the Billiardroom downstairs. I shall be quietly in my own drawing room above.

Now please come; even if as late as seven o'clock.

In haste, your friend,
C. F. Woolson.

To William Wilberforce Baldwin (Morgan)

Villa Brichieri
12 Bellosguardo
Saturday evening
[1889]

Dear Doctor Baldwin.

My sister would like, if possible, to see the Flower-Corso tomorrow afternoon. She desires me to ask whether you could come here in the morning? She will be in readiness at any hour between nine and three. I believe the Corso does not begin until five? In haste, cordially yours,

C. F. Woolson.

To Samuel Mather (WRHS/Mather)

Villa Brichieri
12 Bellosguardo
Feb. 27th, [1889]

My dear Sam.

I sent you a message in one of Clara's letters, saying that the cheque had come safely, & that I was much obliged. And I also sent thanks for the books. But both of these were meagre acknowledgments. I now write to say that I was delighted to be remembered regarding the books. I thought it most kind of you; &, most of them, I had especially wished to see. When I asked you, I did not mean new books, exactly; I imagined you & Flora as buying the new novels of the day, often in paper covers,—just as we used to buy them at Cheerful Corner. My idea was that when you had read them, you might send some of them to me. I do'nt suppose you care to hear—at length—what I think of them. It is dangerous to ask a writer of novels about novels! He may swamp you with the ocean of his words. The truth is, that, to a writer, the subject is so vast,—really his whole life's interest—that if he is to tell you what he really thinks, he will almost never get through. He can go on for days. This is the reason, I think, why writers like to be with writers, painters with painters, & so on; the subject of their art is to them really inexhaustible, & they never tire of it. But others do! All this is apropos of your asking me my opinion of "Robert Elsmere."[1]—You will notice that I abstain from giving it! I will merely say that to me there is nothing the least new in it, from cover to cover. It is but Matthew Arnold's opinions, a little widened. I have read (~~yes~~ several years ago) every word M. Arnold has written. I am so very fond of his poetry, that I thought I would try his prose. I did not like it much. His exquisite style goes with him everywhere, & his delicate humor. But he did'nt know himself, exactly, where he stood. "Robert Elsmere" is well done ~~as~~ in a literary way, I think. But probably that is not what you were thinking about. If you and Flora will come over here, I will talk books with you by the ~~hour~~ hour—before my Bellosguardo fire on my Tuscan hilltop.

I was glad to hear about your Xmas; and that you are all well. Can it be possible that the baby goes to school? It seems incredible that he is old enough. I have hardly got used to the fact that Livingston is old enough to go.

I always hold on to you & Flora being fond of Italy. All my other relatives and old friends prefer Germany. Clara & Clare are enjoying their stay here, after a fashion, I think. They find the house—especially their own rooms—warm & comfortable, & they appreciate the skill of my cook—who is a real chef. They are amused, too, with the society here. But I fear the rest passes unseen; they dream of Vienna & the opera; & the blue mountains and soft blue skies here cannot compensate them for the absence of Wagner. At least such is my idea. It is natural, of course, that I, who cannot hear, should care so much for what I can see. I sometimes wonder—as I look from my north windows & see the blue Apennines, range upon range, and from my south windows and see the fair valley of the Arno dotted with villages & overhung with castles & old towers on the spurs of the hills—I sometimes wonder how I shall feel if shut up again in a street. A wide space of air & sky,—a beautiful view—both have grown so dear to me—cut off as I am from so much else. Last Saturday, Clara & I gave thé-dansant.[2] In reality Clara gave it, but of course my name was on the cards of invitation with hers. The large brilliant room downstairs was turned into a ballroom; it is a beautifully proportioned room with vaulted ceiling, & the elaborate frescoing—though old—is in good taste, & clean. We had a white dancing-carpet put down, & all the doors & windows draped in fresh white. Palm trees in the four corners; & the immense old fire-place filled with magnificent flowers, & the long mantelpiece banked with roses. Then we had a large central chandelier of crystal & four gilt columns supporting candelabra, besides side lights. 200 wax candles in all. In one corner were the musicians (excellent) concealed by shrubbery. This room was darkened & ~~lightened~~ lighted from the beginning. The rest of the house was only lighted at five & a half. We had five large rooms open, besides; one containing the Buffet, which was supplied by the best man here, Doney.[3] My own salon upstairs was also filled with flowers, & lighted with wax candles. We had one hundred and fifty people; they began coming at three; and about forty stayed & danced until eleven,—though the hours on the cards were "three to seven." Of course we asked them to stay. We could not attempt a regular evening party so far in the country. So we did this. Clare, in a beautiful Vienna dress of the palest green, danced constantly, & looked very sweet, & shyly happy. Clara wore an elegant dress of satin, lace, & fur, also made in Vienna. She herself danced all the evening. We had any number of Countesses & Counts & Marquises &c. Titles abound, you know, in Italy. But it is useless for any of them to run after Clare. Clara wants her to go out a little; but she has no ~~interest~~ wish to have her marry over here.

You do not speak of Florida; so I suppose none of you are going down this year? Your letter from the Ponce de Leon, I still keep as a memento—much as I dislike to think of the "improvements" that have changed my dear sleepy old town. I wonder if I shall ever see it again! Mr Washington still keeps it up; almost every week I get some reminder from him. The best reminder just now is his son Harry, who is spending some days in Florence after a long stay in Greece. He tells me that all the orange-trees at East Angels are growing finely, & will be in full bearing in two years more. Yes, there is no doubt, Sam, that I take solid comfort in you. In this very Ponce de Leon letter, you say "If it were only situated near the Fort & the sea!" That is just what I should have said. I am afraid—I am afraid it is a good deal spoiled down there. I do'nt believe my "unknown river" is unknown any longer. (You have probably forgotten a very early article of mine of that name.)[4] But Mr Washington writes that his place, "Bella Vista" (to which "East Angels" belongs) is really the wildest part of the coast, now. It is 20 miles south of St A., & below the southern inlet of the Matanzas river; & directly on the ocean. How like the ~~stories~~ story of Aladdin's Lamp is the wealth of the Standard Oil Company—who supply the world with lamps of a more prosaic description. Mr Flagler as you describe him—giving away horses & yachts—why does'nt he give me "East Angels"? And this reminds me: if you ever see Mr Ryder the photographer, will you make some pleasant speech to him about his letter to me. Say that I received it, & that I am pleased to have been so honorably remembered. He wrote to me, saying that he had done a large crayon portrait of me (from the Harper picture) for the Centennial Exposition at Columbus last September.[5] I have not time to write to him now.—You never told me (I have put in a new quill. I am ordered to use quills, as steel pens are said to act, after a time, on the nerves of the arm.) whether you went to the Indian River, & how you liked it. Some one has written us that Col. Payne is down there with a yacht this winter & that Mel Hanna is with him.

Someone also wrote that you & Flora were to give a beautiful musicale. I should like to hear about it.

Where is Jennie Chamberlain now? Was Will Chamberlain divorced from his wife & Molly C. from her husband, or not?

I go back again to your St. A. letter. I can't defend the South. All you say of it is perfectly true. My case was a peculiar one. I was so wearied out with care that the absolute tranquility and sleepiness of St A. (as it was then) & of the whole South, was like balm to me. I consider that my dear Father died of care. And I was sore with the pressure of anxieties. To come suddenly to a place where business did not exist, where no one spoke of it,—was to me just then like Paradise. I dare say all that is altered. The whole South, Florida included, has waked up since then. And probably I should hear business talk in plenty now in the halls & parlors of the Ponce de Leon Hotel. You wo'nt understand this. But you would if you were a woman, & had been through the cares that I have been through.

In speak of Tolstoi. I do not think Tolstoi is insincere. But I think him insane; in a mild form. His 16 children leave him, one by one, as soon as they are old enough. They cannot stand "les idées de papa."[6] His farm-hands have to do over again all the work he does on the farm; & the shoes he makes no one can wear. Even if they could, why should he take the bread from some poor shoemaker's mouth? He had better employ his ~~educ~~ education & talents in a way suited to them, I think.

My best love to Flora. And kisses for the little boys. Tell Targer that I hope to write to her before very long. I am very busy with proofsheets. In fact I am excessively busy all the time—with writing & the house-keeping.

What a delightful thing was that yachting trip of yours last summer! Kate described it in one of her letters. Times change! Flora Payne & I used to think it great fun to take my row-boat at the Foundry, & row up the Cuyahoga River, & have tea on the bank somewhere. It was really coffee—not tea; we used to take our provisions with us. Now she is entertaining grandly in Washington; & I live on a Tuscan hill!

I am glad you liked the opening of Jupiter Lights. It is different from my other stories, because shorter, & full of action, with almost no description. All the South Carolina incidents (in the 2^{d} N^{o}.) are from life. There is—farther on, an account of a Fourth of July celebration, which is exactly like those we used to have in Cleveland before you were born. Principally fire-engines! The old-fashioned kind before ~~the~~ steam was used.

There is excitement here before a project of "improving" the old part of Florence. That means tearing down the most picturesque parts & replacing the ancient towers & palaces with new modern blocks. Ouidà has been writing eloquently to the London Times about it. For once I agree with her.

My best love to your father & mother. And my regards to Mrs Stone. Is little Miss Pointer glad to be at home again? She struck me as so homesick, last winter. Her friend Miss Alcock, with Mr Alevely, came to our tea. I never see any Clevelanders. Apparently they do not come to Florence.—Who is the minister to Italy? And to England? Colonel Hay? You had better take one of the foreign posts yourself.

Affectionly yours,
C. F. Woolson.

Notes

1. An 1888 novel by Mary Augusta (Mrs Humphrey) Ward.
2. thé-dansant: late afternoon gathering with tea and dancing
3. Doney was known as one of the best caterers in Florence.
4. Woolson published "A Voyage to the Unknown River" in *Appletons' Journal,* May 16, 1874.
5. The Columbus, Ohio, Exposition was held in 1888. The illustration of Woolson done by photographer James Ryder was taken from the photo that accompanied an installment of *East Angels* in *Harper's New Monthly Magazine,* March 1886.
6. les idées de papa: papa's ideas. Tolstoy had only thirteen children. The error in the first sentence of this paragraph is Woolson's.

To William Wilberforce Baldwin (Morgan)[1]

Sunday
April 6th, [1889?]

Dear Doctor,

The two children of the gardiner (whose rooms adjoin my sister's, downstairs) are ill. As it may be fever, will you please come up to-day and look at (& prescribe) for them? I cannot be content until I know what is the matter.

In haste, as ever cordially
Yours C.F.W.

Notes

1. Apr. 6 was on a Saturday in 1889; however, 1890, when Apr. 6 was on a Sunday, is unlikely because Woolson was in Egypt. "Gardiner" is Woolson's spelling.

To Mrs William Wilberforce Baldwin (Morgan)

Villa Brichieri
12 Bellosguardo
April 15th, [1889]

Dear Mrs Baldwin.

Next Sunday (Easter) is my last reception day for that season; if you should happen to be drifting, do look in upon us. The Doctor too, if possible. But I suppose that is impossible; I must wait until a less busy season.

Cordially yours,
C. F. Woolson.

To Daniel Willard Fiske (Cornell)

Villa Brichieri
12 Bellosguardo
May 13th, [1889]

Dear Professor Fiske.

From day to day, I have hoped to tell you that my niece was here, and that I should be so glad to bring her (and myself) to see your library. But she lingers in Paris! She now promises to arrive early next week. I will let you know when she comes, and as she remains a month, you can select your own time for our call upon you, among your treasures—which I long again to see—perhaps for the last time—if you really go to Egypt—happy man! I will bring the photographs when I come. I have looked them over twenty times, with admiration & envy. If I could but go!—With my love to your Mother, I am as ever, your friend,

C. F. Woolson.

To Daniel Willard Fiske (Cornell)

Villa Brichieri
12 Bellosguardo
May 21st, [1889]

Dear Prof. Fiske.

My niece has come. On Thursday, between four & five, I hope to bring her to call upon Mrs Fiske, who, however, must not stay at home for us, if she has another engagement; we will take our chances of finding her, and, if we miss her, we will come again some other time. We are to be at Mme Villari's at five. Is it absolutely useless to ask you to dinner? Wo'nt you really come some day next week? It would give me so much pleasure.

Cordially yours,
C. F. Woolson.

We will come to your Library any afternoon you may appoint, after Thursday next.

To William Wilberforce Baldwin (Morgan)

Villa Brichieri
12 Bellosguardo
June 9th, [1889]

Dear Doctor.

I enclose 740 francs; will you please let me know that it reaches you safely?

Come in whenever you can.

Cordially yours,
C. F. Woolson.

To Katharine Livingston Mather (Benedict/CFW, 305–7)

Villa Brichieri
Bellosguardo. Florence
1889

. . . I suppose to the last moment of my life I shall never be able to hurry one line of my literary work—no matter how much I should like to do so. No matter how hot it is, nor how many mosquitoes, that must still move with the same absolute slowness and regularity.... What a long sigh I shall give when the last line has gone. After I finish the proof, I shall do a little in the way of preparing the house for the people who will be coming to tramp through it, day by day, sent by the Brichieris, who will pull every wire to rent it again. . . . All the Boott and Duveneck things have departed—except Mrs Browning's chair, which Duveneck has presented to me. . . . Duveneck . . . urges my going to Paris, and promises to do everything if I come. Miss Poynter wants me to go to Tours with her and see all the old Châteaux. I much wish to see Chartres, Rouen and Amiens, and also Rheims and Laon; also the "Church of Brou"—Matthew Arnold's—at Bourg.[1] I have always been trying to get there from Geneva, but have never accomplished it. . . .

Miss Greenough is feeble. Her 80th birthday came on the 22d. Her cook, whose name is Angelo like that of mine, died suddenly of heart failure last week, and Mary H. was much distressed lest Miss Greenough should find it out.[2] Especially when, according to Italian custom, the confraternity came with torches to take him away. But all passed off safely; they set the clock forward, had dinner earlier, and brought in lamps earlier, so that the light within the house kept her from seeing the glare of the torches outside. Then to keep her from hearing the tramp of feet, Mary H. talked and talked. She told me the next day that she had never talked so steadily in her life! . . . However, all went safely, and poor Angelo was carried away, covered with flowers, and followed by all the cooks of Florence, carrying torches, with a big banner. . . .

It is tiresome weather now. I shall be glad of a change. I went out and looked at the lunch table to-day, and felt, suddenly, that I could eat nothing. I sent for Angelo, and came back to the writing-room. Presently Angelo appeared.

"Angelo, I don't like those things I ordered for lunch, and I do'nt know what I do want. You must think of something yourself. When it is ready, Paolina can call me."

"Oui, Mademoiselle." He disappears.

In twenty minutes I am called. To the dining-room I go, and find the whole table freshly set, and a completely fresh lunch, freshly cooked, of three courses and a sweet, beautifully served.

Such is the advantage of having a real "cook"—one who knows his art. I am never so "fussy" except when I am tired. . . . But I must stop now and go back to "Jupiter." . . .

Notes

1. Matthew Arnold published "The Church of Brou" in 1853.
2. Probably Mary Huntington.

To Unknown recipient (Benedict/CFW, 273)

[1889?]

Certainly there is nothing like Venice in June. There is a sea-breeze all the time; always the fishing boats with their coloured sails, floating to and fro; the pictures in the churches and galleries are deliciously rich and beautiful; and the motion of the gondola is indescribably soothing to any one who is sad or tired. . . .

To Unknown recipient (Benedict/CFW, 402)

[1889?]

I have one evening caller—Horatio Brown. . . . He lives here with his mother, and is engaged in deciphering the Venetian Archives. Also he has written a good deal about Venetian History. . . . I like him very much. He is a splendid oar, and rows all over the lagoons.

To Samuel Mather (WRHS/Mather)

Address "Villa Brichieri, 12
Bellosguardo" all
summer. Letters are
forwarded if I am not there.
Hotel Britannia
Canal Grande. Venice
July 6th, [1889]

My dear Sam.

Your note, containing the cheque, came safely, and I am much obliged. I sent it to Macquay and Hooker, Florence (the letter had been forwarded to me, here), to be added to my account with them. In this connection, may I ask you to do me a favor? I should like to have my account at the Savings Bank (S. H. Mather's), closed. If there is any money there for me, please send it to me; and then close the account. It was opened after my father's death, so that there might be a place ready to receive any moneys coming to me from the sale of the Milwaukee lands, &c. But as all the land is now disposed of, there will be nothing more coming in. And I can ask your father or Will to send the interest money on my bonds directly to me, when due ~~comes in~~ (as you do with the Grand Rapids interest); and not bother the Savings Bank—which gains nothing from me as a depositor, because I always draw out very soon. I shall be greatly obliged if you will attend to this little matter for me, when you have a spare moment, as I much wish to have it done at an early date.

Your last letter was a charming one from Delaware Water Gap. I reply also from a watery place—Venice. Kate left me a week ago, feeling that she must be in Schmalbach, not only because Mrs Hoyt would be waiting for her, but also because her rooms were engaged from July 1st.[1] I enjoyed having her with me more than I can express. She is very little altered from the Kate Targer of Cheerful Corner, after all; she is the youngest person for her age whom I have ever known. And to the Aunt—who is getting on in life, and reminiscent, (not to say melancholy)—there is much to bring back the old days when hearing her fresh voice again, & listening to her bright cheerful talk. I was very sorry that her late arrival (the last of May, instead of the first, as I had hoped,) prevented me from showing her something of Florentine Society—which is amusing in its way. She said she cared nothing about seeing it, & was glad to escape it. All the same, I am sure it would have amused her. But, by the 20th of May, everything stops;—even the garden-parties are over. Kate saw Florence itself very thoroughly—for a first visit. And she seemed to enjoy it; as also this enchanting water-city, where she had ten days at her disposal; filled pretty full—as you may imagine! I saw her off a week ago, and have had letters from Lucerne, where she is spending some days with her friends the Parmelers, before going to Schmalbach.

It is a very great regret to me, Sam, that you & Flora could not have come to Florence while I am a householder there. Clara and Clare have been; and now Kate. Your father and mother; you & Flora & the two dear little boys—these are the ones I want; & the only ones. The ties of blood-relationship grow closer as one grows older, and it would have made me very happy to have you and your wife under my own roof, and also the two little boys, whom I long to see; I cannot reconcile it to myself at all, that I do not know <u>our</u> children! The villa is simple, and even rough; but it commands one of the loveliest views in all Italy. I fear I must give it up at the end of the year, as it is too expensive for my small means. It has been a pleasant episode—the having it. It will be just three years—when I leave it. I have not yet fully decided as to my plans—as I need not give notice to my landlord until the last of August. If I leave Florence, I may go to Sicily, or Algiers, or Egypt. But nothing is fixed. I am very tired, having been writing hard all winter; and now I shall rest for a month or so. I have always been extremely fond of Venice, and shall hold on here a while longer, before returning home. I have still Miss Quincy with me. She goes to the Dolomites on Monday next. She is one of the handsomest girls I have ever seen;—in the Juno style. I know a good many residents here, so I shall not be lonely.

I always rely upon you & Flora to like & love "Italy" as <u>I</u> do! (This makes it particularly hard that <u>you two</u> could not have come over while I am at Bellosguardo!) I cannot recall whether or not you came to Venice the year you came to Sorrento? I think not. The summer—up to August—is the time for Venice; that is for those who love to float. I float, & float, & float! Never tired of the exquisite dreamy beauty, & silence, of the fairy water streets. By moonlight & starlight, at dawn & at sunset—there is always a new color, a new vision;—something more lovely than before. I brought some books with me;—but I have not read a line. I have an old gondolier, who is a figure from one of Carpaccio's pictures; he & I (when Mabel Quincy goes), are to do some long still voyages together—to the distant islands here & there,—each the seat of some old monastery, or ruined church. Why are you & Flora not here to go with me?

But you have other pleasures, and perhaps equally great ones—in your new yacht—in which I take much interest. There is no summer entertainment, in my opinion, half so delightful as yachting. And I dare say the excitement of the real sea—with big waves and salt freshness—makes up for the palaces and campaniles of the tamer Adriatic! Now and then a yacht puts in here; & I never fail to make my gondolier take me close to it, & all round it, so that I may see the appointments, & perhaps, the glorified beings who own it!

Of course Kate & I talked much of you; that is, I questioned, & Targer answered. So many little things, interesting to me, are not told in letters. It seems to me that you & Flora lead a delightful life; that you have almost no drawbacks; and many pleasures. You speak of coming abroad next year; "or perhaps the year after." Now that "perhaps," I don't altogether like! Send me, this summer, some more photographs of the little boys. I have nothing very late.

I see that the Hays are in Paris. Alas! I never see them any more; like so many other Americans, they come only in the summer, & never come South. I was interested in your description of Flora Whitney's daughter. Flora is always Flora! (I mean Flora Whitney, of course.) She is always rather erratic. In her defense I will say one thing: she always puts Will Whitney first; I mean, above her children. I have the belief that her principal wish is to please her husband; & if a sudden trip to Europe (which he desires) is hampered by "the children,"—over go the children! This is, however, only my own idea of her. I have only seen her twice in 18 years; so there is not much left of our old schoolgirl friendship. I used to like her because she was original; and because she was not malicious or petty. But she has a crowded life, and I dare say has forgotten my very existence. "Out of sight, out of mind," with her. "In sight," and she is delightful. So I found her to be at Baden-Baden, five years ago. (Or was it six?). My gondola waits, & I must go. I will write again before long. With much love to Flora & the boys, yours affly,

C.F.W.

Notes

1. Woolson probably means the spa at Schlangenbad, which she names in the letter below and which was a site for the treatment of women's nervous disorders.

To William Wilberforce Baldwin (Morgan)

Hotel Britannia
Canal Grande. Venezia
July 13th, [1889]

Dear Doctor.

I was delighted to hear from you. I think it is the first time you have written ~~to me~~ without being drummed up to it by some urgent letter from me! This, of course, makes me happy. Especially as I was feeling that I had seen next to nothing of you for a year; that really made part of my general dissatisfaction with Florence,—or rather with the life that has fallen to my lot there, for the past eighteen months. I came very near leaving the place; I mean I had almost decided, the last time I saw you, to give notice, in August, that I should not take the villa another year. But the quiet rest in this enchanting place, has restored my lost peace of mind, as well as of body, and it now looks as though I *should* take it on. I am very fond of Bellosguardo. I am so glad that it seems pleasant to you too—as you drive up there to overlook the good work in this beautiful old villa. Abominations or no abominations—the view from Mr Boott's garden is divine. I hope no one will ever "improve" that open grassy space.

I have had a lovely three weeks—though the first two were rather active—with the girls to chaperone. Miss Quincy looked *so* beautiful in a gondola. We spent all our evenings afloat, *&* she never wore her hat. Every one admired her. She has now gone to the Dolomites, and my niece has gone to Schlangenbad to join my sister and Clare. I am always happy in Venice, which I think the most beautiful place in the world. I float; and float. I wish you were here afloat too! The warm salt air ~~is~~ just suits me. I wear muslin dresses and a broad brimmed hat, and shoes a size too large, and the result is cool tranquility. To-night, as the moon is full, I am going, alone, (with two gondoliers, so as to go fast) away out in the lagoon to an island called "St George of the Sea Weed." There is nothing special to see, I believe, but an old shrine; but it will be a voyage of three or four hours far out on this lovely moonlit water, away from the town. I go alone from choice. But I would take *you*—if you were here.

Tell Miss Greenough that Mr and Mrs Curtis have been exceedingly kind, and have invited me a number of times both to their beautiful palace, & enchanting garden. I do'nt know which I like the most, Mrs Curtis or her husband. Both are the salt of the earth, and I number them among the very most agreeable friends I have ever made. This pleasure I owe to Miss Greenough.

The Queen is here—and enlivens us with her four-oared gondola, and her yacht.—[1]

Alas! Walter Noyes is not here. Do you remember him? I liked him so very very much, and think of him often, as I float by his old home.

Ritter and his fiancée have been here.[2] I think Ritter still lingers, though. Miss A. has gone. Duveneck remains on a point of coming. He has been on the point ever since he landed, two months ago.

My people are at Bayreuth this week, and for a long stay. Bayreuth and Bliss are with them synonymous terms. I do'nt see when your own stay at Villa Castellani begins? Never? I have not fixed a date yet for returning, but shall be guided by circumstances. As long as this fresh sea-breeze blows as splendidly, I shall be in no hurry.

My love to your wife, and a kiss for the boys.

As always, your attached friend,
C. F. Woolson.

Notes

1. Queen Victoria.
2. Possibly novelist J. P. Ritter (1857–1920).

To Edmund Clarence Stedman (Columbia)

Villa Brichieri
12 Bellosguardo. Florence
August 10th, [1889]

Dear Mr Stedman.

Your letter finds me still on my Tuscan hilltop, detained by the book-proof of "Jupiter Lights," which must be corrected before I can go to Switzerland.[1] I was so glad to hear from you again. I am always hoping to be able to write you a real letter, and not a hurried scrawl. It is well to hope; it keeps us going; but it causes one to live in illusions for the leisure for the letter never comes.

I send you, by the same post, two of the latest photographs that have been taken of my ugly face. One—(in the White Lace cape)—was the original of the Harper's Weekly portrait, of Feb.—1887—(I think). The other (also a Venetian photograph though copied in New Haven) is considered the best.[2] This sent, not long ago, to the Scribner's for that magazine "Book Lore?," as they asked for something. A note to the Eds. of A. L. goes at the same time with this. I am delighted to have you make the selection; it is an honor for me. Let me, in this connection, beg you to wait for the book form of "Jupiter Lights"—if you intend to read the story. I will order an early copy sent you. It is much shorter than "East Angels," with a good deal of action, & no description.

I received, by my sister, such a delightful letter from you. It lighted up not only the day, but the year, by its cordial kindness and remembrance. It made me feel that you do not forget.

I do not forget, either. But so many persons do!

You must never let my letter be anything like "a reproach" to you, even though years pass, and they are not answered. I know so perfectly, so comprehendingly—to the furthermost inch—how full your days are, & how many many demands are constantly made upon you. When you can write—even but ten lines—I shall be so very glad. But no matter how long you may be silent, I shall always perfectly understand it; & not attribute it to change, or forgetfulness. On these terms, then, we'll start out on another ten years. For do you realize that ten years (& more) have passed, since we have met?

I follow your life as well as I can, through others, & by means of the Magas. & newspapers. My sister tells all she knows. I congratulate you on the New Hampshire cottage (I was born in N.H.); and I am thankful, so gladly thankful, that you and your wife have had the strength to live through the heavy troubles which a strange unaccountable fate has seen fit to send you—you who deserved them so little! Surely another life is the only solution to the cruel riddles of this one; if I did not believe this with all my heart, I could not endure to live.

We get—we readers—far too little from you. "The Star Bearer" was very beautiful. But it is saddening to have no others. And it is not right; no, it is not. A poet must not be silent; if ever man has a mission,—a message to poor humanity—it is the poet.

I suppose you have been giving your leisure hours to that great job—the Library of A. L. Of course it will be by far the best thing of the kind in existence, or ever to be in existence. We wo'nt curse it (we readers); we'll like it for itself, & rush to buy it; all the same, it will be a happy day for us when it is all done, & our poet emerges again.

Do'nt say you are growing old; I do'nt believe it! You will never be old; it is impossible. This reminds me that my latest intelligence of you & Arthur was from Mrs McPherson, who spent last winter in Florence; I saw her often, & she spoke with much interest & affection of you all.[3] Clara has just met her again (last week) at Bayreuth.

In your letter, you touch upon the vexed questions of realism & idealism. How much I should like to hear your ideas upon the subject! Would that we could meet again, upon the Florida beach; and have a long walk & talk! Over here, one reads so constantly French, Russian, Spanish, & Italian novels, (& now Norwegian too—in Ibsen) that one can't be much of a partisan about anything; the field seems so wide, & there's something good in all. I am a realist. But that does not make me believe that only bad, or commonplace, characters, exist. I know to the contrary. As to my

Margaret in "East Angels" (to which you allude), I have known just such a woman; & more than one. Take your own life, & your wife's; where can be heroism greater than yours?

After three years here, it is probable that I shall give up the villa at the end of this year. It has been a beautiful life, & I leave it only because I want to have a little of Venice. My hope is to take an apartment there next year, & try the water cure in its most fascinating form. (Not that I need a cure—weighing as I do 145 pounds!) To have put a few years of Venice into one's life, will be to have wrestled so much from darkness. I spent June there, & it was unspeakably beautiful. I remember that you like Venice, too. My sister & Clare spent the winter with me. And they were followed by my other niece, Kate Mather. My sister goes home next spring.

I have never received such a lovely Easter remembrance as your wild-flowers. They actually make me home-sick! Though they came from the Rocky Mts, they are the same flowers which I used to gather, when a girl, on the dear little northern island of Mackinac—where we spent our summers. When I come home, I shall spend a summer there, before settling down to a winter residence in Florida, & July, August, & Sept, in Cooperstown—which is my plan. But perhaps you will be able to come & see me in an old Venetian palazzo, with a gondola lying at the water-washed steps, before you do the same when I am in a little coquina house, overlooking the Florida beach? I hope so. My address, up to Nov. 15th, is that at the head of this letter. After that, Macquay & Hooker; Via Tornabuoni, Florence—as I am not quite sure where I shall be. Give my love to your wife. And my best regards to Arthur. And, believe me, always, your unchanged friend,

C. F. Woolson.

Notes

1. *Jupiter Lights* (1889) was serialized in *Harper's New Monthly Magazine* from Jan. to Sept. 1889. Woolson went briefly to Venice after she completed the book version of the novel, then returned to Florence. It is unclear if she also went to Switzerland.

2. The lace-collar photograph also appears on the cover of *Harper's Bazar*, Feb. 3, 1894.

3. Arthur was Stedman's son; Mrs McPherson was probably the wife of U.S. Congressman Edward McPherson (1830–95).

To Samuel Mather (WRHS/Mather)

Villa Brichieri
12 Bellosguardo
Florence
August 13th, [1889]

My dear Sam.

Perhaps you have wondered why you have not heard from me?

The truth is, I have been so overcome by your letter of July 22^{d}, that I have not known how to write. There was so much that I wished to express, that I should have expressed in spoken words if you had been here in person, that I have not known how to begin.

I was standing at my upright desk, correcting the book-proof of "Jupiter Lights," when the letters came in as usual, about ten o'clock. I have grown so tired, so unexpectant, that I let them lie where they were; I did not even look at the addresses. At last I went to the table, and took them up; yours, of course, first, as soon as I saw it was from you. I began reading; but could not believe that I had ~~heard~~ read aright, and went over the words again. And then, when I realized what you meant, tears came, and the happiest feeling that I have known for years.

Independent of the cheer and help, I was proud that it was my own nephew who was doing so beautiful a thing; that it was the little boy whom I have always loved, who, grown to manhood, has done this generous act, and done it too in such a delicate kindly way that it doubles the benefit.

I am glad that I have lived to see such a thing,—such noble kindness. And it comes at the right time. I am afraid I had become almost discouraged, Sam. I had got behind, and was drawing on my capital. This—though not wholly my own fault—was very depressing, especially as I was all the time working as hard as I possibly could over my writing. The feeling was rapidly taking possession of me—"It's of no use!" A feeling of hopelessness for the future.

But now, thanks to your letter, courage has sprung up again, and I feel inspired to take hold anew.

I shall give up the villa on Dec. 1st, and draw in my expenses. I shall try both to save and to earn, and devote my energies to laying up, gradually, enough to give me a fixed income (which I have never had, beyond \$$470^{00}$ a year) which, though not large, will enable me to feel easy about the future. The hopelessness has gone, and that is everything. For we cannot really live without hope.

I intend to store my household things here in Florence. I have no especial plan for the winter, as yet. Clara & Clare wish to be with me, wherever I am, as they go home in the Spring.

I have a vague hope of living in Venice sometime, for a while. I think that to put a little of the enchanting place into one's life, is just so much mental riches. Mrs Curtis (Kate will tell you who she is) says that she can get me an apartment there for half the price I pay here. And life there is cheaper, and "society" much smaller, & more lazy & tranquil; no calls, & no "days"; much less rushing about. Besides, after this Florentine experience, I think I should know how to manage better; I should not allow myself to accumulate such a long visiting list. Clara writes—and my neighbor, Miss Greenough, says—that it will be just the same wherever I go. But I do'nt think so. Florence is a place where people come to spend the winter; it has a large resident society of English & Americans. Letters of introduction (the cause of half my trouble) are always given for Florence & Rome. But rarely for Venice. In Venice there are but half a dozen English & American families; when you have said the Curtises, Mrs Bronson, Sir Henry Layard, Horatio Brown (author of "Life on the Lagoons") & his mother, & the Princess of Montenegro—you have said it all. Now in Florence there are hundreds. I have a vision of myself in some decayed but noble old palazzo, with a gondola waiting at "the wave-washed steps."[1] I, who hate horses—why, I was made for Venice! Perhaps the next time that Kate comes over, or that you & Flora come—you will find me trying this beautiful water cure.

Kate's visit was extremely pleasant to me—cast down at heart though I was; her affectionate manner & unfailing bright cheerfulness did me a great deal of good. She was much liked by everyone who saw her; she was admired for the bright face, and her <u>very</u> pretty figure, as well as for her pleasant ways and evident unselfishness. Mrs Curtis (Venice) told me that she had not for years seen a girl who was to her so attractive. In Venice, Kate was by the side of Mabel Quincy of Boston (~~who~~ of whom I took charge at the request of her relatives here), and Mabel is one of the handsomest & most statuesque of tall maidens. All the same, our Targer well held her own; and the most desirable youth of the band who were dancing attendance, Lionel Byrne, an Eton & Oxford man, & a nice fellow, admired Kate more than he did Mabel. He was introduced to me by my neighbor & intimate friend, Lady Hobart, & I see that he is not going to let the clue drop, as he keeps writing from England. Young Parmelee's evident devotion, I do'nt know whether Kate has confided to her family or not; if she has not, do'nt betray that I have told!

Give my dearest love to Flora. I did not know that there were expectations for September. But if N° 3 approaches in good looks the two little boys whose photograph has just come, you will have a remarkable family. I think it is the prettiest picture of two little boys that I have ever seen. Both faces so handsome, so intelligent, & so particularly <u>attractive</u>, each in its own way. I wish I could see the children!

I shall order a copy of "Jupiter Lights" sent you. The Harpers write that it is considered "the strongest thing" I have done,—& I suppose a publisher's opinion simply represents the collected opinion of many readers; I hope so. It is certainly unlike my other books; I set out to write a story which should be full of action, and without much else; it was only, for its interest, upon the way the action was presented. This is what I tried to do; I do not know whether I have succeeded. Among the letters I have rec^{d}, was one from a man living at Cheboygan, opposite Mackinac; he said it was too bad that I did not know that there were no mines of any kind on Bois-Blanc Island. That everybody <u>there</u> knew that there were none, & this was a fault in my "otherwise deeply interesting & thrilling narrative." I chose

"Bois-Blanc" as a name, at random; I know Bois Blanc Island well, but there has never been any town there at all. I wished ~~only~~ a French name, in token of the early French explorers, who have left French names all along the lakes. In the book-proof I have changed "Bois Blanc" to "Port aux Pins."

I am much obliged to you for attending to the Savings Bank matter for me. I had an especial reason for wishing the account closed. This I now suppose to be done? I return the order, signed.

Macquay & Hooker allow from two to three percent interest.

We have just had a hard shower, & the valley beneath my window is rejoicing; the grapes are nearly ripe everywhere. It is, of course, warm. When I have finished the last of these proofs—but there is a good deal yet to do—I shall go somewhere for change of air for a little while. Then I shall return & break up.

Clara writes that she is going over to Southhampton herself with Kate. Then the two Claras go to Vienna, & will join me, later, after I am free.

Best love to all at 544.

Most Affectionately yours,
C. F. Woolson.

Notes

1. Woolson is quoting James's essay on Venice (*Century*, Nov. 1882), later collected in *Italian Hours* (1909).

To Henry Mills Alden (WRHS/Benedict)[1]

Villa Brichieri
12 Bellosguardo. Florence
Aug 23d, [1889]

My dear Mr Alden.

Being unable, owing to a temporary lameness, to stand at my upright desk today, I seize the time to scribble, seated, a letter to you. (I am so unaccustomed, now, to writing seated, that I always ~~feel as if~~ think that my handwriting must show how awkward I feel!) On the upright desk, lie the last sheets of the Book Proof of "Jupiter Lights," at which I shall go to work again early tomorrow morning; they will go to New York in a few days, and then, but not till then, shall I draw a free breath. To finish with "Jupiter" now—do you really like it? Please read the book-form of it, sometime, before you answer. I should like also to know, if possible, what Mr Joseph Harper thinks of it—in case he has read it? I thought of writing and asking him to tell me; then I feared it would seem pressing. But if you know, you can tell me. Remember that I want honest opinions, even if severe; they are the only ones that are useful to me. The reason I ask for this is that I am receiving letters from literary friends, who say that it is the best thing I have done. Do you think so? You speak of my saying that it was written "hastily"; this only applies to the final weaving together of the sentences, which was done almost always at night, between midnight and dawn; the story itself was all written long ago—according to my custom; the plot, scenes & characters all carefully written down. But the weaving together—the sentences in which all this has to be finally expressed—this was done during the past year, and, owing to the fact that my house has been incessantly full of visitors, both staying with me, and coming up for the day from town, I have been forced to do it almost all in the night—to the great wear and tear of health and nerves.[2]

Notes

1. Pasted into Woolson's *Jupiter Lights*, London: Sampson Low, 1889. Another letter fragment also is pasted into this volume, obviously from a much earlier date and perhaps to Elizabeth Gwinn Mather, Dec. 4, 1874. It reads:

> Now I am going out to walk on the pine barrens, and see the sun set. With love to all,
> I am, yours affectionately,
> Constance F. W.

2. An unconnected legible portion of the original manuscript reads "faults caused by."

To William Wilberforce Baldwin (Morgan)

Richmond. England
Oct. 7th, [1889]

My dear Doctor Baldwin.

I suppose that by this time you are all back in Florence—the three handsome little boys, their mother, the governess, and all the servants; and that the autumn season is fairly opened, with everybody returned or returning; and the whirl of your busy life has begun again. Your vacation was an immensely short one—for I myself saw patients arriving at your door (Villa Castellani) well into August. And I consult[ed?] you (as a physician), the first of September.—When one has such a beautiful home as you have, one suffers—even in the best hotel. And so you found it. I myself have missed my own servants; my own easy chairs; my own things. Still, the change has been of great service; I feel much better, and at last I begin to feel rested. I am staying here for a little while, before I go to Paris—where I shall spend most of October. The great park is the attraction—with its splendid oaks, & miles of green turf, elastic under the foot; deer; running streams—and all the charm of English scenery. I walk from five to eight miles every day. I often see your friend, the Princess Mary, who lives at the White Lodge, across the Park; I do'nt know whether it was there that you visited her, or at her house in town?[1] What a pity you are not here now! Then you would be driving in the Park with her; and I should be walking humbly on my feet; & you would, perhaps, bow to me; & thus I too should have a gleam of royalty. The other day when I came in, her carriage had happened to stop before my door; she was talking to a young lady on the sidewalk. I thought of saying, "I know Dr Baldwin, of Florence."

From my windows, I have the celebrated Richmond view, with the Thames, and miles of green trees & church spires, with Windsor in sight, & Hampstead & Highgate. I can walk to Kew Gardens; to ever so many other interesting places, only a mile or two distant.

I have made a very leisurely progress northward, stopping a number of times to rest, & see Cathedrals. I shall do the same going back.

I saw Henry James in London, & we talked of you. I gave him an account of your new house, in which he was much interested. He sent you his love, and wished me to ask you why you never come to London? He looks remarkably well, having lost flesh; he is writing hard, & seeing many people—as usual. I do'nt think he will go to Italy this year. But he longs to do so in the spring.

Do'nt trouble to answer, as I shall be back so soon. Of course you will not betray to any Florentines, that I am leaving the villa in order to escape too much "society." It sounds so ungracious, and also pretentious—a thing I abhor. I shall say that I am leaving in order to try Venice for a while; after that, Rome. I never intended to live in Florence long; I am going back to my own land for my permanent home. But, as long as I stay abroad, I shall not ~~be~~ wish to be very far from you; I shall probably remain in Italy.

Ibsen is much talked of here. You were the first to lend me his plays. "A Doll's House" was given in London, last June. It is interesting; I have been re-reading it. I should like to write a play. I will come to you for a plot!

I am writing to Miss Greenough. Give my love to Miss [Langmin?], and all those friends who ask about me. If you see the Murrays, tell them how sorry I am that I shall not again see the General. I am following his friends, Miss [Cardin?] & Miss [Lanlie?], to Venice!

Goodby. My love to your wife.

Always your attached friend,
C. F. Woolson.

Notes

1. See appendix for Princess Mary of Teck.

To Samuel Mather (WRHS/Mather)

The Terrace
Richmond. England
October 16th, [1889]

My dear Sam.

From Kate's letter, just received, I learn that you & Flora have a little daughter. How glad I am that it is a daughter, and that Flora is doing so well. I send you both my dearest love, & delighted congratulations. And I pray that an especial blessing may be given to this little girl—my dear little grand-niece. You must both be very proud and very happy—with three such children. It is the greatest possible pleasure to me to think of you in your happy home.

I hope to hear from you very soon.

I got away at last—after finishing the Book-proof of "Jupiter Lights." The change was needed, & has been very refreshing. I had reached that kind of mental fatigue when nothing seemed right; if I went out to walk, I wished I was at home again; if I stayed at home, I was haunted by a restless desire to go out; no chair was just right; even the beds were all wrong, & prevented (so it seemed) my sleeping. If I felt hungry, no sooner had I reached the table than my appetite fled, & I could not eat. I could not read; nor write. But I am glad to say that all this has passed away; I sleep long long hours, & walk six or eight miles every day in the lovely parks with which Richmond is surrounded. Have you ever been out here? The view is magnificent, & Richmond Park is two minutes from my house door. It is 8 miles round, with superb oaks, & browsing deer. I have been three times to Windsor Castle & Park, (also near) & Eton. And I also go to Hampton Court & Bushey Park, & to the beautiful Kew Gardens. And to Wimbledon Common. And I have myself rowed on the pretty little Thames, with its cultivated air! The neighborhood, as you know, is full of old historic houses—such as Lyon House, one of the seats of the Duke of Northumberland, with the stiff-tailed lion of the Percies on the top of the gates; Ham House, just below me, with all its legends (I often spend an hour or two in the charming "Ham Walks," along the Thames under the great elms). York House, where Queen Anne was born &c &c.[1] I walk & drive in every direction. The weather has been divine; warm; a red sun in a mist; colored trees & dropping leaves. It reminds me of our (more beautiful) Indian summer. Tomorrow I go to Stoke Pogis the Scene of the elegy.[2] I wish Kate were still here—to go with me to all these places. Very soon now I start southward, stopping two days in Paris to see the pictures at the Exposition; then to Florence to break up at the Villa.[3] Charming as Bellosguardo is, there is no pang in my heart about leaving it. This is because I feel that it would be impossible for me to lead any other kind of life there, than the one I have led; people are too much accustomed to coming up, & expecting to be received, & entertained. But in Venice I can arrange it differently. I shall be out of the Villa on Nov. 30th. Clara & I are at present writing about winter plans. It is not quite decided, yet, where we shall be. Clara expects to go home in the Spring.

"Jupiter Lights" will come to you in book-form; I hope you & Flora will re-read it in that shape. Perhaps you have been waiting for that?

Have you read Ibsen? His plays are much talked of here.

And have you read Lemaitre's "Les Contemporains"?—essays ~~on~~ about writers of the day? I dare say you have. I think them very interesting & clever. A modern Sainte Beuve.[4] But perhaps you are more interested in the modern Germans? My love to Kate; I have rec[d] her letters & shall answer soon. It would be safer, after this, to address to the care of Macquay & Hooker, Florence; until I send a winter address. My best love to your Father & Mother; I was very glad to get your Mother's letter.

I am having all the funny English things to eat; the loaf in the shape of the Queen's crown; the apple tarts; the omnipresent colly-flower; the buns; the solid banks of beef. For a change, it amuses one. And the elastic green English turf & misty air refresh~~es~~ me, after the long bright hot, Italian summer. All the same, I know that when I get over the Alps again, & begin to see the white oxen the detached campaniles against the blue, blue sky, the vines swinging from tree to tree,—I shall feel the old thrill, the old charm. You & Flora must come to see me in Venice!

Poor Mrs Burnett has been thrown from her pony carriage; concussion of the brain. They say she is improving. She has cast her fortunes with the McClure newspaper syndicate, & has taken a house in London, as well as this place in the country where she now is.—

Do you wish to see another romancing likeness of my ugly face? Get Scribner's October Book Buyer. I have not seen it myself. I never answer requests for photographs unless the Harpers advise it; in their case they did so advise. Harry James tells me that Col. Hay's daughter is a strikingly handsome girl; he saw her when the Hays were in London. I get glimpses of Harry J. when he is not off somewhere, paying visits.

I am already planning another book.

My best regards to Mrs Stone. And a mountain of love to you & Flora & the handsome boys, & the wee girl.

Affectionately yours,
C. F. Woolson.

Notes

1. Queen Anne (1665–1714) was born in the York House wing of St. James Palace.
2. Thomas Gray's "Elegy Written in a Country Churchyard" (1751).
3. The Paris Exposition began in Oct. 1889.
4. Jules Lemaître's second volume of collected essays, *Les Contemporains,* was published in 1889. Woolson is comparing him to French literary critic Charles Augustin Sainte-Beuve.

To Harper and Brothers (McGill)

Richmond
Oct. 18th, [1889]

Office Messrs. Harper & Brothers.

If Mr Osgood is not in town, will you kindly drop me a line, as the enclosed note to him is an invitation to dinner.

Miss {C. F. Woolson

Monte Rosa
The Terrace
Richmond
London. S. W.

To Henry Mills Alden? (WRHS/Benedict)[1]

[November 1889]

Nov. 15th, as all letters will be immediately forwarded to me, wherever I am.

I give up the villa on Nov. 30th. Yes, farewell to beautiful Bellosguardo! I shall have been here three years when I leave. The place in itself has no fault; it is ideal. But there are too many people! The first year, all was heavenly. The second, my life became perturbed. The third has been really terrible. (These confidences are for you alone, of course, as they sound ungenerous & even pretentious, if read by the uncomprehending.) Bellosguardo, to begin with, is a sort of show place; all the guide-books speak of its magnificent view. The tourists & strangers, therefore, drive up here, and, if they can get a letter, or card of introduction to anyone living in one of the four or five villas here, they do it. And naturally, I suppose. As Florence is a place where people come to spend the winter, they generally bring letters of introduction, just as they do for Rome; and as they do not do for Naples or Venice. Owing to these facts, and to my having begun in the wrong way (being by nature hospitable and fond of having a pleasant house), I have ended by having no time at all to myself. It has worn me out, nor do I see any other way out of it than to flee. So away I go on the 1st of December. Of course I shall miss the view terribly. And I shall miss the semi-home. But there is really nothing else[2]

Your beautiful serene way of looking at life has always been my envy and admiration. I am myself so constantly & freshly overwhelmed by the (apparent) cruelty & injustice of life that I can seldom attain that sort of peace. Now & then a divinely fair landscape (such as I have here), lifts my soul above earth's griefs for a while.—(Let me add that I am perfectly aware that the cruelties & injustice are only for a time. I have perfect faith that some day we shall know why we suffered so here).

Notes

1. Pasted into Alden, Henry Mills, *Magazine Writing and the New Literature*, New York: Harper's, 1908. The second portion is identified as being to Alden; the first is also likely to him.

2. The sentence stops with no period. It is impossible to tell if a portion of the letter is missing.

To Samuel and Flora Stone Mather (WRHS/Mather)

Nov. 20th, [1889]

Dear Sam & Flora.

Now that I am giving up the villa, it will be necessary to dispose in some way of the accumulations of representations of my pug nose! This last is not the "Book Buyer" copy; but still a new one done for "The Library of American Literature."[1] They have just sent me five of the "proofs before printing—" if that is the term; can you help me by taking one? I send it to my little grand-niece. I wrote to your mother yesterday, with messages to you. This is but a hasty postscript. Much love to Flora.

Yours affly,
C.F.W.

Notes

1. E. C. Stedman's *Library of American Literature* (1890) included Woolson's poem "Yellow Jessamine" (1874).

To Henry Mills Alden (WRHS/Benedict)[1]

Villa Brichieri
Bellosguardo. Florence
Nov. 21st, [1889]

My dear Mr Alden.

Many times I have wished to write to you, since receiving your two delightful letters. But the whole year has been a busy & breathless time (until the past six weeks), full of toil and anxiety, without a moment's respite. I have never had so steadily hard a year. This came from many causes, which I will not expatiate upon here; "at evening time, there shall be light," &, when October arrived, some light came for me.[2] Having finished the book proof of "Jupiter Lights"(my last story), I went north, to England. I had a longing to see green grass & big oaks, & a misty sun, after a whole summer in the white light of Italy. I established myself at Richmond (near London, you know), & I did nothing but walk & sleep. I believe a long walk is now the greatest indulgence I can give myself! I do so love the open country, & beautiful scenery, & also the exercise. But it takes a great deal of time!—Two minutes from my gate was Richmond Park, with its 8 miles of turf, & magnificent trees; & deer; five minutes by R. R. took me to Hampton Court & the splendid horse-chestnuts of Bushey Park. In 15 minutes I could (& did, often) reach Windsor, with the Park & Castle; & Eton. Also Stoke Poges; and Kew Gardens & Wimbledon Common were within easy walking distance. The weather was an English imitation of our Indian summer,—the best England can do; warm air; a red sun in a mist; slowly dropping leaves. The Thames wound at my feet, pretty & silvery; I often walked along its green banks for miles. Historic houses of all kinds were near at hand, from Pope's villa at Twickenham to the remains of Richmond Palace where Queen Elisabeth died.[3] There I had all the amusing English dishes; the everlasting "mutton cutlets," "apple tart," & [“]colly-flower"; the Queen's loaf; the constantly proffered tea. After the dainty French cooking of my excellent man, Angelo, & the daily black coffee, the bucolic dishes of England were funny. But I enjoyed everything. And did nothing but walk & walk & walk; & sleep & sleep & sleep. Then, refreshed both in body & mind, I went over to Paris, & had a week of the Exhibition. It was a brilliant week; again the weather was kind, & the sun shone every day, & all day. I spent the best lighted hours among the pictures[4]

Notes

1. Pasted into Alden, Henry Mills, *God in His World*, New York: Harper's, 1890.
2. Woolson is quoting Zechariah 14:7, a passage about hope in the coming of the Lord.
3. Alexander Pope was buried at Twickenham Church in 1744; Queen Elizabeth died at Richmond Palace. The misspelling is Woolson's.
4. The excerpt ends mid-sentence.

To Samuel Mather (WRHS/Mather)

Villa Montanto
Bellosguardo
Dec. 8th, [1889]

My dear Sam.

I left my villa yesterday, and am staying for a few days with Lady Hobart. Then I go down to town, & from there, according to the present plans, I start next week for Brindisi, where I meet Clara & Clare, who come by an Austrian Lloyd steamer from Trieste; thence we all set sail—over classic seas—for Corfu!

I never dreamed that I should see the Ionian Isles. Once so near, I may get as far as Athens!

At present Clara & Clare are blockaded in Vienna, where they appeared to have carried an American blizzard; I have heard nothing as the wires are down, & there are no trains; I can only hope that they are well. They had thought of Abbazia as our wintering place—a sort of Istrian Cannes, I believe. Corfu was also named, and I jumped at it. Corfu is historic, poetic; it is on the way to Egypt, or Constantinople, or Athens, as well as to the lands of the Arabian Nights and the realms of my childhood's dreams! I cannot leave Bellosguardo en route to these fairy places, without expressing to you, my dear Sam, the great pleasure it is to me that I owe the possibility, even, of seeing them, in a great measure to you,—the little boy to whom I used to tell the fairy tales which had been often inspired by what I had read of these very countries—(which I never expected to see). I hope it will add another pleasure to your Christmas to know that life is easier and brighter (through you) to me.

Clara has proposed Egypt. But that would be expensive, and I don't wish her to pay all my share.

Corfu for the winter, and a week or two in Athens in the spring—this will be enchantment enough for me.

Give my dearest love to Flora; Kate writes that she is looking so well. A kiss for the boys, & for the little—Flora?[1] I want a photograph as soon as possible.

I sent you word that the interest money (on my bonds) had come safely. You have now all my small affairs in your charge—except the literary part.

This is Hawthorne's villa, you know. Here he wrote "The Marble Faun"; he gives an account of his life here in the "Italian Note Books," and he introduces the villa & its old tower into the romance as the home of Donatello.

I hear most eulogistic accounts of you from Clevelanders. The accounts come through different sources. I am so delighted that all goes so very well with you.

I am ~~writing a~~ beginning a letter to Kate, which will be the last from Bellosguardo.

Affectionately yours,
C. F. Woolson.

Notes

1. Woolson later learns, to her delight, that the Mathers named their baby daughter Constance.

To William Wilberforce Baldwin (Morgan)[1]

Hotel Milano
Via Arretain
Sunday, Dec. 15th [1889]

My dear Doctor.

I should like to pay my debts before I go. You have not forgotten, I hope, that I have consulted you twice, since I came back from Paris; and also there was our [?] at the dentist's. Please let me have a mem. of account.

These are but small matters compared with the large debt for kindness of all descriptions; this I can never pay. I should like so much to see you before I go. I know your time is precious; but if you can, look in to say goodby. Of course if I am in the house, I will see you at any time; but I may be out. If you could come Tuesday evening at eight, I would keep all others away. Will you send me word? I leave Wednesday morning.

Most cordially your attached friend,
C. F. Woolson.

Notes

1. The Morgan dates this as 1888, but December 15 was on a Sunday in 1889.

To William Wilberforce Baldwin (Morgan)[1]

Hotel Milano
Wednesday
[Dec. 18th, 1889?]

My dear Doctor.

I did not—last night—thank you for the kindness of that last note of yours; I shall always keep it; it is one of the most beautiful notes I have ever received. I can't bear to say good-by. But it is really only au revoir, as I fully expect to return to Italy for several years in Venice. My love to your wife.

Always your attached friend,
C. F. Woolson.

Notes

1. The envelope appears to read Dec. 18, 1888, but this was a Tuesday; Dec. 18 was on a Wednesday in 1889.

To Samuel Mather (WRHS/Mather)[1]

Jan. 5th, 1890

My dear Sam.

Your welcome letter of December 6th, bringing the news of the naming of the little Constance after me, reached me at Corfu, and made me very proud, and pleased. I am much touched that you and Flora have done this; it is an especial pleasure and gratification to me; and I send to the little girl a real blessing and benediction, which will, I believe, accompany her through life; the good deeds of the parents are visited upon the children, as well as the bad ones.—I must have a photograph of my namesake as soon as possible, and I wish that she may inherit all the good there is in me (not much!) and nothing unfortunate. May she be blessed! "Yea, and she shall be blessed."[2] Give my dearest love to Flora; I thank her very much for this sweet act. I am sure she must be enjoying the presence of a daughter with a keen and new delight. After all, little girls are awfully nice!

The boys must be much interested. I laughed over the fund accumulated by Amasa's contributions. They must be—from all accounts (& from their photographs) the most darling little chaps! I wish I could see them.

I sent you a short letter from Florence, the last from the villa. After my visit with Lady Hobart, I went down to town, packed, closed up all the last things, & then started—(before daylight on a cold wintry morning)—for—the Orient! (I like that word; one can roll the r. so finely!). I went first to Ancona, where I passed the night in one of the big, bad, old-fashioned inns of Italy; then the next morning began the enchantment of the entirely new journey down the Adriatic coast to Brindisi. The railway runs very near the sea all the way, and the scenery reminded me of that between Salerno & Paestum, when I made my memorable journey, with Flora & yourself, to the great tawny temples on the shore. The train was an express, "carrying the Indian mails." You do'nt know how those words stirred my imagination. The other passengers were English, going out (they always go "out") to India. At lunch and dinner we all talked—as people do in lonely places—& you do'nt know what a sensation it gave me to hear the names of "Alexandria," "Suez," "Constantinople" & "Bombay," bandied about as though they were Canton and Masilon. But I, too, bore my part, if you please. When an English lady asked me "Are you going on to-night," I was proud to answer "Yes." Then she said, "To Alexandria?" "No," I replied; "mine is the Constantinople boat. I am going to Corfu." I hope my elation did not show too much in the tones of my voice. At half past ten that night I reached Brindisi, & went out to the Austrian Lloyd steamer (which was lying off the town) in a small boat rowed by four bandits who howled & roared all the way. On the steamer I found Clara & Clare who had come from Trieste; Clara was suffering from the all-prevailing influenza; (but she is well again now.) We sailed across the Adriatic & the next afternoon reached Corfu—where we spent nine days. The scenery is I think the finest of the kind which I have ever seen; when I say "of the kind," I mean sea & islands, & mainland, with mountains, near at hand. Imagine the Bay of Naples multiplied by ten, with half a dozen Capris, &, instead of Vesuvius, the Bernese Alps rising from the deep blue water. The town is like Mentone; that is, the "old town" of Mentone. Our stay there was delightful—though the hotel is not good. Then we went—by a Greek coasting steamer—through the Ionian Sea, touching at nearly all the islands, Paxos, Cephalonia, Zante, &c. Then across to Missolonghi; then to the Greek mainland town of Patras. The voyage was to me enchanting—though the steamer was very bad. But as the weather was perfect, one could get along by being all the time on deck. The picturesque effects of the Greek & Albanian peasants on board, & their remarkable costumes & luggage; the wonderful scenery, & the embarcations & dis-embarcations at all the little island-ports by means of small boats—this was something I can never forget. Of course the Odyssey had to be quoted! Again the old regret comes up that I am not a good classical scholar! I have all the books; but only as translations. As we sailed by Paxos, I thought of the voice heard crying, "Great Pan is dead!" In fact, I thought of everything poetical & classical which I had ever read, from Homer to Childe Harold. At Missolonghi of course it was (besides Byron) "T'was midnight; in his guarded tent—," for Bozzaris is buried there. But basta![3] as the Italians say; you—& little Constance too—will be tired of all these old-fashioned quotations.

Our landing at Patras was something remarkable. After getting down the ladder over the ship's side into the tossing row-boat, already filled with our luggage, we set off for the shore, Greeks, in their white petticoats, perched on all our trunks. It was dark & rough, & ~~the~~ as the steamer was moored at some distance out, our voyage was a long one. But though we bobbed about like a cork, it was better than the landing, where a crowd of yelling natives awaited us. In their eagerness to secure our bags, they almost tore us limb from limb. If it had not been for the little Dutch landlord of the Holet de Patras—who quietly knocked down three of them—I think we should have had to run for it! One Greek dragged me by the arm towards the other hotel. Once in our rooms, these howling brigands disappeared. The landlord said "They are still half barbarous." And it is perfectly true. The next morning, it was almost as bad when we took the train for Athens. Again we were surrounded by a yelling fighting crowd of Greeks, so that the hotel porter was obliged to <u>beat</u> them off with all his strength. The little Dutch landlord was again our guardian angel; he stationed a policeman at the car door, & the policeman too was obliged to use his fists! This railway is a new thing, & the Greek boatmen hate it; they used to have everything their own way. I can well believe that real brigandage still exists in Greece! I ought, however, to add that we did rather an adventurous thing in taking that little coasting steamer without any man with us,—even a servant. Hereafter, we shall keep to the main routes, and the big boats.—

From Patras to Athens the train brought us in eight hours. The scenery all the way was magnificent & strange; the intense blue of the Gulf of Corinth, the bare rocky mountains, often—as in the case of Helicon (Matthew Arnold's Helicon!) covered with glittering snow; &, in the plain through which we rushed, nothing but currant fields, all being tilled by ballet-dancers![4] For the voluminous short white kilts of the Greek peasants—the men—are exactly like the skirts of ballet dancers, save that the material is twilled cotton. (I now learn—what I dare say you already know—that the currants of commerce are not our red currants at all, but a dwarf grape, which took its name originally from Corinth. The vines are as short as grape vines.) Over all—mountains, hills, water & plain, shines the extraordinary Greek light, which <u>is</u> all they say of it; & over all lay, in layers & shadows, the wonderful

Greek colors, which are all the poets paint them. You & I, Sam, think the colors of the Italian mountains very lovely; imagine the same softness, with six or eight other shades, besides the violet blue; in Greece the same velvety effect is tinged with yellow, with gold, with dark red, with peacock green, and with iridescent brown—besides the violet blue.

The light is more pellucid than anything I have ever seen. No wonder the Greek intellect was so clear! I cannot get rid of the idea that I have reached another star, much higher in space than our earth, & that I am riding along through the empyrean in quite another & more brilliant air. But basta! again. You & Flora will say, "Aunt Connie is quite wild."—

As I write, it comes over me, "Did Sam come to Athens?" My impression is that you did not. If you did, excuse my long descriptions.—I have been here now four days, & shall remain another week. It will take that amount of time to see what we wish to see. I spare you detailed accounts of Athens itself, as we have all read them a hundred times, & seen countless pictures and photographs. But I must add that one afternoon spent on the Acropolis under the portico of the Parthenon—with that landscape spread out below—is worth all the pictures, & all the poetry, ten times over; it is really indescribably solemn & beautiful.

From Athens—(catch your breath; I do!) we sail for Alexandria, going directly to Cairo, where we settle down for six weeks or two months, according to the weather. Clara & Clare will see as much of the Nile as they care to; I shall see the pyramids &c, & I may go as far as the 1st Cataract. But Cairo itself is a vision of color & picturesqueness. I have letters to everybody—if we care to use them—including Eugene Schuyler & his wife—whom, however, I already know. From Cairo we go to Constantinople for a few days; then by the Black Sea, to Varna, Bucharest, Belgrade & Vienna. This return journey was planned for Clara by people in Vienna; she wished to spend some time in Vienna in the spring, & they showed her, that, once in Egypt, it was no further, & no more expensive, to return via Constantinople & the Black Sea, than by the Adriatic & Trieste, as she ~~came~~ had come.

Now Sam, is'nt this an Arabian Nights trip for me? It is almost too good to be believed in. I never expected to see these far countries. And now—thanks to you first, & to Clara second (she gives me my two voyages,—(to Alexandria going; & from Alexandria to Constantinople, as we come back), I am to have this immense pleasure—before I am too old to enjoy it. Why—I shall gather impressions enough, & store up memories enough, for all the rest of my life.—In Cairo itself—once there—I am hoping that living will be no more expensive than it is anywhere.—Think of the excitement of sailing through all that island-sea—with Melos, & Paros, & Naxos! (I do'nt suppose you remember Henry Mather's favorite song, "When I left the shores, O Naxos?"[5] But here I go—off into poetry again!)

Epiphany, Jan. 6th

We have just come in from a long drive, which included many interesting places. We scrambled up Mars Hill—among other things. To day the wind blows—though it is not cold—and with it comes the white dust, which I see must be one of the chief faults of Athens.—We are very near both the King's Palace, & the smaller one where the Crown Prince lives with his young bride.[6] Poor child—I hope she is not homesick. (So far from home.) Both palaces are guarded by soldiers in petticoats, over which are worn military coats.

The only letters we have had here are your Xmas cards, which gave us much pleasure. I recd the newspaper slip with Count [Keraley's?] allusion to Cooper. I have now been abroad ten (or is it twelve?) years, & I can truthfully say that the only American author universally known in France, Germany, Italy, Austria, & Switzerland, is Cooper. Old, thumbed translations, in the language of the country, I have found everywhere—; even in small villages.

I am much interested in your lakeshore house, and hope that I shall see it before long. I do'nt think it will be next summer, though your cordial invitation is tempting. Clara has had a plan for my going home with her. But I am not quite ready yet. After this wonderful trip, I want to settle down & do some steady work, keeping at it for a year at least—though not at night—as I did when doing "Jupiter." I am sure I shall come home for good before long, as I am rapidly approaching a time of life when travel becomes irksome, & a chimney-corner the dearest place on earth. Already I feel as if this was the last long-journey I should take.—I hope with all my heart that I shall be able to visit you & Flora in the new country home; I remember Coit's, & its natural advantages. En passant—Mollie's name "Harrywold" I do'nt admire much. Why didn't she call the place "Brothers." As though it were "brudern." I know a place in Italy called "The Sisters." (Perhaps "brudern" is not correct. I mean "the brother" in German.) I should think it wd. be ever so nice to have the two places adjoining, so that the children can play together.[7]

I envy you the Angelas. I had never seen anything of Millet, until I visited the late Paris Exhibition, where were several of his pictures; but not the Angelas. I had some charmed moments before Millet, Bastien Lepage.[8]

Affectionately—dear Sam & Flora—yours,
C. F. Woolson.

Notes

1. This letter is written on stationary from Grand Hotel D'Angleterre, Athènes, Grèce; Woolson underlined Athènes, Grèce.

2. Ecclesiastes 24:4.

3. Woolson is quoting Elizabeth Barrett Browning's "Aurora Leigh" (1856) and alluding

to Byron's "Childe Harold" (1855). The second quotation is from "Marco Bozzaris," a poem by Fitz-Greene Halleck (1790–1867). *Basta* is Italian for "enough."

4. The reference is to Matthew Arnold's poem "Consolation" (1852).

5. Henry Mather was Samuel Mather Sr.'s brother. The song lyric to which Woolson refers is probably "When I left thy shores O Naxos: an original Greek air," lyrics by Lord Byron, with a musical arrangement by William Staunton (published by James L. Hewitt & Co., Boston, nd).

6. See appendix for Constantine I of Greece and Princess Sophia of Prussia, whom he married in 1889.

7. Woolson is commenting, "in passing," on the name for Mather's summer home, which eventually was known as "Shoreby" or for a home next to his.

8. Woolson had visited the Paris Exposition in 1889, where, as she tells Mather, she did not see Millet's painting *The Angelus* (1857–59). Like Millet, Jules Bastien-Lepage (1848–84) painted scenes of rural life.

To Samuel Mather (WRHS/Mather)[1]

[1890]

& Corot—especially the latter. Give my love to the Hays. I have never yet reached Scotland—where they go—& where your friend has bought his family castle; but I hope to, sometime. I once met in London the Scotch baronet—(the name escapes me—) who is among their hosts in Scotland; he was calling upon Alice James, & had brought her some beautiful flowers. Why do'nt you buy & restore (since Castles are the fashion among you) the beautiful "Berry Pomeroy." My grandfather (<u>your</u> great-g.) was a Pomeroy; that is near enough—the having the same name.[2]

I'll hurl no more Ibsen at you, if you reply with "basic hearth process" & "ship-plate."[3] (I can't imagine though, what the "dolomites" have to do with "a bath"—dry as they are; so deathly dry.)

I do'nt know whether you & Flora are Browningites? Browning was so important a person in Italy, thus his death has come near to me, though I have not met him. He always spent half of the year in Venice, where his most intimate friends were the people I know there. I had a letter from Mrs Curtis (one of them), only a few days before his death, describing his having read aloud, from the Ms., many of the poems intended for his new volume, before a small circle of friends in her drawing room, ten days before. It seems sad that his life-long wish could not be granted,—to be buried beside his wife, in Florence. But the cemetery has been closed for years, & it wd. have required an Act of Parliament to open it. Some one (in the London Times) suggested that an appropriate epitaph would be

"Never the time, & place,
And the loved one, all together!"

I dare say Pen & his wife (I mean the son) were gratified by the offer of Westminster Abbey.[4]

Clare & I have just had some tea—to wash the white dust out of our throats. Clara still scorns tea; but Clare imbibes it with her Aunt. Clara went down to the Piraeus yesterday, to look at the Egyptian steamer whose sister-craft we are to take next week. She pronounces it "so-so." We take Cook's tickets, & deliver ourselves up to Cook, generally. He runs Egypt now entirely, having all the steamers, & all the good dahabeyahs, & everything.[5] Willard Fiske says that there is no use in trying to get on without him there. Kate will tell you about Willard Fiske. He has spent many winters in Egypt, & has learned Arabic, besides digging up a Coptic church, & buying the finest known Scarabeus. I intend to buy a small scarabeus for twelve shillings, & have it set as a ring—just for association's sake. I hope I shall hear from Flora & from you before long. You can address either to Cairo, or to London. I really think London is safer, because if we do not like Cairo, we may not stay there. Still—both addresses are safe enough. The London one is the same old

"c/o Alliance Bank
High Street. Kensington
London. W."

I renewed my associations with them in October; I have always kept a small balance there, & they are very attentive to me.

The Cairo address is

"c/o Crédit Lyonnais
Cairo
Egypt"

Macquay & Hooker, Florence, also know where I am, always. Best love to all at 544; a kiss for the boys & little Constance; & my regards to Mrs Stone.

Notes

1. This fragment of letter to Samuel Mather Jr. begins on page 8. It was likely written shortly after Robert Browning's death on Dec. 12, 1889, and before Woolson sailed from Corfu for Egypt.

2. Berry Pomoroy Castle is in Devon, England. Woolson is joking about Mather's connections to her mother's Pomeroy family.

3. These are steel forgery terms.

4. Elizabeth Barrett Browning died in 1861 and was buried in Florence. Pen or Penini is the nickname of their son Robert. The quotation is from Browning's poem "Never the Time and Place."

5. Dahabeyahs are large sailing ships or royal barges.

To Henry Mills Alden (WRHS/Benedict)[1]

Cairo. Egypt
Jan. 17th, 1890

Dear Mr Alden.

Does'nt that heading stir your imagination? It stirs mine, I assure you.

After leaving my Tuscan hill-top (—with great regret on many accounts, but with relief as regards the many visits one has to receive there—) I met my sister at Brindisi, &, together, we journeyed across the Adriatic to the beautiful island of Corfu. Here we spent Xmas, and ten more days. The scenery is the most beautiful of its kind that I have ever seen. After that, we made a tour among the Ionian Isles; and, one starry night, I thought I heard the cry, "Great Pan is dead!"[2]

Then we went to Missalonghi; & across the blue bay of Corinth to the Greek town of Patras, where we took the railway for Athens; for there is now a railway! At Athens, we remained two weeks. And, at every step, my regret grew keener—that I am not a classical scholar! I have, of course, all the books; but only in translations. How you would enjoy Athens! I continually thought of you. I will not attempt to describe, as you have read all the descriptions; I will simply say that the Acropolis with the Parthenon lifted up against the blue sky, is the most beautiful thing I have ever rested my eyes upon; & that the Greek air is the clearest in the world;—"forever treading the clear pellucid air," is a quotation which was constantly in my mind. In addition, the colors of the Greek mountains are wonderfully varied & lovely. The modern town of Athens is new & ugly; much like Munich. The Museums are interesting; but as yet but beginnings; they cannot compare with the galleries of Italy—whose chief treasures in marble have been stolen from helpless Greece! As to the Schlieman collection, I thought it wonderful—until I came here![3] The Mycenian relics are supposed to date back to about B. C. 1000. But here in Egypt we can see many things that surely date back to B. C. 5000.

Our voyage from the Piraeus to Alexandria was charming; for the first day, we sailed among the beautiful Cyclades; some of them are but a mountain-peak in the sea. At Alexandria began the vivid local color—in the hues of the scanty garments of the Arabs, Egyptians, & negroes who swarmed up the sides of the ship after our luggage; for the landing is made in small boats. We came on to Cairo, after seeing Pompey's Pallas, and here we have established ourselves for a long stay.

If I should ever begin to tell you how fascinated I am, it would take ten sheets. So I will not even begin. But all—all—is far better than I expected; the architecture is more fantastic; the Nile more solemn; the people queerer; the flowers more luxuriant; & the Bazaars more extraordinary—than I had dreamed. So far, we have no plan about going up the Nile. I dare say I shall get as far as the first Cataract and of course see the Pyramids & the Sphinx, Memphis & Thebes.

Curiously enough, the sights,—actual sights—of the millions of orientals—there in Africa, Syria, &c.—has increased the feeling. I knew they were there, before I saw them; but there was no realization of them in my mind. Now, I can picture to myself also the swarms of humanity in India and China. And as I was greatly struck by the intelligence & dignity of the oriental character, I can't look down upon them as I used to,—from a superior Anglo-Saxon standpoint. That is the trouble of traveling widely over the world, and living for years in foreign countries; one inevitably loses one's old standards, and comfortable fixed prejudices and opinions.

I shall do no travel sketches in future. They take an immense amount of time, and, when done, what are they! It is a pity, for if I could put down the joy, the heavenly delight which the strangeness & beauty of the East gave me, it would be a book of heaven! Even now, whenever I think of Cairo, of Corfu, of the islands of the whole route from Naples to Jaffa, & Athens, I am again intoxicated.

Notes

1. Pasted in three sections into Woolson's *Mentone, Cairo, and Corfu*, New York: Harper's, 1896. The last two paragraphs are separate from each other and from the rest of the letter. The last paragraph was likely written after Woolson's return from Cairo.

2. The quotation is from Elizabeth Barrett Browning's "The Dead Pan" (1844); Browning was quoting Plutarch's *De Defectu Oraculorum (On the Failure of the Oracles)*.

3. Woolson is referring to a collection gathered by archaeologist Heinrich Schliemann (1822–90), whose name she spells with only one *n*.

To William Wilberforce Baldwin (Morgan)

Cairo. Egypt
Jan 18th, 1890

My dear Doctor.

Best wishes for you and yours, for 1890.

1890 seems such an old date, that it is appropriate to be writing it in the shadow of the pyramids.

Do you know where I am? I can scarcely believe it myself!

I met my sister and niece at Brindisi as I expected, and from there we went to the beautiful island of Corfu. Then to Athens, where we spent ten nights. Then here. This is best of all. I could not begin—in a brief letter—to describe Cairo. But you know that my imagination is active! Well—my imaginations of Egypt,—vivid and highly colored as they were,—fall far below the reality. The picturesqueness of everything, the queerness of everything, the solemnity, the age, the color—all is extraordinary.

The climate, however—at least that of Cairo—is disappointing. It is not warm as I so longingly hoped it would be. I do not mean that it is cold; the thermometer stands at 58° (Fahrenheit) out of doors. But I do not call that warm; and I am again thrown back upon my old belief that Florida has the best winter climate in the whole world. There it is warm, as I know by the experience of eight consecutive winters. And thither I shall betake myself for a permanent abode when the days of my travels are over.

I dare say we shall remain in Egypt two months. Then we go to Constantinople; and from there, via the Black Sea and Varna to Bucharest and Belgrade; then Vienna.

I shall feel much richer in regards to impressions of life and oriental color, after that wonderful trip.

I hope you are all well. I should like nothing better than an hour of chat with you at the moment! Why can't we have all we want in the world, instead of constantly having to give up either the time, or the place, or the friends? "Never the time, and place/And the loved ones all together!" sang Browning.[1] And it is pretty true. I do'nt regret Florence; but I do regret you.

Athens was extremely beautiful. And "the Isles of Greece, the Isles of Greece" were even lovelier than I expected.[2] We saw them all, for, after leaving Corfu, we made a tour among the Ionian Isles; and between Athens and Alexandria, we passed through the Cyclades.

I suppose you are tremendously busy, as usual. And I know you are doing quantities of good, day by day. I shall never forget my long three months of illness, when you not only cared for me physically, but cheered me mentally by your visits. Is the wind whistling at Bellosguardo, I wonder.

I give you no address on purpose, as I do not want you to be bothered with the idea of a reply—occupied as you are. I will write again, later; and then I will give an address. Clara & I both send our love to your wife. Pray believe me always your attached friend,

C. F. Woolson.

Notes

1. Robert Browning composed "Never the Time and Place" (1883) in memory of his wife Elizabeth Barrett Browning.

2. Byron published his poem "The Isles of Greece" in 1819.

To Samuel Mather (WRHS/Mather)[1]

Cairo. Egypt
Jan. 31st, [1890]

My dear Sam.

I received your letter enclosing the draft, and am warmly obliged to you. I feel a little guilty at not being at work here; but, so far, it has been impossible—there has been so much to see. I am divided between the intense wish to see all, and appreciate all;—and the feeling that I ought to be putting upon paper one or two promised short stories—which are already written in my brain. I am afraid nothing will get into shape until all this excitement is over—as it will soon be.

I don't know what Clara has been writing to Cleveland on the subject of "Cairo." But I, at least, am fascinated & charmed. Clara has not been well here, & indeed we have all suffered severely from the lack of fires—to which we are not at all accustomed. I had at last to go to bed and stay there for a week—with a sharp attack of that excruciating pain in the right shoulder, which I have not had for a year & a half. The chill of my bedroom brought it on. Clara has not been sent to bed; but she has been miserable all the time & still is; she thinks it is malaria. The truth is that she is never really well in a southern climate, & I think this last experience will cause her to give up trying it again. She was never well in Florida; & it has been the same here in Italy; & now Egypt. This acts upon her spirits, & she finds Cairo perfectly detestable, & has but one wish: namely—to get away. So she is going to hurry it a little, & get back to Vienna earlier than she had intended when we first came. We go up the Nile, probably, next week, for a short trip. Then to Port Said, & to Jerusalem for one week. Then I think Clara & Clare will sail directly for Trieste—by the way they came, & return to Vienna. This at least is the present plan. But it may be changed.

In the meanwhile, I am now well, & the weather is much warmer, & I am fascinated with Cairo. As this is the case, and as southern climates agree with me, I wish much to stay on here through March. I am here, & it is a long journey to get here; it seems a pity not to stay & see it thoroughly, when once on the spot.

When I suggested this to Clara, she was dumb with surprise that I should wish to stay. "If you & Clare should go north & leave me alone here," she said, "I should become a howling dervish in a day!" (This was apropos of our having been to see the dervishes.) I don't know how we shall arrange it. But I long to stay, & I don't want to face the winter again so soon; & it would be winter in March. Yesterday I saw Eugene Schuyler—whom I have often seen in Florence. He is Consul-General here, but not yet confirmed—much to his annoyance. I am loaded with letters of introduction to people here, given me by Prof. Fiske of Florence (whom Kate knows); already we have seen some of these people, & I can see the others (one of them is the Dean of the English Church) whenever I please. All this is apropos of my staying on a while—the question which just now fills my mind, & therefore I write about it; though it wo'nt be very interesting I fear, to you. If I do stay, I leave, when I do go, by one of the big ships of the P. & O. Line, going from Alexandria straight to either Brindisi or Venice. Clara has given up Constantinople. She takes me up the Nile instead. I think I told you that she presents me with my voyage from Athens here; & from Alexandria to Italy, whenever I return.

Yes, I must repeat that to me, Cairo is fascinating. I wo'nt fill pages in describing what everybody describes; but I will simply say, generally, that the domes & fantastic minarets, the oriental lattice-work over the carved windows, the narrow streets of the old quarter with their rich & variegated color, the Bazars!—the gardens & roses—are wonderful. Then, whoever [blot] drives out, away from the town—there is the same low sky, bending down to meet a vast level plain, with the great river, & the tall palms; when I say "the same," I mean the same effect that I used so to love in Florida. The Florida palmettos, it is true, are not so beautiful as the palms of Egypt; & the broad St John's has no wonderful old temples; neither is the landscape diversified by the solemn strangeness of the pyramids, which rise above all else. Still it is a flat southern country with a southern sky; there is resemblance enough to bring Florida strongly to my mind. If I do stay on, I shall go straight to England when I leave, & settle down, somewhere in the country, for six months, & perhaps a year, of steady work. It has been a good deal of a change to jump from a house, & into trunks! But I do'nt regret what I have done. Care is worse than a little discomfort & I had far too heavy a load of the former, during my last 18 months in the lovely villa. I am sorry about your friend, [blot] Perrin. I should have enjoyed a longer stay in Athens; but we could not spend the winter in two places. Athens was beautiful. It was also sad—those exquisite ruins & that ugly, bustling completely modern town. Its great defect is the all penetrating white dust. Athens = dust. Cairo = mosquitoes! But I am used to the latter, coming from Italy. I live in an atmosphere of Persian Powder—just as I did in Florence during the summer; I burn it on a tin plate [blot] destroys the pests.

Afternoon comes in your little letter, saying that the roof will be on in time to finish the Lakeshore house in the spring, & renewing your kind invitation to me. It is most kind, & I am touched at your doing it so cordially & earnestly. But I am not ready, yet, to come home; I have too much literary work planned out for this summer, & in fact for the whole year. Thanks to you, I feel in better spirits & better courage, & I now wish to try hard to make & put aside enough to give me a regular income upon which I can live, in a quiet way, without care & anxiety. If I am ever to accomplish this, now is the time. I am not growing younger, & I literally have not a moment to lose. My heart is set upon this.

A year ago, I had given [blot] hope of it. But now hope [blot] in again.

I am waiting for a picture of my little Constance. Give her a kiss from me. Much love to Flora. I should like so much to hear from her—when she has time to write. Cousin Fanny Cooper writes with so much pleasure about your gift; Cousin Sue, in her old age, has the great gratification of seeing both her life-long wishes accomplished; the orphanage is built, & the Hospital in [blot] since the Corning-Clarks [blot] (no relation to the Hyde-Clarks) have given $25,000 as an endowment, & Mrs Carter's children (as a Memorial of her) ten thousand for the building—which will be a simple one. Cousin Sue has worked at these two projects for forty years![2] The Watsons of Buffalo, with Marion Pease, are calling upon Clara as I write. Stanley is here, & we gaze upon him with all our eyes.[3] He has a fine face.—The French Broad is worthy of a chateau, I think. Love to all at 544. Tell Kate I have just had a long letter from Prof. Boucher.

Affly yours,
C.F.W.

Notes

1. The letter is written on stationary from Hotel Continental, Cairo.
2. Among Susan Fenimore Cooper's philanthropic causes were an orphanage, a hospital, a school for under-privileged children, and a home for poor families. The Corning-Clarks were the Alfred Corning-Clarks (1844–96); Alfred founded Singer Sewing-Machine Company. Mrs Carter was Jane Averell Carter (1841–88).
3. Explorer Henry Morton Stanley.

To J. B. Gilder (McGill)

Cairo. Egypt
Feb. 5th, 1890

My dear Mr Gilder.

I wonder whether my far away gratitude ever makes itself felt over your desk, like a perfume in the air? It should. And it would, if the new science of transmission of thoughts, were more fully developed. Do you realize that for ten years you have given me the Century? It is a very great kindness, and a great generosity. A hundred times I have wished to write and tell you how much the gift is appreciated; but always I have been forced to give up the pleasure by either press of literary work, or a lame arm—the latter a great bother. This winter, at last, I am doing nothing save enjoy; so now I can have the enjoyment of saying that I think you one of the kindest of men, and I send you most hearty thanks. I am devoted to the Century, admiring it and liking it with all my heart. How many times, when I have been tired and out of sorts, it has arrived in its fresh brown covers, and helped me to pass the day pleasantly.

After three years of housekeeping at Bellosguardo (Florence), I have given up my villa there. I have always been hoping that you would turn up in Italy, so that I could ask you to come to see me. Will it be any better when I am established in Venice? I am hoping to take an apartment there, before long; I adore the place, and why not have what one likes, after all!

This winter—as you have seen by the headings, I am in oriental lands; and much excited by all I am seeing. I feel opulent; proud; rich; almost arrogant! I have been to Corfu; I have sailed among the lovely Ionian Isles; I have been in Athens! Now I am here; and I go to Jerusalem—to Constantinople. Finally I close with the long voyage from Alexandria to London, touching at all sorts of romantic places.

I remember when I thought a voyage from Cleveland to Mackinac very wonderful!

All the same, my real heart is in my own land,—in Florida. (this heart that I have in Italy & Egypt, is a supplementary one).

You wo'nt expect me to describe Egypt. The Century has already had the best article on the subject; (the one with the likenesses of the Pharaohs). And, recently, Bubastis. As a personal impression, I can say that the amazing color & picturesqueness, the beauty, the marvels, are more wonderful even than I had dreamed. I shall spend the whole spring here.

This note asks for no answer. I know what a burden answers are, & beg that you make no effort about this. But if, next year, you come to Venice, pray let me know, that I may see you. Perhaps Mrs Gilder will come with you? Poor Venice—& our friends there—they are all mourning for Browning; he was the bright star of that horizon.

I hope you are well; and I send you the best good wishes for 1890.

Cordially your friend,
C. F. Woolson.

My regards to Mrs Dodge.

To Samuel Mather (WRHS/Mather)

Hotel Continental
Cairo
Feb. 25th, 1890

My dear Sam.

I have just sent you a cable dispatch, saying that the Hale cheque, which you sent me the last of December, has been lost, & asking you to stop its payment. I have also telegraphed the loss to the Alliance Bank, London, as I think the cheque was on that Bank. The Manager of the Crédit Lyonnais here (our bank) says that this is all that I can do.

All this time I have not cashed that cheque; but intended to do so on my return from the Nile trip. Yesterday morning (Feb. 24th), at Assiout on the Nile, where we left our Nile steamer to take the train for Cairo, the purse containing the cheque disappeared. There was no money; only the cheque. My money was in another purse. We have telegraphed & searched; but I fear that some Arab secreted the purse, & then, finding that there was only a piece of paper, (which he could not read), he threw it away. I hope the money is not really in danger, owing to this wretched accident? As the purse was lost, in a remote place, yesterday, & as I telegraphed early this a. m. to you, & to London, I am trusting that all is safe—though a great bother to you, I fear. The Crédit Lyonnais here, also took a mem. of the affair, in case any attempt should be made, here, to forge my name. But I do'nt think there is anyone in Assiout clever enough to do this!

I have also telegraphed to London for money for myself, & of course Clara can be my banker until I am supplied again. So all is well.

It is a very provoking piece of business. And I am annoyed at myself for not having carried the cheque (as usual) in an inner pocket. I can only say that henceforth I always shall. I have had almost no contretemps of this kind, large or small, in ten years of travel abroad, and the eight preceding years of travel at home.

Our Nile trip (barring this termination) was enchanting. It made an immense impression upon me; as indeed all Egypt has. I think the great vast desert impresses me the most; it is like a sea of arrested waves, & the color varies from silver to golden red. The Nile is magnificent, & the palms & processions of camels on shore are like the old Bible pictures. Then the tombs & the ruined temples are more perfect, & more wonderful, & more interesting than the descriptions would lead one to expect. I only went as far as Thebes—for Karnak to me is the most beautiful of all the temples. Clara & Clare went on to the first Cataract. They do not like Egypt as I do! I hope that I may come again—some day.

We are all well, & excited with all we are doing & seeing. At the present moment, the Watson Pease party of Buffalo are urging Clara to join them for the Jerusalem trip, which begins next Saturday, the first day of March, & lasts until the 10th, when Clara & Clare sail for Europe. I come back to Cairo, and remain until the heat drives me away. I dare say I shall write some "Impressions" of the winter's travels—though from Franklin Square comes a request for "another novel as soon as possible." They also write that "no novel of recent years has been more favorably received than Jupiter Lights." As this is from the publishers, who take the business view of a book's success, and who never deal in flattery, I think we can believe it.

I suppose it will be safer, after this, to address

"Care Alliance Bank
High Street. Kensington
London. W"

This is but a hasty note on business; I will not attempt a description of all I am seeing & enjoying. Suffice it to say that all is perfectly fascinating; & that I feel much stirred; and twenty years younger.

My dearest love to Flora, and a kiss for the boys & for my dear little namesake. Kate (I have had a letter from her this a. m.) writes that she is (the little Constance) very pretty & sweet, & that each day she grows more so. I was much troubled to hear how ill all had been at 544. My love to all; I shall write soon. Here it is like June at home; in the sun it is too hot. The streets are sweet with the odor of violets. At Luxor (Thebes) the jasmine was intensely sweet.

Altogether, this has been a wonderful winter!

Affectionately yours,
C. F. Woolson.

To Joel Chandler Harris (Emory)

Care Alliance Bank
High Street. Kensington
London. W. England
Cairo. Egypt
March 11th, 1890

Dear Mr Harris.

For nearly six months, I have been carrying round with me—all over the world, as one may say—an old copy of Balford's Magazine, which contained a line that gave me great gratification; my wish has been to write to you and say so. The line was this: "and I like C. F. Woolson's stories." It was signed—Joel Chandler Harris.

I think it is safe to say that among the many thousands of Brer Rabbit's admirers, there is no warmer one than I. I have been in the South (eight years) long enough to appreciate the absolute perfection of the dialect; but it is not alone the dialect; it is the exquisite fun and humor; and the negro at his best, both photographed and phonographed exactly. The book (the first one; the only one I have) is a classic. ~~It~~ In our family, it has become the vade mecum.[1] I think you could scarcely read aloud a line, without my being able to give you from memory, the following one. It was sent to me when it first came out, by a southern friend; and, in all my wanderings, whatever else I leave behind, I never leave that. You can imagine, then, the pleasure I felt when I read that its author "liked" C. F. Woolson's stories!

If you come abroad during the next three years, pray enquire for me in Venice. I have been living in Florence; but now I am going to try Venice for a while,—after this wonderful winter in the East. In the end, however, I am coming home; to live in Florida.

I am sending this letter, rather vaguely, to "Atlanta." But anyone in Georgia, or in all the South, must know where to find you.

Cordially yours,
C. F. Woolson.

Notes

1. vade mecum: the thing that always "comes with me."

To Flora Stone Mather (Benedict/CFW, 362)

[1890]

A funny scene. Eugene Schuyler gave a sort of housewarming on the Coptic Easter Monday, which is also the Arab festival called "Smelling the Zephyr." I went and met, among others, a Mrs Benedict who has lived abroad for years.[1] She asked me to come to her parlour that night (she was staying in our hotel), and I went. As I entered, the piano was sounding forth the strains of "Tenting on the Old Camp Ground." Miss Benedict was playing, and her mother, her cousin, Mr Corliss, and Elihu Vedder, the artist, who was with them, were singing in a chorus the old familiar words. From that we passed to the "Star Spangled Banner," "Rally Round the Flag," "Marching Through Georgia," and all the others. It was so funny—under the shadow, as it were, of the pyramids . . . I believe the reason was that the songs had just come, and that little Miss Benedict, who was born abroad, had never seen them . . .

Notes

1. Miss Benedict is probably a relation to the George Benedict family. As Americans, these guests are singing classic American tunes and patriotic songs.

To Samuel Mather (WRHS/Mather)

(c/o Alliance Bank
High Street. Kensington
London. W.
England)
Cairo
April 17th, [1890]

My dear Sam.

The picture of little Constance gives me much pleasure; she is such a beautiful child! And she appears, too, the picture of health, which is such a comfort. She has such bright expressive eyes, and such a remarkable noble head; the way it rises above the eyes, promises much. From their photographs, the three children appear to have much individuality, and, so far as I can gauge, they do not resemble each other; Livingston's expression is that of sweetness & thoughtfulness; Amasa has merriment, and energy; and here comes my little namesake, whose baby face, even now, has a character all its own. I send my dearest love and a kiss to all of them.

I have thought that I should hear from you. I have heard nothing since my letter of Feb. 25th about the lost draft. I recd your telegram, sent to Mr Schuyler; he repeated it to me at Jerusalem. I am hoping that the money has not been lost; in fact, I have felt pretty sure from the beginning that there would be no trouble about it—(save the bother to you, and the delay to me)—because I do'nt think there was anyone on the little steamer—or at Assiout—with intelligence or craft enough to try to make use of it. The Arab who secreted the purse, probably threw the bit of paper away. Still, I shall of course be anxious until I hear from you.

I do not know how regularly Clara corresponds with Will or Kate (I have heard from no one at 544); but I dare say you know, that, after our Nile trip, we went to the Holy Land, sailing from Port Said to Jaffa, & driving thence to Jerusalem. From Jerusalem, we went to Jericho and the Dead Sea. Then we hurried back to Jaffa to catch the steamer for Alexandria, as Clara & Clare were to sail from that port on a certain day for Venice, en route for Vienna. Jerusalem was beautiful & interesting in the extreme; this I had not expected as regards the town itself, for it is, as you know, entirely modern; there is nothing left of the Bible town save the underground foundations of the Temple. But the church of the Holy Sepulchre is as rich in color & architecture as St Mark's, Venice, & very much larger. It was very interesting to see the Russian pilgrims; they had come—over a thousand—all the way from Russia to spend part of Lent, and Holy Week, in Jerusalem, & they were always in & about the church; they were poor peasants, who had walked a good part of the way, & their devotion was intense; they knelt & kissed the stones, sobbing. I afterwards saw many of them on their way to Jericho, on foot in that great heat, carrying their poor beds (rugs) & their food, on their backs.—One has to turn away from many superstitions which seem to me to mar Jerusalem; they insist upon showing so many false things; the prints of Our Lord's feet; relics of all kinds which are utterly impossible. This very church of the Holy Sepulchre is supposed to cover the site of the Crucifixion; the Lord's grave; the spot where St Helena found the crosses; the tomb of Adam! and many more impossibilities. It is the same everywhere. But one can turn away from all that & look at the landscape, which is unchanged; this hill was the site of the old Jerusalem, & yonder is the Mount of Olives; Bethany & Bethlehem are near. Best of all, this is the same sky (& this the same general aspect of the land, with its stony hills, its olive trees, its brooks, its wild flowers in profusion. I did not go to the shore of the Dead Sea; I saw it plainly—its whole expanse—from the top of the queer little inn, at Jericho. What will you say when you hear that I went on horseback to Jericho? I can scarcely believe that it was I. But I had been about so much on donkeys in Egypt, that I thought that I might perhaps venture it. Alas, it was not the same thing! Do'nt ask me how I arrived at Jericho; but think of Lady Hester Stanhope.[1] It was too hurried & too hard a trip for me; I suppose we tried to do too much, as we had so short a time. But Clara & Clare enjoyed every moment of it, and I am glad that I went, tired though I was; it is a great deal to have seen Jerusalem. I came back to Cairo & went to bed with that old tiresome pain in my right arm & shoulder. But it only lasted a few days.

I came back here because I am greatly fascinated with Cairo, & I had not seen half of it. I have been here alone for six weeks, & I am not yet satiated with the oriental architecture & color. I am now, however, ready to go at last. And I find it very difficult to get away! I had no idea that there would be trouble about getting passage so late in the season. But Prince Eddie has been staying here, on his way to England, & there have been gayeties—opera, races, balls &c for him, and I suppose that has kept people on. Besides, now is the time of the summer flight from India. I have been doing my utmost to get away for a week, without success. I will keep this letter open until something definite has been arranged. I am thinking a little of taking the long voyage entirely by sea (to England) via Malta, Gibraltar, & the Bay of Biscay), as with my heavy luggage, it will be much cheaper.

I have thought a good deal about remaining here; Cairo people spend their summers (the well-to-do) in Constantinople; I am told the climate is charming. I could go there; & then return here for another winter—as I am so greatly fascinated with things oriental; I am on the spot, and it is not likely that I shall ever get so far away again. I have excellent introductions for Constantinople from Lady Hobart, and also (best of all) invitations from some of her friends to visit them on two of the beautiful Greek islands!

But I have given up this plan. I feel that it is too far away; and I also know that I should never be able to do any steady work, with all that beauty to see—any more than I should if I were to come home this summer, and be with all of you; I see myself playing with the baby by the hour, & telling all my old fairy stories to Amasa & Livingston! No, if I am to get my finances into shape, I must give myself to steady work, in the most quiet & unexciting place I can find.—

I have made Mrs Oliphant's acquaintance here; she is a pleasant-faced little old lady, fat, & bright eyed; a mixture (in looks) of Queen Victoria & the Miss Horners of Florence (whom Kate knows). She has invited me to visit her at Windsor. I listened to her, (& secretly studied her) very intently; I was curious to find out the secret of the amount of work she produces; she has written about forty novels, & still turns them out at the rate of two or three each year! I think I discovered part of the secret: she writes—but she does nothing else. A capable maid does everything for her; she does not put on her own bonnet, nor shoes. A young niece sees people for her; her son arranges every thing she does. She did not even know her own route to the Holy Land. She has gone there to write a book about the country, & how much time do you suppose she thought sufficient for her observations? Two weeks. I have been in Cairo two months and a half,—longer even than that; yet I feel that I could only risk some slight "impressions." It is true that I am not a Mrs Oliphant!

As I said before, I have had no news from any of you, so have nothing to answer. Clara's letter of this morning, an hour ago mentions that Kate had written, speaking of her father's illness. I am so sorry, & so grieved about it. I have no particulars, but I suppose it is that he has not recovered from the attack of some time ago. Give him my dearest love & sympathy, and do write me how he is.

My love to your mother; I am going to write to her as soon as I can. At present I am tired, & troubled about the difficulties of my journey. It has been summer here for two months.

Tell Kate that I rec^{d} a letter recently from Lionel Byrne at Eton; he had heard from Berenson that I was in England, so he sent a note to the Alliance Bank, asking me to come out to Eton, & "accept such hospitalities as a bachelor can offer." He lives in one of those beautiful old houses which I used to admire last autumn. I think Eton a lovely place, & if Kate & I were in London this spring, we would go out there & have afternoon tea with him. He used to be Master at Clifton College; but that was only temporary. Though he is a Master, he was stroke in the "Varsity" boat, when at Oxford; he is devoted to boating.

Stanley has been here all winter; he only left a week ago—to begin the round of festivities awaiting him. There is another side—; not to Stanley's courage & heroism, which are great—but to this whole business of central Africa. It is a race for power between England & Germany, with other nations also trying to have a slice; & poor Egypt deputed by all. Egypt, at present, is virtually an English province; and I do'nt believe that the British lion will ever let go.

I hear you have had Miss Edwards in Cleveland. The old Boulacy Museum here, has been moved to a palace at Ghiseh, & the treasures are now at last well housed. Brugsch Bey, the director, is one of my friends here, & often comes to see me. He is the hero of the great Deir-el-Baheri adventure—the finding of the ~~Pha~~ mummies of the Pharoahs. He was let down into the shaft by a rope, you remember, & entered the tomb-chamber alone; it is exciting to hear him tell of it. He says he was so overcome—when he recognized the names on the coffins—that he had to go back &

~~be signaled~~ signal to those above to haul him up; he was afraid he should faint away down there in the thick air.

Eugene Schuyler I often see. It is too bad, that, all this time, he has not been confirmed. Can't you do something?

My best love to Flora. I should like so much to hear from her. I hope that she will be able to write to me this summer, when I am grinding away in England alone. Henry James has gone to Italy for four or five months; so I shall not see him. He goes first to Venice; then to some Italian mountain top.

Somebody has taken the pains to send me, very carefully directed, a N.Y. Evening Post, ~~with~~ containing a savage attack upon Jupiter Lights; as the Post & the Nation are the same, the article will go into the Nation also, I suppose.[2] I seldom see reviews of my books, friendly or unfriendly; & I do'nt much care about them—because they are not sincere. But this Post attack touched me a little, because I think it <u>may</u> come—in spirit—from Mr Howells, who, strange to say, has turned from a friend to an enemy. He is powerful; & he is on the spot; & he dislikes with a vengeance! When he does dislike. It is the one painful spot in my literary life, because I used to like him so much, & trust him. I usually try not to think of him; it is only when something occurs unexpectedly—like this arrival of the Post—that my mind goes back to the subject.

For the world is wide and there is room for all; the best courage is to do one's best as bravely as one can, & let the rest go.

My regards to Col. & Mrs Hay. Are they coming over this summer? I have not decided as to the part of England I shall select; perhaps it will be Scotland, and "the beautiful, beautiful Dee."

I hope you will write soon & tell me all about Flora, the children; and the new house on the lake.

I am now going out to [beard?] Gaze & Cook in their dens, & insist upon a cabin for <u>something</u>!

April 18th

After great difficulty I have secured a cabin by the Italian steamer to Naples tomorrow, from Alexandria. It is the Rubattino line, but the name of the steamer I do not know. I do not like Italian steamers; but there was nothing else to be had. Mr Schuyler tells me that <u>he</u> likes the line very much, & always chooses it when possible. I go to Naples & very likely shall keep on by sea to Genoa. From there I must go by train to London. I ought to arrive there by the 28th or so.—I am sending to the little Constance a small remembrance with my dearest love; Clara will take it; she & Clare sail May 10th, and already they are expecting me in England.

"The way to Egypt is long & vexatious," Homer says; in my case, it is "the way from Egypt"[3]—Good by with best love to all.

Affectionately yours,
C.F.W.

Notes

1. Lady Hester Stanhope (1776–1839) was known for how widely she, though a woman, traveled.

2. The review appeared in the Dec. 29, 1889, New York *Post* and in *Nation,* March 13, 1890. The *Nation* review is reprinted in Torsney, Cheryl B., ed. *Critical Essays on Constance Fenimore Woolson,* New York: G. K. Hall, 1992: 55.

3. Book IV of the *Odyssey.*

To Daniel Gilman (Johns Hopkins)

Continental. Tuesday
[1890]

My dear Mr Gilman.

I should like to go, of all things. But I have two engagements, one for four o'clock, the other for half past four; they promise nothing, alas!, in the way of entertainment; but they cannot be postponed—much to my regret.

I will look in at the New Hotel at half past five. If you have not returned, I will come again at six. Do'nt hurry back; the great thorn tree & garden are so interesting. The obelisk is rather spoiled after bazzars.

In haste, yours,
C. F. Woolson.

To Henry Mills Alden (WRHS/Benedict)[1]

(c/o Alliance Bank
High Street. Kensington
London W. England)
Llandudno. North Wales
May 11th, [1890]

My dear Mr Alden.

My last letter to you was written at Cairo. Immediately after that your book came, and I embarked for England, or rather for Genoa; a voyage of seven days, passing Crete, the lower part of Italy, Sicily (we stopped at Messina), and entering the Bay of Naples and that of Leghorn. The weather was beautiful, and it was a beautiful, quiet, silent voyage, for I spoke to nobody. Why? Because I was so taken up with your book.

It was my companion all the way, and my only one, and I can scarcely—in a letter—tell you the impression it made upon me. That impression is profound. It is the most beautiful book I have ever read; by that I mean the most full of beauty. I envy you the state of mind in which you wrote it; I wish that I, ~~could~~ too, could enter in. Perhaps I shall—for already the book has made a change in me, though as yet it is a slight one. The trouble with me is that I am constantly knocked down—as it were—by a horror of the cruelties of life; did you ever see a small insect, trying to climb a wall, and always, sooner or later, falling to the floor—only to begin again? That is I. If the cruelties do not happen to me personally (though many of them have happened, and continue to do so), they happen to some one within my sight; and then down I go again mentally, overwhelmed by the view of so much dreadful, & helpless, & often innocent (or comparatively innocent), suffering. I ca'nt get over it,—as the saying is; it keeps me down.

To me then, constantly depressed, comes this message of yours, & fills me with wonder and admiration. You must let me say, as a parenthesis—that it might be just as wonderful and beautiful a message coming from a man of another kind of life, but that in that case I should not care for it; what gives it especial force with me is your daily patient toil, which has gone on in what seems to me the most magnificent way, ever since I first knew you; how hard you work, I might not, perhaps, have fully appreciated (since you yourself never speak of it), if it had not been for a well-known N.Y. literary man, who explained it to me ten years ago, adding that such responsibilities & labor as you had—(in connection with the magazine)—would kill any ordinary man. In the midst of this laborious life, you have preserved all your sweetness of mind, & you have written this extraordinarily beautiful gospel. It is a miracle.

During a call made upon me last year, in Florence, by Mr T. S. Perry, of Boston, I, not knowing that he was the original leader of the Tolstoi clan, in the U.S., mentioned (simply as a subject for conversation) some stories which I had lately heard concerning him (Tolstoi); (I think I have told you some of them?).[2] Mr Perry did not believe these stories; but presently he exclaimed that even though they were proved to be true, even though worse were true & Tolstoi proved to be a bad man, or a hypocrite, it would make no difference in his admiration for what he had written. He did not care what Tolstoi was as a man (though he believed him to be all that is noble); in his private life he might be anything, do anything,—; but it would make no difference in the ~~worth~~ value and beauty of his message to the world. Of course I do not quote verbatim; but I have given the substance.) Now I could never have said that; it makes all the difference in the world to me whether the writer of a message to mankind is, in his private life, a courageous man, an energetic man, an unselfish sincere man,—or not. And the great moral that I draw under your book (as one adds up a sum in addition), is the to me splendid fact that you have kept all this beauty of soul (which the book displays so unconsciously) through a life of labor, and daily devotion to tiresome unrelenting details; that you have unflinchingly held to all this; and yet that the dust of every day has not dimmed your vision, nor the grasping sordid hands on every side, dragged you down. This is but a parenthesis. But I could not help inserting it.

I have read the book through twice. But I shall read it more times than that. One of your sentences, in the Introduction, seems to me the keynote of the whole: "In loving one another, we find God." This is to me both beautiful and true; for love is unselfish, and it gives a delight (even when it exists only on one side) which seems to me almost the only real pleasure one can have in this existence.

In addition to its beauty, the book is full of common sense; every now and then [excision] sentence appears which might take rank as a maxim; or be quoted by even the most practical unimaginative person. These clear strong sentences bring one up short—if one has been indulging in too many fancies and dreams.

This is much like you in real life, by the way; how often have you brought me up, either in speech or in a letter, in exactly the same way!

In much of the book I agree with you even now. Perhaps Fate may be good to me, and, in time, open my ears to the rest. It would be such peace!—I wish you could have stood with me, this spring, upon the Mount of Olives; could have walked through the streets of Jerusalem. It is true that they are not the ~~same~~ old streets; but the site is the old one. One might think that if there is nothing [?] site, one gains little by seeing it with the actual eyes. But this is a mistake. The sky is the same as of two thousand years ago; the formation of the hills the same, & all the colors of the landscape; a strange feeling comes over one, in spite of all one can do; I think I have never had stranger feelings than those that came over me as I rode across the stony hills where John the Baptist preached, on our way to the Jordan, & the Dead Sea.

Traveling—the actual seeing of far countries and their customs—gives one a much wider vision; it then becomes very difficult to go back to the narrow ~~views~~ ideas which one once had, & which one's best friends, perhaps, still retain. Your book is so broad that it is a comfort as well as a pleasure to read it—after over ten years of world-wandering and observation, which a strong curiosity about mankind in general & its different ways of thinking, still keeps up.

The style of the book (I mean its literary style)—I think faultless. But this does not surprise me; you have always had the clearest & loveliest style; your simplest note shows that. Oh the wider page of this volume, it flows on with often such a beauty that one sighs with satisfaction!—I mean that one does if one cares much—as I do—for a beautiful expression of thought. I am so tired of the common-ness of much of the literary manner of the day. Authors seem trying to show which can be the most commonplace. They hold our noses down to the grindstone. They tie us down to words and phrases as deadly dull as the deadly dull streets & people to which, for the most part, they confine us. They would do well to study your pages, where one splendid sentence follows another with a beauty which lifts the heart. In the communion service (Episcopal) there is, you know, this command, from the priest: "Lift up your hearts!" And the answer from the congregation; "We lift them up unto the Lord." Your sentences lift us up unto the Lord.

If I have a fault to find with your book, it is that it has not a more especial message for the sad, the suffering, the despairing. I understand this, because I have always, from the first of our acquaintance, been struck with your—shall I call it optimism? (It is not the exact word.) And not only was this feeling in you sincere, but you lived up to it. You always said that you were happy; and I could never discover that you were in the least un-happy. Apparently, you were perfectly free from depression of spirit. The serene, the happy, will love your book at once. But those of us who (like me) are weighed down by a sense of the difficulties, & cruelty, of life,—we shall have to search a little for our message; that is, your message to us. I do'nt doubt but that we shall find them.

Cheltenham
May 20th

I did not send off my letter from Llandudno, because I wished to read the book over again. This I have now done, and I am going to give myself the pleasure of jotting down some of the things that have especially struck me. In the first place, I am much struck with your fairness. In Part II of the Introduction, this is conspicuous. Also in all of Part XVIII of the Introduction. Again in the last half of Page 31. And about the Nirvana, Page 33–4. And the last half of Page 55 (that is the opening of XXX). And page 99.

Then there are so many striking ideas! Often, you just touch upon them, & then leave them. Yet they are sometimes so new, & so vast—that they leave one startled. For instance, leaving "the field of his mere understanding"; (Page XIV of Introduction). The idea that there is another field & a higher one, makes one pause. Is there such a field? Can there be?[3]

How remarkable, too, "a plea for Nature & for all her embodiments however grotesque or faultful—thus absolving the ideal from formal perfectness."

And what a striking conception on Page eleven & Page 13, that the dispensation we call Christian is not the only dispensation of grace! When one has been in Egypt—the jumping-off place of history—one comes to believe in ages and ages of human existence; one loses one's way, & all one's ~~old~~ standards and measuring lines. One cannot come back to one's old beliefs, & it is exasperating to be asked to come back. Such an idea as that which you have expressed above becomes, therefore, very real; & a pleasure.

Then, too, I am greatly struck with something on Page 58 that "mortal frailty, divinely purposed," has no connection with sin. The whole of this page is wonderful. And[4]

If one can believe it—& why should'nt one?—it would explain part of that which I call life's cruelty.

Then again on Page 162—"The freedom of the kingdom to a freedom from ethical obligations; from what the world calls conscience." How that sets one to thinking! And perhaps that too touches upon the point of "cruelty"—which has always troubled me so deeply.

Another idea that is startling is expressed at the top of Page 206; can it be that this is the key to the future?—and that constantly-more-complete organization is not the key? Pages 210, 211, 212 belong to the same (striking) class as the sentence I have already spoken of on Page 58. If one can believe all this! If! Then how much simpler & easier does life become! It is like a door suddenly opened into the light.[5]

But I must not tire you.—As for myself I have by no means finished my reading of this book. I shall often look into it.

I cannot stop without again mentioning the style; all of page 250—but especially the close.

And how I do agree with Part III of the Introduction; and above all with its concluding paragraphs.[6]

I left the cold Welsh coast, and came down here, where I shall probably stay for some months. Please continue to address the Bank (as at head of letter) as usual; as that is always perfectly safe. I am in the midst of a green country, with several old castles within walking distance, & three cathedrals near—Hereford, Worcester, & Gloucester. After the constant company and visits of my Florence life, and after this wonderful oriental winter, I am well content to have some perfectly quiet months in which to catch up with myself, and set my mind in order.

I wrote to you from Cairo. I do'nt know whether you will care to answer that letter? But I wish, much, that you ~~will be~~ have been able to. Nothing outside, however, will make any difference in the regard of your old friend,

C. F. Woolson.

Notes

1. Pasted into Alden, Henry Mills, *God in His World,* New York: Harpers, 1890. Throughout the letter, Woolson is discussing this book.

2. Probably writer Thomas Sergeant Perry (1845–1928), a friend of Henry James.

3. Woolson marked up her copy of Alden's *God in His World*. In the passages she mentions

here, Alden speaks about the spiritual power of nature (II, 31); the power of the imagination to perceive the divine (XVIII); the wisdom of the concept of Nirvana, or freedom from all life concerns and all consciousness (33–34); the connection between God and nature in paganism (55); the power of feeling over logic (99); and the rightness of God's plan (XIV).

4. A portion of the letter is missing here.

5. Alden's ideas in these pages focus on life's difficulty and on human frailty as, nevertheless, leading to heaven.

6. These sections focus on the power of art and the imagination.

To Katharine Livingston Mather (WRHS/Mather)[1]

4 Promenade Terrace
Cheltenham. England
June 12th, 1890

My dear Kate.

. . . I have now gone to work again, as they are anxious for another novel (at Franklin Square,) and, before beginning it, I must exorcise the ghosts of Cairo and Corfu, by finishing some "Impressions" of these two fascinating places, which I began while still in Egypt. These "Impressions" have bothered me dreadfully. The notes and manuscripts I wrote in Cairo, would make a large book, instead of two Magazine articles. It has been difficult to select what to leave out, since every item about Cairo is, to me at least, deeply interesting. On the whole, Cairo is the most beautiful and fascinating place I have as yet seen. One does not love it in the tender way one loves Italy. But one is, (or at least I am,) completely absorbed in its strange charm. It is, I suppose, simply the oriental color. And this is probably the reason why I admire Venice so much; it, too, is very oriental. I have spent two weeks here, writing about Cairo, for nine hours a day. You must read the poor curtailed "Impressions," when they come out, sometime, in Harper's. The making of the illustrations takes so long, that I suppose this won't be before next winter.

I think I told you that after my return to Cairo, I saw a great deal of Professor Pierce, of Harvard. He went, afterwards, to Constantinople, and his letters from there are so enthusiastic that I feel I must see that beautiful place. He is not the least enthusiastic, ordinarily; but his Constantinople letters are like poems. He, too, is fascinated with the East. . . .

Cheltenham is, I think, going to do very well, for the summer at least. On the left of the Promenade, (which is a mile and a quarter long) are excellent shops; on the right, behind a second row of trees, is Promenade Terrace, where I stay. I have a drawing room, with dining-room behind it. Then, on the floor above, I have a good bed-room with dressing room attached. I live as we did on Sloan[e] Street, the landlord waiting at table, and his wife being the cook. The only difference is that I buy everything I eat, myself; they merely cook and serve. The house is charmingly clean, and the furniture and linen very fair. . . . The other day I walked to Prestbury, a wee village two miles from Cheltenham. It was on a week-day, and I reached there about six p.m. Presently I saw a magnificent white flag high in the air, and soon discovered that it was flying from the gray stone tower of a very picturesque and ancient Norman Church, standing in its old churchyard. The flag had upon it four red fleur de lys, and a royal crown. I have no idea why. The door was open and I went in. Here I found a choir of twenty surpliced boys, and five priests in vestments, going through the evening service, with all sorts of ritualistic ornaments, banners, crosses, incense, and flowers; a congregation of ten persons. Now who in the world pays for all that in this very small rural village? I am told there is Morning and Evening service there every day in the year. In the quiet little main street I came upon an old cottage with a deep thatch, and very clean white curtains in the little windows; above, under the thatch was this inscription, "The gift of Ann Goodrich to the Religious Poor, 1720." A Trinity Church Home of nearly two hundred years ago. . . .

Affectionately
C. F. Woolson.

Notes

1. The letter is in a typed transcription at WRHS. Portions also appear in Benedict/CFW, 344n.

To Samuel Mather (WRHS/Mather)

4 Promenade Terrace
Cheltenham
(Gloucestershire)
England
June 12th, [1890]

My dear Sam.

The more I look at this picture of little Constance (at six months old), the prettier I think it is! It is the most charming and darling picture of a baby, that I have ever seen. I am so anxious to see her—dear little girl! I keep her smiling face on my table, & often, often, look at it.

I have just written a long letter to Kate, & this is but a line of thanks to you for the picture. I have settled myself here—probably for the summer, & hope to do ever so much writing. They ~~write~~ send me very satisfactory letters from Franklin Square, & are urgent for another novel. So I suppose I shall do some more fiction. But I must have a try at a play, too.

Send me a photograph of your Lake Shore house when it is completed; I am very much interested in that house. I am afraid I am growing very old—for I dwell so much on the past. How often we used to drive out to the different lakeshore places to spend the day. Often we took you & Kate with us. I have a subscription at Mudie's (the only way to get books in England), &, the other day, I got Walpole's Letters.[1] Do you know—I liked them! This marks an advance in age: no young person likes Walpole; I myself have never had the patience to read much of him before. "Eheu, fugaces!"[2]—I hope Flora got my letter? My love to her, & a kiss for each of the babies. Here is an idea for your Lakeshore garden: "Beware! Beware! Scolopendriums & Polypodiums set here!"—This is set up on a big board in a garden, two miles from Cheltenham. Sure enough, the harmless ferns of that name were mildly growing below! But I suppose, to the rustic, it meant some terrible new kind of man-trap & spring-gun. Good-by.

Most affectionately yours,
C.F.W.

Notes

1. Editions of Horace Walpole's letters began appearing in 1818. Woolson has probably been reading an 1891 edition.

2. Woolson is quoting Horace's Ode II:14; "Eheu, Fugaces" roughly translates as "the years fly by."

To William Wilberforce Baldwin (Morgan)[1]

4 Promenade Terrace
Cheltenham
Aug. 17th, [1890]

My dear Doctor.

I hear that you are in London, and I write this line to say how much delighted I should be, if you could spare the time to come to Cheltenham. It is true that the place is dull, and that I have no longer a Tuscan view, and a skilled cook; also, that the journey is three hours long. But your welcome from me would be of the warmest; it would be a very great satisfaction and pleasure ~~for me~~ to see you,—without waiting for the time when I, too, return to Italy. Do'nt you think you can do me this favor?

The hotel here—The Queen's—is not bad; and it is very near me. I should, of course, expect you to dine with me every day, and to give me your evenings. Then we could take some drives. Rural England is always green & pretty. I have a sitting-room in which we can sit and talk, and a little dingy diningroom, in which we can dine. I long to hear all about you and yours; and about Florence; and Italy. Let me know if I may expect you, and when.

I had, last year, the great winter of my life. Nothing has ever so much impressed me as Egypt; even now I am still excited about it. I feel like another person—so broadened in mind by an actual look into the strange life of the East. Of the many people I saw while absent, & of the few I have seen since returning, no one has appeared excited on the subject but myself! For me, Egypt was wonderful and beautiful beyond words.—I wonder if you know anything of Eugene Schuyler's last days? He wrote me about the last of June, from Cairo. He died in Venice, I see; so he was at least in Italy, poor fellow! How he longed for Italy, & hated—hated—Egypt!—Do you wish to take some flowers from The Holy Land to Mrs Thompson? But no; I will send them by Mme Villari, later. Mrs T. asked me to get them for her. My best love to Mrs Baldwin when you next write.

Send me a line; & I hope much that it will say you are coming. With all [?] good wishes, I am your attached friend,

C. F. Woolson.

Notes

1. The envelope reads c/o Henry James, Esqre, 34 DeVere Gardens, Kensington. London W.

To William Wilberforce Baldwin

Promenade Terrace
Cheltenham
Sept. 7th [1890]

Dear Doctor.

When I saw the account of the accident in my morning's paper, I said to myself, instantly, "Could that have been the Doctor's train!" You had not, in your letter, mentioned the exact time of your departure; so I tried to tell myself that my fears were but the reflection of the constant horror of railway accidents, which is always with me—I think you know why?[1]—(Though, oddly enough, I am never afraid for myself when traveling. It is only about others that I am haunted.) But a note from Henry James tells me the dreadful story. What a shock it must have been to your nerves! I am thankful that the horror was so soon followed by the arrival at home, so that the pleasure of seeing the family—those little boys you were so homesick for—effaced other pictures.

I hope you found them all well? Give my best love to Mrs Baldwin.—I should like to be arriving in Florence myself! However, at last summer has come, in this singular climate; yesterday and to-day have been warm and sunshiny, & I am haunted by the vision of the old trees in Richmond & Windsor Parks, as I saw there last year at this time. I may grow homesick too; but alas! only for trees,—not for active bright eyed little boys, like you.

To see you was a great refreshment to me. The next time, I hope the scene will be Venice—which is better than a provincial Promenade.

I have laughed a dozen times over the description of the breakfast given by the Microbe killer. Was the name Leather?[2] That adds to it.—Why do'nt you jot down the amusing, and the strange, and the interesting episodes that dot your life, so that, later, you can bring them out as your Reminiscences? I mean much later; when you are an old man. I am sure you have already enough to fill a volume; the few which you have barely outlined to me, in casual conversation, were extraordinary.

Give my love to Miss Greenough, when you see her; & to Miss Huntington. I hope to be able to write to Miss Huntington very soon. Tell her, please, that I have been bothered with a lame wrist.—I saw three ripe figs here, the other day. They were 9 pence each; nearly a franc! I should like to step into my villa again! But only as owner. No Brichieris. With all sorts of good wishes I am, ever your attached friend,

C. F. Woolson.

Notes

1. Woolson draws on this accident for her story "In Sloane Street" (*Harper's Bazar*, June 11, 1892). Her brother-in-law George Benedict was killed in a train accident.

2. Louis Pasteur's (1822–95) recognition that the tanning process of leather involves microbes led to his discoveries on microbial disease.

To Katharine Loring (Beverly)

4 Promenade Terrace
Cheltenham
Sept. 19th, [1890]

Dear Miss Loring.

Your very amusing letter about the beans, would have been answered long ago, had it not been for a tiresome lameness in my wrist. Work long behind-time had to be done in spite of the lameness; but the pleasure of writing letters had to be postponed. The wrist is well now, I am glad to say.—

Your letter took me back to the days that are no more. My father was a New Englander (New Hampshire), and cherished a secret love for baked beans. My mother, a genuine daughter of New York, would not smile upon this fancy. Still, occasionally we had the celebrated dish,—though it was never right because not prepared in an earthen pot; I think nothing would have induced my mother to purchase the proper pot; she regarded beans much as Lady Agnes (Tragic Muse) regarded

Art;[1]—namely that it (the dish) is pardonable only as long as it's bad. Probably this attitude of hers explains why I ~~was~~ am so uncertain about the soaking, etc; for, in other matters, I was carefully instructed; I wonder if you can make better cake than I can!—I must tell you why I wished information. The street cries of Cairo are so over-described that one dares not give them, in spite of their charm. In writing some light Impressions of that enchanting town, I could not resist putting down one, which is less known. The best beans came from Embebeh, a suburb beyond Boulak (where the great Cairo Museum used to be). The Cairo bean-seller chants daily as follows: "Help, O Embebeh; help! The beans of Embebeh are better than almonds. Oh-h, how sweet are the little sons of the river!" The last phrase refers to the soaking in the Nile water which is required before the baking.—I wished to imagine a Boston huckster crying out, "Help, O Beverly, help! The beans of Beverly are better than peaches. Oh-h! How sweet are the little sons of Cochituate!"

Another remembrance of my childhood is "Old Hartford Election Cake." Do you know anything about that delectable compound? It used to be sent, in a tin case once a year, to my brother-in-law, Mr Mather, the direct descendant of old Cotton & Increase.[2] I think my mother scorned even that; she preferred the crullers & oleykoeks of her own home.—In connection with cake, I shall never forget the masses—banks—of the richest plum cake (real black cake or wedding cake) which the southern girls with whom I passed my time at school, devoured in the winter. It was the French school, Mme Chegaray, New York, & there were but three northern pupils. To the Southern girls came, by express, large boxes containing four & six large plum cakes, thickly iced. Each girl had this quantity,—made by those wonderful black cooks of old. They thought nothing of eating solid wedges, weighing a pound or two, every day.

I see that you are well instructed about Boston, its rivers, & its suburbs. If I am ever so happy as to spend a year there, will you go with me to Watertown—to dig up the bones of my ancestor?[3] We are in the habit of calling him, familiarly, "the original Thomas." He is buried at Watertown, and his age is marked on his venerable tombstone. The date throws his birth back almost to the Mayflower, & yet no such name is to be found in the small, carefully kept lists of those early days. My father amused himself for years in hunting records both in England & New England. At last he discovered a charming trail; the name was not Woolson, but Wollaston, & our American forefather was one of the "Merry Mount" colony (Quincy), and an Episcopalian—of course abhorred by the Puritans, who perforce changed the name, & creed of the one forlorn little boy Thomas, left in their hands. But further search upon this trail revealed the fact that the gay Capt. Wollaston became a buccaneer, & was hanged on the mast of Virginia, later! Since then we have let it alone.—See how your letter, with its Boston aroma of streams & beans, has set me off!

I thank you warmly for reviving my spirits (crushed by Miss Greenough & Mr Boott) about piece bags. Do not local habits & local ways amuse you? To me they are full of entertainment. I was encamped—as it were—for years before the ways and phrases of Southerners, after the war.

I write to-night to ask whether you cannot give me two or three days here? I should be so very glad to see you. I feel ashamed to ask you to take so long a journey for so little; Cheltenham is deadly dull, & I am in dull "apartments"; no longer have I a Tuscan villa; I have not even a Richmond view. But we could go over to Gloucester (15 minutes), to see one cathedral; & to Worcester (one hour), to see another. If you could come, it would give me great pleasure.

I am (in asking you) counting upon the chance that the bedroom below me will be free. Today it is occupied. But I have an idea that the lady is merely settling her boy at school & that she will not remain.

How could you know (when you sent me the circulars about the medical education of women) that you were striking a chord? It is a fact for the Psychical Society.[4] (I know no word so terrible to spell as that adjective! It is'nt in my dictionary & I have to guess at it each time. I never write it twice alike.) I'll tell you if I see you,—I'm medically educated—if you please;—up to a certain point, that is. Have you ever dissected a calf? (I mean a four-legged one.) Have you ever had a large French Manikin pursuing you in your dreams? Have you ever strung together a real skeleton?—seriously, I think the plan an excellent one. It opens a new field for women, & one that belongs to them fairly; one for which they are fitted. But do insist that they shall be educated with the students of the other sex, and not kept by themselves; it is the only way, in my opinion, to widen the feminine mind. Do not suppose from that that I think the feminine mind inferior to the masculine. For I do not. But it has been kept back, and enfeebled, & limited, by ages of ignorance, & almost servitude.

Give my love to Miss James. I hope Tunbridge—if she decides upon that—will prove pleasant. Cheltenham has its advantages; good air; quiet; the numerous small conveniences of a town inhabited chiefly by retired East India officers, & Civil Servants;—and low prices. It is larger than Leamington; 50,000 inhabitants. I liked Leamington because, in ten minutes, I could get beyond the town. There is nothing here like the lovely "old road" to Warwick. I do not know how long I shall stay. I am even now, a little breathless still, after my delightful & exciting, but very fatiguing winter, in Athens & Egypt. It was the most wonderful journey that I have ever made; and the most wonderful winter I have ever had.

Are you reading Kipling?

I hope Mr James has given a good account of me? If he mentions me as "worthy," let me know in private, that I may think of a revenge. Curiously enough he considers it a complimentary adjective, I believe!

I have always felt very guilty about having burdened you with that large doll, for my little godson, Francis Duveneck. Mr Boott writes that Duveneck himself—the papa—is staying at Waltham with the Lymans; he has been ill, & has gone there to recruit.

—An entrance here of Elliot, my landlord, with my six books from Mudie's. (I have six each week.) Perhaps the list will amuse you,—the reading of a Cheltenham spinster—"Praeterita" by Ruskin. "Beauchamp's Career," by George Meredith. The Correspondence of Wagner and Liszt. "The Byzantine Empire," by Finlay. "The World as Will & Idea," by Schopenhauer. And "Beautiful Jim," by "John Strange Winter!"—I am reading the "works" of all these popular ladies—Edna Lyall, Marie Corelli, the "Winter" woman, &c.[5] It is very edifying.

A week ago, I had the big volumes of the Researcher of the London Psichycal! Society. Are you interested in such things? Prof. Peirce (James) writes me that all the recorded facts are illusions. Good night. I am now going to enrage myself over Ruskin; I hate him; & hate's very enlivening—when one is shut up in a British Promenade.

Cordially Yours,
C. F. Woolson.

Notes

1. A character in Henry James's *The Tragic Muse* (1890).

2. The Samuel Mathers were actually indirect descendents of Increase and Cotton Mather.

3. Woolson published a satirical sketch "The Bones of Our Ancestors" in *Harper's New Monthly Magazine,* Sept. 1873.

4. The American Society for Psychical Research was founded in 1885. William James was a founding member.

5. In addition to the well-known writers and composers, Woolson refers to George Finlay, author of *A History of the Byzantine Empire*; John Strange Winter (1856–1911), romance novelist and author of *Beautiful Jim* (1881); Edna Lyall (1857–1903), the author of eighteen novels; and Marie Corelli (1855–1924), who was a musician before turning to writing.

To William Wilberforce Baldwin (Morgan)

Cheltenham
Oct. 5th, [1890]

My dear Doctor.

I was relieved to hear from you, and to know that you had not suffered from the dreadful shock.[1] You have so much vitality—and youth also—that they have helped you to forget the scene. As for me—I cannot see the curtains of a sleeping car without a sick feeling. I have told you why.

You must send me a photograph of the three little boys when you get a good one. Have you ever thought of having them taken in a row one behind the other, in profile view; full length, standing on the floor close together, as though they were in position to play the old-fashioned game, "Open the gates as high as the sky?" I have a picture of the four grandchildren of Mrs Carter of Cooperstown (whom you knew), taken in that way, & it is the best & most lifelike children's group I have ever seen. One of the boys could have his head turned toward the spectators.

Do'nt hope for the beauty of baldness—with that thick hair of yours! The most you can hope for is the silvery hue, twenty years later; & it will be very becoming. I still advise notes for those Reminiscences. But wait until you are seventy-five at least, before you publish them, because otherwise some of the most remarkable events & episodes would have to be left out, as the actors would still be alive. It's amazing how people live on! I was on the point of publishing some leaves from a most charming Diary, written by my dear mother sixty years ago, when by chance I learned that some of the New Englanders (about whom her delicate wit had played), were alive, & actively reading everything in all the magazines, & papers.[2] I still believe you'll write for publication other things—besides the Reminiscences.

I have been making some charming excursions to lovely places in this neighborhood. The weather has been beautiful—strange to say. Henry James came down here & stayed two days; & we went to Worcester; I suppose you hear from him!—I may go to the south coast for the winter. Or perhaps to Paris. I have been up to town for a little amusement, also.—I must not forget to say that I have not touched that mixture since you disapproved of it.[3] But I have strictly contained the diet, & I have lost another five, more; seven, pounds since you left! I shall never have any sympathy for corpulent females (after this) who pretend that they would do anything to be thinner. There's no starvation in this diet, for plenty of meat is allowed. It is simply a sacrifice of the <u>nice</u> things.—Much love to Mrs Baldwin & best regards to your sister. Always your attached friend,

C. F. Woolson.

Notes

1. See letter to Baldwin dated Sept. 7, 1890.

2. Woolson's niece Clare Benedict includes some of Hannah Woolson's writing in volume 1, *Voices Out of the Past of Five Generations*, 3 vols., London: Ellis, 1929–30, 1932.

3. Some scholars believe that Woolson's fear of drugs was well founded and that she became addicted at the end of her life.

To Samuel Mather (Anderson)[1]

4 Promenade Terrace
Cheltenham. England
Oct. 9th, [1890]

My dear Sam.

Your telegram fills me with grief. He has gone then—your dear father. I did not in the least expect it, though I knew that his strength was not what it had been.

You loved him deeply, and I know how you are mourning for him now. He was always so fond of you, and proud of you. And, during these later years, your children have been so much to him.—

We can all look back upon his life with love and pride. And through our tears, we can at least feel that, for him, all pain and infirmity have ended.

It is a deep grief to me, now, that I did not go home this summer to see him. A sentence in one of his letters (sometime ago) haunts me: "Shall I ever see you again? I fear not; you are wedded to Europe." This is one of the sorrows so often associated with death;—that we did not do—or say—something that we might have done. But we must try to remember that our sorrow does not reach him; earthly grief does not enter there.

I thank you so much for sending me the telegram. It would have made me feel dreadfully sad not to know it until all was over at home. Now, I can be with you in thought at least,—day by day.—My best love to Flora. I was very glad to have her letter, for I do not hear half enough about the children. I like details about them; and Flora gave me some. I shall stay where I am until December at least; so letters can come directly here. The Alliance Bank, Kensington, is always safe, too. They repeated your telegram to me, instantly. And then forwarded the dispatch itself, by mail.—My dear Sam, in this great sorrow, you have the warm sympathy of your affectionate Aunt,

C. F. Woolson.

Notes

1. Portions of this letter appear in Benedict/Voices, 85n. Benedict also includes a passage from the Oct. 31, 1890, to Sam Mather at the end of her excerpt.

To Samuel Mather (Anderson)

4 Promenade Terrace
Cheltenham
Oct. 31st, [1890]

My dear Sam.

I thank you very much for your thoughtfulness in both telegraphing and writing to me. It would have been a pain to me ~~to~~ not to have known of your dear good father's departure at the time, but only long afterward. As it was, I could feel with you in spirit, and the tears that kept rising in my eyes, during the hours when his earthly remains still lay in his home, under his own roof and among you all, and during the day of the beautiful and solemn funeral, made me feel one with you. I wish I could have been there in person. If I had gone home for the summer—as at one time I talked of doing—I could have been there. The tie that bound me to him ~~is now~~ was (with the one exception of Clara) the oldest I had left. Many early memories are associated with him, when I, myself, was a child; and then, as later, he was the same kind, generous brother. I have not the recollection of a look, word, or accent from him, during that long stretch of years, which was not full of benevolence, and consideration, and goodness.

I am thankful for your sakes that you were all with him during the last hours. You are spared the eternal regret that comes, when it has been otherwise. There is something extremely solemn, I think, in the death of a father, or mother; the children are touched to the inmost heart, & it is a moment like no other; face to face we then stand—with the great mystery.

But, God be thanked for our firm and beautiful belief in immortality. We shall see them again; & they and we shall then be freed forever from all the imperfections & clogs of this lower life.

As men, you and Will have the noblest heritage in such an example as your father's life.

My letter to him was literally drawn from me, by some feeling which I cannot explain. Kate had written that he was less strong; and she mentioned that he was "pale and thin." But she added some reassuring words as to any immediate danger. But I could not rest until I had written, though I myself had no anticipation whatever of anything more than a gradual decline, perhaps. I had some pressing work ~~on~~ to do, & my lame wrist was very weak; yet I could not feel a moment's tranquility until I had written to him. I said to myself, "—he does not wish to hear from me, as it will be only another letter on his mind when he is tired; another letter to answer." But, all the same, I had to send at least a loving message. And I did. He knows, now, that I have always loved him dearly.

It must be the greatest blessing to you and Will that you were always the best of sons to him. Even though separated from him so much and for so long times, how often have I heard him speak of his two boys with the fondest pride, and love.

My love to all at home. I shall write to them again soon.—Yes, I have missed your letters, lately. But I have understood your silence, and I knew it was not in the least caused by forgetfulness, but simply by press of many occupations, most of them highly important. Flora sent me a delightful letter in the summer giving what makes the grand-aunt happy and amused,—namely details about the children, & stories of the things they do and say among themselves. My little Lady Constance is immensely admired; her photograph, I mean. My summer visitors have been Mr Boott of Boston, Henry James, Dr Baldwin of Florence, and Prof. Peirce of Harvard, and Miss Poynter (author of "My Little Lady.");[1] each one of these has taken the photograph to the window & gazed at it a long time; they have all said it is the prettiest picture of a baby which they have ever seen. My best love to Flora, and kisses for all three of the children. Tell Flora that I was much obliged for Miss Guilford's book; & I intend to write to Miss G. soon.

I look back over this letter, & I now add that I thoroughly believe you have put off writing to me from that Puritan conscience that says duty first pleasure afterwards. You have that sort of conscience, I know. I, too, have a little of it; & it has spoiled some pleasures that I might have had! A lonely old maid would be wiser, I suppose, if she should take all the pleasures she can get! But a young husband and father of a family—I do'nt know whether the same advice should hold? Ask Flora.—

Good-by, my dear boy. (For you will always seem a boy to me; do'nt mind; I wo'nt call you one to others.) I dare say I shall remain here for the present, as I have ever so much literary work on hand, & do not wish to travel. If I find the climate bad for me, as Dr Baldwin feared it would be, I may be forced to go to the Continent. But I hope not. You can address directly here. If I leave, I will make arrangements about letters.

Affectionately yours,
C. F. Woolson.

Notes

1. Eleanor Poynter published *My Little Lady* in 1872.

To Samuel Mather (Anderson)

4 Promenade Terrace
Cheltenham. England
Nov. 4th, 1890

My dear Sam.

I have your letter of Oct. 20th, and I return the certificate signed; (I hope correctly signed?).

I also send your Father's receipt for my Bonds. I think this a proper moment for me to understand clearly the situation of my small affairs. Will you, therefore, be so good as to tell me about them, some time between now and the close of the year? Then I will re-enter the items in my account-book, and begin 1891 with everything in good shape.—

First, as to the Bonds which were held by your Father.[1] You probably know that I was obliged to ask him to sell two of them, during my last year in Florence; he did so, and sent me the money, viz: two thousand dollars. I suppose, therefore, that I now have only the four Bonds of the "Cleveland, Tus. Valley, & Wheeling R. R.," for one thousand dollars each, (interest at seven per-cent, payable Oct. 1st, and April 1st), as I think the Bonds he sold were the two of the "Lake View Cemetery." Is this correct?

Second;—as to the Bond of the "Street Railway of Grand Rapids"; you say, in this last letter that I keep that. Is the interest at six per cent, & at what *dates* is it due? The Bond, I suppose, is for one thousand dollars?

Is it possible that the stock, which you described to me in the beginning as "thrown in," (with the Bond), has been sold by you for "about forty dollars" a share? Is'nt this a good deal of a miracle? I dare say it is *you* at the helm. How wonderful and delightful it must be to make money! How many shares of stock did I have? The certificate says ten; does that mean ten, actually? You say not all the payment is to be made in cash; how much is in cash?

I am now anxious to live, if possible, on my income, and take the next five or ten years—before I am really old—to write, and to invest the money earned by my pen, instead of spending it, as I have done heretofore. Now or never! I have no longer a house to take my time & to cause expenses; I can adapt my living to what I have. But first I must clearly understand what that is. I have, in addition to these Bonds, a (varying) sum per annum from Harpers ~~on~~ from the sale of my books (not counting the next things); what we call our per-cents.

You have so many important business affairs on your mind, Sam, that I feel that you ought not to be bothered with little things, like my Interest money, &c&c. Now is the time to advise me what is best to do. Can't some agent collect & remit to me? The Kensington branch of the Alliance Bank has asked me, or rather the Manager has suggested—that I might give them some money to use. But they give but a low per-cent, &, in reality, I know nothing about them. I should prefer to trust my affairs to you, if you will take the general oversight of them; I mean if you *can* take it,—with all the big affairs you have on hand? But the small details, I do not like to trouble you with. Let me know what is best.

I should like, if possible, to have the Interest money sent to me at regular dates; twice a year, I suppose? It is going to be close sailing at best, and therefore I must have regular dates, so as not to be anxious. For when I grow anxious, I cannot write. And my whole plan for the next ten years, depends upon a good deal of writing.

When you have time, please answer these little questions. You can send the Interest already due, or soon to be due, whenever you please. After I hear from you, I will then let you know whether I need the additional money which has been made (in this Arabian Nights way) on the "thrown in" stock. Perhaps, however, there was no cash paid?—

I wrote to you a few days ago, in answer to your letter of Oct. 9th. I am hoping to hear soon, from some one, how your mother is; for I think the loneliness is greater (for the first year) as time goes on. At first, the void is not fully realized.

My love to Flora, & kisses for the boys, & Little Lady Constance. I congratulate you on the name Shoreby.[2] It is, to my mind, the best at Glenville; I think it excellent.

I have had a delightful letter from Col. Hay, with the beautiful edition of his poems; I am waiting until he reaches Washington—to send my answer.[3] You can address here (as at head of letter), as I have decided to remain at least until January. Perhaps longer. It is dull. But the house is comfortable & warm, and the quiet will be the very atmosphere for writing. I had one farewell row (farewell to autumn) on the river Severn. I went over to Tewkesbury (15 minutes by train), got a nice boat, & rowed down the river to "the oldest Saxon church in England," as the guide books call it. The day was warm, with the trees colored (not the colors of home, though!), & I enjoyed the excursion greatly. Dear me! it was not much like the Tuscararas, & the flat-bottomed "Fligende Hollander."[4] All the same, the autumn colors along the Tuscararas was much finer. I have had some rows on the Avon, which joins the Severn at Tewkesbury. There is a beautiful old Abbey at T.—& then I also go to Gloucester & Worcester, to see the Cathedrals. I am never tired of the English Cathedrals. Gloucester is but fifteen minutes distant. I go over for the afternoon service very often.

I see you have a type writer. Do you dictate? I wish I could, to save my worn-out wrist. I have my mss. copied now. But I fear I never can learn to dictate.

Affectionately yours,
C. F. Woolson.

Much love to all at 544.

Notes

1. The recent death of Samuel Livingston Mather prompted Woolson to seek greater financial advice from Samuel Mather. She had relied on her nephew in the past for advice on the sale of her Wisconsin property and the investment of her money at 6 percent interest.
2. Mather's summer home.
3. John Hay's *Poems* was published in 1890.
4. Fligende Hollander: Flying Hollander.

To Katharine Loring (Beverly)

4 Promenade Terrace
Cheltenham

Sunday
Nov. 16th, [1890]

My dear Miss Loring.

I answered your telegram last evening, and wished much to write also. But it would have been useless, I was told, as there is no delivery in London on Sunday mornings.

I am so glad you are coming. It is very good of you; for Cheltenham is dull and London is always delightful. I used to like it dearly, even when the fog was thick, and there was no daylight to speak of; I think it the most interesting town in the world.—

I did not write on the tenth (the date you had mentioned), because I had heard from Mr James that Miss James was not so well, and that Tunbridge had been given up; so I have been waiting,—with the hope that you would let me know when you could come. Give my best love to Miss James. I congratulate her upon her decision to remain in town. The only reason that I, too, am not in town, is that I have undertaken a long piece of literary work, and this unexciting atmosphere is just the place for it. Especially as my head and imagination have not, even yet, recovered from the extraordinary delight and excitement of last winter and spring in the East.

I liked Nurse Bradford most particularly; she is a very pleasant combination of youth, intelligence, and capability, with (what is almost the best of all) a perfectly tranquil manner.

Please let me know, by letter or telegram, the hour of your arrival, as I enjoy going to the station; it is an event. I am a little distressed that I have only a dreary room for you; an Englishman from India has stepped into the apartment downstairs which I intended for you; and as he has been in the house before, and is to spend the winter, I could not keep him out. There is one advantage in his presence,—he has a little dog who comes up often to see me. I am devoted to dogs, and in constant grief over my Florence dachshund, Pax. I had to leave him behind, because he really does not belong to me, but Lady Hobart, of Villa Montanto (Hawthorne's), Bellosguardo. Pax has just written me a long letter in verse; dictated it, that is, to Miss Mary Huntington of Villa Castellani.

I had my day on the river Severn, and it was perfectly lovely. The trees were all colored, and the air as warm as summer. I went over to Tewkesbury at noon, and, getting a very nice little boat & good boatsman, I was afloat by one o'clock and floated until dark. The Saxon Church at Deerhurst was charmingly rural. But best of all were the Indian Summer day and the voyage. I had planned for another excursion of the same kind on the little winding Avon; but the weather was not right for it, & Miss Poynter, who was here then, does not adore boats as I do. Now it looks as though there had never been any leaves on the trees at all!—But still, if it does not actually rain, we can go to see the two cathedrals of Gloucester and Worcester, and the old Abbey church at Tewkesbury; the new marble table in the Abbey to Dinah Maria Mulock (Mrs Craik), reminded me that Tewkesbury is scene of that beloved story of my youth, "John Halifax"; the story whose hero is not a man at all, in spite of his name; but a good, pious, elder-sisterly woman, attired in trousers and a coat.[1]

I shall not dream of letting you go when your brief two nights are over; you must make up your mind to a longer stay than that. I shall take a vacation while you are here, and shall enjoy it hugely; especially as a long winter is opening before me, with no Nile in it,—no Athens. I shall stay here if I can; I mean if the weather does not affect my throat. If it does I shall go to Paris. Au revoir, then.

Very cordially yours,
C. F. Woolson.

Notes

1. Novelist Dinah Maria Mulock Craik published *John Halifax, Gentleman* in 1856. She was married to publisher George Craik.

To Samuel Mather (WRHS/Mather)

4 Promenade Terrace
Cheltenham
Dec. 15th, 1890

My dear Sam.

This morning comes your note of Dec. 6th enclosing the draft for £16.9.2. I am much obliged for the trouble you took in getting it off at a busy time. You will tell me what money it is, wo'nt you? when you send the answer to the letter I wrote on Nov. 1st. I hope ~~it~~ that letter reached you safely? It contained your Father's receipt.—The papers say there has been a panic in the U.S.—I hope it did not make you trouble?

You speak of Parnell. The political state of things here is exciting & strange. One has to live in England some time & know well a good many English people of the better class, to thoroughly understand the situation. I could write pages to you about it; (or talk hours). But it would take too much time for me to write it, & for you to read. All sorts of things,—ideas, beliefs, prejudices, &c&c, never get into the papers at all. Yet they influence everything. We are the purest nation in the world; that is generally my inward comment, after listening to English talk. I really think the conservatives would burn Gladstone at the stake if they could; their hate is intensely bitter. Even ladies tremble, & their cheeks grow pale with rage, when his name is mentioned. (I mean the "conservative" women.)

I sent a little book to my namesake last week. Another photograph of her is requested. My love to the little boys. I hope Flora is well? And I send you all my very best wishes for a happy Xmas.

It is bitterly cold here, &, for a week, we have only had three hours of daylight each day. I must think of the past—past Xmas-times; & not dwell on the present. I bought a copy of Dickens' Xmas Carol the other day (all my books are in Florence), to help me through. I am never tired of it.

Affectionately yours,
C. F. Woolson.

To Samuel Mather (WRHS/Mather)

4 Promenade Terrace
Cheltenham
Dec. 15th, [1890]
9 p.m.

Dear Sam.

I have mailed three hours ago a brief reply to your note of the a.m. And now, twelve hours behind that note (of yours), comes your long letter from Lakewood, which should have preceded it! You will wonder what I meant. So I dispatch this line to catch the other if I can, & explain it.

I will write tomorrow in answer to all you say. Your letter is a <u>delightful</u> one.

Now I shall ring. Elliot will appear—with the inscrutable gravity of an English servant. (He is my landlord, but acts as servant; he has been a butler, & now takes lodgers.) "Elliot, please have this posted at once."

"Yes mum. It's snowing hard, mum."
"Get a boy who's not afraid of snow."
"'Tubby shore, mum."
Exit Elliot.

In tearing haste,
C.F.W.

To Samuel Mather (WRHS/Mather)

4 Promenade Terrace
Cheltenham
Dec. 18th, [1890]

My dear Sam.

You must have been surprised by my recent letter! I only hope the postscript sent three hours later, caught up with, and explained it. If I had waited a little, the mystification would not have occurred. But I have a habit of writing immediately, when there is a cheque, or anything about money. You remember that with the draft, you wrote only a line or two. I knew you would explain later. But, at the time, I had no idea what money it was.—Your nice long letter from the Laurel House (which came by the next post) gave me great pleasure. You & Flora can never tell me half enough about the children. Can I be growing old? I have always liked children, have'nt I?; how many stories have I told you, for instance, in days of old? Seems to me I also remember plays at Xmas times? Yes—I have supposed that I was always a child-lover. Since your day, Clare, too, has appeared, and grown up, & I seem to remember all sorts of tableaux arranged for her with great labor, her dolls being the performers. And yet somehow I take a greater pleasure than I did in all these, in hearing about your boys, & my little namesake, now! Flora's letter of last summer was charming; it contained details, & anecdotes that made me laugh,—and feel proud of my relations. In this recent letter of yours, I was much interested in your description of Livingston's visit to Middletown; his 100,000 questions; & his eyes as big as saucers. When you can, send me more pictures of them all.

My best love to Flora. I am so glad the change did her good. There is, in my opinion, nothing so good as change, when one is tired, or a little out of sorts. How many times has it proved so in my own case. But it's far nicer to have someone declare that you must go, & take you off just a little against your will, than to go along (for your own "good") when you do'nt, at heart, wish to stir.—

I am very much obliged, Sam, for your promise to send me a statement of my affairs at home. I wish to enter everything in my account-book, and then make a new will. There is now no more Milwaukee land left, & all is simple. I wish to put down just what I have, & the numbers of the Bonds, &c. There is interest due on the R. R. Bonds. All the interest, I should like to have sent to me at regular dates; twice a year will do. With this (thanks to you), and the regular per-cents from Harpers yearly, I wish to live. If I can only manage to do this, I see no reason why (if I ~~live and~~ keep well) I should not be able to make & invest enough money to keep me comfortable (without writing) after eight or ten years more. I am besieged with offers for novels on all sides. The latest is the syndicate to ~~whom~~ which Howells has just sold a novel for ten thousand dollars.[1] But, as you know, the Harpers have the first bid on all my work. I feel sure that they will let no one outbid them. And they not only take everything I can do, but urge me to do more. For instance they wish me to make a volume of travel sketches of the East, instead of the two Cairo articles alone, which I have sent them. I have thought that so long as they were so cordial and paid such high prices, it was better for me to continue with them, than to attempt business relations with syndicates; as I have no one to manage business for me. Mrs Burnett has cast her fortunes entirely with one of these syndicates. But I hesitate. (Poor Mrs B. has lost her eldest boy. She is a devoted mother & she will be in great grief, I know.) So now you have my plan. To carry it out depends upon myself. My old brain & hand. Brain is in good condition now, having no longer a weight of daily care. Hand is weak, or rather wrist is. (So you see by this quill pen.) But even now I think the writing can still be read? When Rhoda Broughton was in Florence, she wrote me several notes, & they looked as if half a dozen Daddy Long Legs had dipped their paws in ink, & then danced on the paper.

I look over your letter. No; thanks for the offer, but I shall not need the money you have made for me by the sale of the G. Rapids stock, before it is due. (I now refer to your kind offer to buy, & send me the whole in a lump, should I wish it.) When anything is paid in, it can be sent. It makes my mind easy to have a little balance ~~at~~ on hand here.

Poor Mrs Walton. I did not know she was older than your father. She was always such a handsome stately woman! I was glad to hear what you tell me of other members of your father's family. I remember so perfectly how much Georgie (your mother) liked them all. She had warm feelings, & a great deal of enthusiasm; I can see her now, after her return from her wedding trip, describing to mother, "sister Elizabeth," "sister Kate," "sister Louisa," & all the others.

It is tremendously cold here—for England. I keep warm, though there is no furnace or steam; only grate-fires. This is a hunting centre, & I see the men in red coats, often. If it were only Gloucestershire instead of Bedfordshire, I could perhaps see Jacob Perkins![2] I dare say he will show the British how to do it; it's amazing how the Americans over here exceed the English, ~~in~~ whenever they try to do so. So far, the glory has been won principally by the American girls, & American wives of Englishmen, but this is because American men have not tried.

The papers are full of the financial crisis in the U.S. I hope it does not trouble you? I remember, even now, the two waves, first of sickness-of-heart, then of long depression, that followed the crisis of 1857? We were at Mackinac (I was a schoolgirl), & even up there, people looked white.

Here, the Parnell mess grows deeper. How exultant the Conservatives are, a letter can not describe. It is one broad grin from John O'Groat's House to Land's End.[3] I have now a number of English friends, & among them but one Liberal, Lady Hobart. I dare say she is shedding tears in Florence. At any rate, she has not the heart to write, whereas all the others (who are rampant Tories) fill sheets & send them to me. All the English ladies are politicians, I fancy. At least all I know. In my replies I simply wave the American flag.

I can do so now more safely, since Congress has at last passed the Copyright Law.[4]

I am asked up to town to spend Xmas; but I have declined. I shall have some holly; & a plum pudding as large as a tea-cup. Then, in the evenings I shall read the Xmas Carol.

I sent the boys an old-fashioned fairybook; the same old stories which I used to love myself. The bookseller here assures me that the McKinley law does not tax books. If he is misinformed, & you have to pay a large sum for your own presents, I shall be vexed indeed. Pray let me know. My love to your Mother, and Kate. I have just rec[d] letters from them, & shall answer soon.

Affectionately yours,
C. F. Woolson.

Love to Will

Notes

1. Howells's *A Hazard of New Fortunes* and *The Shadow of a Dream* both appeared in 1890.
2. Apparently, Woolson wanted to reverse the town names because she placed a 1 above "Bedfordshire" and a 2 above "Gloucestershire." However, the transformation seems backwards if Jacob Perkins (?–1849) is the inventor who developed a generator (1824); Perkins's British roots trace to Gloucestershire.
3. The expression encompasses the whole of England, from Land's End at the southwest tip to John O'Groats at the northeast. The apostrophe error is Woolson's.
4. The U.S. House of Representatives passed the copyright bill in 1890; it became the International Copyright Law in 1891.

To John Hay (Brown)

4 Promenade Terrace
Cheltenham
Dec. 20th, [1890]

Dear Col. Hay.

Your beautiful volume has given me a great deal of pleasure. I don't know how many times I have read it through. I have been in this dull place alone (save for occasional visits from friends, of a day or two's length,) since May. And I have revived an old habit of reading poetry for half an hour every evening, just before going to bed. For years I have read Matthew Arnold's poems for ten minutes or so at that time; I don't know whether you care for them? (They are somewhat melancholy. But I am melancholy, too. Of course you are not.) Since your book came, I have added it to my half hour's evening poetry. And I believe I could really repeat to you, from memory, a large part of its contents.

I am glad to have, safely within these covers and no longer fugitive, Miles Keogh's Horse and The Stirrup Cup,—both so magnificently done. I don't know anything better than The Stirrup Cup; it stirs the heart. I have always been fond of Quand Même, and In the Firelight; these I have often repeated to friends. Before your volume came—(to enrich my Cheltenham table with its beautiful binding),

I had the page of the Century which contained the Distichs, hanging (cut from the Maga.) on my wall. I hope to write a short story, some day, upon

> "Unto each man comes a day, when his favorite sins all forsake him,
> And he complacently thinks he has forsaken his sins."—

You say it is amateurish to have ones books printed according to one's own taste, for one's family & friends. If Fate would only turn me into an Amateur! I am afraid I shall be dead before, in the natural course of trade, I can get poor Rodman the Keeper revised. By misunderstanding, the new edition (Harpers) was brought out just as it stood when recovered finally from the piratical Appletons. No one minds it but the author. But oh! how she squirms! The best thing in the book is Sister St Luke, that dear darling beautiful little poem, a gem of perfection.[1]

I have all my life, until recently, been in too much of a hurry to love poetry. Now I find myself going back to it as a cordial and peace-giver. You'll laugh; but (my books being packed in Florence) I ordered the other day a small volume of Milton in order to re-read the Hymn on the Nativity at this Xmas season. What brought it to my mind was the sailing past Paxo (south of Corfu) a year ago; for it was here, you know, that the sailors heard the voices crying "Great Pan is dead." Milton puts it in: "The lonely mountains o'er And the resounding shore—" &c.[2] I see there is a sketch of your life in the last Sunday Tribune.[3] But it does not say whether you have been to the East, &, en route thither, to the Ionian Islands & Greece? Did I write to you from any of those points last winter? I think I did not. But if I did, I know the letter was fairly lyrical! I wo'nt burst forth again (though longing to); but I will just say that now at last I know my own land; it is Egypt. There must be Egyptian blood in me somehow. Nothing I have ever seen or imagined can approach the reality of Egypt, as it was to my eyes. (I ~~put in~~ mark "my," because my sister hated it.) I have never seen anything so solemn as the ancient temples, &c. And never anything so beautiful as the Arabian architecture at Cairo. I understand now why Venice has fascinated me so strongly: it was simply the oriental tinge there. You may say:, "And not Greece?" And I answer, "No; not Greece." Grecian things are too perfect for me. Possibly if I had a classic nose myself, I should enjoy them more. I ought to add that I was not long enough in Athens (only two weeks) to really appreciate the things in the museums. The Parthenon I did appreciate. But in Egypt I stayed long months. I returned thither alone, after the Holy Land, and had a second long stay. You know Arabian architecture &c, having seen it in Spain.

I saw Eugene Schuyler almost daily. He did much to make my visit pleasant. He was far from well, & he struck me as unhappy, although he never said so; on the contrary, he always spoke very cheerfully. But it seemed to me a determined effort on his part to appear as usual. I think he was a deeply disappointed man. He hated

Egypt & could not understand my enthusiasm. He never went near the Bazaars & old quarters; I do'nt think he saw anything, or wanted to. His whole interest was in his new idea of writing fiction, & upon that he would talk for hours. He had plots for novels all ready, & hoped to be able to write them out. He talked of The Bread Winners. And of Democracy. They were to be his models. I did not dream when we parted, that this life, with its troubles, was so soon to be a thing of the past to him. He was a singular man. Kind as he was, & much, very much as he did for me, I have never met a man so rude! (This is for you alone.) I used to flush very often. It was like a slap in the face. Yet he seemed unconscious of it. And I was so sure that he was bitterly unhappy, that I passed it all over. I have written thus at length about him, because I think you knew him? And I was one of the last Americans who saw much of him. I did not leave Cairo until the end of April.

I congratulate you on having completed your colossal Life of Lincoln. It is a great work, and will carry your name farther down the stream of time than we can now see. Lincoln is one of the great names of history, and your Life must always be the standard authority about him. What do you mean by saying that people do not read history? I do. I have read all of the Life that came out in the Century. And if I can ever carry out my hope of an apartment in Venice, with a room for books, with shelves, the whole work will be one of the first which I shall order. I think it extremely interesting, and perfectly done. I read many parts with the old stir of the blood!—The pulse of those great & exciting years which ~~have~~ has made the pulse of later times seem so quiet & dull. The narrative, so simple & powerful, brought all back.

Mr Adams's History I have not read; but I should if it were in the Libraries here. And I shall, as soon as I have an opportunity. Not read history!! Why—I travel with Gibbon. And I am now reading (from Mudie's) J. R. Green's "History of the English People."[4] There are so many Kings buried in the Cathedrals & Abbeys near here, that I felt it necessary to review my old school-knowledge. The beautiful Cathedral of Gloucester is but fifteen minutes from here; Tewkesbury Abbey ditto. Worcester Cathedral an hour. And Hereford, Wells, & Glastonbury within easy reach. Before it grew cold, I used to visit all these places for my afternoon walk. And I had some charming rows on the Severn, & the pretty little meandering Avon.

I have come here to do a long job of literary work. I could do almost nothing in Florence; there were such endless numbers of people to receive, & to go and see. Venice will be much better in that respect. I hated to give up the beautiful Bellosguardo View; it tore me to pieces to do it. But after a struggle to write & attend to social duties at the same time through three long years, I at last recognized that it was impossible. At least, impossible for *me*. This winter here is much like the one I spent in Leamington (when I was finishing East Angels); I see the men in pink, for it is a hunting centre. I go to the local festivals. The latest was a big Conservative powwow, with wax works, tableaux, music, & unlimited tea. The Duke of Beaufort presided, and Sir Michael Hicks-Beach. These things are amusing to an American, do'nt you think so? The present state of politics is exciting. I believe the Conservatives would burn Gladstone at the stake, if they could; I have never seen such hate.[5] But just now the Tories are immensely happy.

I am so enchanted that the Copyright Bill is at last passed.

Snow enough for sleighing here. I hear that my namesake is a most lovely little girl. May she inherit all the good in me & nothing, oh, nothing, of the bad! My love to Mrs Hay!

Sincerely yours,
C. F. Woolson.

P.S.

I have no one here for oh-ing & ah-ing; so desire for sympathy leads me to say "Did'nt you enjoy Kipling?" And "do'nt you dote on Lemaitre?" And "is'nt this new science of hypnotism & telepathy wonderful?"

Notes

1. Woolson had not received the money promised her from Appletons for her collection *Rodman the Keeper* (1880). A portion of Hay's poem "Sister Saint Luke" appears as an epigraph in the book version of Woolson's story "Sister St. Luke."

2. Milton is drawing on a quotation from Plutarch in his poem "On the Morning of Christ's Nativity" (1629).

3. Dec. 7, 1890.

4. Woolson is reading an enormous amount from Mudie's lending library in London: Henry Adams's *History of the United States During the Administrations of Jefferson and Madison* (9 vols., 1889–91); Edward Gibbon's *The Decline and Fall of the Roman Empire* (6 vols., 1776–88), as well as John Green's (1837–83) *Short History of the English People.*

5. The Duke of Beaufort, Henry Charles FitzRoy Somerset (1824–1899), was a member of Parliament; Hicks-Beach (1837–1916) was the leader of the House of Commons and secretary for Ireland. The Conservatives disliked William Ewart Gladstone because of his Liberal policies.

To Mrs. William Wilberforce Baldwin (Morgan)[1]

To Mrs Baldwin,
With kind
thoughts and best
wishes for
a happy New Year
from C. F. Woolson.
Xmas, 1890

Notes

1. This greeting appears on a card with a rose design and decorative font.

To Flora Stone Mather (Benedict/CFW, 362–63)

[1890]

The winter was a magnificent one, and I feel almost gorged with new impressions and Oriental colour. I lost my heart completely to Cairo. I was strongly, oh! so strongly tempted to go to Constantinople for the summer; it is the summer resort of the Cairo people, and the journey is a short one. Then I should have returned to Egypt for another winter. But, after all, enough is as good as a feast; and with Corfu, Athens and Egypt, I had all I could carry! I am even yet a little intoxicated with the beauty and the colour.

In Cairo, I often saw Brugsch Bey; he is the man who discovered the Pharoahs, you know. He has some idea of going to America to lecture. I think the career of Miss Edwards over there has stirred him up. I could see that he did not believe that women could be very profound scholars in anything; though of course he did not actually say so to me. I think we can—only our education must begin a hundred years before we are born—as some wit has said. By this I mean that it will take several generations of study and training before our girls can equal our boys in scholarship; or rather before our women can equal our men.

A daily companion during the last weeks of my stay in Cairo was Prof. Pierce of Harvard. I have just had a letter from him, written at Constantinople, and it is amusing to see how completely fascinated he is with Oriental life. I do'nt think he has ever been excited before! but now his time has come, and though he is over fifty, he is almost Byronic in his enthusiasm and the expression of it. Well—I cannot laugh at him; for I am the same!

To Katharine Livingston Mather (Benedict/CFW, 35)

[1890?]

Did I tell you what an extraordinary letter B sent me? It was from his wife to him and all about "Jupiter Lights." It was the most remarkable literary letter I have ever read. . . . I find that for years he has written all the reviews of French books for the Nation. . . . [1]

Notes

1. An anonymous review in *Nation*, March 30, 1890, is reprinted in Torsney, Cheryl B., ed. *Critical Essays on Constance Fenimore Woolson* (New York: G. K. Hall, 1992): 55.

To Samuel Mather (Anderson)[1]

4 Promenade Terrace
Cheltenham
Jan. 21st, 1891

My dear Sam.

Your letter, enclosing the draft for the three hundred dollars, came safely; and I am, as always, very much obliged. I should have written earlier if it had been possible; I have been prostrated by the cold weather; I dare say you have seen what an arctic winter we are having here? One must go back a hundred years to find one like it. I am never more than half alive, when it is very cold. Dampness does not trouble me; nor what is called relaxing, or malarious air; heat never makes me ill. But let the air grow really cold, and down I go towards the gates of death; no matter how bright the sun may be nor how clear the air.

These last phrases do not apply to any sunshine or clear air here; do'nt imagine it. We have not seen the sun for two months. However, the telegraph tells us that there is deep snow in Naples, and that soldiers are snowed up in Algiers. Cairo is not mentioned, but I dare say they are shivering there—where there are no fireplaces at all—much more than we did, last winter. I had an amusing letter from Mr Warner (Dudley) not long ago; he wrote from Florence, & said he was colder than he had ever been in Hartford in his life; he and Mrs W. were simply half dead. They had expected to take a villa there; but they could'nt stand it and were going directly to Egypt. Since my own stay in Egypt—(the most fascinating country I have ever seen)—I have made up my mind that we have, in Florida, the best winter resort in the world for those who wish to escape all cold air. But the upper Nile (where we did not go) is warm, also. And of course it has a charm which Florida cannot have.

I look back to my first page & see that I have complained too much; I have not been in the least seriously ill; I have merely been limp & spiritless owing to the cold. This morning it is milder, & now life will go on again. My rooms have been warm during the daytime. But as there are only grate-fires in the house, the air—during this unusual winter—becomes cold during the night.

I have your letter of Dec. 24th, giving me the numbers of the four Tuscarawas R. R. Bonds. I have just finished putting everything down in the one small account-book which contains a statement of all my affairs. I intend soon to make a new will, & shall probably send you a copy, or the will itself, to keep in your safe. In this connection, I will mention that there is, in your father's safe, in a flannel bag, some silver of mine. It may be marked with Charlie's name; I bought it of him in 1880. The rest of my silver is in a safe in the charge of the Society for Savings—(S. H. Mather's).

When you kindly offered to advance me the $400 you have made for me out of the Grand Rapids R. R., I told you that it was not necessary; I could wait until the regular payments were made in six, nine, & twelve months.

But I do'nt think I can do without the regular interest money on my Tuscarawas R. R. bonds. When I made my estimate about living expenses for the present, I included that interest money as part. It amounts to $280.^{00} per annum. For the first time since I came abroad, I am now trying to live on what I have, instead of relying upon the chances of what I make. I have never tried before, because I knew it was impossible; I didn't have enough even to try. But now, thanks to you, I think I can manage it, as I have no house, & no longer feel obliged to see so many people. The $140—then, (the coupons due on the Tus. Valley R. R. last Oct.), had better be sent to me here.

I see you thought of taking this to add to the one thousand dollars now free (i.e. the proceeds of the Grand Rapids Bond), in order to make a new investment for me. I am sorry about it. Can't you take the same amount from the money coming in, later, from the stock of the Grand Rapids R. R.?

I am glad, to have you do whatever you think best with the one thousand dollars (that originally came from Iron Ridge.) It is "lucky money" in your hands. In the first place you & Kate gave me a good part of it. Since then, you have turned it over & almost made fifty per-cent to add to it; (it reminds me of the time when you were the magician in our Xmas play!). Buy the Republic Iron Co. stock if you think best, now. Or wait a little longer. I leave it all, only too gladly, to your judgment. It's good of you to take so much pains to help me, Sam. Do'nt think that I do'nt appreciate it. I do so deeply that I can't talk much about it. Some day, I dare say you will know how opportunely you came to my rescue. I have no superstitions left; but I do believe that the little girl over there, who bears my name, carries a blessing all unconsciously; it comes to her from what you have done for me.

The photograph interested me greatly. Of course I knew Constance at a glance; there are not two Constances. Her bright-eyed, eager, intent little face, and her beautiful hands, are unique. She sits enthroned like a little Princess in her royal baby-wagon, & the big dog guards her nobly. I did not know you had a dog. You may remember my delight in dogs? I miss Pax so much that I am tempted to get a dog here; as I am often rather lonely. (Pax is the dog I had at Bellosguardo). Amasa, I knew at once; every photograph I have had of him, has had the same merry expression like a brilliant sunbeam. Livingston I puzzled over; I could not realize that that big tall boy was yours. I thought he must be a Hay, though he did not look at all like the Hay children I saw in Paris. Alice Hay of course I knew. And the little boy sitting in the foreground has Col. Hay's forehead and something of his eyes. So then I went back to the tall boy behind the wagon. "Can it be Livingston? Has Flora a big son like that!?" The eyes began to hold my attention; I put a paper over the hat & shoulders, & left only the face; & then at last I saw that it was the same little boy, who, as baby and little child, had come to me in photographs) growing larger & larger, but always with the same earnest eyes. He is certainly a very handsome lad. He is a very distinguished-looking boy. But; dear me! Sam—, it was only the other day that you & Flora were at Sorrento, with no boys at all. It's startling to me to see Livingston.—All the same it's the best thing in life; it's the only thing worth living for; this is the sincere belief—& the result of the observations—of one who has never had it! You and Flora have a family to be proud of.

The beautiful Hiawatha gave me especial pleasure. I love to have American books and I have very few. Hiawatha was the poem I knew by heart (portions of it) when I was a school-girl.[2] It is associated with those romantic days when we had a summer cottage at Mackinac, & the first original writing I ever did was a "poem" (heaven save the mark!) an imitation in the same style. It was for a little ms. newspaper which we amused ourselves with one summer, & my associate editor was Col. Spaulding. I hear he is abroad (Italy) with his wife and handsome children, & that he has become a rich man. I am very glad. He deserves good fortune, for he always was a good fellow. The glamor that the war threw over the young officers who left their homes to fight, made me fancy I cared for him. But I see now that it was never a serious feeling. This was the time when my old friend, Flora Payne, fancied she cared for Gen. Hazen. You will be amused by these reminiscences. But of course they are for you & Flora alone.—The illustrations of the Hiawatha are beautiful.—I see, through the circulating Libraries, all the English books; and people send me most of the French & Italian things. But American books I cannot get, without sending over to buy them. Some are republished here; then I see them. It is well, however, for me not to accumulate many books, I suppose, (much as I love them) while I have no house to put them in. All my Florence books are stored; I have'nt them with me here.

Your Xmas was a quiet one I know, & no doubt you had many thoughts of the one who has left you for another life. But they were all pleasant memories. I was glad to have the excellent likeness you sent. My own Xmas was solitary; in the evening I read Dickens' Xmas Carol. I hope the books I sent, have made you no trouble about duty? There is a mysterious silence from Clara, about one I sent to her, that makes me fear you have all been pounced upon by McKinley for fifty percent taxes.[3] I laughed to read of Livingston's stealing out at dawn, to investigate his stocking. As to the taste of the boys for soldiers,—I like an Army officer's life, you know. I have always liked it. It has its hardships, I suppose. But all the officers I have known here seemed to me free from care. It is true that there is a temptation toward drink. But that is not confined to the Army. Think of the tragic case of Fred Phinney. My love to all at 544. I hope to write to them soon. I expect to write (—for the public) very steadily now, so I shall not be sending long letters. Yes, I suppose I shall remain with the Harpers, for I fully agree with all you say; I have the same ideas. Yet it is a temptation to be offered large sums down. The same syndicate that pays Mrs Burnett $5,000 a year, & takes all she writes, is now sending the most urgent letters to me. They are, so far, preliminary letters; but they are very earnest and urgent. Two other syndicates have also written. And the agent of another intends to come here to Cheltenham, to see me personally, I hear. I have written to keep him off, if I can, as I have really nothing to say to him. I shall keep my contract with the Harpers, as they have always treated me extremely well; most generously in fact. If the time ever comes when I have produced more than they care to take, then I shall be honorably free to look elsewhere. This has been always my difficulty—i.e. the slow rate at which I write. Howells, as you have seen perhaps, has recently sold a novel to a syndicate.

Yes, I was immensely amused by your tale of Oliver & Gunn. You ~~must remember~~ may not be aware that, years ago, I knew Oliver very well indeed; & Gunn I knew slightly personally, but I knew him very well by reputation; "the rain upon the roof" of his house at Clinton Park; his affection for the Lake [captain?]; &c&c these were some of the romantic tales about about him that I heard before I left Cleveland. I did not know he cared for Zoar.[4] Poor Zoar!—does it still exist? As I look back now, I see it was the romantic side of my father's nature that was pleased with the little Tuscarawas community—father had so much romance. It had but little to feed upon in Ohio. How often I have thought of him as I have wandered about the old world; how he would have enjoyed it.—To go back to Gunn—& Capri; it's ever so funny, Oliver scuttling away, & Alexander left, perforce, to enjoy the romantic alone. What has happened to break up their friendship? Tell me, sometime.

You closed your letter by saying that your back ached. Let me warn you; for, since you & Flora were at Sorrento, I have had many a miserable day from an ache of that sort. Yours may not be the same at all, however. Mine comes from too much use of the right arm in writing. Nothing stops it but an absolutely motionless rest of hours, & sometimes of days. A violent case can be much mitigated by electricity. It is much better now that I always write at a stand-up desk.

The gentleman down-stairs has just come back from a hunt, in his scarlet coat. He has splendid horses, & is here for the hunting-season. He has the lower floor, & I the two upper ones, & this is all the house (it is not a large house); so we are very tranquil & quiet. I sally out every afternoon & do my marketing; the man of the house, (a ci-devant butler—) waits; his wife cooks.[5] It is really this easy, private system of living that keeps me in England. I detest a public table whether of pension or hotel & I like to have three or four rooms; yet I do'nt want to have the care of keeping house at present. Here I have a large sittingroom, fairly furnished, & a dining room behind it. A good bedroom above, with a dressingroom; & plenty of closets & wardrobes & presses.—I have no fixed plans, & it is not necessary to make any. That is the one advantage of having no fixed place of abode. My best love to Flora. Tell her I bought a little pot of clematis the other day, because it reminded me so strongly of Sorrento.

Affectionately yours,
C. F. Woolson.

Notes

1. Portions of this letter also appear in Benedict/CFW, 46–48, 50–52, 368.
2. Longfellow's "Hiawatha" (1855); the love story of Hiawatha and Minnehaha, was written in unrhymed iambic tetrameter.
3. Before he became president in 1897, Republican Representative William McKinley advocated raising taxes to a historic high level.
4. Cleveland business man Alexander Gunn moved to Ohio's Zoar Community where he tended his garden in retirement. The double "about" is Woolson's.
5. The ci-devant, or former butler, was probably someone who had left domestic employment to run a boarding house.

To William Wilberforce Baldwin (Morgan)

4 Promenade Terrace,
Cheltenham
Jan. 25th, [1891]

My dear Doctor.

Jack's smiling little picture, with the bright eyes, plump little bare feet, and firmly grasped toys, is delightful. It brightens the room. He is a handsome little lad, and the personification of health and intelligence. I am very glad you are to have no more anxiety about him; but only joy and pride. And so there is another boy? I know he is a fine fellow. Give him my love, and tell me his name. And give my very best love to your wife, fitting indeed do you call her "the dove;" she is one of the smartest of women.

I have purposely delayed answering your very welcome letter of Nov. 20th, as I know how very little time you have for outside correspondence, and I did not wish you to be haunted by the idea of an unanswered epistle; for it is sometimes like a ghost. But you must never feel so about letters to me. Write when you can, and I will do the same. When we can't, we won't. In any case, I am sure we understand each other. Lately (during the eight weeks of very cold weather) I have had twinges of the ache that stops my pen. But only twinges; the big pain you have exorcised.

The weather has been unspeakably bad. But apparently it has been bad everywhere. Yesterday the mild air returned again.

And so you have seen my villa, [“]a palace of pure gold floating in the sunset sky,” as you climbed to Bellosguardo. Do you appreciate what a beautiful phrase that is? A person who studies words for themselves, can not help noticing it. It is a true description, too; how often I, coming back from town in one of [Scarlata’s?] carriages, tired & dull, climbing the same hill, have seen that house stand out like some of the bulwarks of the Celestial City, in Pilgrim’s Progress. Its site, at exactly the top of the hill, gives it a look, sometimes, of being in the sky. Would that I could have stayed there! The place was made for me,—with that magnificent view sweeping away in all directions. I mean that in such a spot only can I be happy. Back to Italy I shall certainly come, if I live. But I may seek a less crowded society than that of Florence.

I suppose you are as busy as ever? I saw you quoted in my Daily News the other day; it was your opinion about the fever that was given.

You ask about Henry James’s play. It was given for the first time, not long ago, with immense success. He was called before the curtain by acclamation at the end; cries for “Author,” “Author,” that would not down. So at last, very unwillingly, & very red (so I hear) he came out & bowed. As it was a beginning, his first, it was thought best to try it first in the provinces. But it goes up to London in the autumn. In the meanwhile, he has written another, (not founded on any of his stories) which is very striking. I dare say he will write others. He is well, or was the last time I heard; but the feeble state of Miss James, who has seemed to be almost in a dying condition for months, is a great depression, of course, to the brother. I have’nt kept many of the press-notices of “The American”; but I enclose a few about the first night, & I send you Smalley’s allusion in the “Tribune.”[1]

My sister & Clare come over early in the Spring. It is probable that I shall then go to the Continent. But I make no plans; let me at least take the one advantage that belongs to a houseless state, namely the being able to follow Fancy in whatever direction she may permit.

I have had several little trips; & several visitors here. But I often sit by my big English fire, & think of Florence; of the trees & the bridges; the Palazzo Vecchio, and the Duomo, and Giotto’s tower. I must come back to Florence before long, simply as a tourist; I could stay a month without making a call, or doing any writing,—simply seeing again all the beautiful things & places at my leisure; it would take a month, at least.

I hope you are well? My regards to Miss Green. I hear that you have recommended an American lawyer, who shows signs of being able to help Miss Greenough & the Curtises of Venice, in the Henry Huntington business.[2] I do’nt get this item from Florence, so please do’nt let Miss Greenough know I have heard about it.

Every good wish, my dear Friend, for the new year, for you & yours, from yours ever,

C.F.W.

Notes

1. James's play *The American* opened on Jan. 3, 1891, in Southport; George Smalley (1833–1916) reviewed it in the New York *Tribune*. See Lyndall Gordon, *The Private Life of Henry James: Two Women and His Art* (New York: W.W. Norton, 1998); Gordon cites *Mrs. Vibert* as the second play.

2. Ellen Greenough Huntington owned the Villa Castellani; her daughter Mary inherited it in 1893. Henry Huntington, who may have failed to inherit money, was Mary's brother. Miss Green may have some relationship to James's friend, historian John Richard Green.

To James R. Gilmore (Johns Hopkins)

Cheltenham. England
Jan. 30th, 1891

Dear Mr Gilmore.

I do'nt think I could do it myself. But as Mr Arthur Stedman (son of Edmund Clarence Stedman) has recently prepared a short account of the little there is to say, I dare say he could give you all the information necessary. Mr Stedman's address is, I believe, 137 West 78th Street; New York.

I send my best wishes to "Edmund Kirke," for this vast undertaking.[1]

Very truly yours
C. F. Woolson.

Notes

1. Edmund Kirke was James R. Gilmore's pseudonym. Woolson apparently is referring to a biographical sketch of herself in E. C. Stedman's *A Library of American Literature* (1890) to which his son Arthur contributed.

To Katharine Loring (Beverly)

4 Promenade Terrace
Feb. 5th, [1891]

My dear Miss Loring.

It is kind to ask me again. I, too, have seen the announcements of the "Last Nights." I am also curious to see "The Dancing Girl." And Letty Lind's dancing at the Gaiety; I pore over the theatre attractions in the Daily News![1]

All the same, I shall not allow myself to come up to town at present. Do you know that phrase, "It's dogged that does it"? & Dogged I must be, here in Cheltenham, if I am to accomplish several things that I am trying to do. But it is unspeakably dull. I think I have never been in a place as deadly; except Ventnor. Leamington was dull, also; but one could get out of it in fifteen minutes, in any direction; and the malls (once outside), were infinitely prettier.

Give my love to Miss James. I hope, for her sake, that it is as springlike in London as it is here.

I envy Bruno his trip to Paris. I am determined to spend, before long, a whole year in Paris; (with the exception of six weeks in the heart of the summer). You, who know so many things,—do you happen to know of a place there, or in the immediate neighborhood, where I could establish myself as I am established here? A private table, and three or four rooms? Not in an hotel, if possible. I ask it not for present, but future use.

I am much disappointed that Kipling's novel is so poor.[2] And I see, (though I have not seen the article itself) that he has been abusing everything American, with the same old English tirades against the accent & the hotel-clerks. I do'nt suppose he talked with anyone but shopgirls. And as to the hotel clerks, I could match them with tales of the "Manageresses" of the large English hotels. I shall have to give up Rudyard for the present. Perhaps, by and by, he will fulfil the promise he has made; then I will admire him again. After all, I see now that it was the Eastern atmosphere that charmed me most, in his short stories. I am bitterly homesick for the East.— Now here is the sheet filled, & I'm on the point of taking another! I wo'nt. You are the only woman I have ever known who could leave off in the middle of a sheet.

Thank you ever so much for your cordial invitation. It has cheered me up greatly. I love to be remembered.

Sincerely yours,
C. F. Woolson.

Notes

1. Letty Lind (1861–1923) performed burlesque and, by the 1890s, musical comedy. Arthur Henry Jones's *The Dancing Girl* debuted at Haymarket, Beerbohm Tree's Theatre, London in 1891.

2. *The Light That Failed* (1891).

To Samuel Mather (WRHS/Mather)

4 Promenade Terrace
Cheltenham
Feb 23^{d}, [1891]

My dear Sam.

Just a line to acknowledge the safe arrival of the draft for $140—, interest-money on R.R. Bonds. There will be another $140—, due, I suppose, on April 1st.

All is well here. Dull but healthy. No Egypt, Athens or beautiful Corfu. No Venice. But a stodgy fairly-comfortable English sittingroom; quantities of paper and ink. English mutton to eat. And gray English air outside. The severe cold is over.—This year I shall try to see the primroses. I have never been in England, until now, at the right time. I mean the wild primroses; acres of them.

I hope all is well with you? Love to Flora. I shall write to her, in reply to her delightful letter, before long. Kisses for the children. Yours as ever,

C. F. Woolson.

To Mrs. William Wilberforce Baldwin (Morgan)

Easter Monday
1891[1]

My dear Mrs Baldwin.

The lovely anemones from yourself and the Doctor, came just in time for Easter, and made me long to take the first train to Italy! It is very cold here with dreadful winds. The anemones look as if they had been gathered this morning; perfectly fresh & charming.—

I hope you are well? My love to the new baby, and the little lads. My sister arrives here in April. She always sends her love to you when she writes. With warm thanks for your very welcome gift, I am yours as ever,

C. F. Woolson.

Notes

1. Easter Monday in 1891 was on March 31.

To Samuel Mather (Anderson)[1]

4 Promenade Terrace
Cheltenham
April 11th, [1891]

My dear Sam.

Thanks for your promptness in sending the Tuscarawas Interest money. Owing to you, I have at last a tranquil atmosphere in which to write. I am reading (from Mudie's) the Life and Letters of Monckton Milnes Lord Houghton. He was such a splendid friend of the north in the War of the Rebellion, that I have always liked him. In one of his letters he says, "How different the development of Goethe would have been, under adverse circumstances! And how much Carl August had to do with his genius, in giving it the peaceful, prosperous air in which it delighted to grow."[2] Do'nt imagine that in quoting this, I am comparing myself to that stupendous creature,

Goethe! But "a peaceful air" to grow in is sweet indeed to any kind of a writer; as I suppose it is, also, to a painter or sculptor, even if not of great powers. I except musicians (i.e. composers,) because they appear very often to enjoy every kind of irregularity in life; theirs is the genius nearest to madness.

I am delighted to hear that there is a chance of Kate's coming. I want to see her very much. It wo'nt be long now,—if she does come; less than a month to wait. This is a good starting point for excursions. I am thinking a little of changing my abode sometime this summer, and going down to Cornwall. The climate is the warmest in England, the scenery very pretty. I have about exhausted this neighborhood. Tristram and Iseult are still hanging about Cornwall, I believe.[3]

Your letter was very interesting to me. As usual, I was especially tickled by the report of the children; the story of the boys sitting up late, and sure they were not sleepy, is good. I really think it is well to let children do as they like to satiety, once in a while. Mother tried it once with me about going to school, until I begged to go again.

You must have enjoyed your architectural trip. Your way, yours & Flora's, of getting off for these little changes of scene, is admirable. There is nothing I believe in more than just such things as that. Yet how few people understand it! Sometime when you are writing, please give me the pronunciation of Bryn Mawr. I have never dared attempt it. It is almost as bad as an English family name; I think I have had so many mishaps in that line, that I no longer attempt to pronounce any English name save Smith, until I have heard it done by an Englishman.

—I met the Gilmans in Cairo last year; Eugene Schuyler told them I was there, & they very kindly came to see me. Are'nt you living on the very spot where the old Woolsey house stood? Mrs Gilman is not the Woolsey I used to know as a child; it was a younger sister, I think. They asked me to drive out on the desert with them.—Oh, Sam—if you could see the desert! I dare say you will. To me, it had an inexplicable charm. But I must not begin to pine for the wonderful East, when I have engaged to do two years of steady work here. I have never heard of the Rev. Mr Goucher and his taste for Ravenna architecture. How strange! Yet I like it, too. I'd give a good deal to see a campanile again. You will think me very discontented. I have been upset a little by the chance (offered to me) of getting Lady Hobart's Villa "Montanto" for summer, for almost nothing at all. It is an enormous old place (13th century) (I mean enormous for me)—with an old battlemented tower, & the splendid Bellosguardo view. The walls are so thick that it is cool. And there is a large garden. She would lease everything where it stands, & I should simply take her place. I "am not going a step," as the children say, or used to say. No more housekeeping for me, until I have earned more money. But the offer unsettled me for a day. The evenings up on top of that old tower, with the vast landscape darkening slowly round me,—what an atmosphere for a novelist! Hawthorne wrote the Marble Faun there one summer, you know. Perhaps one could catch a breath of his spirit.

Flora's holding out so well on that journey, fills me with admiration. I could'nt have gone through the half. And it's no use to place ~~it to~~ the inability to advancing age. I could'nt have done it at twenty! I am going to write to Flora before long. But I have it on my conscience to say without [?] delay that Brugsch Bey did not mean so much that Miss Edwards was not a very learned person, as that, in his opinion women, (all women) were not adapted for deep learning or scientific knowledge of any kind. Is'nt that the German idea of women? Brugsch is a German. Now Flora—& I—do'nt agree with him.

You can't possibly tell me too much about the colleges; or anything else. I do'nt come home,—no; (the reasons are strong against it); but I always feel a little hurt, and forgotten, and left out in the cold, to know so little of all that goes on there. I am in a wild state of confusion of mind; for instance, as to the situation of Adelbert College, and the Case School.[4] I know the old St Clair Street; & Euclid Street beyond the toll-gate; I used to know every house on both (or in both as they say here) for many miles. But where those colleges are, I have no idea.

I am just now (very late) reading Bryce's "American Commonwealth."[5] What do you think of it? It is certainly interesting.

I am going to see the primroses this Spring at last. I have never yet seen them in their full glory. I hope to make a foray into the Forest of Dean, for the purpose. It is not so large as the New Forest, but very pretty, I am told; oaks and beeches. In two hours I can reach a place called the Speech House, in the middle of the forest, where the "Verderers' Court," is held.[6]

I look back over what I have written, before closing, and I see that I have alluded to advancing age. How absurd of me to do so, when my contemporary is one of the gayest dancers in New York! But Flora Payne was always a remarkable person.

With love to your wife, and kisses for the children,—especially for my dear little namesake—I am yours affectionately,

C. F. Woolson.

Notes

1. Portions of this letter also appear in Benedict/CFW, 39, 50, 297n, 368–69.

2. Sir T. Wemyss Reid (1842–1905) published *The Life and Letters* of poet Richard Monckton Milnes in 1890. Karl August (1757–1828) was the Grand-Duke of Saxe-Weimar-Eisenach.

3. The legend of Tristram and Iseult about the tragic love affair between a Cornish knight and an Irish princess is part of the Arthurian cycle and is set in Cornwall. Many variations survive including an opera by Wagner, which debuted in 1865.

4. With a donation from Flora Stone Mather's father Amasa Stone, Cleveland's Western Reserve College became Adelbert College in 1892. It is now part of Case Western Reserve University.

5. Viscount James Bryce (1838–1922) published his three-volume *American Commonwealth* in 1888.

6. The Verderers' Court began in the thirteenth century as a court to try minor offenses. By Woolson's day most of these offenses were related to environmental issues.

To William Wilberforce Baldwin (Morgan)

4 Promenade Terrace
Cheltenham
July 15th, [1891]

My dear Doctor.

I have been wondering whether you were not coming to England this summer? I am sorry you are to have so short a stay in the green foggy land. Shall you come back, via England? I am on the point of leaving Cheltenham; the men come to pack my books, pictures, and the few articles of furniture which I have here, in a day or two. I am going to Oxford. And yet I cannot be sure of the exact date of my going. I should be so delighted to see you if you can possibly manage it, either here or at Oxford. The only way, however, will be for you to telegraph me, if you have a day to spare for either journey. You can telegraph to my address here (as at head of letter), & I will make arrangements to have the message repeated to me, if I have gone. Whether I am surrounded by dust & trunks here, or ditto at Oxford, I shall be happy to see you and happy to welcome you as though the scene of meeting were Villa Brichieri on the tranquil hill. I wish I were to be in town. But town is crowded just now, as the brilliant Emperor-haunted month bends toward its close.[1]

Henry James is in Ireland; to remain, as I understand, until August. He had no intention of going away, as his sister's condition grows worse and worse. But the influenza prostrated him and he was ordered to the sea-coast for recovery. (This seems to be the universal course in England. Do you approve of it?) I think he had a bad attack, though it did not affect the throat or lungs; only the head, with fever. He appears to be almost well now, & greatly interested in the glimpse of Ireland. Perhaps you have heard from him? His letters are no doubt forwarded to him directly, from De Vere Gardens.

I have had a delightful spring. My sister & Clare, & my second niece, Kate Mather, came over the first of May, and, making this house their headquarters, amused themselves with excursions in every direction, many of them by coach, & on horseback. I joined in a good many, & saw some charming spots. I went, for instance, away down to Penzance in Cornwall,—the very Land's End. Also to Exeter to see the Cathedral. And to Wells, ditto,—the most interesting spot in England, I think. The Bishop's palace has a moat & drawbridge! I came near taking a small house in Wells. But my people thought it too remote & too dull for a long stay. It is a hard place to get to. Then I have been several times up & down the lovely valley of the Wye,—seeing Tintern Abbey, Chepstow Castle, & best of all, Raglan Castle,—the finest ruin so far that I know in England. Another time we all went to Berkely Castle on the borders of Wales; that day Henry James was with us, having come from town for the purpose, & we had great fun. Do you see Parsons' beautiful drawings of the Warwickshire Avon, in Harper's?[2] Well—I have been seeing the Avon in a rowboat. I never could tell you, in a letter, the charm (to me at least) of following the pretty & historic little stream from Evesham to Tewkesbury—where it joins the Severn. Then, at the last, I accompanied my people up to town, where we did a great deal in the way of amusement. I came very near leaving England, & going with my sister to Germany, &, later, to Vienna. If I had happened to write to you ten days ago, I should probably have told you decidedly that I was going to the Continent for good. But there was trouble about securing the sort of rooms I wished, with (always the difficulty on the Continent, unless one keeps house) a private table. Just at that time I went to Oxford for a few days; I have always loved the place, & it struck me anew as enchanting. So I changed my mind after all, and Oxford is to be my next (temporary) abode?

A letter comes in from my sister this a.m, asking if you are to be in Vienna this summer. She goes to Bayreuth for the whole Wagner season, &, after that, to Vienna (in September), & she hoped to be able to consult you there. She will be disappointed.

I am so sorry to hear, my dear friend, that depression has haunted you. I know so well what it is myself! Nothing but sheer courage from day to day keeps me going. But you have not the great drawback, & the lonely life, that are my lot; and while I do not, & would not, in the least attempt to say that life ought to be easy for you (for the heart knows its own bitterness & cannot always explain it), yet I have hoped, that, taking all things together, the good in your lot overbalanced the other part. It is a great thing to be young, & courageous, & brilliant, & you are all that, & more. We have all watched your career with admiration & keen interest. But life, I suppose, is always a contest to the end. When we read the biographies of even the most successful (to the world's eye) men, we always find that behind the scenes there was a steady grind going on all the time, with any number of hard, very hard things to bear, & quantities of private discouragement. I am sure you are very courageous. Life is not worth living at all, without courage. (I am quite determined never to outlive my own.) You say you have fought the blue devils. Well,—I am sure you have worsted them!

I should like to see your four boys. Be sorry for the people who have no such loving cheer. (I have not even a dog to wag his tail when I come in!) There is nothing like the cheer that children give. My love to your wife. I heard great things of [Monnetin?] when I was in Genoa; such pure air, they said.—

One of Henry James's plays I have seen,—The American. It is excellent. It is to be produced in London in the autumn very brilliantly. Another is to be played, later, at Hare's Theatre, The Garrick. The Miss Robins who made such a success in Ibsen's "Hedda Gabler" in London, is to be the "Claire" in the "American" & Compton, who does Newman, is an excellent actor.[3]

I still hope to return to Italy to live. To Venice. Everything points that way. In the meantime, I may possibly take another eastern journey, and see Constantinople next winter. But that is not decided.

To Kansas. I have never been there. I should like to go home for six months & re-dip myself in the old atmosphere. My relations came very near buying back the sturdy, & rather ugly, old stone house in Cooperstown, which was built for my grandmother & given to her on her wedding day. It was in the market for a low price, & they thought of securing it & giving it to me. This may be my end yet. But I should like to get in some years of Venice, before I retire to Otsego county.

Let me know your plans. If you cannot manage the time for a journey into the interior now, perhaps you can stop on your way back? Then I shall be settled, & not in confusion. With best regards & all good wishes, I am, yours as ever,

C.F.W.
"c/o Alliance Bank.
High Street. Kensington.
London. W."
is always a sure address.

Notes

1. Woolson is probably referring to high-level visits and the politics surrounding an impending alliance between Germany, Austria, and Italy.

2. Alfred Parsons, 1847–1920.

3. Woolson may be referring to *Mrs. Vibert,* which was never produced. John Hare (1844–1921) was both an actor and the manager of the Garrick theater. The American actress Elizabeth Robins (1862–1952) was also a writer and a suffragette. See appendix for Edward Compton.

To Samuel Mather (WRHS/Mather)

(c/o Alliance Bank
High Street. Kensington
London. W.)
Cheltenham
July 18th, [1891]

My dear Sam.

The draft for sixty-one pounds, &c, came a day or two ago, and I am very much obliged for it. This morning arrives your letter of July 6th. I am delighted by what you have accomplished with the Iron Ridge thousand dollars. You have, virtually, doubled it, have'nt you? It seems miraculous to me. When you say that it can be relied on to pay "6% yearly on its par value of $100^{00} per share,"—do you mean that it pays interest on $2,000? It still seems too good to be true. Perhaps it pays on $1400? That also is wonderful.

I write but a few lines, as I am in the midst of upheaval here. I have waited to finish a Ms. first. I go to Oxford next week, and I feel sure that it is a wise choice. When I went over there (across country, via Chipping Norton,) the other day, dull season though it was the place looked very fascinating. I have always liked it. But now I shall have it, as one may say, in my pocket; I can sit in the lovely St John's Gardens (do you remember them?), & walk in Christ-Church Meadows; &, best of all, row on the Isis & Cherwell. I walked to Iffley along the bank of the river, & row-boats were darting about, with ladies of all ages rowing; so that I shall not be conspicuous, if I take an oar,—as I used to be at Lake Leman. I have not, as yet, secured good rooms; only temporary ones. But I hope to find better ones, later.[1] Direct, please, "Alliance Bank," as at head of letter.

I am disappointed about seeing Col. Hay. Just after my letter to Flora, I was laid up for nearly two weeks with the tiresome lame shoulder. As soon as I could be about again, I wrote to Col. Hay, hoping that in some way—Oxford perhaps, where I was going in a day or two—I could see him. But my letter must have just missed him. I heard of him, through Henry James. But I wanted to have a talk with him, greatly.—

I am glad to learn, from your letter of today, that Flora is so much better. Who is the remarkable Dr who ordered complete rest? I have the firmest belief in a long rest of that sort, as the best of all possible remedies. Especially the hours of rest in bed; the early retirement & the late getting up. Yet, simple as it seems, I have almost never known it prescribed, or kept up, excepting in some establishment for a rest-cure. It can quite as well, & much more pleasantly, be done at home. I have never known of any physician who prescribed it,—admirable as it is; & this makes me ask, who is Flora's doctor? You know—when there is no actual necessity—I don't consider it safe for people to "keep up"—no matter how they may feel. For women it is dangerous. In fact, is dangerous for everybody. My best love to Flora. I hope that by this time she is ever so much better. She must not think of answering my letter; I can wait. But send me pictures of the children, when you have new ones taken. I really think very often of that little girl who bears my name.

Love to all at 544. I have rec^{d} Kate's letter, & will answer from Oxford.

Affectionately yours,
C. F. Woolson.

I thought seriously of breaking up entirely & going back to the Continent; Schmalbach first, then Italy.[2] But it seemed foolish to leave so comfortable a country when I wish & intend to be so closely occupied. Venice must wait. Or rather I must.

Notes

1. Woolson moved from 13 Beaumont Street to Oriel Street, then to larger quarters at 15 Beaumont Street.
2. Probably Schlangenbad.

To William Wilberforce Baldwin

13 Beaumont Street
Oxford
Saturday
July 24th, [1891]

Dear Doctor.

I have just telegraphed to you. I arrived here last night, and I shall be delighted to see you whenever you can come. Choose your own time, and stay as long as you can. Please give me notice of several hours in advance, however, that I may not be in Mesopotamia. (There really is a Mesopotamia here; it is a lovely walk by the river.) It is a very poor way to ask you to come here, and yet I have no house to receive you in, properly, & no dinner to offer. These rooms, which I have taken temporarily, are too small, and the cooking is of the most primitive, watery, British description. I shall hope to find a better place, now that I am actually here. If you should stay at the Randolph Hotel, you will be very near my place. I stayed at the Randolph when I came over to look for rooms, and was very comfortable.

I wonder if you have received the letter I sent to you in the care of Brown, Shipley, & Co,—It was written in answer to your first from Florence. If it has not turned up, please inquire for it. Not that it is in the least important. But I don't like to have letters left about the world; and I have heard several complaints lately about carelessness as to letters, at Brown & Shipley's office.

I found your note here, upon my arrival. I think you are very fine with your London tailors & bookmakers! The English (the men) certainly, as a whole, are the best-looking & best-dressed men in the world (except the Austrians as to looks);

and I suppose the tailors have something to do with it. But as to women—they are not, as a whole, well dressed,—though they, too, are often handsome.

Let me know when to expect you.

Yours most cordially (though in haste),
C. F. Woolson.

To Katharine Livingston Mather (WRHS/Mather)[1]

Oxford
July 26th, 1891

My dear Kate.

I am really here at last; and Oxford seems more beautiful than ever. It is now 8 p.m., and Dr Baldwin, who came down from London to spend Sunday with me, has just said farewell, and hurried off to take his train back to town. As we walked nearly four hours this afternoon, I will not go out in the lovely long English twilight, as usual, but sit here and scribble a letterette to you. You know the comical English fashion of attaching "ette" to all sorts of things, as a diminutive? . . . Yes, I remember Mason Bey.[2] I met him once only; at a small party which Eugene Schuyler gave in Cairo, on the Egyptian festival called "Smelling the Zephyr," a sort of May-day. The people go out to the country gardens to smell the roses. It was Schuyler's first entertainment at the Consulate, and so I turned out, as he had been to see me daily for five weeks, with either a large bouquet, or a pile of new books, sent by his "Kavass" in his glittering gold costume.[3] It was an afternoon tea, and a very hot day. The tea was iced, and I sat in the window, and Schuyler paraded man after man, whether they liked it or not, before my chair, and made them talk to me. I then weighed 165 lbs. and I was very much heated, and I had no thin clothes, (having left them all at Florence;) so Mason Bey's idea of me, is of a red-faced porpoise. As he has married (according to your description) a stoutish person himself, I do not feel so wretched about it. He is a cousin of Mary Lee (General Robert E. Lee's daughter), and that is the reason he talked to me. I know Miss Lee. He came abroad after the war, because he was such a rabid secessionist that he would not stay at home! He belongs to the Mason family of "Mason and Slidell" fame. But he was a brave officer in the Khedive Army, and he has been a great explorer in his quiet way. He explored, for instance, years ago, that lake in Africa where Stanley finally met Emin Pasha.[4] Poor Schuyler, you know, gave but that one opening entertainment. He died in Venice about six weeks later. . . . Oh, Kate, it is so lovely here. The great quadrangles of the twenty-one Colleges, all so beautiful and so different; the lovely college gardens; the two rivers and little row-boats; the beautiful country all about. I have endless pleasure before me. I am dying to get settled. Imagine me in a row-boat, (with a boy to help) paddling about these half dozen little rivers, under the trees all the way!

Affectionately,
C. F. Woolson.

Notes

1. The letter is in a typed transcription at WRHS. Portions also appear in in Benedict/CFW, 361–62n. The final paragraph appears in Benedict/CFS, 369 under the date Aug. 23, 1891.

2. Alexander McComb Mason came from an aristocratic Virginia family and fought on the side of the Confederacy during the Civil War. He was part of the Mason-Slidell family, who were involved in a mission between the Confederacy and England that was stopped by the Union Army. After the war, during which he was imprisoned, he explored Egypt for its ruler Khedive Ismail (1830–95). A "bey" is a high-ranking officer or government official.

3. A "Kavass" is an armed authority.

4. Governor of Equatoria, Africa, Emin Pasha (1840–92) was a both a doctor and a naturalist.

To William Wilberforce Baldwin

13 Beaumont Street
Monday morning

Dear Doctor.

I enclose a letter which has just come for you. I hope you are well, and I hope also that the fresh cool rain we have had here, reached London also. This morning the air here is delicious. I enjoyed your visit, greatly. But you must come again later, when I am more at home here.—My love to your wife when you write. I send best wishes for your journey.

Always your friend,
C.F.W.

To Katharine Livingston Mather (WRHS/Mather)[1]

15 Oriel Street
Oxford
August 23^{d}, [1891]

My dear Kate.

. . . I am in a picturesque house, four hundred years old, belonging to Oriel College. It has pleasant low-browed rooms, and big oriel, (or bow) windows, gay with flowers. Its great attraction to me is, that it looks out on a quaint little quadrangle where there is no traffic. On one side of this quadrangle is the Canterbury Gate of

Christ Church; at the end is Corpus Christi, and all the left side is Oriel College. It is therefore the essence of old Oxford. The cooking is excellent; if I could only spend the winter here, I should be delighted; but alas! the whole house is engaged, years ahead, to University men, and I must turn out at term-time, early in October. I am perfectly captivated with Oxford. I have had some lovely afternoons on the two little rivers;—far up the Cherwell under the trees,—it is enchanting. Then the old gardens of the Colleges are ideal. And all the beautiful towers, façades, gateways, Chapels, &c&c. And the Bodlein Library. . . . There is a big bull-dog in the house, whose name is Oriel Bill. He insists upon spending the evening in my sitting-room. I don't mind that, as I like dogs; but when he jumps heavily into my lap, I have to protest. He is almost as large as I am. I put him down; and then, as apology, he offers me his paw. He goes out to walk with me every day. I wish you were here, Kate, Oxford is so lovely.

Affectionately,
C. F. Woolson.

Notes

1. The letter is in a typed transcription at WRHS. Portions also appear in Benedict/CFW, 369–70.

To William Wilberforce Baldwin (Morgan)

15 Oriel Street
Oxford
Sept. 7th, [1891]

My dear Doctor.

Welcome back. I hope your mother has had a comfortable voyage? For I have heard from H. James that she is with you; how delightful for you, and for her! How she will enjoy seeing your boys! I send her my best regards, and I wish very much that I could see her. Can you not both stop at Oxford en route for London? You will remember that you promised me a second visit. I am in a low-browed little house, five hundred years old, belonging to Oriel College. It overlooks a quiet quadrangle with the façade of Oriel on one side, the Canterbury Gate of Christ Church on the other, and Corpus Christi at the end. It is the essence of old Oxford, and I like it greatly. I am very near the old-fashioned "Mitre Hotel," in the High Street—in case you like old-time inns, as many people do. I should be delighted to see Mrs Baldwin and yourself if you can stop. Let me know by telegram in advance—that I may not be five miles away on one of my long tramps.

Oxford is—to me—an enchanting place. Yet I am homesick for Italy, as it has rained here almost daily since you left.—I received your note from London, and the goodby word from the "Majestic" with its delightful account of your railway journey with the English schoolboys. Wo'nt you be happy to see your own, though! I should like to witness that meeting.

I shall be curious to hear how the U.S. struck you—in comparison with Italy. Climate for instance, & the life generally. Your testimony will be valuable, because you are, in spite of your long residence abroad, a warm patriot, just as I am. My sister is under the care of the specialist in Vienna, to whom you introduced her. Frank Loring has been here, &, a few hours after he left, came (unexpectedly) Mr Richard Greenough, his brother-in-law. They do not love each other, you know! Supposing they had met here. I hope you will have time to see Miss James. Last accounts of her were bad. With all good wishes, yours as ever,

C. F. Woolson.

To William Wilberforce Baldwin (Morgan)

15 Oriel Street
Oxford
Sept. 11th, [1891]

My dear Doctor.

I sent a letter to Queenstown to meet you upon arrival. But I see, by the morning's paper, that your steamer did not stop there, owing to thick weather. My letter contained a message of welcome back, and my best regards for your mother. And I also asked—(and now repeat the inquiry)—whether I could not have the pleasure of seeing you here again, and not on a Sunday, so that you can have a glimpse of the picturesque colleges? Is not this possible? I hope so. Oxford is really very near London. In my Queenstown letter, I urged your stopping here with Mrs Baldwin, en route to town. But I suppose you are already in the great metropolis, so that chance is lost. Wouldn't your mother like to have a glance at Oxford? I should be very glad to see her. The old-fashioned "Mitre" hotel is very near my present abiding place; but if it were for the day only, Mrs Baldwin would of course stay with me.

Please let me know, by telegraph, if you are coming, and send it half a day in advance, please, as I take long daily walks, miles in the country.

I hope you are well? How delighted your mother will be to see your boys!

With all good wishes, yours as ever,
C. F. Woolson.

I received your letters written before you sailed; one in town, the other from Queenstown. I am curious to hear how the U.S. struck you—in comparison with Italy; i.e. climate, & the life, generally. Are they in as much of a hurry as ever?

To Samuel Mather (WRHS/Mather)

15 Beaumont Street
Oxford
Oct. 16th, [1891]

Dear Sam.

Thanks for the draft. You can have no idea how your promptness in sending on this exact day, makes my life comfortable!—I have moved into my winter quarters (as above), and now you can send directly here. I dare say I shall not stir again, until I am ready to go back to Italy. Oxford suits me perfectly. It is ideally lovely & interesting in many ways. The colleges & college-gardens enchant me. Also the boating on the two pretty little rivers. Then I am so near London that I can see more of life and the world than I could at Cheltenham. I can come & go in an hour—when I wish to. And as I have at last learned how to travel 3d class (as all the English do), it's but a trifling expense. So, on the whole, I think I am in the right niche at last.—My new rooms are very comfortable. My landlord is the "Manciple" of Exeter College. (The word vaguely conveys to <u>me</u> only an idea of a mysterious insect, looking like a stick, or twig, who assumes, with his thin legs, attitudes of prayer!) But, in Oxford, it means simply a steward. So I shall hope to live well! When birds are cheap & good, & the college indulges, then <u>I</u> shall have birds, I suppose. I shall let supply my table.[1]

I wish you could have had all "Cairo" together. Suspend judgment until you have read the 2d part. There will be—sometime—one article on "Corfu & the Ionian Sea." That's all. They were anxious that I shd. fill a volume, to be called "Sketches in the East." But I did not stay long enough in the Holy Land or Greece to feel justified in writing about them. The "English Library," the new Continental rival of Tauchnitz, is bringing out my books, newly set up & corrected (by me). I will send you the vols., later.—This is not a letter. I am much pressed & hurried, so only send at present this scrawl. Much love to Flora & the boys. And 40 kisses for my little girl.

Yours affly,
C.F.W.

Notes

1. Woolson omitted a direct object in this sentence.

To Katharine Livingston Mather (WRHS/Mather)[1]

15 Beaumont Street
Oxford
October 20th, 1891

My dear Kate.

. . . I had to leave my Oriel bower when term began, as all the rooms were engaged by under-graduates of Oriel and Merton Colleges. I am now in my winter quarters. My landlord is the Manciple of Exeter College (a "Manciple" is a steward). I am more and more enchanted with Oxford every day! . . . I went to a first night at London of "The American," Henry James's play. A first night in London is like a reception. All the best seats are given to friends, to critics, and to persons of distinction; full dress necessary. I put on my best, and we looked well enough, but were nothing to the others; pink satin, blue satin, jewels of all sorts, splendor on all sides of us. The house was packed to the top, and the applause great. Mr Balestier pointed out to me some of the celebrities; all the literary and artistic people were there, and many swells also. Mr Balestier is the young American writer, now living in London, who has written a novel in partnership with Rudyard Kipling, which is to be in the Century this winter.[2] When the performance was ended, and the actors had been called out, there arose loud calls "Author" "Author." After some delay Henry James appeared before the curtain, and acknowledged the applause. He looked very well, quiet and dignified, yet pleasant; he only stayed a moment. The critics have, since then, written acres about the play. It has been warmly praised; attacked; abused; highly commended, &c. In the meantime, it continues to draw, and is now in its fourth week, and going on. It is, as you know, simply the novel "The American" dramatized. Compton, who plays Newman, is excellent. The whole play a great success. . . . [3]

The sun is shining, and I am going to take the long walk of the "Scholar Gypsy," the scenes of Matthew Arnold's two poems, "The Scholar Gypsy" and "Thyrsis." Both of them I have long known by heart. I go through "the two Honkseys" and up to "Childsworth Farm." And "the tree! the tree!" is a landmark all the way. . . . [4]

Affectionately,
C. F. Woolson.

Notes

1. The letter is in a typed transcription at WRHS. Portions also appear in Benedict/CFW, 371–72.

2. *The Naulahka* appeared in *Century* from Nov. 1891 to July 1892. See appendix for more information on Wolcott Balestier.

3. *The American* debuted at Opera Comique in Southport on Jan. 3, 1891. Edward Compton played the part of Christopher Newman.

4. Woolson is quoting from "Thyrsis" (1866), a poem Arnold wrote in memory of Arthur Hugh Clough; the poem reads "Hinkseys," not "Honskeys." He published "The Scholar Gypsy" in 1850 and refers to a "scholar gypsy" in "Thyrsis."

To William Wilberforce Baldwin (Morgan)

Wednesday evening
[Oct. 21st?, 1891]

Dear Doctor Baldwin.

I think it well that you should know immediately that I went before the Pretore today & swore that Mrs Launt Thompson had never told me, either in speech or in a letter, that Julia [Sciaccu?] "would sell her daughter for one hundred lire." This is all they asked me, & I answered an emphatic "no."—Finding that Mrs Thompson is too ill for me to notify her of this, I notify you. (You will remember that the letter I received, was not in her handwriting, & had no signature; was literally anonymous. Moreover it contained no such statement.)

Yours ever,
C. F. Woolson.

To Flora Stone Mather (Benedict/CFW, 373–75)

Oxford
[1891][1]

I have had a long walk this beautiful Indian summer day; I went first across the fields, beside a little brook, to a rustic ferry over the Thames, or rather over one of its branches. A cord hangs down from the tree; you pull it, and it rings a bell in the ferryman's house on the other side; then he comes over in his punt and takes you across for a penny. On the other side is one of Matthew Arnold's "two Hinkseys," namely, South or Ferry Hinksey. I looked in at the little ancient weather-beaten church, then I crossed by a field-path to North Hinksey—"the Tree, the Tree!" being in sight all the way, so that I could not "despair"—even if I had wished to (which I did not). I don't know that you care for Matthew Arnold's poetry? To me it is very dear and especially the two poems about Oxford; "Thyrsis" and "The Scholar Gipsy." Finally, just as dusk fell, I stopped at the cathedral on my way home, and attended the beautiful choral service. I sit close to the organ, for I love to hear its rolling chords. The cathedral was crowded, and as all the undergraduates of that particular college (Christ Church) are obliged to wear surplice when attending service, the nave and choir seemed (with the many choristers in addition) to be full of white-winged figures.... Then I came home in the fog, and found my kettle boiling on the trivet attached to the grate in the sitting-room, and the little low tea-table all ready with the jap teapot that has a cup inside, so that there shall be only an infusion of tea, and no tannin. I therefore instantly made a cheerful cup. And now I am writing to you by my blazing fire.

All this is to give you a picture of my life here. I think you were right in saying that you felt convinced Oxford would be more satisfactory to me than any place outside of Italy. It is. I had a good deal of difficulty in getting pleasant rooms, as in term-time almost everything is engaged for the colleges; I find that about half of the undergraduates live in lodgings, and not within the gates. However . . . I have at last obtained a very nice place with sitting-room, dining-room, trunk-room and a bedroom above, all cheerful, and with big English coal fires. My landlord is the Manciple of Exeter, and so I fare well as regards the table. Then I go to town in an hour, and that gives more variety than I had or could have at Cheltenham. Yesterday, for instance, I went to town by invitation ... to the Lyceum matinée to see the Daly company in "As you Like It" ... Rehan is a delightful Rosalind and I smiled to see Lewis as Touchstone. I remember his beginnings at Cleveland ages ago....[2]

Notes

1. Benedict incorrectly dates this letter 1892. See letter to Kate Mather dated Oct. 20, 1891.

2. The American actors in this performance of Shakespeare's *As You Like It* (1623) were Ada Rehan (1857–1916) and James Lewis (1838–96). Benedict omitted the period after *As You Like It.*

To William Wilberforce Baldwin (Morgan)

15 Beaumont Street
Oxford
Nov. 10th [1891]

My dear Doctor.

Just a line to say that I send you, by the same post, the magazine, with a little more "American" literature,—for I know you are interested.[1] After you have read them, possibly Miss Huntington might like to see them.—

But please do not say anything of my having sent them, when you write to James himself. He does so hate anything like blowing the trumpets; & already he is weary of all this talk about the play.—What D. C. Murray says in the "Contemporary," is pretty true; the acting by no means equals the writing! Still, the public appears to like it greatly. Tomorrow is the 50th performance, & the ascension is to be celebrated. I did not write the article in "Murray's magazine."[2] I have no talent for critical writing. Miss James has had it read aloud to her, & likes it greatly.

I keep you posted, privately, because since your letter, I know that you are interested.—

Weather lovely today after a great gale. My sister & Clare have come & gone. They landed in N.Y. yesterday. My sister says you are better than any of the specialists. And she calmly told the Vienna man, & the other one in London (I do'nt remember the names) that "Dr Baldwin had done more good than anyone else." She had weeks of treatment in Vienna, & did not appear much better. But, possibly, she has been at least saved from a worse condition. I dare say she has. The trouble is not bad. But hangs on. You will, I know, be glad to hear that the drums are really doing me some good. I shall continue their use. I am settled for the winter very comfortably. But I pine for Italy. With love to Mrs Baldwin I am your friend,

C. F. Woolson.

Notes

1. Woolson is writing about reviews of Henry James's play *The American.* She enclosed the following notice from the evening paper, *Pall Mall Gazette*:

> Royalty has especially favoured "The American" at Opera Comique. Within the past three weeks there have visited the theatre the Prince of Wales, the Duke and Duchess of Fife, Prince Albert Victor, Prince George of Wales twice, and the Duke and Duchess of Teck.

See appendix for names and titles of royalty.

2. *Murray's Magazine* was published by the John Murray Publishing House from 1887 to 1891.

To William Wilberforce Baldwin (Morgan)

15 Beaumont Street
Oxford
Nov. 15th, [1891]

My dear Doctor.

Last Saturday evening, the 14th of November, witnessed the 50th performance of "The American" before a crowded & brilliant house. I was present, so I know. The play has been greatly improved, & now goes extremely well. I enclose slips. Please remember not to betray to H. James himself when you write, that I have sent you these extracts & magazines. He can't endure any appearance of puffery. I think he is over sensitive about it; but we must take him as he is.—I hope Mrs Baldwin is better? Give her my best love. You will, I know, be interested in hearing that the ear drums really seem to be doing me good. I am afraid to count too much upon it. But people tell me I hear them more readily than I did before using them. I shall keep on now with them very carefully. I have not been careful heretofore.

In haste, but with much regard, yours,
C.F.W.

To Linda Guilford (WRHS/Mather)[1]

[1891]

. . . Your book gave me great pleasure. The first time I read it, I sat fascinated over its pages for half the night; how it revived the past! I had not until then, realized that the Seminary—the place where I had the benefit of your teaching was, for you, but one of a chain of schools, or rather, an episode in the one school whose scene was occasionally changed, though not its spirit. . . .

For myself, I feel that I owe you much. The pains you took with my crude compositions; the clearness with which you made my careless eyes notice the essential differences between a good style and a bad one; your praise, when I (not very often) deserved it; your discriminating, careful censure, which did me more good than all—these were, and still are, invaluable to me. I must have tried your patience, and I might, no doubt, have profited much more than I did, from your teachings. But it was the start you gave to the faint taste which enabled it later to grow in the right direction. (At least I hope it is right).

So many thoughts rose when reading your book. One was my (still fixed) impression of the immense size of the Water Cure Woods.[2] I have travelled far and wide over the world since then; but I really think I have never found any forest so wild and so vast as the Water Cure Woods! Another will amuse you. It came later—this impression—but still it is of the past. You remember the reverence we had for Prof. St John; when I was beginning to write a little, I was much put out and annoyed by a fashion of that day in the U.S.—namely, the exalting of stories for children to a place which it did not seem to me belonged to them. I thought that they had their own sphere, and that it was a very high one. But Shakespeare still existed, and Milton; the great historians, the great essayists, the great writers of fiction. But in the U.S. at that time, one would almost suppose to hear the talk (it is true that much of it was done by mothers) that the writers for children were greater than all these. I was spending the winter in New York, and Prof. St John came to see me; (it was almost the last time I saw him)—the conversation turned toward literature, and I had to hear fully an hour's eulogy of Miss Alcott's "Little Women"—which I, too, liked but could not place above all else in the world. I smile, now to think how sore I felt about it;—that my demi-god, the Professor, should have followed the crowd in this respect. This reminds me to ask if you have read "The Life & Letters of Miss

Alcott?"[3] I was greatly impressed by the book. What heroic brave struggles. And what a splendid success.—

Do not fancy that I admire Tolstoi; (you quote him in one of your letters). I do not in the least, save as a novelist. As a man, I dislike him. And I think him half mad. I know much of his life from a lady who lived for years in his family. He wears a colored shirt,—& and makes shoes in his drawing-room; he digs in his fields. But the drawing-room & and the house are very handsome (Mme Tolstoi has a large fortune); he makes the shoes so badly that no one can wear them,—he only spoils so much leather; and the farm-laborers are obliged to do over, secretly, all the work he does in the fields. What good does it do to anyone on earth, for him to go barefoot?—He was notoriously immoral for years; after that, when he had married, he had so many children that I dare not, from memory, say just how many; but it was something like twenty two.[4] Mme Tolstoi, being strong and very rich, has lived through it. She has had nothing to do with her children, for nurses & tutors & governesses were provided, and took entire charge; the large house was like a colony. This is a nice record for an Apostle who has lately preached to the world, in his old age, that all men should live like monks! The "Kreutzer Sonata," which contains this doctrine of his, is (in the unexpurgated edition) the most indecent book I have ever read.[5] I write all this, because I have the idea that there is a very incorrect idea of him abroad in the world. That is, the English-speaking world.

Who are the "college boys" to whom you so kindly read my story, "Peter the Parson[”]? What college? Did you enjoy the California trip? I am so sorry I did not see that country before coming abroad. I did see the South very thoroughly, as I lived there for years with my mother. The Middle States I know, and the seaboard. But not California. I must go thither before I settle down in Florida, which is to be my home when I come back . . .

What shall I tell you of myself? Last year, I saw Egypt, Greece and the Holy Land. Now I am bent upon going to Constantinople and to India. My next housekeeping will probably be Venice—the place I love best over here.

I am no handsomer than of old. . . . I walk five miles a day; I am very well; and immensely interested in the great movement of life everywhere. I must add that I no longer know how to spell! (I fear you have noticed that already!) The many small differences between English and American spelling now confuse me—reading constantly, as I do, the English papers and magazines. Then, too, the similar words in French and Italian; neither "agreeable" nor "amiable," can I spell without a dictionary (I have just looked into one!) One becomes polyglottish in spite of all one's efforts. The funniest thing is the English "Society" slang. We used to be so carefully taught not to say "ain't"; here, duchesses say it . . . My regards to Mrs T., if she remembers me. At the Seminary, I remember I was much impressed by the name of a sister of hers, as she pronounced it: "Italia Beatrice." There were romantic horizons to me in that name! Since then I have lived much in Italy itself. But it still remains fully as beautiful and romantic as it seemed in imagination then in Kinsman Street.[6]

Notes

1. Pasted into Woolson's *Anne*, New York: Harper's, 1882. Portions of the letter, sometimes with no surviving original, also appear in Benedict/CFW, 37, 41–44.
2. The Water Cure Woods were in Cleveland, Ohio.
3. Ednah D. Cheney's *Louisa May Alcott: Her Life, Letters, and Journals* was published by Roberts Bros. (Boston) in 1889. Alcott published *Little Women* in 1868.
4. Tolstoy had thirteen children.
5. The *Kreutzer Sonata* was published in 1889.
6. Woolson attended the Cleveland Female Seminary on Kinsman Street.

To Samuel Mather (WRHS/Mather)

15 Beaumont Street
Oxford
Jan. 21st, [1892]

Dear Sam.

I had intended to write you a long letter; in fact had begun one, which was to have accompanied one I was writing to your mother. But I have been ill, & so now I will send a card without further delay, to say that the cheque came safely, and that I am ever so much obliged. I do'nt see how I get that extra thirty, exactly? I had one thirty in Oct. Has that 2d thousand you created begun to pay me interest so soon?—I am saddened to think of the two aunts gone.[1] But they have met so many of their loved ones in the next world!—Here all is gloom. For 100 years there has not been such sincere mourning.[2]—The tragedy is heightened because the mysterious malady is as bad as the plague. It is raging all over England. Very bad in Oxford.—I hope you have all escaped?—My illness was severe, but short. A strange & terrible pain in the head. The Dr does not know what it was, but I fancy the artificial drums I have been wearing produced it in some way. For two or three days I was almost delirious with the pain. I am well now. But weak. Love to Flora. I recd her pretty Xmas remembrance, & your dear little American book. That is the sort of book I need, & the one I like best.

Yours affy,
C.F.W.

Notes

1. Samuel Livingston Mather was one of nine children; the aunts are his sisters.
2. Prince Albert Victor died in Jan. 1892.

To William Wilberforce Baldwin (Morgan)

15 Beaumont Street
Oxford
Feb. 5th, [1892]

My dear Doctor.

It must be telepathy! Here am I, ill; wishing for you. And behold your letter arrives; though, busy man that you are, you are not in the habit of writing, save when you must.

I have had no influenza, though it has raged so severely in Oxford that for the first time in living memory, term has been postponed. I have been afflicted with a pain in the head which at times has been simply infernal; I can use no milder word. I wo'nt go into all the details. The doctor here thinks it is purely "neurotic," which means "neuralgic," does'nt it? I, (with American conceit) take the liberty of differing—a little. No doubt it is neuralgic. But behind the neuralgia, I think there was inflammation of some sort. One night, I thought I should be mad, or dead, before morning. This terrible pain is now at an end. But there remains a constant ear-ache, which is hard to bear. This is now the fourth week. My own idea is that those artificial drums (I spoke to you of them, I think?) have done some harm, somewhere. But I am improving; & with the aid of tonic medicine by day, and sleeping draughts at night, I am creeping back to strength again. How I <u><u>have</u></u> wished for you!

England has been like one continuous funeral. The ravages of the Plague on all sides; the cold, and bleak fogs; & the tragic death of Prince Eddie, have put the whole country into black. As an outsider, I can bear witness to the sincerity of the sorrow for the poor young fellow, who had (after, as I hear, years of waiting,) secured at last the girl he loved. Perhaps <u>you</u> know more of the story than I do; you may have heard why there was so long an opposition to his choice? It is so pathetic that I am hoping that Princess May really loved him, & that she is mourning for him now sincerely. You must tell me, sometime. At any rate, the situation has struck the English heart, and there has been no such genuine national sorrow for a hundred years.—

I am glad to hear that you and yours have escaped the Plague; or rather have escaped its worst poison—for you yourself appear to have been in the clutches. <u>You</u> would, however, never give up unless you were struck prostrate!

Give my best love to your wife; and my regards to your mother and sister. I wish I, too, were in Italy!—

Think of Miss Greenough having the influenza—when she was so far from strong to begin with! Give her my love. And also to Miss Huntington. I want to write to them; & will as soon as I am stronger.

In the intervals of pain, I make plans: 1st I wish to see India, & go round the world! 2[d]: I wish to go home for one year, & see how it strikes me. A year could be charmingly divided; the summer between Mackinac; my nephew's lovely country place on Lake Erie, "Shoreby"; & dear little Cooperstown. Then Florida for the whole winter.—If I like all this, I'll stay. If I do'nt, I'll bring over my silver, linen, books, etc, & settle in Venice forever. What do you say to these ideas? With many thanks for your kind letter, yours as ever,

C. F. Woolson.

Feb. 6th

This letter did not get off last night, so I'll add a little more. I think I feel a little better to-day, though I shall not feel sure until I have had sleep without the aid of narcotics. I shall—for my own entertainment—put in two of this English doctor's prescriptions for you to look at. One is a tonic. The other a medicine for the daytime, which I take to be quieting—though of course I do'nt know. Will you sometime let me have them again? This illness has been, & still is, so depressing to me, that it is only by constant reading—forced reading—and by sleeping draughts that I get on at all.—

That sounds rather bad, does'nt it. And probably I don't really mean it. Very likely if the house should take fire, I should be the first to make a desperate effort to escape! But I need'nt explain, for you already know what a crybaby I am about pain.

I must tell you a piece of news: my very pretty second cousin, Julia Smith, has written to announce her engagement to a young Episcopal clergyman. He is a very good fellow, and has been in love with her for several years; I have known of it, but I did not feel sure that Julia herself would elect to fill the difficult position (difficult in the United States; not in England) of a clergyman's wife. However, she writes me a very sensible letter about it, & she tells me that she is very happy, & perfectly satisfied. As she is now 27, she must know her own mind.—

The delightful letter you wrote me in November, I did not answer out of regard for your crowded winter hours & days. Now that I have a (vague) notion of going home, your mention of "an island camp in Lake Champlain," & an eagle, set me to dreaming of whole days (January days, too) spent out of doors in Florida, & great eagles sailing over our heads far above in the blue. You'll see that I'm homesick & tired. I fear I am. Your troop of little boys are always there to amuse you. But I have no little boys. My nephew (a trump) has just sent me a photograph of his two, with their little sister "Constance"; lovely children. This is a lure to draw me over seas!

No, I do'nt think my Cairo articles were half so good as they should have been. I had not space enough to put in anything but facts. And in the East, facts are only half. Yes indeed, you would appreciate the East. To me, there is nothing to approach it. I am dying to go again; to go to the 2^{d} Cataract. Thence to India.—

"On the road to Mandalay,
Where the old flotilla lay,—

Ship me somewhere east of Suez, where the best is like the worst"—as one of Kipling's ballads has it.—I am not quite sure where Mandalay is! But so long as it's "somewhere east of Suez," I'm satisfied. Fancy! Rudyard Kipling, strange genius, after abusing Americans right & left, has married a little American girl, with neither beauty, money, nor breeding; (a capable little woman no doubt). But he might have married anybody. I rather admire the way he has insisted (against the wishes of all his family) in wedding the girl he loved. Though I think it a pity, on general principles, as he is not yet twenty five.[1]

Mrs Burnett's new play just withdrawn in London was a dead failure. She was foolish enough to take a theatre herself, in order to produce it, & so I suppose she must have lost a good deal of money. It ran less than three weeks.—It was called "The Showman's Daughter," & was (all the papers said) so old-fashioned that one might easily have supposed it to have been written fifty years ago. It was a so-called "domestic drama," & very sentimental & weak. I put in this bit of news because we have discussed Mrs B., & her literary ideas, several times together.

Of the James family, you know directly from themselves. Miss Loring has just mentioned having cured her cook with your directions as to influenza. Alice lives, and even enjoys, for every now & then I get a witty message from her. If she had any health, what a brilliant woman she would have been. Henry J. has not, so far, had a second attack of the Plague. But both of his servants have had one, and life in De V. Gardens has been a good deal mixed. As I write, the pain has begun again—like a knife—in the left ear. I wonder if you would send me a prescription for a sleeping draught that won't hurt me? Something I could always use, if necessary. I cannot long stand this sort of pain.—I am thinking of going to Schlangenbad for the summer. What do you say to that? Regards to all who remember me. Yours as ever,

C.F.W.

Excuse a dull letter. I still suffer constantly.[2]

Notes

1. From Rudyard Kipling's "Mandalay" (1892). Kipling had recently married Caroline Starr Balestier, the sister of his publisher and collaborator, Wolcott Balestier.

2. Woolson wrote on the envelope, "I feel better today."

To Samuel Mather (WRHS/Mather)

15 Beaumont Street
Oxford
Feb. 8th, [1892]

My dear Sam.

I sent you a card to say how much obliged I was for the cheque. Now I will try to forget pain in a letter to you;—a reply to your kind and delightful invitation of Jan. 11th. To have done with the blue part first, let me say that I am still suffering from the pain which attacked me a month ago. But it is now much less severe, so that I bear it better. (I have not much fortitude about pain, you know!) The English doctor here, a clever young man, thought the whole affair was neuralgia. "Neurotic" was his word; that is a malady of the nerves of the head. I did not, in my heart, agree with him. And I think it is now pretty well decided that it has been a slow gathering in the inner ear, first on the right side; & now on the left. I say "inner," because there has been no sign of anything visible anywhere. The first two weeks I let the thing run on, with a few remedies of my own. But the intense pain forced me to send for a doctor, & though he has accomplished nothing else, he has given excellent prescriptions for sleeping-draughts, so that I get through the nights. Today, as yesterday, I am putting on linseed poultices every 15 minutes, & in spite of a low state of depression, my reason tells me that in all probability in a few days more, this left-side ache (a rather stab) will be over, & well, just as the right side now is.—The loss of time preys upon me worst of all. I try not to think of it. I read & read. And when I can no longer do that, I even play solitaire! If you & Flora could have peeped in half an hour ago, and seen me seated on the rug, with the kettle on a trivet attached to the grate behind me, & all the materials for the linseed poultices assembled on a tray at one side, while I, with tear-stained face, was drearily playing solitaire on an atlas propped on my knees, you would have laughed, I am sure. I never play games, you know; so when I play solitaire, it is desperation indeed. The tears are not serious; it is only the pain that forces them out. I too can even laugh (at intervals) at my own forlorn situation.

However, one side of the head is now perfectly well, & I have good hopes of the other. I will send you a rejoicing little card the moment I am free again.

I do not remember whether I told you (I think I told your mother) that for several months I have been trying some artificial ear-drums. They certainly improved my hearing. But I attribute all this pain to them; I think they made the real drums very sensitive; & then I took cold, owing to receiving a long call when my shoes were wet.—

I am so much obliged to you, Sam, for your cordial invitation. It does me ever so much good to get it just now. I can't come this summer simply because every well moment must be given to finishing the novel, which begins in a serial in Harper's Magazine next December. I have already postponed it a whole year, owing to the tiresome condition of my health; never really ill, I may say, sadly enough with truth, that for a year I have not been really well. Unless I wish to make the Harpers lose all patience with me, I must keep my engagement fully & promptly this time. Therefore it is not by any means the moment for a home-coming, and a visit to you. How much writing do you suppose I should accomplish if my dear little Constance was within my reach; you & Flora might give me twenty writingrooms—but I should be out of them every five minutes to look at the boys, & see how they were amusing themselves! Instead of constructing fiction for the American public, I should be recalling fairy-tales for the Shoreby private infantry. So I cannot come this summer. But, do you know, Sam—I have a plan. It is vague. But still it is more a plan than any I have had for ten years. I have long hoped (as you know) to go to housekeeping again, in Venice. Lately the idea has come to me that before I do that, I'll go home for a year. I want to see all of you at Cleveland, first of all. Then I should like once more to see Mackinac. Then a few days at Cooperstown for mother's sake. Then a winter in Florida. After that, it will be time enough for Venice. I have set no dates for all this. Because first, as a standing-point, I wish to do a certain amount of literary work.—Nothing less could possibly content me.—I am hoping that my health will improve. And all the doctors say that it will. They all, however, advise me to live in a warm climate.

This darling little picture of the three children is perfectly enchanting. It is the prettiest child-picture I have ever seen; each child so charmingly natural. Constance looks brimming over with fun; her mouth is all ready to burst into laughter, & also her bright eyes. She is a very pretty little maiden, & I take the greatest interest in her pretty cloak, bonnet, & muff, & little fur robe on the sled. The boys are also beautiful figures, artistically. I am much struck by the strong likeness of Livingston to you. It is the first time it has seemed to me so very marked. The picture as a whole gives me great comfort & satisfaction; I have framed it & put it on my mantel piece.—

I have been, & still am, very proud to tell my friends that "my nephew has just written, inviting me to come home & spend the summer with him." Especially so (as regards England; for I must confess I have put the brag into my recent letters to Italy, also!), ~~for~~ because recently in reading "The Principles of Psychology," by Prof. Wm James (of Harvard) I came upon a sentence something like this; "under these circumstances, it is best to express an emotion of benevolence, if it rises within us; it is best to do something that one would not otherwise do, as for instance to give a penny to the crossing-sweeper; or to yield up one's seat in a horse-car to an old man; or to speak genially to one's aunt."!! I sat down and scratched off a note to Alice James, the Prof.'s sister (who is in London), demanding to know what that meant! We have been writing back & forth about it ever since; & though it is in joke (she is very witty), yet I have been astonished to find that she considered her brother's illustration a perfectly good one! Heavens—is that the usual idea of aunts? Why—the only importance I have is that of an aunt; it is only through nephews & nieces, & now grandnephews & niece if you please, that I keep in touch with the actual life of the day. Poor Miss James is slowly dying of cancer. But everything that can be done for her, has been done in the nicest way. She preferred to be in London, so as to be near her brother; so a very pretty little house was taken for her in Kensington near him; her devoted friend Miss Loring lives with her, & the three excellent servants & a trained nurse.—[1]

I knew you would feel the loss of the last two remaining members of your father's family.[2] I too admired Mrs Walton the most, though I had in reality seen more of Mrs Burnham and Mrs Thomas Mather. As families go, it is very seldom that so many brothers & sisters live through middle-age & into old age together. I have always thought the Mather constitution an excellent one on the whole. Ours (your mother's) has'nt half its staying power. Still, I think that with care, ours may also last long. But care is necessary.

I am glad to hear your good report of Clara & Clare. I hear often from them. But I like also to hear an outside word. I am extremely desirous that Clare should have happy years just at this time. Nothing can make up to a girl the free-from-care gay, lighthearted period after school is over, & before marriage. The period must not last too long, or it loses its charm. But never to have had it at all, is to have missed something peculiarly bright & happy; something always delightful to remember.—

England has been dreadful—; the influenza, the cold, & fog, & the death of Prince Eddie, have combined to make the days very dismal. The mourning for the young Prince has been the most genuine national sorrow for a hundred years. He was not personally well-known; but all England was interested in the way he has stuck to the girl he loved. At last they let him have his heart's desire. And then came death! Now the country is all agog on account of the danger of the Duchess of Fife's coming to the throne. Nobody wants that, & so there will be uneasiness until Prince George is married.—

My best love to Flora. Kisses to the children. Tell Kate, please, that I rec[d] her letter just after I had mailed one to her mother. But I shall write to her soon. Love to her, to your mother & Will.—A letter received this winter from Solon Severance, praises you & Will in very high terms. How comes it that I hear from Solon?[3] He came to Oxford in the summer, called upon me, but did not get in, as I was ill.

Hence notes. Have you heard that Cousin Caroline Phinney died in Jan.? She was the sister next to cousin Sue Cooper.

Yours affly,
C.F.W.

Notes

1. William James published *Principles of Psychology* in 1890. Alice James died just a month after this letter on March 6, 1892. The brother near her was Henry.

2. In her letter to Mather dated Jan. 21, 1892, Woolson refers to the death of his paternal aunts.

3. Solon Severance (1834–1915) was a Cleveland banker and philanthropist.

To Samuel Mather (WRHS/Mather)

15 Beaumont Street
Feb 15th, [1892]

Dear Sam.

A few lines on business. I am looking over my accounts for the past and coming year, and in order to see exactly what I have to depend upon, I need more light upon the Minnesota Iron Stock.

In July, 1891, you bought for me 20 shares of that stock, at 70. But at the time, I had in your hands only 1188^{16} to pay for it. You wrote that you hoped to collect enough from the Grand Rapids to complete the payment. Did you succeed in this? You also wrote that you thought the Minnesota could be relied upon to pay six per cent of its par value of 100^{00} per share. And that the payments were quarterly; i.e. Oct. 1st, Jan. 1st, April 1st, July 1st. Last Oct. with my railroad Interest you sent me 30^{00} of Minnesota. And also on Jan. 1st. It appears therefore that you have either succeeded in completing the purchase with the Grand Rapids money, or else you must have advanced the money that was required for it, yourself. Will you please let me know? And whether I can, or can not, rely upon the 30^{00} Minnesota, four times a year?

If you did succeed in completing the purchase from the Grand Rapids money, then you have performed the miracle of actually turning one thousand dollars into two thousand. Besides getting six percent interest for the two thousand! This looks magical to the aunt.

However, I started you as a magician early in life.

At last, to-day, I feel better, though there is still a steady earache in one ear. To-morrow I hope to take up my novel again, & Oh! how glad I shall be that this dreary, enforced, pain-filled vacation is at an end.

The charming picture of the children continues the light of the room. It is snowing outside, & foggy at the same time. But my very nice landlady has just brought me a pot of white tulips, & another of lilies of the valley, to cheer me up. Various kindly friends have offered to come & stay with me. But I declined all (save one who came in spite of me), as I have not been able either to talk, or to hear. The lady who came (English), has now departed. But I hope soon to be myself again. Much love to Flora & the children. And to all at 544.

Affectionately yours,
C. F. Woolson.

To Samuel Mather (WRHS/Mather)

15 Beaumont Street
Oxford
Easter Tuesday [1892][1]

My dear Sam,

Your draft comes promptly & I am greatly obliged. I will write before long in answer to your delightful letter. I am not well, or I would write to-day. There is an irregular action of the heart, which, though not painful, is sometimes rather distressing. The Dr, however, does not think it important, & I dare say it is not. I shall do better no doubt when it is warmer. It is bitterly cold here now, with the dreadful English Spring East wind.—For your Easter, take the thought of all you have done for me; it ought to add to your happiness. It would, if you could see how much it adds to mine.

—Your "Ruddy" items were of great interest. I have not seen him; but I know much of his engagement & wedding. The latter I regretted for his sake,—simply on the general principles of his being so young &c. But they tell me he is not attractive, personally. But how he can write sometimes. "The Man Who," for instance.—[2]

Love to Flora & the dear little ones.

Affly,
C.F.W.

Notes

1. Easter in 1892 was on Apr. 17, so this letter was written on Apr. 19.

2. For Woolson's reactions to Kipling's marriage, see letter to Mather dated May 20, 1892, and letter to Baldwin dated Feb. 5/6, 1892. Kipling published *The Man Who Would Be King* in 1888.

To Rebekah Owen (Colby)

15 Beaumont Street
April 28, [1892]

Dear Miss Owen.

I suppose you will reach Museum Road to-day. (How cold it is!) I write this line to ask whether you, and your sister, and Colin, could come to tea on either Tuesday or Wednesday afternoon (next week) at five? If you can come, will you let me know on which afternoon I may expect you? I hope Colin will bring his doll.—My sister sails on May 3[d], and will arrive here, I suppose, about the 10th.—Thanks for your attempt to find primroses. I have been gathering fritillaries in the Iffley Meadows; but no primroses.—I had a charming walk last Saturday nearly to King's Weir, and back for tea at the Godstow bridge.—With regards to your sister, I am, yours very truly,

C. Fenimore Woolson.

To Samuel Mather (WRHS/Mather)

15 Beaumont Street
Oxford
May 20th, [1892]

My dear Sam.

Your letter of March 6th was a comforting one. I am so forlorn when ill,—so downcast and disheartened—that words of sympathy and affection like those you wrote, cheer me greatly. I have had a very trying winter, and even now I feel far from strong. First, it is one thing; then another. Nothing ~~very~~ serious; but serious to <u>me</u> because when I am not well, I cannot write well. I am beginning to think that Dr Baldwin was right when he warned me, two years ago, that the English climate was bad for me.—

To day is the second race of "The Eights," & we are going. Yesterday was the first. I have not wished to make acquaintances in Oxford, as all the ~~time I can get~~ well moments I have <u>must</u> go into this new novel. However I do know a few persons, & now I am glad that one of them happens to be the wife of a "Head"; namely Mrs Woods, the wife of the President of Trinity College. My gladness is of course on Clare's account, & yesterday we went to Mrs Woods at Trinity to tea to meet some pleasant people in her beautiful drawingroom, & then we all went down through the green Christ-Church Meadows to the Trinity Barge, where we had seats on top to see the races. It is a lucky thing to get a seat on a Barge; each college has one; a sort of river club-house. Of course these are private invitations. If you do'nt know any one, & get no such invitation, then you have to take your chances with the great crowd on the tow-path, or hire a boat & creep, at a safe distance, behind the procession. The race was very amusing & comical (to me, at least) with the "bumping," & frantic yelling of everybody, & the different (23) College yells. Mrs Woods, or rather the

President, has given us seats on Trinity Barge for the whole week of races—"Boat Week"—& we are going again today. If Clara would stay through "Commemoration," I could get ~~her~~ invitations for her and Clare to a good many things including some of the College Balls. But she thinks she must go on June 10th.—Oxford is very pretty now. But not warm enough to please me. English Springs are so cold.

I have been a good deal stirred up, lately, by ~~three~~ four letters from Harry Washington offering me his beautiful apartment in Venice, at a low rent.[1] Harry is the son of my old friend Mrs Washington of Florida. The two Washington boys are well-off, and rather erratic about travelling & collecting all sorts of curiosities. By "erratic" I only mean that they appear to have no taste for settling down. Since they were graduated at Harvard, they have been all over the world. One of their "collections" has been this handsome apartment at Venice, which is now filled with oriental & other bric-à-brac; I believe there are one or two mummies! The boys go home for six months &, hearing that some time I hope to go to Venice, they wrote to offer the place to me. Well—I was "struck all of a heap" (as I once to my joy, heard a Boston Dana say)! But I had at last the fortitude to decline. For I <u>must</u> finish my novel before I can go anywhere. I have written to Harry to ask whether he would let it, for a year, at any future time? But I know he wo'nt, as he is passionately fond of Venice himself. He thought I wanted it for this summer,—which was a mistake. I will send you one of his letters (you need not return it) as it may amuse you; he is such a good specimen of one sort of American boy. I ought to explain that Harry's mother (now dead) was the best friend I have ever had, outside of my relatives. She taught these two little fellows (they were little then,) to think of me as a sort of aunt. Hence all these letters; for Harry never lets his apartment. He only proposes to do so now, because he has heard that <u>I</u> want one.

You do'nt know how greatly interested I was in all you wrote of Ruddy & his wife,—especially in the amusing language of Mr Adams. I have longed to hear Mr Adams talk ever since Flora gave me those entertaining accounts of him at Sorrento. But now alas! I never shall. It is only old friends who will take the trouble to speak in a trumpet. One day last winter, when I was lying here on the sofa, with my head swaddled, & only a little chink of light in the room, a telegram was brought in. Miss Poynter was here; she had come up from town (London[)] to see how I was. <u>Mrs</u> Poynter, her sister-in-law, is Ruddy's aunt,—as three sisters married, respectively, three painters, namely Burne Jones, & E. J. Poynter, & Kipling père. I opened the telegram, which read "Have just given away Ruddy's bride, C. Balestier, at All Souls. Present only Gosse, Heineman, & self. H. James."—I read this aloud in great surprise. And Miss Poynter, <u>white</u> with astonishment, took up the block & wrote, in big letters, "I am <u>flabbergasted</u>!" I have never heard her use any such word in my life; she is very precise in her language.—She had to write, as it was at the time when everything had to be written to me. Up to the last, the Kipling relatives hoped that the match would not come off; they looked higher for the gifted boy, & were inflexibly opposed to the idea of Carrie Balestier, who is older than Ruddy, plain-looking, & ordinary. Ruddy, however, was as inflexible as they, & he married the girl he loved whether or no. The reason there was no one else present was that Mrs Balestier & her younger daughter, & Mrs Gosse, were all in bed with influenza! Henry James, Gosse, & Heineman were present as friends of poor Wolcott Balestier, the brother. Wolcott was the only one of the family I knew.[2] I ought to add that the Kiplings, & Poynters, & Burne Joneses, have been sensible enough to make the best of it. They now say that Carrie will make an excellent wife, & that she is a very good woman-of-business, & will see to Ruddy's affairs & keep him straight.—She has straightened him a little already, for his recent letters to the London Times have not had any of the unpleasant & petty digs at America & Americans, which used to annoy me so.—

I heard of you at Lakewood. And I suppose you are now at Shoreby. Give my best love to Flora, and a kiss for each of the children. In all probability, I shall stay quietly here all summer. But I am allowing it to be supposed that I am going to Germany with Clara; so please do not contradict this, if anyone should, by chance, ask you. I am not well enough to see people; & many come to Oxford during the summer.

I have had a charming letter from Col. Hay, about "Dorothy." I was much pleased to hear from him. And sorry to hear he had been ill. Mr Boott writes that there has been such a demand for the song ("Through the long days") that Ditson's salesmen in Boston have been amazed.

Everyone who comes in, admires the picture of Constance on her sled, with the two boys. You have certainly had the prettiest pictures of your children,—all of them—that I have ever seen. So picturesque, & also so natural.—

Excuse scrawling. I have now learned to hold my pen between my little finger & the one next to it, to relieve the hand. I also write with the pen between the second & third fingers.—

The rumor here is that Prince George is to marry May. They would like to postpone it for two years. But the nation is so nervous about the Fife succession that this may force it forward. Princess May has a hard position to fill, just now.

It looks as though I should be in England through a general election. It will be an exciting one. I only know one English woman who is a liberal, & that is Lady Hobart. All my other friends are rabid Tories, & their hate of Gladstone is extreme & intense. Who will win at home? You must explain to me, when we meet, the subject of Protection & Free Trade. For I suppose you are a Protectionist?[3] Civil Service Reform is the only hobby I have left, from the many old questions of 15 years ago. Now for the river, & Bra—zen—Nose!! which was the loudest shout yesterday.

Love to all at 544. I shall write to Kate soon. I want to write to Flora. But will wait until I am alone again.

Affectionately yours,
C. F. Woolson.

Notes

1. Henry Washington's letter below is archived in the Mather collection at WRHS. The letter also includes a sketch of his apartment.

Palazzo da Mula
San Vio 725
Venice
May 13th, 1892

Dear Miss Woolson.

Over a month ago I wrote you a letter from Athens but as I sent it to an address of which I was not at all sure, I fear very much that it has never reached you. I had the Alliance Bank in my mind as your address, but latterly a terrible fear has been growing in me that London & Westminster Bank is your right address—So I shall send this there and also a note to Oxford in the hope of reaching you. I wrote you in regard to my apartments here, as my brother told me that you had expressed a wish to take them for the Summer—I should be most happy to hand them over to you after my departure from here,—about June 1st. In fact it would be doing me a great favor to have ~~you~~ them occupied, and there is no one whom I ~~she~~ would have more gladly than yourself. But perhaps it would be as well to give you a short description of them—They are on the Secondo Piano—"Piano nobile"—and front on the Grand Canal—The Palace is well situated—on the south side of the canal—which makes the place cool in Summer—just below the iron bridge—above the Palazzo Davio and almost opposite the Pal. Barbarigo where the Curtis's live—a splendid situation—from the big balcony one gets a fine view down the Canal and along the Riva Schiavoni—It is only about ten minutes from the Piazza—and a traghetto is almost opposite—A sketch plan is subjoined. The rooms are quite large—the three front ones being about 25 × 16 feet, and the long hall 60 × 25—The "sitting room" is well furnished—and with a lot of curios, bric a brac &c—being in fact a place for the rubbish I collect on my travels—also with a lot of rugs and hangings—the three bedrooms are all furnished with the necessary furniture—beds chairs &c—But I haven't bothered much with them—one must take things slowly—and then one is so little in them—There is a kitchen above the small hall on the left—but I never use it—taking only my morning coffee at home, and eating at the restaurants—Hence I have no kitchen furniture—but this you could easily get—and I would most gladly take it off you afterwards when you are through with it—It would be a blessing and, in fact, as living and house prefer, I should be utterly lost when brought face to face with the complicated problem of buying pots and pans—There is also running water and some of the window improvements—and altogether you could be very comfortable here—In regard to the rent I should be most happy to hand the place on to you for the summer for nothing—but of this we can talk later—I shall certainly not accept much for it as the it is really a kindness to me to have it occupied while I am gone—Please let me know as soon as you can about your plans and whether you think of coming here or not, as I may leave before June 1st, and would have to fix things up a bit—I have a pretty good gondolier—and also had last year a capital man to attend to the rooms, make the coffee—a first rate valet or butler—he has at present a temporary place elsewhere—but if you wished him could leave, I think—[Grist?] is not here now, you know, went back to America many years ago where his mother died shortly after his arrival—He is hoping to come out soon again—but his coming is always problematical—My brother is not with me—having left yesterday for Africa with a friend—He had a pleasant, though archeologically not a successful time of it in Greece, and I spent some three weeks in Asia Minor, collecting lava and studying volcanoes—I expect to leave for home before the middle of June—sailing from Hamburg. If possible I shall take—or make—a chance to see you and Mrs Benedict & Clare in Oxford—but I really fear that it will be impossible—as I must get on soon to America. We'll see one another anyway in the fall I hope—It is some years since we last met and I trust you are all well—I only wish I could have the pleasure of a long talk with you, but am afraid it will be impossible—Pray give my warmest love to your sister & Clare and believe me

Your loving friend
Henry Washington

Written across margin of first page: Please address c/o Banca Credito Veneto. Venice—

2. William Heinemann (1863–1920) was a publisher. Woolson omits the second "n." See appendix for other names.

3. In the 1892 U.S. presidential election protectionist Republican Grover Cleveland defeated incumbent free trade Democrat Benjamin Harrison.

To Katharine Livingston Mather (WHRS/Mather)[1]

15 Beaumont Street
Oxford
May 21st, [1892]

Dear Kate.

I am very sorry you have not been with you during the past three weeks; for the weather has been pleasant, and Oxford so pretty and green and fresh; and my (few) friends have sent delightful invitations . . . We finished up the gaieties of "Boat Week" by an afternoon on the Balliol Barge, as a change from the Trinity. The "Boat Week" means the seven races of the twenty-four crews of eight-oars each; each College has a crew, and the contest is for the position known as "Head of the River."[2] It has been very amusing, and the scene most animated, with the crowds of ladies on the barges, and the bands of music. To-day we go to a garden party at Trinity. Clara and Clare go next Wednesday; and I go with them to London for one Wagner

Opera (Seigfried), and then return to Oxford for a summer of very steady work.[3] I took a lovely walk along the Upper River (Thames) to Godstow (Fair Rosamund's Convent) where we had tea at charming ancient Inn on the bank, "The Perch." . . . [4]

Affectionately yours,
C. F. Woolson.

Notes

1. The letter is in a typed transcription at WRHS. Portions also appear in Benedict/CFW, 372–73. The error in the opening sentence is Benedict's.

2. CFW adds this note from an unidentified Woolson letter about the boat races: "We were on the Trinity barge when Magdelen 'bumped' Brasenose, now Magdalen has the honour of being 'Head of the River' until next summer. We have also been to hear some of the debates by the undergraduates. Earl Beauchamp spoke, and was most charming in manner, speech and looks." Earl Beauchamp is probably the 7th Earl Beauchamp, William Lygon (1872–1938), who became a Liberal Party politician and whose career was threatened by enemies who wanted to make his homosexuality public.

3. *Siegfried* (1876) is the third of Wagner's *Ring* cycle.

4. "Fair Rosamund" was the subject of an 1861 poem of that title by Dante Gabriel Rossetti. Rosamund was a mistress of Henry II (1133–1189); she was rumored to have been murdered by Henry's wife Eleanor of Aquitaine (1122–1204) but actually retreated to a convent.

To Henry Mills Alden[1]

June 30th, [1892?]

I am very much obliged for the two cheques. They make my summer easy, and enable me to finish my novel with a mind freed from anxiety. Perhaps I ought to give you a sketch of the story? It is about a man, this time; I mean the man is intended to be more important than the woman. I have not decided, as yet, whether to call the story boldly by the man's name: i.e.

"Horace Chase"

For I have always criticised a little the security with which woman undertakes to describe the masculine mind! For instance: "Adam Bede," "Felix Holt," Daniel Deronda," and of late "Robert Elsmere," and "David Greene."[2] I may, therefore, shrink from calling my story after that fashion. "A Husband" would do excellently in French; i.e. "Un Mari" but I doubt whether it would do in English; what do you think?

Well, Horace Chase is a plain American business-man who has made money, and will probably make more. I omit all the details (which serve to show how everything comes about in a natural way). He marries a girl of nineteen, he being thirty-seven, or eight. She thinks herself in love with him. Later, she becomes fascinated with another man, who is nearer her own age. This second man is not really in love with her; it is only through her own folly and wrongheadedness that she comes to believe that he is. She finally runs away to join him, but finds him (without his seeing her, or being in the least aware that she has followed him) with another woman,—namely the girl he is going to marry; he is with this girl (to whom he is betrothed) and her mother. (And it may be mentioned that his marriage follows soon afterwards.) Meanwhile the wife's flight has been instantly discovered by her sister, who follows her; finds her on the mountain nearly dead; & gets her to a farmhouse for the night. The husband, who has been in California on business, returns and follows them to this farmhouse, not suspecting in the least the truth. The wife is upstairs, asleep at last—confronted unexpectedly by the husband, the sister, with the inspiration of love, invents upon the spot a perfect explanation of why they are there; i.e., she and her sister. The husband accepts it without hesitation, and sets down to rest by the fire until his wife wakes. The sister meanwhile, starts upstairs, wakens the wife, tells her that her husband is below, and repeats to her what she has told him. Then she urges her not to contradict the story, and her arguments are 1st: that it (the truth) will make him implacably hostile. 2^{d}: that she, the wife has actually done no wrong, since no one on earth knows the motive of her flight, & no one has seen her; and the man whom she intended to join has not the least suspicion of her intention, and will now never know it. 3^{d}: that she (the wife herself) is now cured of her belief that this second man had ever cared for her, and, in his heartlessness, her own love for him—such as it was—will vanish, has already vanished.

To these arguments the young wife's reply is simply to rise, and go down to her husband—followed by the trembling defeated sister.

The wife then tells the exact truth. Not because she is brave or high-minded. She is neither especially. But because she feels that she must tell it, and therefore the sooner it is over the better.

And when she has got it out (in a few brief phrases), Horace Chase says something like this. 'Go?' (For she has offered to go.) "Why, where should you go but home? Come back, poor child, and we'll do the best we can. I do'nt know that I have been so perfect myself, that I have any right to judge you."

The whole book, as you will see, lies in that last sentence. Do you think it impossible? I do not.

I must mention that there are no cave scenes; the infatuation of the young wife with the second man is sketched very lightly, and not dwelt upon.[3] For, in my own mind, Horace Chase is the principal personage. He is a careful study from actual life, although, even in his case, I do'nt describe so much what he thinks, as what he says, and does. The date is 1873–1876. The two scenes are Asheville, North Carolina (in the mountains), as it was at that time. And St Augustine, ditto. Both places mentioned by name, and described realistically. There are minor characters, and a good deal of fun in the first parts. Will you let me know what you think of the plot?

Notes

1. The excerpt from this missing letter about *Horace Chase* is quoted in John Dwight Kern, *Constance Fenimore Woolson: Literary Pioneer* (Philadelphia: University of Pennsylvania Press, 1934): 93–94. A shorter excerpt is reprinted in Rayburn S. Moore, *Constance F. Woolson* (New Haven: College and University Press, 1963): 111–12.

2. *Adam Bede* (1859), *Felix Holt* (1866), and *Daniel Deronda* (1876) are all by George Eliot; *Robert Elsmere* (1888) and *David Grieve* (1892) are by Mrs Humphrey Ward. The title error *David Greene* is Kern's.

3. Woolson is alluding to a cave scene during a storm in her novel *Anne* (1882), where one of Anne's suitors first discovers his interest in her.

To Samuel Mather (Anderson)

15 Beaumont Street
Oxford
July 15th, [1892]

Dear Sam.

The cheque has come safely, & I am glad to have it.—It is so cold here that I have had a fire for ten days. In fact, the fire has only been out for about seven days; seven collected from the whole time. I am over my head in the new novel, & much interested in it, myself. I write 8 hours a day, walk 3, & sleep the rest of the time. I do'nt dine until 8, p. m., after my long walk in the country. By halfpast nine, I am in bed—to rise again at six.—Meanwhile all sorts of people send me notes "Care of Alliance Bank," asking where I am, &c&c. Save in especial cases I (for the first time since I came abroad) make no reply whatever! I had to take what physicians call "heroic" measures, for I was so behind-hand, owing to months of wretched health that it was that, or failure to keep my contract.—

Kate sent me a delightful description of your beautiful garden-party. How I should have liked to see it.—Her account of Constance was very captivating.

Of course the three must have come bravely through the measles?—

My best love to Flora. I do'nt remember whether I told about my meeting Mrs Humphrey Ward? I think I did; but if I did'nt, I will write Flora about it, later. Does Flora care for Mrs Ward's books. I do'nt (privately). But I was curious to see the woman who had made a fortune by one volume. She has just bought an estate in Surrey, with a park & deer.

—Last night a big torch-light procession here to celebrate the Liberal gains. They hooted this block, because here, next door to me, stayed the Tory candidate,

Sir George Chesney. The Chesneys have gone, but I think the crowd thought I belonged to them somehow, & they groaned & roared as they passed. For I was out on my balcony, looking on, as this English election has been a great sight from the beginning.—My excellent little landlady is a warm Tory; had it not been for her feelings, I should have waved my red shawl (Liberal colors), & then I should have had a round of cheers.—Shall you elect Harrison this time?[1]

Good-bye. I long to leave England, as I am never well here nowadays, & that makes everything dreary. But I must finish this book first.—Write when you can & tell me about the children.—Ruddy Kipling has written a very unpleasant & very untrue letter to the London Times about New York,—"little cad" indeed,—as Adams called him.—

Have'nt you had Shoreby photographed? I should like a copy; if you have.

In illegible hands, yours affectionately,
C.F.W.

Notes

1. In the 1892 British Parliamentary elections, Conservative Tories won the most votes but not enough for a majority. Tory Sir George Chesney (1830–95) won a seat. In the United States, Democrat Grover Cleveland defeated incumbent Benjamin Harrison in the 1892 U.S. election.

To Unknown recipient[1]

[1892]

The other day I met Mrs Humphry Ward; I mean I was invited to meet her. Although I seldom accept invitations nowadays, I did accept this; I was curious to see this fortunate woman. She looks very much like the portraits: fine eyes, not handsome, but plenty of force. I should say she takes herself and her books with intense seriousness, as very important influences in the world of to-day. There is a pretty story told of her. She fell in love with Ward, and early broke her heart about him. For she had no money at all—in England a sine qua non;[2] I mean that money is—and as he had none, his friends were strongly opposed to his saddling himself with such heavy responsibilities young as he was. He was an undergraduate of Brazenose; and, later, a Fellow. Finally he did marry "poor Mary," as people were calling her. And now behold his reward!

Now that I have scribbled this gossip, I seem to remember that I have already written it to your wife! If I have, forgive me. You see one doesn't meet Robert Elsmeres every day. Did I also tell that I had my purse snatched out of my hand upon coming from the opera? I went to town with Clara for one night, and this happened!

Such a strange sensation in wrestling with a criminal! He bent back my fingers, one by one. A good deal of money was in the purse, also.

Notes

1. This letter fragment was published in J. Henry Harper, *The House of Harper* (New York: Harper and Brothers, 1912): 486.

2. sine qua non: without which there is nothing.

To Unknown recipient (Wisconsin)[1]

Oxford. England
Aug. 10th, [1892?]

Dear Sir.

I have received your two letters; your having taken the trouble to get English postage stamps (for the last), is something that no one else has done! I am shy, always, about writing any paragraphs concerning myself, for I dislike the tone of so many that are published about others. I cannot believe that the public is in the least interested in the personal affairs of literary people;—to them an insignificant class. But as I am unwilling to pass as ill-tempered, I say—relying upon your promise to give nothing as coming directly from me—that I shall probably spend the rest of the summer and the autumn at Oxford, and that I am writing a novel.

Probably, in any case, this trifling item is too late for your purpose.

Very truly yours,
C. F. Woolson.

Notes

1. The letter is possibly to L. E. Jones, to whom Woolson wrote on Nov. 4, 1893.

To O.F.R. Waite (Claremont)[1]

15 Beaumont Street
Oxford. England
August 15th, 1892
O.F.R. Waite, Esqre

Dear Sir.

I have your note of May 24th. With regard to the sketch of the life of my father, Charles Jarvis Woolson, I should like to write it myself. But I cannot do it at present. Will you kindly let me know the latest date possible, for this ms.? Also its length, i.e. about how many words? We have never had any likeness of him which was satisfactory, & therefore we prefer to have no portrait. If I find, by your reply, that it will be impossible for me to prepare the sketch myself, owing to lack of time, I may be able, perhaps, to get a family friend to do it.—

Please let me know about how many words you prefer to have in the sketch of myself; & the latest date for that, also. A friend will prepare it.—

I was born in Claremont, but my parents left the place when I was a baby. I spent a few days there when a schoolgirl; & that is all. But I know both New Hampshire & Vermont well, from my father's loving descriptions; he never liked the West; he was always homesick for the hills of New England.—

With best wishes for your undertaking,
I am, yours truly,
Constance Fenimore Woolson.

Notes

1. Waite was Claremont's Episcopal minister and compiler of its town history. Apparently, Woolson did write her father's biography.

To Katharine Livingston Mather (WRHS/Mather)[1]

15 Beaumont Street
Oxford
October 2[d], 1892

Dear Kate.

. . . I took, at last, my long talked of trip down the Thames in a small steamer, to see the scenery. It was very pretty, but a little too cool for perfect enjoyment. I ought to have gone in August; but did not feel like taking even one day off till a good deal of copy had actually started to New York. I only went as far as Henley; then I went by train to Cambridge, which I have never seen; the same day to Ely for two hours, then back to Oxford; all in one day. Fortunately the day was divine, and I enjoyed it beyond words. I had no idea Ely was so magnificent. Between Henley and Cambridge I made a little pilgrimage to Stoke-Pogis, where Grey is buried. "The curfew tolled the knell of parting day" while I was there; perfectly beautiful.[2] I walked for two hours in Stoke Park (private park), where there were three hundred deer. The leaves were colored, and all was so tranquil and sweet; it did me good.—Now I am back, and tomorrow I take up my work again, refreshed. . . .

Here comes the tea tray, now I shall make tea, and drink a big cupful of it; then a walk of five miles, as it is a cold day; then home to dinner at half past seven; then bed; then tomorrow to work again. I send dear love to you all.

Affectionately yours,
C. F. Woolson.

Notes

1. The letter is in a typed transcription at WRHS. Portions also appear in Benedict/CFW, 375. There are two typed versions at WRHS: the first is dated Oct. 2, 1892; the second is dated Dec. 22, 1892 and missing the last paragraph. Given Woolson's comment on the weather, the October date seems most likely.

2. Woolson is quoting Gray's "Elegy Written in a Country Churchyard" (1750), which he based on the cemetery in Stoke Poges.

To Samuel Mather (Anderson)[1]

15 Beaumont Street
Oxford
Oct. 14th, [1892]

Dear Sam.

This morning comes the cheque for the dividend on the Minnesota Iron Company's stock, & the C.T.V.& W. bonds, also. I am much obliged for your promptness in sending it; this promptness is a great help to me.—

I have been hoping to hear from you. But I well know how many things there are to take your time & attention. Kate sent me a description of the beautiful party at Shoreby. I wish I could have seen it. She says that Constance looked so pretty & winning. She mentions (what I did not know) that the little girl indulges in baby talk, & that the boys never did so indulge. I think it is time for another picture of the three. The group of the two manly little brothers, & the sister on her sled, has been admired by every person who has entered my sittingroom. My friend here, Mrs Woods, has two little boys, but no little girl; she wishes her boys were as fine & strong as yours. Her two are sweet; but delicate in health.—The mention of her reminds me of Tennyson's funeral yesterday at Westminster Abbey (for Mrs W—'s father is Dean of Westminster). Perhaps you will be interested in seeing the order of the service? I did not get it from her, however, but from Henry James, who was one of the procession. He writes me that the effect of "Crossing the Bar," as sung in absolute perfection by the Abbey choir, was something extremely beautiful.[2] The "One clear call for <u>me</u>!" was like an angel's voice from on high.—I have always thought the poem itself one of the most touching & perfect things Tennyson ever wrote.—I am told, too, that the music for the last lines; "I hope to see my Pilot face to face, When I have crost the bar,"—was magnificent.—

Well—the summer is now over. It is cold & wet, & almost dark enough this morning for lamps. I have struggled along, since Spring, with health that has been rather uncertain. However, I am glad to say that I think I shall now be better, & better. After getting off a goodly portion of my new novel, which begins as serial in

"Harper's" in January, I took three days of vacation & change. At last—after talking about it for a year—I went down the Thames on the little steamer, to see the pretty scenery; then I made an expedition to Stoke Pogis; then I spent the last day at Cambridge, with a look also at magnificent Ely. I had no idea Ely was so superb.—I am now at work again.—

I do'nt want you to have a cold! But the fact is, that you have written to me, several times, the most delightful letters when you were shut up owing to one of those infections. Let me ask, by the way, whether you have at such times tried inhaling benzoin? To me it is the most satisfactory & soothing of remedies. I have a small china inhaling jug; I put in about a teaspoonful of tincture of benzoin, & fill up with boiling water. Then I sit down, take a book, & read & inhale for half an hour or so. I generally cure a cold in that way, very soon.—

Give my love to Flora. I have heard nothing for a long time that has seemed to me so charming as her naming her work the "Guilford Cottage."[3] I mean the building she has created. Such an act as that,—all too rare nowadays—makes me sigh with a full satisfaction. So kind; so graceful. Miss Guilford must have cried with joy.—She wrote me once a long time ago (I mean Miss Guilford) a most interesting letter; she was visiting the Hays, with Mrs Stone. I have answered it mentally twenty times, for it contained food for thought. How I wish that Edison would ever finish & let us have the phonograph (is that the name?). For then, in the evening, I could talk ~~with~~ to you so easily, & send off the cylinder the next day.[4]

Flora's last letter to me was from Washington. Miss Edwards (about whom she wrote) has died, & I have been interested in the revelation that she left, among other legacies, $2,000 a year to ~~be~~ found a chair of Egyptology, somewhere. Meanwhile a public appeal was made for her, after her return from the U.S., on account of "poverty," & she was put on the ~~pension~~ public pension list with the printed reason "insufficient means of support."—The queer things the English do, sometimes! When Mrs Dinah Mulock Craik died, there was some comment in the newspapers upon her having kept always her public pension, which was given her when she was poor, although she had long been very well off, & died rich. Mrs Oliphant wrote to the papers, defending her friend, & explaining that she (Mrs Craik) always gave the whole pension away each year in charity. Just as though the being-able to give a goodly sum of the public money away each year, as her own private charity, was all right!! I have been told that Mrs Oliphant herself who is now very well off, clings tightly also to her own pension; for she, too, has one.—

By the way, if Flora has time, I should be interested to know upon what grounds Gail Hamilton believes Mrs Maybrick to be innocent.[5] The American petition was presented here recently, & the Home Secretary declined to interfere. If you read the whole testimony at the trial (as I did), I am sure you must be convinced of the woman's guilt. I could have pardoned a sudden, impulsive murder, perhaps; but never the slow, cold, calm, torturing poison, day by day.—

I had a delightful letter from Col. Hay in the summer. He spoke so kindly of "Dorothy." That gave me much pleasure. Mr Boott (who is now over 80) came to Oxford in July to see me. He was greatly pleased (& so was I for his sake) because there had been so much demand for "Through the long days." He told me that the clerks at Ditson's, the music publisher, Boston, were astonished by the call for "that old song," as they phrased it, which had been reposing undisturbed on their shelves for years. Both the words & music are to me very beautiful. But the song needs the interpretation of a true artist.—

What shall I tell you about? Myself, I suppose. For when I hear from you, it is about you yourself, & Flora, & the children, [but?] I wish details of all sorts. Well, there is nothing exciting in my life. I have taken scores of beautiful walks this summer, all over Oxfordshire and Gloucestershire & Berkshire. I go by train several miles, here and there, & take my walks in a new region every day. Being alone; I confine myself to the highroads & the little villages; I do'nt go off through solitary footpaths &c. I generally make straight for the little grey church overgrown with ivy; I almost always find the door unlocked (a beautiful custom, which I wish could be followed everywhere) & within, there is ~~almost always~~ generally some quaint old tomb of an ancient worthy, life-sized, & clad in armour, with his wife beside him in a ruff. Occasionally these effigies are of alabaster, painted. Then I prowl about the village, looking for the queer little alms-houses "for three poor men, and three poor women," &c. Then I get a cup of tea at the rustic inn. It is always served in the same way; an enormous loaf, a pat of butter, orange marmalade, & water cress. I never touch anything but the tea. But there is no use objecting to the other things; it is the custom to serve it in that way, & in that way you must have it, or not at all. Then I come home by train to dinner at 8 p.m.[6] But these jaunts were taken in the long summer days. Now all is wet & cold.

Perhaps you will be interested in hearing the name of my new novel? I sent to New York, with a sketch of the plot, three or four possible names. They were not good, & I was aware of it; but could think of nothing better. Mr J. H. Harper then suggested "For better, for worse."—Should you not have supposed that it had been already appropriated? I looked through all the Mudie lists, &, strange to say, it is not there. So that is the title. I may tell you, in confidence that the Harpers pronounce the sketch of the plot "captivating." They are always so nice to me.—

The Columbus celebrations at home must have been imposing. I am—something,—a Member of some Committee—in the World's Fair.[7] Honorary, I suppose. I presume you know Mrs Farmer? She has written asking me to send an article on American novelists for a World's Fair book she is compiling. But I have not a moment of time for it.—Tragic, is'nt it, the illness of Mrs Harrison. The report over here is that the end is near.—If Blaine had not been so treated by his party, I should say that the death of Mrs Harrison would elect her husband—from sympathy.[8] But "sympathy" did nothing for Mr Blaine. His story seems to me as tragic as any in Plutarch.

Clara has seen Flora Whitney's daughter at a reception at Mrs Fred. Grant's, Vienna. This is the girl you & Flora found at Lakewood, in a semi-deserted condition. The desertion apparently still continues, & I am afraid I cannot find any thing more to say in defense of my old friend. She, by the way, is still learning the German & going to parades on tops of coaches. She is my age! She must have a large amount of courage.

On glancing over my letter, I see that I have not said <u>why</u> I disapprove so much of all these people (yes—even my dear Matthew Arnold, alas!) keeping their pensions when rich. (M. Arnold never <u>was</u> rich, & that makes his case not so bad.) It is because the sum set aside for such purposes, & paid by the British tax-payer, is small & rigidly limited. If these persons would give up what they no longer need, there would be more for those cases which are in reality pressing.—

Here comes old Domenico, the Italian image-seller. He has established himself & his basket opposite the house, & now he is steadily gazing at my windows! He is over 80. I talk to him in Italian, & occasionally buy a sixpenny plaque. I say to him "Come sta" & "Fa bel' tempo oggi," & he responds with a radiant Italian smile. When I go out to post this, I shall give him a penny and remark: "Credo che avremo della pioggia."[9] He speaks English, but we both pretend that he doesn't know a word. Good-bye with love to you both, & kisses for the children.

Affectionately yours,
C.F.W.

Have you changed your address?

Notes

1. Portions of this letter also appear in Benedict/CFW, 45–56, 49, 50, 367–68, 377.

2. Tennyson's poem "Crossing the Bar" (1889) was sung at his Oct. 1892 funeral.

3. Now part of Case Western Reserve University, Guilford Cottage was built in 1892.

4. Thomas Edison (1847–1931) developed the cylinder phonograph from ideas sparked by his previous inventions, the telegraph and the telephone. It was first introduced in 1892.

5. Writer Gail Hamilton joined many who argued for acquittal of Florence Maybrick (1862–1941), an American socialite who in 1889 was accused of poisoning with arsenic her unfaithful British husband, James. Maybrick was found guilty and spent fifteen years in prison.

6. CFW incorrectly identifies this section of the letter as being written from Cheltenham.

7. The 1893 Chicago World's Fair.

8. Benjamin Harrison won the 1892 Republican primary over James Blaine (1830–93), who never formally declared his candidacy, but lost the election. Harrison's wife Lavinia Scott died on Oct. 25, 1892. Woolson's reference to Blaine's "tragic" story may refer to charges of corruption leveled against him.

9. Come sta: How are you; Fa bel' tempo oggi: The weather is fine today; Credo che avremo della pioggia: I think we will have some rain.

To Unknown recipient (McGill)[1]

Oxford
Nov. 22^{d}, 1892

My dear Friend.

I was very glad to hear from you, & I should have written to thank you for the little book, if I had had a stronger wrist. It is still weak from overwork, so this can only be a note. But it carries much love to you & Nellie, and every good wish for the new year which will soon be upon us. Here, at this season, all is dark; constant & heavy lead-colored fogs; almost no daylight at all. The old year dies in gloom. With you I suppose the sky is clear and bright.—

The little book was just what I wanted; thank you so much for sending it. I shall order Harper's Magazine to be sent to you during 1893, as my new novel will run through most of the year. Perhaps you already take the magazine. There is not time to ask. So if you have two copies, you will be tired of the sight of it!—Give one away.—

Clara & Clare have been paying me a visit. They left yesterday for New York, where they will spend the winter. I shall remain in England a while longer; then go to Italy. The old address ("Care Alliance Bank. 88 High Street, Kensington. London. England.") is always a safe one.

I was greatly interested in your account of Asheville. I spent five months there in 1873, <u>or</u> 1874—(I cannot remember which), with mother at the Eagle Hotel in the Main Street; <u>then</u> the only hotel in the place. The people we know best were the Rev. Mr Buel & his wife (now dead) who was the daughter of Bishop Atkinson, (who has also gone). The Bishop was an <u>enchanting</u> man. Then we knew Gen. Martin & some of his family. The General is dead. I should like to hear of them, or of Mr Buel. Do you know them?[2] We knew many more (for it was a very small & sociable society in those days); but I have forgotten the names. I went up many of the mountains. And when we left, we drove along the French Broad & over the mts into Tennessee. It was in Oct., with colored leaves. An expedition of several days. Magnificent scenery.—And how I used to botanize. I suppose now the woods are no longer at the very door?

I remember Mrs Osgood well. She dined with me with the Miss Reynolds, who are intimate friends of Clara's.[3] If she is again with you, give her my love.

Has the old name "Beaucatcher" been changed to "Beaumont?"

The mountain scenery of western N.C., is the most beautiful I have ever seen in America. I have not been to California, but I have seen everything else our country has to offer.—Of course there is no resemblance to Switzerland. But it is quite as beautiful as many parts of the Tyrol. I am so happy for you that you have it to look at, & the ferns & flowers.—

This is a poor letter. But it is all my wrist will allow. I will write you when it is better. Love to you both.

Affectionately your old friend,
C. F. Woolson.

Notes

1. The letter is possibly to E. C. Stedman; Nellie may be his coeditor of *Library of American Literature* (1888–90), Ellen Hutchinson.

2. Woolson is referring to Episcopal minister David Buel; the Episcopal Bishop of North Carolina, Thomas Atkinson (1807–88); and Confederate General James Green Martin (1819–78).

3. The Miss Reynolds are likely daughters of Mr. and Mrs. Daniel Reynolds (Susan Adelia Baird), who had an exquisite home in Asheville.

To Samuel Mather (WRHS/Mather)

15 Beaumont Street
Nov. 24th, [1892]

Dear Sam.

Your letter & the photographs have come, and I am very glad to have all three. It has seemed a long time since your last letter. But when you do write, I must acknowledge that you send an epistle that is worth having! Give my especial thanks to Flora for the photograph of yourself, & tell her that I think it not only handsome, but remarkably distinguished. (Of course I don't tell you this; only Flora.) The picture of the children I like greatly. The sled group was extremely picturesque; but this shows so clearly the three faces that it is very satisfactory to the aunt. They are three faces full of beauty, character, & expression. I am proud of them.—

This is not an answer to your letter; I reserve that for a leisure hour, farther on.—"For better, for worse," has been used, after all. By the prolific Miss Braddon. The Harpers have probably announced "Horace Chase"; but I don't know. I cabled "The better way." But I fear it was too late. I shall hold on here until I have sent the last sheets.—I really am better at last. I mean in health. I have never had such an excellent landlady as now; she keeps such splendid fires, & watches over me like a trained nurse. It appears that she has a great admiration for literature & considers it "a privilege" to see to an authoress! At least so she told Mrs Woods.—I am hoping that my long illness last winter was due to those unlucky ear-drums.—Your letter suggests many things. But I must not stop to say them now.—With much love to Flora, & kisses for the children, yours affectionately,

C.F.W.

To Katharine Livingston Mather (WRHS/Mather)

15 Beaumont Street
Oxford
Dec. 27th, [1892]

My dear Kate.

Your letter, containing the generous & most welcome Xmas present, reached me on the 20th, in time to make me cheerful for the rather lonely season. I must not, however, dwell too much upon the loneliness, since it is—as far as ordinary acquaintances go—my own choice. I do'nt care for the usual festivities & always flee from them. I remember twice, in Italy, taking a journey merely to be "out of town," as the easiest way of declining invitations to dinner &c. Here, in Oxford, I have had no trouble, for I frankly told the people I know that I like best to spend the day alone. This is true,—so long as I am out of my own country. The day to me is haunted by old memories; many of them are the very ones you invoke, when you speak (in a way, too, that was very touching to me) of the things we used to do at Xmas time. It was to us the great festival of the year, & as everything was done for us when we were little, so it seemed to me right to pass on the legend & do everything that was possible for the next generation; that is Charlie, & you, Sam, & Will. If I were at home now, no doubt I should be restless unless I could be employed about something Xmas-y connected with Sam's & Flora's little ones.—Christmas is associated, too, in my mind with the Gordons; your mention of Mr G's will reminds me of it. For several years, they took part in the church trimmings, which were always carried in so energetically & gayly by the Carter family in the Sunday School building, with coffee & mince pies kept hot on the big stove. Charlie G. & his tutor, Mr Fay, were always there. I am pleased to think that Mr Gordon remembered Grace Church. And, in addition to the pleasure, of many sorts, which your letter has given me, there is an especial comfort in hearing of your Xmas offering in memory of father & mother, to whom Grace Church was so very dear on Emma's account.[1] Again I say to myself that you, as a family, keep warm my failing belief in goodness, in this selfish world. You probably have no idea how you—I mean your father &

mother, Sam, Will, & yourself,—have stood, all unconsciously to yourselves,—like a dam across a stream of pessimism within me, which would otherwise have swept over everything, like a flood! However, I am determined (even if I am disposed to pessimistic vein), not to give way to spoken gloom; surely if father was always brave & cheerful, I, with so much less to do & to bear, should be able to be the same.—

And, in fact, this Xmas—what with the relief of Clara & Clare's arrival safely to New York; & my good progress with this new novel—; & your delightful letter, I have got on fairly well. In the evening (Xmas Eve) I read Dickens' "Xmas Carol," & Milton's "Hymn on the Nativity," as usual. And kept the vigil quite alone by the fire.—

Give my dearest love to your mother. I was so glad to hear from her. I had not your anxiety about the Spree, for, the first I knew was Clara's telegram from Queenstown,—"Safe."[2] Then, when I got the details, I was very much alarmed, lest they should break down & be ill, one or both of them, on the return voyage. We lived in a grove of telegrams for two or three days. But they assured me they were well, & that they much preferred to sail at once, & have it over. Clara's letter, written on shipboard, from day to day, & mailed upon landing, was the most graphic account of all the horrors of the scene, that words could possibly paint. I dare say she has told you, or written to you, the same?

Your account of the "Home" reception interested me very much. Such a satisfactory way to raise the money. The rooms, to me, would be full of memories of the Carters. Grace, & Mary & Hyde with their children, are in England; they have taken a house in Warwickshire for the hunting (for Hyde), & they are coming to see me.—But they do'nt of course can't remember anything about the old days at "The Rectory," to which I was referring.

Is it thought that Miss Walton is satisfied with $2,000 a year? Had he given her other property also? I mean primarily Her house, for instance?—The Waltons too, Lily & Tom, were old Grace Church people.

Your letters this winter, Targer, have been very especially interesting to me; the account of your Thanksgiving; of Baltimore & the Convention; & many other things—not forgetting, (never forgetting) H.O.T.! And your reading "In Memoriam to Dr. Bolles"![3] I wish you would write often. The truth is, I do get so dreadfully tired over the writing for Harper's that my hand will scarcely follow my guiding sometimes. It is really quite out of shape now, & I fear all my right side is somewhat distorted, too. It pains me a good deal when I am very busy—as I am now. Did you see Petie Trone in my new story?[4] Also the flying squirrel; do you remember him? And the Franklin ditty was ours; we used to sing it at Cheerful Corner to His Gram.—

"Mother Woolson thinks,
That George Carter,
Mr Rich,
Gabriel Bennet,

And the Minister in the "Minister's Wooing,"

Are per-fec-tion!"

Poor mother had tried to read aloud "The Minister's Wooing" (Mrs Stow) & G. W. Curtis' "Trumps"; in the latter is a certain rather goody-goody Gabriel Bennet, & she incautiously let us see that she approved of him. So we invented this chant, & we sang it to her for years![5]

Good-gracious! Kate. What set of Dickens of ours did Will take to Marquette? We never had any, except a very poor cheap fine-print edition, that father gave me on my 12th birthday, & which I read to rags, before I was 20. My last remembrance of it is Sam's reading one of the dismembered volumes, in torn sheets, when he was about 15.—Do you mean to tell me those books still exist?

By the way, you never answered my question about John Hay's dress at the Shoreby party. The reason I asked was for my own education. I am exceedingly cautious not to allude to the garments in which my men appear (in my fiction), because I am so deeply ignorant as to what they do, & do not wear. It seemed to me that what he wore was the usual thing. Yet evidently you did not think so. Please enlighten me. I asked Clara, & she thought it was the tall hat that was unusual.

Roy Keese writes that Sam is "A very fine fellow." So "20 questions" is evidently at rest.—

Mel sent me a paper with account of his yacht. Very handsome it must be.

Mrs Woods continues a very kind friend. I dine with her now & then. I am going to spend part of your present in a bonnet, & it is the Dean of Westminster Abbey who recommends the milliner from whom I expect to buy it!! That is a little stretched. But the rec. really comes from the Deanery.—I'll now stop scribbling. With dearest love to all,

Yours
C.F.W.

Tell Sam I recd his letter & the photo; & I intend to melt soon. Best love to Will, & Fanny Gwinn Mather.

Notes

1. Woolson is referring to Grace Episcopal Church in Cleveland, where Woolson's brother-in-law Rev. Timothy Carter was rector before he became ill.

2. Clara Benedict was a passenger on the SS *Spree* when it sailed from Bremen to New

York on Nov. 26, 1892. On Dec. 3, it had to be towed to Queenstown because of a broken shaft and hole in its bottom. When the *Umbria* ran into a similar problem, the steamship *Gallia* refused it help.

3. Tennyson's poem (1849). *H.O.T.* may read *H.O.A.* The reference is unclear.

4. Pete Trone was Woolson's childhood dog. She is referring to passages from her book in progress, *Horace Chase* (1894).

5. Woolson is discussing Harriet Beecher Stowe's novel *The Minister's Wooing* (1858–59) and George Curtis's novel *Trumps* (1861). She misspells Stowe's name.

To Unknown recipient (Wisconsin)[1]

[1892]

She was rich.—The only other quest (made by a woman) that strikes me as equally charming was made through several years by lady of Rome, an artist; she visited every spot in Italy where Dante went.—Some of them now very remote & inaccessible places. And she made a beautiful sketch of each one. A few of these sketches were published in the "Century," but only a few; they were charming.

According to the N. Y. papers, the Tory "Saturday Review," I must tell you that Gladstone's journey down to the Isle of Wight yesterday to kiss hands upon his appointment, for the fourth time, as Prime Minister, was an immense ovation. The splendid old man (84) deserves it, I think. But how the Tories hate him! For whom are you voting this time? As I am, theoretically, a Free Trader & a Civil Service Reformer, I hardly know what I am; probably a "mugwump."[2]—Oxford is beautiful. I often row on the Thames.

Yours sincerely,
C. F. Woolson.

Notes

1. The fragments appear to be from a single letter.

2. The Mugwumps were Republicans who supported Democrat Grover Cleveland against James Blaine in the election of 1884.

To Samuel Mather (Anderson)[1]

[Oxford
Jan. 1893]

To Samuel Mather

him comfortable.—He (Roy) is a good man. And one of the plainest looking human beings I have ever laid eyes on! Clara & I both look a good deal like him!!—

Roy's mother was very handsome. But the elder Keese was very plain. Roy's wife has just written me a Xmas letter, & she mentions that the body of Fred Phinney had just been brought to Cooperstown to be placed beside that of his dear old mother. Do you remember Fred? He had one of the finest minds I have ever known. I mean he was, to my sense, wonderfully clever. But he had a wretched puny body that always disappointed him. He took to drink & for years has been a care & grief to all. Poor Fred.—

I was much interested in all you wrote about Cleveland's election.[2] I need to have these things explained to me;—I have been away so long. Theoretically, free trade seems beautiful. But literary people, you know, run to theories; "litery fellows," à le Simon Cameron.—[3] The most amazing thing you say is that Oliver Payne contributed money to elect Harrison. I had supposed that he & Whitney were one & the same on all questions.—

You ask me where I am going. Nowhere at present. I must first finish this book. I have the most perfect landlady here; the best I have ever had in my life. She was a Church school-mistress, & is very nice as well as competent. She is extremely devoted to me, & watches over me like a trained nurse. She is always cooking little extras to tempt my appetite, & when I am ill, as now, she is a miracle of goodness. She comes into my room two or three times in the night to keep up the fire. I shall never find anyone so devoted again. As long therefore as I am still laboring over this book, it is wiser to stay where I am. But my intention is to leave England without fail next Spring, & go to Italy. Probably Venice, as I like it better than any other place.—I may not attempt housekeeping immediately. But I can try a winter there at an hotel, to see how the climate suits me.—

The photograph of the children gave me the greatest pleasure. The sled group as a whole is extremely picturesque. But all the same the three dear little heads together, each one so bright, so handsome & happy, gave the old aunt much satisfaction. It seems to me as though your children "take" better as photographs than any children I know. Many kisses to them, & much love to Flora. I wish I could have been present when she dedicated Guilford Cottage.[4] What she said was in my opinion far the best that was spoken on the occasion; simple, dignified, touching.—

Much love to your mother, Kate, & Will. Excuse this scribbling. It is growing dark & I must stop. Have you read Rudyard's Barrackroom Ballads?[5] I am quite wild over "Manalay," & the last; "L'Envoi."—But of course it is the longing for "The East" that appeals to me.

"If you've 'eard the East a-callin',
You won't never 'eed naught else."

And in L'Envoi—the refrain

—"the old trail, our own trail the out trail—
The trail that is always new."—

I heard part of a letter from Ruddy read aloud the other day. He spoke very sweetly of "Another, who will be dearly welcome." (I see it has come;—a little girl), & the whole letter made me forgive him—a little—for the horrid things he said of New York. He had been to N.Y., by the way, & had seen Henry Adams, whom he admires greatly. Funny—his settling down in Brattleboro! His mother (Mrs Kipling) has not yet forgiven his American marriage.—

Goodbye.—
Affectionately Yours,
C.F.W.

P. S.

They say, you know, that a woman always puts the most important item in her postscript. For once the saying is true, for I take this fresh sheet to say how glad I am to have such a good photograph of you. And I am much obliged to Flora for suggesting your sending it. I think it by far the best likeness of you I have ever seen. And the only change the fourteen years have made, is that you are handsomer. I think you are a handsome man, Sam. And you also look very vigorous & strong.—It is not, however, so long—for I saw you at Sorrento. How many years is it? I have ceased to recall dates, so I do'nt know.

It is now evening; a damp thaw outside, & I feel much better. Almost well.—Let me warn you that I do'nt write Clara the little ups & downs in my health. She has had enough to bear—with her dreadful "Spree" anxieties. And in reality, the cold is nothing serious.—I was much alarmed about her sailing again so soon, for I feared she would be ill on the voyage. But she felt that she could go then, but not later. And I partly understand that feeling. Since the Spree, there has been the Umbria terror. I hardly know what to think of the Gallia.—I must tell you that the newsboys in Oxford were calling here in the loudest tones: "Mr Moody on the Spree!"—For Mr Moody had held a series of revival meetings <u>here</u> just before he sailed.[6]

Do you ever think of Sorrento? And poor Fiorentino? I have sometimes thought of returning. Marion Crawford lives there, you know. But the place is almost too small for a solitary person like myself; it is not quite safe for long walks.—At Venice, too, I should have more society. And with my fear of horses & my love of boats, Venice seems a better place.

Goodbye again.

Notes

1. Only this fragment, clearly written to Samuel Mather, survives.

2. In the U.S. presidential campaign of 1888, Republican Benjamin Harrison defeated incumbent Grover Cleveland, a Democrat. In the election of 1892, Cleveland defeated

Harrison to become the only president who served two terms that were not consecutive. One of the major issues in these elections involved high tariffs.

3. Simon Cameron (1799–1889) was a U.S. Senator and Lincoln's Secretary of War, though he had to resign the Secretary's position under allegations of corruption.

4. Flora Stone Mather gave a speech at the dedication of Guilford Cottage in the fall of 1892.

5. Rudyard Kipling's collection *Barrackroom Ballads* was published in 1892, the year his first daughter, Josephine, was born. His home Naulakha was in Brattleboro, Vermont. "Manalay" is Woolson's spelling.

6. See letter to Katharine Livingston Mather dated Dec. 27, 1892, for information on the *Spree.* Born in Massachusetts, Dwight Moody (1837–99) conducted mass revivals throughout Britain and the United States.

To Samuel Mather (WRHS/Mather)

15 Beaumont Street
Oxford
Jan. 9th, [1893]

Dear Sam.

I will first explain the formidable enclosure of type copy. The sheets form part of my new novel "Horace Chase," & I send them to you for advice, &, if need be, correction. It is confidential. As you & Flora are one, what goes to you, goes as well to her, of course. Outside of you two, I think only those at 544 need know. Not that the subject, or the secret, has the least importance, or even interest, to anyone save myself. But, on general principles, all the details concerning the making of novels had better be left in the vague.—

What I need your advice about is, first, this: Is the conversation given in the pages enclosed, natural? Is it possible? Is it, in short, good? I must premise that Horace Chase is a self-made man. He has had only the free-school education of the U.S., & even that was cut off at the age of fourteen. He is not intended to be in the least illiterate; he does not hopelessly murder his English. But he has not had further educational advantages than those I have mentioned. He is not a speculator; all his money has been honestly made. But he has been a daring, keen, man of business, trying now first one thing, & now another, & always with success. I intend him to be a man of extraordinary genius as regards money-making. As I said above, he is not at all dishonest; but he is sharp & keen as steel, &, where money is concerned, there is not a soft spot in him.

He has married this beautiful young wife; he ~~is 3~~ was 38 when he married, but he looked much older. He is now over 39.—He is very much attached to his wife, & very good to her, & to all her family. In the true American way, he is very generous. I may mention that he is at heart a noble creature—as the close of the story will show. But, all the same, where business is concerned, he is as inflexible as iron. He is not intended to be what is called "a good man." On the contrary, he has had shady spots in his past life; I mean by that, that he has been more or less irregular in his private ~~life~~ relations.—

Walter Willoughby, the other speaker in the dialogue, is a young man of 28, one of a well known family in New York. A family not so conspicuously rich as the Astors; but still with a reputation of the same sort on a smaller scale. Walter himself has very little money, & he is determined to make some. Two of his rich uncles, Nicholas & Richard Willoughby, have put him in, as junior partner, in the firm of Willoughby, Chase, & Co. But Walter is not satisfied with that. Willoughby, Chase, & Co, own a line of steamships, running from N.Y. to Savannah, & Charleston. The firm, however, is, reality Horace Chase himself, who manages the whole business, the elder Willoughbys only contributing some of the capital. Horace Chase however has a dozen other interests besides this steamboat firm. At the time of this conversation (1874), he is about embarking in a new business in California,—"a big thing."—If I could have got at you, I should have taken your advice, & then said more clearly what the big thing was. As it is, it is left in the dark. The only big Californian business I know anything about, is sugar, & it is more connected with the Sandwich Islands, after all, than with California,—though I believe Claus Spreckles is a Californian, is'nt he? But I thought Col. Spaulding would be too much amused by my making use of sugar,—![1] which is the business in which he has made all his money.

The first point I want your advice about is the colloquial style of Chase's talk. He is meant to use all the slang expressions which men of that sort certainly did use, in 1874. For I used to hear them myself.—I do'nt mean that it is important that Chase should use only the slang that was current in 1874. People wo'nt stop to think about that. But, as you read it aloud (read it to Will, & let him criticize, too), does it sound natural? If there are expressions that appear to either of you to jar, or to seem far-fetched, or "too much so," or "not enough so," will you change them, & put in improvements? The copy I send has been printed expressly for you, so you need not save it, or take any pains about keeping it in good order. You might write your suggestions on other sheets of paper, & connect them with the type copy by corresponding numbers. Or any way you like.—

Wolcott Balestier (now dead, you know) came to see me a year ago, & I think he came in reality entirely on account of a character in "Jupiter Lights." Hollis.—He told a mutual acquaintance that he wanted to see the woman who knew enough of the undercurrent of common American life to set down so exactly the character, & above all the talk of a man like Hollis. He said that women generally shirk those men (in literature), & write about every other kind of American on earth,—including Yankees, Negroes, Tennessee mountaineers, &c&c—but never the plain, slangy, unpoetical, tobacco-chewing creature, who forms, in reality, a large part of the population. I was much pleased by this testimony of Wolcott's.—But Horace Chase is not intended to be a Hollis. Horace Chase chews no tobacco. He is a "plain" American—yes. But he is a Napoleon in finance.—He is however, slangy. So please review his talk, & give me your very best advice.—

Rhoda Broughton (who is my age) sends all her young-man talk (after it is written) to her nephew, who is a young army-officer. He revises it "up to date"; & they say that his corrections give to her masculine conversations that air of perfect naturalness that adds so much to the amusement of her readers.—

The second point upon which I need your advice is Chase's threat to Walter,—as to what he intends to do in case Walter's boast (that he can induce his uncle to come forward with a large amount of capital) proves a false one. I have made him (Chase) say that he will, virtually, sell out of the steamboat firm in a way that will injure it; & also that he will run down some stock that Walter owns. But I feel very uncertain about these methods, I confess! Please tell me just what you think.—

You will see upon reading the conversation, that Chase really would like Nicholas Willoughby to go in with himself, & David Patterson (another successful man). Yet he does'nt feel sure that Walter has with his uncle the influence he thinks he has.—

Please send your ideas, & whatever occurs to you in connection with the whole subject.—You do'nt know how much obliged I shall be. The part containing this conversation has gone to N.Y. But it is not to appear until the May number of the magazine, so I can still change it.—It is Part 5 of the novel. There are 8 (or perhaps, by dividing, 9) parts in all.—

I hope all this wo'nt bore you & tire you too much.—It will be very good of you to help me with it.—

I write with a steam kettle filling the room with its soothing vapor. Do you ever try steam kettles? I have a terrible cold, but the doctor says that if I stay in the house & take care, all will go well. One lung is a little affected; but only a little, & the cough is already much better. I am enveloped in linseed. But there is no fever, & so no danger. The weather has been very cold (a rare thing in England), & I am always wretched in cold weather. There has been skating all over England, & as that is a rarity, there has been great rejoicing. But the ice & snow are always fatal to me. To day there is a thaw, & so I feel much better.

I received your delightful letter in November, & was interested in every word of it.—I am glad to hear that your remedy for colds is staying indoors. A still better thing is staying in bed! But it is tedious. The handsome young German emperor, you know, deliberately stays in bed for a whole day, or two days, even when the cold is only a slight one.—[2]

The name "For Better, for Worse" had to be given up, because one of Miss Braddon's bears the title, & the whole English edition could have been confiscated. The English ed. is to be published here by Osgood, McIlvaine, & Co. I am to receive fifteen percent on sales.—I get $3,500 from Harpers for serial publication in the Maga. As it is so short a novel (half the length of "E. Angels"), that is considered a good price. I do'nt like these short novels. After this, I shall either write only short episodes,—one dramatic event, & not a history of lives—; or else I shall write novels & have them appear as books, & not as serials at all. It is the serial form that ties me & cramps me. And yet that is the form that pays best.—

Roy Keese writes that you are "a fine fellow." So you won his heart. Poor Roy has had some hard things to bear. You knew, I suppose, that after he was middle-aged & more, he lost fifty thousand dollars? He was not brought up to do anything, as he was an old only child, & his health was delicate; his father thought he had left him enough money to make[3]

Notes

1. Both Claus Spreckels (1828–1908) and Col. Zeph Spaulding ran sugar cane businesses in Hawaii. Woolson misspells Spreckels's name.

2. Wilhelm II.

3. The remainder of this letter is missing.

To Samuel Mather (WRHS/Mather)

15 Beaumont Street
Oxford
Jan. 17th, [1893]

My dear Sam.

Your note, enclosing the draft for sixty-seven pounds, one shilling and five pence, has just arrived, and I am greatly obliged. I send, also, many thanks for the Christmas book, which reached me the other night, when I was feeling ill, owing to a tiresome cough. Like most persons who live alone, I was making quite too much of my pains and aches! But in beginning to read The Oregon Trail, and in looking at the fine illustrations, I actually forgot all about my illness.[1] That is the sort of book that does me good while I stay abroad; i.e. something wholly American. It is to me a fascinating narrative. I have never seen that wonderful country, alas! But I did see prairies in all their splendid wildness; (you were with us,—a baby a few months old). And I did see thousands of wild Indians gathered at La Pointe for their payment a few years later.—

I hope my type copy has not bothered you too much?[2] Send your advice & corrections (do'nt take any pains; just scribble your ideas with a pencil) as soon as you can. For everything for magazines is put in type long ahead, &, at best, your corrections have to cross the ocean to me, & then re-cross to New York, & that makes a long delay.—With love to Flora & the children, I am yours affectionately,

C. F. Woolson.

P. S.

I forgot to say that my cough is better. The doctor has examined my lungs twice, & reports only a slight "wheezing." Since then, thanks to care & his remedies, even that has vanished. It all came, probably, from the unusually cold weather we have had here.—

Notes

1. Francis Parkman's last revision of *The Oregon Trail* was published in 1892.
2. See letter to Mather dated Jan. 9, 1893.

To William Whitney (LOC)

15 Beaumont Street
Oxford. England
Feb. 25th, [1893]

Dear Mr Whitney.

You were so kind to me at Baden-Baden, when I myself was suffering acutely from grief, that I cannot refrain from expressing my sympathy now.[1] You do not need it,—you will have countless similar messages; and, in addition, all words will seem to you vain. But for my own sake—as I cannot from this distance send flowers—let me send a few words of affectionate remembrance of my childhood's friend.

She was the most brilliant girl I have ever known. In the old days at Cleveland, she, more than anyone else, gave a charm to our small society there; she lighted up the room when she entered. And this not in her own house only, but everywhere; if Flora came, we knew that our evening would be full of interest. I was no companion for her; as I look back, I can see that I was very immature mentally, in spite of the fact that I was several months older than she was. But at least I appreciated her,—I knew that no one else approached her. I used to enjoy deeply the long talks we had together in her room, when she expressed her ideas of books, and people, and life, with so much wit, power, and originality. I prized also the afternoons when we went out rowing together in a little boat I then had. Often, as I lived so near, I used to meet her walking down Euclid Avenue; it was always a pleasure to see her walk,—for her step was so firm and graceful,—her bearing so unapproached.

I left Cleveland soon after her own departure, and, since then, our lives have been widely separated. But from a distance I have watched her brilliant career. It was the fulfilment of the promise of her girlhood. Her death has been a great shock to me. For I have always thought of hers as the type of a happy lot,—so admired, so valued, so surrounded by love, and by everything that this life can bestow. Yet she is taken, and I am left. It seems so strange, and wrong.—I was much attached to her, and I am one of her sincerest mourners.

If Col. Payne is with you, please give him a message of sympathy from me. And I send the same to Senator and Mrs Payne, and to Mrs Bingham.

Truly your friend,
Constance Fenimore Woolson.

Notes

1. Woolson is referring to the death of her brother Charly in 1883. William Whitney's wife, Flora Payne Whitney, died on Feb. 5, 1893.

To Richard Watson Gilder (McGill)

15 Beaumont Street
Oxford. England
March 11th, [1893]

Dear Mr Gilder.

My friend, Mrs Woods, has asked me to write, inquiring whether you would look at a story (which she has just completed) with a view to its appearing in the "Century," as a serial? If so, she will send it to you, type-copied, for your consideration. In length it is, she tells me, half as long again as her tale, "A Village Tragedy."

I dare say you have read that powerful little masterpiece? It made a deep impression in England. Literary people here, are, I think, looking to Mrs Woods for something remarkable. As "The Speaker" said of her not long ago: "She is the one woman-writer in England to-day, from whom something great many be expected." She has not shown me her new story; but I know that she has been engaged upon it for a year past.

You may already know who she is?—The daughter of Dean Bradley of Westminster Abbey, & the wife of the President of Trinity College, Oxford.—

She wishes me to ask whether the appearance of her story in "The Century" would bind her to any particular publisher in England, for the book-form? Or whether she would be free to choose her own?—

As I am going very soon to Venice, perhaps you would reply directly to her:

"Mrs Woods.
Trinity College.
Oxford."

If, however, you prefer to write a line to me, you can always reach me, by the following address:

Miss C. F. Woolson.
c/o Alliance Bank.
88 High Street, Kensington.
London. W.

I take this occasion to send you, again, very warm thanks for "The Century." Its arrival, month after month, gives me great pleasure,—greater, probably, than you know. It is such a token of friendliness; and I have been abroad so long, that I prize such remembrances deeply—I hold on to them. Then, in itself, it is so interesting & beautiful.—I am afraid you did not collect, as a volume, that wonderful series of drawings & text, describing a pilgrimage to all the places ever visited by Dante?—"Colonel Carter of Cartersville" is a delight to me, from the first word to the last; I now have it in book-form.—The Napoleon document in the March number is a great treasure. I read month by month, Wolcott Balestier's novel, with melancholy interest. The last time I saw him (just before he went to Germany—never to return), he told me about it, & we had some joking talk about our running side by side in 1893,—he with "Benefits Forgot," & I with "Horace Chase."—[1]

I had thought a little of coming home for the Chicago Fair. But Venice calls me strongly this Spring—after the English gray skies & everlasting rain.—So I shall probably "pull out, pull out on the old trail." Perhaps I shall find you there?

Sincerely yours,
C. F. Woolson.

Notes

1. Woolson's *Horace Chase* (1894) ran in *Harper's New Monthly Magazine* from Jan. to Aug. 1893; Wolcott Balestier's *Benefits Forgot* (1892) ran in *The Century* from Feb. to Oct. though it had already been published in book form.

To Samuel Mather (Anderson)

15 Beaumont Street
Oxford
March 14th, [1893]

Dear Sam.

I am so much obliged for your excellent corrections. Especially for your advice upon the point I felt most doubtful about, namely Chase's threat. It did not seem to me reasonable—as I wrote it. Yet I did not quite know how to correct it. Now—by the addition of only one brief phrase—you have made it all that could be desired. I wish very much that I could have been near you, through the whole process of putting this novel together. It is the first to me, you know, that I have called a book—or even a short story—by the name of a man. And in fact I did not intend to do so, this time, as you know. "For better, for worse." "The Better Way," & others, were my choice. "Horace" came last on the list. But when we slipped up about the first title, there was no time to consult me, & the Harpers selected H. C.—My only solace is that the story appears to be liked, so far. They write me this from Franklin Square very decidedly. And I hear it from other quarters. I hope it is true?—I hurried off your corrections (each one was a great improvement, in my opinion) as fast as possible. They went to N. Y. an hour after their arrival here. The Ed., however, (whom I had warned as to what I was doing) has written that in any case I was too late for the serial form; it was already in press. But of course in the book form, I correct as I please. I am still cherishing a hope, however, that the corrections did get there in time, after all; or that they stopped the press. They have done wonders for me in times past; I mean in the way of waiting for my ms. I am always late, & always making them trouble. They treat me with the most intense courtesy & kindness, & have from the first.—

I am pretty low in health, so excuse all. I am not worse, however, than I have been at the end of my two preceding books. I have still two Parts more to finish. There will, after all, be nine parts. I am now, by Dr's orders, on a modified form of rest-cure (you know how I believe in it?); as much rest as is possible under the circumstances. I write, but I do absolutely nothing else. And I go to bed at six p.m., & rise at 9 a.m.—Then I have very nourishing food; & quinine, phosphorus, & iron.—I shall pull through all right, now.—Grace Carter really was the one to bring this about. She came here to see me, & instantly said "Cousin Connie, I am perfectly shocked at your looks. I never saw any one so changed. You look like death." And so on. I have taken her to task, since then, for saying it. But she declares she is glad she did, as it made me send for the Dr, and try to take care of myself.—You must not think ill of her. She is a noble sort of woman, & very devoted to me. But she is astonishingly frank, sometimes!—

What really keeps me up, is the thought of Venice, Sam.—I do so long to see Italy again, & I am sure the climate is far better for me than this.—I have about decided to go down May 1st (if I have finished H. C. by that time). Harry Washington has hunted up a small furnished apartment there, on the Grand Canal, next to his palace. And Mrs Curtis (whom Kate will remember) advises it, & says it will do (temporarily) very well. Mrs Carter has written a lovely letter, offering to do anything & everything.—This place would be only a temporary perch for two or three months. For if I should stay in Venice, I should take an unfurnished apartment, so as to use my things now packed in Florence.—

I have been terribly shocked by Henry Sherman's death. I was expecting him here.—And the story of Flora Whitney's last years—now revealed—have made a deep impression.—As in her life, so in her death, she was like no one but herself.—

Clara says you thought I had finished H. C. last Oct. In one sense, the whole book was finished more than a year ago. I always write out the whole plot, in every detail, first. Often this takes as much time as to write the book. Then each character is written out, & the amount of paper it covers, for each, is as much nearly as the whole book.—Then come the scenes—at equal length. And finally pages & pages of conversation; incidental only; things that might be said.—All this takes nearly 2 years! Then comes the terrible putting together; the fitting in the parts. If it were not a serial, it would not be half so much labor. But as I have only a certain fixed amount of space (which I know beforehand), I must first manage to tell my story. And all the rest must be brought in, condensed, to the best advantage. I am aware that I take my work hard. But we must all do as we can, & the only way I can write at all, is to do my very best. Something in me makes me take these enormous pains.—My best love to Flora. And kisses for the boys, & my little Constance. Tell Kate, I'll write to her later. I have only to-day—as a sort of vacation (having got off some ms. on the Aurania), & then tomorrow I start on again.—Much love to your Mother.

Affectionately yours,
C.F.W.

Love to Will.

To Katharine Livingston Mather (WRHS/Mather)[1]

15 Beaumont Street
Oxford
March 20th, 1893

My dear Kate.

. . . I am sending a photograph of the Sheldonian Theatre here (not a "theatre" at all, but the circular hall of the University) on the occasion of the "Grand Old Man's" visit, this winter.[2] It is an amateur picture, but perhaps you can make it out. The under-graduates were to be admitted by the iron gate. There were only 700 seats placed at their disposal (the rest of the theatre was filled with graduates from all over England, and Dons), and there are between three and four thousand under-graduates,—so you may imagine the fight to get in. The gate was not opened until two p.m., and before ten a.m. Broad Street was entirely blocked by under-graduates, waiting and wrestling for a place. When at last the gate was opened, only one half of it was swung back, and the youths thought they were not fairly treated. So they swarmed up the immensely high iron railing. I was on the other side of the street; I never saw such a funny sight! About twenty-two men were seriously injured by the spikes, and I don't know how many pairs of trousers impaled! I saw the G.O.M. arrive in the Dean's carriage. He is a wonderful old man. . . .

Last evening the President of Trinity spent an hour here, and he wore his splendid silk gown and mortar-board, as other men wear hat and overcoat. . . .

Affectionately,
C. F. Woolson.

Notes

1. The letter is in a typed transcription at WRHS. Portions also appear in Benedict/CFW, 376.

2. William Gladstone.

To Samuel Mather (WRHS/Mather)

15 Beaumont Street
March 30th, [1893]

My dear Sam.

This morning when they (or she) came in at seven o'clock, to make a little fire & bring the hot water, they (or she) deposited a letter by the side of the cup of beef-tea with which my day begins.—. I looked at it languidly; that is with languid curiosity; for I get so many epistles whose contents are disappointments, such as requests for autographs, circulars, & advertisements. The next thing I saw, in the dim light, was the picture of the Hotel Métropole on the envelope.—And, finally, I distinguished your handwriting. And then the old lady capered out of bed, threw aside the window-curtains, &, with the silk handkerchief which she wears as a nightcap all askew, read & re-read the welcome pages. The beef-tea was not touched, or needed; the letter was a far better tonic.—

I had felt a pang,—& really a sharp one, too—when I heard, from both Kate & Clara, that you & Will were to be on this side of the ocean, & yet I should not see you. Of course I understood it. In fact I comprehended perfectly the whole situation; & also the very pleasant and convenient trip you had arranged for your short time ashore. But that is all in the past now, & your new idea seems to me a far better one. You will laugh & say "Naturally!"—But though I can't deny that I'm "in it" (i.e. the new plan), still I really think that perfectly enchanting tour through France—beginning with the Mentone excursions which are still like yesterday's memories to me—Castellan, Ste. Agnese, Gorbio, &c; & then the coach-drive; & then those places which I have for 14 years longed to see—Arles, Nimes, Avignon, Aignes-Mortes, Carcasonne—& then, further north, Tours, Blois, & Chartres—and Paris;—why this, I think simply perfect, and far better.—I send this to Paris, & I hope to have a line from you, or a telegram, very soon. Give me all the time you possibly can. If you could spend the night here at the Randolph Hotel, which is very near this house,—then you could dine & spend the evening with me. Please let me know. Or if you do'nt want to spend the night, there is a train leaving Oxford at 9.25 p.m. (after dinner), which reaches Paddington Station, London, at 10.45 p.m.—Only if you take that train, I shall hope that you will give me some hours in the afternoon also, as there is so little time after dinner when anyone takes that train.—

Think of it, Sam—I have not seen you since that winter at Sorrento! And Will I have not seen since I said goodbye to him at home!—It seems too good to be true, that I am so soon to see you coming in this very door.—

You must be prepared to see me a good deal changed. I looked very well while I was stout. But now that I have lost some of the flesh, I have also lost the stronger look. And just now I am very tired over "Horace C." But that is temporary. (I shall consult you again about his talk.—)

I hope to go to Italy as soon as I have sent off the last pages.—I have taken a small furnished apartment in Venice for 3 months from May 10th.—Harry Washington got it for me, & my friend Mrs Curtis says it is a clean house. The padronna is honest & tidy. She cooks for me if I desire. The house is a small place—, not one of the old palaces. But the situation is the very best part of the Grand Canal. I'll go down & try it for three months,—to see if its old charm still remains with me. For of course if it does'nt,—it is not Venice's fault, but my own.—I have a good many friends there, you know.

I suppose you have both seen Oxford? If not, it is worth a look. (But I am afraid I shall be very selfish about sparing you, or letting you ~~escape~~ look). It is vacation now, you know, & the 4,000 amusing youths in flannels are all gone. They only keep their terms half a year.—

Well, I wo'nt write more, but will mail this immediately, & then wait for tidings from you.—Your coming here is the best news I have had for many long months, & makes me very happy. With dearest love to you both, Sam,

Yours affectionately,
C.F.W.

To Samuel Mather (Anderson)

Friday night
April 7th, [1893]

Dear Sam.

You had not been gone two minutes when I remembered that two small presents I had for the children had been forgotten. Mr Philipps (my landlord) took them to the post office; he is there now. He will inquire if there is a possibility of their reaching you, & if there is, he will mail them. They are trifles; a wee thimble for Constance, & some little things to be painted, for the boys.—

I did'nt hear half enough about Flora. Give her my love, & tell her how much I should like to see her. This meeting with you (all too brief) has recalled our Sorrento days; & especially some of the walks I had with her there along the walled lanes; I wonder if she remembers?—Those walls with tufts of ferns & flowers in the crevices of the stones.—

It was a perfect joy to see you & Will. And yet I feel very sad to-night; sad & lonely. Yet it is, after all, a pleasant sadness, for I feel that the old ties have not been in the least weakened by all these years of separation; but are still the same.—I did not speak of your dear father, because I <u>could</u> not (I mean I did not speak of his having gone.) But as I looked at you & Will, I thought of him many times.

It was a great pleasure to me to see how remarkably well you are looking, Sam. Everyone has told me so, & it is true.—

I thought Will also looking very well indeed. He has such a fresh color, & his eyes are so blue! I do'nt remember that they used to be so blue. He is a handsome fellow. Tell him to keep an eye out for Grace.—(And she can help to keep the fire burning in the home altar for she has about $200,000, I believe.)

I have thought of forty things I wanted to say, & to hear. But it is difficult sometimes to speak of one's deepest feelings. You have done so much for me, my dear Sam, that I always feel as though you ought to know how much. Yet I can't quite write it down.—I was so unhappy that last month or two 3 years & a half ago in Italy! And at the very moment when I was at the lowest, you came to the rescue just as if you had known it! And yet you <u>could</u> not have known.—Well, good night & good-bye. I shall post this immediately so that it will perhaps catch the tomorrow's Cunarder via Queenstown.—Excuse pencil.

Love to all at 544.
C.F.W.

To Rebekah Owen (Colby)

15 Beaumont Street
Saturday
April 16th, [1893]

Dear Miss Owen.

I am so very closely occupied that I fear I cannot come to you, as you kindly suggest. But I want to see dear Lord Colin before I go. Would you and Miss Owen come with him to tea next Thursday, or Friday, as suits you best, at five? Or on

Tuesday of the following week, at the same hour? Would you please let me know, as I am going back and forth to times at present, on account of the dentist! and the dressmakers.—I hope you did not think me too bold in taking Colin out? I am so fond of dogs, and understand them so well, that I felt sure all would go smoothly. He looked so mournful tied up in Mr W's yard.—I rejoice that he is with you again. His eyes, the first day I saw him, were so heartbrokenly sad! With regards to Miss Owen, believe me, yours sincerely,

C. F. Woolson.

To Rebekah Owen (Colby)

[1893?]

Dear Miss Owen,

Lord Colin has been much happier at Dog Tray I think than he has at the other places. I was going to keep him to dinner (he has dined twice with me); but now that I know you have returned, I hasten to send him, as I know it will make him so very happy.—I myself go to town tomorrow. I hope to see you before I finally leave Oxford, two weeks later.

In haste,
C.F.W.

To Unknown recipient (WRHS/Benedict)[1]

1893

I am beginning to plan for Venice. And I find that I am still capable of joy! I thought it was at an end, as far as this life was concerned; I have been so out of health & tired for so long, long a time, that I have grown resigned to monotony & pain. But—somehow—as the letters arrive,—about "apartments" on the "piano nobile," or "secondo"; & the talk of the "water-door"; & the rent to be so & so, "servizio & biancheria" included (servants & linens)—the old thrill appears.[2] I am thinking a little of taking a small furnished apartment on the Grand Canal for a month or two,—just as a rest.—The other day I even got out my Italian grammar again, & propped it open in the old way on the pincushion. When I lived in Italy before, I always learned an irregular verb when I dressed & undressed!—You'll see from all this that my spirits are rising a little?—

With best love to all,
C.F.W.

Notes

1. Pasted into Grandgent, C. H. *Italian Grammar*, Boston: D. C. Heath, 1889.

2. The "piano nobile" is the main floor in an Italian house; the "secondo," the second main floor. "Servizio & biancheria" are, as Woolson notes in parentheses, servants and linens.

To Samuel Mather (Anderson)[1]

15 Beaumont Street
Oxford
April 29th, [1893]

My dear Sam.

Your letter has come, with the Bill of Exchange, and I am very much obliged. Particularly so for your advancing the Interest on the Railroad bonds, due October next. (For it *is* October interest, is'nt it? This second $\$140.^{00}$? It is called, in the type-written letter, "July coupons." But, as I understand it, it must ~~be~~ mean October coupons).—The advance is very welcome, as I am breaking up here, and have the usual final bills &c to pay.—

I saw the newspaper accounts of the arrival of your fine ship in New York, and the reception of the descendents of Columbus, speeches, &c. I hope the descendents looked dignified and Spanish? I am so glad to hear, ~~that~~ from ~~your~~ this letter, that all were well at home,—Flora and the children, and your mother & Kate.—Clara I know is extremely tired. There is no use my finding fault with the way she lives; no doubt she does the very best she can. But if she could only have a first-rate competent woman to do all the packing &c&c, I should be relieved from a good deal of anxiety, sometimes. She has had maids. But they come & go, & that is tiresome. I believe it is not easy to get good ones in the U.S.—All I mean by this is simply that she (Clara) is not really strong, & she always keeps up; she never goes to bed & stays there, as I do when I feel ill.

I still sit here by the hour going over all you & Will said, & the whole visit. It was so *delightful* to me to see you. And so sweet and dear to find that I have still a place in your hearts.

This note carries much love to you all. It is short* because I am in the last pull uphill of *Horace Chase*, which will finally be finished next week! I can scarcely believe it myself.—I was much pleased to see that the Harpers did stop the press for your corrections. They are in, all right, in the last Number, & oh! such an improvement.—

There is a little skirmish here between the English publishers to get hold of the English edition. This is good news for me, for it shows that the story is liked.—

I do'nt know just when I shall get off for Italy. But the "Alliance Bank. 88 High Street, Kensington," is always a safe address. I put in the number of the street because it (the Bank) has changed its name to the impossibly long title of "Pare's Banking Co. & the Alliance Bank."—

I shall send my heavy trunks by sea, & a box of books, &c.

I have already written a description of the *un*furnished apartment offered me in

Venice, for the year. If I want to keep house there at all, it is the place for me. The most perfect situation in Venice, and one of the most beautiful old palaces, and, best of all, these kind and influential friends over my head, so that in case of any trouble, or illness, it would be so safe; like living in the same house with them. They have succeeded in getting the refusal of it until I arrive. At least they hope they have—. But Italian landlords are slippery.—The Curtises have the whole splendid top; the piano nobile & the floors above.[2] Then, under them, the Countess Pisani has three quarters of what is left. The remaining quarter is the place I can have. There are four little balconies on the Grand Canal, and also a water-door, ditto.—I sit & think about it. And long for some one to talk it over with.—I am a little afraid of the responsibility. But I can pay my rent ($470.^{00}) for three years, and furnish simply—(I have a good deal, you know, stored in Florence), and still have $1300 to add to income; I mean that the Horace Chase money will do this. And this estimate does not include the money that will come to me from the sale of the book-form—which will no doubt be $1,000 more.—

(You see I am "talking it over" with you by mail!)—

I think I ~~shall~~ should be very happy in Venice for a while. There is a good deal in that.—And the climate is better for me, no doubt, than this.—I think I could write another novel there with less toil.—

You will see that in all this, I am giving up the being near my kind friend, Mr James. I do'nt know what made me tell you & Will that last message of his sister to me—that touched me so much. But I suppose it was simply the relief of having some of my own family to talk to, after being so long alone. I felt that I could say anything to you, without having to think whether it was safe or not, wise or not, prudent or not.—But ~~he~~ Mr J. will come to Italy every year, and perhaps we can write that play after all.—

The weather here has been so extraordinarily warm that it seems alarming! Nothing like it on record.—

I must now go on with my last pages. Love to Flora, & please send me a good likeness of her to put with yours—which I think so good.—Kiss the children for Aunt Connie.

Affectionately yours,
C.F.W.

*Not so very short, after all! [Woolson's note]

Is it "Perry-Payne Building?" or "Western Reserve Building?"

Notes

1. Portions of this letter also appear in Benedict/CFW, 36.

2. Woolson did not stay at the Curtises' Palazzo Barbaro in Venice, so these rooms must have been withdrawn. She did, however, maintain a strong connection with the Curtises.

To Rebekah Owen (Colby)

15 Beaumont Street
Tuesday
May 9th, 1893

My dear Miss Owen.

I am off on Friday for London; thence to Venice. If I should look in on Thursday afternoon, between three and four, could I see you all, and say goodbye? ("All" means Colin.) I have an engagement for tea at five, which forces me to suggest an early hour. Will you please send me a word of reply? Tomorrow I go to town, & today I have men here, packing things to go to Venice by sea.—As for Colin—he is the most wonderful dog I have ever seen. His intelligence is perfectly astonishing. I had no idea of bringing him to dine with me, for I thought you might not like it. But simply his eyes,—his speaking pathetic human eyes, when I turned to leave him—absolutely compelled me to take the leader again and bring him home with me. He just stood motionless, and looked at me. "Can you have the heart to leave me here?"—that was all he said.—I do'nt wonder you love him. He is a person. I am sure he has a soul.—With regards to Miss Owen, I am, yours sincerely,

C. F. Woolson

To William Wilberforce Baldwin (Morgan)

Casa Biondetti
San Vio 7th
Venice
June 16th, [1893]

My dear Doctor.

I have long been wishing to write to you.—But I was far from well, during my last months in England. And then, just as I was starting for the continent, I was prostrated in London by a sharp attack of influenza,—my first; (almost everyone else has had a second, and even third).—The attack was short,—with no symptoms but high fever. The London doctor, however, seemed to have no doubt as to its nature.—I still feel singularly weak. But now that the long journey is over, I dare say I shall gain strength.

In your last letter you asked: "Are you never coming back to Italy?"—Here I am, you see.—I have taken this small apartment temporarily, while I look about for something else. For I really think I shall stay here for a while; I have always adored Venice,—with its soft sea-air, and quiet. Everyone is lazy here; and the resident English and American society is so small, that there is no danger of ~~the~~ one's time being taken up by it. You have no idea how much these long hours in the floating gondola rest and refresh me. I love the motion of a boat. It takes, with me, the place that driving does,—for as I am timid where horses are concerned (having been run away with and terribly injured when a child), driving is no pleasure.—

Is there no hope of your being here this summer? I would be so glad to see you. And you have also other friends here, I am sure. Mrs Bronson, for one, I happen to know.—Your April letter gave me much pleasure. I think—(I have always noticed it—) that we have a good many moods in common. More than once you have outlined phases of thought, which, word for word, I have recognized as also mine. Particularly is this true when you allude to depression; the "amazing wilderness of gloom," of which you speak in this last letter, brings the tears to my eyes.—For how often am I too lost in some dark land.—And your next remark—that your only relief has been a "grim & desperate will to be resolute,"—and to do your best day by day, waiting meanwhile for the light which will surely come—how that spurs me! I must take fresh courage from it. The fact is that simple courage seems to me to sum up all the virtues of life.—There was an old phrase which my father (a New Englander) sometimes used,—namely "Keep a stiff upper lip."—That's it.—

There is no use in our advising other people; for we do not know all the circumstances of their lives; there are always some which they do not (perhaps cannot) tell. Each heart knows its own griefs, or aches, or disappointments, & my own heart knows mine. But where you are concerned, my dear friend,—at least one can say to you that your eminence in the profession you chose, is great, and constantly growing greater; there is, & there will be, no limit to it. At your age, to have risen so high in a profession that ranks so high,—surely that must be a pleasure? And in another way,—to be so much liked, and valued, and admired, by so many persons,—persons whose trust in you is complete, and whose love for you is sincere,—that also is a rare thing in world of cynics, and mistrust.

—Yes,—I know you have five bonny children,—four fine little boys and one daughter. I wish I could see them all. I have never forgotten Fritz, he will soon be 8—and the visits he used to make me, with you, during that tedious illness of three months at Bellosguardo—What changes there! In private I want to say that I was astonished that your dear old friend Miss Greenough did not leave a legacy to your children. It was to me a disappointment,—for I had fancied that she would certainly do it, and I should have liked it as a token of her affection for you. Her affection for you was undoubted, and was the strongest feeling she had. <u>You</u> did'nt want the legacy,—I can well understand that. But on general principle, I wish she had done it.—Her money, however, was not hers to leave; only her savings. And she has always had in her mind Mrs Huntington's children. As things have turned out, it is Miss Greenough who provides for Mr Henry H, I suppose.[1] And that was the duty which always haunted her.—

I was much amused by your description of the English royalties; "the wise, little, fat red-faced Queen," and the daughter, "discontentedly representing her at Bazaars, &c." And the tame cat of Battenberg.[2] You would have distinguished yourself in literature, Doctor, if you had turned your attention in that direction. Which reminds me to say that I hear that Bourget and his wife are on the point of sailing for the U.S.—(Perhaps you already know this?) What will they do there? Is'nt it funny!

I saw Henry James in Paris on my way down. He came back from Switzerland to see me, & for the four days I was there, he amiably took me out to his galleries, theatre, &c. He is now well. But he has had gout this winter, & has suffered a good deal. I dare say that Prof. James told you?—

Have you yet learned to be idle? Idle with mind, as well as body?—In short to rest?—A short rest each day, and a longer one each year,—that would be perfect.—(I preach what I can't practice myself! However I'm trying to learn.)—

I have at last declined an invitation from my nephew to go home in August, and accompany him to the Chicago fair.—I half promised to go, when he came to see me at Oxford in April.—It was, and still is, a great temptation. But I do not feel strong enough.—

How & where is our mutual friend, Mrs Launt Thompson?—

I suppose Mary Huntington and her party will be here soon.—

Are you going to move to England and be Court Physician to future Royalties? After all, May will probably be Queen.—[3]

Give my love to your wife when you write. And my regards to Miss Baldwin, whom I hope to see some day.—And believe me, unchangeably, your attached friend,

C. F. Woolson.

Notes

1. See Lyndall Gordon, *A Private Life of Henry James: Two Women and His Art* (New York: W. W. Norton, 1998); Gordon believes that Woolson did not like Miss Greenough. Ellen Greenough Huntington owned the Villa Castellani; her daughter Mary Huntington inherited it in 1893. Henry Huntington is probably Mary's brother. For further information on the Greenoughs and Huntingtons, see Nathalia Wright, "James and the Greenough Data," *American Quarterly* 10 (1958): 338–43.

2. Queen Victoria's daughter Alice was the mother of Princess Louise of Battenberg, Germany. Princess Alice's daughter Beatrice married Prince Henry of Battenberg. Henry is probably the "tame cat."

3. Princess Mary of Teck.

To Flora Stone Mather (Benedict/CFW, 377–78)

Casa Biondetti
Venice
July 1st, 1893

... Here the weather is delicious; it could not be more perfect. And the tints of the sky and the sea; the splendid outlines of the old palaces as they rise from the water; the coloured sails of the fishing boats; the gondolas, the music and the flags (it is a festa)—all this is as gay and enchanting as ever.

My little apartment has the best possible situation with views both up and down the Grand Canal. It is not far from the Salute Church. I have five windows on the Canal, and I spend most of my time looking out of them. I have a fair-sized salon, a small dining-room, two bed-rooms, and a little room on the roof, where there is always the sea breeze and a splendid view. The woman of the house cooks for me and cooks very well, too, and this floor has a very nice and pretty little Italian maid. ...

Have you read any of the books on Italy by J. Addington Symonds? He died this spring in Rome, and Mrs Symonds who is here (they used to spend their summers here) wants me to take his gondolier ... He has lived with them for 18 years, and Mrs Symonds has pensioned him; perhaps the fact that I know her might make him anxious to please me. For one thing I suppose he knows every out-of-the-way fresco and bit of carving, and interesting church, not only in Venice, but for ten miles around. For Symonds was always afloat. In Venice your gondolier not only takes you out in his gondola (which floats at all times at your door), but goes to market and waits at table, blacks shoes, and brings up wood, &c&c. ...

It is all so lovely! Yesterday I went over to have tea with S. in his enchanting hall. The sea breeze blew through the great room, and the gondoliers, in white and gold, waited upon us. Then I came back and joined Miss Felton on her balcony where we watched the gondolas pass, and all the flags and banners, until a friend sent in to us a great basket of roses and another of strawberries ...

To Katharine Livingston Mather (WRHS/Mather)[1]

Casa Biondetti
San Vio 715
Venice
July 2d, 1893

My dear Kate.

... I am here at last, as you see. I got away from Oxford very late, and very tired. I stopped in London to go to the dentist's, and was taken down with a sharp attack of influenza; my first experience. There was no symptom at all but high fever, but the London doctor, whom the Hotel sent for at 4 a.m.! seemed to have no doubt as to the nature of the malady. I haven't got back my strength, and I have always heard that weakness and depressed spirits, were the special charms of this delightful complaint. . . . Well, Kate, Venice is to me even more beautiful, more enchanting, than ever; that sums it up. Casa Biondetti is not a palazzo; it is a small house on the Grand Canal,—not on the Hotel side, but on the other; one lives just as one does in England lodgings. I have a gondola, and I am searching for an apartment. The Society here, unlike Florence, is very small. On the floor below me, are two ladies I know, from Boston, Miss Felton, and Miss Lily Norton, the daughter of Charles Eliot Norton, the author, and Professor of Fine Arts at Harvard. Opposite are Miss Huntington and Mrs Quincy of Boston, whose son is now Assistant Secretary of State at Washington. It is warmer than at home, the soft salt air is just right for me. Venice is full, for the bathing season has begun, and there are fêtes, and regattas, and music, &c. I was particularly pleased with what you wrote of "Horace Chase." I don't suppose any of you realize the amount of time and thought I give to each page of my novels; every character, every <u>word</u> of speech, and of description is thought of, literally, for years before it is written out for the final time. I do it over and over; and read it aloud to myself; and lie awake and think of it all night. It takes such entire possession of me that when, at last, a book is done, I am pretty nearly done myself. The little sketch of Jared Franklin, is more or less from life. "Jared," of course, had to be in the story, as one of the reasons why Ruth married Horace Chase; and also Chase's character had to be brought out by contact with another <u>man</u>; (not merely his relations with ladies). What did you think of the drive over the Blue Ridge with the four horse hearse; the scene between Mrs Franklin and Genevieve after the funeral; and the return of Ruth?, and Chase's character through all? I do'nt often write to any one about my literary work, but Will's remarks have drawn me out a little. . . .

July 4th

Looking out of my window this morning I saw Harry Washington's large Star-Spangled waving in the sea breeze, and Miss Felton's little one from her balcony under me; I was so ashamed of having forgotten the great day, that I went out in the gondola, and bought, (for one dollar) a Star Spangled of my own, and it is now flying from my window. I am so tired of changing, and sometimes so disheartened at the thought of all the labor that must be gone through before a new place is any where near comfortable,—that it seems as if, after I am settled this time, I shall never have the strength or courage to move again. It is a curious fate that has made the most domestic woman in the world,—the one most fond of a home, a fixed home, and all her own things about her,—that has made such a woman a wanderer for nearly twenty years. . . .

Dearest love to you all.
C. F. Woolson.

Notes

1. The letter is in a typed transcription at WRHS. Portions also appear in Benedict/CFW, 52, 379.

To William Wilberforce Baldwin (Morgan)

Casa Biondetti
July 7th, [1893]

My dear Doctor.

I am very sorry. But I fully understand.—No mosquitoes <u>here</u>.—(It is true I sleep under a net.—) I promised Mrs Curtis that if I did not go out with you to day (to Burano, &c), I would come to her at 4.30, as she has a small tea.—I shall be sitting <u>here</u> by myself, from half past three to half past four;—if you could pay me a visit then, needless to say I should be delighted.—In any case, come as often as you <u>can</u> during the remainder of your stay. If you will send word beforehand, I will certainly be at home.—

Yours as ever,
C.F.W.

To William Wilberforce Baldwin (Morgan)

Casa Biondetti
San Vio 715
Venice
July 20th, [1893]

My dear Doctor.

The darling little beastie has just come, and it gives me the greatest pleasure;—You probably have no idea how much.—I am going to wear it daily, and I feel sure that it will give me all sorts of profound Egyptian thoughts. I have been reading a book, which asserts that houses in which persons have lived, become, after a time, permeated with their thoughts, in case their thoughts were powerful enough, &c. So this little amulet must certainly be full of ancient influences, and <u>I</u> shall feel them.—

The book, by the way, is very remarkable as containing the only working hypotheses I have ever seen in regards the strange facts of telepathy, hypnotism, &c. I don't know whether you are interested in such subjects? (I am). If you are—get this book. It is called "The Law of Psychic Phenomena," & is by an American named T. J. Hudson.[1] My copy is borrowed from Mr Quincy, or I would send it to you.

I am hoping to hear from you.—We miss you very much.—I have seen Mrs Bronson & Edith several times, and they are very kind. I think Mrs B. seems decidedly better. At any rate, she went to Torcello the other morning, in the Eden steam launch, & walked all about. She looks brighter, too.

Mary Huntington also has improved, & goes out. She says she owes it to you.

I took tea with the Montebas yesterday & they too sounded your praises.

No apartment yet. 8 new ones on hand. The owner of the Brandolin-Rolta (which you approved of) has raised his price to 3,000 fr. So that is lost.

It is very cool here now. A great change in the weather. Last night there was a splendid spectacle on the Grand Canal. Today I go to St Francisco del Deserto, a far-away island. Then I turn up at seven p.m. at Burano (where I wanted to take you), for dinner, to meet the Fulton & Quincy party, who arrive thither from another direction. Then all home [by?] moonlight.—If you were here.—But probably you are among the high cool mountains, and consider Venice very "lowdown."

How are the children? Give my regards to your sister, whom I hope sometime to visit.—

Mrs Curtis enjoyed your call very much. The honeymooners have sailed for home, and the splendid Barbaro now contains only the master & mistress.—

People are beginning to engage rooms "for September and October." And I am trying to make up my mind whether I'll go away for August, or not. My friends are writing from Tegernsee (near Munich), to urge me to come there. But I like Venice. Adieu. Let me hear from you.

Always your attached friend,
C. F. Woolson.

Notes

1. *The Law of Psychic Phenomena* (1893) by Thomas Jay Hudson (1804–1903) included chapters on hypnotism, crime, and the subconscious.

To William Wilberforce Baldwin (Morgan)

Casa Biondetti
Friday evening
[1893]

My dear Doctor.

How sorry I am to have missed your visit. I think it so very kind of Mrs Bronson to come to see me. I was out with Mr and Mrs Curtis, looking at an apartment which tempts me somewhat; for it is a beautiful house. On the other hand, it is not on the Grand Canal.—I don't want to miss you again; and if you will send word, any morning, that you will be here in the afternoon (naming the hour), I will certainly be at home. I have a gondola, and the gondolier of the late J. Addington Symonds; if you would prefer to float with me rather than spend the time in this little house, you have only to name your hour, and I will come for you with much pleasure.—

Will you please give my best regards to Mrs Bronson. I was coming to see her with Mrs Curtis. But I won't wait for that.

Always your attached friend,
C. F. Woolson.

To Katharine Livingston Mather (WRHS/Mather)[1]

Casa Biondetti
San Vio 715
Venice
August 20th, 1893

My dear Kate.

. . . I have just been in my gondola to the floating bath in the harbor, but there was such a crowd of bathers that I could not get in. On Sundays the Lido is so thronged with excursionists from mainland towns, that bathing there is not pleasant. So behold I have no sea-bath at all to-day,—and I will take the time to write to you. I have been a good deal depressed in spirit all summer, but no one knows it, for I do'nt let it be seen. I dare say part of it is the result of the influenza; another, is the constant work, for I am still doing the Book proof of Horace Chase, and shall not be able to finish it before September 10th I fear. I am now called at 4.30 every morning, and then, after a cup of tea, I sit (in a dressing gown) and write until 9.30, when I have breakfast. This is to get the cool hours for work. Then I dress and go on writing until 4 p.m., when I go to the Lido and take a sea-bath. These baths are, to me, quite perfect; the best I have ever had, because not at all cold. The water is soft, and the little waves lift one up so lightly that I almost swim. I go out as far as I can, and just float and float. Then home to dinner at 7.30, and all the evening I am out in my gondola. I had some idea of going away for a few weeks; to the Venetian Alps,—but I am so busy that unless I feel ill, I think I won't stir. It is warm, but not unbearable; 80° is the highest, and there is always a sea breeze. Nothing in the world can be more beautiful than the lagoons in the evening. Then my special friends are here, Mr and Mrs Curtis, and Mrs and Miss Bronson are not going away at all.

My news is that I have taken part of a furnished house for eight months, from September 10th. The house is almost opposite the Casa del Desdemona, and is a nice one, though not a romantic palazzo. It belongs to an English General, who comes here for his summers; his winters are spent in the Riviera, where he has another house. He has offered two floors of it, for $40 a month. For this sum I have two salons, a winter bedroom, a large dressing-room, a summer ditto; dining-room; kitchen; and three servants rooms; and excellent furniture. He is Lieutenant General de Horsey. He invited me to tea, to make the final bargain, and entertained me with much magnificence. Forty years ago, he went to the United States and took the trouble to go to Cooperstown and spend two days, on account of his great admiration of Fenimore Cooper's novels; he knows them by heart. His brother, Admiral de Horsey, of the English Navy, was one of the few who were invited to the dinner which the Prince of Wales gave to the German Emperor at Cowes, last month.[2] I took this house because it was a good bargain, healthy, comfortable. And I have not yet found the ideal apartment, with gothic windows on the Grand Canal, and a rent of nothing at all! It seemed wise to try a winter here. The General's big house has plenty of room, and I shall probably send for my Florence things, and have, (oh, joy!) my beloved yellow chair; my stand-up desk, and my own sheets. . . .

August 21

Well, Targer, this letter did not go off; so I will scribble a little more. It is pretty hot to-day, 88°, in fact quite sizzling; but I shall stick it out if I possibly can, and at any rate, I must do so, until the proof is done, for they are waiting for it, both in New York and London. The Regatta came off on the 9th of August, and was by far the prettiest thing I have ever seen. The race is between the different clubs of gondoliers; but the prettiest part is the sight of the Grand Canal, decorated from end to end; everybody hangs out brocades, armorial bearings, and flags and flowers; and the barges of ideally beautiful shape, in gilt and white, with swans for prows, and long velvet hangings trailing in the water behind. Each of these boats has twelve men, dressed in medieval costumes, who row, standing. I first saw the preliminary parade from the splendid Barbaro. Then, I went, by invitation to the Rezzonico Palace (that is Browning's), whence one has a fine view of the finish and the prize giving. A splendid collation was served in the sumptuous dining-room, and all the nice Venetians were there; among them the English clergyman in a long black tightly fitting garment (cassock?) which came to his heels. He is young and handsome, and dances and plays tennis, they say. . . . I will add one short story, and then close. The Empress Frederick of Germany, (the "Vicky" of queen Victoria's books) was here for a short time this week. She was on her way to Homburg from Greece, where her daughter, the Crown Princess, has just been confined. The English dispatch-boat which brought her from Athens, was bound for Trieste; so she got off there; but she is so devoted to Venice that she came here by train, in all the heat, for a few days.

She was incog.—but she did accept one dinner, which was given by the Countess Pisani, whose apartment is under the Curtis' in the Barbaro.[3] Mrs Curtis attended the dinner. (She and her husband, and my landlord, General de Horsey, were the only other guests,—with the ladies and gentlemen of the suite;—for the empress travels with a suite of twelve persons.) Mrs Curtis tells me that the Empress in describing the heat at Athens, said, "I assure you, Mrs Curtis, that all the while I was there, 'Sophy' (the Crown Princess) hadn't a dry thread on!" The phrase struck me as so funny, for an Empress. The Countess Pisani had out all her magnificent old Dresden china dinner service, and her ancient Venetian glass; there were ten different kinds of wine, and ten wine glasses at each plate, and everything to correspond. She was in blue satin, Mrs Curtis in pink brocade; meanwhile, "Vicky" came in her travelling dress, of plain black woolen cloth, without an ornament, and on her head an ugly little travel-worn cap of black lace; she is not only an Empress, but exceedingly rich. It is that sort of thing which made the Germans dislike her, always,—they call her "a dowdy." . . .

P. S. Tuesday morning, Five o'clock

The sun is rising in a thick fog! The first I have seen here. It is refreshing, because not so hot.

Affectionately,
C. F. Woolson.

Notes

1. The letter is in a typed transcription at WRHS. Portions also appear in Benedict/CFW, 380–83.

2. The Lieutenant General is William de Horsey; the British Admiral is Algernon Frederick Rous de Horsey. In 1893, the Prince of Wales was Queen Victoria's son Albert Edward; the German emperor was Wilhelm II.

3. Princess Victoria (Vicky) was the daughter of Queen Victoria and wife of German Emperor Frederick III. The Crown Princess is Princess Sophie who married King Constantine of Greece. Evelyn Van Millingen Pisani and her husband Almorò III Pisani had splendid gardens in Venice.

To William Wilberforce Baldwin (Morgan)

Casa Biondetti
Sunday
[1893]

My dear Doctor.

If the weather is favourable would you like to go with me (no one else) to Torcello tomorrow (Monday), about half-past three? It takes about two hours to go, and the same for the return; this, with an hour at Torcello for the ancient little cathedral &c, and a simple picnic dinner, will bring us back between nine and ten.—

I merely suggest this. But we can just as well go to the Lido, and dine there (at the restaurant), if you like that better? I have no choice as to whereabouts, so long as I have you as company.—If you don't like floating in a gondola, we can simply sit here, and then go and dine at Quadri's in the Piazza.—Will you send me a line tomorrow morning by nine or ten, if possible? And if you select the excursion to Torcello (which is very pretty), I will then send word exactly when my gondola (I shall have two gondoliers so that we can go faster) will arrive at Casa Alvisi to take you up.—

Yours as ever,
C. F. Woolson.

To William Wilberforce Baldwin (Morgan)

Casa Biondetti
Sunday evening
[1893]

My dear Doctor.

I have postponed the excursion to the garden, which, was to have taken place tomorrow. I have, therefore, no engagements all day, and I shall be delighted to see you at the hour most convenient to yourself.—With regards to Mrs Bronson, I am yours as ever,

C. F. Woolson.

To Unknown recipient (WRHS/Benedict)[1]

Casa Semitecolo
San Gregorio
Canal Grande. Venice
Oct. 14th, [1893]

My dear Friend,

Your beautiful photographs (those of yourself) filled me with delight. How lovely they are! And how well you look.—I wanted to write on the instant. But I have been so closely occupied for months with the book-proof of Horace Chase that my eyes and hand were incapable of any other ~~work~~ writing.—At last it is done. Only a few days ago the final sheets went off.—I think I have never been so tired as now! Not ill. Only exhausted. Of course you will ask—why work so hard over book proof! But that is something I can't help doing: I mean that with all my literary work, I am impelled by something stronger than myself to do the very best, absolutely the very best, I can.—I only mention all this now to explain how I have had to defer all pleasure until the toil was over.—It would have been a pleasure to write to you.—

I must add, in truth to Venice, that it has been pleasure of one sort merely to exist here, work or no work. Then I have also had the long evenings on the lagoons in my gondola, when it was too hot to write by lamplight. How I wish you could be here with me now. The weather is ideal and I float for hours daily. I did try to pay a visit or two, the day before yesterday. But one of the ladies said as soon as I entered, "Oh, do let me get you some hot brandy & water! You look so ill."—At the second home, the hostess said: "Do you know I really think you had better not try to spend the winter here. Go to Algiers."—So I have given up visits until the wear & tear of Horace Chase are less visible. Yesterday I floated over to the Adriatic beach (across the lagoons), & walked for 2 hours on the grass-covered dyke, with the soft blue waves rolling in at my feet. I had sent the gondola three miles down to meet me, & when I arrived, the gondoliers had made a fire, & my five o'clock tea was all ready on the beach. Then I floated home among the islands reaching here at 7 p.m.—The weather is still summer. I have taken this home for 8 months, & will write you at length before long and answer your letters & Hello's. My love to the whole of you. I hope your husband—my best friend—is well? Affectionately yours,

C. F. Woolson.

Notes

1. The letter is pasted into Woolson's *Horace Chase* (London: Osgood, McIlvaine & Co., 1894).

To Samuel Mather (WRHS/Mather)

Casa Semitecolo
San Gregorio
Canal Grande
Oct. 31st, [1893]

My dear Sam,

The above Venetian address is mine until May 10th next, when my landlord, Lieut. General de Horsey, a retired officer of the sacred "Guards," returns from his winter residence at Hèyres. The General is a delightful Englishman of about 70. As his health is delicate, he has for many years spent his summer at Venice, and his winters at Hèyres, where he has a second house.—Casa Semitecolo is, I am sorry to say, on the wrong side of the Grand Canal; (wrong for health, not beauty). Do you remember the stately church of the Salute? I am very near it, & ~~exactly opposite~~ nearly opposite the Grand Hotel. One has to live here in order to learn the ins and outs; the other side of the Grand Canal has all the sun in winter, and all the bronze in summer. But I could not find there a small furnished apartment for a short time, so I accepted the General's offer of two floors of his house, and I shall occupy the back rooms, where there is sun.—I pay forty dollars a month for the two floors, furnished. I have a large hall (which is like a salon), a smaller salon, four bedrooms, a diningroom, and three servants' bedrooms & kitchen, besides store rooms. I have an excellent Austrian cook to whom I pay seven dollars a month, & a parlor maid to whom I pay four dollars a month. I put in these last items for Flora, as Venetian housekeeping may perhaps interest her? The cook is really very skilful. But as I do not entertain at all, her talent can show itself only in a very modest way. She complains that it is hard to cook nicely for one. This is true. No roast, for instance, is possible; I mean of good size. I could never eat it up.—I have given myself the rest and pleasure of this one winter of housekeeping. I do'nt look forward, and have made no plans beyond May 1st.

It was well that I did not set my heart upon accepting yours & Flora's invitation for the past summer. For only this month (October) did I finish the last sheet of the book-proof of Horace Chase. I have kept steadily at it, too, for many hours each day, in spite of the heat.—The truth is that I always go through the same round with each book; first, I am always much longer in writing it than I plan to be; second, I always tire myself out; third, the book-proof invariably takes four or five months. Yet, with each new novel, I always think I am going escape these conditions!—

I shall be curious to hear what you think of the Fair? Do not forget to tell me what the children think of it, and what they say. I have not heard of one dissenting voice, either at home or abroad. Even the little evening paper of Venice, which I take for the sake of the Italian, abounds in praise of the "great American Exposition."—To-night as I ate my solitary dinner (for I am writing in the evening), I read in this same handkerchief-sheet the brief telegram: "Chicago; the Fair closed today." I felt a sharp pang that I could not ~~see it~~ have seen it.—But as one grows older, pangs are many. Fortunately one grows more resigned to them, also.—

It is long since I have heard from you. Nothing since Flora's nice letter of invitation—But I know, through Kate, that you have been in N.H.—And also that you went yachting.—And then Chicago.—

I came here, as you know, in May. Having spent the entire summer, I now know how bad it can be! The heat is not killing. For ten days in August it was 86° in the shade; that was the highest. The mosquitoes are no worse than I have seen them at Yonkers. But they last longer. They come in July, and they are still with us;—on the last day of October. Practically, the summer is six months long.—I am now going to try a winter. The Americans & English who reside here, are funny in the way they arrange it; about half of them think the Venetian summer "divine," and always stay here from April 1st to December, and then flee to Egypt, or the Riviera for "the drought winter." The other half find the summers "perfectly terrible." About the first of May, they take flight for the mountains, and the last of October they come back, open their houses, and begin to live again. There are some very pleasant people among both the winter and summer residents; and they have all given me a cordial welcome.—I am, at heart, rather more interested in the unusual person. Don Carlos (of Spain) has just arrived for the winter, & opened his palace not far from me. Then there is a Princess of Georgia! Who in the world (I asked) is "a Princess of Georgia?" But it seems that her husband (now dead) really did reign in Georgia (Caucasus) for a while; his widow lives here in a handsome palace, the Czar having given her a pension. She is young & handsome, & in love with Tirindelli, a young ~~Italian~~ Venetian composer of talent. But she forfeits her pension if she marries, & so all she can do is to follow, in her gondola, when he commands the floating orchestra on the nights of the great "Serenades." Do'nt you call that romantic? Then there is a certain Countess Burchtold, who has been seen by no one for 20 years. She occasionally goes out in a gondola at night. But always veiled. 20 years ago, when her beauty began to fade, she gave a ball, & appeared in all her diamonds. It was her farewell. No one has seen her since, though she has continued to live here.[1]

Did you see Duse? She too is a Venetian. She told a lady I know here that neither her American or London season was a financial success. I was astonished, for I know that no one has so captivated the best class of theatre goers both in the U.S. & in England. Poor Duse told my friend that she feared she must learn to paint her face, wear wigs, & try skirt-dancing to attract "the paying public."—Duse has been here for a month, next door to me. She has now gone to Vienna.

I need not expatiate on the beauty of the lagoons, & the delight I find in floating over them. I have been out every evening. Only this week has the autumnal feeling in the air forced me to give it up. As my proofsheets are done, I can now go out in the afternoon, & I don't know but that I like the little canals almost more than the larger ones. As one glides through them, one constantly comes upon old carved doorways, gothic windows, armorial bearings, shrines, half-concealed gardens, and countless other interesting things.—Do you know those old Italian lamps called "lucerna"? They are usually brass with hanging chassis, one holding a little scissors, another the snuffers, a third a needle for arranging the wick. They are tall & slender with a handle at the top; for they are carried about the house as a lantern is carried. Mr Curtis showed me one the other day, which he thought beautiful. It is antique, & of solid silver. He himself has one already, so he does'nt intend to buy it. But he thought it would be a good purchase for me, as it is for sale at the price, merely, of the silver it contains, namely 390 francs, which is something less than 78 dollars. I smiled (inwardly) at his supposing that 78 dollars would be nothing to me. I mention it now because it came into my mind as I was dwelling upon the picturesqueness of Venice. I could buy it for you, I suppose, if you should take a fancy for it. But in that case I should get Blumenthal, the Banker, to keep it for you until you could come for it, or send.—The houses of all the people I know here are full of the most exquisitely beautiful things I have ever seen. They are all antique, & the furniture is (to my taste) very fascinating. There are old cabinets, carved & inlaid, which are extremely lovely. Such extraordinary "finds" are sometimes made! One gentleman I know here, noticed, in a little obscure baker's shop, an old oil painting. He bought it & it is nothing less than an early Tintoretto! Hung in his beautiful drawing-room, it shines out in absolute splendor.

Another person I know here, while prowling through a bric à brac establishment, took up an old book. It proved to be a copy of Bacon's Essays given by Wordsworth to Tennyson; the inscription in W's handwriting being on the first page. And Robert Browning, who was then in Venice, said it was undoubtedly W's handwriting. The Italian who kept the shop sold it for a franc.—

Then not long ago an acquaintance of mine here found 50 volumes of the wonderfully beautiful editions of the Classics which were (strange to say) printed at Parma in the last century. And among the Latin authors were several English works,—Gray's Poems, for instance. These Bodoni editions seem to me magnificent; the handsomest books I have ever seen. (I allude to the type, size, & paper).—Yet they were sold for a song.—

I must not forget to tell you that I have a little dog. He is a Pomeranian spitz, only 5 weeks old. As he is black, the Dalmatian sailors of whom I bought him (for 4 francs) called him "Moro," or the Moor. So I have named him Othello, the Moor of Venice. His nickname is "Tello."—He is still a baby, & full of tricks. He steals my shoes & stockings, & scampers & dances about like a mad creature. I began by putting him in the dressing room to sleep. But he cried so pitifully that I had to let him come into my rooms, where he cuddled down in his basket contentedly, & was asleep in a minute. These little Pomeranians are very lively & intelligent. In addition to the pleasure of having some one who is glad to see me when I come in, Tello is really a safeguard. As I sit alone in this big Venetian house, he stirs & barks at the least step, or approach. I sit & read after the servants have gone to bed, & no one could move anywhere on this floor, without calling out his high quick challenge.—

The picture of the children is on my salon table, & is admired by all. (I allude to the group.) Kiss the three for me, and tell me all about them. My best love to Flora.—If you think I am not very enthusiastic about Venice (or anything else), it is only because I am tired & not well; I have'nt even yet recovered from that attack of influenza; I am only half myself. Venice is as beautiful as ever; to my vision the most beautiful place in the world.

If I live (and live here), I think I might perhaps write a leisurely volume on the lagoons. Nothing more can be said about Venice itself. But the lovely sweet water-plains all about it,—with their 20 islands, & ancient shrines & churches—of these no note has been taken.—

I will add a Venetian item. The stair-carpet needed rods, & I only wanted small cheap iron ones. So I tried to buy them. Then I discovered that all stair rods have to be made (forged), one by one, to order. Both brass & iron. So I went to the forge & saw them made! one by one. The forge-smith, a thin very dark creature, turns out to be a poet. An improvisatore. And the best in Venice. Sir Henry Layard says he has real genius.—Love to all at 544.—

Affectionately yours,
C.F.W.

Notes

1. Don Carlos VII (1848–1909) of Spain; the Princess of Georgia may have been a member of the Chavchavadze family; Pietro Aldolfo Tirindelli was a Venetian composer; Countess Fanny von Berchtold (?–1912) was a cousin of Austro-Hungarian ambassador to Russia, Leopold von Berchtold (1863–1942).

To Samuel Mather (WRHS/Mather)[1]

Casa Semitecolo
San Gregorio
Canal Grande. Venice
Nov. 20th, 1893

My dear Sam,

I fear you will not approve of a decision I came to last night. You would—if you could get into my skin; for then you would have a clear vision of the constitution of my mind, and the way my thoughts run. But as this is impossible, you will have to take it on trust.

Now that I have reassumed the responsibilities of housekeeping, the accompanying anxieties have turned up again. If you ask, "Why go to housekeeping, then, if it affects you in that way?"—my answer is that even with the anxiety, the pleasure outweighs the pain, for the privacy of a home of my own has become very necessary to my comfort;—a home of my own, no matter how small and plain. I seem to have come to the end of being able to live in other peoples's rooms.—I have got back to cheaper Italy (cheaper than the delightful, but expensive England); I have reassembled my scattered belongings from Oxford & Florence; I have made the necessary first purchases; and now, having settled myself for a while, I find I am beginning to be haunted by the fear that my reserve fund at the Bank here is not large enough to leave me free from immediate care. I have therefore decided to ask you to sell one of my bonds (any one you think best), and remit to me, here, the sum of one thousand dollars. This sum can lie at the Bank here (the Bank of S. & A. Blumenthal), and it will be a backing for me as well as a relief to my mind. Blumenthal will allow me some interest (though nothing like the amount you get for me), and I shall feel safe. ~~It will~~ The presence will ~~be~~ have much the same effect that a low-hung carriage has upon my nerves: with it, I feel that I can jump out if I become frightened, and the knowing that I can, acts as a tranquilizer; I never do jump, & never want to. Whereas in a high vehicle, I never have one moment's freedom from terror.

I hope that you will not be obliged to wait until you can send me an order (or whatever it is) to sign. Let me sign afterwards.

I once asked your father to do a similar thing. He complied instantly (with his prompt kindness), but he wrote at the same time that he did not approve of it; one should not use one's capital, especially when it was so small; it should be carefully saved for the infirmities of age. But one must do, from day to day, the best one can. And my "infirmities" are upon me now; they will not grow worse. (This last sentence means that your aunt is already pretty old!) I hope you will not be shocked if I add that for a long time my daily prayer has been that I may not live to be old; I mean really old.—

But you must not think from this that I am especially sombre just now. On the contrary. I am much more cheerful and serene than I was in England. Venice suits me in many ways, and I think I am going to be happy here.—

There is one—I was going to say "difficulty"; but I am not sure that it is that. Well then, there is one condition here which has both pleasures & bothers connected to it. And that is the wonderfully cordial way in which I have been received. The society is small, very pleasant, &, I fancy, rather exclusive. But they have'nt excluded me; they have called & called again. They climb my long stairs & and establish themselves in my little sittingroom really as though they like it,—which is a surprise to me. If you could see their superb palaces, filled with the most exquisite things, you would share my wonder. But their cordiality and kindness touch me greatly, and I do'nt quarrel with either. Though it sometimes is difficult for me to keep up my end of the tie when there are such big fortunes at the other. I do'nt mean that there is any difficulty materially; it is only spiritually that one feels the difference. Or perhaps "imaginatively" is the better word. They want nothing from me; & as I no longer accept invitations—save to tea, informally—there are no obligations of any sort on my side.—

I have bought a little dog, partly for company, partly as a guard. His sharp little bark I can always hear, & he rouses up at the slightest sound. He sleeps in a basket beside my bed, & he is better than the loudest bell. He is black, & I call him Othello (The Moor of Venice.) You should see me washing him, & projecting Persian Powder into his curly hide with a vaporizer! He is only 2 months old, & very funny. He is biting the buttons of my boots as I write. I bought him from some Dalmatian sailors for five francs. My love to Flora & the children. I am tired to-night, so will stop. Ever, my dear boy, affectionately yours,

C.F.W.

Love to all at 544.

Notes

1. The errors in this letter are Woolson's. There are also a number of illegible strike throughs, suggesting that she found her financial decision difficult, especially given the economic panic of 1893.

To Samuel Mather (WRHS/Mather)

Casa Semitecolo
San Gregorio
Canal Grande. Venice
Nov. 23^{d}, [1893]

Dear Sam,

Your letter has just come with the draft for sixty dollars. It is extremely kind of you to advance it (the dividends). But when were you anything else than thoughtful and kind! Clara has written of the hard times at home. I hope they have not troubled you? I hear (from the rather unfriendly English papers—it's true) that the hard times—American—are the worst for 30 years. Can this be so?—I wrote you a day or two ago. Nothing to add. Or rather so much to add that I do'nt even begin. I mean that Venice is so beautiful, & the life here so picturesque, that I could write a volume.—To-day, for instance, comes an intensely grateful note in German-English from the Princess Hatzfeldt.[1] She is an Austrian, &, in her beautiful apartment, holds a sort of salon each week. She has been growing deaf, to her bitter grief. An English lady asked me to ~~send~~ lend her one of my trumpets. I did so—& the Princess is quite wild with joy; it is touching to see her gratitude. I have ordered one for her from London, & in the meanwhile she uses mine; (I have two). So now the whole Hatzfeldt household, which includes nieces & nephews &c is at my feet. And with it, all the Austrian society. It's a pity that I do'nt care for society. But I feel old, & tired, & indifferent.

I know what you mean by the effort of writing letters. I go through the same feelings, & often postpone because I have no time to write a letter of any length. Let us both give up our old superstitions on the subject, & relegating long & interesting & well-written letters to either the Lost Arts, or the Next World, write in their places frequent notes of three pages; (like this).—Love to all & kisses to the children.

In haste, yours most affectionately,
C.F.W.

Notes

1. See appendix for Princess Hatzfeldt, the American-born Clara Elizabeth Prentice-Huntington.

To L. E. Jones (Brigham Young)[1]

Venice
Nov. 24th, 1893

L. E. Jones, Esqre

Dear Sir,

I have revised the above, and have taken pains that the new version should be no longer than the old one. Hoping that it will prove satisfactory, I am,

Yours truly,
C. F. Woolson.

Notes

1. See letter addressed to Dear Sir on Aug. 10, 1892.

To Clare Benedict (Benedict/CFW, 383–87)

Casa Semitecolo
San Gregorio
Canal Grande. Venice
December 3d, 1893

I begin a letter in the interval after tea and before dinner—which I have set apart for letter-writing in the short space that remains to me before I begin another novel on January 1st.[1] If no one comes in, it is a peaceful time. I have, however, a good many callers, and I have told everybody that I am almost always at home by dark . . .

My "peaceful moment" to-night would be rather more peaceful if Tello did not insist upon lying on my lap. As he is a good deal larger than Tiny Polliket, (though not so large as Packim) he makes writing rather difficult. He is tired and is taking a nap. We went in the gondola to the Adriatic beach, and had a long walk on the shore of two hours, and he ran and ran, and carried sticks in his mouth which were longer than himself. Then in addition he had to fight all the coast-guards who patrol the beach; he showed his teeth at each one, to their amusement. So now he is resting, and I am writing under difficulties. I have your letter after you had heard I had bought him—you ask for description. Well—him id kinnin. But him id'nt good! Him growl, and fight everybody and everything but me! Him tear to pieces every single thing he can get hold of, and then, when we find him in the midst of the ruin he has wrought, he wag 'em tail, perfectly triumphant. Him id now exactly three months old. Him birthday wad September 1st. He sleeps in my room in a basket, and although I did not think of it when I bought him, he is an excellent guard for me. He rouses at a step or the slightest sound, and his sharp little bark I always hear. As he lies at my feet in the evening, I can tell merely by the pricking of his ears, if any one has even passed through the hall outside the closed door. These Pomeranians are celebrated as watch dogs; not for their size, but for their acute attention and loud bark. . . . He will guard me better than a servant . . .

I am beginning to feel rather more rested, and the apartment is at last in order. I shall now have five months of quiet and comfort in it. There has been a good deal to do, and I have been far too impatient about it. But now all my things from Florence are unpacked and in place, and the necessary things bought. . . . I live on the south side of the house, where I have a pleasant sunny little sitting room, a small warm dressing, and sunny bed-room. The north side of the house on the Grand Canal I do not now use. Here is the big bedroom and dressing room I occupied when I moved in in September, and here I shall put you and Mamma when you come. The view is splendid. In the spring, too, we can use as a salon the long hall which also opens on the Grand Canal with a balcony . . .

Night before last I actually went to the theatre. Edith Bronson took me. It was done principally to show me the theatre, and how things are managed, &c so that if I ever care to go my myself, I can do it easily. It was an Italian company, one of Dumas fils plays—"Denise"; I didn't care for the play itself, but the acting was very good. The Italians are to me the most natural actors in the world. It comes out, the same trait, in Duse.[2] Edith B. told me that she had twice seen Duse in "Denise," and that when she played the part every one was breathless . . .

By the way, she (Edith B.) asked me to write in her precious little album, in which she has only very nice names—Longfellow, Lowell, Browning, Tennyson and lots more. I'll scribble what I wrote. Her pet dog's name is Tubby ben Toufou (the son of Toufou, her mother's Japanese dog).

"Precious booklet made for Edith,
Famous names, and verses sweet,
Only one thing more it needeth,

To be quite complete—;
There should be a verselet, clearly,
(Tiny painted portrait, too),
Of the friend she loves most dearly,
  Tubby ben Tou-fou!
Stalwart little Tubby,
  Eyes so leal[3] and true,
Loving, faithful, dauntless, chubby
  Tubby ben Tou-fou!"

I enclose a note from Princess Hatzfeldt—Yes, I have got to Princesses! When Lady Layard called upon me, I felt quite fine. But Princesses are better than Knights and their "ladies" . . .

It is now after dinner, Tello has waked up and come climbing up on my lap. I have given him a bone (I keep bones on all the tables), two sticks, and the envelope of your letter, and I hope he will let me write. I notice that he is beginning to have a little doggy smell. But it's a very nice smell, don't you think so? . . .

Tello is biting the penholder. I put him down, and took up your letter, when, happening to lift my eyes, I saw that he had climbed up on the sofa, got the silk cushion Henry James gave me, jumped down and was carrying it off under the table, but it is bigger than he is! . . .

Love to Mama. Will write to her soon. Tello chend him love.

C.F.W.

Notes

1. No record exists that Woolson started a new novel and no other letters to Clare Benedict survive.

2. Alexandre Dumas, the younger, wrote *Denise* in 1885; it was produced at the Goldoni Theatre in Venice. Benedict (385) adds this excerpt from a Woolson letter, where she describes actress Italian actress Eleonora Duse.

> About Duse . . . She again sent her agent to me last week, for she is so in hopes that I will take the apartment she still has on her hands—the top floor of beautiful Casa di Desdemona . . . So I again went to look at it. The one room on the Grand Canal is perfectly beautiful, with the exquisite balconies, and a divine view. . . . Her red silk is still on the walls, and ever so many of her other hangings and decorations.

3. leal: faithful.

To Samuel Mather (Anderson)

Casa Semitecolo
San Gregorio
Canal Grande
Dec. 10th, [1893]

Dear Sam.

Your long delightful letter has just come, and I send a brief reply at once, because I feel impelled to. For I am afraid you have been disturbed by the request of my last letter?—But though it is a necessity that I should have that thousand dollars here as a backing & to relieve the strain of anxiety, matters are not so bad as my request may lead you to suppose, for this next twelve months will bring me the book-profits of my last novel, both in the U.S. & in England. Other money is also owing to me in England, from the "English Library"—(the new rival of Tauchnitz). But in the meanwhile I want to feel peaceful, so I hope you have already sent me the proceeds of one of my bonds.—For I need it.—Banks have been failing in Italy at such a rate that I hardly know whether to trust the thousand with Blumenthal or not. Mr D. S. Curtis—who was a banker himself, formerly in Boston, & who is a ~~very~~ rich man (it is called "very rich" in Italy; but American ideas are so much more extensive that I rubbed out the "very"), tells me that he (Blumenthal) is perfectly safe. Mr Curtis (who is one of the kindest friends I have ever had) took me to Blumenthal's & introduced me, & asked B. to give me the same advantages & rates as those he himself enjoys; & this is very nice for me.—

I don't at all know whether I shall stay in Venice after my lease here expires. It depends upon the cost. I keep account, week by week, & by May 1st I shall know exactly what it amounts to.—I have heard of a small apartment in a good situation which I can get for 250 dollars a year.—I am going to look at it.—I look at everything; it is all interesting. Your letter was perfectly delightful to me. I have felt your long silence more than you know.—

I am dreadfully shocked to hear of the insanity of Clarence King.[1] Yes, I know him. I met him once in Paris, & saw much of him for a few days. He remains in my mind as an example of one of the most agreeable men I have ever known. Also he seemed to me exquisitely kind. He took me to the Comedie Francaise, with the Hays, & his sister, & I was much touched by his thoughtfulness in other ways; he arranged it all so that I should enjoy it, & understand.—It must be a great grief to Colonel Hay.—Do send him a message of sympathy from me. It is heartfelt.—

As to the Lucerna—I will have a sketch made of it, with its exact dimensions, & send to you. Then you can see whether you really like it.—I thought that perhaps you would remember the shape? But I fancy you do'nt? They are Tuscan lamps. I have two ordinary brass ones in use in the house now. To my eyes they are very picturesque.

The story of Oliver Payne & Col. Zeph made me laugh.—It is quite true that Colonel Zeph knew both Oliver & Nathan very well in old times.—Oliver may not like him, ~~&~~ that is all right ~~&~~ in that case his withdrawal on the Calais boat was all right. But if it was owing to his desiring to know only the ultra fashionable;—that is unpleasant. I never thought Oliver Payne snobbish. He never used to be.—Col. Zeph has been reputed to be a rich man for ten or fifteen years. But he is of a speculative nature.—I should like to see him again. If I could get him alone, I dare say we should have a very friendly and funny talk. But, meanwhile, we should both be inwardly thinking, "Great heavens—what an escape I had!" It was only the glamor of the war that ~~made~~ brought us together. Every girl wanted to have a soldier-lover in those intense years, and every soldier (especially the volunteers) was wrought up to the highest point of excitement & romance. I remember Judge Spaulding's making a splash at a public meeting in Cleveland, shortly after Col. Zeph had gone to the front with his regiment; he said "And if it is to help save his dear country, I am willing to have my son brought back to his home on his shield!"—And we all wept.—Now it sounds rather funny,—as shields are not common on the battlefields of today, and Zeph was always rather stout.—As to the lagoons—(you speak of them), I am greatly fascinated with them. At this season the whole magnificent long line of the Dolomite Alps fills the entire north & northwestern sky. They are glittering with snow, & as superb as the Bernese peaks from Berne—the Monch, the Eiger, & the Finsteraarhorn; I dare say you remember these latter? If I stay here, I think I shall write something about the lagoons. I have learned to row gondolier fashion, as that is a good way to get exercise here. It is now cold, but not at all bitter. Splendid sunshine & no wind.—

I am deeply sorry that I missed the Fair. Evidently there will not, in my life time, be anything so beautiful again.—Love to Flora & Kisses for the children. I have scratched this in haste as it is evening & I ought not to write by lamplight. I am saving my eyes as I begin another novel on January 1st.

Yours affectionately,
C.F.W.

Notes

1. King was put into the Bloomingdale Asylum in New York in 1893. He was released in January 1894.

To Katharine Livingston Mather (WRHS/Mather)[1]

Casa Semitecolo
San Gregorio
Canal Grande. Venice
Dec. 13th, [1893]

Dear Kate.

The gondolier has just brought me your letter of Nov. 27th & I will take this peaceful hour before dinner to at least begin a reply. It is dark now at five, & I don't have dinner until seven, so that gives two quiet hours, in case no one comes in. A good many people do come in (at present). But almost all of them leave Venice immediately after Xmas for about 6 weeks; that is for the worst of the winter. Some go to the Riviera, some to Rome or Naples.[2] They tell me that in Jan. & Feb. there is an icy fog here which is depressing. But I don't believe it is so bad as the icy winter-fogs of Oxford & Cheltenham, which sometimes went on unbroken for 10 days. And I am not afraid.—Your letter told me what I have wished much to know—namely how your mother enjoyed her trip to Chicago? I think her going was a really great event, & I have been anxious & eager to hear about it ever since Clara's letter mentioning that she had gone. I am so glad she saw the especial things she cared to see. And in spite of the disheartening illness that followed, I am sure the journey will be a most interesting thing to think of for many months to come. I know that often it now happens with me that I have to spur myself up to go somewhere,—even if it is no more than to the Lido, here. I don't feel in the mood, perhaps. Very likely I feel depressed, & I say to myself that fifty Lidos won't do me any good! But when I actually go, I always brighten up. The sea, & sky, & splendid line of the Dolomite Alps (now visible in the north & north-east; one almost never sees them in summer),—all this cheers me, & the causes of depression for the time grow less, & even disappear.—Give my dearest love to your mother, & tell her I was really acutely interested (over here in Venice) in her expedition. I am so glad you wrote.—It was nice too, that Will met her in Chicago and spent Sunday.—I did not know that Mrs Bolles had passed away. I remember her as such a sweet woman, long ago. How many years of being an invalid she has had! I hardly know another ~~care~~ case like it.—Mother was delicate for a good many years. But she did not have such frequent & severe attacks as Mrs Bolles had. Give my love to Mary Bolles & the doctor, and much sympathy.—

I was interested in hearing about your new watch. I like marked watches. In fact I like inscriptions. I like them on silver, & even on furniture. It gives such an interest, and value.—

You speak of a snowstorm. Here it has not, so far, been at all wintry. It is cold enough to make a bright open fire pleasant. But not in the least bitter. To-day, when I went with my little dog to the Piazza for a walk, a military band was playing, & people were not only walking up & down, but sitting in front of the café's you remember, taking coffee. It is true that the Piazza is like a large hall, or drawing room.—I am watching the climate with much interest to see how it compares with that of Florence, & England.—

You speak of Thanksgiving. I thought of you all. Here, there was no sort of mention of it. In Florence there used to be one or two dinner parties. Grace Carter wrote me that she was invited to eat Turkey in Munich. Grace writes often. She has seen Mary, & she gave me an exact account of the interview.[3] Mary seemed well, save that she looked rather pale. She was dressed in a sort of wadded wrapper—the only thing they can make her wear. She said, "Well, Grace, where have you been all this time?" But without dwelling upon it, or as though she cared much. She spoke of her children in the same way; that is, she mentioned them; but with no distress of mind. Her thoughts changed rapidly, she veered from subject to subject, talking constantly, but without connection. Her voice is weak from this constant talking. Grace hoped that the visit would have some effect. But it did not. The nurse repeated the next day that Mary had not alluded to it.—Grace thinks that Mary's having been unwell lately—(for the first time since she became insane)—is a good sign. I hope it is. But somehow I feel rather discouraged. Hyde, having been to Cooperstown to look after <u>his</u> hops & his farm has now returned to England where his children are staying with his mother & sisters. He wishes to be within reach of Grace's telegram—in case there should be a marked improvement in Mary.—Grace, meanwhile, stays in Munich, & busies herself with her music & German. She likes Munich; all the same I should think she must have some lonely sad hours.—

To-day I had, to my surprise, a letter from Paul Carter! from Zoar. If he is in Cleveland still, do tell him how much I enjoyed it. I really did, for he told me all about the Zoarites, & the changes there, &c. I shall certainly answer the letter, though I may not be able to do so immediately. He tells me that a Cleveland man named Gunn is looking at Zoar. This cannot be Alexander, can it?[4]—

My apartment here is all in order at last, & very comfortable. My little sitting room has a large open fireplace (an unusual thing in Italy) with a most picturesque hood & high mantelpiece in the old style. All my things from Florence are here & they make the rather bare house look cosy. I have a sittingroom, bedroom, & dressing-room on the south side of the house, away from the Grand Canal. I do'nt like this. But as the house faces due north, I had to move from the northside, as in Italy the sunshine is highly important in winter. The bedroom & dressing room are heated by the funny Venetian stove made of plaster! They are small, & ugly; closed. But they heat well. Then I have a tolerable diningroom, & big hall. The hall, being fireless, is only to look at. At the front are the big rooms I occupied when I moved in, in September.—I look, rather vaguely, at other apartments, for my lease here expires May 10th. But I really have no plans. I am keeping exact accounts, this winter, to see what housekeeping here costs. Sometimes I think that as I have re-collected all my things from Florence & England, & paid a good deal to accomplish it,—& as I like Venice so much, I had better stay on here for some years. I have had to buy a good deal to make this apartment comfortable, & all that would tell in furnishing one for a term of years. Your hundred dollars bought my nice bed & marvelous feather pillows; my wardrobe, & bureau & little table, & other things. It is plain walnut furniture, but very nice, & a _great_ comfort to me. Clara seems to have the idea that I am not satisfied with the bed. But this is a great mistake. It is a delightful bed, & I am _very_ thankful for it every night. It is not the brass bed I have dreamed of. But few of us ever realize our dreams! Mother, throughout her whole life, longed to have no teatable set, but tea passed around with thin bread & butter. She lived to be 70 & never was able to carry out her dream. Thus it will be with me & my brass bed—though I shall not live to 70,—waiting for it.—

On January first I begin to write again, so after that date, my letters will be scarce again. For the last month, I have felt better & more rested, so I dare say I shall get on all right.—The publication of _Horace Chase_ in book-form, has been delayed by the long time it took me to revise it. I have ordered a copy to be sent to your mother, & I hope you will re-read it, as it is now made clear & intelligible. To write a serial is difficult; for only just so many pages are allowed in each number of the magazine, & the story must stop at the end of a certain fixed time. This hampers me, & in the book-form I spread out a little, & give myself more space & ease. The story will be published in London at the same time it is published in N.Y.; that is in January.

Society here is to me delightful. The circle is very small (unlike Florence), & it is either lazy, or exclusive—as you prefer to call it; the members do'nt trouble themselves to run after strangers, or transient visitors. I have never been so kindly received as here. But there are few young people. It is essentially a society of older persons—quiet persons; people who have retired from active life, & are taking their ease.

I will close (for it is now after dinner & I must not tire my eyes any longer), by an account of an expedition I made yesterday with Edith Bronson, to see some unfurnished apartments; (for I look at everything; it does no harm to look).—one was the 2^{d} floor of this magnificent Palazzo Pesaro, on the Grand Canal, below the Rialto bridge. Here are ten or 12 superb high-ceilinged rooms with great balconeys on the Grand Canal & a ~~superb~~ splendid view. All in perfect order. I can have this for three hundred dollars a year! It is owned by the Duchess of Bevilacqua who sent me word that she would make all repairs, & do any little thing I wanted, without expense.[5] The objections to this ideal place are two; one is that with the very high ceilings, I could not heat it in winter. The other is that such large rooms require much furniture. But think of such a perfect place, with marbles & stucco, & balconeys & view—for 300^{00} a year. If I were intending to go away for the 3 months of winter, as so many do, it would be perfect.—What a place for you to come to, & make me a visit! Perhaps you remember the big Pesaro?—Another apartment (very different) is by the side of the clock-tower of the Piazza San Marco. Do'nt you remember the clock tower with the two giants on top that strike the hours. These rooms are beautiful, & look straight down the Piazzetta to the water, with San Giorgio Maggiore opposite. Of course they also command the whole Piazza, San Marco, & the Doge's Palace.—

Finally, there is a small palace on the Grand Canal round the bend where the Foscari Palace is; it is some distance down, but by no means so far as the Rialto. This little palace has pretty Gothic windows, & little balconeys, & a water door, & there is an apartment in it (the first floor) which is only $200.^{00}$ a year. It is a small place, but excellent situation & with sun.—At present the Count Grimani with his mother & sister live there. The Count who is about 30, has very small means, & he has fallen in love with a young Italian girl who has no money at all. So much in love is he that he is going to marry her in spite of her having no dot—a very unusual ardor for an Italian. And therefore he cannot pay even 200 dollars rent, but is obliged to move. So that is where my chance comes in. Could I get any sort of a house at home for 200 dollars a year?—But though I look at many apartments (for the search is amusing and gives me glimpses of Venetian interiors which one would not otherwise see), I have no plans beyond May 10th.

Your letter about Mrs Homer Brown threw light upon a subject which had puzzled me. The Brown husband is a painter. I believe she met him in Paris.—Harry W.'s marriage was a grief to me. Not that I know anything against Miss Beckworth, who is a pretty girl. But as I greatly dislike Mrs Brown, I can't help associating the two sisters together. Mrs Brown is a pushing, common, metallic sort of woman. She is not received by the best people here. This is not on account of her history, which is not known. It is on account of herself; everyone thought her common, & let her drop. She laid seige to Harry W,—and has won the day; he has married her sister! As to Clare & Harry—they never fancied each other. It was for years Mrs Washington's dream, & she used to talk about it. But that is the very way to set a boy against it. Then, on the other side, Clara does'nt like Harry, I think. And Clare has always been calmly indifferent.—Did Mr Homer get the divorce? Harry W. thinks that <u>Mrs</u> Homer got it, & without difficulty, as Homer had treated her so badly. I have also heard that Homer had to pay her a large alimony. Is this true?

Christmas evening

This letter did not get off, my dear Kate; so I will scribble a little more and post it tomorrow. The weather is perfectly beautiful. Yesterday, Christmas Eve, I went to the Lido in the gondola, & walked for two hours on the Adriatic beach, with my little dog, Othello, the Moor of Venice. It was so warm that I sat for some time on the grassy embankment of Fort St Niccolo, looking at the blue water, the blue sky, the snowy Alps in the distance; and, on the sea, the many red sails. To-day I have been strolling in the Piazza San Marco crowded to the doors. Flags flying on the three great flagstaffs before the church, and the two enormous banners of St Mark floating from the church itself. I am invited tonight to a Christmas party at Lady Layard's. This is the palace which has such a beautiful collection of pictures. I have declined, & shall sit alone by my fire & read Dickens's Christmas Carol & Milton's Hymn on the Nativity, & think of those who are gone.—This morning Mrs Bronson sent me a beautiful pearl & gold pen; & other pretty things have come in from these kind Venetians.—

My latest new acquaintance is Princess Olga of Montenegro. She asked Edith Bronson to bring her to call upon me; so they came day before yesterday. I have always wanted to go to Montenegro, & Olga tells me it is very easy now; one goes to Fiume opposite Venice, & thence by steamer one day down the Adriatic. Olga's father was King. At his death, a nephew succeeded to the throne, & the widow & her little girl came to Venice to live. The elder princess died last year, & Olga now spends her time with relatives—sometimes here, sometimes in Russia, sometimes with her cousin, the present ruler of Montenegro. Like all Russians she is wonderful about languages. She speaks English perfectly as regards all she says; the only thing is that she has a slight foreign accent. It is a very small accent. She speaks half a dozen tongues in the same perfect way. She is about 28, small, dark, not pretty, but very interesting. She asked if she might come "very soon" again, so I think she means to pursue the acquaintance. The Czar has settled a pension upon her. I do'nt know whether all this interests you? It does me; I like to see unusual people.—

I send again, this Christmas night, much love to your mother. I wonder if she would be amused by one of my "Horace Chase" letters. I get many, & some are very funny. You need not return this. Please destroy it.—I went to get one Christmas card to send to my devoted Oxford landlady (the nicest little woman!), when I discovered a view which shows this house,—though rather vaguely. [excision] I'll send it to your mother in [excision] another envelope. Good-bye, Targia. Much love to Will.

Affectionately,
C.F.W.

Paul Carter could'nt have eaten more than the Thompsons?

Notes

1. Portions of this letter were typed and used in Benedict/CFW, 387–91. My transcription is from the original.

2. CFW footnotes the following excerpt, from a different Woolson letter: "Pretty soon my visitors will diminish, for this winter more than ever before, 'the 400' are leaving Venice for the worst of the weather. You must not suppose that the number of people I know here is large, but the same persons call often, ('The 400' of Venice consist of about 25 or 30)." Woolson is joking about New York society's elite 400, the number who were invited to Mrs. Caroline Schermerhorn (William Blackhouse) Astor's (1830–1908) balls purportedly because that was the capacity of her ballroom.

3. Probably Mary Gayle Carter Clarke.

4. As a child, Woolson had vacationed at this German religious community in Ohio. Alexander Gunn published *The Hermitage-Zoar Note-book and Journal of Travel* in 1902.

5. Duchess Donna Felicita Bevilacqua La Masa (1822–99) willed her palazzo to the city of Venice.

To William Wilberforce Baldwin (Morgan)

Casa Semitecolo
San Gregorio,
Canal Grande. Venice
Dec. 17th, [1893]

My dear Doctor.

I have been intending to write to you ever since your visit. And now I am led to making the intention a reality by a letter, just received, from Henry James, in which he begs me to find out whether you have suffered by all the dreadful bank failures in Florence? He seems to be apprehensive that the disaster of Macquay & Hooker will cause you loss? I hope not, with all my heart. But, as I remember Florence, there were no other banks save Macquays, Der Firenze, the Credito Mobiliare, & Wagniere. And all these have collapsed. Do let me know that all is well with you?—If I had been in Florence, I should have lost by Macquay, though not much. There was where I kept my money. Have many persons lost?

I took tea at Casa Alvisi yesterday, & have not seen Mrs Bronson look so well in many months. She was beautifully dressed, and her <u>kind</u> voice and manner were to me delightful. She has a genius for kindness. Edith has actually spurred me up to going out in the evening; I went with her, not long ago, to the Goldoni, to see an Italian company play "Denise."—[1]

I have just come in from a long expedition in the gondola. This time I had the men row across the lagoon to the mainland & then I landed, & walked for an hour. The afternoon was beautiful, & all the Dolomite Alps were visible, glistening with snow. So far, the Venetian winter is angelic—compared with my three last winters in England!

I take more pleasure than you would dream possible, in the scarab you gave me. For years I have wanted one. And then I was fool enough to give away the three I bought! But now I have a better one than those were; it is really a beautiful specimen—

So you read Shakespeare up in the mountains? I like that. I always mean to do it, too; & in fact I generally do read a play through each month. This winter, I am rich in books as I have Mrs Curtis's library, & also that of Mrs Skinner, at my disposal. I go with the gondola & get 40 books at a time. The Curtises are in India. Mrs Skinner (whom you met here that afternoon) goes to Egypt in a few days. She has been a great traveller;—is the only woman (white) who has visited the Great Basin. And she went thither alone! She is 74, & now goes to Egypt by herself.—

I wonder if you have heard how Miss Huntington is? I have not,—as I have not written.—

Excuse this torn sheet. This rough-edged paper often has these gaps.—

My love to Mrs Baldwin, & a kiss for the children. With all sorts of good wishes for this New Year, I am, my dear Doctor, your attached friend,

C. F. Woolson.

Notes

1. Alexandre Dumas, the son, (1824–95) wrote *Denise* in 1885. It was produced at the Goldoni theater in Venice. Carlo Goldoni (1707–93), for whom the theater is named, is credited with moving theater into a realistic mode.

To Samuel Mather (Anderson)

Casa Semitecolo
San Gregorio
Canal Grande. Venice
Dec. 20th, [1893]

Dear Sam.

This morning comes your letter, with the draft and certificate. Thank you greatly for having attended to the matter with such promptness; you must have done it on the very day my letter was received. I shall get some one to witness my signature, and then re-endorse the certificate in this envelope.—

I have now in your care, have'nt I?—only the four thousand dollars' worth of Railroad Bonds? I ask because I am making a new will.—I owe you for the interest you very recently advanced on these Iron Shares just sold. This sum please deduct from the interest on the Railroad Bonds, which will be due on April 1st. And do'nt I owe you also for part of the purchase-money of these Minnesota shares? It seems to me that you advanced something. Please let me know, when you have time, for I should like to have a clear idea, this winter, of all my affairs.

I disliked to call in this money. I suppose you know that, without my writing it. Perhaps I may be able to send it back to you for re-investment before long; more than that sum is owing to me from publishers. Correspondence is now going on about a new edition of my earlier novels in England. And also a Continental edition of "Horace Chase." The latter book, made late by my long summer toil here over the proofs, will be published simultaneously in the U.S., & London, in January. To-day comes a letter from the Harpers, suggesting that I should let them make still another volume of my earlier short stories. (I tremble a little about this!) And a volume of my Italian stories will be out in 1894.[1]—So there seems to be a good market for my wares.—

Dec. 21st

I went to the Consul~~ate~~ to get him to witness my signature, as it was the easiest way. The Consul was out. In 14 years I have never found an American Consul in. The Vice, however, was present & wrote his name. He is a German Banker, & he is also the German Consul. I may mention that I have never met, over here, a Vice Consul of the U.S. who was an American; these sub officials (who do all the business) are always foreigners, because the Consul never can speak a word of any language but his own!—

Venice remains perfectly beautiful to me, even in winter. So far, the winter has not been at all cold. I take long walks and rows every day. On Tuesday I went in the gondola down the harbor to the little coast village of [Malamosso?] where I often go; here I landed, and walked for two hours on the grassy dyke, which borders the Adriatic. The sea & sky were as blue as in July, and there were 40 red sails in sight. In the northwest, the whole long line of the Venetian Alps & Dolomites was visible, seeming almost near enough to touch. The Alps were as beautiful and snow-covered as the Jungfrau.—

The society here, too, pleases me much. It is small & not at all hurried. The people are tranquil, and make no demands upon anybody's time. It is true that almost all of them are rich. To those who are not rich, the constant atmosphere of wealth sometimes becomes oppressive; depressing. But I do'nt think that would ever be the case in Venice, just because of the very tranquility of the society. Nobody is ambitious. The pushing people either do'nt come here, or, if they do, do'nt get in.— Everyone has been surprisingly kind to me. They climb up my stairs & stay hours. They invite me—though I seldom accept.—(I like better to have them come here.) An invitation has just arrived for a Christmas party at Lady Layard's. This is the

Palace that has such a superb collection of pictures. I do'nt think I shall go, as I ~~have~~ prefer, nowadays, to spend my Christmas alone by the fire, thinking of the past. You and Kate & Will fill a large share of these Christmas visions. Also, I recall the dear ones who have gone from earth.—

Christmas cannot be itself without the voices of children. Yours will be delightful, I know.—

You may be interested, perhaps, of hearing of a new acquaintance I have just made; that is Princess Olga of Montenegro. Are'nt you curious about that odd rocky little Kingdom, with its one port & inaccessible situation? I am. Olga's father was King. After his death, a nephew took his place, & his widow & daughter came to Venice to live; they are pensioned by the Czar. The elder princess died last year, & Olga is now alone. She is about 30, highly cultivated, & very pleasant. She is dark and small; not pretty but very interesting. She asked to make my acquaintance, & came to call upon me with Edith Bronson. Such people interest me.—But I am afraid I shall not be able to get hold of Don Carlos, the Spanish pretender! He is here now, & I know he goes often to the Bronsons. But they give delightful little dinners, & Don Carlos likes that.

The other day I had a long letter from Cousin Fanny (Mrs Richard Cooper), again asking if I was never coming home? Lovely as Venice is, I am sometimes homesick, & I have seriously thought of packing all my things next spring & sailing by the Italian line for N.Y., with the intention of living in Cooperstown. But I suppose the winter there would try me, & I should not be able to travel. And then also I suppose I could not get any sort of a house for the rent I pay here? Here three hundred dollars a year gets a good apartment. Here, I can get a capital cook for seven dollars a month; a waitress for four dollars, ditto. I wrote these items to Cousin Fanny, & asked her how they compared with prices at Cooperstown?—Clara declares that I should be very unhappy, if I settled down forever in a place like Cooperstown.—But I do'nt think so. My only fear would be that after 14 years abroad, I should not know how to conform, perhaps, to all their ways, & they might not like it. Good night & goodbye. Dearest love to all.

C.F.W.

Notes

1. Woolson died just before the publication of the book version of *Horace Chase* (1894). Both her collections of Italian short stories were published posthumously, *The Front Yard* in 1895 and *Dorothy* in 1896. Some of her last letters to Samuel Mather suggest that financial worries may have contributed to her probable suicide; however, Harpers' continued interest in her work suggests that she still could make money from her writing. No will was ever found.

To Arabella Carter Washburn (Benedict/CFW, 392–93)

Casa Semitecolo
Canal Grande. Venice
December 25th, 1893

. . . My Christmas Eve, the afternoon, was spent alone. It was a perfect day with brilliant sunshine, blue sky and sea. I started in the gondola at two o'clock and went over to the Adriatic beach. Here I took a long walk with my little dog beside the lovely sea. There were innumerable red sails in sight. Finally, I went to the very end of the point, entered the fort, and asked permission to sit for a while on the grassy ramparts, overlooking the water. Venice, like a fairy city, rose in the distance, and in the north-north-west, the whole long line of the splendid snow-covered Alps and Dolomites was clearly visible. If I should go home and live in Cooperstown, should I be homesick for all this?

To-day, I have been to the Piazza. Crowds of people, all with happy faces, for the Italians require so little to make them happy! San Marco crowded to the doors. The banners flying on the church and the great Italian flags streaming forth from the tall flagstaffs where once floated the standards of the tributary provinces. It was so warm and bright that I could not wear my fur cloak; I needed only a jacket.

I am invited to-night to a beautiful Christmas party at Lady Layard's, but I prefer to sit alone by my fire and think of days that are gone . . . I often think that though I stay abroad, I seem to remember better than any one else. All the others have forgotten the old personages, but I haven't. . . . I have taught myself to be calm and philosophic, and I feel perfectly sure that the next existence will make clear all the mysteries and riddles of this. In the meantime, one can do one's duty to try to do it. But. . . . if at any time you should hear that I have gone, I want you to know beforehand that my end was peace, and even joy at the release. . . .

Now I am going out again for another walk through the beautiful Piazza.

To Henry Mills Alden[1]

[January 1st, 1894?]

I have given up my broken sword to Fate, the Conqueror. . . . I am finishing up the fringes and edges of my literary work, for I feel that I shall do very little more. Of course, this feeling may change. But at present it has full possession of me; I am profoundly discouraged. . . . If I could go into a convent (where I didn't have to confess, nor rise before daylight for icy matins), I think I could write three or four novels better than any I have yet done. But there are no worldly convents. So I'll write my new effusions on another star, and send them back to you by telepathy.

Notes

1. Excerpts from missing letter or letters quoted in an obituary by Alden in *Harper's Weekly*, Feb. 3, 1894: 113. Reprinted in Rayburn S. Moore, *Constance F. Woolson* (New Haven: College and University Press, 1963): 148.

To Harper and Brothers[1]

Venice
Jan. 17th, 1894

Messrs. Harper & Brothers:

Dear sirs,—In the list which I sent you some time ago with the names of the persons to whom I wished copies of Horace Chase to be sent, I do not remember whether I included "F. E. Boot, Esq. 747 Cambridge Street, Cambridge, Mass."

If I did, no matter; if I did not, please forward the copy as above.

This letter is dictated, as I am in bed with influenza.

Truly yours,
C. F. Woolson.

Notes

1. This letter, quite possibly the last Woolson wrote, appears, with the misspelling of F. E. Boott, in J. Henry Harper, *The House of Harper* (New York: Harper and Brothers, 1912): 487. According to Rayburn S. Moore, the book version of *Horace Chase* appeared just ten days after Woolson's death on Jan. 24, 1894; see *Constance F. Woolson* (New Haven: College and University Press/Twayne, 1963): 116.

Undated Letters

It is impossible to date precisely these letters, which are often fragments that Clare Benedict pasted in volumes relating to Woolson or that she included in her three-volume *Five Generations*. They are arranged here in an order that represents letters from the United States; letters from Europe when Woolson arrived in 1879 to 1886 when she moved to Bellosguardo Hill, Florence; letters from 1887 to 1889 when she left for Greece and Egypt; letters from 1889 until her death in 1894. Letters that could be from any of these time periods are listed at the end. Within this chronology, letters are placed alphabetically by recipient.

LETTERS FROM THE UNITED STATES

To Elizabeth Gwinn Mather (Benedict/Voices, 253; Benedict/Abroad, 750)[1]

I send by Mother some specimens of autumn leaves, which I hope will retain their colours for a few weeks. They are not as gracefully arranged as I could wish, and they do not look half so lovely as they did lying on the ground in the forests, but I have at least preserved them, while their mates are withered and brown.

Everything still looks beautiful around the lake, but it has reached that stage when the cold rains are hourly anticipated. Imagine me in my little room looking out on the "Vision" all alone, and send a letter to cheer me up. It is about five months since we came here. It does not seem half that time.

Notes

1. The letter appears to have been written from Cooperstown, probably at the beginning of the three years the Woolsons stayed there after Charles Jarvis Woolson's death in 1869 and George Benedict's death in 1871.

To Katharine Livingston Mather (Benedict/Voices, 253; Benedict/Abroad, 750)[1]

Mother and I had a lovely peaceful day at the Three Mile Point last week. The County Fair was being held in the village and the inhabitants of the surrounding towns were pouring in from all directions, so we escaped, and rowed up the still Lake to the Point, which was entirely deserted, and so quiet that two wild ducks on their way South stopped and played about in the water all day. The trees are tinged a little, with here and there a bright red branch; all the trees at the Grove are coloured.

Notes

1. The letter appears to have been written from Cooperstown, either at the beginning of the three years the Woolsons stayed there after Charles Jarvis Woolson's death in 1869 and George Benedict's death in 1871 or during one of Woolson's frequent visits in the 1870s.

To Samuel Livingston Mather? Arabella Carter Washburn? (Benedict/Voices, 245; Benedict/Abroad, 743)[1]

[March 187?]

So many rich people here—Aspinwalls, Stewarts, Rhinelanders, Astors, &c.[2] I look at them with much interest . . . people who have been enormously rich for several generations, and who have had time to cultivate themselves. In every case I notice that those who are the richest are the quietest, both in dress and manner.

And after all I do'nt see but that Mother has just as good a time when she puts on her bonnet and her blue veil and goes walking peacefully on the sea wall, as her next door neighbour, Mrs De L. N., who with all her millions can do no more.

And it also seems to me that Clara and I have quite as good a time as the Misses R. Contentment has a great deal to do with it, I suppose; and as regards myself, I really think I grow more contented every day. I am twice as satisfied and contented as I was ten years ago, which is a very fortunate thing for me, isn't it? I had a birthday last week, you see, and hence these reflections. . . .

Notes

1. Benedict identifies this letter with two different recipients, Mather in *Voices* and Washburn in *Abroad*. The last paragraph is only contained in the Mather excerpt. In the nineteenth century, some writers copied the same letter to different recipients, but this does not appear to have been Woolson's habit.

2. Edith Wharton's mother was Lucretia Rhinelander Jones.

To Samuel Livingston Mather (Benedict/Voices, 247)[1]

This winter we have rooms right on the water, only the narrow roadway separating us from the old sea-wall. Mother and Clara have two bedrooms, a little parlour, and an overhanging piazza, Spanish style, the whole second story front, and I have a large room under the roof, the whole top of the house, with six dormer windows. As I sit by my table, I can see the old fort, the sea wall, the harbour, and right over Anastasia Island out to the sea; miles and miles of blue, with the surf breaking near the shore. It is even better than Mackinac. What more could be said? At night, I have the flash of the lighthouse opposite my window. The grandees are arriving and we are beginning to breathe that tiresome atmosphere of gold dust and ancestors which has oppressed us for two long winters. I always feel like a fraud when I go sailing with, say, six or eight incomes of six figures and the like. And then the ancestors. "Her mother was a so-and-so, you know," and "his grandfather was a Van something." The only thing we have to fall back upon is Fenimore Cooper, our one little anchor out in the crowded harbour. They have it now that Mother was his "only sister." We let it go so!

Notes

1. This letter would have been written in 1875 or '76, the second and third years Woolson was in St. Augustine.

To William Gwinn Mather (WRHS/Benedict)[1]

My dear Willie,

When I was about your age, Father gave me a set of Dickens'. If these books afford you half the pleasure that mine gave to me, it is all I could ask. I suppose there has been scarcely a week in all these long years when I have not taken them up; and the interest has never failed, although the old volumes are tattered and torn.

Notes

1. This typed note is pasted into Charles Dickens, *A Christmas Carol* (Boston: Osgood, 1876), a book Woolson gave to Clare Benedict and which she inscribed "To Clare from Aunt Conny Dec. 25th."

To Arabella Carter Washburn (Benedict/Voices, 273)

I am surprised and pleased to hear that any of the Zoarites had the charity to ask after me. Did you not hear how enraged they were over "Happy Valley"? I wrote to poor David and from his answer I could see how much dissatisfaction was felt at my description. I was truly sorry, not because I ever care to go there again, but because of the care-less times I have enjoyed there with you and the thousand associations with Father . . . I hope that you will continue to go down to Zoar occasionally and tell me how the valley looks. I am sincerely glad to hear that people are not angry with me.

To Arabella Carter Washburn (Benedict/Voices, 325)

I amuse myself all day long and enjoy every moment. But then I am countrified enough to be interested in what I see. . . . It is impossible in a letter for me to express how very much I enjoy New York. . . . I am so exceedingly (perhaps excessively) fond of music and good acting that I fairly revel in the superb orchestras, magnificent architecture, beautiful faces and delicious voices I find at Booth's Theatre, the Academy of Music, &c. The Philharmonics have begun, and next week the Academy of Design opens. New York is overflowing with attractions, as stars of every magnitude have come to shine in the New World; among others, four dancers so beautiful and graceful that for the first time I realise the meaning of that hackneyed phrase—"the poetry of motion." If this keen sense of enjoyment lasts all winter, I shall have a new pleasure every day . . . I am just like a prisoner let loose. I enjoy an opera as much as I did when I was here a school girl—can I say more? . . . Jefferson is playing "Rip Van Winkle," and the night we went, there was scarcely a dry eye in the house.[1] Great men fairly sobbed and in the funny parts, the same persons would shout with laughter. I am as bad as any of the rest.

Notes

1. Beginning in 1859, Joseph Jefferson (1829–1905) became famous for his dramatization of Washington Irving's "Rip Van Winkle" (1819).

To Arabella Carter Washburn (Benedict/Voices, 325)

After a little ecclesiastical sight-seeing, I presume I shall settle down on Old Trinity.[1]

Notes

1. New York City's Trinity Episcopal Church.

To Arabella Carter Washburn (Benedict/Abroad, 621)

If he looks half as wise and scornful as little Clare did when two hours old, he will frighten you.[1]

Notes

1. Woolson is referring to the birth of Washburn's child.

LETTERS FROM EUROPE, 1879–86

To Jane Averell Carter (Benedict/CFW, 32)

. . . I think the best way really to enjoy a great gallery like the one in Dresden, is to go often, but never stay more than a half-hour at a time. I think "gallery fatigue" the worst I know, for it is of both body and mind. The Dresden gallery seemed to me extremely rich and beautiful. . . .

To Miss Emily Vernon Clark (Benedict/CFW, 27–29)[1]

. . . How can you say George Eliot was unhappy? I think that she had one of the easiest, most indulged and "petted" lives that I have ever known or heard of—considering that she was a woman without a fortune (which always make the personal life easy), and without the least beauty, in fact, very plain. From first to last, she did exactly as she pleased—law or no law, custom or no custom! Lewes adored her; I heard all the details in London. She was surrounded by the most devoted, personal, worshipping affection to his last hour. True, she earned the money for two, and she worked very hard. But how many, many women would be glad to do the same through all of their lives if their reward was such a devoted love as that! Then, with a very short interregnum, this plain woman of sixty inspires with the same worshipping adoration another man, one who is spoken well of by all the world; a man of excellent mind and character, with a fortune of his own, handsome, strong, only forty years old.[2] And up to the last moment of <u>her</u> life, his love continued unchanged, all the stories to the contrary notwithstanding. I heard the undoubted facts, testimony of eyewitnesses of their life together, &c. I think you are right in saying that she "needed a staff to lean upon." My own idea is that she could not live without the adoration her nature craved. But my point is that she always had it! She got it, whether or no! And the one thing I have against her is that after getting and having to the full all she craved, then she began to pose as a teacher for others! She began to preach the virtues she had not for one moment practised in her own life. Like Rousseau's writing "Emile," after sending all his own children one by one to the "Enfants Trouvés"![3] As to what you allude to—the tone of her letters and journals—to me all that seems but the bodily weariness of such constant literary toil; and (alas!) the melancholy which seems to me to belong to all creative work in literature, or almost all. Her success as a literary artist was enormous . . . and she had the exquisite pleasure of lifting the man she loved and all his children into ease and prosperity by her own efforts. I don't think she ever felt, or was haunted by the slightest touch of remorse for what she had done; it alienated all her own family—the brother she had loved so fondly while a girl—but all this was as nothing to her compared with her love. She had that sort of nature. . . . She did work very hard; . . . All I reiterate is that throughout her toil, she had the atmosphere she craved constantly round her. Thousands of women work as hard (in other ways) and finally die (as she did) of their toil, without it.

Notes

1. George Eliot died in 1880, so this letter was written after that date.

2. Eliot lived openly with philosopher and critic George Lewes (1817–78). In 1880, she married John Cross, a banker twenty years her junior. During their honeymoon, Cross either jumped or fell into the Grand Canal, Venice; he survived but died of natural causes later that year.

3. Rousseau published *Emile* in 1762. He convinced his lover, Thérèse Levasseur, to give their children, possibly five in number, to the orphanage Enfants Trouvés.

To Mary Benedict Crowell (Benedict/CFW, 33)

I cannot help liking the English—some of them, I mean. I am quite fascinated by their sincerity. They really do tell the truth plainly, and this is a great novelty. If it lies between evading a little, or hurting your feelings, they calmly hurt your feelings. Yet I think at heart they are real friends, if friends at all.

To George Pomeroy Keese (WRHS/Benedict)[1]

Clare's "education" has now become the important point. Her mother worries over it. I don't. The child is by nature a thoughtful & industrious student in her youthful way, & very intelligent. I don't know that she has her mother's quickness; but she has all the Benedict thoroughness. Like a certain aunt of hers, too, she wants to go to the root of a thing! The myriad questions she asks remind me all the time of my own! She speaks French quite nicely, has made a good beginning at music, &

is always one of the best scholars in English at every school she attends. I think that will do.

Notes

1. Fragment pasted into Frances Hodgson Burnett, *The Little Lost Prince* (Edinburg: Andrew Eliot, nd). A portion of this letter also appears in Benedict/Abroad, 39.

To George Pomeroy Keese (Benedict/CFW, 31)

I have several theories about "foreign travelling," and one is that only excitable young people or persons absorbed in some one subject like painting, architecture, or sculpture, can really enjoy a hurried, busy tour. They may pretend to! For my part, I have seen so many tired-out American parties, worn with fatigue, pale with "sight-seeing" (which is the most killingly hard work I know) that I turn my head when I see them coming and look in another direction. Half the time they do'nt know they are so tired! Have no suspicion of it. The English take things more slowly; are never excited, and always see to it that their "dinner" is good, and plenty of time given to it! The result is that with their fine, robust physiques they never have that used-up air. For my own part, nothing shall ever make me join, even for one week, an American party of "sight-seers." They might be my dearest friends, and I should still refuse. But O! the delight of seeing Venice, Florence and Rome slowly, at your leisure and unimpeded! . . .

To George Pomeroy Keese (Benedict/CFW, 38)

I have often thought that I should like to come back and make a little home in Cooperstown. The climate is the great objection. Perhaps, if I am ever obliged to stop walking, I can come there. If I am to be shut up in the house, I could be there as well as anywhere. The great point of these southern climates to me is not the warmth indoors. No house I have ever seen in Italy or Florida, can approach the comfort of one of our northern houses in winter. But I can walk out for long hours every day, without the least irritation in my throat, when at the south, that is all there is to it.

To Unknown recipients (WRHS/Benedict)[1]

I get a quantity of praise of "Anne" continually from all sorts of sources. But perhaps there is also dis-praise, which I do not hear!

Yours,
C. F. Woolson.

Yesterday I was sitting before my fire, with the Ms. of my new novel on my lap; not doing much, and rather depressed, I think; feeling the cold, and feeling, too, just a little lonely. The servant knocked, and brought me a newspaper, the address in my sister's handwriting. I opened it rather languidly, thinking she had sent me, from Paris, the details of the election. I was interested in the election, of course—; still—. But it was not the election at all. It was a "Cleveland Herald" with a half-column of editorial announcement of "Anne," headed with what I suppose is a quotation from you in the November maga. It is all very well for the "Cleveland Herald" to say nice things about the daughter of a former citizen; but what takes my breath away is what you have said! Do you realize what a tremendous commendation you have given me! I began to tremble as I read it; and am trembling still!

Notes

1. These two fragments do not appear to be from the same letter. They are pasted into Woolson's *Anne* (New York: Harper's, 1882). The internal references to *Anne* (1882) and to an election suggest both fragments were written sometime between 1882 and 1884.

LETTERS FROM EUROPE, 1887–89

To Clara Benedict (WRHS/Benedict)[1]

If any one should come to-day, will you please say that I am not very well. I like that better than "busy."

C.

; it is a great moment when the last word has been written, & the pen drops! There is an excitement about it like nothing else; and a joy.

Notes

1. Two fragments are pasted into Woolson's *Horace Chase* (London: Osgood, McIlvaine & Co., 1894); the first is clearly identified as a note to Clara Benedict, written while Woolson lived at the Villa Brichieri, Florence, between 1887 and 1889.

To Flora Stone Mather (Benedict/CFW, 300–301)

We are a little excited at Bellosguardo just now because Prof. Willard Fiske of Cornell, is talking of buying the Villa Castellani, where Miss Greenough and the Bootts live. . . . Eugene Schuyler has been here twice, visiting Prof. Fiske. I think him very entertaining. . . .

The King does try so hard to do his duty and all his duty. This winter we are to have plenty of royalties, the King and Queen of Würtemberg have taken a villa on the other side of the valley; the Queen of Servia has a villa near Fiesole; and the poor German Crown Prince—such a handsome, stalwart man—has arrived in Venice with his family, and is to spend the winter in Italy—they say here, but I do not believe it, as Florence is so cold. . . .[1]

I expect to have a very busy twelve months, and shall not have much time for letters. All the more reason why I want to receive them! . . . There has just been an addition to my family. A nightingale—a present. He is supposed to sing "ravishingly." I shall listen hard.

Notes

1. See appendix for King Umberto I of Italy; King Charles I of Germany and his wife Queen Olga Nikolaevna; Queen Draga of Serbia; and Crown Prince Wilhelm, later Emperor Wilhelm II, of Germany. Benedict's spelling is Servia.

To Katharine Livingston Mather (Benedict/Abroad, 39)

We stopped to look at the two leaning towers there, and to see the St Cecilia by Raphael.[1] The two towers make me far more nervous than the famed Pisa one. . . . The Pisa tower you can stand at a safe distance from and gaze at in astonishment, knowing that if it should fall while you are looking at it, not a piece would strike you. But the Bologna towers are in the heart of thc town and lean in different directions, so, no matter where you stand, you feel unsafe. But they are wonders, and the St Cecilia is as lovely as I hoped she would be. It gives me a strange feeling to see at last the original of such a famous picture.

We stopped at Ferrara to see the cathedral, castle and Ariosto's house.[2] The cathedral is a little like Peterborough, although the marble-stucco façades of the Italian churches seem so sham-like.

Notes

1. Raphael's *The Ecstasy of St. Cecilia* (1514) is in the Pinacoteca Nazionale, Bologna.
2. Poet Ludovico Ariosto (1474–1533) died in Ferrara.

To Harriet Benedict Sherman (Benedict/CFW, 29)

Anthony Trollope's Autobiography, yes, I have read it.[1] It gave me such a feeling! Naturally I noticed more especially his way of working. What could he have been made of! What would I not give for the hundredth part of his robust vitality. I never can do anything by lamplight, nothing when I am tired, nothing—it almost seems sometimes—at any time! . . . And here was this great English Trollope hauled out of bed long before daylight every morning for years, writing by lamplight three hours before he began the "regular" work (post office and hunting!) of the day. Well, he was English and therefore had no nerves, fortunate man!

Notes

1. Trollope published his autobiography in 1883.

LATE LETTERS FROM EUROPE, 1890–94

To Linda Guilford (Benedict/CFW, 367)[1]

I am now going out for a long walk, I have been rowing, during the autumn, on the Avon; Shakespeare's Avon. Such a pretty little river, winding among the soft green English fields. Flora Payne and I used to row on the meandering Cayuhoga. I am afraid we cannot row there now.[2]

Notes

1. This letter was likely written in 1890 or '91 when Woolson lived in Cheltenham.
2. Woolson is referring to the increasing industrial pollution of this Ohio river, which first caught fire in 1868. The correct spelling is Cuyahoga.

To Flora Stone Mather (Benedict/CFW, 48–49)[1]

I am thinking a little of taking lessons in drawing or painting. Since music and so many other enjoyments have been taken from me, it would perhaps be wise to extend the horizon a little on a side still open.[2] I shall never be able at this late day to paint any sort of a picture; but by taking lessons (as I have a great love for colour), perhaps I can, in time, derive a larger enjoyment from galleries, from pictures of all kinds. It is a serious thing to have no great pleasures, nothing that one greatly enjoys. And, as I grow older, I am inclining towards the opinion that it is a duty to be happy, provided one is not selfish about it for melancholy, unhappy persons make everybody about them very uncomfortable. These are fine ideas. It isn't always easy to live up to them! However, I'll get a little doggie, and take lessons in water-colour. And I can always read Matthew Arnold's verses—even if he <u>does</u> write, occasionally, such terribly unmusical bits as; "As the punt's rope chops round."[3] It was in a punt, I suppose, that I used to row on the Avon last year—nearly up to Christmas.

Notes

1. This letter was written in 1891 or after when Woolson had left Cheltenham.
2. Woolson is referring to her increasing deafness.
3. The quotation is from Arnold's "The Scholar Gypsy" (1853).

To Flora Stone Mather (Benedict/CFW, 52)

Oh, yes, I always like books. I have given up trying not to accumulate them! I have a bookcase here nearly full. The truth is that they are my companions. Where other people are talking, I must read. Fortunately, I have always been intensely fond of reading, and the older I grow, the more curious I am about the modes of thought and literature of other countries. The Russians and the Spanish fascinate me, and now that I have had a glimpse of the East, I am curious about Persian and East

Indian writers. My interest will outlast me; when I am 80 (if alive) I shall probably be trying to get hold of the sacred books of the Chinese or of Thibet!

To Flora Stone Mather (Benedict/CFW, 367)[1]

Gloucester is charming. I have explored it from end to end during the year that I have passed here. Gloucester itself, being but fifteen minutes distant by train, is a great resource. I could almost draw the cathedral from memory, inch by inch. The New Inn is charmingly quaint. . . . I can reach the Severn and Avon at Tewkesbury very near here. There is a delightful old Abbey there. I am always prowling about, and then concluding the afternoon by a cup of tea at some old-fashioned country inn. I am sometimes very homesick for Italy—under these grey skies. But generally, I am so busy that I do not think of it.

Notes

1. This letter was written in 1890 or '91 when Woolson was in Cheltenham.

To Flora Stone Mather (Benedict/CFW, 50–51)

Mrs Sutherland Orr's "Life of Browning" is thought rather disappointing here.[1] Mrs Orr was one of his intimate friends (I mean women-friends). . . . Browning's life was largely dependent upon many of such friendships. I mean that it was so after his wife's death. Very masculine himself, he yet enjoyed the society of ladies more than that of men. He said that women were more appreciative than men, and less vain! . . . I heard much about the Brownings when I lived in Florence; many items, anecdotes, and stories are still to be picked up there from the mouths of people who saw them daily. Browning died famous; but there were long years of his life when he was utterly neglected by the public, and even regarded with contempt. Fortunately for him, his own belief in himself was robust and never faltered. In addition, he had the advantage of an inherited income large enough to live upon, so that he had no care. I think all Lives written while contemporaries are living, must necessarily be disappointing; there must always be more or less reticence or timidity on account of the feelings of others . . .

There is much talk in London about "Plain Tales from the Hills," and "Soldiers Three," by a young fellow named Rudyard Kipling. . . . They are original and strong. . . . They do not, in my opinion, equal Bret Harte's early tales. My love to the Hays. I wish much to write to the Colonel to tell him how magnificent I think his Lincoln. . . . I have both enjoyed and greatly admired every word of it.[2]

Notes

1. Mrs. Sutherland Orr published *The Life and Letters of Robert Browning* in 1891.

2. Kipling's collections *Plain Tales from the Hills* and *Soldier's Three* were both published in 1888; John Hay and John Nicolay's *Abraham Lincoln: A History* was published in book form in 1890.

To Flora Stone Mather (Benedict/CFW, 35)

I took the winter, the odd moments of it—for letter-writing, and wrote to almost all my old friends, whom in some cases, for years, I had neglected. . . . The answers are beginning to come, and, as a general thing, they make me sad. It is so evident that they were more or less of an effort. Of course, I can expect nothing else, as I have been away over ten years. To most people that seems half a lifetime! But, as I never change myself, it does not seem so to me.

To Katharine Livingston Mather (Benedict/CFW, 33)[1]

Boston people—I mean those that belong to the old families there—are like nobody but themselves. I have had to learn their ways slowly, inch by inch, just as I have the ways of the English. They are quite as unlike other Americans as the English are unlike all Americans. I have been surrounded by Boston people ever since I came to Italy, and after burning my fingers a good many times, I have at last succeeded, I think, in comprehending them. They are cold, cold, cold, but only in manner, and on the outside. They are stiff. They never gush, and hate gush. They have an inborn belief that Boston "ways" are by far the best in the world, and <u>secretly</u> they think all other ways vulgar. Having accustomed myself to their immense serenity about themselves and their views, I now know how to take them. And I can see, too, their really good points which are many. . . .

Notes

1. This could possibly be written as part of the July 2, 1893, letter to Kate Mather where Woolson mentions Boston.

To Unknown recipient (Rollins)[1]

Here in Oxford I have been comfortable, because I happen to have such a nice landlady. She was a schoolmistress, & she is not only very devoted & kind, but really nice & refined. As her husband is the steward of Exeter College, I can occasionally get dishes from the college cook, as well as a waiter.

of the [excision] the splendid piano [excision] ~~an~~other floors above it. Then, underneath half of their part, is the apartment of Countess Pisani, one of the ladies-in-waiting of the Queen of Italy.—Countess P. has about three quarters of this lower floor. The [excision] is the

Notes

1. Two fragments pasted into Alden, Edward C. *Alden's Oxford Guide* (Oxford, Alden & Co., nd). The first fragment was written during Woolson's stay in Oxford between 1891 and 1893; the second, when she arrived in Venice in 1893.

UNDATEABLE LETTERS, WRITTEN PRIMARILY FROM EUROPE

To Henry Mills Alden (WRHS/Benedict)[1]

you will certainly come when I have at last realized my dream of a cottage in Florida. I had a letter, yesterday, from the kind friend who has begun the place for me.[2] Tired of waiting for my consent, he has begun without it. He has bought six acres, south of St Augustine on the sea, & his men are now clearing four acres of it for an orange-grove. The rest—with its great live-oaks & palmettoes—is to be left for "the cottage." So you see the oranges will be growing! I pay nothing now. If I am ever able to buy it, I am to have it at base cost price, no matter how much the value may have risen meanwhile. This prospect pleases me warmly. And gives an additional zest to my temporary residence here.

In Florida I too can have "a garden,"& "strawberry beds." I adore a garden, & have never outgrown the excitement of finding dear little "new potatoes" in the warm brown earth.

Notes

1. The fragment is identified as coming from a letter to Henry Mills Alden and is pasted in Woolson's *Rodman the Keeper: Southern Sketches* (New York: Appleton, 1880).

2. A handwritten note identifies the friend as probably Mr W. H. Nell of New York, "a great comrade of Miss Woolson's when she was in St Augustine."

To Jane Averell Carter (Benedict/CFW, 36)

I sometimes think that if Clara would give up and go to bed once in a while, it would be better for her, but she always keeps up, and always tries to be bright and cheerful, and so people have got into the habit of expecting her to be always so.

To Elizabeth Gwinn Mather (Benedict/CFW, 19)

It is entirely a new experience for me to go among entire strangers in a strange city for so long a time. Fortunately, I do'nt know what it is to be lonely.

To Flora Stone Mather (Benedict/CFW, 46–47)

The Thetis and Bear—do I remember them?[1] I should think I did. I was in London during the fitting out of whichever one it was that was sent by the English

Government for that Arctic search. The whole responsibility of properly preparing the vessel for Arctic seas rested with Commander Caspar Goodrich, U.S.N. . . . He used to come in (at my lodgings) in the evening, perfectly worn out with his toil . . .

Notes

1. The ships *Thetis* and *Bear* explored the Arctic in 1882–83; however, they became locked in ice and the crew attempted an overland retreat. When they were eventually rescued, eighteen men had died.

To Flora Stone Mather (Benedict/CFW, 36)

I have the firmest belief in simple and complete rest. It is better than medicine; better than anything. I am convinced of it.

To Flora Stone Mather (Benedict/CFW, 45)

Robert Louis Stevenson plays with tin soldiers, and makes great forts of sand and clay to this day! The funniest part of it is that he has no children; he plays these soldier games with his wife!

To Flora Stone Mather (Benedict/CFW, 45)

Frank Crawford, you know, has selected Sorrento as his home; lately I have heard that his health has given way from over-work. I don't know whether this is true, but I should not be surprised if it were, as his literary production has been enormous.

To Flora Stone Mather (Benedict/CFW, 49)

Girls do so need a more thorough education! I never hear, or, rather, I seldom hear, one of my own sex talk long without noticing the lack of broad, reasonable, solid views. . . . But I am sure that education is all that is required. I do not think the feminine mind inferior. . . .

To Flora Stone Mather (Benedict/CFW, 53–54)

If you had lived alone as I have done for so many years, you would appreciate better, no doubt, the exquisite pleasure it is to feel that one <u>is</u> welcome. One gets to doubt it a little, as one grows older, when there are not the defences and bulwarks of one's own family to fall back upon.

To Flora Stone Mather (Benedict/CFW, 39)

You got to the Berkshire hills . . . did you see Fanny Kemble's grave! I am told people ask for it every summer, but the majestic old lady is as well as ever, and able to entertain all the clever men in London, night after night.[1]

Notes

1. Actress Fanny Kemble did not die until 1893.

To Katharine Livingston Mather (Benedict/Voices, 120; Benedict/Abroad, 671)

. . . I will not close my letter, dear Kate, without referring to the desire I have to arrange and publish—probably added to one of my own books—a few of the pages included in the MS. volume of her "recollections" that Mother bequeathed to you.[1] I have always thought that those of them that are not of a private nature, ought to be published; they are so very charming; they have a simplicity and reality of style that is very remarkable, and that my best efforts can never approach. And besides, the descriptions of country life in New Hampshire at that day, are very interesting. Of all the numerous "Recollections" and "Letters" I have read in the past ten years, I have found none more charmingly written than Mother's. And that this is not simply my love for her memory, is proved by the fact that all the Cottage Coopers fully agree with me. And they are excellent judges.

Notes

1. Benedict's *Voices Out of the Past* contains many of Hannah Woolson's "Recollections."

To Harriet Benedict Sherman (Benedict/CFW, 29–30)[1]

I value so much the picture of your father which came to me at Christmas. It took me back so pleasantly—even if sadly too—to the days when he used to come down to St Clair Street. I was beginning to write a little and his encouragement and interest were everything to me. I don't believe I should have gone on if I had not had them behind me just at that time. He was always very kind to me, and in just the way I needed. I was so despondent, and the future looked so dark, yet I wouldn't betray how I felt. They were hard years for me, and your father was my mainstay.

Notes

1. This letter could possibly have been written in the United States. Sherman's father was George Benedict, Woolson's sister Clara's father-in-law and editor of the Cleveland *Herald*. St. Clair Street is in Cleveland.

To Arabella Carter Washburn (Benedict/Voices, 244; Benedict/Abroad, 743)

This is a fearful scrawl. But I cannot write letters any more. I can hardly spell, and my sentences come out all wrong. The truth is, I work so hard over my magazine work that when I do stop, I lose the use of my hands. I have just sent off fifty pages of manuscript, and took a holiday especially to write to you.

. . . . Don't fancy I am sad all the time. Oh no. I am much too busy and too full of plans of all kinds. But at times, in spite of all I can do, this deadly enemy of mine creeps in, and once in, he is master. I think it is constitutional, and I know it is inherited.

To Unknown recipient (WRHS/Benedict)[1]

I have seldom if ever heard of anyone who was able to combine the virtues of charity & non-interference! Many people give to those poorer than themselves, & give freely & generously. Sometimes they start themselves to be able to do this. But very seldom do they, or can they, keep themselves from criticizing or disapproving of the way in which their bounty is spent, provided it is not exactly the way they would have selected themselves. Whether consciously or unconsciously they cannot refrain from disapproving. The utmost they can accomplish is to do this silently. Often it is not silently. They appear to think that the possession of tastes that differ from their own is a crime. And to believe that if any one borrows money, he must at this same instant have no tastes of his own; he must buy them, or destroy them; it is his duty to change his entire nature if he borrows. To find the person who can give, & at the same time refrain from all criticism upon the way in which his gift is spent, ~~is~~ would be tremendously difficult! The moral of all this of course is; never borrow! Live on a crust if necessary. Then you are a free man, & your tastes are your own affair.

I go down so far myself in the depths, when anything happens in my family—I become so ill with grief—that when a friend is stricken in the same way, I can only add my tears to his. And that is useless. [I]t seems to me one of those (many) incomprehensible sorrows before which we must bow; but which remain a mystery.

How anyone can doubt the existence of another life as a solution to the riddles & sufferings of this—how anyone can doubt that & live—be willing to live on day after day—I cannot understand.

Notes

1. Two fragments pasted in Benedict, Clare, *Constance Fenimore Woolson* (London, nd.). This volume also contains some notebook entries in Woolson's hand and a copy of a New Hampshire military commission for Thomas Woolson, dated Sept. 12, 1803.

To Unknown recipient (WRHS/Benedict)[1]

Tell the Royalty lovers at the College that the Queen bowed to our little Clare, not long ago! The child had run forward, and hurried up a flight of steps to get a good view, when the scarlet liveries came in sight. I suppose her Majesty was amused by the eager smiling face. Clare colored a deep crimson when the Queen bowed; and primly and shyly nodded her little velvet bonnet and golden curls.

Notes

1. Fragment pasted into Clare Benedict, *European Backgrounds* (Edinburg: Andrew Elliot, 1912).

To Unknown recipient (WRHS/Benedict)[1]

Dear Miss Guilford—She was never like anybody but herself. I owe much to her. She used to take the greatest pains with me out of school hours, as well as in; I mean when I was at the Seminary.

Notes

1. Pasted into Woolson's *Two Women* (New York: Appleton, 1890). This letter appears to be about, not to, Linda Guilford, who did not die until 1911.

To Unknown recipient (WRHS/Benedict)[1]

I shall never be able, however, to change my tendency to make a definite picture (whether of persons or scenes), when I am writing. I see life in that way. I shall never be "vague," simply because I am neither vague myself, nor do other people appear vague to me. Nor do lives appear "vague." But tremendously (& alas! oftenest disappointingly) vivid.

About reviews in general, I have grown rather indifferent. Because I have gradually learned, year by year, that very few of them are sincere; the majority are founded upon some other motive than the one which appears upon the surface.

Notes

1. These unidentified fragments appear to be from the same letter and are pasted into Woolson's *For the Major* (London: Sampson Low, 1883).

To Unknown recipient (WRHS/Benedict)[1]

to give a description of the interpretation of two or three women upon a picture. Then the mind of the parasites who created it,—painted it. He had not a single one of their ideas, & would have loathed them.

I sometimes throw up my arms with a weary movement, & wish I had a lighter load of care! But I suspect that is what our life is intended to be,—a discipline.

With much love yours, lamely,
C.F.W.

Notes

1. These two fragments were pasted into Woolson's *The Front Yard and Other Italian Stories* (New York: Harper's, 1895). The first, on lined white paper, is a notebook entry that Benedict transcribed in CFW, 146. The second appears in CFW, 53.

To Unknown recipient (Benedict/CFW, 53)

There is a new theory, "working hypothesis" they call it, which seems to explain many mysteries. It is that we have two minds, one which we feel, another which only makes itself known at moments. I am shy about talking on such subjects to people who are not interested or who are not intelligent for they confound the purely scientific with the "spiritualistic" beliefs. My only interest in these researches is a scientific one, and I think we are on the eve of great discoveries.

To Unknown recipient (Benedict/CFW, 53)

I have been thinking so much of you—since I heard the sad tidings. . . . What should we do if this life were all we had—so almost constantly full, as it is, of pain and sorrow. . . . I loved my own father so dearly that I know how you will feel—are feeling now. . . . Do not grieve. All is in some way for the best, ordered by One wiser than we can ever be. . . .

To Unknown recipient (Benedict/CFW, 54)

How any one can doubt our immortality, I am at a loss to conceive. A future existence seems to me the only solution to the riddle of the present one—this present one with its bitter disappointments, its heavy cares, its apparent injustice to so many. . . . Yes, we shall live again—and go on living, and then, if we have been faithful here, we shall be happier . . .

To Unknown recipient[1]

not be able to send you anything at present. But I see, by the brilliant list of contributors you have recently published, that you have probably, all you can use. You have certainly the best names.

With good wishes, and thanks for your remembrance, I am,

Yours very truly,
C. F. Woolson.

Notes

1. Only this fragment of a letter survives from an unknown archive.

Addendum of Letters

For the sake of her own and her correspondents' privacy, Woolson apparently burned numerous letters she received from other people. Many scholars also believe that Henry James burned letters written to her when he helped clean out her apartment at the Casa Semitecolo after her death. The few letters to survive and surface are reprinted below and provide a rare glimpse into the other side of her correspondence.

Touching upon Woolson's final days and also included here is the January 31, 1894, letter of Marie Holas to Samuel Mather, which describes Woolson's death. Finally, of particular interest to scholars, Woolsen's March 2, 1882, letter to Katharine Livingston Mather illustrates the changes to Woolsen's original letter that Clare Benedict made when she typed the transcription and published the letter in CFW.

From Mrs. George Pomeroy[1]

Cooperstown

When your Mother was here, she told me you wished much to obtain some relic in the shape of an autograph of her Uncle Fenimore. In looking over some family letters, I found one which I think may meet your wishes as it has the advantage of containing on one side a short letter also from your cousin, author of "Rural Hours."[2] Of course, your Uncle Fenimore's letter contains allusions to family matters, as all his letters to me naturally do; but I think the one now sent can create no disturbance, for one of the parties is gone, the other probably will not long survive, and the matter commented upon between Messrs. B___ and P___ will not be understood by any but those immediately interested. I rely upon your prudence, Constance.

I think Uncle Fenimore's letter will interest your Mother from what he says of your Sister Georgiana, it was in an answer to a remark of mine that she was not as handsome as her sister Emma.

Notes

1. Benedict/Voices, 44. Mrs. Pomeroy was Woolson's maternal grandmother.
2. Susan Fenimore Cooper published the first of nine editions of *Rural Hours* in 1850.

From Clara Urquhart Potter (WRHS/Mather)

Tuxedo Club
Tuxedo Park
Oct. 15th

Dear Madam.

May I include your "Kentucky Belle" in a collection which I am thinking of publishing?[1] I recited "Kentucky Belle" last summer on the Royal yacht "Osborne" for the Empress Eugenie, at the especial request of the Prince & Princess of Wales, who admire the piece more than anything I had the honor of reciting for them.[2] By allowing me to include it in my collection, you will confer a great favor, upon your sincere admirer,

Cora Urquhart Potter.

Notes

1. Potter included "Kentucky Belle" (1873) in her book *My Recitations* (1887).

2. The French Empress Eugenie (1826–1920) was the wife of Napoleon III (1808–73). The Prince and Princess of Wales were Queen Victoria's son, later Edward VII, and Alexandra of Denmark.

From Harper & Brothers[1]

February 1882

Dear Miss Woolson,—

Anne amply confirms Mr. Alden's good opinion of it. In its serial form it has been so satisfactory to us that it becomes our grateful duty to express in some substantial way our appreciation of the story by increasing the amount originally paid for it. In pursuance of this purpose we enclose herewith:

I. An additional one thousand dollars (by draft on our London agent for £204–18–5) and

II. An agreement to pay you royalty on the sales of the story in book form. If this agreement meets your approval, please to sign and return it, and we will send you duplicate with our signature.

We heartily congratulate you on the success of the story, so well deserved, as shown by the cordial reception of it by the press during its appearance in our Magazine. And better than the praise of the press is the appreciative sympathy of thoroughly interested readers in all parts of the country. We hope that we may continue to be the honored means of your communication with these readers, and that your appearance before them may be frequent.

Notes

1. This letter is printed in J. Henry Harper, *The House of Harper: A Century of Publishing in Franklin Square* (New York: Harper and Brothers, 1912): 484.

From Edmund Clarence Stedman[1]

November 1882

You know of my trouble, flight from beautiful Venice to arid, sordid, fiery New York in midsummer. A sudden and perilous misfortune brought me home. Instead of finishing my book abroad,—of seeing Italy and Spain,—of seeing you with your green new wreaths of laurel,—I have passed a half-year of really desperate gambling, here, and have but just retrieved the disaster that brought us home. A half-year almost wasted, and gone out of one's brief life. A should say quite wasted, had I not managed to write my essay on Emerson; no light matter! 'Twas finished last month, but will not come out before the March *Century*.

Notes

1. The letter is printed in Laura Stedman and George M. Gould, M.D., eds., *Life and Letters of Edmund Clarence Stedman*, 2 vols. (New York: Moffat, Yard and Co., 1910): 1:576–77. Stedman's "misfortune" involved serious business and financial problems.

From Edmund Clarence Stedman[1]

November 12th, 1882

Of course I read "Anne" seriatim—you never write a line that I do not read at once. You could not have felt more concerned than myself in its quality, in its reception. All in all, I considered it a beautiful work—an epochal stage in your career as a creative writer. And I will say at once that I agree with those critics who think the original, faultless, creative manner and standard of the first half of the novel in certain respects superior to the remainder. It seemed as if you threw a sop to Cerberus, or adopted a mistaken form of continuance, in relying somewhat upon realistic plot and counterplot for the disposition of your characters.[2] Your true self, your highest and most creative standard, are found in the early portraitures; in the ideal and growth of your large-moulded heroine. But as a first novel, "Anne" is a noble effort, confirming me in my early belief that you can and will produce masterpieces, and become our foremost writer of imaginative prose. And you were amazingly fortunate in the backing given you by your powerful publishers.

* * *

I have just got the *Harper's* containing the opening of your new novel—which I expect to like better than I like its rather inconsequential title.[3] You are now *sure* of your audience; take your time, do *not* overwork, do not strain your eyes, do not be afraid to lie "fallow" for long periods—meditating great rather than *many* novels. You have only yourself to maintain, and have not ______'s excuse for bringing out a new book every half-year. Your imagination is more *creative* than Howells's or James's—follow your own vent, give us life and passion and color, and do not, like them, overdo your "analysis" and "subtilties." Their novels are clever, dexterous; let yours be free, imaginative, dramatic, human, and not without poetic elevation.

Notes

1. The letter is printed in Laura Stedman and George M. Gould, M.D., eds., *Life and Letters of Edmund Clarence Stedman*, 2 vols. (New York: Moffat, Yard and Co., 1910): 2:347–48.
2. The reference to Cerberus, a multi-headed dog who guards the gates of Hades, is used to criticize the complicated detective-style plot at the end of *Anne* (1882).
3. Because this paragraph is an excerpt, it is impossible to know which novel Stedman is referring to.

From Edmund Clarence Stedman[1]

September 2, 1889

I must write this letter before "the Tuscan vines and olives" surrender you to the haunts of the Edelweiss. In truth, I have been hesitating whether to write briefly, and at once, or to wait until my eyes permit me to say all that I should think might interest you. . . . One can dictate business letters, but when Constance Woolson receives a typewritten letter from me—I say with Sir John Manners—May the Lord forget me! (Sheridan, I think, said "Never—He'll see you d___d first!")[2] These presents are, then, to thank you warmly for your letter of August 10th, and with specific warmth for the two photographs, which have come in perfect condition. Like you, I prefer for our use the profile view, though 'tis a pity 'tis slightly blurred in photographic *re*production from the (N.H.) original.[3] Our best engraver, who already has it in hand, tells me that he can make the outline a little clearer, and I hope to send you some "proofs before letter" of a satisfactory picture. Now we were congratulating ourselves that we should issue a fresh picture of you—having chosen the one unused by *Harper's*—when comes a request to my son Arthur, from *Scribner's*, to write a brief biography or sketch of C.F.W.—to accompany a portrait of you in the October *Book-Buyer*, from the "profile portrait"! So, being forestalled, I can only avenge myself by getting up a nicer portrait than theirs. Well, my chagrin will not creep into Arthur's sketch you may be sure, and it is tempered by the fact that the rivalry all increases the fame of my most honored woman-friend.

Now, as to your verbal "representation" in our portentous but (I trust) enduring "Library." Mistress E. Hutchinson and I *each* have the veto-power as editors.

That is the way we get along. Of course I defer greatly to her taste in the matter of her fellow-crafts*women*. We long since agreed to represent tale-makers, when practicable, by complete "short stories," in preference to taking chapters or episodes from their *novels*. Of course your greatest work is in your novels. But when we find a perfect and dramatic short-story, which is so rare, we both rejoice and jump for it. The *best* short-stories, since Hawthorne, with American themes and atmosphere, are yours and Bret Harte's. I *hope* you have not lived long enough yet to undervalue your "Peter the Parson" or "The Lady of Little Fishing." I have lately reread them both, and think more highly of them than ever.

But to change the topic. Never tell me again that you are a "realist." That word, and "romancer," are merely terms. I wish you could see my Preface to the (revived) issue of Mrs. Stoddard's novels. I will enclose, as least, a copy of one portion of it, show you *my* briefly stated view of the realism-romanticism conflict. It amounts to nothing except that all "school" conflicts are *stimulating*—as was that of Hugo's romanticism with the classicists, when *Hernani* was produced.[4] You are what God made you—a woman of taste, industry, insight, *plus* genius; and *your* so-called realistic method is charged no less with passion and imagination. 'Tis a poor workman who can't use any tool. Forgive this digressional preachment. I think you must have returned to the graye goose quille of the romance-period, by the change in your handwriting. It has become veritably Byronic in its vigorous abandon, and I scarcely recognized it at first.

So there is one full-brained person left who *believes* with her "whole heart" in another life? Of late I have not met another. All mankind and womankind have lost their Faith, and like Young Goodman Brown, our end is gloom—and our life *Omar-Khayyamicism*. A quotation in Mallock's "New Republic" states the case exactly: "They have taken away our Lord, and I know not where they have laid him." Poetry? I write perchance one poem a year—when I absolutely can't help it: that's all. You like "The Star-Bearer"? 'Tis my one stained-glass poem. "Peter the Parson," you know. But didn't you see the crowning honor and pleasure of my magazine-life; to have my ballad of Morgan, superbly illustrated by Pyle, *next* to *your* story in last December's *Harper's*? At last, for one month, *we* were mated! And 'twas a live ballad, too; and Tom Aldrich said there *was* one excuse for Alden's putting it in a Christmas issue,—it had the word "Jesu" in it. I wrote recently a poem to go with Fortuny's "Spanish Lady" in the *Century*. Perhaps I'll send it to you this Fall.[5] Otherwise, not a line for *myself* in a year past: but letters, letters, and reading second-rate American "literature" have made me weary, poor, and gray. This year, I am earning a scanty living down-town and going like a slave *every* afternoon to the "Library" office—you see we are rushing the work through the press, under contract. My "leisure moments." Why it has taken *all* my time for some years, bad cess to it! . . .

My wife loves you, and we often speak of you. *Can* it be ten years! Well, you have had an ideal life, and I am content to know it. Laura has stayed in this hot town all summer to take care of Arthur and me. 'Tis our last year of thraldom. "Kelp Rock" is rented to strangers.[6] We are alone in New York—not a friend left in town. If I live through, and don't lose my vital powers, as I have lost my money and eye-sight, I shall try to enter upon a philosophic afternoon of life.

Notes

1. The letter is printed in Laura Stedman and George M. Gould, M.D., eds., *Life and Letters of Edmund Clarence Stedman*, 2 vols. (New York: Moffat, Yard and Co., 1910): 2:139–41. Portions of the letter also appear in Benedict/CFW, 555.

2. The reference is to Irish playwright Richard Sheridan (1751–1816) and, probably, to British soldier and politician Sir John Manners (1721–70).

3. Stedman is referring to a photograph he was seeking for his eleven-volume *Library of American Literature* (1888–90). A photo of Woolson appeared in the March 1886 issue of *Harper's New Monthly Magazine*, and a new one appeared as the cover of the February 3, 1894, issue of *Harper's Bazar*. Woolson's story "The Lady of Little Fishing" (1874) appeared in Volume X of Stedman's *Library*.

4. Victor Hugo's (1802–85) play *Hernani* opened in 1830.

5. Stedman refers to the following: Hawthorne's "Young Goodman Brown" (1835); Persian poems translated by Edward Fitzgerald (1809–83) as *The Rubaiyat of Omar Khayyam* (1859); William Mallock's (1849–1923) novel *The New Republic* (1877); Stedman's own book-length poem *The Star Bearer* (1888), illustrated by Howard Pyle (1853–1911); and Mariano Fortuny's (1838–74) painting *A Spanish Lady* (1865). The Woolson story referenced in the Dec. 1888 *Harper's New Monthly Magazine* is "The Front Yard."

6. Stedman's summer home in New Castle, New Hampshire.

From Harper and Brothers[1]

July 27, 1892

Dear Miss Woolson,—

I showed Mr. J. Henry Harper your sketch of the new novel, and he agrees with me in thinking it captivating. The husband's attitude to the wife in the final situation does not seem at all impossible, though not so commonplace as to lack nobility. It is probably more just than noble. Mr. Harper suggests as title "For Better, for Worse." How do you like it? It seems to be better than "Horace Chase" or "A Husband" or "Chase, Willoughby & Co." It has also a deep meaning from association with the marriage service of the church.

I will try to give you a large space for your first instalment, but it may be impossible, as Dr. Conan Doyle's will run at the same time, and each part of it will make from 25 to 30 pages.[2]

Yes, I read *A Village Tragedy*. It is a strong story, but over-sad, without relief.

Sadness has its place in art. If it is quick, as in the Niobe group, the tragedy needs no justification.[3] The tragedian may sweep the stage through the sharpness of Death before the curtain falls. Death unties all knots, and *is* a release. But the slow gathering of mephitic vapors about an imprisoned soul—*that* is different and leaves no way out, unless a great light appears, and we are made sure that, after all, there is Hope. This unrelieved pessimism has the same effect upon the reader as is produced by materialism—imprisonment with no escape.

Notes

1. This letter is printed in J. Henry Harper, *The House of Harper: A Century of Publishing in Franklin Square* (New York: Harper and Brothers, 1912): 485–86.

2. Arthur Conan Doyle's *The Refugees* ran in *Harper's New Monthly Magazine* from Feb. to June 1893; Woolson's *Horace Chase* (1894) ran from Jan. to Aug. 1893.

3. See letter to Richard Watson Gilder, March 11, 1893, for Woolson's request that he consider publishing Margaret Woods's *A Village Tragedy* (1888) in *Century*. In 1875, Thomas Davidson published *A Short Account of the Niobe Group*. Many classical stories and sculptures draw on the myth of Niobe, whose pride Apollo punished with the death of all her children.

From Marie Holas to Samuel Mather[1]

Venice. Jany 31st, 1894

Dear Mr Mather.

Miss Carter asked me to write & let you know all that has happened in the last days of the life of Miss Woolson. I had been introduced to her by her friend Miss Bronson, on the 15th of Jan. Miss Woolson was then in bed with influenza, but as on that same day, I wrote under her dictation to Mrs Benedict, the doctor said it was a mild case, & having spoken myself with him, he told me it was indeed a very mild one. Miss Woolson had no fever at all, & had only a little bronchial catarrh. Miss W. had been unwell since the beginning of the year, & had gone out in the 13th although the Dr had said she had better not, the weather being then very cold. She walked in the Public Gardens on the snow, & that was the cause. She was obliged to stay in bed again. She was quite alone & felt lonely, troubled by the cares of housekeeping & for that reason I was introduced to her, to relieve her from every care that might have troubled her in her present state of health. On the 15th, 16th, & 17th she was in very good spirits, spoke to me, dictated many letters, & said she was much better than she looked. Now & then, she moaned & when I looked at her, thinking she felt bad, she smiled & said it was her habit of doing so—I was not to be frightened; that all her life she could not bear the slightest physical pain & as it did her good to moan or scream, why she felt a comfort in doing so—and the same she said to the doctor. During those three days, she ate a little more, without the feeling of nausea she had had before. I ordered her meals, & on the 17th at breakfast she told me that for the first time, for many days, she was looking in the dish, to see whether there was something more for her to eat. She spoke of death as one who does not fear it, & said one must be prepared for it. She wished to make her will, & told the Dr he must let her know when he thought she was growing worse & let her not die without one.[2] She told the same to me, adding that for the first time in 20 years she was without a will, & wanted to make one as soon as possible. That she considered very wrong what people often did, to leave such an important matter to the last, & sometimes were too late. She mentioned even her dog, for which she wanted to provide. She told me also, that in case of her death I must not let her to be buried in the cemetery of Venice, as she hated the place, & the only place where she could rest in peace was the cemetery in Rome—She threatened me in case I did not tell her relatives what her wishes were to let me have no peace after her death. It was useless, she said to cable to her relatives in case she were worse as it would give them only pain, as they could not come at once; but if she was to die, then I should have to cable to you & to Mrs Benedict, to let you know, so that you might take your time & come here. As she had the house till the 10th of May, she wished everything to be kept as it was, the house closed & put under seals until you or Mrs Benedict came to look after her things & dispose of them, according to her will.

But, of course all these things were said half joking, & when I asked her why she spoke thus, she answered 'We Americans are fond of joking & we do so, even on our death bed—' So I joined her in the joke, & asked her not to frighten me too much after death, & promised to do all she wished for—

When I left her on the 17th at night, she was in very good spirits, & told me, when I went to her on the following morning, she would be up, & waiting for me in her drawing-room. On the 18th instead of seeing her up, as I expected[3] I found she had great pains in her bowels & said she had suffered dreadfully in the night, & had taken laudanum to quiet the pains. I sent for the Dr who ordered morphia, with something else, & that soothed the pains. I left her in the evening later than usual. She was much better, sat in her bed, & read her letters & newspapers—When I went to her the next morning she had been worse in the night had vomited very much & in showing the Dr the vomit, he wondered & said it was a bilious attack. He asked her if she had had anything that had troubled her more than usual. She answered there was not a person under the sun that had more cares & troubles than herself for many years. She added, that every time she had finished writing a book, she felt for months afterwards a great nervous prostration. And that now, she was suffering from it, having finished her last novel Horace Chase—at the end of October, & that consequently, it required some time before she could be herself again. That same day she had fever—39.3—She gave me all her keys (she had given me all the money she had at home the second day I was with her) & said 'Do as you like, but please don't trouble me about anything.' She vomited still but the pains were almost gone & had no more fever. Although there was nothing alarming in her illness, the Dr said it was better a nurse should be called for the nights—Miss W. did not like it at first, therefore her maid was settled for one night in her dressing-room. That was on the 20th. But on the 21st a trained nurse was called. I gave her the instructions I got from the Dr & in the morning, took her place for the day—Since the 20th Miss W. spoke but little even to me, & when I was taking her trumpet to tell her something, she said she would rather not listen. Miss Carter had written she wished to come here, & when I asked her why she would not let her come, she said it was useless. But on the 22nd in the evening she told me to wire her to come—& in the meantime she gave me yours & Mrs Benedict's addresses She told me to call the American Consul when she would tell me, to make her will—that there was a model in a box where she kept some papers, I should have to look for it—(This paper was found after death, but has no importance) On the morning of the 23rd she was much better, took some milk & did not vomit at all. But she was very weak. She asked the Dr to give her something strong to make her sleep & said 'If I sleep today, I shall be quite well tomorrow, but if I don't sleep, I shall be dead—' According to her wishes, the Dr gave her laudanum. Then she told me that if any telegram was coming, I was to open it, answer if necessary, but trouble her not with it. At 1 o'c she asked me to send to the Dr & ask him to allow her to take some more laudanum. I got his answer & gave it to her. When I received Miss Carters telegram I waited for a moment, when she wanted to speak to me, & told her—'Good news, Miss Carter is coming.' 'Well, well,' she said no more—In the evening when the Dr came, she asked him for some more laudanum, & begged him besides to make her an injection of morphia, which he decidedly refused to do, for he said, she was so weak, she could not bear it, & never awake again. She would die in her sleep, & he would be responsible for her death. Then she asked me to change her position in the bed, to turn her & put her head on the other side, & so I did, with the help of the servants—I arranged her blankets, her pillows & cushions; she wished the door, windows, shutters, & curtains very well closed so that the slightest ray of light could not pass through—Then as I took the trumpet to speak to her she said 'I am so comfortable please let me alone.' I went out, after having prepared everything that might have been necessary for the night so that the nurse could have all at hand, & had not to leave the patient for one moment. I went away at 9 o'c having left Miss W. as quiet as possible. At 1 o'c in the night, her gondoliers came to fetch me, saying, she had jumped out of the window—Horror-struck, taking hardly time to dress, I ran to her house—but when I arrived, she had just died. The Dr told me she had lived three quarters of an hour unconscious, moaning slightly when they touched her. He said, she had died from internal commotion of the brains & bowels, & had lost all sensibility almost immediately in the fall. I asked the nurse, how it was she had left her, she said, Miss W. had been very quiet, & called her at a quarter past 12, wanting to know the time. Then asked for some milk, but refused to drink it in the cup she handed to her, & sent her to the dining room to take another of pink china. She wanted that one & no other. The nurse went, & when she came back, she found the window opened, & the bed empty. This is the sad relation of the last days of Miss W's life—Nothing gave ever to suppose that she had such a sad purpose in her mind, nor can I think she had it, as she sent for Miss Carter, & was going to make her will, that same day. Many people speak of death when ill, & Miss W's illness was not such as to give any kind of anxiety. Had I had the slightest idea of what happened, on my own accord, I should have cabled to you, & wired much sooner to Miss Carter—I told Miss Carter every wish of Miss Woolson's & now her remains are at rest, in the cemetery in Rome. I am at your & Mrs Benedict's orders for all that is in my power to do. If there is any other information you wish to ask from me, I shall do my best to satisfy you. I shall always be too glad to be of any use to you. Believe me

Yours truly
Marie Holas

Notes

1. I am grateful to Molly and Connie Anderson, who shared their handwritten copy of this letter with me. The letter is also reprinted in Lyndall Gordon, *A Private Life of Henry James* New York: Norton, 1998: 267–70. Edith Bronson secured Holas to help Woolson during her illness.

2. No will was found, nor is there any indication of why Woolson did not have an earlier will with her in Venice.

3. Gordon inserts a comma here in brackets, changing the meaning to what Holas probably intended. Throughout, I have reproduced Holas's punctuation and lack of punctuation.

From Woolson to Katharine Livingston Mather (WRHS/Mather)[1]

Hotel Bristol
Sorrento. Italy
March 2[d], 1882

My *dear Kate.*

It is a long long time since I have written to you. But all last summer I knew Clara could report the little there was to tell of my quiet life at Engelberg, &, as she seems, to me, to have scarcely stopped going to Cleveland about once a week since, I have felt that you knew all that was important. There is'nt much that is "important," except that I am very well. (I consider that important not for itself so much as the other side of it, namely, how dreadful it would be to be ill over here alone!) My health amuses me quite a good deal, because it is so absurd. Every year proves to me more & more decidedly that it is entirely a matter of warmth; so long as it is warm, really warm & not any make-believe of it—I am well, & remarkably well. The instant it becomes cold, I am wretched. Sometimes the wretchedness takes one form; sometimes another. Sometimes a doctor would give it this name; sometimes that. But the point is that the moment it is warm, all the wretchedness; no matter what serious & dignified name it may have borne, vanishes into nothing & never comes back until the weather is cold again.—The Sorrento winter, now over, has been much warmer than the Mentone one was. And of course much warmer than the Roman one last year. None of them approach however the climate of Florida.

It happened quite provokingly that during the two weeks Sam & Flora were here, we had our coldest weather for Sorrento. I suppose they will never believe that it was summer up to about the time they came (with two or three times when the "tramontana," or north-wind, blew, for a day or two) & that it grew immediately warmer after they left. To-day is like warm June at home. No—they will never believe it, but will always maintain that Cannes has the best climate. When they were at Cannes, people were fairly fanning themselves here! But I am quite well, aware there is no use trying to convince them. We were at Mentone during the coldest winter known on the Riviera for 20 years. Everybody told me so, & even showed me tables of the average temperature for 19 seasons. But I still am perfectly sure that it is never really warm at Mentone; that its glittering sunshine has always an east wind concealed in it; & that one's hands always chap there; & that the chimneys always smoke. I shall think this as long as I live!

Sam & Flora's visit was perfectly delightful to me. I have been so much by myself since Clara went home that to see dear & familiar faces, & hear home-talk, was the greatest possible pleasure. They were both so kind & agreeable & charming to their "Aunt Connie," that she felt *quite brightened up by their visit.* I am only afraid that what was so delightful to me, may have been rather dull for them—for *there really is nothing to entertain people in Sorrento. There is always the beautiful Bay to look at; but that is all. However, Sam & Flora are so congenial, & so perfectly happy in each other, that perhaps the dullness of Sorrento did not trouble them.* I think Sam is quite a good deal changed since I said good-by to him at New York. He has broadened out generally, looks a good deal older. He was the same dear good nephew to me that he has always been, & while he was here, I quite stopped taking care of myself, & <u>rested</u> in the very fact he <u>was</u> here—if you know what that means! I have taken care of myself so long, & for so many years also was the one who had the direction & responsibility of the journeys South & back with Mother, that I have the habit of feeling always the weight of more or less care—like the people who go about with always a frown between their eyebrows. Well—while Sam & Flora *were here, I let the care go, leaned back in an easy chair, & laughed & enjoyed everything.*

They took a parlor with me, & had their meals served there—in which I joined. I think it possible they did this on my account, as they knew I was not going to the table d'hote. I meant to have told them in advance that it was not at all necessary to do this, as my objections to a table d'hôte are principally contained in the fact that when I am alone, it is not agreeable. All last winter, when I had Miss Clark with me, we went to the public table. But Sam had made his arrangements before I knew of his intention; &, to tell the truth, it was so much pleasanter that I was very glad to have it so. One of the results of having lived about the world in hotels & boarding houses for so many years, is, that I have'nt a particle of curiosity left about "people," & never want to see them if I can help it. I want to see my friends. I do'nt want to see strangers. I shall never forget my surprise—& how I then realized that this was my own peculiarity, in which all others did not share—when Miss Dana said to me in Florence last spring—"O, do you know Father & Mother have taken a fancy to have ~~their~~ our morning-coffee upstairs—as you do. I am so sorry." I looked at her in wonder. "Why?" I said. [“]Why are you sorry?" "O—because I like to see the people," she answered frankly.

You do'nt know how charmed I am with my new niece. I have always thought her very agreeable—as I presume you remember. But now that I have seen more of her, I think her brilliant, & not only that, but very lovable & winning too. I do'nt know when I have heard anyone talk so well—& all without the least attempt,—just in an easy natural way. She told a number of the best sort of stories, & in the way that is so delightful to me—I mean leaving out the unimportant details with which so many people will persist in clogging a story, & thus tiring you out before the point comes. For a person who does'nt talk well herself, & who ought to be grateful when people try to entertain her, Constance Woolson is certainly a most obstinate & ungrateful woman—in that she is so easily tired, & hates so deeply to be bored! She ought to go out & live somewhere in sack-clothes & ashes! Her only excuse is that she does try extremely hard to conceal her ingratitude; I do'nt know whether she succeeds!—The point of this is that Flora—in addition to my natural interest in her as Sam's wife—was perfectly delightful to me in herself. I have met no lady so agreeable in many years. (I was going to say "girl"—for so she seems to me; but you young people are always so indignant when I let you see how youthful you are in my estimation.)

I quite reveled too in all Flora's pretty things—beginning with her "Princess Dagmar" cloak, & ending with the little sewing case you gave her. That cloak is superb—is'nt it? Also the velvet dress. I quite insisted upon seeing everything, & she read me the list of her presents, & described them, so that on the whole I at last feel as though I knew something about my nephew's wedding. The ring Sam gave her, I greatly admire; it is a beautiful gem. Of course the bracelet I still only know from description. I have a great taste for nice things, although I do'nt know much about fashions, shopping, & dressmakers; & I enjoyed all Flora's things almost as much as though they had been my own. Sam showed me, by the way, the very nice dressing-gown you gave him. It is a beautiful piece of cloth, I think.

We had a delightful excursion together. I did not go with them to Capri, but I was very glad of the opportunity to go *to Paestum with them, as that is something I could never accomplish alone, & I never join "parties." Sam arranged it all in the most charming & easy way, so that the excursion generally considered the most fatiguing in the vicinity of Naples, was not the least so to us, but on the contrary without flaw. We left here, in a comfortable carriage, & drove along the beautiful road, overhanging the Bay, to Pompeii. It was a lovely bright day, &, taking a guide who spoke English, we went through the wonders of the uncovered city, my first visit; Sam & Flora had seen it before.* [As everybody knows all about Pompeii from pictures & descriptions, I will only say that the reality exceeded my anticipations. I had no idea the walls of the houses were so high or so well-preserved; that it was so little like a ruin, & so much like a modern Italian town. In fact, take off the roofs & upper-stories of any one of the closely-built Italian towns of to-day, empty the houses of everything, & banish all the people, &, you have Pompeii. There is also another & important difference: Pompeii is scrupulously clean;—while all the Italian towns are—well, come over & see! The narrow streets, well-paved, stretch away in all directions, with their lines of silent houses; overhead in the blue sky smokes old Vesuvius. But it is almost impossible to realize how so large a town could have been so deeply buried.—I said it was like any modern Italian city, but I mean only in its general aspect, viewed from a distance, or as a whole. When you enter the houses, you see at once the well-known peculiarities of Pompeian building & decoration.—Leaving Pompeii, we took the train to Salerno, a picturesque old place on the Gulf of Salerno, south of here. Here we spent the night comfortably, & the next morning started on our grand day's excursion to Paestum, to see the Greek temples—the one thing in Italy, south of Rome, in which I have felt the deepest interest. Beside these temples, even the Coliseum is modern. They were built by a colony of Greeks 2400 years ago, & are considered the finest specimens of Greek architecture in the world, save those at Athens itself.] *The Coliseum was built 1800 years ago.* (Very likely you know all this, are smiling at my putting it in!) [We left Salerno in a carriage drawn by 3 horses abreast, Italian-fashion, at a pleasant hour in the morning; no getting up at dawn if you please—as the people have to do who make the excursion from Naples. The day was divine]—*in fact* the only absolutely perfect day we had while Sam & Flora were here. [Warm, with the sky & sea oh! so blue (the road runs along the shore) & that soft haze over the purple mountains which is to me the feature of an Italian landscape. It was a drive altogether of 52 miles—there & back. We passed through a number of small villages, & as it was Carnival-time, the whole population was enjoying itself, with masks & processions, & much dancing of the Tarantella. This road has been always a favorite haunt of Brigands. Only lately has it been considered safe for travelers. Ten years ago, Taine, who was visiting Naples, could not go to Paestum at all, although he waited a month for a safe time, & would have taken an escort. The thought that we were passing along the road where real Brigands so recently hovered, quite added to the enjoyment of our drive. We looked up toward the near mountains, & imagined them sallying down from their strongholds, & retreating thither with booty & prisoners! No one assailed us, however. We even met two armed patrol men. "United Italy" has been very determined with her Brigands. Those who are not hanged are sent to one or two desolate islands, far out in the Mediterranean, where they have a fine opportunity to meditate, & earn their living in Adam's way!—After a while the great columns of the temples began to loom up against the blue; we rolled through an old gateway between the crumbling town-walls, &, passing the few houses of the modern village, drove directly to the "ruins." But "ruins" they can hardly be called, so perfectly are they preserved. Roofless of course,—but the great solid yellow-brown stone pillars standing as evenly & firmly as ever.] *I don't know whether you care about architecture—but will say that the Temples are Doric.*—[I was not in the least disappointed in my first sight of Greek columns. Indeed—the temple of Neptune seemed to me the most perfect building I have ever seen. I mean in pure simple beauty.]—*We had our lunch in the "cella" of the Temple, looking out on the soft sea on one side, on the hazy mountains on the other. Sam invested in two little vases, supposed to be "antique," & formed "in tombs," & in a collection of coins, also supposed to be antique—the cleaning of which I am now attending to here with breathless interest. I am sorry to say that, so far, they seem to be entirely copper, & that I greatly fear no inscriptions will come out distinct.* But no one is to be allowed to say they are not at least "antique," & when I am home with one set as a scarf-pin, you are to pretend you have never heard that such things are made by the thousand in Naples, & buried by deceitful Italians in order to take in credulous pilgrims from a western world. <u>Some</u> of the coins one sees are undoubtedly genuine; thus why not these? *After, gazing & gazing at the beautiful proportions of the temples from various standpoints, we went to a tower on the old-wall, to get a general view, & here Sam got up a sort of platonic flirtation with a very handsome peasant girl who opened the door for us.* She tried to sell Sam a ring, whose stone she said she herself had found near the old-wall; but Sam preferred to admire her bright eyes & blooming cheeks. (Flora has not these!) *We reached Salerno again at dusk, having had a most enchanting day. The next day Sam had planned to go to Amalfi, & on donkeys to Ravello; but a wind came up so we did not do that part, but came home.*[2]—Just here comes a letter from Flora—at Rome. The first I have had from them since they left. (They were here two weeks & 4 days) So—I see it was written at Rome & mailed at Assisi—where I too so much want to go! Are they having a good time, though!

I am not going to be much alone after this—shall I say, I "fear"? That does'nt sound very nicely, so I'll change it & say that I do like to see people if they will only understand things & not keep me all the time "apologizing" but I am so busy.[3]

a pretty one in Rome—palest pink & quantities of white lace; slippers & little cap to match. The lady was supposed, of course, to have slipped it on hastily, upon coming in from her drive—just to drink her tea in,—before beginning to dress for dinner; but I know she took a solid hour to arrange it!

I get such numbers of letters about "Anne,"—I wish I could show them to you. I am sure they would amuse you. Every mail brings them, & some are quite remarkable. One of the latest is from Judge Tourgee (who wrote "A Fool's Errand," you know) & he not only says nice things about the novel, but quotes Whittier as saying the same. I ought to explain that Judge T. is writing to me about contributing to his new periodical, "Our Continent"; probably he would not have written to me about "Anne," alone.[4] This is in confidence, of course. I [was] much distressed to hear such bad news about Mr Howells. Is it true? I mean that his health is so broken? What do you hear?

Well—I must stop. Tell your Mother, with my dearest love, that I never notice the Bay—or an Italian landscape anywhere—looking especially fair, without thinking of her, & of the time when we took Italian lessons at Farilla. I am extremely fond of Italy—I cannot deny that. I must not forget to put in that Sam gave me my Paestum excursion. I—who count so carefully all my outings—would have hesitated a long time over the expense of it, I fear.

From what you & others write, I think Cleveland must be a gay place nowadays; something going on all the time. Enjoy it all. Take all the good of it. I am so glad that you are so well.

Tell your Father that I use his present, the audiphone, a great deal now, for conversation. I have learned all its "ways," & found it very useful back in Florence & here. When I am the least tired, it rests me to take it; then I do'nt have to "listen" so much,—but the words come to me. By the way—why did no one ever tell me Flora sang? I think she has a remarkably sweet voice; not powerful, but very agreeable. She sang some of the "Patience" songs for me.[5] She wo'nt like it that I am speaking of her voice. Her own idea seems to be that she can't sing at all.

Give my love to Will. His handwriting is growing so like his Father's that before long I shall hesitate over them! I think I have thanked him for his photograph before this; if not, I do so now. It is good; but does not flatter—to say the least. He must try again. I want the very best looks of my friends in their photographs. Did Sam write you, by the way, that when Mr Goodrich was here, he saw a photograph of your Father & one of Garfield on an etagère in Sam's parlor, & said "Ah—Blaine & Garfield, I see."[6] Mr Goodrich, Lieut. Com. in the Navy—came over to see me one day, the Flagship the "Lancaster," having stopped at Naples for a week. He is a "Roman" friend of mine, a nephew-in-law of the Mrs Washington of whom you have heard me speak. The Goodriches had an apartment in Rome last winter.

This Xmas I was quite proud—I had 20 Xmas cards. Will's "cherub" is the centre-piece. Two Birthday ones have just come; so I do'nt feel "forgotten" any more.

I feel that I know a great deal more about you all, now that I have had so many long talks with Sam & Flora; sometimes all three together; sometimes with one of them alone. Talking tells more than letters can.

The next one I expect to see is you—on a similar tour!! Then I shall hardly have returned to my usual quiet when along will come Will! I'll welcome you all; I only wish I had an Italian villa in which to receive you. [Good-by. Love to all.]

Yours affectionately,
C.F.W.

Notes

1. Because both an original and a typed version of this letter survive, it provides a good index of variations among Woolson's original, the typed version, and the version collected in Benedict's CFW (263–65). In the case of this letter, the typed version omits a great deal: pages of the original letter that Woolson numbered 10 to 13 are missing. Woolson's original letter is the source of the transcription above: Bracketed passages appear in both CFW and the typed version; italicized portions appear in the typed version but not in CFW; Benedict also made minor changes when she omitted material, especially when she needed to supply a transition.

2. The typed version of the letter ends here with "Lovingly C. F. Woolson."

3. Pages 10–13 are missing.

4. Albion Tourgee's 1879 *A Fool's Errand,* set in the Reconstruction South, was enormously popular. The weekly magazine *Our Continent* ran only from 1881 to 1884.

5. Songs from Gilbert and Sullivan's 1881 opera *Patience.*

6. Secretary of State James Blaine (1830–93), who had run against Grover Cleveland in the 1876 election, delivered the eulogy at the assassinated President Garfield's funeral.

Appendix of Names

This appendix includes the lesser-known or personal names that Woolson mentions more than once in her letters, as well as the names of all the people with whom she corresponded. Woolson often commented on British, Italian, German, Russian, and other royalty. For ease of location, names of royalty are grouped together under one heading.

FREQUENTLY USED FIRST NAMES

Amasa: Amasa Stone Mather
Charly: Charles Jarvis Woolson Jr., variously spelled Charley and Charlie
Clara: Clara Woolson Benedict
Clare: Clare Rathbone Benedict
Constance/Connie: Constance Mather
Flora: Flora Stone Mather
Kate: Katharine Livingston Mather
Libbie: Elizabeth Gwinn Mather
Livingston: (Samuel) Livingston Mather
Sam: Samuel Mather
Will: William Gwinn Mather

FAMILY, FRIENDS, COLLEAGUES, PERSONS OF INTEREST

Adams, Oscar Fay (1855–1919): Writer and speaker on literature and architecture
Alcott, Louisa May (1832–88): Woolson was sometimes impatient with how writers like Alcott increased the pressure on women to write for children's markets.
Alden, Henry Mills (1836–1919): Writer and editor at Harper's with whom Woolson corresponded, especially about her response to his book *God in His World* (1890)
Aldrich, Thomas Bailey (1836–1907): Writer; Woolson's editor at *Atlantic Monthly*
Angelo: Woolson's cook and servant at the Villa Brichieri in Florence
Assunta: Woolson's maid at the Villa Brichieri in Florence
Averell, Jane: See Carter, Jane Russell Averell
Baldwin, Dr. (1850–1910) and **Mrs. William Wilberforce:** Dr. Baldwin was the preferred physician of many British and American expatriates. Among Baldwin's patients were Henry James and Alice James, whose cancer he diagnosed.
Balestier, Carrie (1862–1939): See Kipling, Carrie Balestier
Balestier, Wolcott (1861–91): Brother of Carrie Balestier Kipling; worked with Kipling on the novel *The Naulahka* (1892)

Barrett, Lawrence (1838–91): Irish-American actor

Benedict, Clara Woolson (1843–1923): Woolson's younger sister with whom she traveled throughout the South and Europe

Benedict, Clare Rathbone (1868–1961): Woolson's niece who lionized her after her death, compiling *Five Generations* (1930/32), a three-volume biography of the Woolson-Benedict families. Benedict cut and pasted many of Woolson's letters into various books owned by her or by Woolson. The second volume of *Five Generations, Constance Fenimore Woolson,* contains excerpts from many of Woolson's letters and notebooks as well as some of her literary work.

Benedict, George, Jr. (1840–71): Coeditor of the *Daily Cleveland Herald* and Clara Woolson Benedict's husband, who left her a young widow when he was killed in a train wreck

Benedict, George, Sr. (1812–76): Clara Woolson Benedict's father-in-law and owner of the *Daily Cleveland Herald.* Woolson wrote "Letters from Gotham" for this newspaper in the early 1870s.

Benedict, Harriet (Hattie): See Sherman, Harriet

Berenson, Bernard (1865–1959): American expatriate art historian, who lived in the Villa I Tatti in Florence. The Villa is now Harvard University's Center for Renaissance Studies.

Bingham, Mrs.: A member of the Payne-Whitney family

Black, William: Woolson complained that the general public preferred writers like Black to George Eliot.

Boardman, Mabel Thorp (1860–1946): National Secretary of the Red Cross

Booth, Mary (1831–89): Editor of *Harper's Bazar*

Boott, Elizabeth (Lizzie): See Duveneck, Elizabeth Boott

Boott, Francis (1813–1904): American expatriate composer who lived in the Villa Castellani in Florence. Henry James drew on this villa and Boott's relationship with his daughter Lizzie for his portraits of Gilbert and Pansy Osmond in *Portrait of a Lady* (1881). Woolson used John Hay's poem "Through the Long Days," set to music by Boott, as a refrain in her story "Dorothy" (1892).

Bourget, Paul (1852–1935): French novelist and intellectual. He and his wife Minnie were particular friends of Edith Wharton and Henry James.

Bowen, John Eliot: Editor of *The Independent*

Bowker, R. R.: Founder of *Publishers Weekly.* Woolson valued his literary criticism.

Boyesen, Hjalmar Hjorth (1848–95): Norwegian-born professor of Germanic languages at Cornell and Columbia. Boyesen was a prolific writer of fiction, essays, and reviews, including a review of Woolson's *Rodman the Keeper* (1880).

Bracken, Mrs.: A resident of Florence who offered her apartment to Woolson. Woolson refers to her servant Ansarro in several letters.

Braddon, Mary Elizabeth (1837–1915): British novelist

Bronson, Edith (1861–?): Friend of Woolson's in Venice and member of Daniel and Ariana Curtis's circle at the Palazzo Barbaro. Bronson found a secretary/companion, Marie Holas, for Woolson during her last days in Venice.

Bronson, Katherine de Kay: A friend of Henry James from Newport and mother of Edith Bronson. The Bronsons lived in the Casa Alvisi in Venice.

Broughton, Rhoda (1840–1920): Welsh novelist whom Woolson knew in Florence

Brown, Ford Maddox (1821–93): British painter

Brown, Horatio (1854–1926): Author of several books on Venice and a biography of John Addington Symonds (1895)

Brown, Jane Russell Averell (1860–1919): See Carter, Jane Russell Averell

Brugsch Bey, Emil (1842–1930): Younger brother of Egyptologist Heinrich Karl Brugsch Bey (1827–94), Emil was assistant conservator of the Boulak Museum in Cairo. He photographed a cache of royal mummies discovered in Luxor.

Buchanan, Robert (1841–1901): Scottish writer whose poetry Woolson did not find interesting

Bunce, Oliver Bell (1828–90): American novelist and contributor to *Appletons' Journal*

Burlingame, Edward L. (1848–1922): Editor of *Scribner's Monthly*

Burne-Jones, Edward (1833–98): British Pre-Raphaelite artist

Burnett, Frances Hodgson (1849–1924): The author of *Little Lord Fauntleroy* (1886) and *The Secret Garden* (1911). Woolson reviewed Burnett's *That Lass o' Lowrie's* (1877) in *Atlantic Monthly* (Sept. 1877).

Burroughs, John (1837–1921): Naturalist and essayist whose work Woolson tired of. A supporter of the controversial Walt Whitman, Burroughs published *Notes on Whitman* in 1867.

Byrne, Lionel: For a short time, a Master at Clifton College, Eton, Bristol, England

Cabanel, Alexander (1823–89): Painter whose works include a portrait of John Hay

Campbell, Helen: A cousin's cousin's daughter

Carpaccio, Vittore (1460–1525/26): Venetian painter

Carter, (Anna) Grace (1841–98?): See Carter, Jane Russell Averell. Grace Carter helped to arrange Woolson's funeral. Woolson refers to Grace as a "cousin," but the exact relationship is unclear.

Carter, Arabella: See Washburn, Arabella Carter

Carter, Emma Woolson (1833–52): Woolson's sister who married Rev. Timothy Carter. Both died shortly after their 1851 marriage.

Carter, Jane Russell Averell (Mrs. Lawson, 1841–88): Childhood friend. Her husband joined Charles Jarvis Woolson's stove business around 1857 and in 1869 committed suicide. Some of their children were (Lawson) Averell, (Anna) Grace, Jane Russell Averell Carter Brown, and Mary Gayle Carter Clarke. Woolson also mentions a Paul Carter.

Carter, (Lawson) Averell (1869–1925): See Carter, Jane Russell Averell

Carter, Rev. Timothy: Husband of Emma Woolson Carter; brother of Arabella Carter Washburn; brother-in-law of Jane Russell Averell Carter

Chadwick, Admiral French Ensor (1844–1919): President of the Naval War College and author of *Temperament, Disease, and Health*. The Chadwicks lived above Woolson on Sloane Street, London, in 1884.

Chamberlain, Jennie (1865–1959): William and Mary Chamberlain's daughter. Woolson also mentions a Robert Chamberlain from Cleveland and a Mollie Chamberlain.

Chamberlain, William (1837–1920) and **wife Mary:** Friends from Hudson, Ohio

Chapman, A. W. (1809–1899): American botanist. Woolson's copy of his *Flora of the Southern United States* (New York: Ivison, Blakeman, Taylor, 1872) is at Rollins College. It contains a section written by D. C. Eaton as well as Woolson's notes on where and when she found particular ferns.

Chegaray, Madame Eloise: Owner of the prestigious girl's school in New York City that Woolson attended. The girls called Madame Chegaray "Tante," a name Woolson used for Anne's mentor in her novel *Anne* (1882).

Cherbuliez, Victor (1829–99): Swiss novelist whom Woolson quotes in French in a Feb. 12, 1882, letter to Henry James

Clark, Henry and **Emily Vernon Clark:** Their relationship is unclear, but both are possibly related to the Corning-Clark family of Cooperstown that founded the Singer Sewing Machine Company.

Clarke, George Hyde (1768–1835): New York agriculturalist who built an estate, Hyde Hall, on Lake Otsego in Cooperstown. Clarke had an affair with James Fenimore Cooper's sister-in-law Ann, the wife of Richard Cooper. Although he had a wife and children in England, Clarke married Ann shortly after her husband's death. Woolson sometimes spells his name "Clark."

Clarke, Mary Gayle Carter (1862–1929): See Carter, Jane Russell Averell. Sister of Grace Carter and wife of George Hyde Clarke (1858–?). Mary's mother was Jane Averell Carter.

Clossen, Julia: Family friend from Cleveland

Clough, Arthur Hugh (1819–61): Woolson especially liked Arnold's poem "Thyrsis" (1866), written in memory of Clough, his fellow poet and friend.

Compton, Edward (1854–1918): British actor who played the part of Christopher Newman in Henry James's *The American* (1891)

Cooper, (Anne) Charlotte (1817–85): James Fenimore Cooper's daughter

Cooper, Fanny (Maria Francis, 1819–98): James Fenimore Cooper's daughter

Cooper, James Fenimore (1789–1851): The novelist was Woolson's great-uncle. Woolson's mother, Hannah Pomeroy, Woolson was the child of Cooper's sister Ann. Woolson often refers to the Coopers' residency in Florence at the Villa St. Ilario.

Cooper, Susan Fenimore (1813–94): James Fenimore Cooper's daughter and one of the "cousins" Woolson admired. The author of *Rural Hours,* Susan was a well-known nature writer and advocated for policies that preserved nature and promoted village improvement.

Craik, Dinah Mulock (1826–87): British novelist and poet. Craik's *A Woman's Thoughts About Women* (1858) offered cautions against extending romantic friendships between girls into maturity lest they impinge upon adult heterosexual marriage.

Crawford, Francis Marion (1854–1909): American novelist who also wrote about Italy and India

Cross, John Walter: American banker, who, though he was twenty years her junior, married George Eliot

Crowell, Mary Benedict: Relative by marriage of Woolson's sister Clara Woolson Benedict

Curtis, Daniel and **Ariana:** American expatriates who owned the Palazzo Barbaro in Venice. At the end of her life, Woolson delighted in being able to borrow books from their extensive library.

Curtis, George William (1824–92): American essayist and novelist. Curtis defended Henry James against criticism over his charge that Hawthorne was parochial.

Curtis, Ralph: Daniel and Ariana Curtis's son, who studied art with John Singer Sargent

Cushman, Charlotte (1816–76): American actress who, like Clara Urquhart Potter, recited Woolson's poem "Kentucky Belle" (1873)

Dana, Richard Henry (1815–1882): Woolson was fond of the elderly Dana, a member of a well-known Boston family and the author of *Two Years Before the Mast* (1840). Dana's son Richard married Longfellow's daughter Edith. Woolson also refers to a Miss Dana.

D'Aubigné, Agrippa (1552–1630): French poet

Daudet, Alphonse (1840–97): French novelist whose work Woolson knew well

Daudet, Ernest (1836–1921): Brother of Alphonse Daudet and also a writer

Della Robbia, Andrea (1435–1525): Italian artist known for his Madonna paintings in Florence

Dickinson, Anna (1842–1932): American abolitionist and suffragette, whose attempt at acting and playwriting (*Crown of Thorns,* 1877) was a failure

Disraeli, Benjamin (1804–81): British politician and Prime Minister and author of the novel *Lothair* (1870), which Woolson read

Dodge, Mary Mapes (1831–1905): Editor of *St. Nicolas Magazine* whom Woolson described as obviously literary in her appearance

Donatello (1386–1466): Florentine sculptor

Doré, Gustave (1832–83): French-born illustrator

Duse, Eleanora (1858–1924): Italian actress whom Woolson met during her last months in Venice

Duveneck, Elizabeth Boott (Lizzie, 1846–88): The daughter of Francis Boott, Lizzie lived with her father in the Villa Castellani in Florence. Their relationship and their Villa have been identified as the model for James's Gilbert and Pansy Osmond in *Portrait of a Lady* (1881). Lizzie's marriage to the Catholic and poor artist Frank Duveneck came under much criticism and might serve as some basis for Woolson's story "Dorothy" (1892). Duveneck was Lizzie's art teacher and she was herself an accomplished artist. She died shortly after the birth of her son; Woolson was godmother to the boy.

Duveneck, Frank (1848–1919): American artist and husband of Lizzie Boott Duveneck

Eaton, Daniel Cady (1834–95): Professor of Botany at Yale with whom Woolson exchanged letters and fern specimens

Edwards, Amelia (1831–92): Novelist and Egyptologist

Eggleston, Edward (1837–1902): American novelist best known for his Hoosier novels about Indiana

Farnian, Miss: Solicits Woolson to write stories for children

Fawcett, Edgar (1847–1904): American writer whose career Woolson followed

Field, Kate (1838–96): American actress and journalist

Fiske, Daniel Willard (1831–1904): Linguist and librarian at Cornell University

Flagler, Henry (1830–1913): Oil magnate responsible for bringing the railroad to Florida and for building St. Augustine's Ponce de Leon Hotel (1888)

Flash, Henry Lynden (1835–1914): New Orleans poet whose work Woolson disdained

Flaxman, John (1755–1826): English sculptor

Fouque, Baron Friedrich de la Motte (1777–1842): Author of *Undine* (1811), a fantasy romance. Woolson resisted those who urged her to write in a similar vein.

Fromentin, Eugene (1820–76): Painter and writer whose one novel Woolson did not appreciate

Garibaldi, Giuseppe (1807–82): Italian revolutionary

Gilder, Joseph B. (1858–1936) and **Jeanette L. (1849–1916):** Brother and sister who founded *The Critic*

Gilder, Richard Watson (1844–1909): Brother of Joseph and Jeanette Gilder and editor of *Scribner's Monthly*, which later became *The Century*

Gilman, Daniel (1831–1908): Librarian at Yale and first president of Johns Hopkins

Gilmore, James Robert (1822–1903): Editor of *Continental Monthly* and compiler of a biographical encyclopedia. Gilmore also wrote Civil War novels under the pseudonym Edmund Kirke.

Giorgione (Giorgio Barbarelli de Castelfranco, 1477–1510): Venetian painter

Gladstone, William (1809–98): A four-time Liberal Prime Minister of Britain, Gladstone supported Charles Stuart Parnell in his efforts to achieve Home Rule for Ireland.

Goodrich, Casper (1847–1925): President of the Navy War College. Woolson was godmother to his son Wolseley Goodrich, who died as a child.

Gosse, Edmund (1849–1928): Poet and critic. Woolson also mentions Gosse's wife Ellen.

Gray, Asa (1810–88): Harvard Professor of Natural History and author of *Elements of Botany* (1836), a book Woolson consulted

Greenough, Miss Laura (?–1892): The elderly Miss Greenough, a relative of the Bootts and sister of Richard and Horatio Greenough, lived on Bellosguardo Hill in Florence.

Greenough, Richard (1819–1904): Younger brother of Horatio Greenough (1805–1852); Richard sculpted a bust of Woolson.

Guercino, Giovanni (1591–1666): Italian painter

Guilford, Linda (1823–1911): Woolson's teacher at the Cleveland Female Seminary

Hale, Edward Everett (1822–1909): Pastor of Unity Church, Worcester, Mass., and of South Congregational Church, Boston. Woolson sent him a few early manuscripts for publication in his magazine *Old and New*.

Hamilton, Gail (1833–96): Pseudonym for Mary Abigail Dodge. Woolson disliked her attack columns in the New York *Tribune*.

Harper, Joseph: With his brothers James, John, and Fletcher, publisher of Woolson's work under the Harper and Brothers imprint

Harris, May: A close friend of Woolson's sister Clara Benedict, Harris wrote an appreciation of Woolson in *The Saturday Review of Literature* (1929). Clare Benedict includes this and excerpts from Clara's letters to Harris in *Five Generations* (1929–30, 1932).

Haskin, Major: A fern collector whom Woolson knew in Charleston, Haskin was likely a Civil War officer from Ohio and a friend of D. C. Eaton.

Hawthorne, Julian (1846–1934): Woolson's sister Clara, to Woolson's delight, dined with this son of Nathaniel and Sophia Hawthorne.

Hay, Clara Stone (1849–1914): Wife of John Hay and sister of Flora Stone Mather

Hay, John (1838–1905): Hay married Clara Stone, the sister-in-law of Woolson's nephew, Samuel Mather. Woolson's frequent correspondence with Hay reflects her enthusiasm for the biography of Lincoln that he coauthored with John Nicolay (1832–1901). Hay was Lincoln's private secretary, an ambassador to Great Britain, and Secretary of State in the McKinley and Roosevelt administrations. Woolson speculated, correctly, that Hay was the author of the anonymously published novel *The Bread Winners* (1884).

Hayne, Paul Hamilton (1830–86): Woolson carried on a long correspondence with this Southern poet, whom she never met in person. Her letters suggest that Hayne sent her copies of poems he was working on but had not yet published.

Herbert, George (1593–1633): British poet and clergyman whose church at Bemerton, near Salisbury, Woolson visited in 1884

Higginson, Thomas Wentworth (1823–1911): American minister and abolitionist, remembered now for his support of Emily Dickinson's poetry

Hobart, Lady: Likely a descendent of the British essayist Lord Henry Hobart

Horner, Susan (1816–1923) and **Joanna (1823–?):** Authors of *Walks in Florence and Its Environs* (1873). The eldest sister Mary (1809–?) was married to geologist Charles Lyell (1797–1875).

Horsey, Algernon Frederick Rous (1827–1922): British Admiral

Horsey, William de: Lieutenant General in Venice from whom Woolson rented her last residence, the Casa Semitecolo

Houghton, Henry (1823–?): Founder of Houghton publishing company. Houghton later partnered with Melancthon Hurd.

Howells, Elinor (1837–1910): Wife of William Dean Howells

Howells, Mildred (1872–1966): Daughter of William Dean and Elinor Howells and editor of *The Life in Letters of William Dean Howells* (1928)

Howells, William Dean (1837–1920): Woolson's connection to Howells was primarily through his editorship of *Atlantic Monthly*. Her correspondence with and about him reveals both admiration and frustration, but she sympathized with his lack of privacy in Europe when many admirers sought his attention.

Howells, Winifred (1863–89): Daughter of William Dean and Elinor Howells

Huntington, Ellen Greenough (1814–93): Sister of Horatio and Richard Greenough. Huntington's brother, Henry Greenough, was Francis Boott's brother-in-law.

Huntington, Henry Greenough (1848–?): Son of Charles and Ellen Greenough Huntington

Huntington, Mary: Daughter of Charles and Ellen Greenough Huntington; she inherited the Villa Castellani in 1893.

Hurd, Melancthon: See Houghton, Henry

Hurlburt, Miss: Possibly a relative of Illinois Congressman Stephen Augustus Hurlburt (1815–82)

Hutchinson, Mrs. Ellen Mary: Coeditor with E. C. Stedman of *Library of American Literature* (1888–90)

Ingelow, Jean (1820–97): Woolson published a poem about this British poet and novelist, "To Jean Ingelow," in *The New Century for Women*, July 8, 1876.

Irving, Sir Henry (1838–1905): Actor whom Woolson saw perform in *Romeo and Juliet* with Ellen Terry

James, Alice (1848–92): Sister of Henry and William James. Although no correspondence between Woolson and Alice James survives, they did exchange letters.

James, Henry (1843–1916): Woolson met James in 1880 and, thereafter, they became close friends and correspondents. Some have speculated that Woolson was in love with James, while others find this unlikely.

James, William (1842–1910): Woolson was especially interested in William James's work in psychology. In addition to his sister Alice, Woolson also mentions William's wife Alice.

Jarvis, James Jackson (1818–88): American art collector

Jones, Lawrence Evelyn: British memoir writer

Keenan, Matthew (1837–93): Vice President and Trustee of Wisconsin's Northwestern Mutual Life Insurance Company. Keenan was involved in a land sale for Woolson.

Keese, George Pomeroy: Woolson's first cousin on her mother's side, Keese donated toward building St. Agnes Chapel at the Christ Episcopal Church in Cooperstown.

Keese, Roy: Woolson's first cousin on her mother's side

Kemble, Fanny (1809–93): British actress

King, Clarence (1842–1901): Woolson was fascinated by this member of the Hay/Adams Five of Hearts group. King was an explorer and the first director of the U.S. Geological Survey. In 1888, several years after Woolson's association with him, he secretly married Ada Copeland, a black woman, and lived a double life under the name James Todd.

Kipling, Carrie Balestier (1862–1939): Wife of Rudyard Kipling and sister of Wolcott Balestier, who worked with Kipling on his novel *The Naulahka* (1892). Woolson, like many others, was interested in and dismayed at Kipling's marriage to the twenty-nine-year-old Balestier when he was twenty-six.

Kirke, Edmund: See Gilman, James Robert

Landor, Walter Savage (1775–1864): Woolson wrote extensively to E. C. Stedman about her struggle to appreciate Landor's poetry.

Lanier, Sidney (1842–81): American poet from Georgia whom Woolson first heard about through his writing on Paul Hamilton Hayne

Layard, Sir Henry (1817–94) and **Lady Layard:** British archaeologist, historian, and diplomat and his wife

Lee, Mary (1835–1918): Daughter of Civil War general Robert E. Lee (1807–70)

Lee, Vernon (1856–1935): Pseudonym for British writer Violet Paget, whom Woolson met in Italy. See also Robinson, Agnes Mary.

Lemaître, Jules (1853–1914): French playwright and critic

Levorati, Ernesto (1880–1920): Italian painter born in Padua, outside Venice

Lewes, George Henry (1817–78): George Eliot's partner in an open marriage

Litchfield, Grace Denio (1849–1944): American poet and novelist

Loring, Frank: Brother of Katharine Loring

Loring, Katharine (1849–1943): Longtime companion to Alice James

Mabie, Hamilton Wright (1846–1916): Mabie was on the staff of *Christian Union* and, later, was Associate Editor of *The Outlook.*

Macquoid, Katherine Sarah: Author of *At The Red Glove* (1885), which Woolson speculated had been written by John Hay.

Mather, Amasa Stone (1884–1920): Son of Samuel and Flora Stone Mather. Woolson often commented on how pleased she was to have photos of the Mathers' children.

Mather, Constance (1889–1969): Later Mrs. Robert Bishop. Daughter of Samuel and Flora Stone Mather. Woolson delighted in the fact that she was her namesake.

Mather, Elizabeth Gwinn (Libbie): Samuel Livingston Mather's second wife. When writing to her niece and nephew, Kate and Sam Mather, Woolson referred to Libbie as their mother rather than their stepmother.

Mather, Flora Stone (1851–1909): Wife of Samuel Mather, and sister-in-law of John Hay

Mather, Georgiana Woolson (1831–53): Woolson's sister, the eldest of the Woolson children, who married Samuel Livingston Mather. Georgiana died shortly after the birth of her second child.

Mather, Katharine Livingston (1853–1939): Woolson's niece, the child of her sister Georgiana and Samuel Livingston Mather

Mather, Samuel (1851–1931): Woolson's nephew, the child of her sister Georgiana and Samuel Livingston Mather. After his marriage to Flora Stone, he and Flora moved to the Amasa Stone house at 514 Euclid Avenue, Cleveland, Ohio. Both Samuel and his father helped Woolson with financial matters. When he died, Samuel was known as the richest man in Ohio.

Mather, Samuel Livingston (1817–90): Husband of Woolson's sister Georgiana. The Mathers lived on "Millionaire's Row," Euclid Avenue, Cleveland, Ohio. Although sources conflict about the street number, maps and Woolson's frequent greetings to 544 indicate that this is the correct number. Woolson also mentions other Mather relations: Mrs. Walton, Mrs. Burnham, Mrs. Thomas Mather, Nellie Mather. The Mathers were indirect descendants of Puritan ministers Increase and Cotton Mather.

Mather, (Samuel) Livingston (1882–1960): Son of Samuel and Flora Stone Mather. Woolson sometimes spells his name Livingstone.

Mather, William Gwinn (1857–1951): Son of Samuel Livingston Mather and his second wife, Elizabeth Gwinn Mather

Meacci, Riccardo (1856–1940): Italian Pre-Raphaelite painter

Mead, Larkin G. (1835–1910): The brother of Elinor Howells, Mead created medallion portraits of Woolson, John Hay, William Dean Howells, and Henry James.

Memling, Hans (1430–94): Dutch painter

Meredith, George (1828–1909): British novelist

Mérimee, Prosper (1803–70): French dramatist and short story writer whose work Woolson found "charming"

Miller, Joaquin (1837?41?–1913): Pseudonym for western adventurer and writer Cincinnatus Heine. Woolson admired Miller's work.

Milnes, Richard Monckton (1809–85): Woolson read Sir T. Wemyss's *Life and Letters* of this poet, which was published in 1890.

Morris, Clara (1849–1925): American actress known for her emotional performances

Morris, William (1834–96): Woolson was advised to read a poet with the last name Morris to develop her writing style. The reference is likely to William Morris.

Moultrie, William (1730–1805): Revolutionary War general from South Carolina

Musset, Alfred de (1810–57): French dramatist, novelist, and poet

Nadaud, Gustave (1820–93): Translator of "Carcassonne," a French ballad that Woolson received from John Hay

Newman, Henry Roderick (1843–1918): Copyist and painter of architecture and flowers

Nicolay, John (1832–1901): Coauthor with John Hay of *Abraham Lincoln: A Life* (1890)

Norton, Charles Eliot : Professor of Fine Arts at Harvard

Norton, Lily: Daughter of Charles Eliot Norton. Norton was living in Venice when Woolson died.

Noyes, Walter: Sometimes referred to as MacWalter or McWalter, Noyes was a classmate of John Hay at Brown and the American Consul in Venice.

O'Brien, John and **wife Charlotte (1812–55):** O'Brien was the Chaplain on Mackinac Island.

Oliphant, Mrs. Margaret (1828–97): Scottish novelist whom Woolson met in Cairo

Osgood, James (1836–92): *Atlantic Monthly* publisher. Although she liked Osgood, Woolson doubted his commitment to marketing her work.

Ouida (Marie (Maria) Louise Ramé, 1839–1908): British novelist. Woolson thought Ouida had power but also that she had "horrible taste" and expected too much attention from lovers.

Owen, Rebekah (1858–1939): Poet who gave editorial advice to Thomas Hardy and Henry Wadsworth Longfellow. Owen and her sister lived near Woolson in Oxford. Woolson often writes about Owen's dog Colin.

Paget, Violet: See Lee, Vernon

Parkman, Frances (1823–93): Author of *The Oregon Trail* (1847–49), which Woolson was reading in 1893

Parnell, Charles Stuart (1846–91): Irish politician who, with the support of William Gladstone, campaigned for Irish Home Rule

Parsons, Julia: Friend from Cooperstown

Payne, Henry (1810–96): Payne was a member of the Ohio Senate and on the Democratic Ohio Electoral Commission in the disputed 1876 election between Samuel Tilden and Rutherford B. Hayes.

Payne, Molly: A member of the Cleveland Payne family and friend of Kate Mather

Payne, Col. Oliver (1838–1917): Son of Henry Payne and treasurer of Standard Oil, which made him one of Cleveland's richest men

Pell, Mr.: Botany enthusiast from Milford, New York

Pell-Clarke, Henrietta (Mrs. Leslie): Sister of Henry James's cousin Minnie Temple

Pennell, Joseph (1857–1926): Illustrator for *Century* magazine

Phelps, Elizabeth Stuart (1844–1911): Woolson stayed in the same St. Augustine hotel with Phelps, but did not become acquainted with her. She was struck with her "mannish" behavior and devotion to dress reform.

Phillips, Barnett: Staff writer for the *New York Times*

Phinney, Caroline (1815–92): Daughter of James Fenimore Cooper and wife of Henry Phinney (1816–75)

Phinney, Frederick (1854–92): Son of Caroline and Henry Phinney

Phinney, Susie (1852–81): Daughter of Caroline and Henry Phinney and wife of Sutherland Irving (1850–81), an insurance broker

Piatt, Sarah M. B.: Poet whom Howells, to Woolson's dismay, published in *Atlantic Monthly*

Pierce, James Mills (?–1906): Professor of mathematics at Harvard. Woolson often spells his name Peirce.

Piombo, Sebastian del (1485–1547): Italian artist

Plum: Woolson's nickname for her niece Clare Benedict

Potter, Cora Urquhart Brown (1857–1936): American actress and niece of Mrs. Launt Thompson. Potter's readings of Woolson's "Kentucky Belle" (1873) made the poem famous.

Potter, Henry Codman (1835–1908): Bishop of the Episcopal diocese of New York. Potter was the brother of Mrs. Launt Thompson.

Potter, Paul (1625–54): Dutch artist

Poynter, Edward John (1836–1919): Artist brother of Eleanor Poynter

Poynter, Miss Eleanor F.: British writer who lived in Florence and whom Woolson considered an especial friend

Preston, Col. John (1811–90): Husband of Margaret Preston and professor at Virginia Military Academy, Preston served under Stonewall Jackson during the Civil War.

Preston, Mrs. Margaret (1820–97): Philadelphia-born poet who became associated with Virginia and the Confederacy

Quincy, Mabel: Bostonian who lived in Venice

Reade, Charles (1814–84): British novelist whose work Woolson admired

Récamier, Madame Juliette (1777–1849): Exiled from France by Napoleon, Récamier sustained a friendship with Madame de Staël and was the subject of many portrait painters. Her letters, which Woolson read while in Geneva, were published in 1859.

Regnault, Alexandre-Georges-Henri (1843–71): French painter

Reid, Christian (1846–1920): Pseudonym for Frances Christine Fisher Tiernan, author of over forty post–Civil War romances. Woolson found her work, like that of many Southern women, too "exaggerated" to be believable.

Reid, Whitelaw (1837–1912): Editor of the New York *Tribune* and author of a history of Ohio in the Civil War

Rideing, William Henry (1853–1918): Travel writer who published frequently on western landscapes in *Harper's New Monthly Magazine*

Robinson, Agnes Mary (1857–1944): A poet, novelist, and scholar of French literature, Robinson was a companion of Vernon Lee. Lee was outraged when Robinson married James Darmesteter in 1888 because he was Jewish.

Rollins, Alice Marland (1847–97): American writer

Ronsard, Pierre de (1524–85): Woolson knew the work of this French poet well enough to quote him at length, in French, in a letter.

Rosa, Salvator (1615–73): Italian Baroque painter

Sainte-Beuve, Charles Augustin (1804–69): Woolson claimed to have read all forty volumes by this French literary critic as background for her story "At the Château of Corinne" (1887).

Salvini, Tommaso (1829–1915): Italian actor

Schuyler, Eugene (1840–90): U.S. Consul General in Cairo

Serao, Matilde (1856–1927): Novelist Woolson read to perfect her Italian

Sheridan, Richard (1751–1816): On September 7, 1884, Woolson saw Sheridan's *School for Scandal* (1777) in Salisbury with Henry James after they had visited Stonehenge.

Sherman, Harriet Benedict (Mrs. Henry): Hattie was Clara Woolson Benedict's sister-in-law. Woolson also mentions several Sherman girls.

Smith, Julia: Woolson's second cousin from Virginia

Southey, Robert (1774–1843): British poet whose admiration for Walter Savage Landor Woolson did not share

Southworth, E.D.E.N. (1819–99): American author of over sixty novels. Woolson disparaged her work.

Spaulding, Col. Zephaniah: Woolson had thought herself in love with Spaulding during the Civil War. After the war, he emigrated to Hawaii where he developed a highly successful sugar plantation. The name is variously spelled "Spalding."

Spofford, Harriet (1835–1921): American novelist

Stanley, Sir Henry Morton (1841–1904): Welsh journalist who with medical missionary David Livingstone (1813–73) explored much of Africa

Stedman, Arthur: Son of Edmund and Laura Woodworth Stedman

Stedman, Edmund Clarence (1833–1908): Poet and author of critical essays that Woolson prized. Stedman collected his essays in *Victorian Poets* (1875) and *The Poets of America* (1885). He also edited with Ellen Hutchinson the eleven-volume *Library of American Literature* (1888–90). Woolson frequently corresponded with Stedman for advice and about literary taste.

Stedman, Laura Woodworth: Wife of E. C. Stedman

St. John, Samuel (1813–76): Woolson's science teacher at the Cleveland Female Seminary

Stillman, Mr. (1828–1901) and **Mrs. William:** An artist and journalist, William Stillman was also the U.S. Consul in Rome.

Stoddard, Elizabeth Drew (1823–1902): Woolson admired Stoddard's "odd strong novels." Stoddard's appearance prompted her to wonder why so many women writers lacked physical beauty.

Stoddard, Richard Henry (1825–1903): American critic and poet who married Elizabeth Stoddard and helped her with her career

Stone, Flora: See Mather, Flora Stone

Strictland, Edward F.: Autograph collector

Symonds, John Addington (1840–93): A British poet and critic, Symonds, though homosexual, lived with his wife in rooms below Woolson in Venice.

Taine, Hippolyte Adolphe (1828–93): French critic and historian

Targer/Targia: Woolson's nickname for her niece Kate Mather. The origin of this nickname is unknown, but it could possibly refer to a Targia or Tuareg woman from a Saharan nomadic tribe. This tribe was matrilineal and venerated strong and beautiful women.

Taylor, Bayard (1825–78): American poet and travel writer associated especially with his journeys to Africa and the Far East. Woolson knew that he often had work rejected for publication.

Terry, Ellen (1847–1928): British Shakespearean actress whom Woolson saw perform in *Romeo and Juliet*

Thompson, Mr. (1833–94) and **Mrs. Launt:** Launt Thompson was a sculptor and his wife, whom Woolson met in Italy, was a sister of Bishop Henry Codman Potter.

Tiernan, Frances Christine Fisher: See Reid, Christian

Timrod, Henry (1828–67): American writer of the South whose life story Woolson found "sad"

Tourgee, Albion (1838–1905): American writer who argued for desegregation in the Plessy v. Ferguson (1896) case. Tourgee wrote an admiring letter to Woolson about her novel *Anne* (1882) and invited her to write for his magazine *Our Continent*.

Turner, Campbell: Woolson's second cousin

Turner, J.M.W. (1775–1851): British landscape painter. Because Woolson had reproductions of Turner's paintings, she found the originals especially beautiful.

Vanderbilt, George Washington II (1862–1914): Grandson of railroad magnate Cornelius Vanderbilt (1794–1877); George had his Biltmore estate in Asheville, North Carolina, constructed between 1889 and 1895. Woolson satirized the Vanderbilt excesses in *Horace Chase* (1894).

Vedder, Elihu (1836–1923): American artist best known for his illustrations of Edward Fitzgerald's (1809–83) translation of *The Rubaiyat of Omar Khayyam* (1894)

Verga, Giovanni (1840–1922): Novelist Woolson read to help improve her Italian

Vernon, Miss: A cousin of Clarence King

Veronese, Paolo (1528–88): Venetian painter

Villari, Madame Linda (1836–1915): British writer who translated a life of Machiavelli (1892)

Ward, Mary Augusta (Mrs Humphrey, 1851–1920): British novelist in whose *Robert Elsmere* (1888) Woolson saw nothing new

Warner, Dudley Charles (1829–1900): American novelist

Washburn, Arabella Carter: The sister of Woolson's brother-in-law Rev. Timothy Carter and one of Woolson's close friends. Arabella married a Dr. Washburn.

Washington, Henry: Washington offered to rent his rooms in Venice to Woolson.

Washington, Mrs. Henry Washington's mother

Weber, Dr. and **Mrs.:** Physician from Cleveland who tried to wean Charly Woolson off morphine

Weber, Ida: Daughter of Dr. and Mrs. Weber who attended the same Paris school as the young Clare Benedict

Westmoreland, Mrs. Maria: Georgia playwright and novelist

Whitney, Flora Payne (?–1893): Daughter of Henry Payne of Cleveland, Ohio, and wife of William Whitney. Their son, Payne Whitney, married John Hay's daughter Helen. Flora was a close childhood friend of Woolson, but in later years they grew apart.

Whitney, William (1841–1904): Secretary of the Navy

Wickham, Gertrude Van Rensselaer (1844–1930): Journalist for the *Daily Cleveland Herald* and writer about dogs

Wolseley, Lord Garnet (1833–1913): British army officer who served in India. He and Woolson were godparents to Commander Casper Goodrich's son.

Woods, Henry George: President of Trinity College, Oxford

Woods, Margaret Louisa (1856–1945): British author of *A Village Tragedy* (1888) and wife of Henry Woods

Woolson, Alida (1845–46): Woolson's sister who died in infancy

Woolson, Ann Cooper (1835–40): One of the Woolson children who died of scarlet fever the year of Constance's birth

Woolson, Charles Jarvis, Jr. (1846–83): Woolson's brother who died a suicide in Los Angeles. Woolson spelled his name variously as Charly, Charley, and Charlie.

Woolson, Charles Jarvis, Sr. (1806–69): Woolson's father

Woolson, Clara: See Benedict, Clara Woolson

Woolson, Emma Cornelia: See Carter, Emma Woolson

Woolson, Georgiana Pomeroy: See Mather, Georgiana Woolson

Woolson, Gertrude Elizabeth (1836–40): One of the Woolson children who died of scarlet fever the year of Constance's birth

Woolson, Hannah Cooper Pomeroy (1808–79): Woolson's mother, the child of James Fenimore Cooper's sister Ann

Woolson, Julia Campbell (1838–40): One of the Woolson children who died of scarlet fever the year of Constance's birth

Worthington, John: Husband of Woolson's relative Jennie Cooper

Royalty

AUSTRIA

Crown Prince Rudolf (1858–89): The Prince and his mistress's apparent suicides at his hunting lodge at Mayerling made international headlines. He was married to Princess Stephanie of Belgium. Princess Stephanie later remarried.

BELGIUM

Princess Stephanie (1864–1945): See Austria/Crown Prince Rudolf

BRITAIN

Prince Albert (1819–61): Husband of Queen Victoria

Prince Albert Victor (Prince Eddie, 1864–92): Son of King Edward VII and older brother of George. Prince Eddie's death made his younger brother heir to the throne. In 1893, George married his deceased brother's fiancée, Princess Mary of Teck, also called Princess May. He was crowned King George V in 1911, making Mary Queen.

Princess Alice (1843–78): Daughter of Queen Victoria and mother of Princess Louise of Battenberg, Germany, and of Beatrice (1857–1944), who married Prince Henry of Battenberg

King Edward VII (1841–1910): Edward was the oldest son of Queen Victoria and the father of King George V and Prince Albert Victor. He married Princess Alexandra of Denmark.

Duchess of Fife, Louisa Victoria Alexandre Dagmar (1867–1931): Daughter of Queen Victoria and wife of the 6th Earl of Fife (1849–1912). Many feared she rather than George V would inherit the British throne.

Leopold, Duke of Albany (1853–84): Queen Victoria's son who died of medically administered morphine

Princess Mary (1847–1953): See Prince Albert Victor

Princess Victoria (1840–1901): Daughter of Queen Victoria and wife of Germany's Frederick III (1831–88)

Queen Victoria (1819–1901): Victoria's sixty-three-year reign encompassed Woolson's lifetime.

DENMARK

Princess Alexandra (1844–1925): Wife of Britain's King Edward VII

FRANCE

de Montijo, Empress Eugenie (1826–1920): Wife of Napoleon III (1808–73)

GERMANY/PRUSSIA

King Charles I (1823–91): Husband of Olga Nikolaevna of Russia
Princess Clara Elizabeth Prentice-Huntington (1860–1928): American-born wife of Prince Franz Hatzfeldt (1853–1910)
Empress Frederick: See Britain's Princess Victoria
Prince Henry of Battenberg (1858–96): Son-in-law of Queen Victoria's daughter Alice
Princess Louise of Battenberg (1889–1965): Granddaughter of Queen Victoria
Princess Sophia (1870–1932): Wife of Constantine I of Greece
Emperor Wilhelm II (1859–1941): Wilhelm also served as the King of Prussia.

GREECE

Constantine I (1868–1923): Husband of Princess Sophia of Prussia

ITALY

Margherita Maria Theresa (1851–1926): Queen consort to Umberto I
Rosa Teresa Vercellana Guerrieri (1833–85): Morganatic second wife of Victor Emmanuel II
King Umberto I (1844–1900): Assuming the reign of Italy in 1878, Umberto was king during Woolson's years there.
Victor Emmanuel II (1820–78): First king of a united Italy
Victor Emmanuel III (1869–1947): Son of Umberto I

MONTENEGRO

Elena Petrovic-Njegos (1873–1953): Wife of Italy's Victor Emmanuel III. She was the daughter of Prince Danilo I Petrovic-Njegos (1826–60) and Princess Darinka Kvekic (1837–92) who had been born in Trieste, Italy. Danilo I was assassinated, perhaps because of his sometimes brutal rule. He was succeeded by Nikola I (1841–1921), the only person who ruled Montenegro with the title King.

RUSSIA

Princess Olga Nikolaevna (1822–92): Wife of Charles I of Wurtemberg (1823–92) and daughter of King Nikola I (1841–1921)

SERBIA

Queen Draga (1861–1903): Lady in Waiting to Princess Natalija Obrenovic. Draga became Queen Consort to Princess Natalija's son King Alexandar Obrenovic (1876–1903).
Natalija Obrenovic (1859–1941): Wife of Prince Milan Obrenovic (1854–1901). She

became Queen of Serbia when her husband declared the territory independent in 1882.

SPAIN

Don Carlos VII (1848–1909): Claimant to the throne whom Woolson saw in Venice in 1893

Index

Woolson's letters to various recipients are listed by first page only and often contain information on the person, on his or her family members, and on Woolson's desire for family photographs. Letters from cities and towns are also listed by first page only and contain information on the place, its weather, Woolson's lodgings, and her walking and rowing excursions.

Professor emerita from Rivier College, Sharon L. Dean is the author of *Constance Fenimore Woolson: Homeward Bound* and *Constance Fenimore Woolson and Edith Wharton: Perspectives on Landscape and Art*. She is coeditor with Victoria Brehm of *Constance Fenimore Woolson: Selected Stories and Travel Narratives*.

The University Press of Florida is the scholarly publishing agency for the State University System of Florida, comprising Florida A&M University, Florida Atlantic University, Florida Gulf Coast University, Florida International University, Florida State University, New College of Florida, University of Central Florida, University of Florida, University of North Florida, University of South Florida, and University of West Florida.